D1607150

DIGITAL HARDWARE DESIGN

DIGITAL HARDWARE DESIGN

JOHN B. PEATMAN
School of Electrical Engineering
Georgia Institute of Technology

McGRAW-HILL BOOK COMPANY

New York St. Louis San Francisco Auckland Bogotá Hamburg
Johannesburg London Madrid Mexico Montreal New Delhi Panama Paris
São Paulo Singapore Sydney Tokyo Toronto

In memoriam
Edward S. Donn
1939–1979

DIGITAL HARDWARE DESIGN

1 2 3 4 5 6 7 8 9 0 D O D O 8 9 8 7 6 5 4 3 2 1 0

This book was set in Melior by Progressive Typographers.
The editors were Frank J. Cerra and Madelaine Eichberg;
the copy editor was Barbara Zeiders;
the designer was Anne Canevari Green;
the production supervisor was Richard A. Ausburn.
The drawings were done by J & R Services, Inc.
R. R. Donnelley & Sons Company was printer and binder.

Library of Congress Cataloging in Publication Data

Peatman, John B
Digital hardware design.

Includes index.
1. Electronic digital computers—Design and
construction. 2. Digital electronics. I. Title.
TK7888.3.P36 621.3819'582 80-10452
ISBN 0-07-049132-1

CONTENTS

PREFACE

This book is intended for the engineer who is interested in the design of digital instruments and devices. It recognizes the changes wrought in the *design process* by the advent of microcomputers and other products of the integrated circuit revolution. It differs from many books in that it develops design capability while focusing upon the larger problem of designing *maintainable* products.

The role of the microcomputer in the design of an instrument or device has become pervasive. This role is described in order to put into perspective the relationship between the microcomputer and the remainder of a design. With a clear view of the opportunities afforded by this relationship, the book concentrates upon this other half of the digital design problem. That is, it concentrates upon the design of circuitry to handle those tasks which require a faster response than is obtainable by an algorithm executed in the software of a microcomputer.

Because of the pervasive role of the microcomputer in the design process, the study of this book is best supplemented by a study of microcomputer hardware and software development plus a study of those input/output devices and considerations which can be handled directly by the microcomputer. This book has been prepared by assuming that the reader will either precede or follow its study with the study of a companion microcomputer book, such as the author's *Microcomputer-Based Design* (McGraw-Hill, 1977). Although one might question which study should come first, this book has been prepared to be useful to readers in either situation. In addition, the characteristics of a particularly versatile *one-chip* microcomputer (Motorola's 6801) are described in Appendix A3 to illustrate the support that a well-conceived microcomputer can provide for instrument design.

With its emphasis upon digital design in a world that has become dominated by low-cost microcomputers, this book breaks away from a variety of design ideas which have been important in the past. Thus, it accentuates the use of gates to implement only the simplest of combinational functions. The complex functions that required the Karnaugh maps or the Quine-McCluskey method in the past arise less frequently in these times when *all* functions can be translated into the software of a microcomputer. For applications in which such treatment is too slow, this book discusses the relegation of combinational circuit complexity to *programmable* devices (e.g., PROMs, FPLAs, and PALs). This approach is justified on the commonly accepted grounds of minimizing package count and supporting maintainability with a regular circuit structure. Likewise, designing complex sequential circuits has largely given way to designing simple sequential circuits and using standard counters and shift registers.

The microcomputer has caused another revolution in the design process. There is no longer any good reason (other than the insensitivity of a designer) for creating a product which cannot thoroughly test itself. If the product malfunctions, it should help pinpoint the source of the malfunction. The techniques of designing maintainability into a product are given solid treatment in this book. These ideas are made concrete by carrying out several iterations on the design of a specific instrument (a "signature analyzer").

The consistent, reliable handling of the timing considerations arising in a design have long been the hallmark of the experienced digital designer. These timing considerations, and the design opportunities they afford, are given extensive treatment. Furthermore, most instrument designs require the careful handling of the communications between real-time circuitry having one clock source and a microcomputer having another. Several alternative approaches are developed.

Because this book considers the design of fast circuitry to augment the microcomputer part of an instrument design, it must address the problem of selecting a suitable family of logic to use for such a design. Throughout the book, the 74LSxxx family of TTL logic (introduced by Texas Instruments and second-sourced by many companies) is used. This follows present industry practice and offers the opportunity to speed up such a design with little modification other than to substitute 74Sxxx parts (or the recently introduced 74ALSxxx or 74ASxxx parts) which serve the same logic function. Such a choice underplays the role of emitter-coupled logic (such as Motorola's MECL

10,000 logic family) for extremely fast designs. It also underplays the role of CMOS logic for slow, low-power-consumption designs. However, concentration on one family of logic offers the compensating advantage of introducing familiarity with a broad range of real devices which can become building blocks for the reader in his or her designs.

Sometime during 1980 or 1981 a new logic symbol standard will be introduced by the International Electrotechnical Commission as IEC Publication 617-12 and by the Institute of Electrical and Electronics Engineers as a *revised* IEEE Std 91/ANSI Y32.14. The *dependency notation* employed in this symbol standard will fill a long-standing need for a way to represent MSI devices like decoders, multiplexers, and counters so that the symbol, by itself, describes the operation of the device. It will go a long way toward clarifying the circuit schematics for an instrument. In this book, we introduce this symbology little by little so that the reader can build up a repertoire of notation ideas without being overwhelmed in the process. By the end of Chapter 2 we will have developed symbols for many widely used devices. For further support, the reader is referred to Appendix A1 which has been prepared by F. A. Mann of Texas Instruments Inc. to describe the main ideas of dependency notation. The reader is also referred to the 1980 printing of Texas Instruments' *TTL Data Book for Design Engineers* (third edition) which includes the dependency notation symbol for every one of that manufacturer's TTL devices.

This book is directed toward a specific goal of engineering studies—the development of creative design capability. Digital design offers a superb opportunity to develop this capability under rather ideal conditions: the specifications of system performance can be made both real and unambiguous; the building blocks to be employed can be easily delineated (e.g., use 74LSxxx parts); and the validity of a simple design criterion permits the student to carry out design while subject to a specific, real measure of the quality of a design. To take advantage of this opportunity, most chapters close with a broad variety of problems having a design flavor.

The book will typically be used in a one-quarter or one-semester course on digital hardware design. As a senior-level text, the book can build upon earlier digital hardware studies and extend these into a strong design framework. As a junior-level text, the book can serve as an introduction to digital hardware studies, leading the student to a solid overview of the implications of digital design in today's environment.

If this book is used by students who are already familiar with logic ideas and logic devices, then Chapter 2 might be scanned quickly to pick up dependency notation ideas. Also, Section 2-12 might be scanned for familiarization with PROMs, FPLAs, and PALs. Chapter 3 lays the groundwork for maintainability ideas which recur throughout the book. Chapter 4 presents a powerful approach for describing and designing the controller portion of fast circuitry. At the same time, it introduces the signature analyzer instrument design which is carried on in Sections 5-4 and 6-1.

One way to use this book might be to accentuate the design thread provided by the signature analyzer instrument design example. For such use, the dependency notation ideas of Chapter 2 might lead quickly to a study of Chapters 3 and 4, followed by Sections 5-1 through 5-4 and 6-1. The studies might then be filled out by selecting from among the remaining sections of Chapters 5 and 6. Such a study might be augmented by obtaining the service manual for an instrument and considering its redesign in light of the maintainability ideas presented in the text. A laboratory accentuating the development of these ideas might employ a personal computer (like that of Fig. 1-18) to fill the role of the microcomputer so that software development can be handled with simplicity and flexibility.

I am grateful for the one-fourth of my life during the past eight years spent working with outstanding design engineers within Hewlett-Packard. Most recently, working with Paul Lingane and Allen Edwards of the Stanford Park Division gave me an appreciation for the signature analysis concept developed and promoted by Hans Nadig, Bob Frohwerk, Tony Chan, Gary Gordon, and Ed White of the Santa Clara Division. For an appreciation of the impact which programmable chips can have in minimizing instrument design cost, I am grateful to Charles Muench of Intelligent Systems Corp. I am indebted to my students at Georgia Tech who have served as mentors through a variety of design activities.

In another vein, I am grateful to Dr. Demetrius Paris for fostering my activities at Georgia Tech and for having the vision to promote my participation in IEEE SCC11.9, the "dependency notation group." Conrad Muller, Fred Mann, and John Russell have each been a vivid example to me of the impact which a dedicated individual can have upon an industry standard. I am grateful to Ed Donn for his insights, his friendship, and the impact of his life upon my life. Eddie planned Chapter 1. The influence of his thoughts pervade Chapter 3. Finally, I fondly acknowledge the many roles my wife, Marilyn, played in the preparation of this book, including the editing and typing of the manuscript.

John B. Peatman

DESIGNING FOR USEFULNESS

1-1 A TECHNOLOGICAL REVOLUTION

"Once upon a time" the applications of digital technology were constrained by the cost, size, and heat dissipation of the technology itself. An early vacuum-tube computer filled a large room. Its air conditioner filled the adjacent room. As shown in Fig. 1-1, product planning meant room filling.

Today, product planning is entirely reoriented. In contrast to being driven by the abilities of technology, today's electronics world is driven by the needs of markets. This world says "if you can define it, you can design it," quickly followed by "but let's make sure somebody wants it."

In a 1979 address, Dr. C. Lester Hogan, vice-chairman of Fairchild, cast light upon our present state by reflecting back to the 1950s. At that time the five leading electronic-device manufacturers were

RCA, Sylvania, Raytheon, Westinghouse, Amperex

Figure 1-1. A 1950s product planning meeting. (Rand Renfroe.)

Since then the *revolution* in electronics technology has changed this list to

Texas Instruments, Motorola, Fairchild, National Semiconductor, Intel

We are just entering another period of technological revolution. Soon, integrated circuit (IC) manufacturers will be able to put a *million* components on a single chip. It is not clear what we should be doing with all of this capability. However, it seems apparent that each of the following IC developments will create significant demand:

1 The development of ever more "powerful" microcomputers, such as the Motorola 6801 one-chip microcomputer shown in Fig. 1-2 and discussed in Appendix A3.

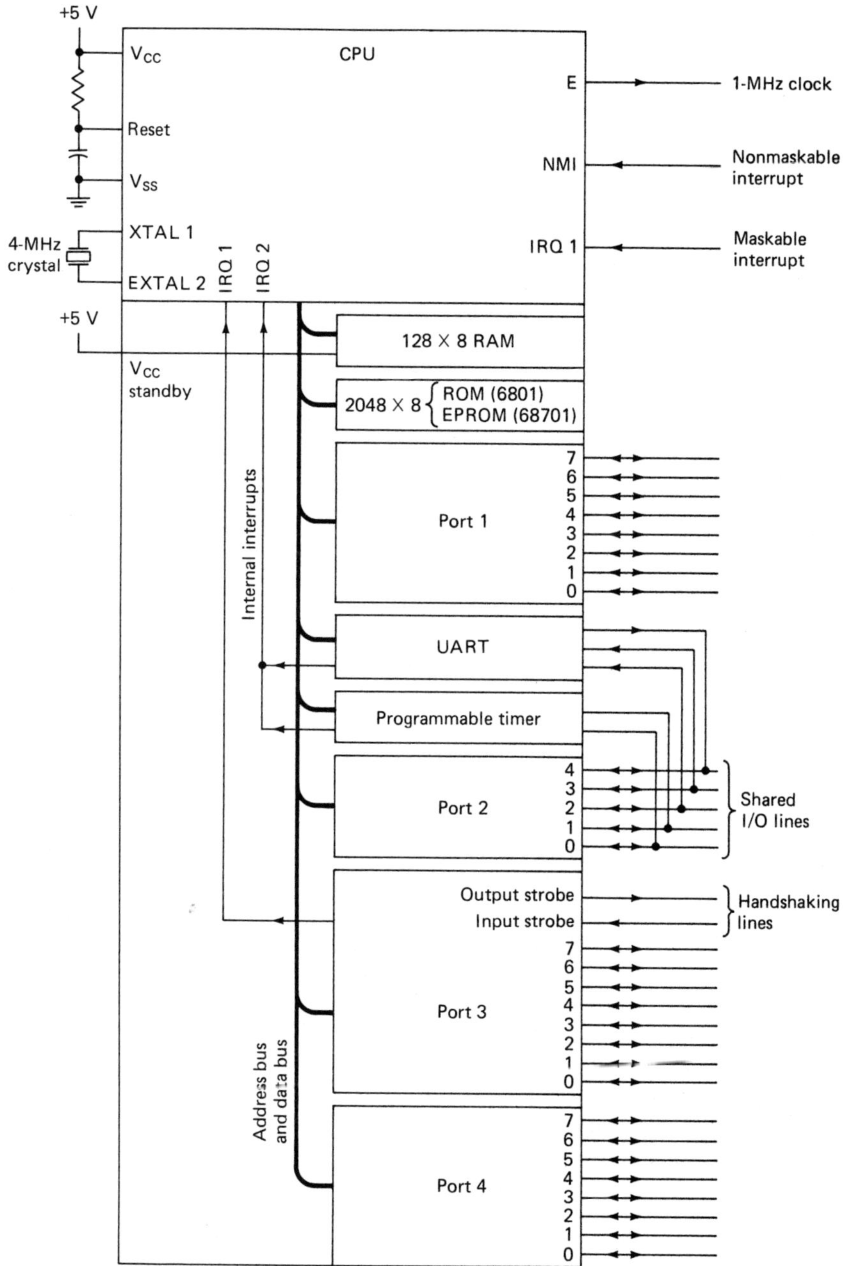

Figure 1-2. *Motorola 6801 one-chip microcomputer. (Motorola, Inc.)*

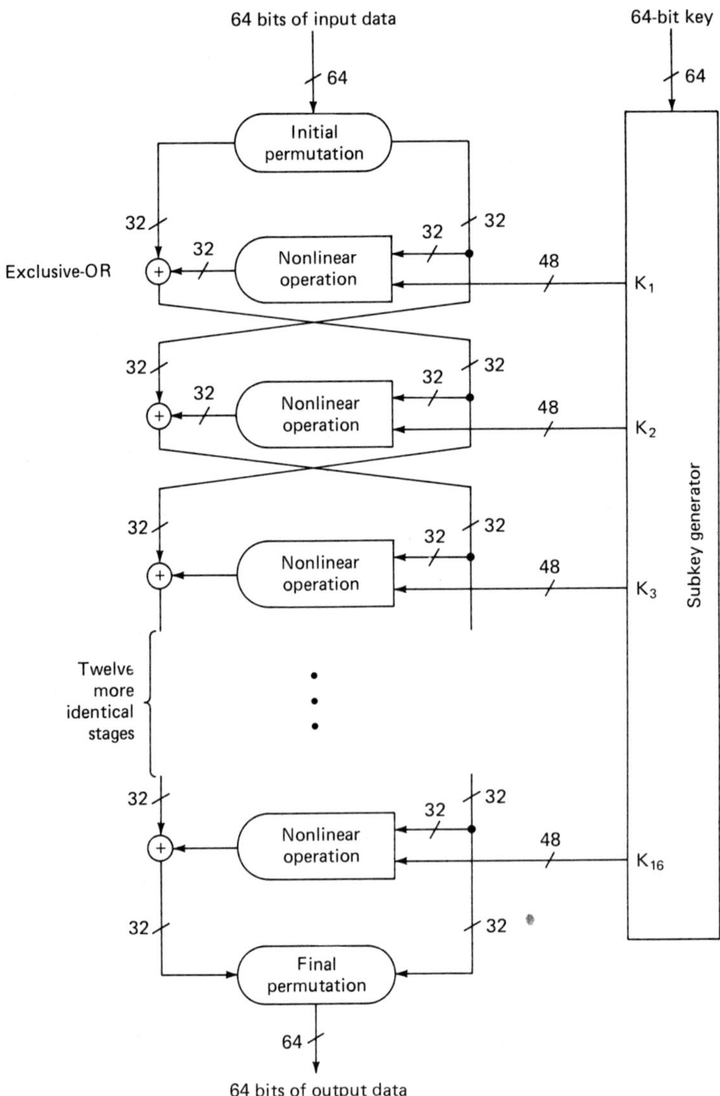

Figure 1-3. Data encryption using the National Bureau of Standards' Data Encryption Standard, FIPS PUB 46.

2 The transfer of any significant part of the microcomputer programming burden from designers to on-chip, "canned" software. For example, the microcomputer of Fig. 1-2 can be expanded into a multichip microcomputer configuration. It might include a "real-time operating system" developed by Motorola and supplied within the 6801 chip itself. The rest of the software would

be developed separately by an instrument† designer and reside in a separate memory chip.

3 The "casting into silicon" of pervasive algorithmic processes. The National Bureau of Standards' "Data Encryption Standard" shown in block diagram form in Fig. 1-3 is one example that has already happened. It supports data security measures for the commercial sector of our society.

4 The inclusion within an integrated circuit of the ability to be queried by another device as to its "health," to test itself, and to respond that it is either working or malfunctioning. "Smart" peripheral controller chips organized around a one-chip microcomputer can include this capability via extra on-chip software incorporated solely for this purpose. Alternatively, chips developed to implement specific algorithms can include the hardware organization, together with on-board testing algorithms, to execute this function.

5 Standardization efforts which permit designers to develop custom ICs without first acquiring in-depth knowledge of IC technology. Programmable read-only memories (PROMs) were a first step in this direction, followed by field-programmable logic arrays (FPLAs), discussed in Chap. 2. A more recent opportunity has been the development of the *master-slice* approach to custom IC design. Here an instrument designer generates an interconnection mask for an array of standard devices within a chip, such as that of Fig. 1-4. With this approach, an IC manufacturer can define most of the critical parameters of the chip, leaving the interconnects to the user. In this way a user with limited exposure to semiconductor technology can produce a specialty IC at relatively low cost.

The list above projects opportunities for dramatic growth at the *integrated circuit* level. Moving to a higher level of organization, we can identify further opportunities for dramatic growth:

1 The identification of smart, replaceable *modules* that can be queried and then test themselves and respond. These modules can include a one-chip microcomputer on a printed circuit (PC) board, a PC board in an instrument, an instrument in an automatic test system, or the automatic test system itself. For example, the instruments shown in Fig. 1-5 are interconnected using the GPIB, the general-purpose interface bus defined by IEEE Std 488-1978.

† We will use the term *instrument* in a general sense to mean any self-contained, stand-alone device, not a rack full of equipment.

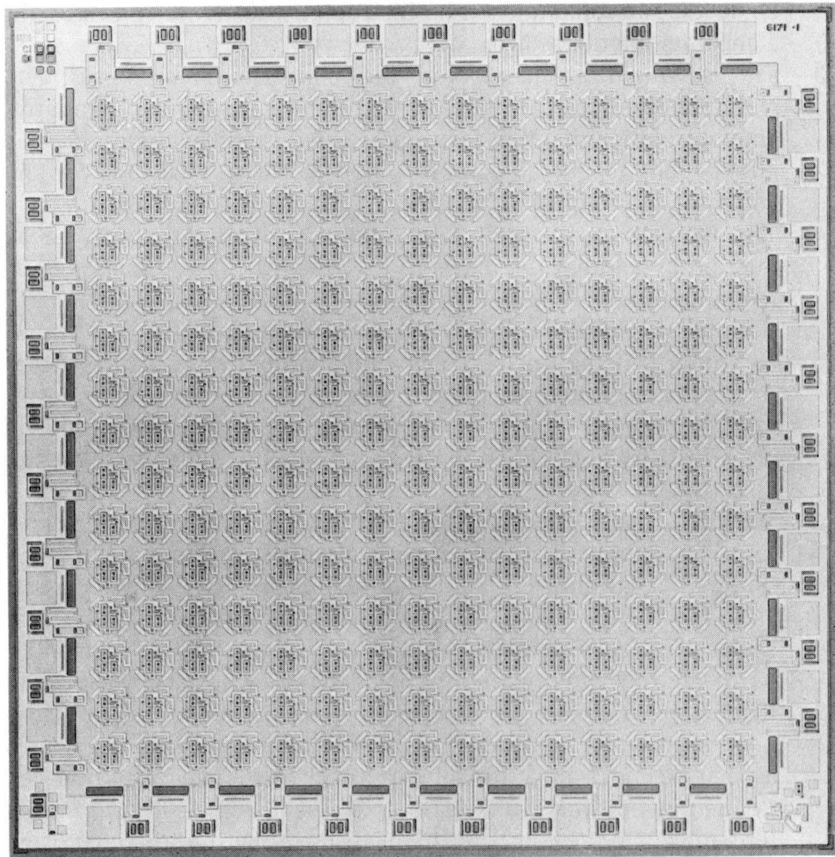

Figure 1-4. Master-slice chip for custom integrated circuits. (Interdesign Inc.)

The programmable controller on the bus cannot only test itself, it can send commands to all instruments on the bus to test themselves and then report back the results. The microcomputer controller within an instrument can likewise test itself and then command any "smart" subsystems (controlled by separate microcomputers) to test themselves and to report back. In this manner, each level in the hierarchy can obtain the self-test information it needs in order to pass along a status report on its health to the next-higher level in the hierarchy.

2 The standardization efforts supporting "concatenation of complexity," illustrated in Fig. 1-6. We use this term to identify different levels of activity, within any one of which a meaningful contribution can be made, but without requiring strong interaction with the levels just above or below.

The general-purpose interface bus (GPIB) serves as a broad

Figure 1-5. Instruments interconnected on the GPIB, general-purpose interface bus. (Hewlett-Packard Co.)

example of the ability of standardization to *create* markets. For example, the sales of test and measuring instruments by Hewlett-Packard for the first half of 1979 showed a 40 percent increase over the corresponding sales during the first half of 1978. John Young, the president of Hewlett-Packard, has reported that one-third of these sales were related in one way or another to the bus.

3 The design of new products which iterate upon the opportunities made possible by other recently developed products. Again to cite the example of Hewlett-Packard, John Young has reported that over half of their sales can be attributed to products *introduced* within the past three years. New product development plays a crucial role in the growth (or decline) of a company's activities. It is probably also true that a company's creative efforts are being counterproductively spent when it tries to create *future growth* through the protection of past accomplishments (via secrecy and litigation). In a rapidly evolving technological world, winning demands continuous creativity.

1-2 TOYS VERSUS TOOLS

A toy is an interesting collection of features, but it does not really do much for you. A tool is a helper. It may even help in ways you did not realize you would need.

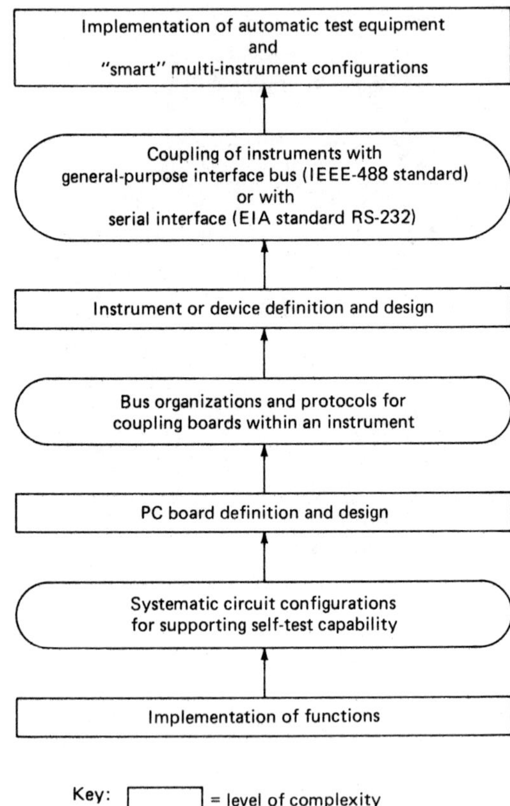

Figure 1-6. Concatenation of complexity—support via standardization.

The characteristics of a tool which are valuable to a user depend upon the nature of the application:

1 *Unknown problems require flexible, general solutions.* For example, the desktop computer of Fig. 1-7 is shown being used to set up and collect data from instruments on the general-purpose interface bus. It can interpret the data and display the results in easy-to-use, graphical form.

As another example, the universal programmer of Fig. 1-8 can be used to program the programmable read-only memories (PROMs), field-programmable logic arrays (FPLAs), and programmable array logic chips (PALs) discussed in Chap. 2. A *family* of devices (e.g., all Harris Semiconductor bipolar PROMs) utilize one generic programming "pak" which supplies the voltages required to program all devices in the family as well as the program-

Figure 1-7. Desktop computer serving as a programmable GPIB controller in an automatic test system. (Hewlett-Packard Co.)

ming algorithm. Then each device in the family (e.g., a 32 × 8 PROM or a 256 × 4 PROM) requires an additional low-cost socket adapter which steers addresses, data, and programming pulses to the appropriate pins.

A third example is the programmable, real-time measurement and control system shown in Fig. 1-9. A user configures the unit with signal conditioning plug-in cards, chosen according to the number and type of analog and digital input signals required by an application. The built-in computer permits a user to program the sampling, and the analog-to-digital conversion, of inputs. This data can then be manipulated into an appropriate information display as well as output control signals. All of the programming is carried out in easy-to-use Basic language. A real-time operating system and a simple set of commands for input/output operations permit concurrent tasks to be programmed easily.

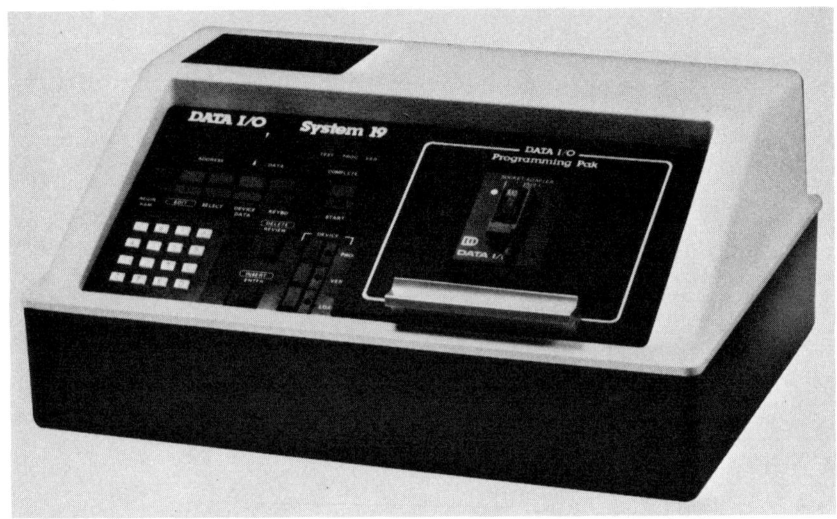

Figure 1-8. Universal programmer for PROMs, FPLAs, PALs, and so on. (DATA I/O.)

2 *Known problems benefit from specific, dedicated solutions.* The battery-powered transmission test set shown in Fig. 1-10 is used to characterize the quality of a telephone line configured into a "loop-back" connection. It transmits a sequence of tones while measuring and displaying either returned tone level, noise level, or frequency.

The cable tester of Fig. 1-11 is a battery-powered, "time-domain reflectometer" specifically designed to identify and locate cable faults to within less than an inch over cable lengths of up to 2000 ft. It is environmentally protected for use in aircraft and ships. In use, it transmits a voltage step and displays the waveform which is returned because of any discontinuities in the line. The waveform characterizes the type of fault (i.e., a short to ground, a break in the line, a short to an adjacent signal line, etc.). The delay dialed in for the waveform is calibrated to yield the distance to the fault.

3 *Heavily used instruments can support powerful solutions.* The spectrum analyzer of Fig. 1-12 can determine the frequency-response characteristics (up to 25 kHz) of devices such as audio tape recorders, loudspeakers, analog signal conditioning circuitry on voice-grade telephone lines, mechanical structures, and rotating machinery. It includes a built-in noise source to serve as a stimulus for transfer function evaluation. It can store, and later recall, either of two spectra for facilitating the comparison of one device with another. It can make unusually extensive use of the

(a)

```
READY

REV

MULTI-TASK BASIC REV 3.00E

10 TASK 1,100
20 TASK 2,200
30 ACTIVATE 1 PERIOD 7
40 ACTIVATE 2
50 STOP

100 FOR I=0 TO 7
110 IF AIN(2,I)>5.6 DOT(5,5)=1
```

HLT RUN
RESET (OVR) CONT (ION)
AUTO LOAD

(b)

Figure 1-9. Programmable, real-time measurement and control system. (a) Front view; (b) close-up of display. (Analog Devices, Inc.)

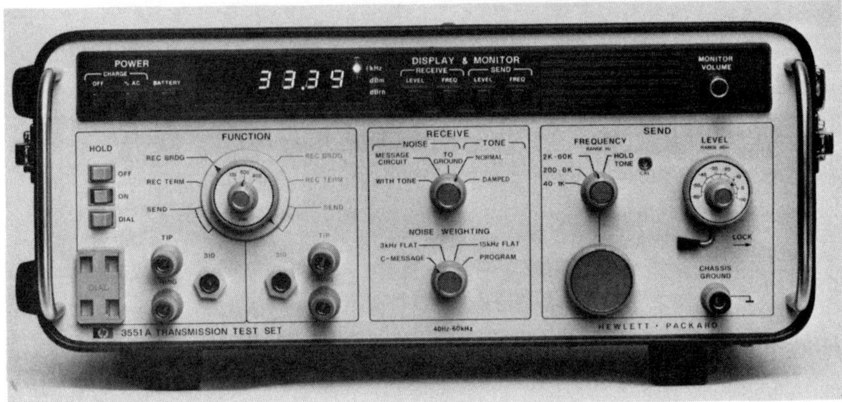

Figure 1-10. *Transmission test set.* (Hewlett-Packard Co.)

general-purpose interface bus (GPIB), permitting a programmable controller to set up its mode of operation, initiate a measurement cycle, collect output data, and write messages on the cathode-ray-tube (CRT) display.

As another example, the typewriter shown in Fig. 1-13 gives

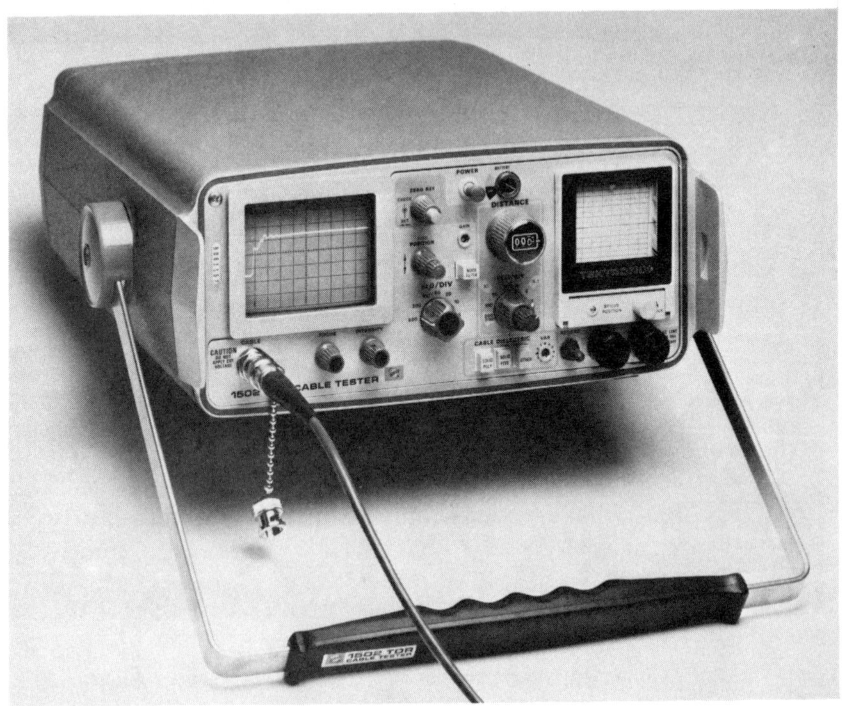

Figure 1-11. *Cable tester.* (Tektronix, Inc.)

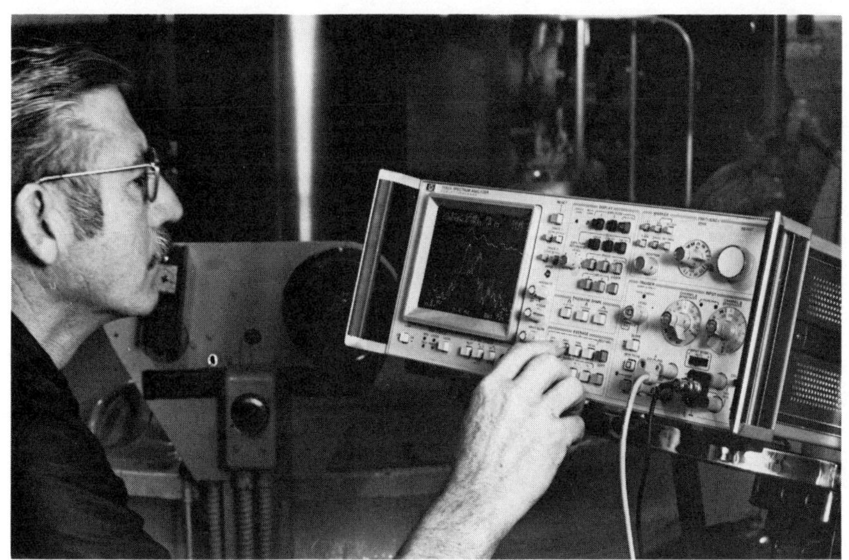

Figure 1-12. *Low-frequency spectrum analyzer.* (Hewlett-Packard Co.)

Figure 1-13. *IBM Model 60 electronic typewriter.* (IBM Office Products Division.)

Figure 1-14. Digital pyrometer. (*Newport Electronics, Inc.*)

electronic support to a secretary's typing function. Pressing the "correction" key backs up the carrier, lifting the typed letters off the page (using the typewriter's memory to recall the previously typed letters). The switch-selectable "automatic carrier return" function senses the end of a line and, at the completion of the word being typed, returns the carrier without help from the typist. If the typist continues to type while the carrier is being returned, the characters are stored and then typed out on the new line. The typewriter can remember the inside address of a letter and subsequently play it back on the envelope. Both centering and underlining are handled automatically upon command by the typist.

4 *Friendly instruments reduce confusion and training.* The hand-held digital pyrometer of Fig. 1-14 employs a platinum resistance sensor to measure temperature with a resolution of 0.1°F and an absolute accuracy of 0.5°F over a range of ±200°F. A flick of a switch yields temperature measurements with a resolution of

1.0°F and an absolute accuracy of about 2°F over a range of −200 to +1470°F.

The computer shown in Fig. 1-15*a* is designed specifically for the business management of small- and medium-sized companies which have, perhaps, not used computers previously. When the computer is turned on, its CRT display requests the user to select a function by pressing one of the "softkeys" located along the

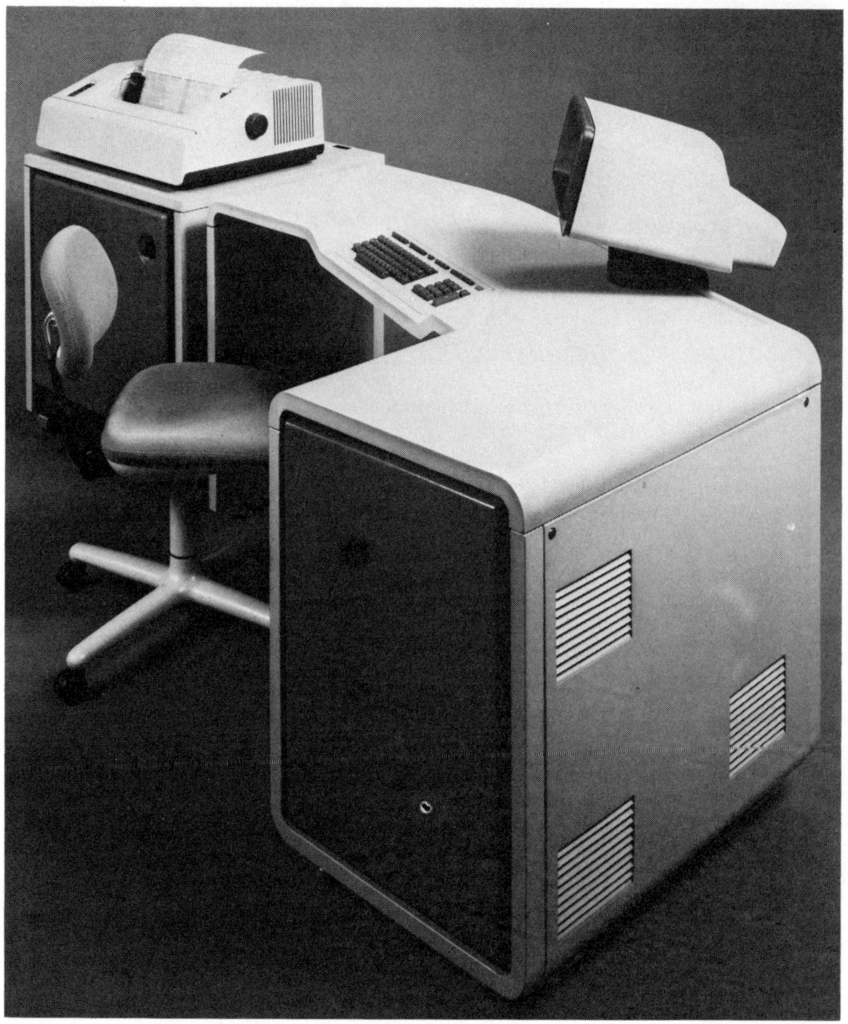

Figure 1-15. Business computer. (a) Complete system.

Figure 1-15 (*b*) Friendly softkeys. (*Hewlett-Packard Co.*)

bottom edge of the display, as shown in Fig. 1-15*b*. In response to pressing ORDER ENTRY, a new display will appear having to do with entering orders. The softkeys will be redefined with new functions appropriate to entering orders. Hence the user is guided through a selected business operation directly and without the potential confusion that can arise with a memorized protocol.

5 *Buried flexibility helps both novices and experienced users.* The logic state analyzer of Fig. 1-16 permits a user to probe up to 16 digital inputs in an instrument under test. By keying in

TRIGGER = ----000000000011

the user selects an input pattern of "don't care" conditions, 0s, and 1s upon which the analyzer will trigger. Then in response to pressing the TRACE key, the analyzer will wait for that pattern to occur and will then collect the bits of data on the 16 inputs during that clock period and the subsequent 63 clock periods. In this manner a user can examine a "snapshot" of activity in the instrument under test.

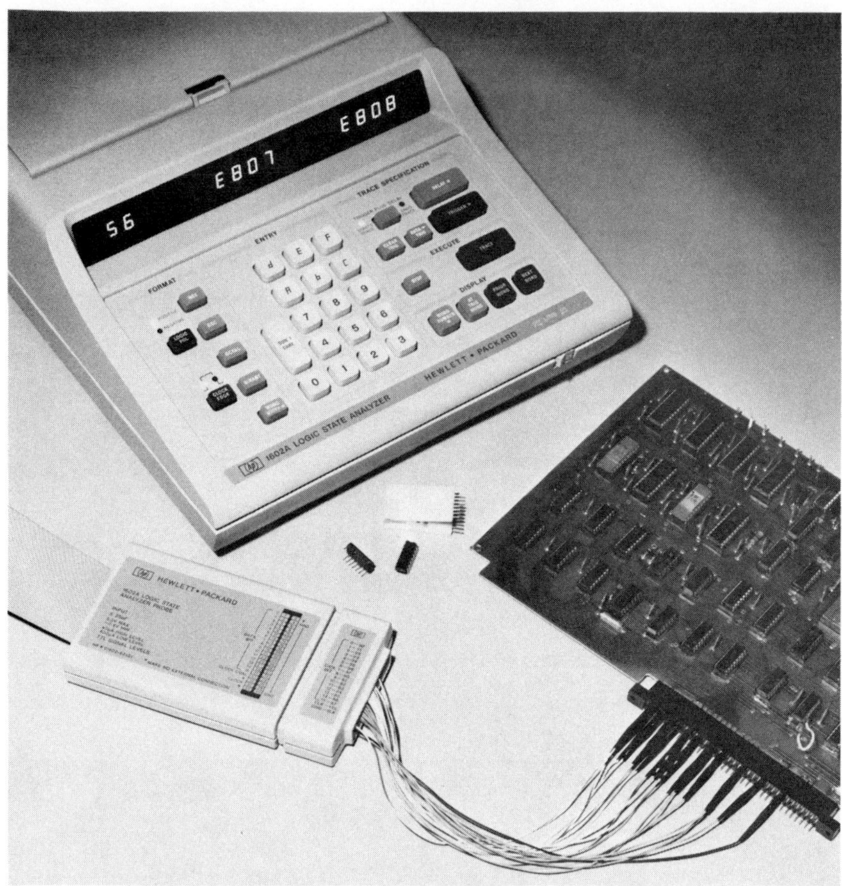

Figure 1-16. Logic state analyzer with buried flexibility. (*Hewlett-Packard Co.*)

A more experienced user can employ some of the buried flexibility of the analyzer (described in the operating manual) to modify this basic function. If instead of pressing just the TRACE key, the user presses the two-key sequence TRACE followed by C, the analyzer will *continuously* collect new snapshots of activity. On the other hand, if the user presses TRACE followed by E, the analyzer will collect only those *events* which satisfy the trigger condition, ignoring the intervening data.

6 *Low-cost add-ons can create dedicated tools out of general-purpose tools.* To troubleshoot malfunctions on the GPIB, the low-cost auxiliary probe shown in Fig. 1-17*a* can be added to the normal probe of the logic state analyzer of Fig. 1-16. The resulting combination is shown in use in Fig. 1-17*b*. The auxiliary

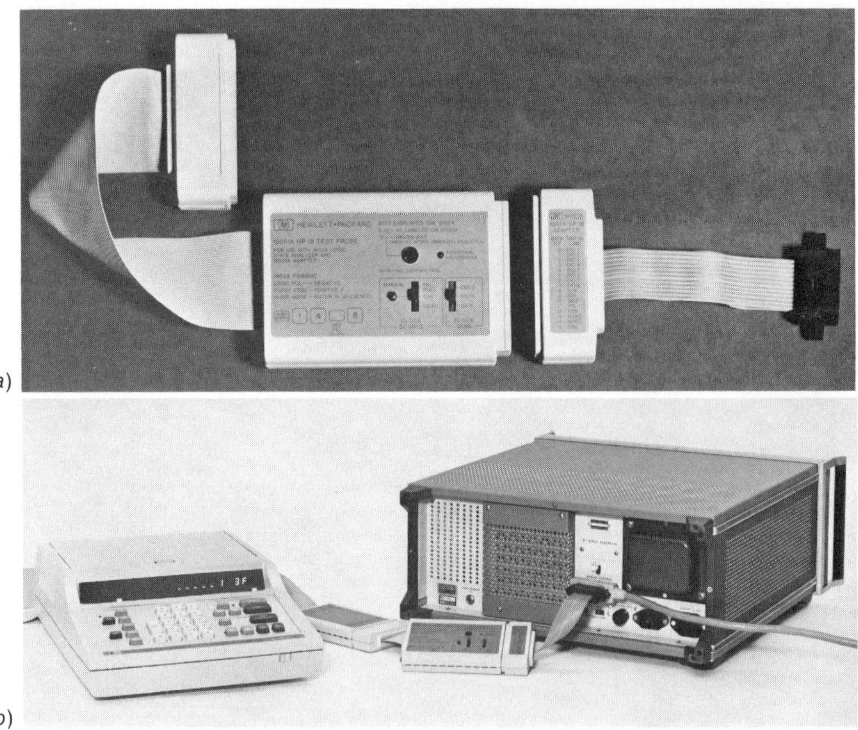

Figure 1-17. *GPIB probe and logic state analyzer combination.* (*a*) *Probe;* (*b*) *in use debugging GPIB.* (*Hewlett-Packard Co.*)

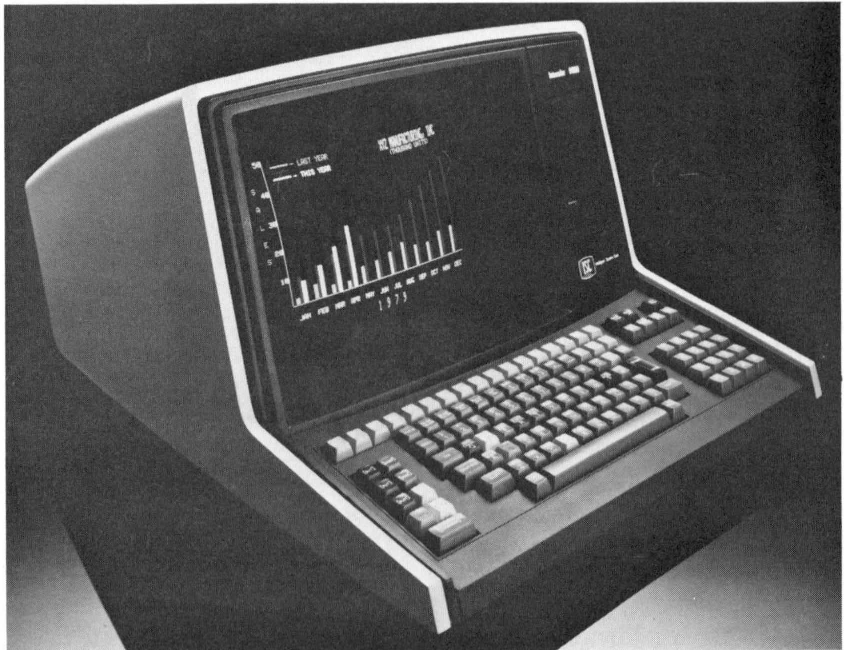

Figure 1-18. *Low-cost computer.* (*Intelligent Systems Corp.*)

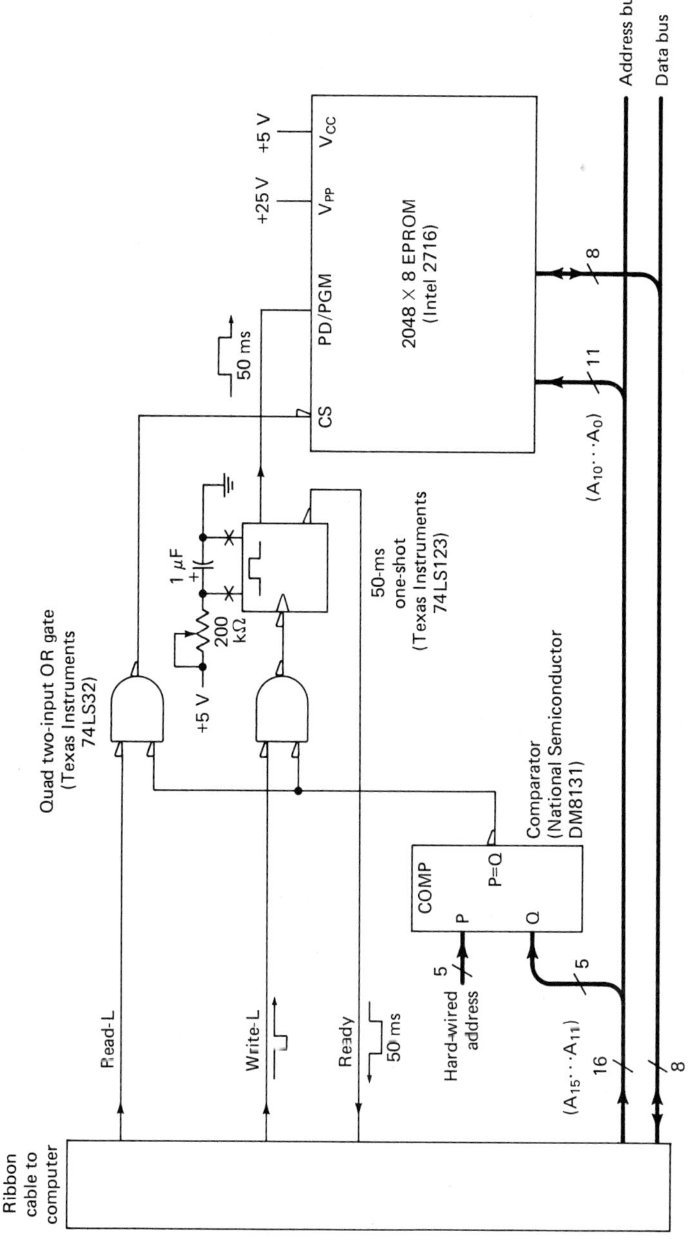

Figure 1-19. EPROM programmer built as a low-cost add-on to a computer.

probe senses when an abnormal "handshake" has taken place between two instruments. It then generates a trigger signal for the logic state analyzer, assisting the analyzer to collect just that data whose interpretation will identify the cause of the problem.

As another example, consider the low-cost computer shown in Fig. 1-18. It includes fast, floppy-disk program entry, color graphic display, "disk-Basic" programming (which permits disk commands to be embedded into Basic programs), and an external connector which makes the central processing unit's (CPU's) signals available for smart add-ons. A programmer† for the popular Intel 2716 erasable programmable read-only memory (EPROM), used for storing microcomputer software, is shown in Fig. 1-19. Because all the "smarts" reside in the computer of Fig. 1-18, it requires only the three integrated circuits shown. Although it is not our purpose here to understand this circuit in detail, we might point out that programming the contents of one EPROM address requires the computer to write the data to memory. The comparator shown detects the address and triggers a one-shot. The one-shot, in turn, generates the 50-ms pulse required to program the EPROM. By also controlling the CPU's Ready input, it causes the computer to "hiccup," keeping the EPROM address and data available for 50 ms.

With this simple hardware add-on, the novice user who wishes to program an EPROM turns on the computer, inserts the floppy disk holding the "smarts" of the EPROM programmer, and presses the autostart key. The computer will carry on from there, giving the user appropriate instructions for entering the EPROM data and for inserting the EPROM in the socket. It can also check that the EPROM is initially unprogrammed and that subsequent programming has been completed successfully, commenting to the user if there are any problems.

† Derived from D. Passey, Low-Cost Processor Package Programs EPROMs, *Electronics*, June 7, 1979, pp. 146–147.

PRELIMINARY CONSIDERATIONS

In this chapter we will consider four topics:

- Codes
- Gating, or combinational, circuitry
- Sequential circuitry
- Microcomputers

Each of these topics will be extended in later chapters; the intent here will simply be to create a foundation for the digital design theme of the book.

We will also develop the use of *dependency notation*† for repre-

† Dependency notation was introduced in the standards document, *Graphic Symbols for Logic Diagrams*, published jointly as ANSI Std Y32.14-1973 and IEEE Std 91-1973. That standard did not include sufficient means for representing important characteristics of many logic devices. Since its publication, these weaknesses have been overcome, step by step. At present, the International Electrotechnical Commission (IEC) is approaching the adoption of a strong, versatile standard, IEC Publication 617-12. An IEEE/ANSI revsion will closely parallel the IEC version. Its features are discussed by F. A. Mann, a member of the IEEE symbol standards committee, in Appendix A1.

senting digital integrated circuits (ICs). This notation aids the interpretation of digital circuit diagrams employing medium-scale integrated (MSI) circuits such as decoders and counters.

2-1 CODES

A *boolean,* or *binary,* variable is one that can take on either of two values. For example, consider the four tires of an automobile. We might represent each tire as being inflated or flat. This information can be *coded* by defining a binary variable to represent the condition of each tire. Then we assign a value of 1 to one of the conditions and a value of 0 to the other.

Example 2-1. Code the conditions of the four tires of an automobile.
First, define variables:

LF = condition of left-front tire

RF = condition of right-front tire

LR = condition of left-rear tire

RR = condition of right-rear tire

Second, assign values:

1 = inflated tire

0 = flat tire

Thus $RF = 0$ codes the condition wherein the right-front tire is flat.

Notice the arbitrariness of these definitions. It is not important what names we give to variables. They can be single letters (e.g., A, B, C, D for the conditions of the four tires), letters followed by numbers (e.g., $T1$, $T2$, $T3$, $T4$ for the four tires), cryptic letter combinations (e.g., the definitions of Example 2-1), word combinations (e.g., left-front, right-front, left-rear, right-rear), or anything else that suits us. It is only necessary to state the definitions we select. It is also necessary to state how we assign values 0 and 1.

More generally, we want to be able to describe variables that can take on more than two conditions or values. Thus for some purposes it is useful to define variables representing the age of people in terms of the five *values*

Infants, children, teenagers, adults, golden-agers

For other purposes we might use values such as

One-year-olds, two-year-olds, three-year-olds, etc.

In describing a neighborhood, we might use values such as

King, Vivie, etc.

A consistent way to handle the coding of *any* set of conditions or values is to assign an integer to each condition and then to represent that integer using a *standard* code. We will consider five such codes:

- Decimal code
- Binary code
- Gray code
- Hexadecimal code
- Binary-coded-decimal code

Decimal code is useful because of its familiarity. If we choose to use decimal code to code a variable, I, which can take on values between 0 and 999, we can use a three-digit decimal code made up of three *decimal* variables (i.e., variables that can take on 10 values),

$$d_2, d_1, d_0$$

The relationship between I and these variables is given by

$$\begin{aligned} I &= 10^2 \times d_2 + 10^1 \times d_1 + 10^0 \times d_0 \\ &= 100 \times d_2 + 10 \times d_1 + 1 \times d_0 \end{aligned}$$

That is, the number 529 is coded by

$$d_2 = 5 \qquad d_1 = 2 \qquad d_0 = 9$$

Binary code is formed in an analogous way using binary variables to code each *bit*. Thus

$$I = 2^5 \times b_5 + 2^4 \times b_4 + 2^3 \times b_3 + 2^2 \times b_2 + 2^1 \times b_1 + 2^0 \times b_0$$
$$= 32 \times b_5 + 16 \times b_4 + 8 \times b_3 + 4 \times b_2 + 2 \times b_1 + 1 \times b_0$$

Example 2-2. How many bits are needed (as a minimum) to code the decimal number 99 in binary code?

Noting that the binary number 1111 · · · 11, made up of n ones, is equal to $2^n - 1$, we can further note that

$$63 = 2^6 - 1 < 99 \leq 127 = 2^7 - 1$$

Consequently, we evidently need *seven* bits to code the decimal number 99.

Example 2-3. Express the decimal number 99 in binary code.

$$\begin{aligned} 99 &= 64 \times 1 + (35) \\ &= 64 \times 1 + 32 \times 1 + (3) \\ &= 64 \times 1 + 32 \times 1 + 16 \times 0 + 8 \times 0 + 4 \times 0 + 2 \times 1 + (1) \\ &= 64 \times 1 + 32 \times 1 + 16 \times 0 + 8 \times 0 + 4 \times 0 + 2 \times 1 + 1 \times 1 \end{aligned}$$

Or, using a subscripted label to indicate the code:

$$(99)_{\text{decimal}} = (1100011)_{\text{binary}}$$

Binary code is useful because it represents numbers in terms of binary variables, which, in turn, can be represented by two-state electronic devices. It is also useful because the power-of-2 *weight* given to each bit leads to arithmetic properties which are easy to implement in digital hardware.

Gray code, shown in Fig. 2-1, is an example of a code which is closely related to binary, employs binary variables (i.e., . . . , g_3, g_2,

I	g_3	g_2	g_1	g_0
0	0	0	0	0
1	0	0	0	1
2	0	0	1	1
3	0	0	1	0
4	0	1	1	0
5	0	1	1	1
6	0	1	0	1
7	0	1	0	0
8	1	1	0	0
9	1	1	0	1
10	1	1	1	1
11	1	1	1	0
12	1	0	1	0
13	1	0	1	1
14	1	0	0	1
15	1	0	0	0

Figure 2-1. Gray code.

g_1, g_0), does not associate a weight with these variables, but has useful properties in its own right as a *unit-distance* code. The unit-distance property means that in going from the coding for any integer I to the coding for $I + 1$, only one bit changes, regardless of the value of I. This property is usefully employed in transferring a coded variable reliably between a transducer and an instrument input. The transducer must be one whose digital output *follows* variations in the analog input without skipping over any integers.

An example of such a device is the 10-bit Gray code shaft-angle encoder shown in Fig. 2-2, which divides one revolution of its shaft into 1024 parts, or quanta. As long as the shaft rotates at a rate less than 12,000 quanta per second (i.e., about 12 rps), the manufacturer guarantees that the output will be accurately read. And as long as the encoder is sampled by an instrument at a rate (samples per second) which is faster than its maximum turning rate (quanta per second), the integers encoded by every pair of successive samples will differ by, at most, one. The instrument can read the encoder reliably *even* at the exact moment when the encoder is changing from one quantum position to the next since only one bit will be changing. Whether that bit is read as a 1 or a 0, the instrument will receive a correctly encoded value of position,

$$g_9g_8g_7g_6g_5g_4g_3g_2g_1g_0$$

Figure 2-2. 2.65-in.-diameter shaft-angle encoder. (Encoder Division, Litton Systems Inc.)

The general structure of an n-bit Gray code can be described by the following scheme:

1 Except for the beginning and ending of the code, bit g_0 alternates two 0s, two 1s, two 0s, etc., g_1 alternates four 0s, four 1s, four 0s, etc., g_2 alternates eight 0s, eight 1s, eight 0s, etc., and g_k alternates 2^{k+1} 0s, 2^{k+1} 1s, 2^{k+1} 0s, etc.

2 The first transition from 0 to 1 for bit g_{k+1} occurs right in the middle of the first string of 1s for bit g_k.

The algorithm for Gray code-to-binary code conversion can be gleaned from Fig. 2-3. Notice that, in this case, $b_3 = g_3$. In general, for n-bit Gray code and binary code

1 The most significant bits are equal:

$$b_{n-1} = g_{n-1}$$

	Gray code				Binary code			
I	g_3	g_2	g_1	g_0	b_3	b_2	b_1	b_0
0	0	0	0	0	0	0	0	0
1	0	0	0	1	0	0	0	1
2	0	0	1	1	0	0	1	0
3	0	0	1	0	0	0	1	1
4	0	1	1	0	0	1	0	0
5	0	1	1	1	0	1	0	1
6	0	1	0	1	0	1	1	0
7	0	1	0	0	0	1	1	1
8	1	1	0	0	1	0	0	0
9	1	1	0	1	1	0	0	1
10	1	1	1	1	1	0	1	0
11	1	1	1	0	1	0	1	1
12	1	0	1	0	1	1	0	0
13	1	0	1	1	1	1	0	1
14	1	0	0	1	1	1	1	0
15	1	0	0	0	1	1	1	1

Figure 2-3. Gray code-to-binary code conversion.

2 Each bit of the binary code can be obtained as follows:

$$b_{k-1} = \begin{cases} g_{k-1} & \text{if } b_k = 0 \\ \overline{g_{k-1}} & \text{if } b_k = 1 \end{cases}$$

where $\overline{g_{k-1}}$ signifies the *complement* of g_{k-1}. That is, if $g_{k-1} = 0$, then $\overline{g_{k-1}} = 1$; whereas, if $g_{k-1} = 1$, then $\overline{g_{k-1}} = 0$.

Example 2-4. Find the binary equivalent of the 10-bit Gray code number 0111000111.

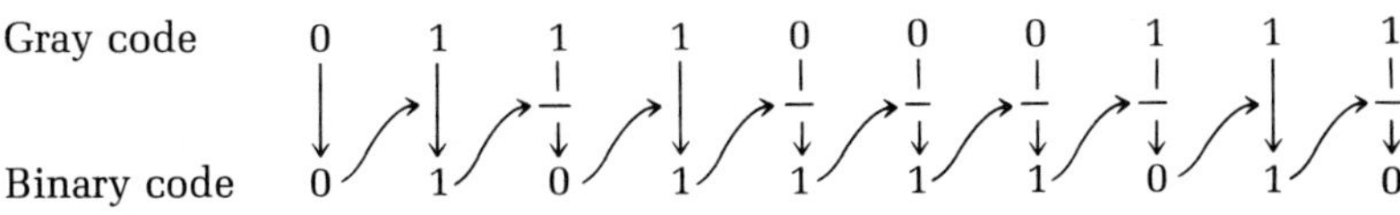

Hexadecimal, or *hex,* code employs hexadecimal digits (i.e., variables that can take on 16 values)

$$. . . , h_3, h_2, h_1, h_0$$

The relationship between an integer I and its encoding is given by

$$I = 16^n \times h_n + \cdot \cdot \cdot + 16^2 \times h_2 + 16^1 \times h_1 + 16^0 \times h_0$$

The usual names given to these 16 values are

0, 1, 2, 3, 4, 5, 6, 7, 8, 9, A, B, C, D, E, F

Their decimal and binary code equivalents are given in Fig. 2-4.

Hex code is useful for providing an alternative, compact representation of a binary number. Thus for binary code

$$\begin{aligned} I &= 2^7 \times b_7 + 2^6 \times b_6 + 2^5 \times b_5 + 2^4 \times b_4 + 2^3 \times b_3 + 2^2 \times b_2 + 2^1 \times b_1 + 2^0 \times b_0 \\ &= 2^4 (2^3 \times b_7 + 2^2 \times b_6 + 2^1 \times b_5 + 2^0 \times b_4) + (2^3 \times b_3 + 2^2 \times b_2 + 2^1 \times b_1 + 2^0 \times b_0) \\ &= 16(8b_7 + 4b_6 + 2b_5 + b_4) + (8b_3 + 4b_2 + 2b_1 + b_0) \end{aligned}$$

whereas for hex code

$$I = 16 \times h_1 + h_0$$

Hexadecimal code	Decimal code		Binary code			
h_0	d_1	d_0	b_3	b_2	b_1	b_0
0	0	0	0	0	0	0
1	0	1	0	0	0	1
2	0	2	0	0	1	0
3	0	3	0	0	1	1
4	0	4	0	1	0	0
5	0	5	0	1	0	1
6	0	6	0	1	1	0
7	0	7	0	1	1	1
8	0	8	1	0	0	0
9	0	9	1	0	0	1
A	1	0	1	0	1	0
B	1	1	1	0	1	1
C	1	2	1	1	0	0
D	1	3	1	1	0	1
E	1	4	1	1	1	0
F	1	5	1	1	1	1

Figure 2-4. Hexadecimal digits and their equivalents.

and we can make the identifications

$$h_1 = 8b_7 + 4b_6 + 2b_5 + b_4$$
$$h_0 = 8b_3 + 4b_2 + 2b_1 + b_0$$

Example 2-5. Find the binary equivalent of the hexadecimal number C5A6.

Hex code	C	5	A	6
Binary code	1100	0101	1010	0110

Binary-coded-decimal, or *BCD,* code employs four binary variables to code each digit of a decimal number using 4-bit binary code. It is useful for representing decimal switch inputs to an instrument, such as those shown in Fig. 2-5. It is also useful for driving a decimal display, such as the four-digit liquid-crystal display of Fig. 2-6.

Example 2-6. Find the three-BCD digit representation of the decimal number 485.

Decimal code	4	8	5
BCD code	0100	1000	0101

2-2 LOGIC FUNCTIONS

In order to express binary, or boolean, variables as functions of other binary variables, we need to *define* several logic functions. The role these serve in boolean algebra is analogous to the role served by ordinary algebraic functions involving addition and multiplication.

Consider first the *AND function* as it relates to two binary variables *B* and *A*. Figure 2-7*a* illustrates two ways to express the alge-

Figure 2-5. BCD-encoded switch. (EECO Inc.)

Figure 2-6. Liquid-crystal displays. (Beckman Instruments, Inc.)

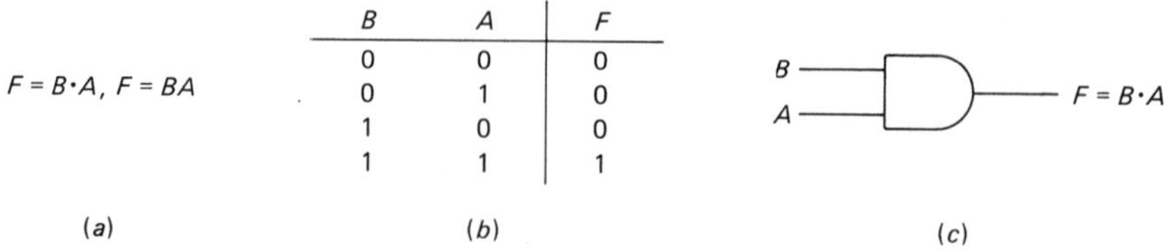

B	A	F
0	0	0
0	1	0
1	0	0
1	1	1

Figure 2-7. AND function. (a) Algebraic representations; (b) truth table; (c) graphic symbol.

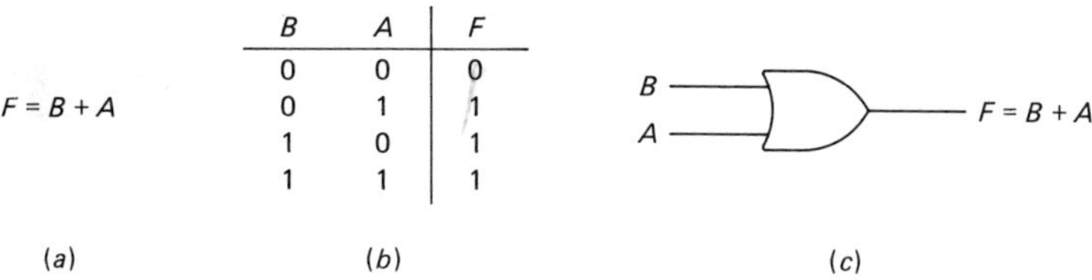

Figure 2-8. OR function. (a) Algebraic representation; (b) truth table; (c) graphic symbol.

braic ANDing of B and A. The *truth table* of Fig. 2-7*b* has nothing to do with truth or falsehood but rather is simply a listing of the four possible combinations of B and A and the corresponding values of the function $F = B \cdot A$. Note that $B \cdot A = 1$ if and only if $B = 1$ AND $A = 1$. The standard† graphic symbol is shown in Fig. 2-7*c*. For three (or more) binary variables, the function $F = C \cdot B \cdot A = 1$ if and only if $C = 1$ AND $B = 1$ AND $A = 1$.

The *OR function*, more properly designated the inclusive-OR function, is illustrated in Fig. 2-8. Note that $F = B + A = 1$ if $B = 1$ OR if $A = 1$ OR both. It is the inclusion of this *or both* condition which leads to the name inclusive-OR. For three (or more) variables, $F = C + B + A = 1$ if and only if one or more of the variables C, B, or A are equal to 1.

The *exclusive-OR function*, illustrated in Fig. 2-9, excludes the *or both* case described in the last paragraph. Consequently, for two variables, the function $F = B \oplus A = 1$ if and only if either input equals 1 while the other input equals 0. The extension to three variables is not immediately obvious. However, it can be derived by considering the sequence of operations

$$(C \oplus B) \oplus A$$

The first column of Fig. 2-9*d* illustrates the function $C \oplus B$, while the second column is an exclusive-ORing between this result and the variable A. An appropriate question is whether

$$(C \oplus B) \oplus A \stackrel{?}{=} C \oplus (B \oplus A)$$

The third and fourth columns develop the truth table for $C \oplus (B \oplus A)$. Since the second and fourth columns are identical in all cases, we have

† ANSI Std Y32.14, referenced at the beginning of this chapter.

$F = B \oplus A$

(a)

B	A	F
0	0	0
0	1	1
1	0	1
1	1	0

(b)

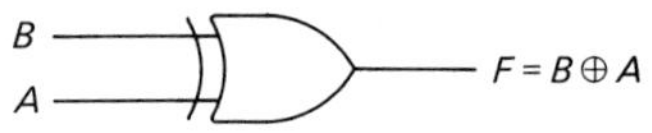

(c)

C	B	A	$C \oplus B$	$(C \oplus B) \oplus A$	$(B \oplus A)$	$C \oplus (B \oplus A)$	Number of variables equal to 1
0	0	0	0	0	0	0	0
0	0	1	0	1	1	1	1
0	1	0	1	1	1	1	1
0	1	1	1	0	0	0	2
1	0	0	1	1	0	1	1
1	0	1	1	0	1	0	2
1	1	0	0	0	1	0	2
1	1	1	0	1	0	1	3

(d)

Figure 2-9. Exclusive-OR function. (a) Algebraic representation; (b) truth table; (c) graphic symbol; (d) derivation of properties of $C \oplus B \oplus A$.

proven this *boolean identity:*

$$(C \oplus B) \oplus A = C \oplus (B \oplus A)$$

Consequently, since the order of operations makes no difference, it makes sense to express the function without parentheses:

$$F = C \oplus B \oplus A$$

The meaning of this function is not as obvious as an ANDing or an ORing of three variables. However, if we count the number of variables (C, B, and A) equal to 1 in each row of the truth table, as has been done in the fifth column, we note that

$$F = C \oplus B \oplus A = \begin{cases} 1 & \text{if an odd number of variables equals 1} \\ 0 & \text{if an even number of variables equals 1} \end{cases}$$

The extension of this analysis to the general case for any number of variables gives

$$F = \cdots \oplus C \oplus B \oplus A = \begin{cases} 1 & \text{if an odd number of variables equals 1} \\ 0 & \text{if an even number of variables equals 1} \end{cases}$$

As a consequence, the exclusive-OR function is a *parity*-determining (i.e., oddness/evenness-determining) function.

2-3 LOGICAL PROBLEM FORMULATION

If we are given the word statement for a problem in which some binary (i.e., boolean) variable is a "wordy" function of some other binary variables, we can make sense out of these words by reexpressing them in a truth-table relationship between independent and dependent variables. First, however, we must define the variables more explicitly. The potency of this technique of first defining the variables and then the function with a truth table is that we avoid becoming overwhelmed by the problem. Rather, we break it down into small, easily manageable steps.

Example 2-7. Obtain a logical definition of a functioning automobile, in terms of whether its tires are inflated or flat.

Our first step is to define variables precisely. We might use the four variables *LF*, *RF*, *LR*, *RR* and their assignment of values

1 = inflated tire

0 = flat tire

made in Example 2-1. Next, we might define a variable *F* to indicate whether or not the automobile is functioning. More precisely, suppose we let

$$F = \begin{cases} 1 & \text{when the automobile is functioning} \\ 0 & \text{otherwise} \end{cases}$$

With these definitions we can begin a truth table and fill in the first row:

LF	*RF*	*LR*	*RR*	*F*	
0	0	0	0	0	(all tires are flat)

Proceeding row by row, we complete the truth table:

LF	RF	LR	RR	F	
0	0	0	0	0	
0	0	0	1	0	
0	0	1	0	0	
0	0	1	1	0	
0	1	0	0	0	
0	1	0	1	0	
0	1	1	0	0	
0	1	1	1	0	
1	0	0	0	0	
1	0	0	1	0	
1	0	1	0	0	
1	0	1	1	0	
1	1	0	0	0	
1	1	0	1	0	
1	1	1	0	0	
1	1	1	1	1	(all tires inflated)

This looks like the truth table for the AND function discussed in the last section. Consequently, we can write

$$F = LF \cdot RF \cdot LR \cdot RR$$

Example 2-8. Utilize truth tables to reconsider the Gray code–to–binary code conversion algorithm of Sec. 2-2.

There we obtained the relationship

$$b_{k-1} = \begin{cases} g_{k-1} & \text{if } b_k = 0 \\ \overline{g_{k-1}} & \text{if } b_k = 1 \end{cases}$$

Translating this into a truth table, we have

b_k	g_{k-1}	b_{k-1}
0	0	0
0	1	1
1	0	1
1	1	0

This looks like the truth table for the exclusive-OR function of the last section. Thus we can write

$$b_{k-1} = g_{k-1} \oplus b_k$$

This, together with the relationship found in Sec. 2-1 for the most significant bits

$$b_{n-1} = g_{n-1}$$

leads to the *implementation* of a Gray code-to-binary code converter shown in Fig. 2-10.

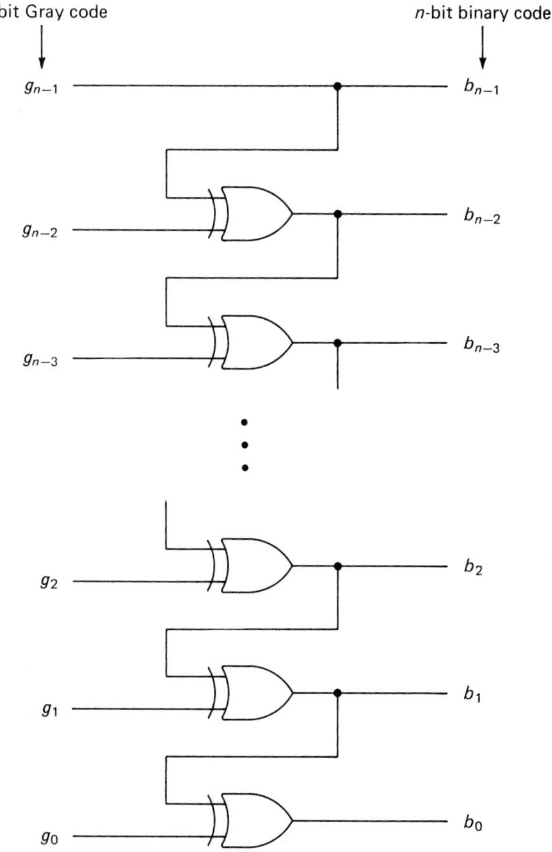

Figure 2-10. Gray code-to-binary code converter.

A real-life problem generally will not have a truth table which is identical to that for an AND function, or an OR function, or an exclusive-OR function. Handling these more general problems is a task that still lies ahead of us.

2-4 VOLTAGE LEVELS AND NOISE IMMUNITY

One of the virtues of the digital world is that it is independent of tight tolerances. Thus the representation of 1s and 0s requires only that when a variable's value is 1, it must be distinguishable from when its value is 0.

The *output* of a TTL (transistor-transistor logic) gate must be in one of the two bands in Fig. 2-11*a* in order to be functioning properly

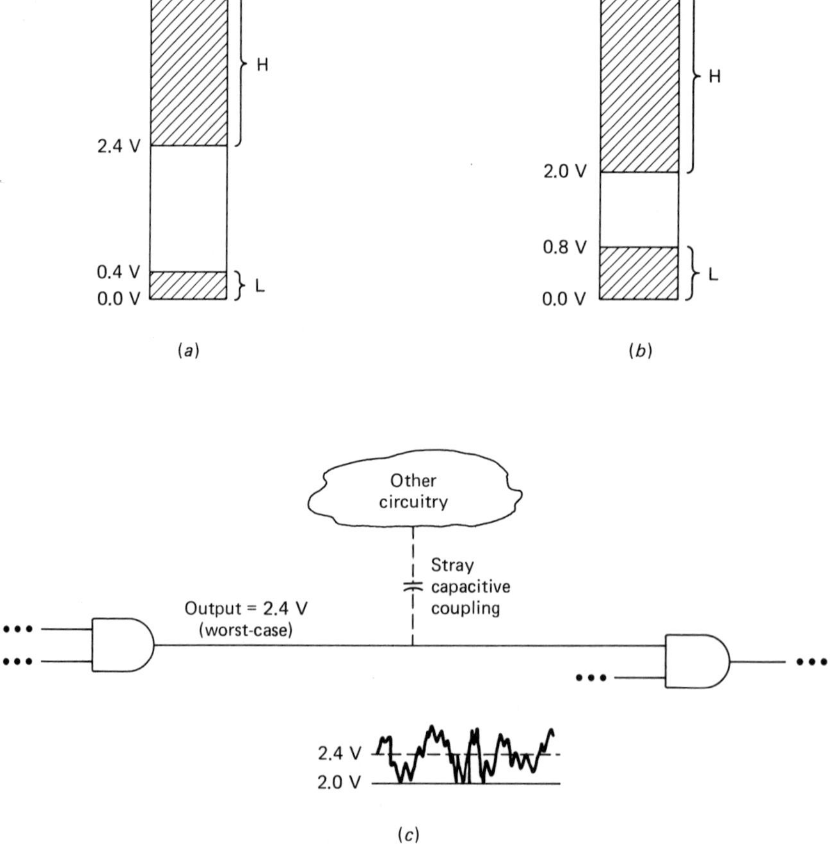

Figure 2-11. TTL guaranteed voltage levels and noise immunity. (a) Outputs; (b) inputs; (c) "H" noise immunity.

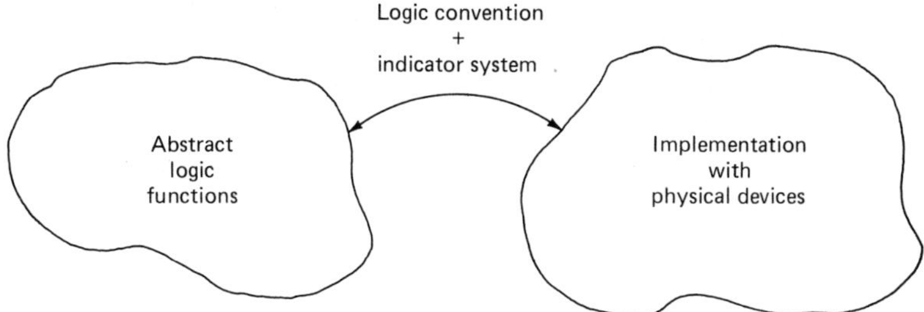

Figure 2-12. Bridging between abstract logic and physical implementation.

and within the manufacturer's specifications. That is, it must be in the band of voltages between 2.4 and 5.0 V (labeled H) when the output voltage is supposed to go high and in the band of voltages between 0.0 and 0.4 V (labeled L) when it is supposed to go low. Now consider Fig. 2-11*b*, which shows that the *input* to a TTL gate is within specification if it is between 2.0 and 5.0 V when it is supposed to go high and between 0.0 and 0.8 V when it is supposed to go low.

The difference between these two sets of specifications gives TTL logic a *guaranteed noise immunity* of 0.4 V. That is, when a gate output is supposed to be high, it will be above 2.4 V. In the worst case, it will have been loaded down to exactly 2.4 V, as shown in Fig. 2-11*c*. Even so, the wire between the gate output and the input to another gate can pick up as much as 0.4 V of peak noise voltage without having the gate input fall below the 2.0-V specification.

2-5 GRAPHIC REPRESENTATION OF LOGIC

We want to translate between the abstract logic functions of Secs. 2-2 and 2-3 and the physical implementations of these functions. The bridge between "abstract" and "physical" is a *logic convention*, supported by a related *indicator system*, as shown in Fig. 2-12. The dependency notation standard supports three possibilities:

1 Positive-logic convention + negation indicator system (○).
2 Negative-logic convention + negation indicator system (○).
3 Mixed-logic convention + polarity indicator system (⊳).

The positive-logic convention is widely used. It consistently defines the more positive of the two voltage levels (H of the last section) as logic 1 and the more negative level (L) as logic 0. A physical device, characterized by a voltage truth table as in Fig. 2-13*a*, is *defined* in positive-logic terms. To do this, a small circle is introduced as a

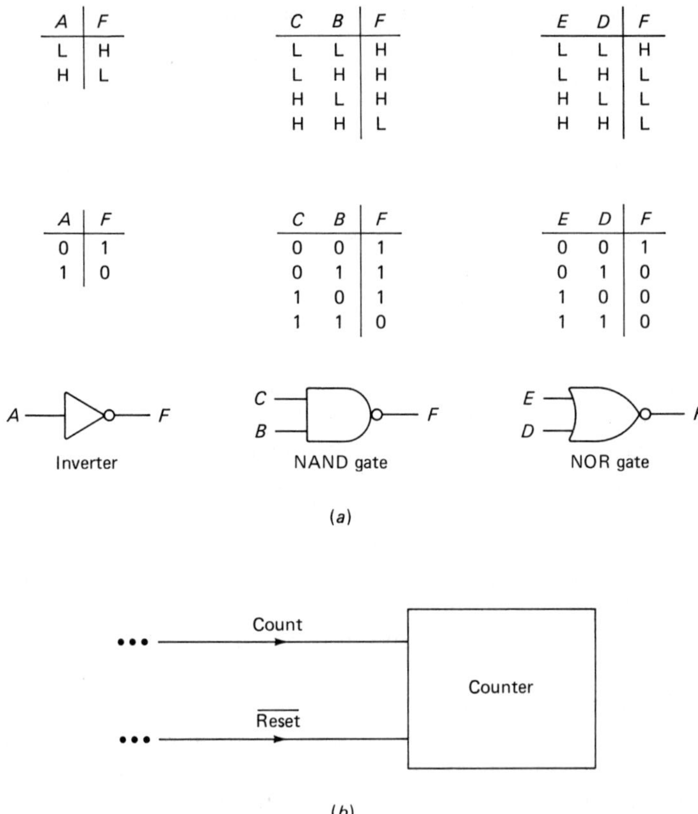

A	F
L	H
H	L

C	B	F
L	L	H
L	H	H
H	L	H
H	H	L

E	D	F
L	L	H
L	H	L
H	L	L
H	H	L

A	F
0	1
1	0

C	B	F
0	0	1
0	1	1
1	0	1
1	1	0

E	D	F
0	0	1
0	1	0
1	0	0
1	1	0

Figure 2-13. Positive-logic convention. (a) Device names and representation; (b) signal labeling.

negation indicator. It complements, or inverts, the logic meaning. This requires the *naming* of the logic functions shown in Fig. 2-13*a*. Thus users of the positive-logic convention describe the gates in their circuits as inverters, AND gates, NAND gates, OR gates, NOR gates, and so on. They label signals in their circuits with positive-logic labels, as in Fig. 2-13*b*. Thus the name "Count" implies that the counter on the right will count when its Count input is high (H), and will not count if its Count input is low (L). In contrast, the $\overline{\text{Reset}}$ input will *not* reset the counter when it is high, but will reset the counter when it is low.

The positive-logic convention is often used to support the definition of devices by IC manufacturers in their data books. For example, we might see a device called a "NAND gate." To bring attention to this use of the positive-logic convention in the naming of a device, some manufacturers will call this device a "positive-NAND gate."

The negative-logic convention (where L = logic 1 and H = logic 0) is rarely used today. As a consistent definition throughout the documentation of a complete instrument design, it made sense in the early days of integrated circuits. At that time, now-obsolete resistor-transistor logic (RTL) was a dominant logic family. Its only memory element during its first years was a flip-flop which was set and reset with low (L) inputs. A negative-logic convention supported a designer's intuition as he or she translated into circuitry the gating functions driving these flip-flop inputs.

The mixed-logic convention permits us to redefine the meaning of logic 1 (as either H or L) at every point in a circuit. This lends support to our intuitive understanding of a complex design. Inputs and outputs of each integrated circuit are defined so as to clarify our interpretation of the integrated circuit's operation.

The dependency notation standard makes use of small triangular *polarity indicators* to define voltage levels for the mixed-logic convention, as in Fig. 2-14*a*. For example, the voltage truth table of Fig. 2-14*b* can be described as an AND gate with active-low output, as shown in Fig. 2-14*c*. Note that the truth table of Fig. 2-14*c*, obtained by substituting H = 1 and L = 0 on inputs and H = 0 and L = 1 on the output, *is* the truth table of the AND function. Similarly, the definitions of Fig. 2-14*d* yield an OR gate with active-low inputs.

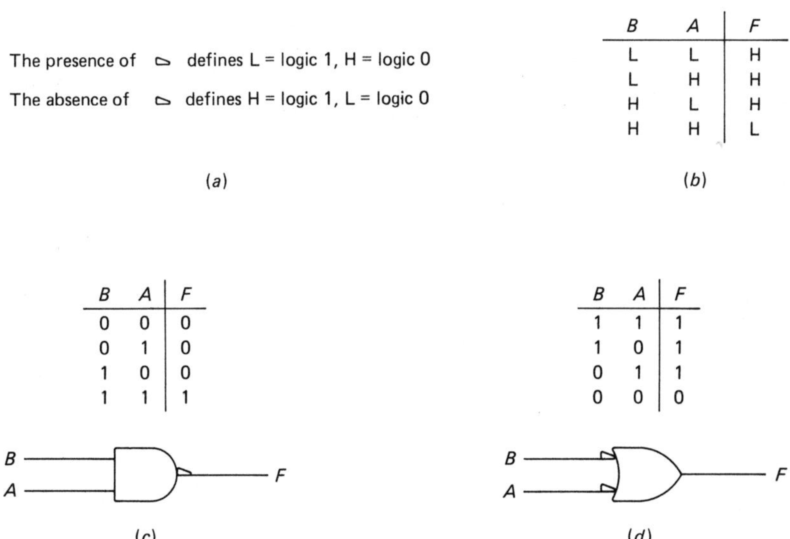

(b)

B	A	F
L	L	H
L	H	H
H	L	H
H	H	L

(c)

B	A	F
0	0	0
0	1	0
1	0	0
1	1	1

(d)

B	A	F
1	1	1
1	0	1
0	1	1
0	0	0

Figure 2-14. Polarity indicators and the mixed-logic convention. (a) Definition of polarity indicators; (b) voltage truth table of a device; (c) definition as an AND gate with active-low output; (d) definition as an OR gate with active-low inputs.

Voltage truth table	Positive-logic convention: Truth table	Positive-logic convention: Symbols	Positive-logic convention: Name	Mixed-logic convention: Truth tables	Mixed-logic convention: Symbols	Mixed-logic convention: Names
A F L H H L	A F 0 1 1 0	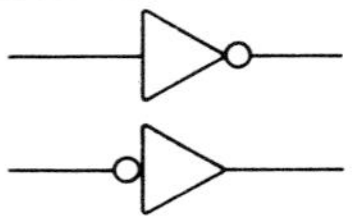	Inverter	A F 0 0 1 1	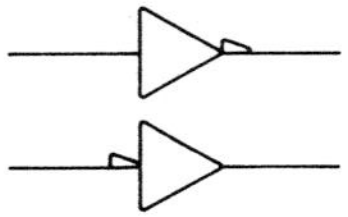	Inverter
C B F L L H L H H H L H H H L	C B F 0 0 1 0 1 1 1 0 1 1 1 0		NAND gate	C B F 0 0 0 0 1 0 1 0 0 1 1 1		AND gate (with active-low output)
				C B F 1 1 1 1 0 1 0 1 1 0 0 0		OR gate (with active-low inputs)
E D F L L H L H L H L L H H L	E D F 0 0 1 0 1 0 1 0 0 1 1 0		NOR gate	E D F 0 0 0 0 1 1 1 0 1 1 1 1		OR gate (with active-low output)
				E D F 1 1 1 1 0 0 0 1 0 0 0 0		AND gate (with active-low inputs)

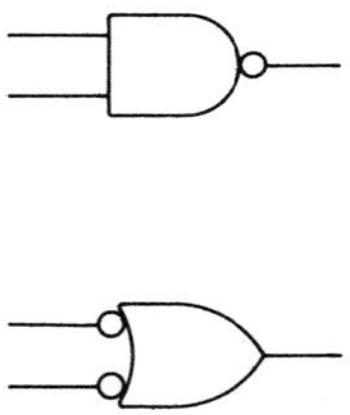

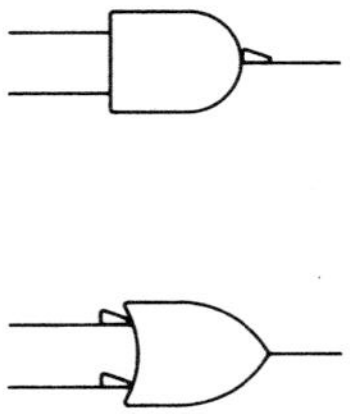

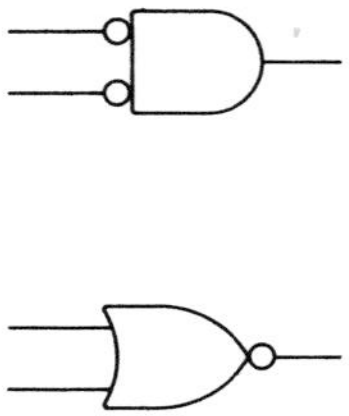

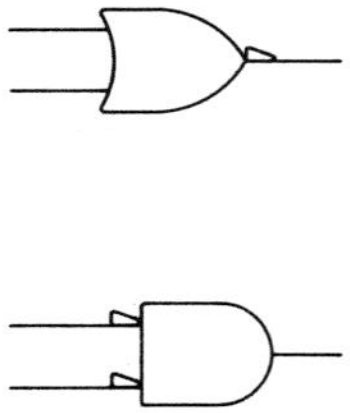

Figure 2-15. *Gate definitions.*

Our name for the device of Fig. 2-14 will depend upon the circumstances in which the name is used. While describing the operation of a circuit diagram employing the symbology of Fig. 2-14*c*, we might talk about the function of the "AND gate." Similarly, the operation of a circuit depicting the device as in Fig. 2-14*d* might lead us to talk about the function of the "OR gate." However, if we are identifying the specific integrated circuit used, we would probably fall back upon the positive-true name and refer to the "74LS00 quad two-input NAND gate." A comparison of the treatment afforded various devices by the positive-logic convention and the mixed-logic convention is shown in Fig. 2-15.

The presence of the small triangular polarity indicators in a logic diagram is a signal to us that the mixed-logic convention is being used. On the other hand, the presence of the small circular negation indicators tells us that either a positive-logic convention or a negative-logic convention is being used. Furthermore, unless the logic diagram is prominently marked "negative-logic convention," the presence of circular negation indicators almost certainly means that the positive-logic convention is being used. In this book we will employ the mixed-logic convention (and the triangular polarity indicators) exclusively.

Each of these conventions provides an alternative way to translate the H and L *logic levels* of a circuit into the 1 and 0 *logic states* used to define the operation of an IC. Furthermore, an *internal logic state* describes the logic state assumed to exist inside a graphic symbol at an input or output. For example, in Fig. 2-14*c* when B and A are both high, the absence of polarity indicators defines these inputs as being in the 1 state. The internal logic state of the output is 1. Finally, the *external logic state* of the output is also 1. We can translate this external logic state of 1 into a logic level of L because of the polarity indicator on the output.

The mixed-logic convention serves to make external logic states match up with internal logic states at all inputs and outputs. Furthermore, when we describe the device of Fig. 2-14*c* as an AND gate *with active-low output*, we are saying that an external logic state of 1 corresponds to a logic level of L.

Signal labeling on a logic diagram employing the mixed-logic convention must identify whether the signal at the labeled point is being defined active high or active low. A *signal-name convention* serves to convey this information. The approach shown in Fig. 2-16 is one which we will employ and one which finds reasonably wide use. In general, we will add −H or −L to a signal name to indicate whether the signal is defined active high or active low, respectively. However, if we omit this postscript, the implication is that the signal is defined active high. Thus if Count equals 1, the input to the counter in Fig.

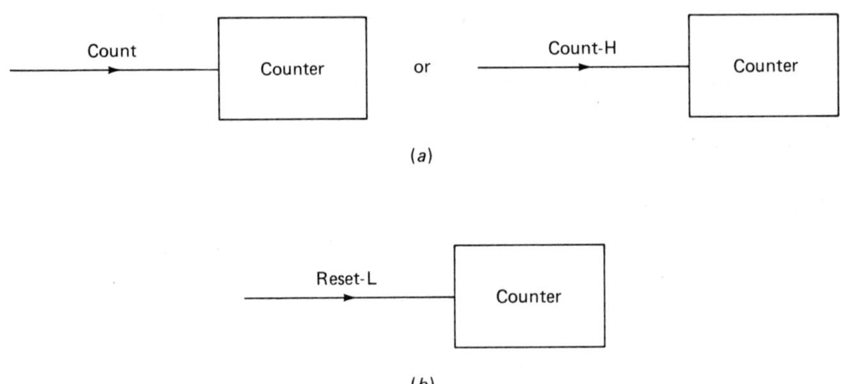

Figure 2-16. Signal labeling for the mixed-logic convention. (a) Active-high definition; (b) active-low definition.

2-16*a* is high. In contrast, if Reset equals 1, the input in Fig. 2-16*b* is low.

On occasion, we will use a label such as $\text{UP}/\overline{\text{DOWN}}$ (or $\text{UP}/\overline{\text{DOWN}}$-H) for a control signal that draws a distinction between two distinct modes of operation. For example, when the $\text{UP}/\overline{\text{DOWN}}$ line is high, the counter that it controls might count up. On the other hand, when $\text{UP}/\overline{\text{DOWN}}$ is low, the counter might count down.

2-6 TTL GATES

The hardware implementation of logic functions can employ any one of several logic families. Throughout this book, unless we have some specific reason to utilize another logic family, we will employ the low-power Schottky TTL (transistor-transistor logic) family.† This is the industry's most widely used family. The originator, Texas Instruments, provides parts having the designation 74LSxxx, where xxx represents a two- or three-digit number which distinguishes functionally different parts (e.g., a package of AND gates from a package of OR gates).

This 74LSxxx family is widely *second-sourced;* that is, the parts are produced by many manufacturers. Also, although the 74LSxxx family is designed to operate over a temperature range from 0 to 70°C, it

† Throughly described in *The TTL Data Book for Design Engineers,* available at cost from Marketing Information Services, Texas Instruments Inc., P. O. Box 5012, MS 308, Dallas, TX 75222.

Family	Typical gate propagation delay (ns)	Typical power dissipation per gate (mW)	Comments
74LSxxx	10	2	Industry-standard general-purpose TTL logic
74Sxxx	3	19	Industry-standard fast TTL logic
74ALSxxx	5	1	Advanced versions of the two families listed above, introduced in 1979
74ASxxx	1.5	22	
74xxx	10	10	Obsolete logic families
74Lxxx	33	1	
74Hxxx	6	22	

Figure 2-17. TTL logic families.

is paralleled by 54LSxxx parts that can operate from −55 to +125°C. It is also a family that shares compatability with several related TTL families developed by Texas Instruments and having characteristics shown in Fig. 2-17.

The basic gate structure of the 74LSxxx family is exemplified by the structure shown in Fig. 2-18*a*. It is one of the four gates in a 74LS00 "quadruple two-input positive-NAND gate" chip. As discussed in Sec. 2-5, a logic diagram (employing the mixed-logic convention) would symbolize each of the gates in either of the ways shown in Fig. 2-18*c*, leading us to refer to it in the logic diagram as an AND gate (with active-low output) or an OR gate (with active-low inputs).

The output of the gate in Fig. 2-18 employs two transistors, Q_U and Q_D, to form what is known as a "totem pole" output. When the output is supposed to be pulled high, Q_U is turned on, providing *active pullup*. When the output is supposed to be pulled low, Q_D is turned on.

This output structure gives a TTL gate a low output impedance, whether it is pulling the output high or low. However, during switching, the off transistor turns on faster than the on transistor turns off. This creates a low-impedance path between the +5-V supply and ground at the moment of switching. If no precautions are taken, a "glitch" will appear on the power-supply line every time any TTL device switches, causing erratic operation of other TTL devices. The cure, shown in Fig. 2-19, is simple. Small (high-frequency) capac-

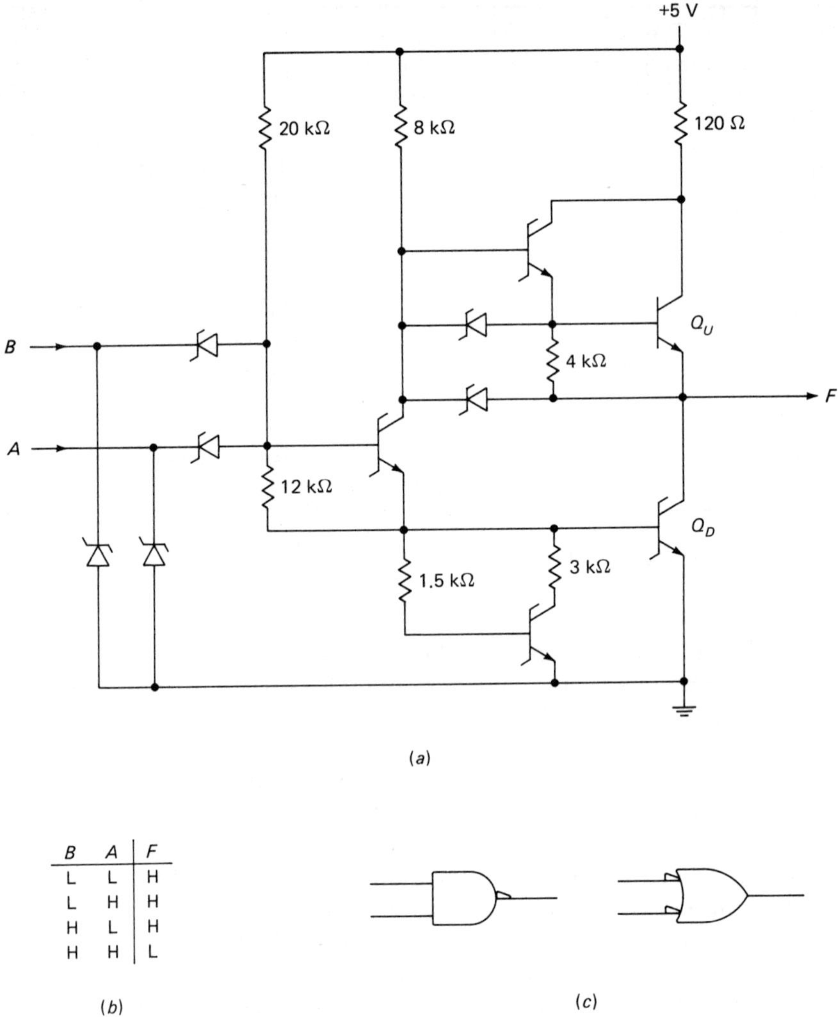

B	A	F
L	L	H
L	H	H
H	L	H
H	H	L

Figure 2-18. 74LS00 "two-input positive-NAND gate." (*a*) *Circuit;* (*b*) *voltage truth table;* (*c*) *symbolic representations.*

itors, perhaps 0.01 μF in value, are "sprinkled" liberally among the TTL logic chips. With one capacitor (wired between +5 V and ground) for every four or five TTL chips, what was a problem no longer exists.

Figure 2-20 lists the variety of TTL gates available with the standard, totem-pole output configuration. The alternate symbols shown arise from alternative interpretations of the voltage truth table, analogous to Fig. 2-14.

Figure 2-19. Use of capacitors with TTL logic. (Intelligent Systems Corp.)

2-7 IMPLEMENTING SMALL FUNCTIONS

In the past, a study of digital design techniques put significant emphasis upon ways to implement, and to simplify the implementation, of arbitrary boolean functions using gates. Today, this has changed, for the following reasons:

1 Before the advent of the microcomputer and of the programmable read-only memory (PROM), designers had *only* gates available for handling the complexity of a design. Today, any complexity at all is almost invariably transferred into one of these components—which handle it easily and well.

2 As we will see in Chap. 3, there are important reasons to minimize the "package count" of a digital design, that is, the number of ICs required. With this as a criterion, complex gating functions can almost invariably be implemented in fewer packages using PROMs.

3 Certain standard gating functions are available as MSI (medium-scale integrated) circuits. When one of these functions is required, the MSI circuit implementation will invariably require fewer packages than will an implementation with gates.

So how do designers employ gates now? They use them for simple functions and they use them intuitively.

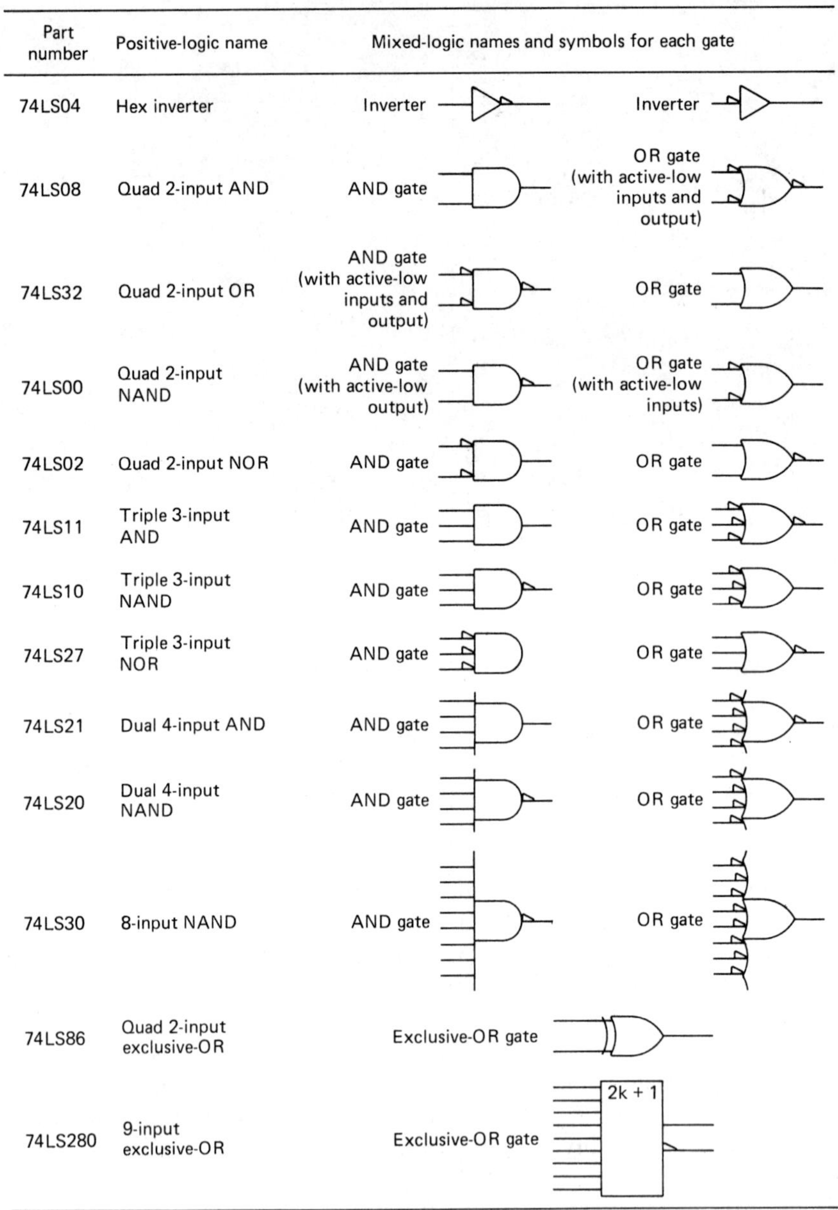

Part number	Positive-logic name	Mixed-logic names and symbols for each gate	
74LS04	Hex inverter	Inverter	Inverter
74LS08	Quad 2-input AND	AND gate	OR gate (with active-low inputs and output)
74LS32	Quad 2-input OR	AND gate (with active-low inputs and output)	OR gate
74LS00	Quad 2-input NAND	AND gate (with active-low output)	OR gate (with active-low inputs)
74LS02	Quad 2-input NOR	AND gate	OR gate
74LS11	Triple 3-input AND	AND gate	OR gate
74LS10	Triple 3-input NAND	AND gate	OR gate
74LS27	Triple 3-input NOR	AND gate	OR gate
74LS21	Dual 4-input AND	AND gate	OR gate
74LS20	Dual 4-input NAND	AND gate	OR gate
74LS30	8-input NAND	AND gate	OR gate
74LS86	Quad 2-input exclusive-OR	Exclusive-OR gate	
74LS280	9-input exclusive-OR	Exclusive-OR gate	

Figure 2-20. TTL gates with totem-pole outputs (14-pin DIPs).

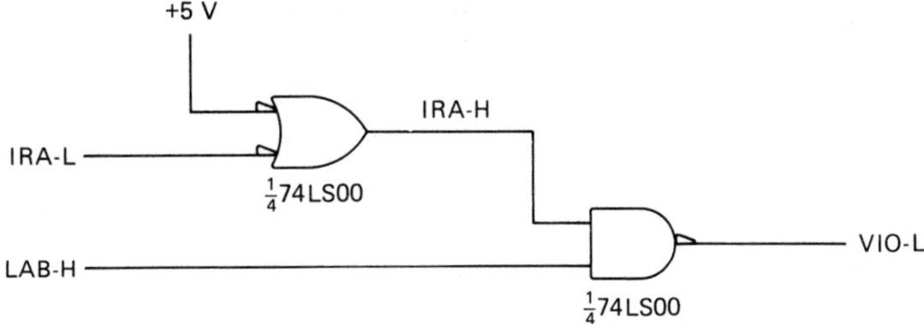

Figure 2-21. Solution for Example 2-9.

Example 2-9. Minimizing package count, generate a signal, called VIO-L, which is to be "active" (i.e., low) when LAB-H is active and IRA-L is active.

A solution is shown in Fig. 2-21 which requires one-half of a 74LS00 package. Notice the use of the gate forming IRA-H. This avoids the use of a separate 74LS04 inverter package.

Example 2-10. After implementing the other functions required in a design, we need to form A7-L from A7-H. We have one-third of a 74LS27 left unused after implementing everything else.

Two solutions are shown in Fig. 2-22. The solution in Fig. 2-22*b* might be preferred because it does not put as much of a load on the A7-H signal, if that is important. We will discuss loading in Sec. 2-8.

Example 2-11. Minimizing package count, generate BWE-L so as to be active when WEN-H is active and when either VRWA-L is active or VROA-L is active.

The solution is shown in Fig. 2-23.

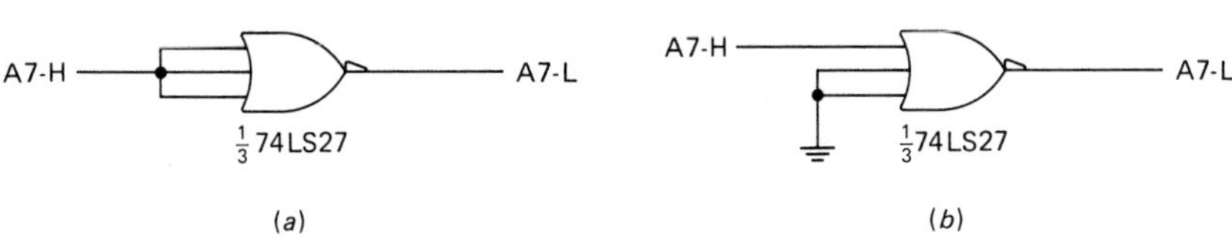

Figure 2-22. Two solutions for Example 2-10.

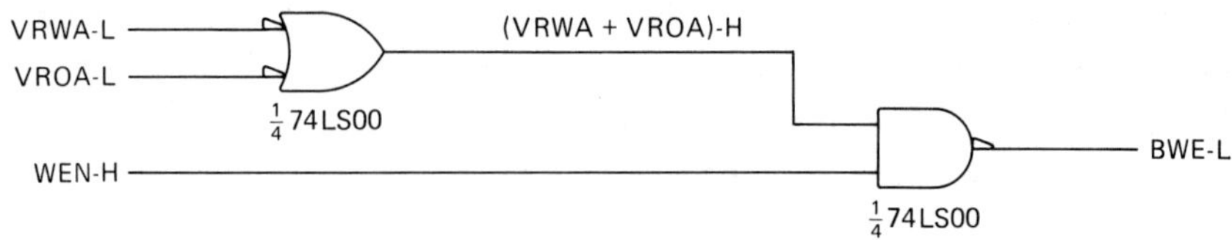

Figure 2-23. Solution for Example 2-11.

Example 2-12. Minimizing package count, generate Test-H from Sense-H and Inv-L so as to satisfy

$$\text{Test} = \begin{cases} \text{Sense} & \text{if Inv} = 0 \\ \overline{\text{Sense}} & \text{if Inv} = 1 \end{cases}$$

Making a truth table, we have

Inv	Sense	Test
0	0	0
0	1	1
1	0	1
1	1	0

We recognize the exclusive-OR function. The solution is shown in Fig. 2-24. Note the use of the extra exclusive-OR gate to form Inv-H from Inv-L.

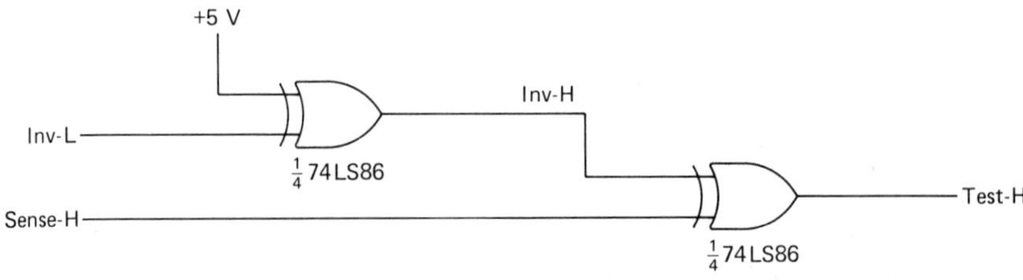

Figure 2-24. Solution for Example 2-12.

If you are aware of "minimization techniques"† and feel nervous about this wholesale bypassing of them, you might do either of the following two things:

1 Study these techniques, using almost any older digital design textbook.
2 Look at the service manual for several modern instruments and convince yourself that designers are indeed using gating circuitry only in rather simple ways.

2-8 LOADING RULES

Loading rules constrain our use of a logic family due to the limited drive capability of outputs. We cannot connect the output of a TTL gate to too many other gate inputs and still expect it to rise above 2.4 V, the level specified for a TTL device when its output is supposed to be high (as discussed in Sec. 2-4). Similarly, we cannot expect an overloaded gate to drive its output below the guaranteed 0.4-V specification when it is supposed to be low.

Figure 2-25 lists the specifications for several TTL logic families. Notice that the currents involved are rather different, depending upon whether the logic level is high or low. An output is described by the current it can *sink* when it is low, and by the current it can *source* when it is high, as shown in Fig. 2-26. We also speak of the *fan-out* capability of a logic family as the number of gates that can be driven by another gate.

Example 2-13. What is the fan-out capability of the 74LSxxx logic family?

$$\text{Fan-out (low)} = \frac{8 \text{ mA}}{0.4 \text{ mA}} = 20$$

$$\text{Fan-out (high)} = \frac{400\ \mu\text{A}}{20\ \mu\text{A}} = 20$$

Since the minimum of these two is 20, the fan-out is 20. That is, a 74LSxxx gate can drive up to 20 other 74LSxxx gates.

---

† Such as Karnaugh maps or the Quine-McCluskey method.

Family	Minimum low-level output current	Maximum low-level input current
74LSxxx	8 mA	0.4 mA
74Sxxx	20 mA	2.0 mA
74xxx ("standard TTL" loading)	16 mA	1.6 mA

(a)

Family	Minimum high-level output current	Maximum high-level input current
74LSxxx	400 μA	20 μA
74Sxxx	1000 μA	50 μA
74xxx ("standard TTL" loading)	400 μA	40 μA

(b)

Figure 2-25. Loading characteristics of TTL gates with totem-pole outputs. (a) Low-level characteristics; (b) high-level characteristics.

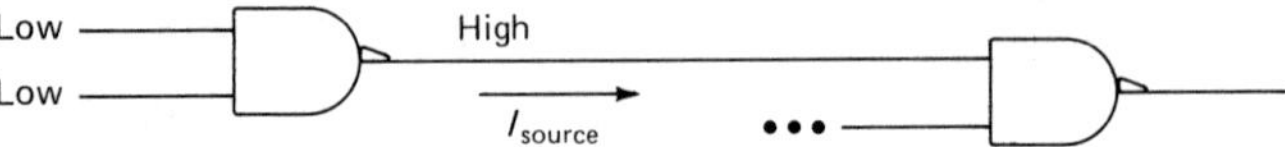

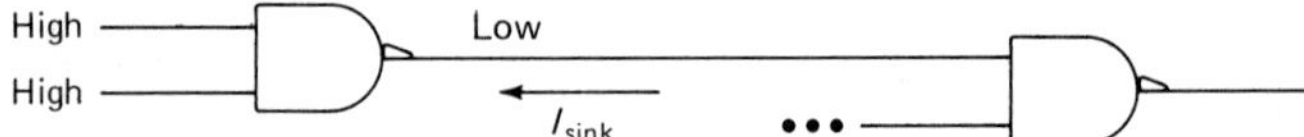

Figure 2-26. Source and sink loads.

Example 2-14. What is the fan-out capability of a 74LSxxx gate driving 74xxx gates?

$$\text{Fan-out (low)} = \frac{8\ \text{mA}}{1.6\ \text{mA}} = 5$$

$$\text{Fan-out (high)} = \frac{400\ \mu\text{A}}{20\ \mu\text{A}} = 10$$

In this case the fan-out is limited to 5 by the low-level specifications. That is, a 74LSxxx gate can drive no more than five 74xxx gates and still be guaranteed to remain within specifications.

Another loading-rule specification becomes important as we try to operate logic near the upper limit of its speed capability. The *propagation delay* of a TTL gate is defined as the time it takes for the gate output to change in response to a change on its input. More precisely for TTL logic, this time is measured as shown in Fig. 2-27. Notice in Fig. 2-27*b* that the propagation delay is actually measured between crossings of the *nominal threshold voltage* by the input and output. The threshold voltage is that voltage on the input that will produce the same voltage on the output. This is slightly lower for 74LSxxx parts (1.3 V) than it is for 74Sxxx or 74xxx parts (1.5 V).

As far as loading rules are concerned, notice in Fig. 2-27*a* that the specification is made with a conservative fan-out of 10. However, the *capacitive loading* used in the measurement may not be so conservative, depending upon how an actual circuit is implemented. For example, printed-circuit-board wiring might be estimated to add a capacitance of roughly 30 pF/ft (for 0.025-in.-width conductor on standard G10 glass epoxy board). Accordingly, the specifications, shown in Fig. 2-28, really assume that the interconnections between parts are equivalent to no more than 6 in of PC-board wiring.

2-9 DEPENDENCY NOTATION: DECODERS

Combinational circuitry encompasses the gating circuitry we have been discussing, together with any other circuits where the outputs are boolean functions of the inputs. In this section and the next, we will consider two types of medium-scale integrated (MSI) circuits which solve two broad classes of combinational problems.

Also in this section, we will introduce *dependency notation*, which graphically portrays the function of an integrated circuit. We can look at a logic diagram expressed in this notation and understand what use each IC makes of each input as it generates each output. Furthermore, we do not have to have an IC manufacturer's book open before us to do this. However, we do have to learn the language of dependency notation before these benefits are available to us. To help with this learning, we will introduce the notation by describing actual 74LSxxx parts. Also, we will include the *pin-outs* of these parts.

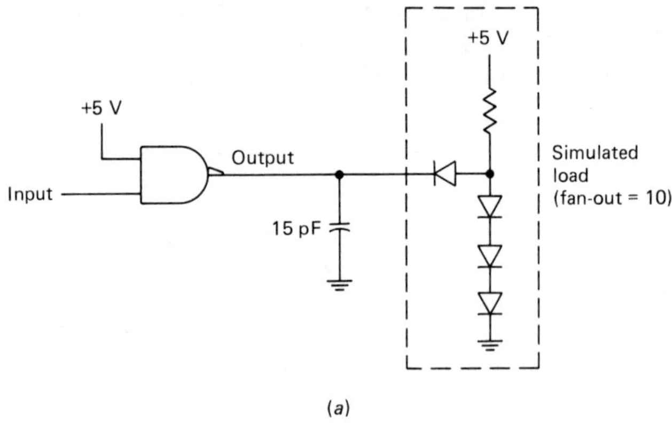

(a)

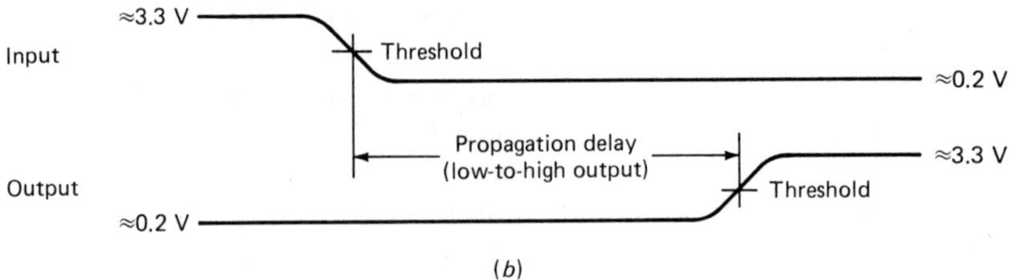

(b)

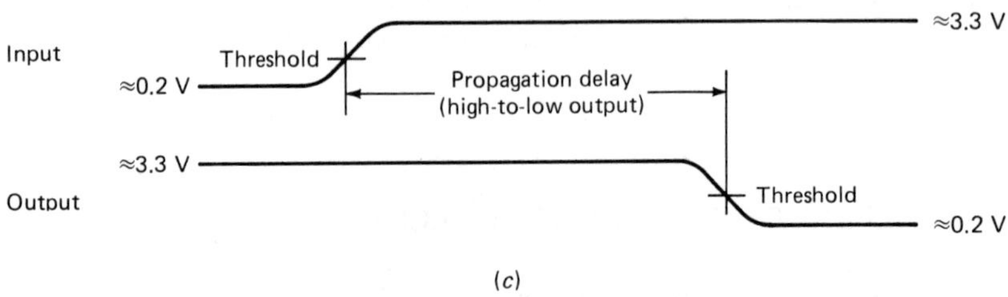

(c)

Figure 2-27. Measuring propagation delays. (*a*) *Test circuit;* (*b*) *measurement for low-to-high output;* (*c*) *measurement for high-to-low output.*

Then, if a question arises as to which pin in a data book description of the part corresponds to one of the lines in the dependency notation symbol, we can use the pin number to make the identification.

To aid the interpretation of logic diagrams, the dependency standard encourages signal flow from left to right, or top to bottom, or both. This is illustrated in Fig. 2-29*a*. In addition, the standard encourages the orientation of dependency notation symbols with inputs on the left and outputs on the right, as in Fig. 2-29*b*.

Family	Maximum propagation delay	
	Low-to-high output	High-to-low output
74LSxxx	15 ns	15 ns
74Sxxx	5 ns	5 ns
74xxx ("standard TLL")	22 ns	15 ns

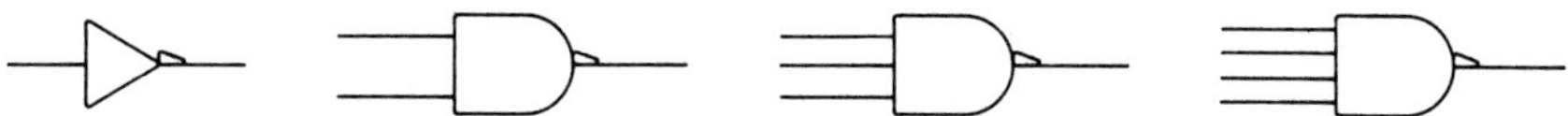

Figure 2-28. Maximum propagation delay for the gates shown, with totem-pole outputs and subject to a fan-out of 10 and a capacitive loading of 15 pF.

Decoders are a fundamental building block for digital design. They are also a fundamental entity for understanding dependency notation.† In this section we will "beat decoders to death," both to gain dependency notation symbols for a variety of 74LSxxx decoder chips and to introduce a variety of dependency notation ideas. Furthermore, we will find that the basic symbol used for a decoder is employed as *part* of the symbol for other types of devices.

The decoder of Fig. 2-30 has inputs on the left and outputs on the right. The X/Y notation at the top designates that this device sums the weights associated with *active* inputs. These inputs are labeled according to their *weights* of 1, 2, 4, and 8. The output whose weight equals the sum of the weights of the active inputs will be active; the other nine outputs will be inactive.

Example 2-15. If pins 15 and 14 are high, while pins 13 and 12 are low, what will the outputs of a 74LS42 be?

Since all inputs are active high, the 1 and 2 weights form a sum of 3. Since all outputs are active low, the 3 output (pin 4) will be low, while all the other outputs will be high.

---

† The symbology standard uses "coder" as a general term for a number of functions, one of which is a decoder.

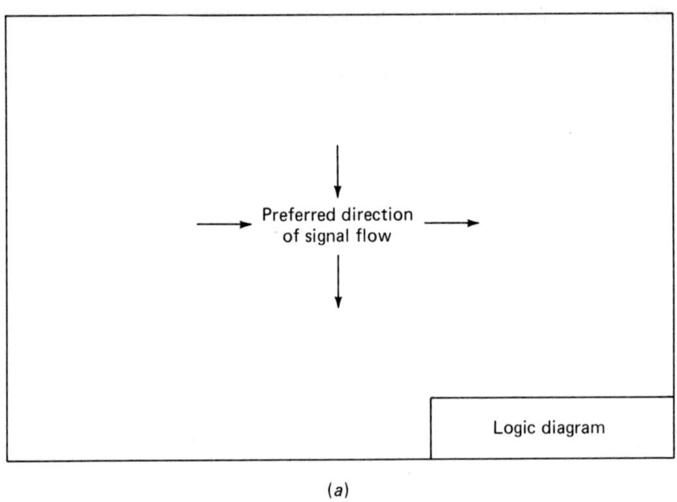

(a)

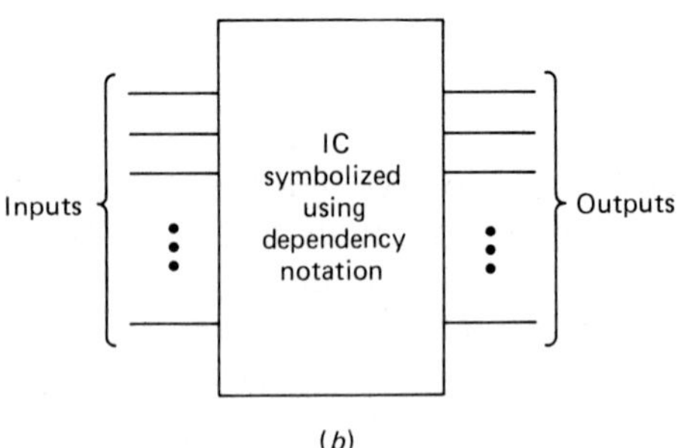

(b)

Figure 2-29. Preferred (but not required) directions of signal flow. (a) Entire logic diagram; (b) individual integrated circuit.

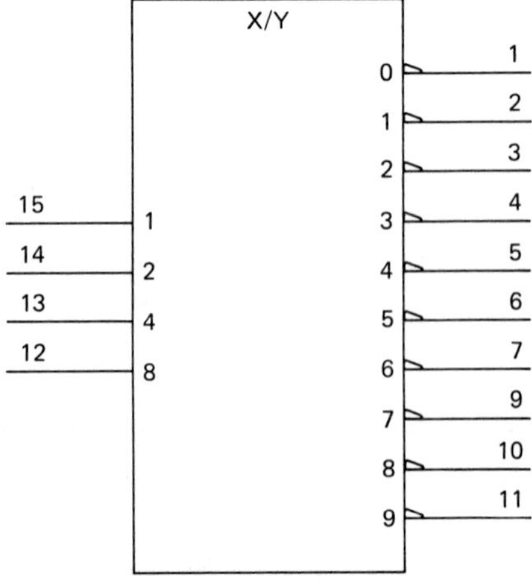

Figure 2-30. 74LS42, 4-line-to-10-line decoder. (Texas Instruments.)

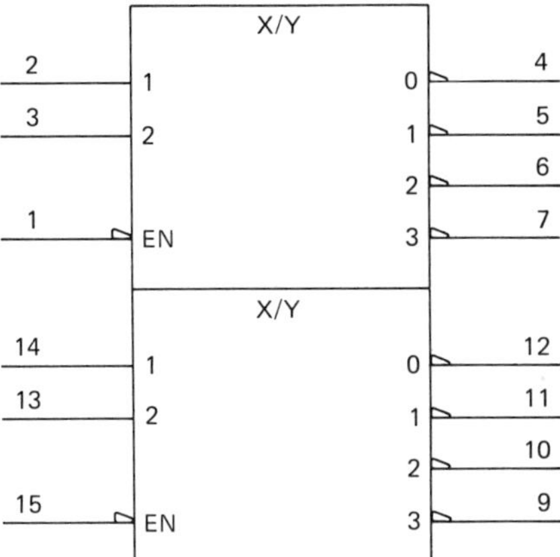

Figure 2-31. 74LS139, dual 2-line-to-4-line decoder, illustrating the use of EN inputs. (Texas Instruments.)

Before moving on to another decoder circuit, we must digress and develop a fundamental label used with dependency notation. The letters EN are *reserved* solely to identify inputs that *enable* outputs. If an input labeled EN is active, all outputs are active or inactive according to whatever else affects them. On the other hand, if the EN input is inactive, all outputs are inactive.

Now consider the dual decoder shown in Fig. 2-31. Even though these two decoders reside on the same IC, they do not interact with each other, as indicated by the horizontal line across the middle of the symbol which divides the symbol into two *logic elements.*† The EN symbol in each logic element signifies that this input must be active in order for any of the four outputs *in the same logic element* to be active.

Example 2-16. What inputs are required to drive pin 6 low on a 74LS139 chip?

The EN input in the upper logic element indicates that this input must be active before any of the outputs of the upper logic element can be active. Thus to drive pin 6 low (i.e., to make it active), pin 1 must be low, pin 3 must be high, and pin 2 must be low.

---

† A *logic element* is a part of an IC symbol having a well-defined logic function and output(s) which are defined functions of the input(s) and variables internal to the element.

The dependency standard actually employs several ways for representing an ANDing of variables. One way is with the isolated gate symbol of Fig. 2-18c. The other ways are used in dependency notation symbols. The EN input is one of these; an "&" enclosed in a rectangular block *within* a dependency symbol is the other. The latter two representations are combined in the decoder dependency symbol shown in Fig. 2-32. In this case the three inputs to the & block must all be active for EN to be active. Similarly, EN must be active in order for any of the outputs to be active.

Example 2-17. What inputs to a 74LS138 are necessary in order for the 6 output to be low?

In order to make *any* output go low (i.e., be active), pins 4 and 5 must both be low and pin 6 high. Furthermore, pins 2 and 3 must be high and pin 1 low to give an "input sum" of 4 + 2 = 6. With these inputs, the 6 output (pin 9) will be low and all the other outputs will be high.

Example 2-18. If all six inputs of a 74LS138 are low, what will the outputs be?

Since pin 6 is defined active high and yet has a low input, the entire decoder is inactive. That is, all outputs are inactive. Therefore, they are all high.

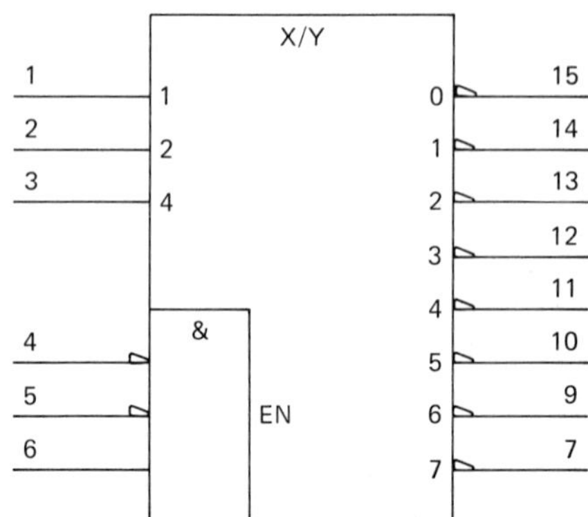

Figure 2-32. 74LS138, 3-line-to-8-line decoder, illustrating the use of the & and EN symbols for ANDing. (Texas Instruments.)

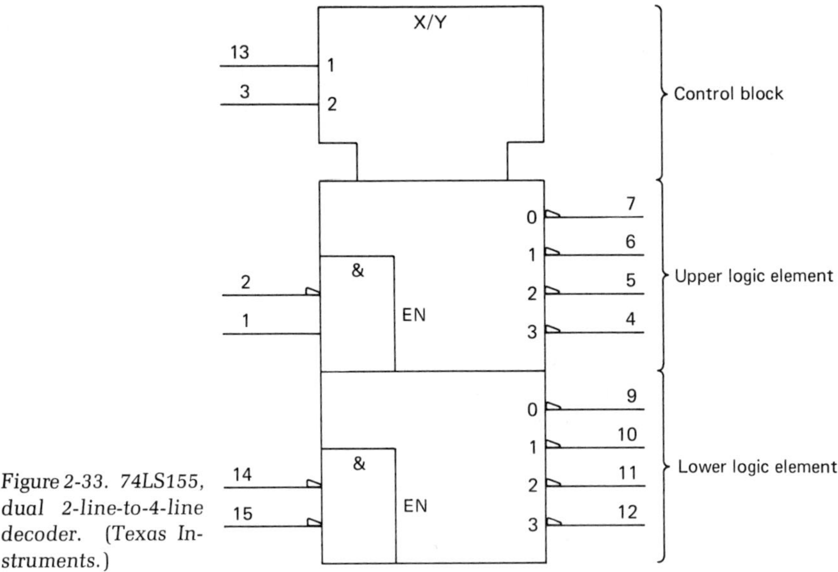

Figure 2-33. 74LS155, dual 2-line-to-4-line decoder. (Texas Instruments.)

One of the strengths of dependency notation is its clear representation of circuits that *share* control inputs. The dual decoder of Fig. 2-33 illustrates this. The standard-shaped *control block* on top includes the X/Y symbol, which indicates the decoder function. Because it is a control block, its function is applied equally to all the attached logic elements.

Example 2-19. If all inputs of a 74LS155 dual decoder chip are pulled low, what will the outputs do?

First, the decoder-type control block has inputs that sum to 0. Consequently, the only outputs that can possibly be active (i.e., low) are pins 7 and 9. However, the upper logic element is disabled by the inactive input on pin 1, so pin 7 will be inactive (i.e., high). On the other hand, both inputs to the & block in the lower logic element are active, enabling the decoded output, pin 9. Thus all the outputs will be high except for the 0 output of the lower logic element (pin 9), which will be low.

Example 2-20. What inputs will drive the 3 output of the upper decoder of Fig. 2-33 low?

First, the weights associated with the active inputs to the decoder-type control block must sum to 3. Consequently, pins 3 and 13 must both be high so that 2 + 1 = 3. Next, outputs of the upper decoder must be enabled with active inputs on pins 2 and 1. Therefore, pin 2 must be low and pin 1 high.

2-10 DEPENDENCY NOTATION: MULTIPLEXERS

All the logic elements employed in the IC symbols of the last section were decoders, identified by the X/Y symbol. As a basic logic device, a multiplexer is identified by the label MUX. To represent multiplexers we must define a fundamental dependency notation mechanism called *AND-dependency*. The letter G is *reserved* solely for implementing AND-dependency. Whenever G is used, it will be followed by a number. Then, any other input or output in the same logic element labeled with this same number is ANDed with the input (or other entity) labeled G.

A multiplexer is shown in Fig. 2-34. The cryptic $G\frac{0}{7}$ really stands for eight AND-dependency symbols:

G0, G1, G2, G3, G4, G5, G6, G7

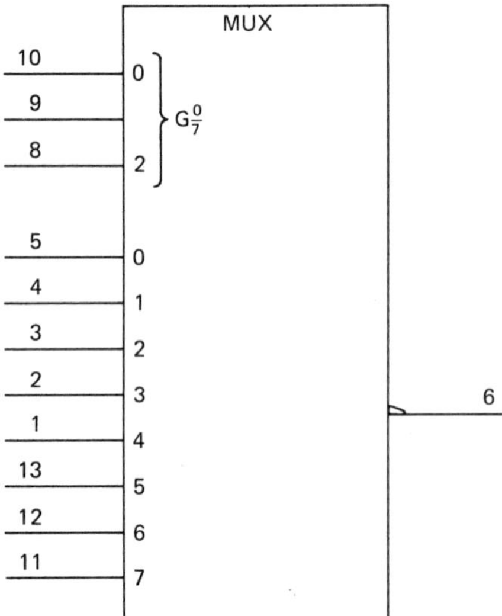

Figure 2-34. 74LS152, 8-line-to-1-line multiplexer. (Texas Instruments.)

One of these is selected by the *binary grouping symbol*, which weights the active inputs on pins 10, 9, and 8 with successive powers of 2 (i.e., $2^0 = 1$, $2^1 = 2$, and $2^2 = 4$). The resulting net weight of the active inputs is *translated* into one of the eight values 0, . . . , 7 defined by the $G\frac{0}{7}$ symbol, making one of these AND-dependency symbols active. More generally, if we had written $G\frac{10}{17}$, a net weight of 0 would have been translated into the lowest of the eight G values (i.e., 10), whereas a net weight of 7 would have been translated into the highest (i.e., 17). This mechanism permits us to translate input weights into arbitrary G numbers. In the case of the multiplexer of Fig. 2-34, the AND-dependency mechanism makes the output active if the selected input is active.

Example 2-21. What inputs to a 74LS152 multiplexer will select the 3 input? How will the output be related to inputs in this case?

To select the 3 input, the binary grouping symbol inputs must sum to 3, so pin 8 must be low while pins 9 and 10 must both be high. This makes G3 active and G0, G1, G2, G4, G5, G6, and G7 inactive. With only G3 active, only the 3 input affects the output. If it is active, the output will be active; otherwise, the output will be inactive. That is, if pin 2 is high (i.e., active), pin 6 will be low (i.e., active). If pin 2 is low, pin 6 will be high. If pin 2 represents a variable with the name INH-H, the multiplexer has made its output equal to INH-L.

The multiplexer of Fig. 2-35 is almost identical to that of Fig. 2-34 except for the addition of an enable control input, labeled EN, and an active-high output. Although there are several alternative ways of representing this IC (or *any* IC) with dependency notation, the representation shown here has the advantage of directly showing that neither output will be active unless the EN input is active. That is, if the multiplexer is disabled (with pin 7 high), pin 5 will be low and pin 6 high.

Example 2-22. What must we do so that the output on pin 5 of a 74LS151 is identical to the input on pin 13?

First, pin 7 must be low so that the outputs can be active. Then to select the input on pin 13, the binary grouping symbol must sum to 6, so that G6 will be active. This requires that pins 9 and 10 be high and pin

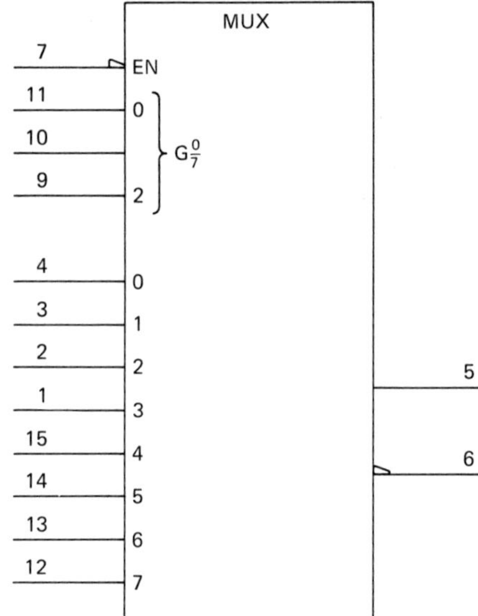

Figure 2-35. 74LS151, 8-line-to-1-line multiplexer. (Texas Instruments.)

11 low. Now, if pin 13 is active, pins 5 and 6 will be active. If pin 13 is inactive, pins 5 and 6 will be inactive also. That is, if pin 13 is high, pin 5 will be high and pin 6 low. On the other hand, if pin 13 is low, pin 5 will be low and pin 6 high.

One last example of a multiplexer is shown in Fig. 2-36. It employs a control block and four logic elements to steer either of two sets of four input lines to four output lines, if the chip is enabled.

Example 2-23. If pin 15 of a 74LS157 multiplexer is high, describe how the four outputs are related to the other inputs.

With pin 15 high, the enable input EN is inactive. Consequently, all outputs will be inactive, regardless of any other inputs.

Example 2-24. What inputs to a 74LS157 multiplexer are required to steer the 1 inputs to the outputs?

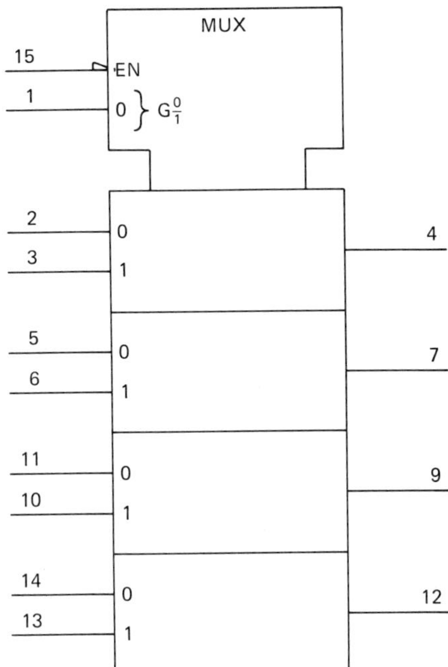

Figure 2-36. 74LS157, quad 2-line-to-1-line multiplexer. (Texas Instruments.)

For the outputs to be active, pin 15 must be low. Then if pin 1 is high (i.e., active), the binary grouping symbol will sum to 1, so that G1 will be active. Thus the pin 4 output will be active if and only if the pin 3 input is active. That is, pin 4 will be high when pin 3 is high, but it will be low when pin 3 is low. Hence the output of this logic element follows its 1 input. The same is true of the other three logic elements.

2-11 OPEN-COLLECTOR AND THREE-STATE OUTPUTS

In Sec. 2-6 we discussed the totem-pole output structure of normal TTL circuits. The following problems have given rise to alternative output structures:

- Bussing
- Expanding

The data bus of a multiple-chip microcomputer configuration is a common example of the use of *bussing*. The central processor (CPU) can drive these lines when it writes data to memory. A memory chip

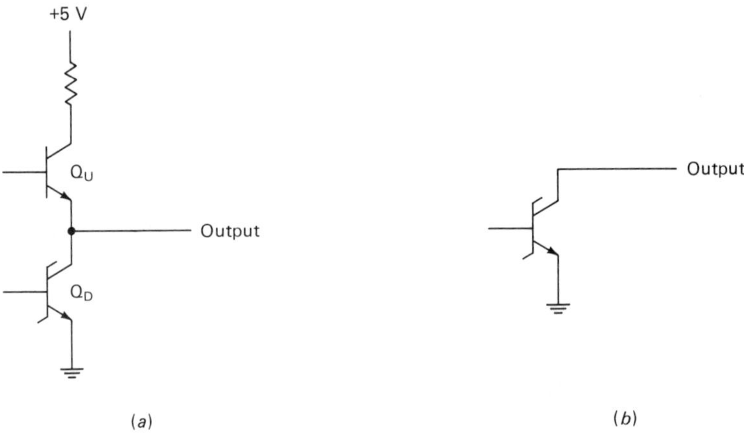

Figure 2-37. TTL output structures. (a) Totem-pole or three-state; (b) open-collector.

can drive these same lines when the CPU reads from memory. With more than one device able to drive the same lines, each must have an output structure that permits its output to be "turned off" when another device is supposed to be driving the bus.

Often a logic function is available to us as an integrated circuit. *Expanding* lets us combine these ICs to obtain a larger version of the same function. This occurs most frequently with memory chips. For example, the programmable read-only memory (PROM) chips to be discussed in the next section come only in standard sizes. If the largest PROM available to us is a 512 × 4 PROM (which has 9 inputs, 4 outputs, and is packaged in a 16-pin DIP), what do we do if we actually need a 2048 × 12 PROM? As we shall see, either open-collector outputs or three-state outputs will help solve this problem.

The TTL *open-collector output* structure is shown in Fig. 2-37*b* in comparison with the normal totem-pole output structure of Fig. 2-37*a*. The pull-up transistor is simply omitted. Consequently, to function properly, a device with open-collector outputs requires external *pull-up resistors*. These might be individual, discrete resistors or one of the SIP (single-in-line package) resistor networks shown in Fig. 2-38. Dependency notation identifies open-collector outputs with an underlined diamond, as illustrated in Fig. 2-39 for several ICs with open-collector outputs.

Sometimes the pull-up resistors used with open-collector outputs are built into the IC. Such an IC is said to have *passive pull-up* outputs. We will identify a passive pull-up output with a "⎐" symbol.

The output stage of a *three-state output* looks like a totem-pole

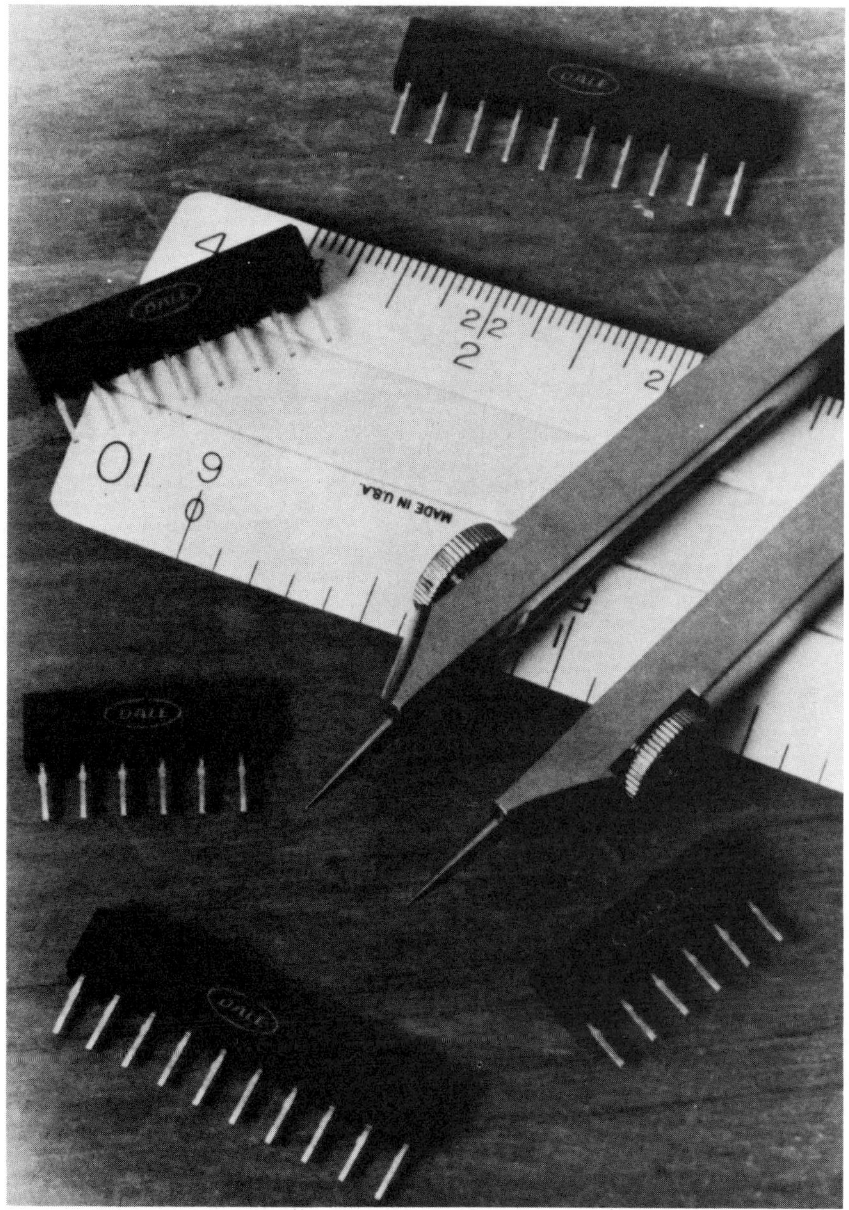

Figure 2-38. SIP resistor networks. (a) Devices.

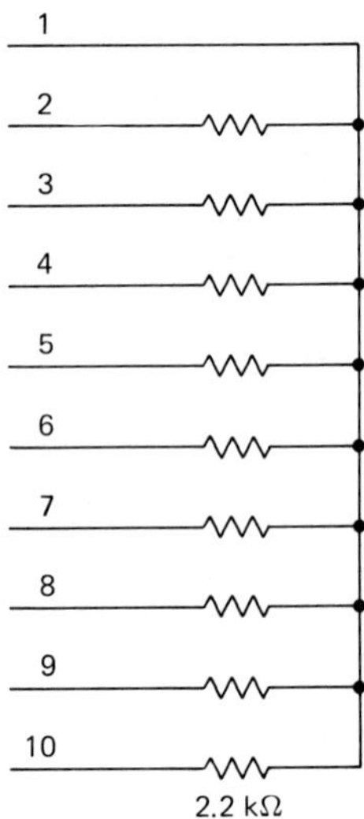

Figure 2-38b. Typical circuit. (Dale Electronics, Inc.)

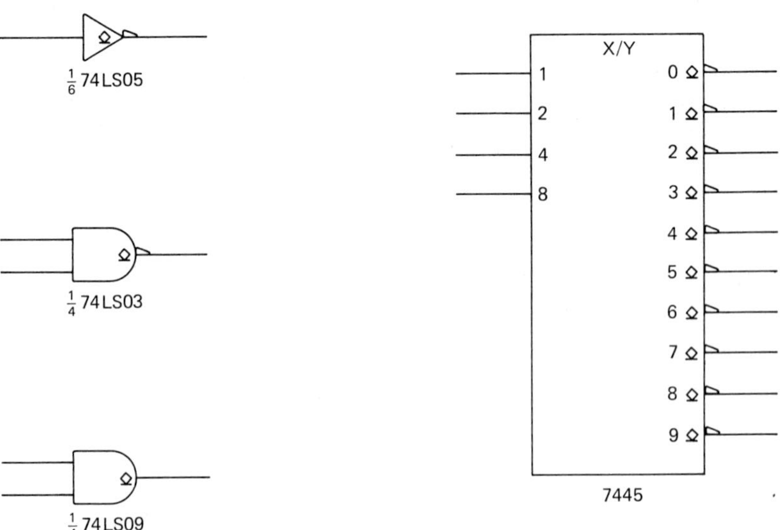

Figure 2-39. Representation of open-collector outputs.

output, as illustrated in Fig. 2-37*a*. The difference is in the circuitry that drives the two output transistors Q_U and Q_D. A device having a three-state output can turn off *both* transistors, putting the output into a high-impedance state. To any ICs connected to the output, the chip looks as if it has been removed from the circuit.

The EN enabling symbolism discussed earlier is defined in the dependency notation standard to handle both open-collector and three-state outputs. If an EN input is inactive, such outputs go to the high-impedance state. Going one step further, the standard also defines *ENABLE-dependency* to handle an enable input which does not affect *all* outputs of a logic element. Whenever EN is followed by a number, any other output in the same logic element labeled with the same number is enabled by the EN input. For example, consider the octal buffers with three-state outputs shown in Fig. 2-40. The upper four outputs are enabled by the input on pin 1 and the lower four outputs are enabled by the input on pin 19. The three-state outputs themselves are symbolized by the inverted triangle shown by each output line.

This 74LS244 illustrates another feature of the symbol standard. The "▷" indicates a device with unusual drive capability. Brackets are used within a symbol to permit concise, descriptive comments to be

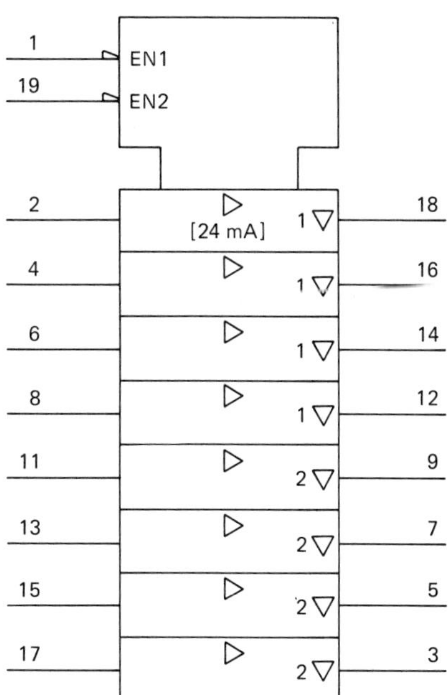

Figure 2-40. 74LS244, octal buffers with three-state outputs. (Texas Instruments.)

made. Thus [24 mA] beneath the ▷ implies that these buffers can drive loads up to 24 mA. If these devices had three-state outputs with normal drive capability, the ▷ would have been replaced by 1.

Example 2-25. Describe the output on pin 18 of the IC in Fig. 2-40 in terms of its inputs.

The symbolism indicates that pin 18 is the output of a logic element having two inputs (pin 2 and pin 1). If pin 1 is high, the enable input, EN1, will be inactive and the output on pin 18 will be in the high-impedance state. If pin 1 is low, the output on pin 18 will match the input on pin 2; that is, it will be active (i.e., high) if pin 2 is active (i.e., high), and it will be inactive (i.e., low) if pin 2 is inactive (i.e., low).

The distinctive-shaped symbol for a three-state buffer is shown in Fig. 2-41. The simplicity of the symbol does away with the need for further labeling.

To see how three-state outputs can be used to aid expansion, consider the two multiplexers of Fig. 2-42, each of which has its output available in both active-high and active-low form. By tying the three-state outputs together and then enabling only one of the chips at a time, we have created a 16-line–to–1-line multiplexer.

As we shall see in the next section, this method is also used for expanding programmable read-only memories (PROMs) which have three-state outputs. Corresponding output pins on the PROM chips will be tied together to form the expanded output. Then just one of the chips will be enabled at a time.

Expansion of open-collector PROMs leads to an identical circuit except that pull-up resistors must be added. All the disabled PROMs will let go of the output lines, which are pulled high by the pull-up resistors. Only the one enabled PROM can override the pull-up resistors, either pulling lines low or leaving them pulled up, so as to achieve the desired expanded PROM output.

Open-collector outputs offer a *further* possibility for expansion which is not paralleled by a corresponding capability of three-state outputs. Consider the 6-bit comparator of Fig. 2-43*a* and note the underlined diamond in the AND gate, signifying an open-collector output that will be turned off (i.e., go to the high-impedance state) when pin 7 is high. In using this comparator, we are reminded by the diamond to add an external pull-up resistor.

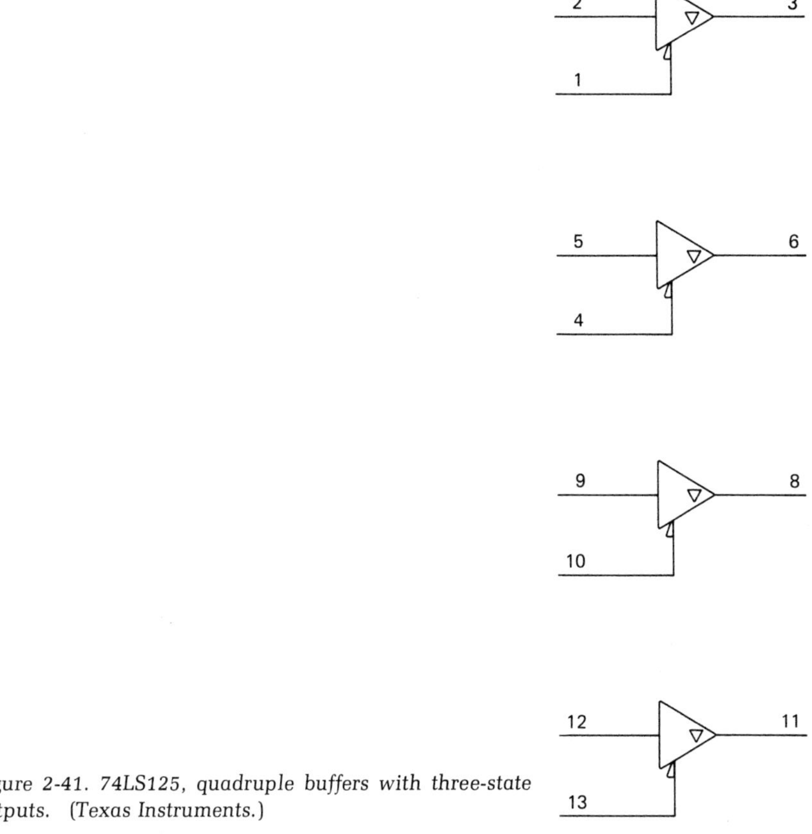

Figure 2-41. 74LS125, quadruple buffers with three-state outputs. (Texas Instruments.)

The dependency notation for this comparator is shown in Fig. 2-43*b*. The two binary grouping symbols define two numbers, P and Q. The output, labeled $P = Q$, is active if these numbers are equal and if the chip is enabled (with pin 7 low).

To expand this comparator, we will enable two of them *all of the time*, even though the active-high outputs are tied together. In general, if two or more *active-high*, open-collector outputs (of enabled devices) are tied together and to a pull-up resistor, the result is logically equivalent to ANDing these outputs together. That is, the resulting output will be active (i.e., high) if all the individual outputs are active (i.e., high). The symbolism for this connection is shown in Fig. 2-43*c* and is called dot-ANDing.

Tying open-collector, *active-low* outputs plus a pull-up resistor together (in enabled devices) is called dot-ORing. These powerful uses of open-collector outputs are summarized in Figs. 2-44 and 2-45.

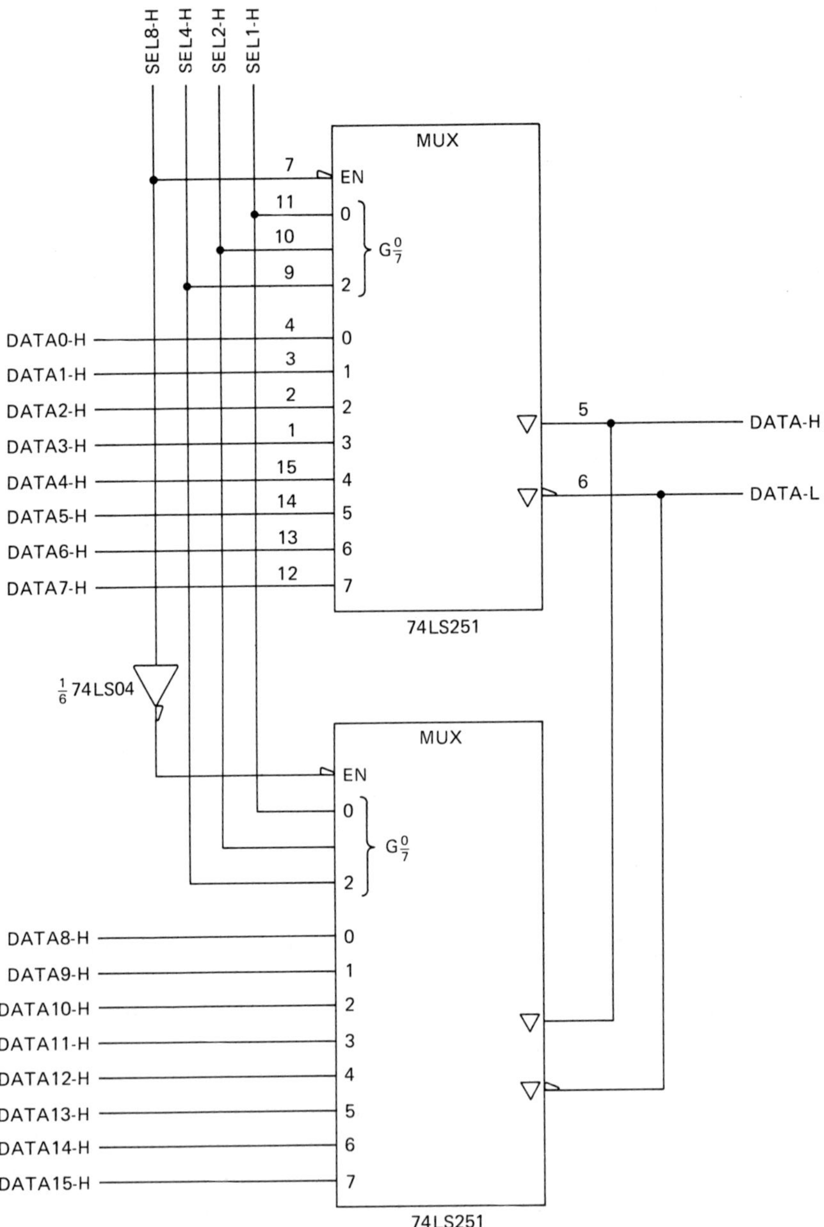

Figure 2-42. Expanding of 74LS251, 8-line-to-1-line multiplexer with three-state outputs. (Texas instruments.)

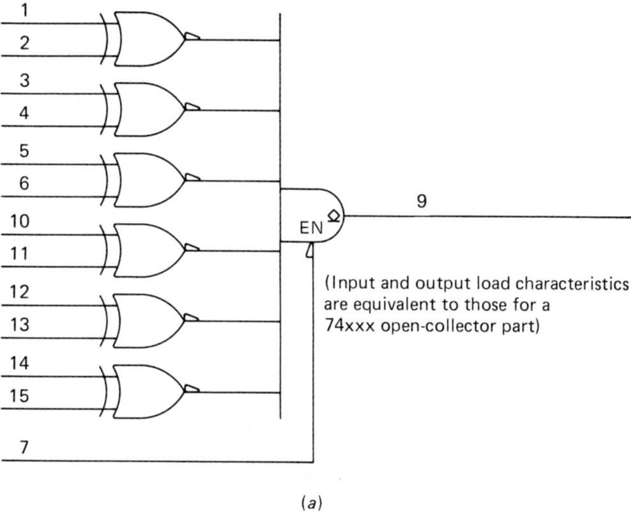

(a)

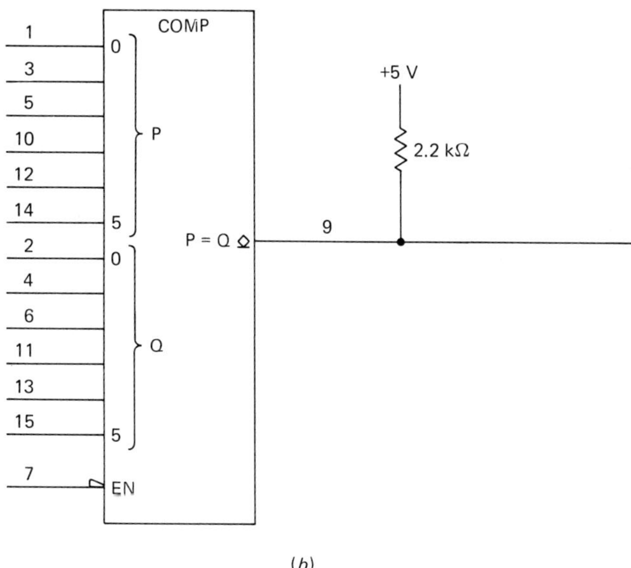

(b)

Figure 2-43. 8160, 6-bit comparator. (a) Circuit; (b) symbol, including pull-up resistor added to output.

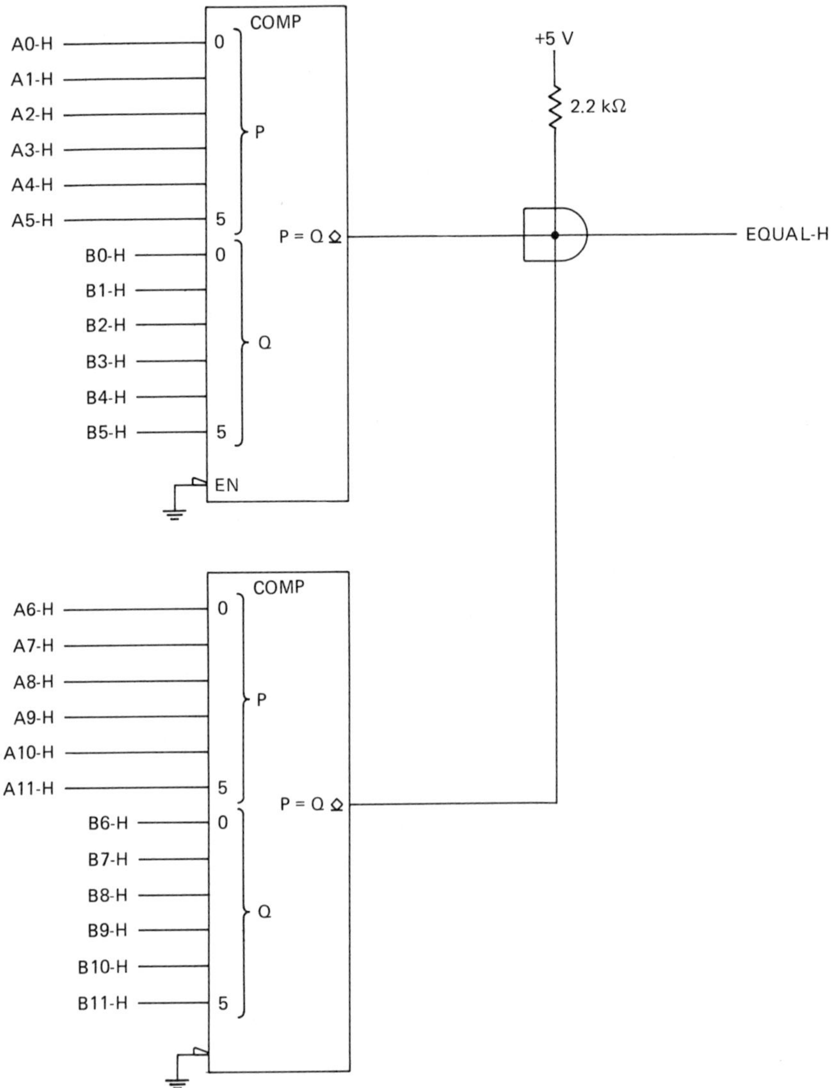

Figure 2-43c. Dot-ANDing of open-collector outputs of enabled chips, for expansion. (National Semiconductor.)

The 8160 part number for the 6-bit comparator of Fig. 2-43 illustrates an interesting phenomenon that has taken place in the semiconductor industry. When Texas Instruments introduced the 74xxx family, they did the industry a favor by introducing a family with high fan-out and consistent loading rules. For example, the low-level input

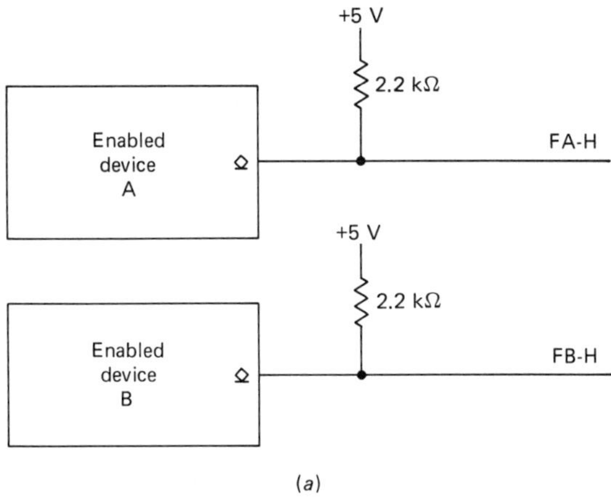

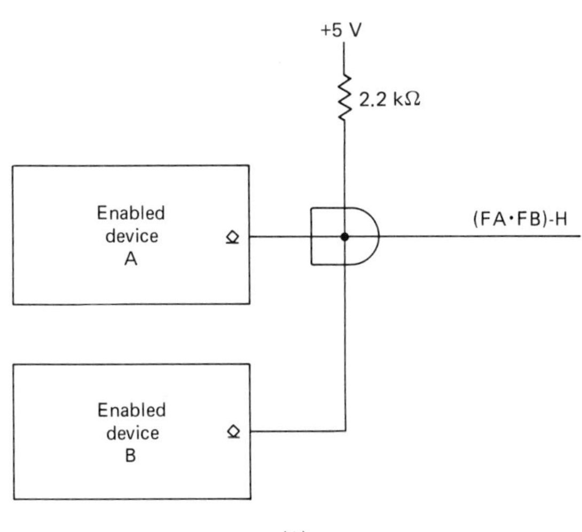

Figure 2-44. Dot-ANDing equivalence for open-collector outputs. (a) Definition of FA and FB; (b) logical result of dot-ANDing.

current of 1.6 mA (maximum) is the specified input current for virtually all inputs of all 74xxx parts. Some other TTL families (e.g., Fairchild's 93xx family) introduced MSI parts which were excellent logical contributions but had inferior loading rules. Eventually, Texas Instruments redesigned many such parts so as to produce logical equivalents but with the 74xxx loading rules and a 74xxx part number. Other manufacturers have also introduced parts that obey the 74xxx loading rules and have assigned 74xxx part numbers to them. *In addition,* some manufacturers (e.g., National Semiconductor, in the case of this 6-bit comparator) have introduced parts that obey the 74xxx loading

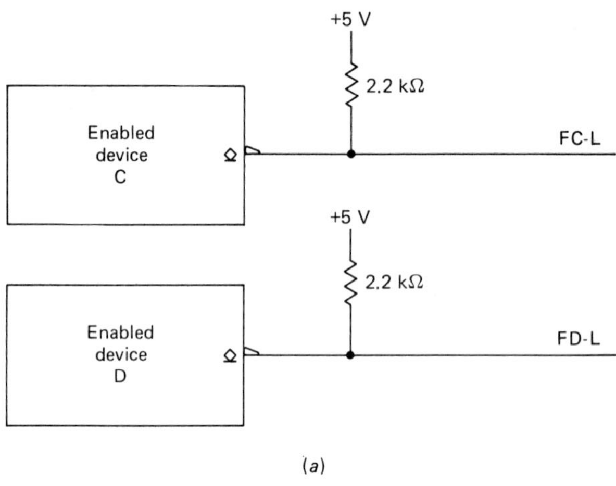

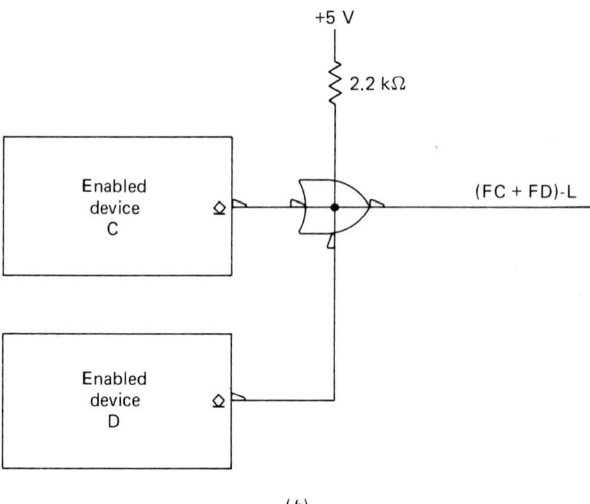

Figure 2-45. The dot-ORing equivalence for open-collector outputs. (a) Definition of FC and FD; (b) logical result of dot-ORing.

rules but then have assigned "proprietary" numbers to them. As designers, we want to be aware of all parts that might be useful to us. Because of this part-number confusion, a guide such as *IC Master*, referenced at the end of this chapter, is invaluable.

2-12 PROGRAMMABLE COMBINATIONAL CIRCUITS

As we carry out the design of an instrument or device, any *complexity* that we encounter will tend to be relegated to a microcomputer incorporated in the overall design. Within the microcomputer this complexity is translated into an algorithm implemented in software. The software is typically stored in one of two devices:

1 *ROM*, or *read-only memory*, mask-programmed by an IC manufacturer from a truth table sent by a customer. ROMs provide the lowest-cost alternative for large quantities of parts. They have the disadvantages of an initial, one-time mask charge of $1000 to $2000, a minimum order of 100 to 500 parts at a time, and a delivery time of 10 to 12 weeks.
2 *EPROM*, or *erasable, programmable read-only memory*, purchased, unprogrammed, from a local distributor. We program it with an EPROM programmer like that of Fig. 1-8 or that of Figs. 1-18 and 1-19. If we want to reprogram it, we first erase its contents by subjecting it to the light of an ultraviolet lamp for about 20 minutes.

For the storing of microcomputer software, both ROMs and EPROMs are normally implemented with NMOS (*N*-channel metal-oxide semiconductor) technology. This yields higher-density, but slower parts than bipolar technology. For example, Intel Corporation's popular 2716 EPROM is a 2048×8 device with a maximum access time (i.e., propagation delay) of 450 ns. This speed is satisfactory for a microcomputer's memory.

Some aspects of a design may require more speed than is attainable with a microcomputer. This will lead to special-purpose circuitry, very likely implemented with TTL logic. The complexity residing in such circuitry will be translated into the contents of a bipolar† ROM or PROM. A bipolar PROM employs fusible links which are selectively blown by a PROM programmer to form the required contents of logic 1s and logic 0s.

In comparison with EPROMS, bipolar PROMs are a low-cost component, as shown in Fig. 2-46. There are several reasons for this:

1 They can employ a low-cost 16-pin plastic package (at least up to 1024×4 bits).
2 The technology of bipolar PROMs is mature, having been introduced in 1970 by Harris Semiconductor.
3 The market for bipolar PROMs is so huge as to benefit from the economies of high volume. In 1979, sales totaled an estimated $150 million. (In contrast, the bipolar ROM market in 1979 totaled an estimated $36 million.)

† The same technology used to produce TTL logic.

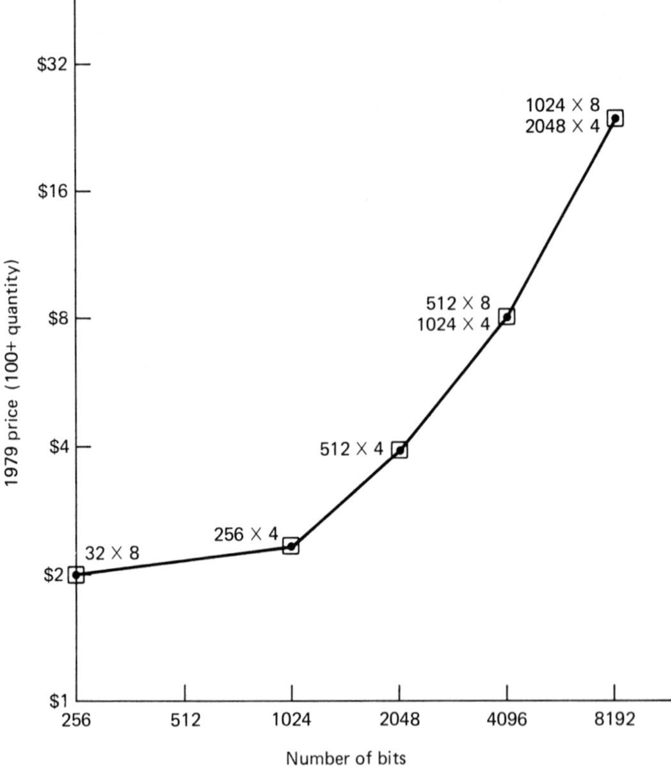

Figure 2-46. Cost of bipolar PROMs.

4 The competition to supply this market is fierce, with about a dozen manufacturers, led by Signetics, Harris Semiconductor, and Monolithic Memories, in 1979.

With manufacturers doubling the number of bits of memory on a chip every year, what is a large, low-yield PROM of today will become the smaller, high-yield PROM of tomorrow. Consequently, the price characteristic of Fig. 2-46 should change with time to include larger PROMs at about the same minimum price now afforded by 32 × 8 and 256 × 4 PROMs. Moreover, with standard 300-mil-wide DIP packages growing in length to include 20-pin and even 24-pin "skinny DIP" devices, packaging economies will encourage the introduction of even larger PROMs. For example, a low-cost 20-pin DIP package can be used even as PROMs grow to 16K × 4 bits (i.e., 65,536 bits).

Another factor that favors the increased use of PROMs is the transformation taking place in how they are programmed. A "smart" programmer, built around a low-cost computer such as that of Fig. 1-18, can provide a versatility unmatched in a dedicated unit. When power is turned on and the "PROM programmer" floppy disk is inserted into the disk drive, a novice can be directed through a sequence of steps which will result in a programmed PROM. A more sophisticated user can take advantage of an editing capability which has been specifically designed to reduce the drudgery of programming large PROMs. For example, if a PROM is to be used to implement rather easily described boolean functions, a "smart" programmer will permit a user to enter these directly. This is a big step forward for a user who in the past has had to recast the form of such data to specify the contents of each PROM address. This can get tedious for a PROM with 1024 addresses!

In some senses, PROMs are the ultimate combinational circuit. A PROM with m inputs and n outputs can implement *any* n functions of those m inputs. Also, a PROM implementation can be a *fast* implementation. For example, if the maximum "access time" of a PROM is 50 ns, then regardless of the function being implemented, we can be assured that within 50 ns after we change an input, the outputs will have changed to the correct new values.

The dependency notation standard uses the term *coder* to include not only the decoders of Sec. 2-9, but also *any* combinational circuit. If the coder is a decoder, its description is given by the numbers within the dependency notation symbol, as discussed earlier. For a PROM we will use the X/Y coder symbol but will also reference a table from within the dependency notation symbol. For example, a 9-bit version of the Gray code-to-binary code converter of Fig. 2-10 is shown implemented with a 512 × 8 PROM in Fig. 2-47. Note that the 512 addresses of the PROM correspond to a 9-bit input because a 9-bit binary number can take on 512 values. The coder of Fig. 2-47 is defined by the boolean functions in PROM Table 1, referenced within the symbol.

Incidently, this provides a good example of the manner in which we should be able to talk to a PROM programmer. A "smart" PROM programmer should let us enter the eight boolean equations directly. A more traditional PROM programmer would require us to recast these equations into truth-table form, as shown in Fig. 2-48.

PROMs are available from a specific manufacturer as a *family*. Within one family we will typically find a variety of sizes (e.g., 32 × 8 PROM, 256 × 4 PROM), each packaged in an appropriately sized DIP. Each size will also typically be available with either three-state outputs or open-collector outputs (with a different part number to identify each of these alternatives). The loading rules for most PROM families make them look more or less like 74LSxxx inputs and 74xxx outputs (i.e., inputs that lightly load whatever is driving them and outputs with excellent drive capability). A PROM programmer should be designed to

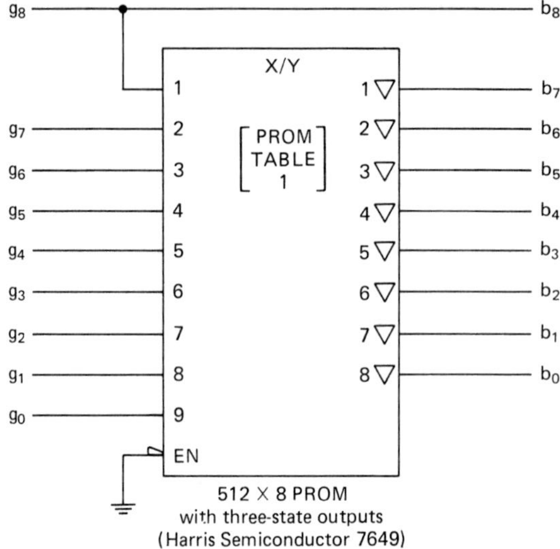

PROM TABLE 1

Outputs		Inputs																
1	=	1	⊕	2														
2	=	1	⊕	2	⊕	3												
3	=	1	⊕	2	⊕	3	⊕	4										
4	=	1	⊕	2	⊕	3	⊕	4	⊕	5								
5	=	1	⊕	2	⊕	3	⊕	4	⊕	5	⊕	6						
6	=	1	⊕	2	⊕	3	⊕	4	⊕	5	⊕	6	⊕	7				
7	=	1	⊕	2	⊕	3	⊕	4	⊕	5	⊕	6	⊕	7	⊕	8		
8	=	1	⊕	2	⊕	3	⊕	4	⊕	5	⊕	6	⊕	7	⊕	8	⊕	9

Figure 2-47. PROM implementation of a 9-bit Gray code-to-binary code converter.

PROM TABLE 1

Inputs									Outputs							
1	2	3	4	5	6	7	8	9	1	2	3	4	5	6	7	8
0	0	0	0	0	0	0	0	0	0	0	0	0	0	0	0	0
0	0	0	0	0	0	0	0	1	0	0	0	0	0	0	0	1
0	0	0	0	0	0	0	1	0	0	0	0	0	0	0	1	1
0	0	0	0	0	0	0	1	1	0	0	0	0	0	0	1	0
0	0	0	0	0	0	1	0	0	0	0	0	0	0	1	1	1
0	0	0	0	0	0	1	0	1	0	0	0	0	0	1	1	0
0	0	0	0	0	0	1	1	0	0	0	0	0	0	1	0	0
0	0	0	0	0	0	1	1	1	0	0	0	0	0	1	0	1
0	0	0	0	0	1	0	0	0	0	0	0	0	1	1	1	1
				⋮		(512 rows!)						⋮				
1	1	1	1	1	1	1	1	1	0	1	0	1	0	1	0	1

Figure 2-48. PROM contents for the PROM of Fig. 2-47.

handle all members of the family, because the programming pulse width and voltage required to "blast" the fusible links will typically be the same for all members of the family. The PROM programmer can incorporate separate IC sockets to handle the different pin-outs of the different family members.

Figure 2-49 shows the characteristics of one popular family (listed in order of increasing cost). *Maximum access time* is the worst-case propagation delay between a change on any address input and the resulting change on any output, with the chip enabled throughout. *Maximum chip-enable time* is the worst-case propagation delay between a change on a three-state control input which enables the outputs and the resulting change on any output, with the address fixed throughout.

Output expansion of a PROM requires that we connect inputs together, as shown in Fig. 2-50. *Input expansion* can employ PROMs with either open-collector outputs or three-state outputs. A decoder is used to decode the address lines that determine which PROM is to be enabled, so as to drive the output lines. This is illustrated in Fig. 2-51. For an application in which we need only one output from a PROM, we can achieve input expansion with a data selector on the output, as shown in Fig. 2-52.

Part number	Configuration	DIP package	Number of three-state enable inputs	Maximum access time (ns)	Maximum chip-enable time (ns)	Maximum power-supply current (mA)
7603	32 × 8	16	1	40	30	105
7611	256 × 4	16	2	40	25	130
7621	512 × 4	16	1	45	25	130
7643	1024 × 4	18	2	50	30	140
7649	512 × 8	20	1	60	40	170
7685	2048 × 4	18	1	70	40	170
7681	1024 × 8	24	4	70	40	170
76161	2048 × 8	24	3	60	40	180

(*a*)

Input loading (low) = 250 μA
Input loading (high) = 40 μA

Output drive (low) = 16 mA
Output drive (high) = 2 mA

(*b*)

All bits are initially programmed high

Programming pulse = 100 μs, 12 V
Programming current = 600 mA, typical

(*c*)

Figure 2-49. Three-state PROM family characteristics. (a) Characteristics; (b) loading rules; (c) programming pulse characteristics.

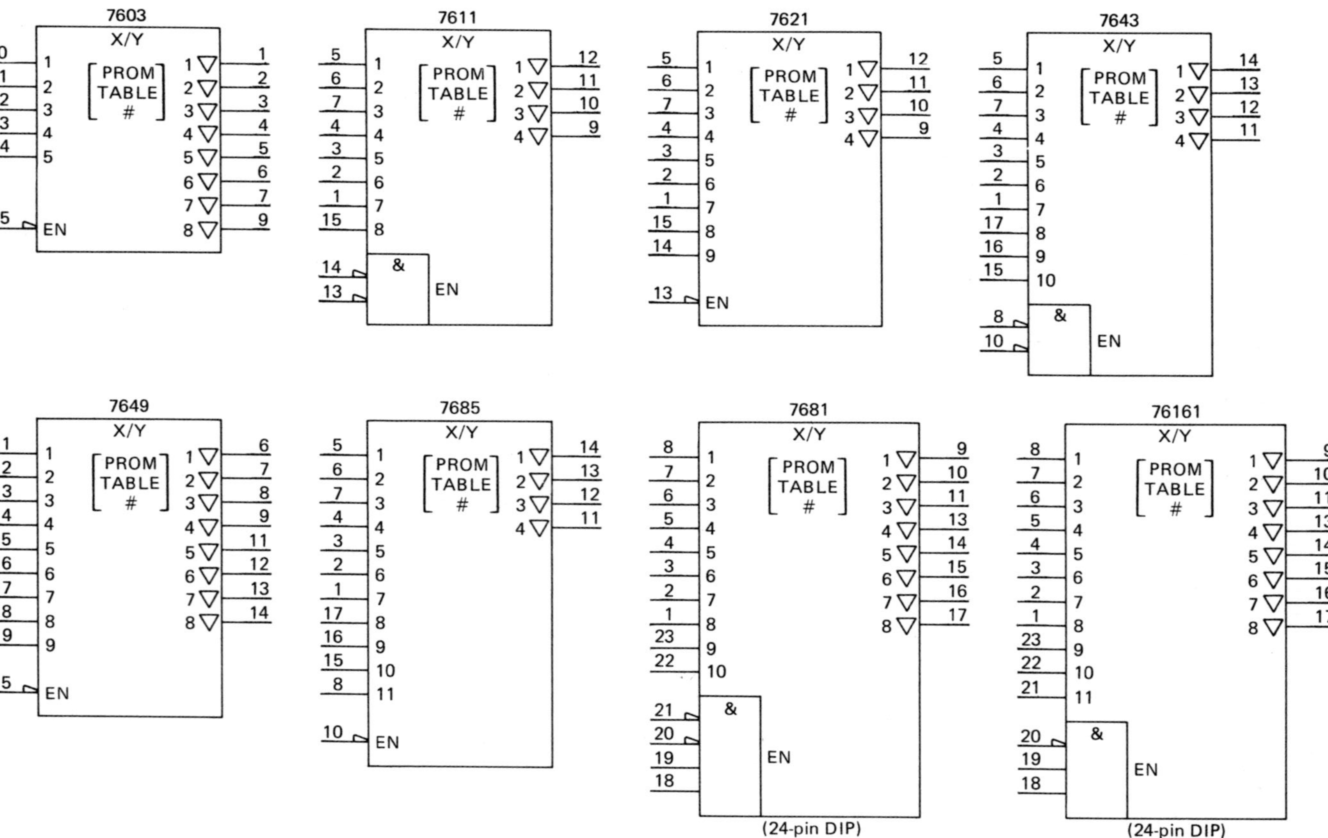

Figure 2-49d. Dependency notation symbols. (Harris Semiconductor.)

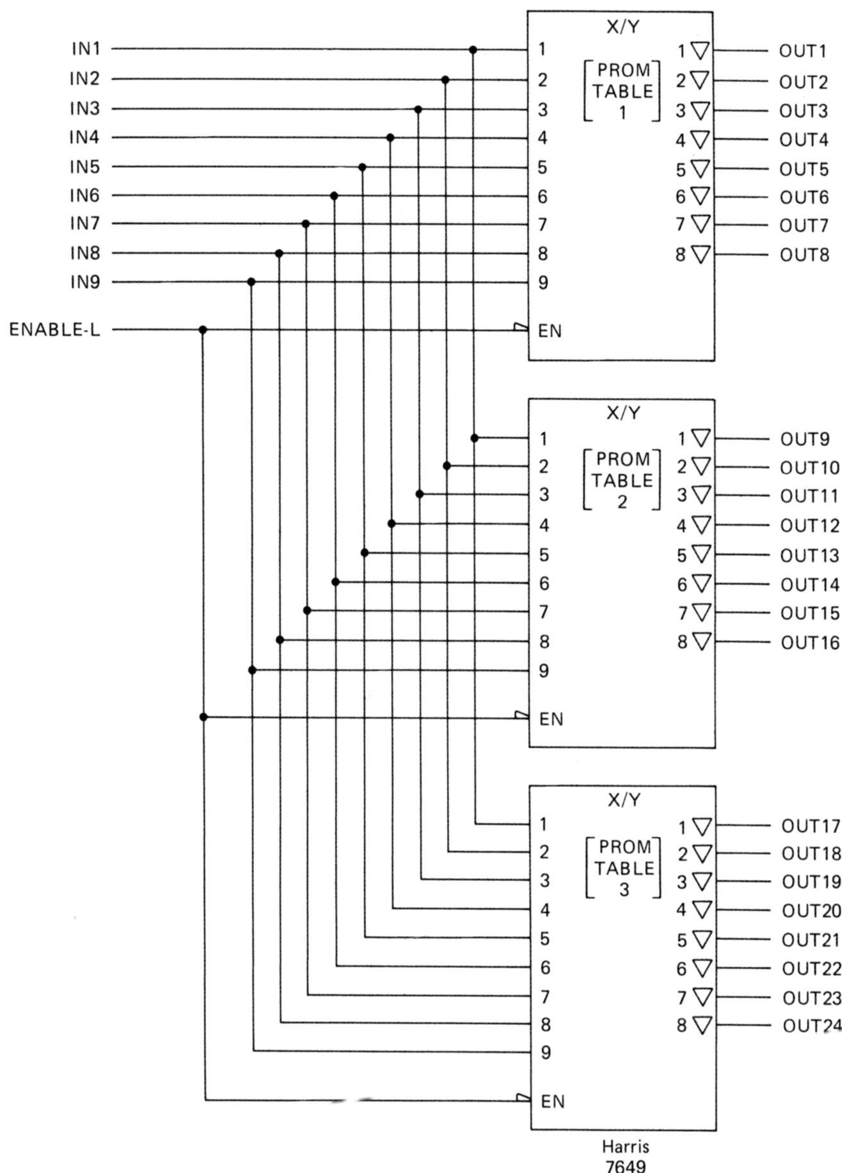

Figure 2-50. PROM output expansion to achieve a 512 × 24 PROM using three 512 × 8 PROMs.

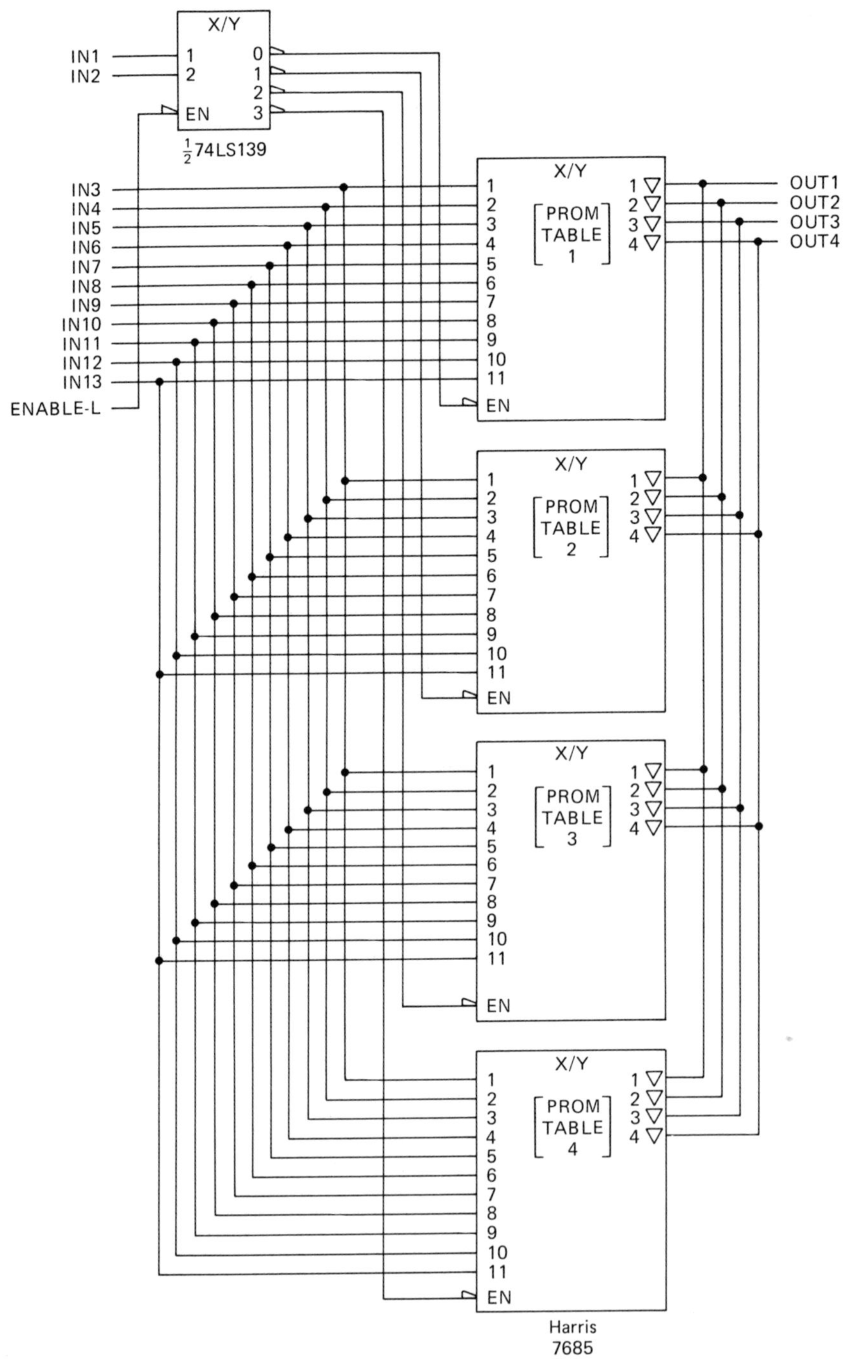

Figure 2-51. PROM input expansion to achieve an 8192 × 4 PROM using four 2048 × 4 PROMs.

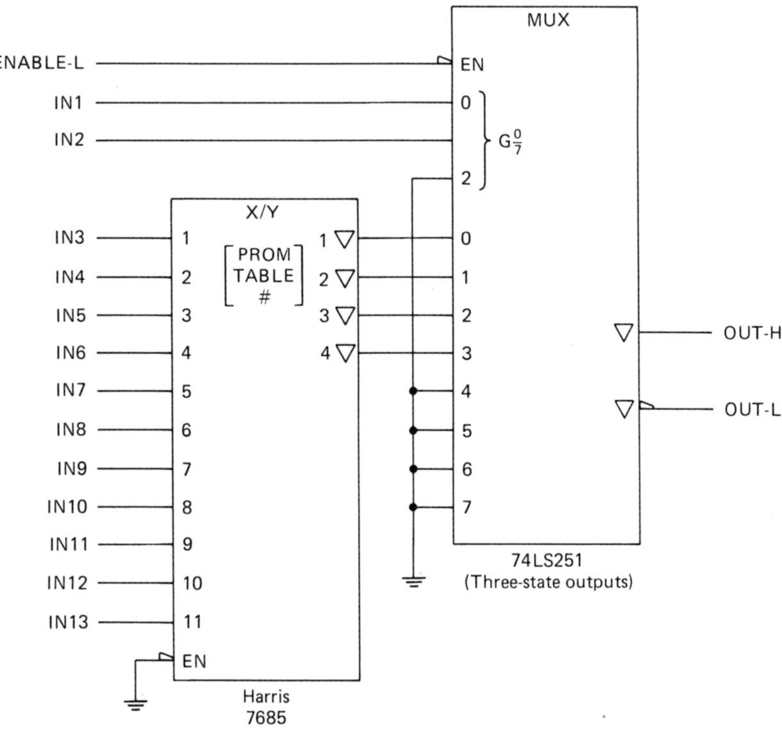

Figure 2-52. PROM input expansion by output contraction to achieve an 8192 × 1 PROM from a 2048 × 4 PROM.

To help with our eventual use of PROMs, Fig. 2-53 is a PROM table which can be duplicated and copies used to list the contents of a 32 × 8 PROM (where a simple *functional* representation of the PROM contents is not available). For a larger PROM, the total PROM table will consist of *several* of these copies. For example, a 256 × 4 PROM requires *eight* of these tables, in which four of the output columns in each table are ignored. The spaces on the left labeled "Function" and those at the bottom labeled "I/O Assignment" are to help annotate the PROM contents in terms of its application. We will see examples of this use later.

PROMs may be the ultimate combinational circuit, but their cost suffers badly as more and more inputs (really, more and more bits) are required. Above some minimum size, cost is proportional to the number of bits, as illustrated in Fig. 2-46. As a consequence, a variety of alternative programmable devices have appeared which offer a user more inputs configured with relatively few fusible links. The trick for a manufacturer is to design a device that can find wide application in spite of a constrained logic organization.

PROM TABLE NO.____

INPUT				
10	9	8	7	6

FUNCTION	INPUT 5	4	3	2	1		OUTPUT 8	7	6	5	4	3	2	1
	0	0	0	0	0	0								
	0	0	0	0	1	1								
	0	0	0	1	0	2								
	0	0	0	1	1	3								
	0	0	1	0	0	4								
	0	0	1	0	1	5								
	0	0	1	1	0	6								
	0	0	1	1	1	7								
	0	1	0	0	0	8								
	0	1	0	0	1	9								
	0	1	0	1	0	10								
	0	1	0	1	1	11								
	0	1	1	0	0	12								
	0	1	1	0	1	13								
	0	1	1	1	0	14								
	0	1	1	1	1	15								
	1	0	0	0	0	16								
	1	0	0	0	1	17								
	1	0	0	1	0	18								
	1	0	0	1	1	19								
	1	0	1	0	0	20								
	1	0	1	0	1	21								
	1	0	1	1	0	22								
	1	0	1	1	1	23								
	1	1	0	0	0	24								
	1	1	0	0	1	25								
	1	1	0	1	0	26								
	1	1	0	1	1	27								
	1	1	1	0	0	28								
	1	1	1	0	1	29								
	1	1	1	1	0	30								
	1	1	1	1	1	31								
I/O ASSIGNMENT														

Figure 2-53. PROM table.

An *FPLA*, or *field-programmable logic array*, is one example of such a device. The logic of an $m \times p \times n$ FPLA is shown in Fig. 2-54, where m is the number of inputs, p is the number of *product terms* (to be defined shortly), and n is the number of outputs. An FPLA is programmed with a PROM programmer (like the ones discussed earlier). Programming consists of three steps:

- Programming the AND matrix
- Programming the OR matrix
- Programming the active level of each output

Each of the p product terms ANDs together any number of the inputs (in either active-high form or active-low form). For example, the product-term PT1 might implement the boolean equation

$$\mathrm{PT1} = \mathrm{IN1} \cdot \overline{\mathrm{IN2}} \cdot \overline{\mathrm{IN3}} \cdot \mathrm{IN4} \cdot \mathrm{IN12}$$

with the function

$$\mathrm{PT1} = \text{IN1-H} \cdot \text{IN2-L} \cdot \text{IN3-L} \cdot \text{IN4-H} \cdot \text{IN12-H}$$

Notice that a product term is not required to be a function of *all* inputs. It can treat any number of inputs as *don't care* inputs, not caring whether they are high or low.

Each of the n outputs is formed by ORing together any number of the (active-high) product terms. For example, output OUT5 might implement

$$\mathrm{OUT5} = \mathrm{PT1} + \mathrm{PT5} + \mathrm{PT32}$$

Furthermore, we can select whether this output is active-high or active-low. For example, we might let

$$\text{OUT1-H} = \mathrm{PT1} + \mathrm{PT2} + \mathrm{PT3}$$

and also let

$$\text{OUT2-L} = \mathrm{PT1} + \mathrm{PT4} + \mathrm{PT5} + \mathrm{PT6}$$

Notice that the output functions can share common product terms (such as the sharing of PT1 by OUT1 and OUT2 above).

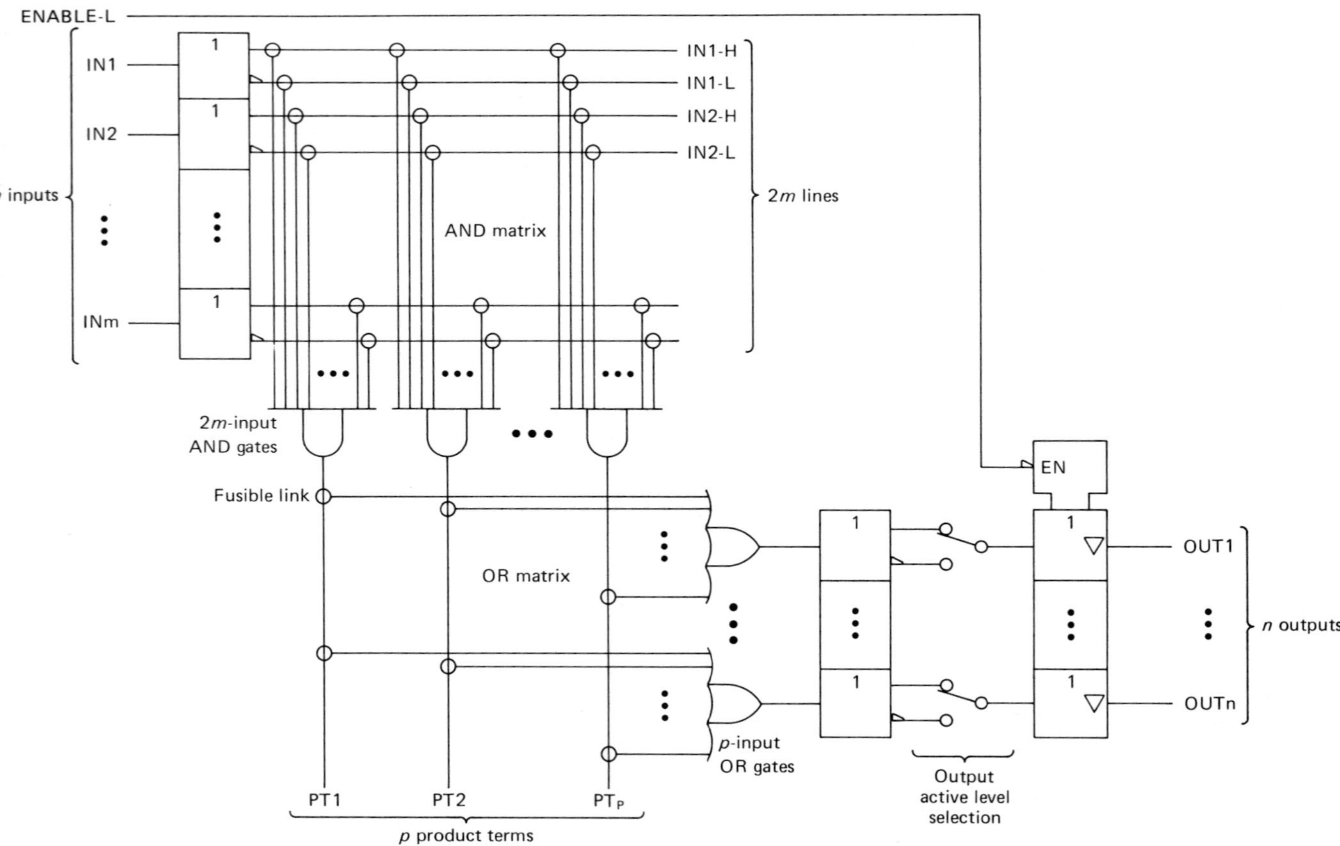

Figure 2-54. FPLA logic organization.

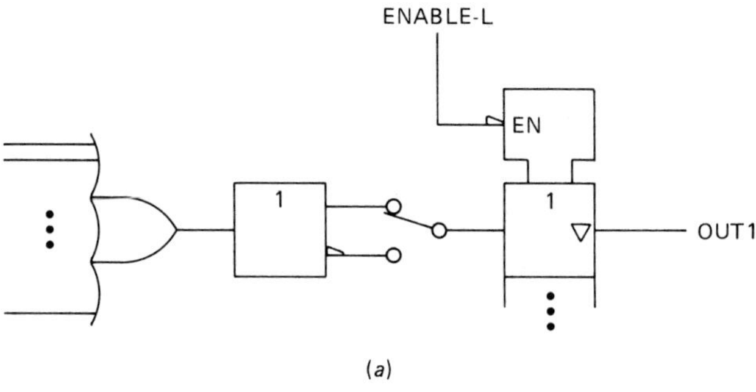

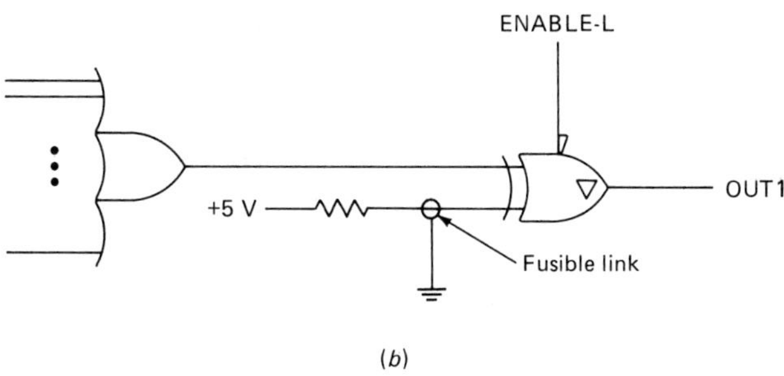

Figure 2-55. Implementations of FPLA output circuit. (a) Logic shown in Fig. 2-54; (b) implementation with a three-state exclusive-OR gate.

Example 2-26. How many fusible links are used in a 16 × 48 × 8 FPLA?

Assume that only one fusible link is required to set the active level for each output. This is commonly done using the circuit of Fig. 2 55.

Output fuses		= 8
AND matrix fuses = 2 × 16 × 48		= 1536
OR matrix fuses =	48 × 8	= 384
		1928 fuses

Example 2-27. How many fusible links would be required in a 16-input, 8-output PROM (i.e., a 65,536 × 8 PROM)?

The number would be 65,536 × 8 = 524,288 fuses! From these two examples, we can see the incentive that has induced semiconductor manufacturers to develop alternatives to PROMs with many inputs.

Dependency notation symbols for four popular FPLAs are shown in Fig. 2-56. The larger Signetics units are especially useful, relative to PROMs, because of the comparison illustrated by the last two examples. Their organization is exactly that of Fig. 2-54 (except that the 82S101 has open-collector outputs).

Just as a truth table can be used to specify the contents of a PROM, so the FPLA table of Fig. 2-57 can be used to specify the contents of an FPLA. We will use the Signetics programming notation:

1	Product terms:	H = active-high input
		L = active-low input
		– = input ignored (don't care)
2	Output functions:	A = product term included
		• = product term ignored (don't care)
3	Output active level:	H = active-high output
		L = active-low output

This table can be duplicated and copies used for the programming of any FPLA with up to 16 inputs, 50 product terms, and 8 outputs. For the Signetics units of Fig. 2-56 (with 48 product terms) we just leave rows 49 and 50 blank. For the Texas Instruments units of Fig. 2-56 (with 12 inputs and 6 outputs), we just leave blank input columns 13 to 16 and output columns 7 and 8.

The Texas Instruments 74S330/331 FPLAs include an interesting programming option for the enabling of outputs. Rather than dedicate one of the 20 pins of the DIP as an ENABLE-L line for all users, they have permitted each user to decide whether it is worth giving up an input line to gain an ENABLE-L line. This option is illustrated in Fig. 2-56 with the dotted-line inputs to either input 12 or input EN. For some applications, it is useful to have an "automatic enable," whereby the outputs remain in the high-impedance state until one of the product terms becomes active. The 74S330/331 supports all of these, as shown in Fig. 2-58. A user must specify one of these four options as part of the FPLA table information.

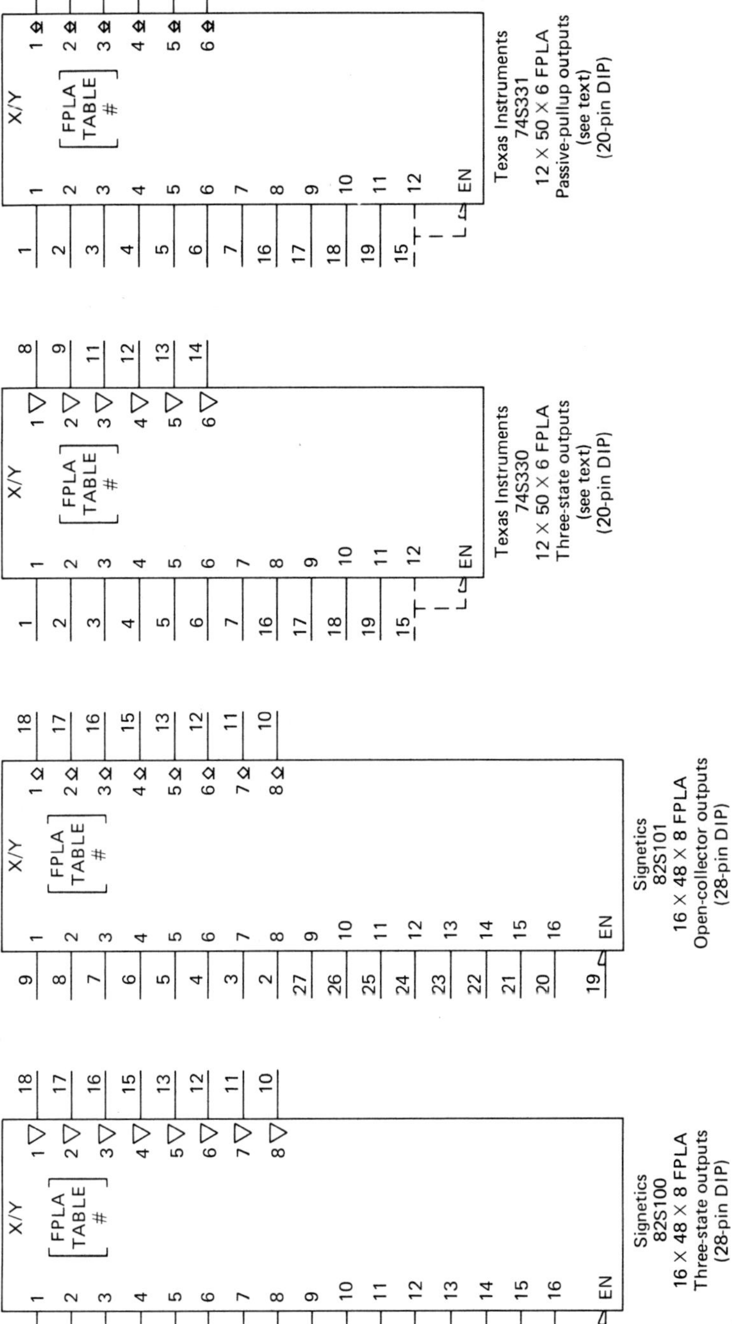

Figure 2-56. Four FPLAs.

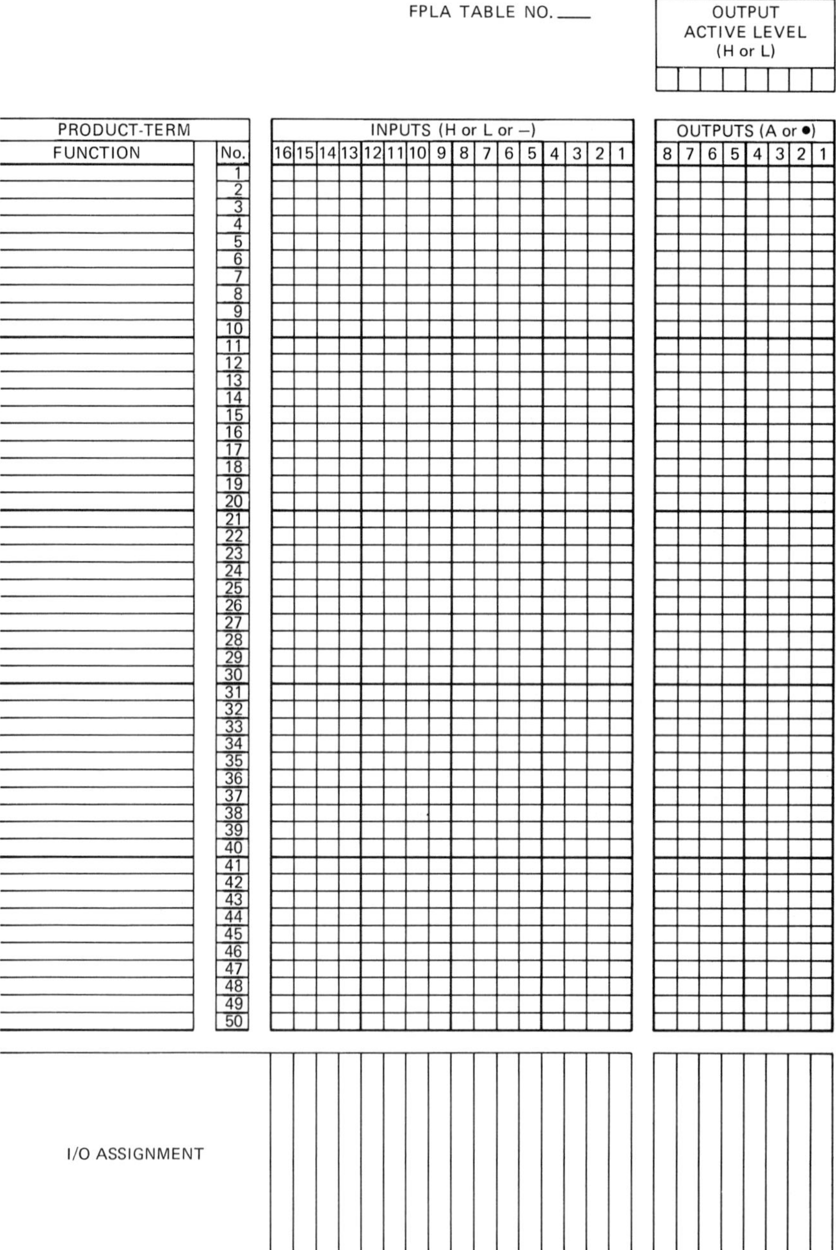

FPLA TABLE NO. ____

OUTPUT ACTIVE LEVEL (H or L)							

PRODUCT-TERM FUNCTION	No.	INPUTS (H or L or –)																OUTPUTS (A or •)							
		16	15	14	13	12	11	10	9	8	7	6	5	4	3	2	1	8	7	6	5	4	3	2	1
	1																								
	2																								
	3																								
	4																								
	5																								
	6																								
	7																								
	8																								
	9																								
	10																								
	11																								
	12																								
	13																								
	14																								
	15																								
	16																								
	17																								
	18																								
	19																								
	20																								
	21																								
	22																								
	23																								
	24																								
	25																								
	26																								
	27																								
	28																								
	29																								
	30																								
	31																								
	32																								
	33																								
	34																								
	35																								
	36																								
	37																								
	38																								
	39																								
	40																								
	41																								
	42																								
	43																								
	44																								
	45																								
	46																								
	47																								
	48																								
	49																								
	50																								
I/O ASSIGNMENT																									

Figure 2-57. FPLA table.

Enable option	FX	Input "12"	FPLA size
E = Always Enable	Always enabled	Pin 15	12 × 50 × 6
AE = "Automatic Enable"	Enabled by any active product term	Pin 15	12 × 50 × 6
DE = Dedicated Enable	Low input on pin 15	Deleted	11 × 50 × 6
AE·DE = AE AND DE	Enabled by any active product term AND a low input on pin 15	Deleted	11 × 50 × 6

Figure 2-58. Output-enable options of Texas Instruments 74S330/331 FPLAs.

An example† of the use of an FPLA table is shown in Fig. 2-59. The specific example employed is not intended to make sense to us here. Rather, it is shown to point out how the three kinds of programming information are entered. The Function and I/O Assignment entries illustrate labeling that can be helpful both when the table is created and when it is subsequently used for debugging.

In Chap. 4 we will see that in spite of their being constrained (relative to a PROM with the same number of inputs and outputs), FPLAs have an organization which is admirably suited for some of our major design tasks. For now, we will worry about two things bearing upon their use:

- Minimization of product terms
- Expansion

Although we downplayed the role of minimization techniques, in general, in Sec. 2-7, nevertheless FPLAs offer an opportunity to use the very simplest of minimization techniques to reduce the number of required product terms. The basis for this technique is the boolean identity

$$BA + B\overline{A} = B$$

(which we can prove with a truth table, if we desire). To use the technique, we first make a (preliminary) FPLA table like that of Fig. 2-59. If the number of product terms required is less than the number in a standard FPLA, we can let this preliminary table be the final table, pro-

† Taken from *Signetics Field-Programmable Logic Arrays: An Applications Manual*, available from Signetics Corporation, Publications Department, 811 East Arques Avenue, Sunnyvale, CA 94086.

		PRODUCT TERM																ACTIVE LEVEL							
		INPUT VARIABLE																H	H	H	H	L	H	H	H
FUNCTION	NO.	I 1	I 2	I 3	I 4	I 5	I 6	I 7	I 8	I 9	I 10	I 11	I 12	I 13	I 14	I 15	I 16	OUTPUT FUNCTION 1	2	3	4	5	6	7	8
Clear Display	1	L	L	L	L	L	L	–	–	–	–	L	H	H	H	H	H	•	•	A	•	A	•	•	A
Clear Accumulator	2	L	L	L	L	H	L	–	–	–	–	L	H	H	H	H	H	•	•	A	•	A	•	•	A
Enter Weight (K-1)	3	H	L	L	L	L	L	–	–	–	–	–	–	–	–	–	–	•	•	A	•	A	•	•	•
Multiply	4	H	L	L	L	H	L	–	–	–	–	H	H	H	H	L	H	•	•	A	•	A	•	•	A
Address Digit 1 (MSD)	5	–	L	L	H	L	L	–	–	–	–	–	–	–	–	–	–	A	•	•	A	A	•	•	•
Address Digit 2	6	–	L	L	H	H	L	–	–	–	–	–	–	–	–	–	–	A	•	•	•	A	•	•	•
Address Digit 3	7	–	L	H	L	L	L	–	–	–	–	–	–	–	–	–	–	•	A	•	A	A	•	•	•
Address Digit 4	8	–	L	H	L	H	L	–	–	–	–	–	–	–	–	–	–	•	A	•	•	A	•	•	•
Address Digit 5 (LSD)	9	–	L	H	H	L	L	–	–	–	–	–	–	–	–	–	–	•	•	A	A	A	•	•	•
Add	10	–	L	H	H	H	L	–	–	–	–	H	H	H	L	H	H	•	•	A	•	A	•	•	A
Enter Bias Digit 1 (MSD)	11	–	H	L	L	L	L	–	–	–	–	–	–	–	–	–	–	•	•	A	•	A	•	•	•
Enter Bias Digit 2	12	–	H	L	L	H	L	–	–	–	–	–	–	–	–	–	–	•	•	A	•	A	•	•	•
Enter Bias Digit 3	13	–	H	L	H	L	L	–	–	–	–	–	–	–	–	–	–	•	•	A	•	A	•	•	•
Enter Bias Digit 4	14	–	H	L	H	H	L	–	–	–	–	–	–	–	–	–	–	•	•	A	•	A	•	•	•
Enter Bias Digit 5 (LSD)	15	–	H	H	L	L	L	–	–	–	–	–	–	–	–	–	–	•	•	A	•	A	•	•	•
Subtract (or add)	16	–	H	H	L	H	L	–	–	–	–	–	–	–	–	–	–	•	•	A	•	A	•	•	A
Enter Weight (K)	17	H	H	H	H	L	L	–	–	–	–	–	–	–	–	–	–	•	•	A	•	A	•	•	•
Divide	18	H	H	H	H	H	L	–	–	–	–	H	H	H	H	H	L	•	•	A	•	A	•	•	A
No Operation	19	L	H	H	H	H	L	–	–	–	–	–	–	–	–	–	–	•	•	A	•	A	•	•	•
Decode BCD '0'	20	–	–	–	–	–	H	L	L	L	L	L	H	H	H	H	H	•	•	•	•	•	A	•	•
Decode BCD '1'	21	–	–	–	–	–	H	L	L	L	H	H	L	H	H	H	H	•	•	•	•	•	A	•	•
Decode BCD '2'	22	–	–	–	–	–	H	L	L	H	L	H	H	L	H	H	H	•	•	•	•	•	A	•	•
Decode BCD '3'	23	–	–	–	–	–	H	L	L	H	H	H	H	H	L	H	H	•	•	•	•	•	A	•	•
Decode BCD '4'	24	–	–	–	–	–	H	L	H	L	L	H	H	H	H	L	H	•	•	•	•	•	A	•	•
Decode BCD '5'	25	–	–	–	–	–	H	L	H	L	H	H	H	H	H	H	L	•	•	•	•	•	A	•	•
Decode BCD '6'	26	–	–	–	–	–	H	L	H	H	L	H	L	H	H	H	H	•	•	•	•	•	•	A	•
Decode BCD '7'	27	–	–	–	–	–	H	L	H	H	H	H	H	L	H	H	H	•	•	•	•	•	•	A	•
Decode BCD '8'	28	–	–	–	–	–	H	H	L	L	L	H	H	H	L	H	H	•	•	•	•	•	•	A	•
Decode BCD '9'	29	–	–	–	–	–	H	H	L	L	H	H	H	H	H	L	H	•	•	•	•	•	•	A	•
I/O ASSIGNMENT		FILTER IN/OUT (1=IN)	STEP COUNT 8	STEP COUNT 4	STEP COUNT 2	STEP COUNT 1	DECODE HALF-CYCLE	BCD8	BCD4	BCD2	BCD 1	COLUMN STROBE 1	COLUMN STROBE 2	COLUMN STROBE 3	COLUMN STROBE 4	COLUMN STROBE 5	COLUMN STROBE 6	DIGIT ADDRESS 1	DIGIT ADDRESS 2	DIGIT ADDRESS 3	DIGIT ADDRESS 4	LATCH CONTROL	ROW DRIVE 1	ROW DRIVE 2	ROW DRIVE 3

Figure 2-59. Example of an FPLA table.

gram the FPLA (perhaps inefficiently), and move on to more enterprising activities. On the other hand, if reducing the number of product terms (if possible) is necessary in order to squeeze them all into one FPLA, the following technique is worth trying:

1 Look for two rows with identical outputs.
2 Now, if the inputs for those two rows are identical except for *one* column which contains an L in one row and an H in the other, the two rows can be replaced by a single row with a "–" in the one column.

Example 2-28. Noting that the eight outputs are identical for rows 1 and 2 of the FPLA table in Fig. 2-59, see if condition 2 is satisfied.

We see that the product terms differ only for input 5, which equals L in row 1 and H in row 2. Consequently, we can replace these two product terms by a single product term having a "−" for input 5. We might rename the function on the left to CLEAR. This new product term will make outputs 3, 5, and 8 active if inputs 1, 2, 3, 4, 6, and 11 are all low and if inputs 12, 13, 14, 15, and 16 are all high. It ignores inputs 5, 7, 8, 9, and 10.

Output expansion of FPLAs can be identical to output expansion of PROMs, as illustrated in Fig. 2-50. We simply tie all inputs of the FPLAs together. On the other hand, as long as a large FPLA costs well over 10 times as much as a small 32 × 8 PROM, it makes sense to *code* the outputs and then decode them with PROMs.

Example 2-29. Assume that an FPLA problem would fit into a single 16 × 48 × 8 FPLA except that it requires 19 outputs. Furthermore, assume that an examination of the outputs required reveals that while 19 outputs are required, less than 32 *different combinations* of 16 of these outputs occurs. Assume that because of the nature of the problem, no more than one product term will ever be active at the same time. Show how to organize this circuit using only one FPLA together with low-cost PROMs.

First, each output combination is coded with a different number between 0 and 31, as in Fig. 2-60*a*. The coding used is irrelevant. Next, this information is used to program two 32 × 8 PROMs which are then connected together as in Fig. 2-60*b* to look like a 32 × 16 PROM. The first three outputs (not coded in the PROMs) can come directly from the FPLA. Note that it is all right for more than one product term to generate the same output combination.

Product-term expansion can be achieved by using FPLAs having open-collector (or passive pull-up) outputs. The FPLAs must be

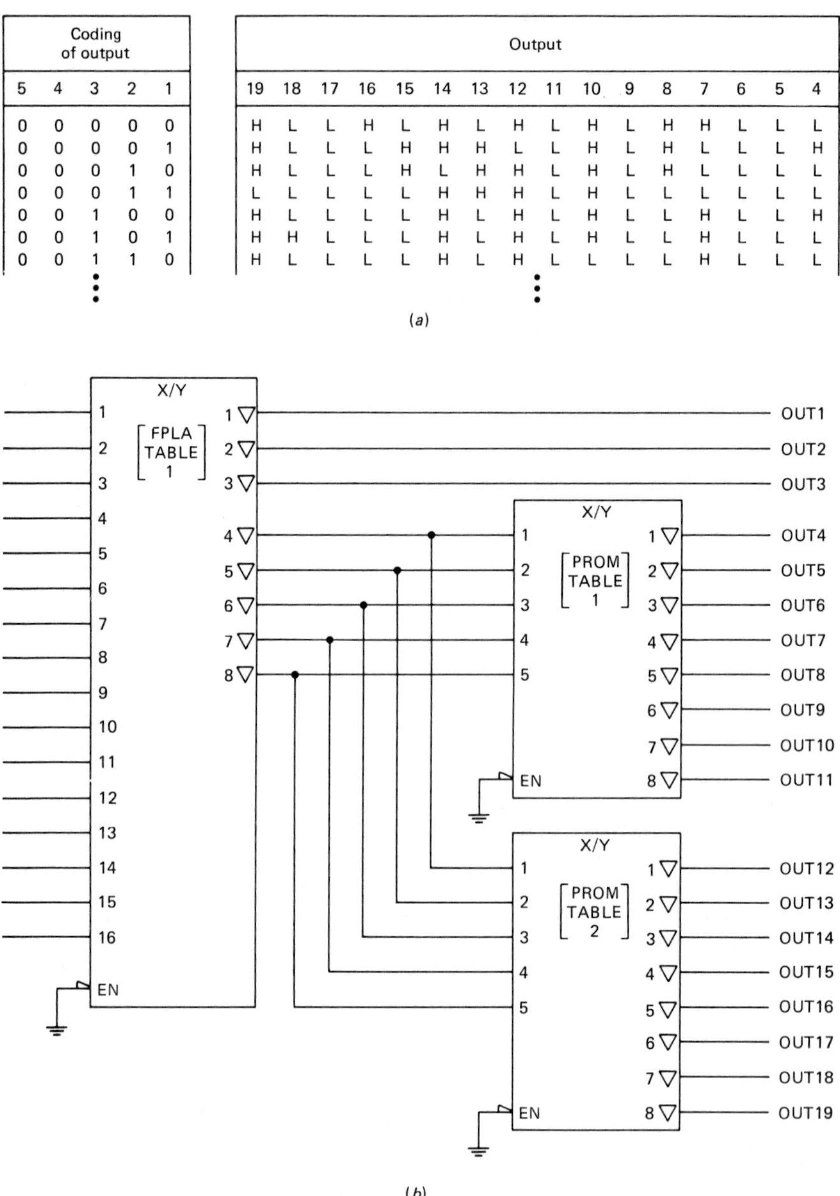

Coding of output					Output															
5	4	3	2	1	19	18	17	16	15	14	13	12	11	10	9	8	7	6	5	4
0	0	0	0	0	H	L	L	H	L	H	L	H	L	H	L	H	H	L	L	L
0	0	0	0	1	H	L	L	L	H	H	H	L	L	H	L	H	L	L	L	H
0	0	0	1	0	H	L	L	L	H	L	H	H	L	H	L	H	L	L	L	L
0	0	0	1	1	L	L	L	L	L	H	H	H	L	H	L	L	L	L	L	L
0	0	1	0	0	H	L	L	L	L	H	L	H	L	H	L	L	H	L	L	H
0	0	1	0	1	H	H	L	L	L	H	L	H	L	H	L	L	H	L	L	L
0	0	1	1	0	H	L	L	L	L	H	L	H	L	L	L	L	H	L	L	L
		⋮										⋮								

(a)

(b)

Figure 2-60. FPLA output expansion via output coding. (a) Coding of outputs; (b) circuit.

enabled all of the time (or use automatic enabling), and the outputs must be defined to be active-low. Then the dot-OR equivalence of Fig. 2-45 applies. An output will be pulled low by an active product term in any FPLA. This connection is shown in Fig. 2-61.

Input expansion of FPLAs is more difficult to implement than either output expansion or product-term expansion. However, the source of the problem that is being implemented with an FPLA may be constrained in such a way as to permit an easy solution.

Example 2-30. Assume that an FPLA problem would fit into a single 16 × 48 × 8 FPLA except that it requires 27 inputs. Furthermore, assume that an examination of the product terms reveals that 16 of the inputs can be selected such that

1. They occur in 31 or fewer different combinations.
2. Because of the nature of the problem being implemented, no two of these combinations will ever occur at the same time.

Show how to organize this circuit.

The combinations of the 16 inputs of interest are coded from 1 to 31. Then one FPLA is dedicated to the job of looking at these 16 inputs and coding each combination of interest as a 5-bit binary number. A second FPLA combines the state of the other inputs with this coded output of the first FPLA to generate the final output, as in Fig. 2-62.

Example 2-31. Assume that an FPLA problem would fit into a single 16 × 48 × 8 FPLA except that it requires 25 inputs. However, assume that because of the nature of the problem being implemented, there are 10 inputs (I16, . . . , I25), no two of which need ever be looked at simultaneously. Furthermore, assume that of the remaining 15 inputs, the state of four of them (I1, . . . , I4) provides enough information to identify which of the 10 inputs (I16, . . . , I25) must be looked at. Show how to organize this circuit.

This constraint is more realistic than it may, at first, appear. For many sequential circuits, we might code "state" information with four variables. If the FPLA looks at this state information on inputs I1, . . . , I4, we can use a 16-input multiplexer (with "select" inputs also connected to I1, . . . , I4) to select whichever of the 10 inputs (I16, . . . , I25) is appropriate to be looked at for each particular state. This is illustrated in Fig. 2-63.

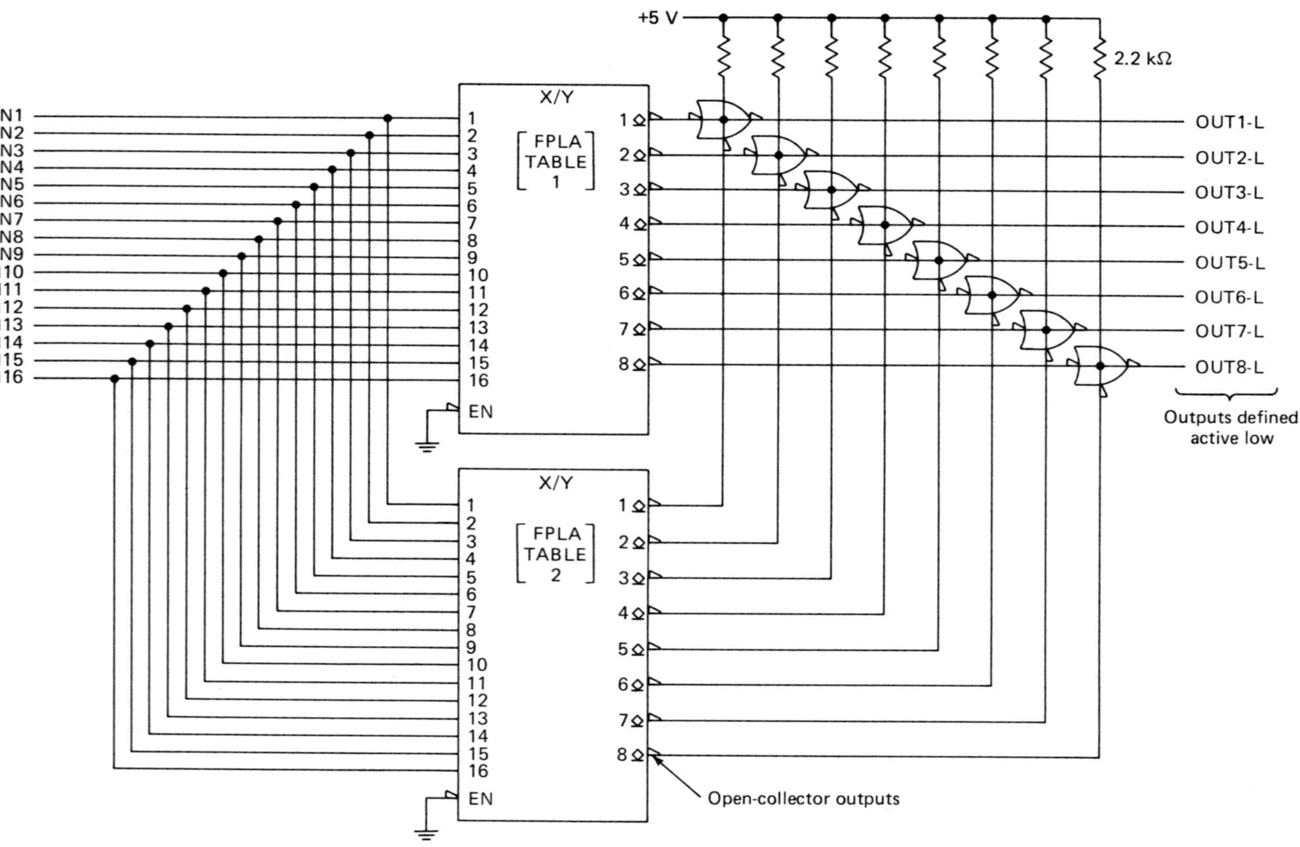

Figure 2-61. FPLA product-term expansion.

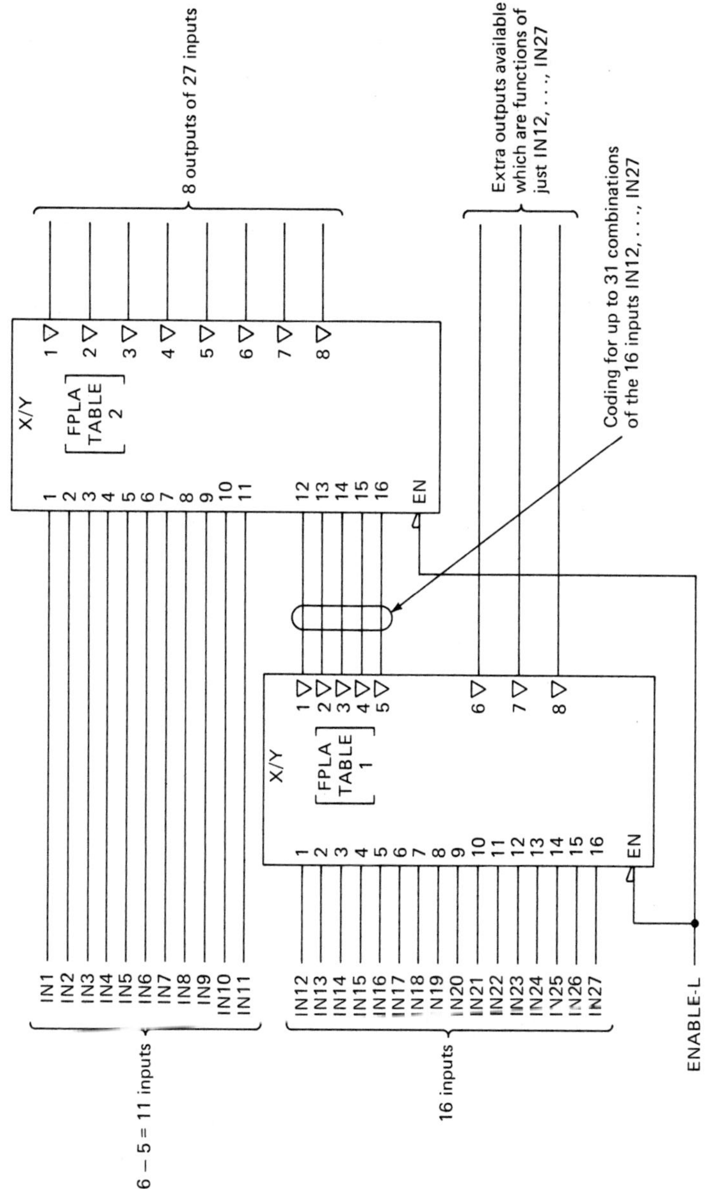

Figure 2-62. FPLA input expansion by coding selected, mutually exclusive input combinations.

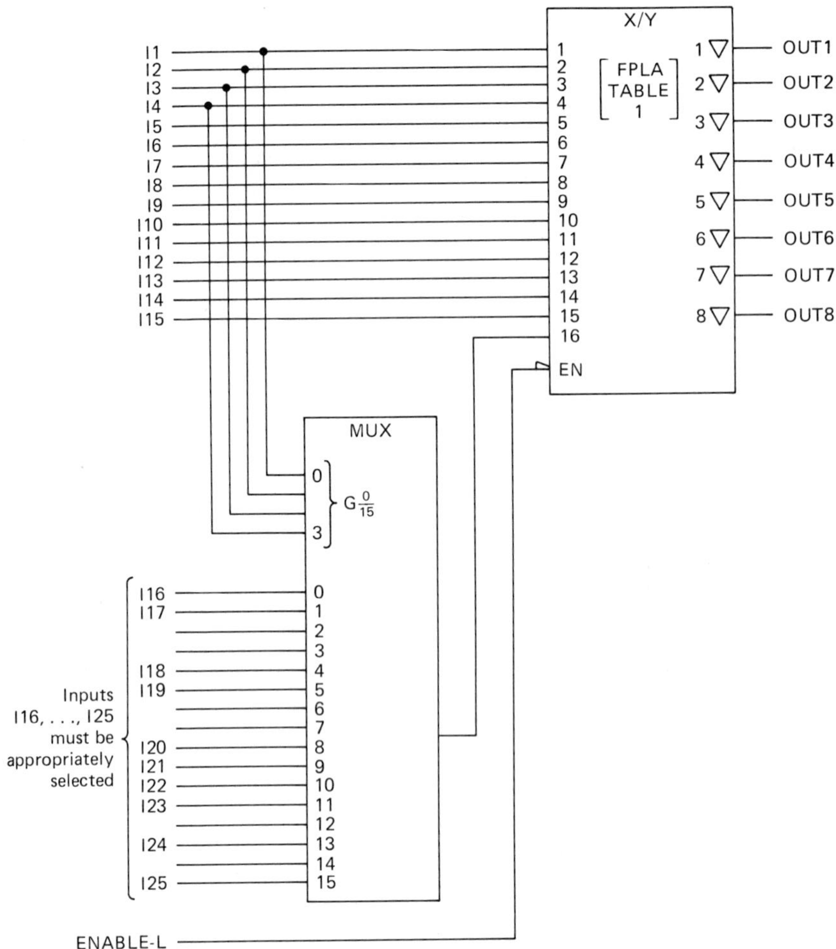

Figure 2-63. FPLA input expansion by selecting mutually exclusive inputs on the basis of other inputs.

The PAL, or *programmable array logic* family of devices, represents another alternative to PROMs. Introduced by Monolithic Memories, the nine units shown in Fig. 2-64 are all $m \times 16 \times n$ FPLAs, where m (the number of inputs) and n (the number of outputs) take on the values shown in that figure. These values give a variety of alternative circuits, each one packaged in a 300-mil-wide, 20-pin DIP. Their totem-pole outputs provide ease of use and fast access time, but preclude expansion.

Figure 2-65 shows programming tables (ready for duplicating) for each of the devices. We see that the outputs and the output active

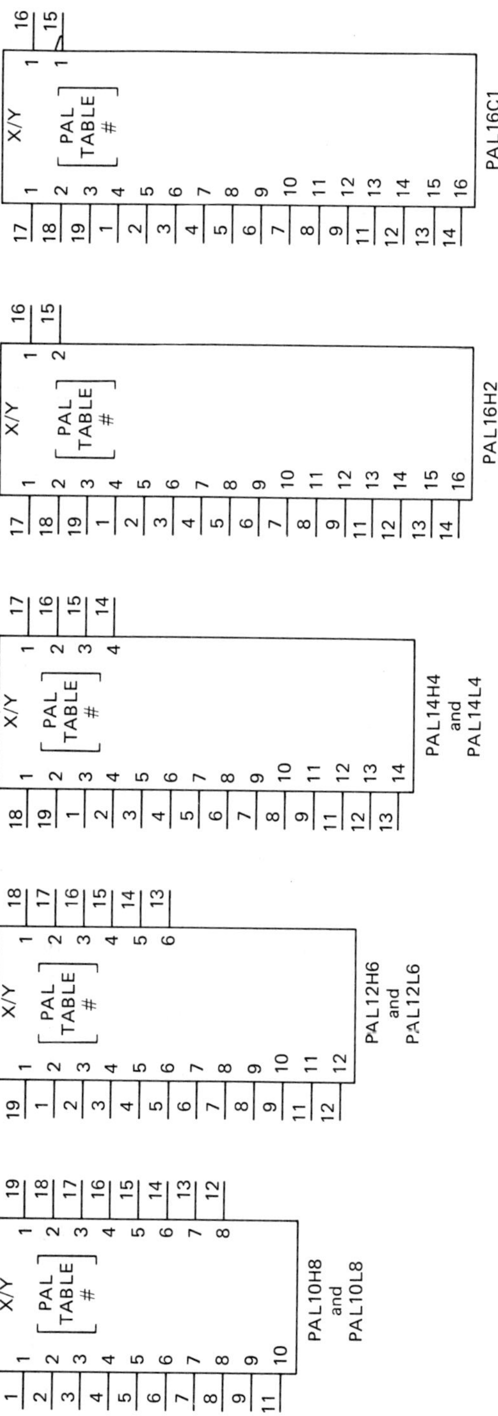

Figure 2-64. *Nine PALs.* (*Monolithic Memories.*)

PAL TABLE NO. ____

CHECK ONE	MONOLITHIC MEMORIES PART NO.	OUTPUT ACTIVE LEVEL							
	PAL10H8	H	H	H	H	H	H	H	H
	PAL10L8	L	L	L	L	L	L	L	L

PRODUCT-TERM		INPUTS (H or L or –)										OUTPUTS							
FUNCTION	No.	10	9	8	7	6	5	4	3	2	1	8	7	6	5	4	3	2	1
	1											•	•	•	•	•	•	•	A
	2											•	•	•	•	•	•	•	A
	3											•	•	•	•	•	•	A	•
	4											•	•	•	•	•	•	A	•
	5											•	•	•	•	•	A	•	•
	6											•	•	•	•	•	A	•	•
	7											•	•	•	•	A	•	•	•
	8											•	•	•	•	A	•	•	•
	9											•	•	•	A	•	•	•	•
	10											•	•	•	A	•	•	•	•
	11											•	•	A	•	•	•	•	•
	12											•	•	A	•	•	•	•	•
	13											•	A	•	•	•	•	•	•
	14											•	A	•	•	•	•	•	•
	15											A	•	•	•	•	•	•	•
	16											A	•	•	•	•	•	•	•
I/O ASSIGNMENT																			

Figure 2-65a. PAL tables PAL10H8 and PAL10L8.

levels have already been programmed, leaving us to define the 16 product terms. Note that pairs of devices (e.g., PAL10H8 and PAL10L8) are identical except that one has active-high outputs while the other has active-low outputs.

Example 2-32. How many fusible links are used in each PAL?

We see from Figs. 2-54 and 2-65 that each PAL has $2m \times 16 = 32m$ fusible links, where m is the number of inputs. Consequently, we find that

PAL16H2, PAL16L2, PAL16C1	each have 512 fusible links
PAL14H4, PAL14L4	each have 448 fusible links

PAL TABLE NO. ____

CHECK ONE	MONOLITHIC MEMORIES PART NO.	OUTPUT ACTIVE LEVEL					
	PAL12H6	H	H	H	H	H	H
	PAL12L6	L	L	L	L	L	L

PRODUCT-TERM FUNCTION	No.	INPUTS (H or L or –) 12	11	10	9	8	7	6	5	4	3	2	1	OUTPUTS 6	5	4	3	2	1
	1													•	•	•	•	•	A
	2													•	•	•	•	•	A
	3													•	•	•	•	•	A
	4													•	•	•	•	•	A
	5													•	•	•	•	A	•
	6													•	•	•	•	A	•
	7													•	•	•	A	•	•
	8													•	•	•	A	•	•
	9													•	•	A	•	•	•
	10													•	•	A	•	•	•
	11													•	A	•	•	•	•
	12													•	A	•	•	•	•
	13													A	•	•	•	•	•
	14													A	•	•	•	•	•
	15													A	•	•	•	•	•
	16													A	•	•	•	•	•
I/O ASSIGNMENT																			

Figure 2-65b. PAL tables PAL 12H6 and PAL 12L6.

PAL12H6, PAL12L6	each have 384 fusible links
PAL10H8, PAL10L8	each have 320 fusible links

These numbers of fusible links are significantly less than for the Signetics 82S100/101 FPLA (with 1928 fusible links, as found earlier) or the Texas Instruments 74S330/331 FPLA (with 1508 fusible links). As we study design techniques in later chapters, we will be looking for ways to squeeze the *complexity* of a design into a programmable chip. We will find that a specific application may favor one device or another because of the number of bits that can be stored, on the one hand, or because of the I/O configuration, on the other.

PAL TABLE NO. ____

CHECK ONE	MONOLITHIC MEMORIES PART NO.	OUTPUT ACTIVE LEVEL			
	PAL14H4	H	H	H	H
	PAL14L4	L	L	L	L

PRODUCT-TERM FUNCTION	No.	INPUTS (H or L or –)														OUTPUTS			
		14	13	12	11	10	9	8	7	6	5	4	3	2	1	4	3	2	1
	1															•	•	•	A
	2															•	•	•	A
	3															•	•	•	A
	4															•	•	•	A
	5															•	•	A	•
	6															•	•	A	•
	7															•	•	A	•
	8															•	•	A	•
	9															•	A	•	•
	10															•	A	•	•
	11															•	A	•	•
	12															•	A	•	•
	13															A	•	•	•
	14															A	•	•	•
	15															A	•	•	•
	16															A	•	•	•
I/O ASSIGNMENT																			

Figure 2-65c. PAL tables PAL 14H4 and PAL 14L4.

Example 2-33. Implement an 8-bit comparator analogous to the 6-bit comparator of Fig. 2-43 using a PAL16C1.

Let the input pairs to be matched be 1 and 2, 3 and 4, . . . , 15 and 16. That is, inputs 1 and 2 must be equal, 3 and 4 must also be equal, and so on. Now define a function called UNEQUAL which is active if 1 is high while 2 is low, or if 1 is low while 2 is high, or if 3 is high while 4 is low, and so on. Each one of the resulting 16 conditions can be implemented with a product term in the PAL16C1. The resulting PAL table is shown in Fig. 2-66.

Now, note that the function EQUAL will be active when UNEQUAL is inactive. Consequently, the active-low output of the PAL16C1 (i.e., pin 15 in Fig. 2-64) implements EQUAL-H, while the other output implements EQUAL-L.

PAL TABLE NO. ___

CHECK ONE	MONOLITHIC MEMORIES PART NO.	OUT. ACT. LEV.	
	PAL16H2	H	H
	PAL16L2	L	L

PRODUCT-TERM FUNCTION	No.	INPUTS (H or L or –) 16	15	14	13	12	11	10	9	8	7	6	5	4	3	2	1	OUT 2	OUT 1
	1																	•	A
	2																	•	A
	3																	•	A
	4																	•	A
	5																	•	A
	6																	•	A
	7																	•	A
	8																	•	A
	9																	A	•
	10																	A	•
	11																	A	•
	12																	A	•
	13																	A	•
	14																	A	•
	15																	A	•
	16																	A	•
I/O ASSIGNMENT																			

Figure 2-65d. PAL tables PAL 16H2 and PAL 16L2.

We will conclude this section with the table of Fig. 2-67, which compares some of the features of the families of programmable chips discussed in this section. The "normalized number of fusible links" column is included to give some measure of bits per unit area (where a 20-pin DIP represents a "unit area"). In particular, it is included as a reminder that the 600-mil-wide Signetics FPLAs take up a lot of PC board area which is offset by the greater flexibility they provide.

2-13 SYNCHRONOUS SEQUENTIAL CIRCUITRY

Up to this point, we have been considering alternative implementations of *combinational* circuitry, that is, circuitry in which outputs are solely boolean functions of inputs. Combinational circuit design represents just one part of the more general problem of *sequential* circuit de-

PAL TABLE NO. ___

MONOLITHIC MEMORIES PART NO.	OUT. ACT. LEV.	
PAL16C1	H	L

PRODUCT-TERM FUNCTION	No.	INPUTS (H or L or –)																OUT	
		16	15	14	13	12	11	10	9	8	7	6	5	4	3	2	1	1	1
	1																	A	A
	2																	A	A
	3																	A	A
	4																	A	A
	5																	A	A
	6																	A	A
	7																	A	A
	8																	A	A
	9																	A	A
	10																	A	A
	11																	A	A
	12																	A	A
	13																	A	A
	14																	A	A
	15																	A	A
	16																	A	A
I/O ASSIGNMENT																			

Figure 2-65e. PAL table PAL 16C1.

sign, wherein circuit outputs are functions of both present *and past* inputs. Past inputs assert their effect through *flip-flops* and other memory elements in the circuitry.

The mechanism that gives order to present and past events is a *clock*. As shown in Fig. 2-68, the rising edges of a clock signal can be used to quantize time into successive clock periods. Outputs of the sequential circuit during the $(k + 1)$th clock period are boolean functions of inputs during the kth clock period as well as being boolean functions of inputs during previous clock periods. We must run the clock at a sufficiently high clock rate to ensure that the sequential circuit can do whatever needs to be done, even if it needs many clock periods in which to do it.

A clock must have *good edges*. Assume that it is the *rising edge* of the clock which distinguishes between one clock period and the next. A "slowly" rising edge can cause flip-flops to change at different

PAL TABLE NO. Ex. 2-33

MONOLITHIC MEMORIES PART NO.	OUT. ACT. LEV.	
PAL16C1	H	L

PRODUCT-TERM FUNCTION	No.	16	15	14	13	12	11	10	9	8	7	6	5	4	3	2	1	OUT 1	OUT 1
Mismatch on 1, 2	1	-	-	-	-	-	-	-	-	-	-	-	-	-	-	L	H	A	A
	2	-	-	-	-	-	-	-	-	-	-	-	-	-	-	H	L	A	A
Mismatch on 3, 4	3	-	-	-	-	-	-	-	-	-	-	-	-	L	H	-	-	A	A
	4	-	-	-	-	-	-	-	-	-	-	-	-	H	L	-	-	A	A
Mismatch on 5, 6	5	-	-	-	-	-	-	-	-	-	-	L	H	-	-	-	-	A	A
	6	-	-	-	-	-	-	-	-	-	-	H	L	-	-	-	-	A	A
Mismatch on 7, 8	7	-	-	-	-	-	-	-	-	L	H	-	-	-	-	-	-	A	A
	8	-	-	-	-	-	-	-	-	H	L	-	-	-	-	-	-	A	A
Mismatch on 9, 10	9	-	-	-	-	-	-	L	H	-	-	-	-	-	-	-	-	A	A
	10	-	-	-	-	-	-	H	L	-	-	-	-	-	-	-	-	A	A
Mismatch on 11, 12	11	-	-	-	-	L	H	-	-	-	-	-	-	-	-	-	-	A	A
	12	-	-	-	-	H	L	-	-	-	-	-	-	-	-	-	-	A	A
Mismatch on 13, 14	13	-	-	L	H	-	-	-	-	-	-	-	-	-	-	-	-	A	A
	14	-	-	H	L	-	-	-	-	-	-	-	-	-	-	-	-	A	A
Mismatch on 15, 16	15	L	H	-	-	-	-	-	-	-	-	-	-	-	-	-	-	A	A
	16	H	L	-	-	-	-	-	-	-	-	-	-	-	-	-	-	A	A
I/O ASSIGNMENT		Pair 15, 16		Pair 13, 14		Pair 11, 12		Pair 9, 10		Pair 7, 8		Pair 5, 6		Pair 3, 4		Pair 1, 2		EQUAL-L	EQUAL-H

Figure 2-66. PAL table for the 8-bit comparator of Example 2-33.

times, in going from one clock period to the next, because of the tolerance on the threshold voltage of their clock inputs, as illustrated in Fig. 2-69. This is called *clock skew* and can cause faulty operation in an otherwise well-designed sequential circuit.

One of the major benefits of the digital mode of operation is its inclusion of a tolerance on all logic specifications such that operation within tolerance yields "ideal" performance (e.g., a logic 1 will not be degraded to a logic 0). In Sec. 5-6 we will discuss the *maximum allowable clock skew* for a logic family and what determines it. As long as the effective clock skew of Fig. 2-69 is less than the maximum allowable clock skew, the flip-flops in a circuit will act as if they have all been clocked by an infinitely fast edge (having zero rise time). For our purposes here, it is only necessary to note that the time involved for 74LSxx logic is on the order of 5 to 10 ns. Needless to say, neither the output of a mechanical switch nor a 60-Hz sine wave makes a very good clock source.

Family	DIP package	Number of inputs	Number of outputs	Number of fusible links	Normalized number of fusible links (see text)	Maximum access time (ns)	Input loading–low (μA)	Input loading–high (μA)	Output drive–low (mA)	Output drive–high (mA)	Maximum power-supply current (mA)
Harris Semiconductor 76xx PROMs — 32 × 8	16	5	8	256	320	40	250	40	16	2	105
— 256 × 4	16	8	4	1024	1280	40	250	40	16	2	130
— 1024 × 8	20	10	8	8192	8192	60	250	40	16	2	170
Signetics 82S100/101 FPLAs	28	16	8	1928	689	50	100	25	10	2	170
Texas Instruments 74S330/331 FPLAs	20	12	6	1508	1508	60	250	50	12	6	165
Monolithic Memories PALs	20	10–16	2–8	320–512	320–512	60	250	25	8	3	90

Figure 2-67. Comparison of programmable combinational chips.

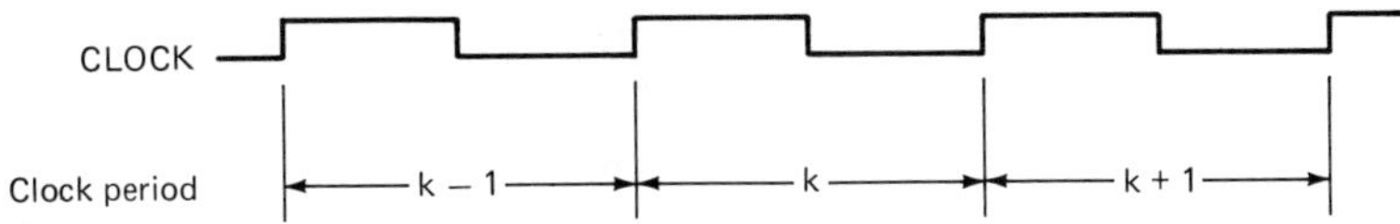

Figure 2-68. Time quantization by means of a clock.

A *Schmitt trigger* is a circuit whose output *snaps* from one state to the other as its input crosses a threshold. It has two thresholds, depending upon whether the input is a rising edge or a falling edge, as shown in Fig. 2-70. It can be used to generate a good clock from a signal whose only fault is its edges. For example, Fig. 2-70*c* illustrates how a slow but stable frequency clock can be obtained from a 60-Hz signal. Figure 2-70*d* shows how one line of an output port of an NMOS microcomputer can be used to generate a clock signal for TTL logic, even though the NMOS part generates relatively slow edges. Figure 2-70*e* illustrates a minimum-cost Schmitt-trigger clock circuit that is satisfactory for applications in which the frequency is not critical. The frequency depends upon the Schmitt trigger's *hysteresis* (i.e., the difference between its two input threshold voltages), which is specified as being at least 0.4 V and typically 0.8 V. Consequently, different PC boards made with this circuit and with the same nominal values of R_x and C_x might vary in clock frequency by a factor of 2 or 3 to 1.

A common way to generate a clock signal having good frequency accuracy and stability is to employ a *crystal* clock. Even without taking special steps, a low-cost crystal like that of Fig. 2-71*a* will yield a clock frequency accuracy of 50 parts per million. The circuit shown in Fig. 2-71*b* is one of the few IC oscillators designed specifically for

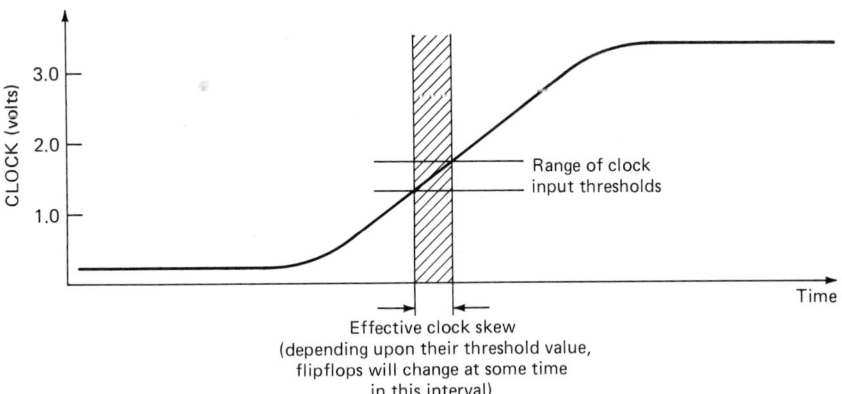

Figure 2-69. Clock skew created by poor rise time of the clock.

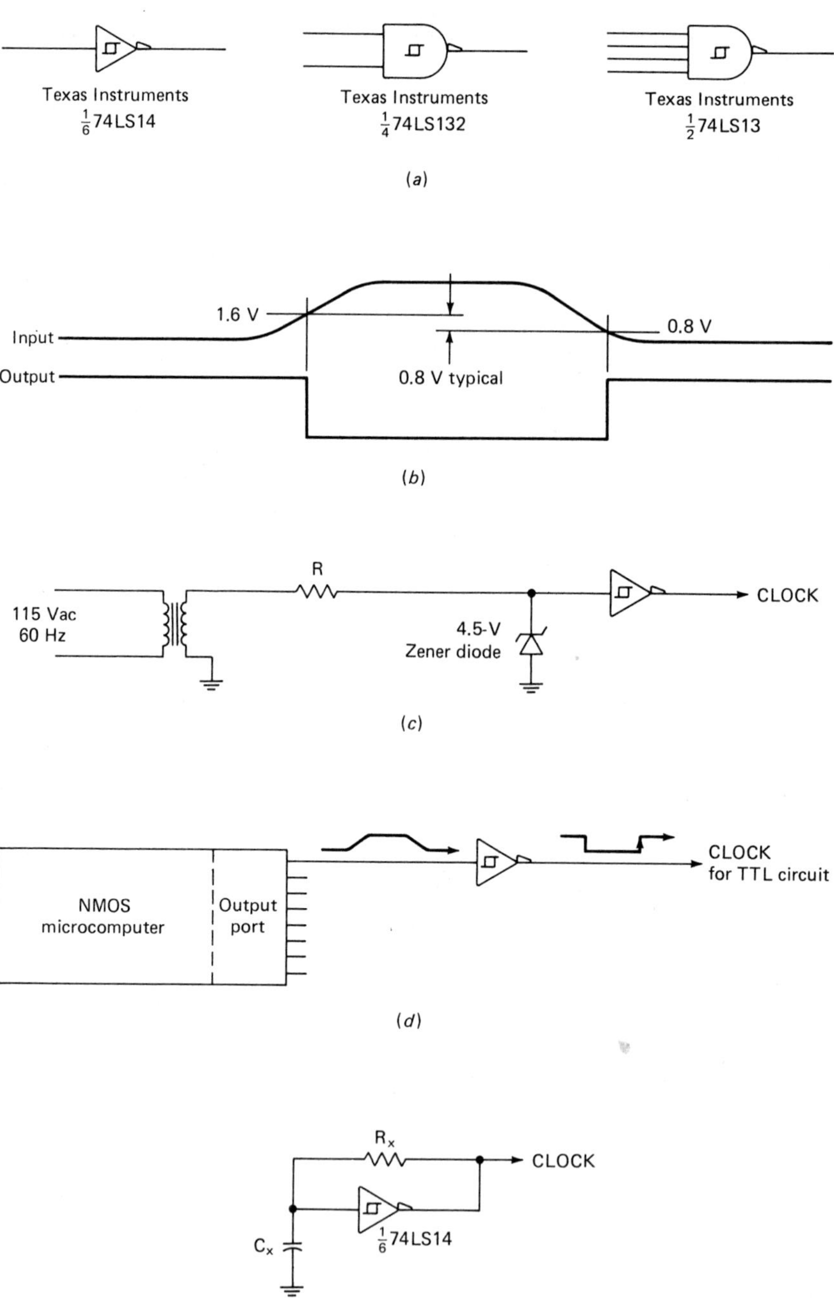

Figure 2-70. Schmitt trigger. (a) Devices; (b) operation; (c) generating a 60-Hz clock; (d) use with an NMOS microcomputer to generate a TTL clock; (e) RC clock circuit.

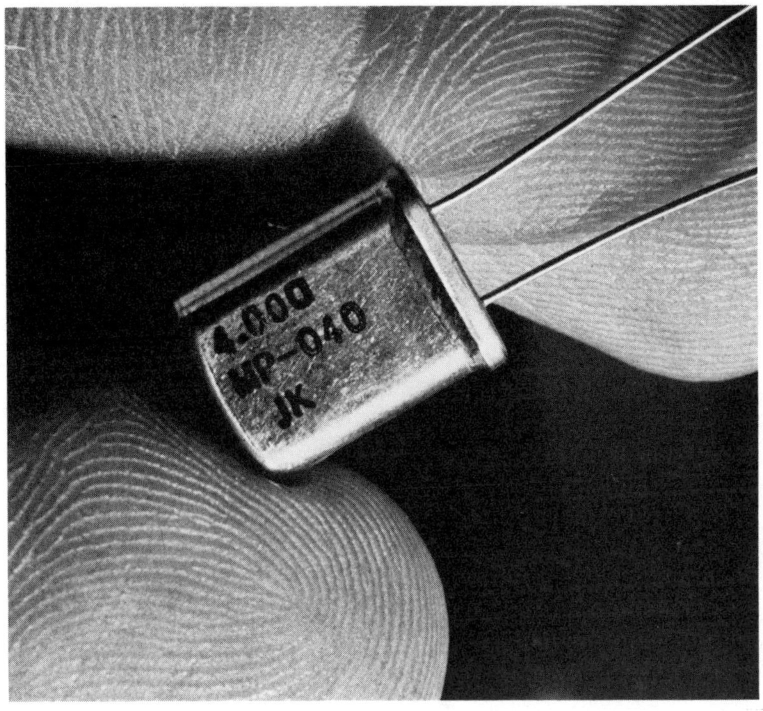

(a)

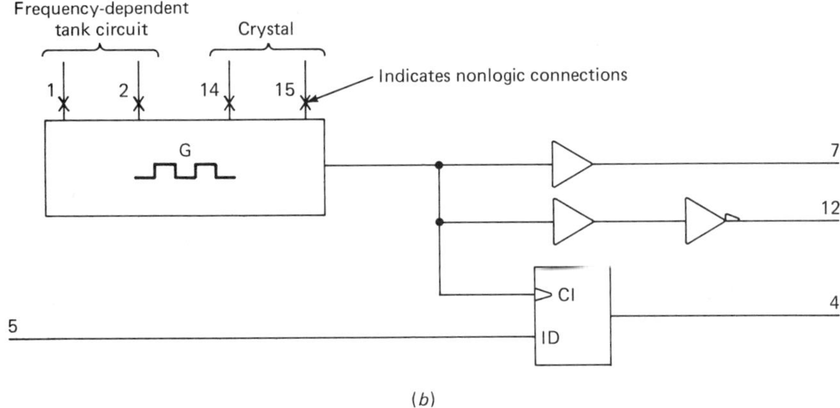

(b)

Figure 2-71. Crystal clock. (a) Low-cost, 0.53-in-high quartz crystal, for 4 MHz and higher (CTS Knights, Inc.); (b) part of 74LS320, crystal-controlled oscillator (Texas Instruments).

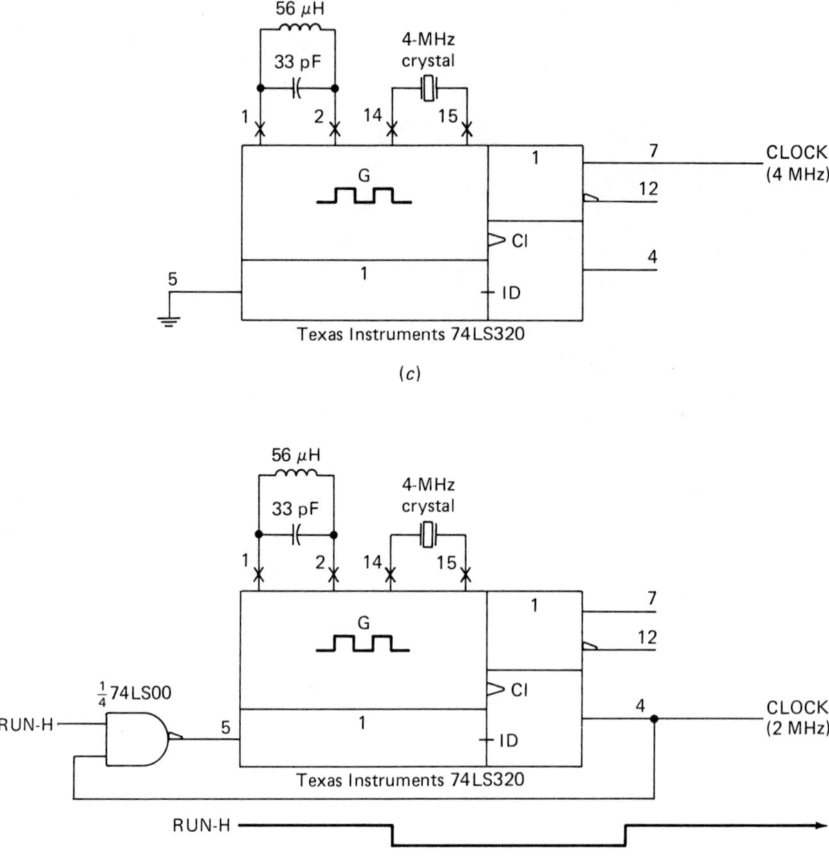

Figure 2-71c. 4-MHz clock circuit; (d) clock with a control input.

crystal control. It can generate an output at the crystal frequency, as shown in Fig. 2-71*c*. Alternatively, it includes a flip-flop, so that with the addition of a single gate, the clock can be turned on and off, using the circuit of Fig. 2-71*d*. This method of controlling the clock will never produce a "glitch," or cutoff clock pulse. Any time the clock output goes low, it will remain low for exactly one-half of the output clock period. If we try to turn it off while its output is low, it will wait until it has been low for one-half of a clock period, produce one last rising edge, and then stop. Notice that the output frequency of this circuit is one-half of the crystal frequency.

While the clock chip of Fig. 2-71 can operate over a range from

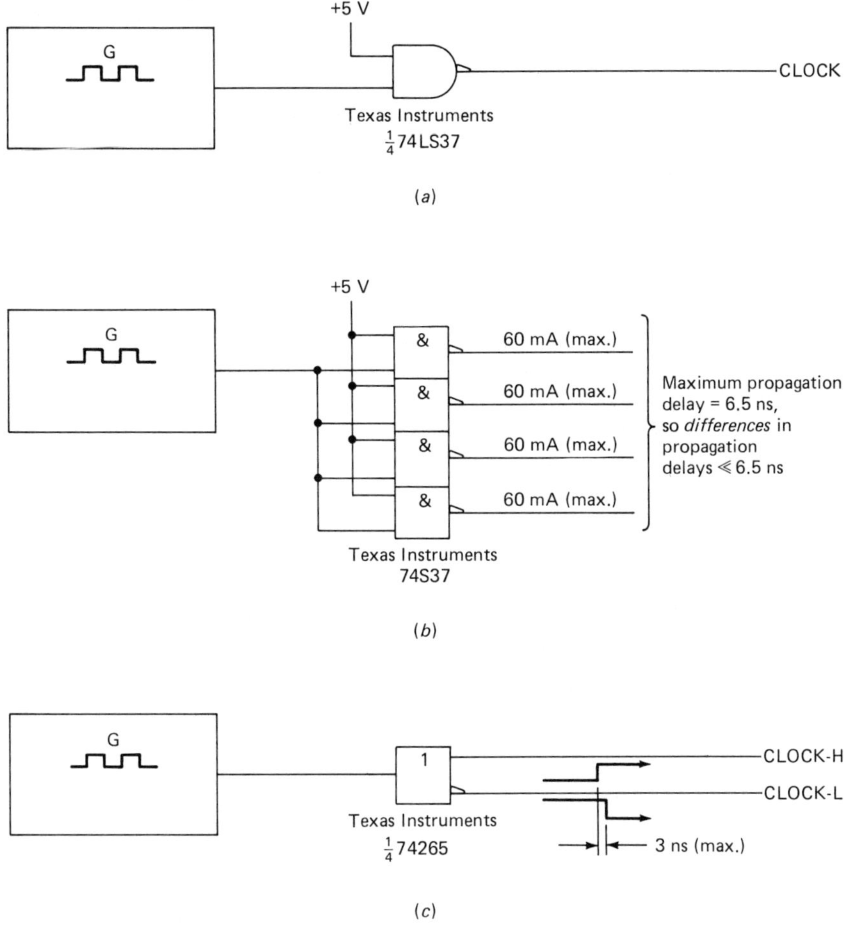

Figure 2-72. Clock drivers. (a) For sink loads up to 48 mA; (b) for sink loads up to 240 mA; (c) where CLOCK-H and CLOCK-L are both required.

1 Hz to 20 MHz, crystals tend to increase in size as the frequency drops below 2 MHz. On the other hand, if the clock rate gets "too high," the logic circuitry will have difficulties keeping up (as will be discussed in Chap. 5). A good compromise for many applications in which the clock rate is not particularly critical is to use a 2.0- or 4.0-MHz clock.

The clock line is likely to be the most heavily loaded line in a digital design. Accordingly, we may use a *clock driver* circuit such as one of those shown in Fig. 2-72. If the clock must be split among several drivers, we must ensure that the rising edges of the driver outputs occur close enough together to avoid clock-skew problems. Usually, clocked TTL chips respond to the *rising edge* of the clock signal. However, if we have a special need to mix in a TTL chip that responds to the falling edge of the clock, the circuit of Fig. 2-72*c* will minimize clock skew between the two clocks required.

A fundamental building block for sequential circuit design is the clocked D-type flip-flop. The dependency notation symbolism for eight of these in one 20-pin DIP package is shown in Fig. 2-73. It indicates that the output of each of the eight flip-flop logic elements is controlled by the three inputs, R, C1, and 1D. Each of these labels is a reserved identifier in the symbol standard. R is used to label a *reset* input; when it is active (i.e., low), all eight flip-flop outputs are reset to their inactive (i.e., low) state. Because all eight logic elements are identical, only the top one need carry any labeling. The C1−1D inputs exhibit *CONTROL-dependency.* This is similar to AND-dependency, but is used to control the input to a sequential device (i.e., a flip-flop), as will be discussed in more detail in Chap. 5. A 1D input becomes active only when C1 is active. The bit of data on this 1D input is stored in the flip-flop and becomes the flip-flop's output.

The *dynamic indicator symbol* (▷) indicates that the C1 input senses a *transition,* not a level. Thus a rising edge (from a clock) on the C1 input will cause the output of each flip-flop to change state so as to take the value that was on its 1D input *just before* the rising edge occurred. In this manner, a sequential circuit steps gracefully from clock period to clock period. Each flip-flop's output during the next clock

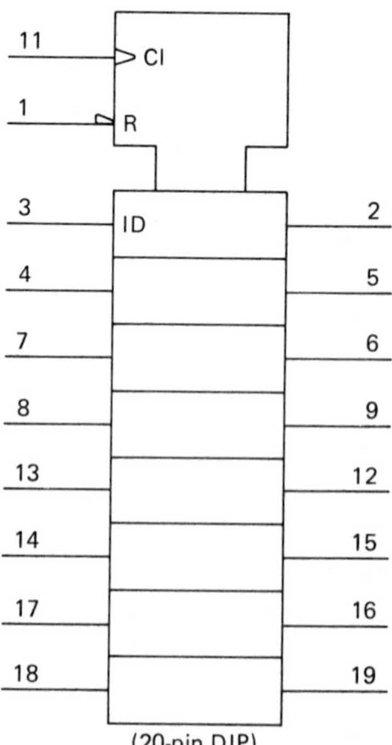

Figure 2-73. 74LS273, octal D-type flip-flop. (Texas Instruments.)

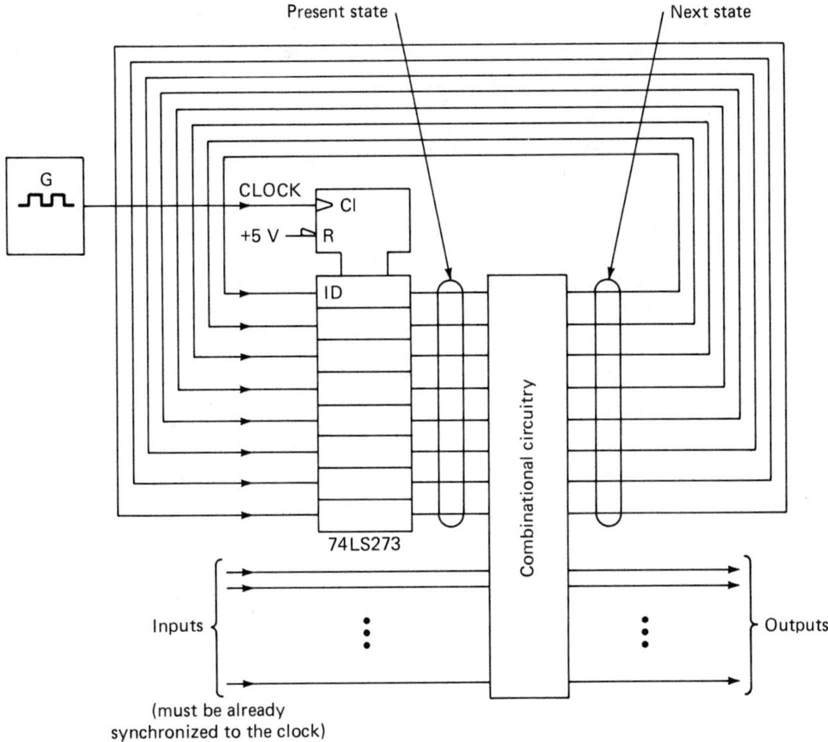

Figure 2-74. Synchronous sequential circuit.

period is determined by the value of its 1D input during the present clock period.

Notice that the R input of Fig. 2-73 *does not* include the dynamic indicator symbol (▷). If it did, this, together with the polarity indicator symbol (⌂), would indicate that the flip-flops reset on a *falling edge* of the R input. But with the dynamic indicator symbol *missing*, R is a static input. When R goes low, it resets the flip-flops. As long as it remains low, it *holds* the flip-flops in the reset state, even overriding the momentary effect of an input on C1 and 1D.

A *synchronous* sequential circuit is represented in one form in Fig. 2-74. The circuit is synchronous because:

1 All the flip-flops are edge-triggered, as indicated by the dynamic indicator symbol (▷) on the C1 input.
2 The clock inputs to all flip-flops are tied to the same clock source, labeled CLOCK.
3 Static inputs to flip-flops (e.g., the R input) are disabled.

4 All inputs are (already) synchronized to CLOCK. Consequently, their changes, when they occur, will only occur *just after* the rising edges of CLOCK.

When a circuit is designed synchronously, we can be assured that circuit "funnies" will not take place. The circuit implementation will behave exactly as it did on paper. In Chap. 5 when we broaden our design techniques to include *asynchronous* sequential circuit design, we will take advantage of circuit capabilities such as the reset input to the octal flip-flop of Fig. 2-73. We will find that, with care, we can design asynchronous circuitry to operate just as reliably as synchronous circuitry. But it will require an extra dimension of discipline.

The circuit of Fig. 2-74 allows circuit outputs to depend not only upon circuit inputs, but also upon the *state* of the circuit. The state information is represented by the states of all the flip-flops in the circuit. In this case the state information resides in one IC, an octal flip-flop. More generally, the state information will reside in flip-flops, counters, shift registers, and any other devices that include memory.

To avoid spurious operation, inputs to a synchronous circuit must be synchronized to the clock. The problem of an unsynchronized input arises when that input changes just (nanoseconds) before the circuit is clocked. This is illustrated in Fig. 2-75. When IN* changes toward the end of the *k*th clock period, the combinational circuit outputs respond to the change to generate new "next-state" information. However, if the propagation delay is different for the two next-state outputs, then when the clock transition occurs, the S1 flip-flop may see its new value (H) while the S2 flip-flop may still be looking at its old value (H). Consequently, a circuit whose next state should be either LH or HL ends up being HH.

We might argue that with a clock rate of 2 MHz, the chance of an unsynchronized input changing during such a critical time is remote. On the other hand, suppose that the *difference* between the two propagation delays of Fig. 2-75 is 10 ns (the typical propagation delay of a 75LSxxx gate). Then for a 2-MHz clock (with a clock period of 500 ns), we have 1 chance in 50 of erroneous operation occurring. Any real system that has this kind of error mechanism lurking, waiting to strike, will look to a user as if it is continuously bumbling. It will experience many errors during the 2 million clock periods occurring every second.

This problem never arises if the inputs to a synchronous sequential circuit come from *another* synchronous sequential circuit (clocked by the same clock). Now, these inputs will change only in response to the clock. All changes occur immediately *after* the clock transition, never before it. This assumes that we are not clocking the circuit so fast that the combinational circuit outputs are still changing when the

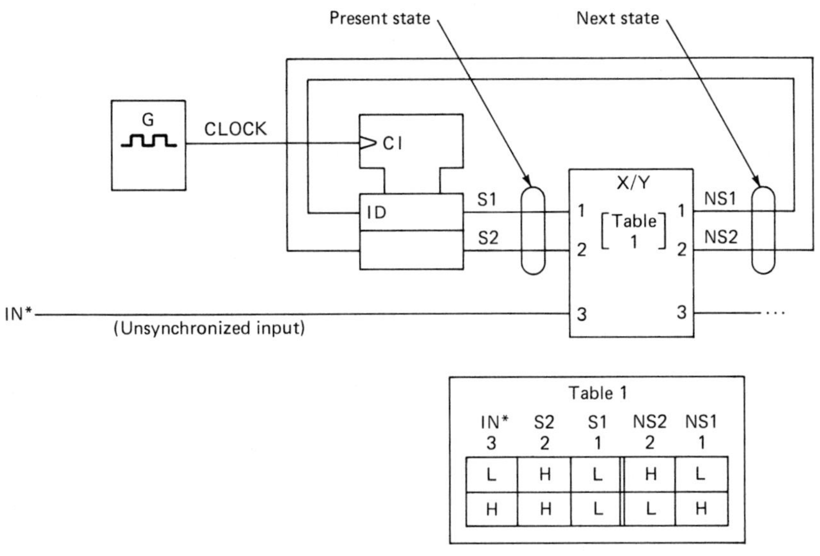

Table 1

IN* 3	S2 2	S1 1	NS2 2	NS1 1
L	H	L	H	L
H	H	L	L	H

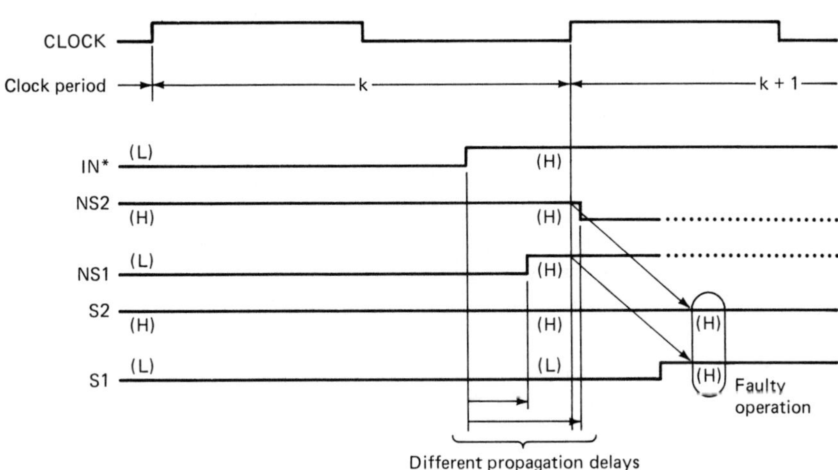

Figure 2-75. Problem with an unsynchronized input.

next clock transition occurs. In fact, it is just this consideration which determines the maximum clock rate at which a synchronous sequential circuit will operate reliably. We will discuss this in Chap. 5.

Unsynchronized inputs to a synchronous sequential circuit are synchronized by clocking them into D-type flip-flops. This is illus-

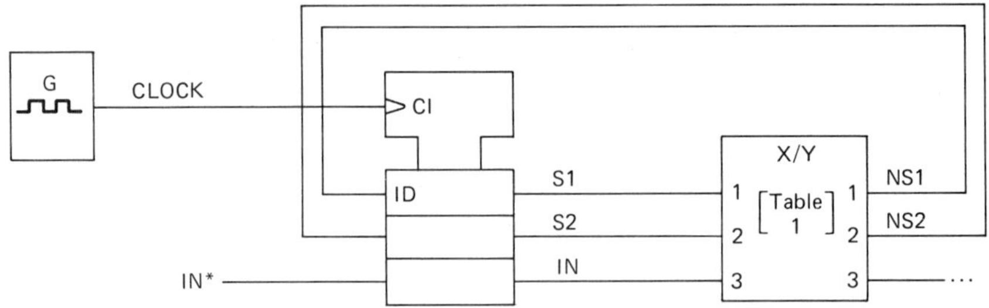

Figure 2-76. Synchronizing the unsynchronized input of Fig. 2-75.

trated in Fig. 2-76. Note that if the unsynchronized input IN* changes just before the clock transition occurs, we are still not sure whether the synchronized input IN will change. However, if the change is not seen at one clock transition, it will be seen at the next one. In *either* case the synchronous sequential circuit that uses IN will behave correctly during *every* clock transition.

Our intent here is simply to introduce the concepts of a synchronous sequential circuit and of circuit state. In subsequent chapters we will employ these concepts within a design context.

2-14 SYNCHRONOUS BUILDING BLOCKS

Any sequential circuit can be implemented with the structure of Fig. 2-74. In fact, we will soon see that there are good reasons for contraining a design to have this very structure. On the other hand, a variety of commonly recurring problems can benefit from the availability of integrated circuit solutions to them. In this section we will consider:

- Enabled flip-flops
- Shift registers
- Counters

We will also consider their symbolic representation using dependency notation.

Variations of the octal D-type flip-flop of Fig. 2-73 are available to satisfy a variety of design needs. Thus three-state outputs have been added in the unit of Fig. 2-77. With pin 1 high, all eight outputs are put in the high-impedance state. As the symbol indicates, we can still clock new data into the flip-flops (since only the outputs are dependent upon EN, not the inputs).

Figure 2-78 shows another variation. In this case, the eight flip-flops do not get clocked until a rising edge on the clock input (pin

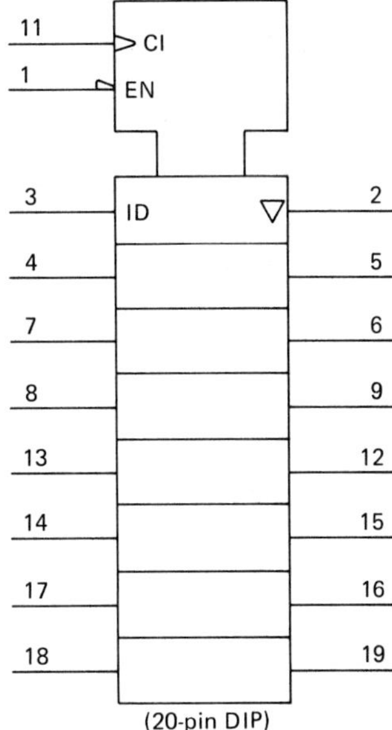

Figure 2-77. 74LS374, octal D-type flip-flop with three-state outputs. (Texas Instruments.)

11) occurs at the end of a clock period during which pin 1 has been held low.

We often wish to convert binary data between *parallel form* (i.e., data represented at different points in a circuit, all looked at during the same clock period) and *serial form* (i.e., data represented at *one* point

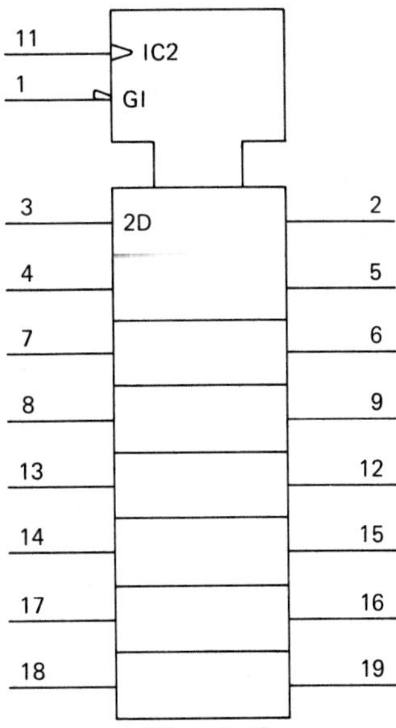

Figure 2-78. 74LS377, octal D-type flip-flop with enabled clock. (Texas Instruments.)

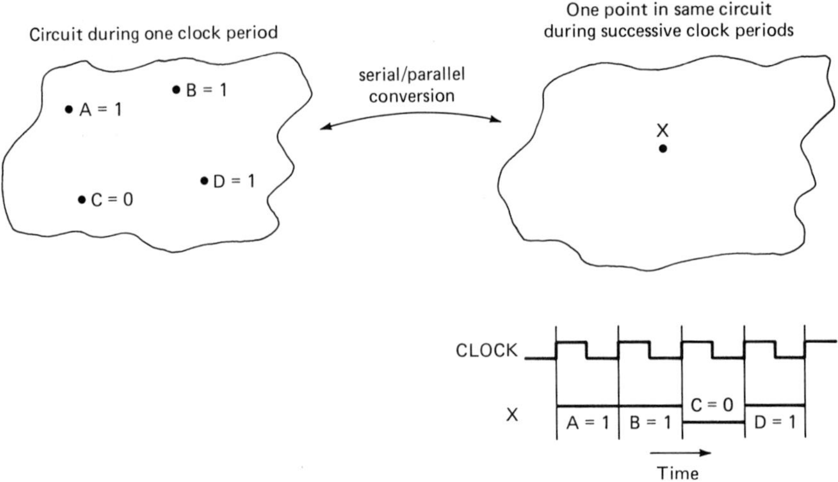

Figure 2-79. Serial/parallel conversion.

in a circuit, looked at during successive clock periods). This is illustrated in Fig. 2-79. A *shift register* is a circuit for carrying out such conversions. The unit symbolized in Fig. 2-80 will convert up to 8 bits of serial input data to parallel form. The C1/→ labeling of pin 8 indicates that this input does two things. When pin 8 sees a rising edge (as required by the ▷ dynamic indicator symbol), the C1 indicates that the data bit formed by ANDing the inputs on pins 1 and 2 will be clocked into the flip-flop with output on pin 3 (because of the C1–1D CONTROL-dependency relationship). The arrow directed to the right indicates that the data stored in the eight flip-flops making up the shift register will be shifted downward when the rising edge of the clock occurs.

The → symbology represents the second of three ways used by dependency notation to represent clock inputs. All three ways are shown in Fig. 2-81. Of course, for falling-edge-sensitive inputs, the symbolism requires an additional polarity indicator symbol (⊳) on the input line.

A more complicated example of the use of dependency notation is required for the circuit of Fig. 2-82*a*. If we try to represent the ORing of the two clock inputs (pins 6 and 7) as such, the symbolism distracts our attention from the normal use of this input. For synchronous design, only one of these will be used as a clock (say, pin 7). As we will see in Sec. 5-7, we can actually use the pin 6 input to enable the clock, provided that we use synchronous design and satisfy a constraint upon the maximum clock rate.

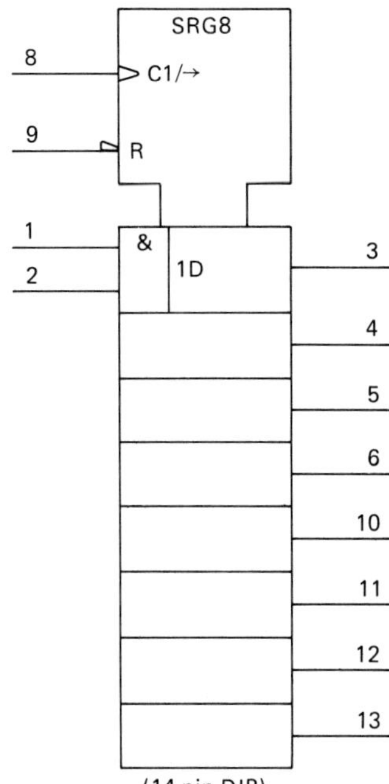

Figure 2-80. 74LS164, 8-bit serial in/parallel out shift register. (Texas Instruments.)

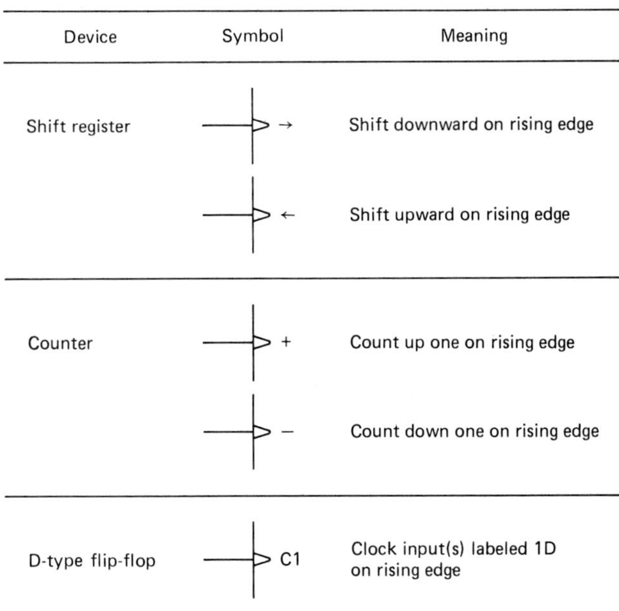

Device	Symbol	Meaning
Shift register	→	Shift downward on rising edge
	←	Shift upward on rising edge
Counter	+	Count up one on rising edge
	−	Count down one on rising edge
D-type flip-flop	C1	Clock input(s) labeled 1D on rising edge

Figure 2-81. Dependency notation symbolism for rising-edge-sensitive inputs.

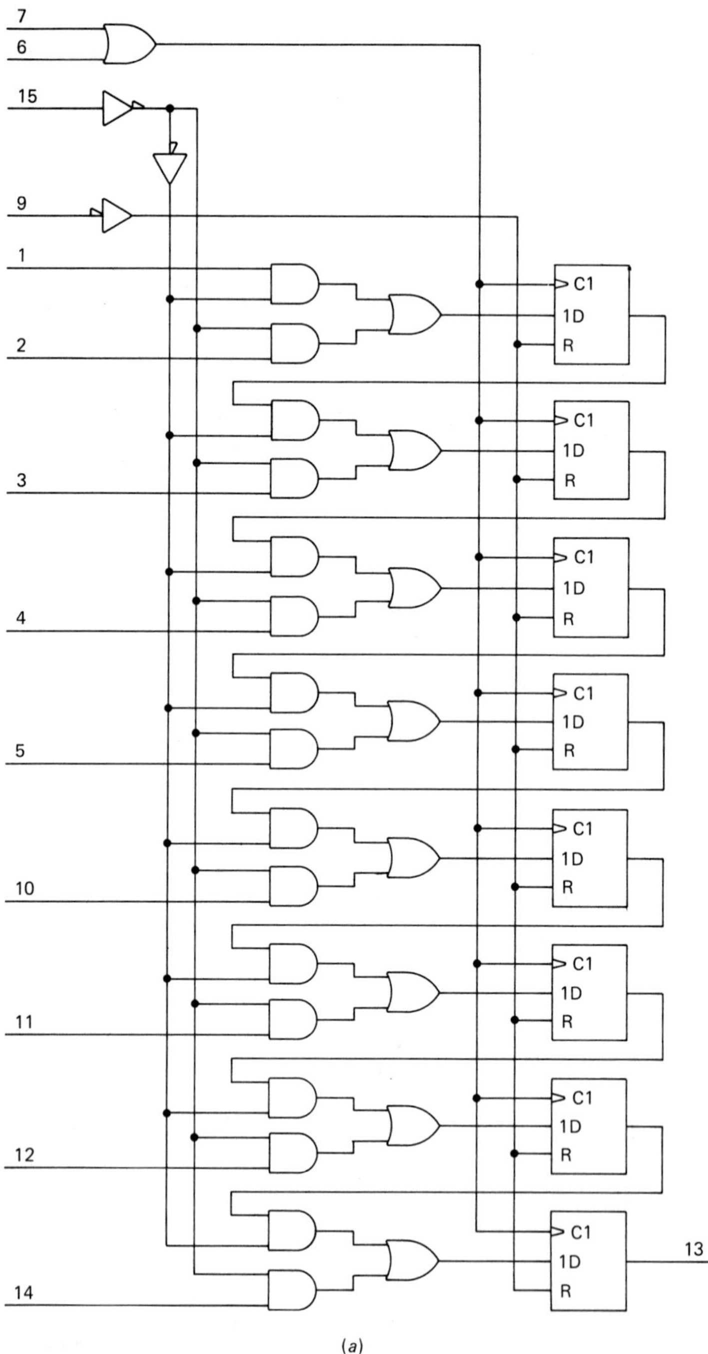

(a)

Figure 2-82. 74LS166, 8-bit parallel in/serial out shift register. (a) Functional diagram.

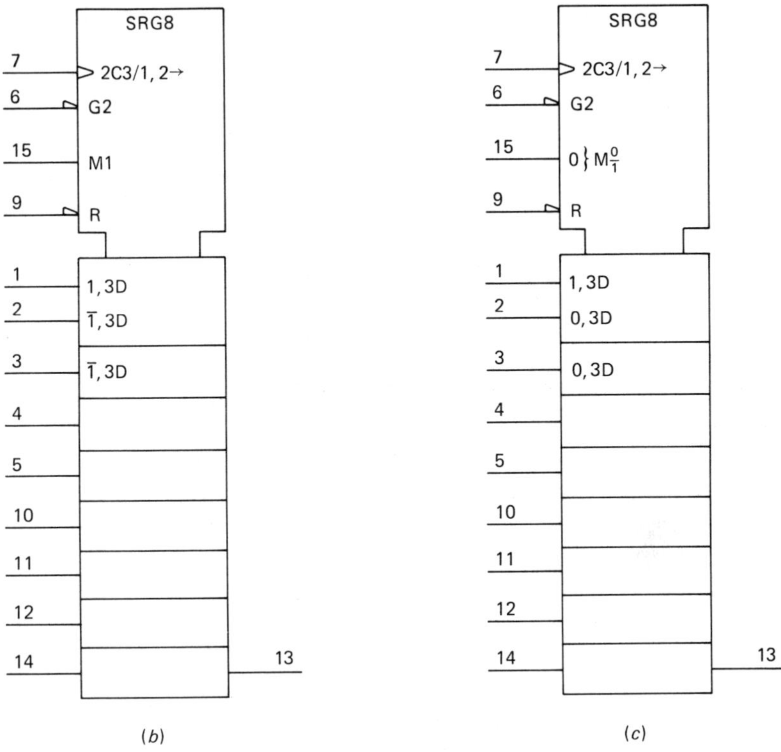

Figure 2-82b. Symbol; (c) alternative symbol. (Texas Instruments.)

The two alternative symbols of Fig. 2-82*b* and *c* show the pin 6 input enabling the clock. Thus the 2C3 labeling of pin 7 says to make C3 active if a rising edge occurs on pin 7 AND if G2 is active (i.e., low). The 1,2→ labeling says to shift the 8 bits of data in the shift register down if pin 15 is high and pin 6 is low when the rising edge occurs on pin 7.

The M1 labeling of pin 15 in Fig. 2-82*b* and the alternative 0}M$^0_1$ labeling in Fig. 2-82*c* introduce *MODE-dependency* to identify the two different modes of operation of this chip, namely shifting and loading. Shifting is invoked when pin 15 is high (and the enabled clock edge occurs). In both figures M1 will be active, enabling all pins that include a 1 in their labeling. Loading is invoked when pin 15 is low. In Fig. 2-82*b* this is symbolized by $\overline{\text{M1}}$ being active, enabling all pins that include a $\overline{1}$ in their labeling. We will prefer the symbolism of Fig. 2-82*c*, wherein the "load" mode is symbolized by M0 being active, enabling all pins that include a 0 in their labeling. Although we might object to the use of a binary grouping symbol with only one input, this is countered by the advantage of *emphasizing* the two modes of the device right in the labeling of pin 15, which controls those two modes.

A *counter* is an example of a sequential circuit whose flip-flops are supported by extensive gating to implement a useful function. Medium-scale integrated circuit implementations of counters are devices of great versatility. For example, consider the 4-bit binary counter of Fig. 2-83. The CTR4 label for the device identifies it as being a 4-bit binary counter. The labeling of pin 9 indicates that it can operate in either of two modes, identified as mode 0 and mode 1. The C4 labeling of pin 2 to the left of the slash says that when a rising edge occurs on pin 2, all C4–4D CONTROL-dependencies will be active. If the device is in mode 0 (as required by the 0,4D labeling of flip-flop inputs), the four flip-flops will be parallel-loaded from the inputs on pins 3, 4, 5, and 6. The 1,2,3+ labeling of pin 2 to the right of the slash says that the counter will count (+) if pins 9, 7, and 10 are all high when a rising edge occurs on pin 2. This labeling takes advantage of G2-2 and G3-3 AND-dependencies, M1-1 MODE-dependency, and the ANDing implied by numbers separated by commas (i.e., 1, 2, 3). The 3CT=15 labeling of the output on pin 15 says that this output will be active when the G3 input is active (i.e., pin 10 is high) AND when the content of the counter is 15. Finally, the weights associated with each flip-flop are shown in brackets.

To illustrate the versatility of this counter chip, consider the 12-bit binary counter of Fig. 2-84. If LOAD = 1 (i.e., if the input la-

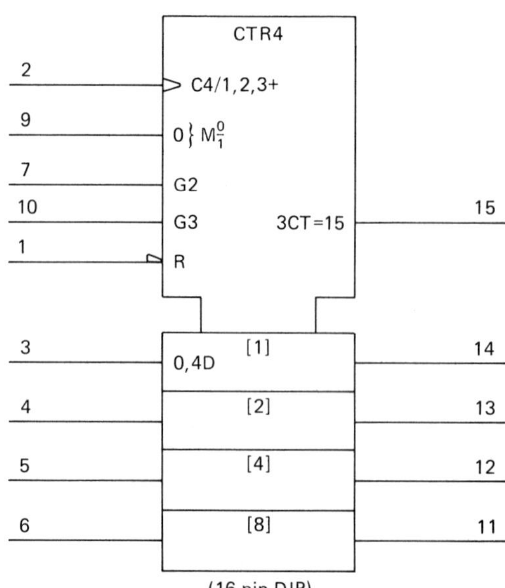

Figure 2-83. 74LS161A, 4-bit synchronously presettable binary counter. (Texas Instruments.)

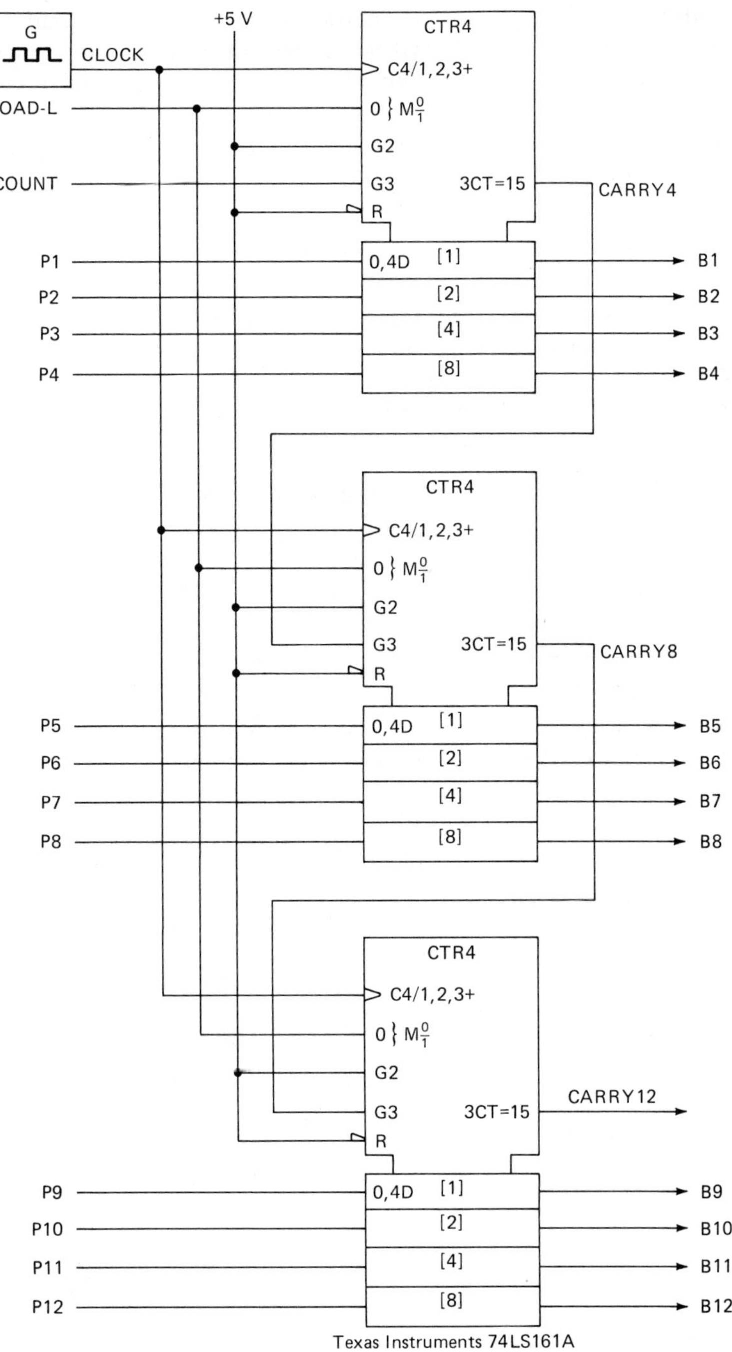

Figure 2-84. 12-bit synchronously presettable binary counter.

beled LOAD-L is low) when the clock transition occurs, the 12-bit number P12, . . . , P1 will be loaded into the counter. On the other hand, if LOAD = 0 and COUNT = 1 when the clock transition occurs, the 12-bit counter will be incremented. Finally, if LOAD = 0 and COUNT = 0 when the clock transition occurs, the counter will remain unchanged.

Example 2-34. Write boolean equations for the four variables labeled CARRY4, CARRY8, and CARRY12.

CARRY4 = COUNT·B1·B2·B3·B4

CARRY8 = CARRY4·B5·B6·B7·B8

= COUNT·B1·B2·B3·B4·B5·B6·B7·B8

CARRY12 = CARRY8·B9·B10·B11·B12

= COUNT·B1·B2·B3·B4·B5·B6·B7·B8·B9·B10·B11·B12

A BCD version of this same counter structure is shown in Fig. 2-85. Notice that the symbol is identical except for its CTRDIV10 la-

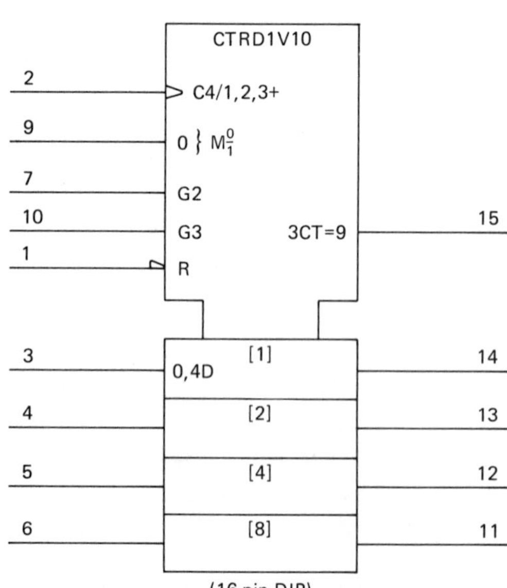

Figure 2-85. 74LS160A, synchronously presettable decade counter. (Texas Instruments.)

beling and its 3CT = 9 labeling of pin 15. When its content equals decimal 9 (i.e., binary 1001) and pin 10 is active, pin 15 will be active (i.e., high). The counter counts from 9 back to 0, as implied by the CTRDIV10 labeling.

Example 2-35. Using 74LS160As, design a three-decade BCD counter, including LOAD-L and COUNT control inputs.

The circuit is identical to that of Fig. 2-84, with the 74LS161As replaced by 74LS160As.

2-15 THE MICROCOMPUTER AS A COMPONENT

As the cost of one-chip microcomputers continues to drop, these devices are becoming the *bargain component* available to digital designers. In addition, those parts of an instrument or device design which can possibly be relegated to a microcomputer (in either one-chip or multiple-chip form) should be, as will be discussed in Sec. 3-3.

Designing the software for any microcomputer, and the hardware for a multiple-chip microcomputer, can be an extensive undertaking. It is not an undertaking we will deal with in this book. Rather, we want to characterize the *role* of the microcomputer, and to understand its *capabilities*. We want to understand how special-purpose circuitry can carry on *reliable interactions* with the microcomputer.

As we look at all of the tasks of an instrument or device design, we try to relegate each one to the microcomputer. If we are thwarted, it will be because:

1 A task must be performed at a *higher rate* than can be handled by the microcomputer.
2 A task may require a *quicker response* than can be achieved by the microcomputer.
3 A task is so *all-consuming* as to leave the microcomputer little time for anything else.

An example of the first kind of task occurs when we try to encrypt data according to the National Bureau of Standards' Data Encryption Standard (DES) (refer back to Fig. 1-3). If we want to execute this algorithm in software, this will set some upper limit upon the rate at which encrypted data can be transmitted. If the required rate exceeds this, the task must be handled in some other way.

Before we act too hastily and design special-purpose circuitry to handle a task, we want to investigate whether the task has already been supported by a specialty chip available from IC manufacturers. If so, the task can be relegated back to the microcomputer in the form of a special-purpose peripheral chip. Some of the tasks that have been supported by specialty chips are:

- DES encryption
- Synchronous and asynchronous serial data transmission
- Printer control
- Keyboard and display control
- Floppy-disk control
- General-purpose interface bus (GPIB) control
- Video display (CRT) control
- Direct memory access (DMA) control
- Tone generation
- Capacitive switch interfacing
- Analog data acquisition

An annually updated guide, such as *IC Master*, referenced at the end of the chapter, is an excellent aid to our awareness of such chips. So are trade journals such as *Electronics, EDN, Electronic Design,* and *Electronic Products*.

The refreshing of a video CRT display, such as that of the computer of Fig. 1-18, is an example of a task that requires *quick response*. First, we might consider an approach that achieves this quick response with a microcomputer and a CRT display controller chip. As the electron beam sweeps across the CRT screen, the microcomputer retrieves data for each character from its read/write memory and transmits it to the CRT display controller chip. This chip turns the electron beam on and off appropriately to generate the image of the characters. The required quick response is achieved by tying up the microcomputer so that it does very little else. Thus the task becomes an (almost) *all-consuming* one.

A separate *dedicated microcomputer* can be employed for handling this task, and one (or more) other microcomputers for remaining instrument tasks. Thus the total microcomputer function is achieved. In this way no one microcomputer has an impossible task. We can use this approach any time we try to relegate several tasks to a microcomputer and one of these tasks consumes so much of the microcomputer's time (or quickness of response) as to degrade the performance of other required tasks. This dedication of separate microcomputers to specific tasks results in our having to handle the *interactions* between these microcomputers as a fundamental task in its own right. It is one that we will address later.

In dealing with a microcomputer as a component, we need to consider each of the following perspectives:

1 How does the microcomputer execute tasks?
2 What is the extent of the microcomputer's resources, and how does this impact the interactions with other special-purpose circuitry?
3 What options exist for reliable data transfer between a microcomputer and special-purpose circuitry?

To execute a task, a microcomputer first acquires any needed input data. Then the algorithmic requirements of the task are executed step by step with a sequence of microcomputer instructions. Finally, the results are transferred out of the microcomputer, perhaps as display or control information. As we try to evaluate whether a microcomputer can keep up with the data rate imposed by a task, we are addressing a problem of software execution speed, which is beyond the scope of this book. We can either develop software expertise ourselves, or gain answers to our execution-speed questions from others.

If we are using a *multiple-chip* microcomputer, the constraint of available microcomputer resources is mitigated. For example, if we need more memory, we add more memory chips. On the other hand, there are good maintainability arguments (which we will discuss in Chap. 3) for organizing microcomputer resources in a one-chip microcomputer if we possibly can. These arguments are so strong that we might prefer to split the tasks of a design among several one-chip microcomputers rather than using a multiple-chip microcomputer, even when both approaches provide workable alternatives.

The resources of a one-chip microcomputer are part of the specifications for the device. For example, the Motorola 6801 unit shown in Fig. 1-2, when operated as a one-chip microcomputer (rather than in one of its multiple-chip microcomputer modes), has the configuration shown in Fig. 2-86, which includes:

- Twenty-four general-purpose input or output (I/O) lines
- Five additional I/O lines which can either serve dedicated purposes or be used as more general-purpose I/O lines
- Two "handshaking" lines for I/O synchronization
- A versatile interrupt structure, with a choice among seven different sources of interrupts
- A UART for automatic, serial I/O

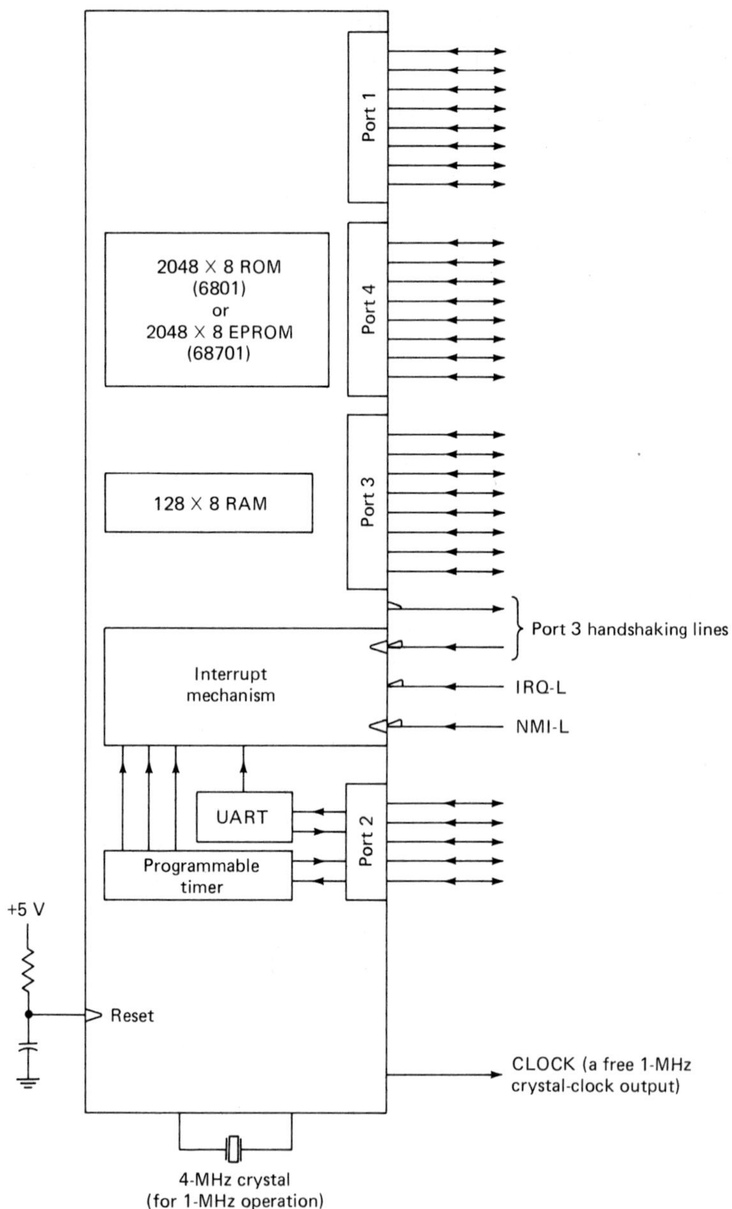

Figure 2-86. Motorola 6801 configuration as a one-chip microcomputer.

- A programmable timer to handle I/O timing (without tying up the CPU)
- 2048 bytes of ROM (or EPROM in the 68701)
- 128 bytes of read/write memory (RAM)
- Motorola 6800 instruction set, augmented by a few new instructions

If the interactions between special-purpose circuitry and a one-chip microcomputer are hampered by an insufficient number of I/O lines, these can be expanded, perhaps with an I/O expander chip designed by the manufacturer specifically for this purpose (e.g., the Intel 8243 I/O Expander for the Intel 8048/8748 one-chip microcomputer).

A programmable timer built into a microcomputer permits it to control the timing of events. For example, in Chap. 4 we will discuss the design of a "signature analyzer" instrument which employs a four-digit multiplexed display. The microcomputer will continuously refresh the display with the help of its programmable timer, as illustrated in Fig. 2-87. If each digit is to be refreshed once every 10 ms (i.e., 100 times/s), the programmable timer must interrupt the microcomputer every 2.5 ms. Each time the interrupt occurs, the microcomputer stops whatever else it is doing, determines which digit is presently turned on, turns it off, turns on the next one, restarts the pro-

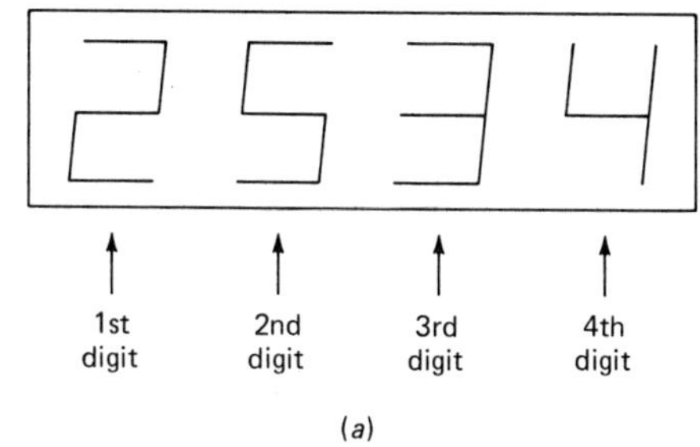

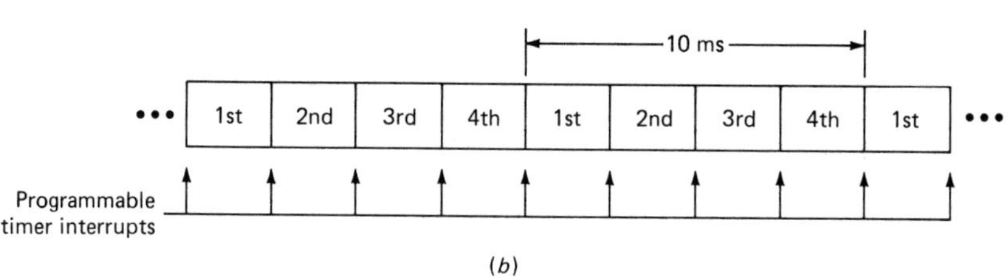

Figure 2-87. Use of a programmable timer to control the refreshing of a four-digit multiplexed display. (a) Display; (b) time during which each digit is turned on.

grammable timer for the next 2.5-ms interval, and then goes back to what it was doing at the moment the interrupt occurred. The programmable timer thus permits the microcomputer to handle the display and to do other tasks as well.

The UART (universal asynchronous receiver transmitter) built into the Motorola 6801 will permit an instrument design to employ several one-chip microcomputers and yet tie up only two pins on each microcomputer chip for communication with another microcomputer. In Chap. 6 we will discuss how this can be carried out.

Just as the interrupt capability of a programmable timer permits the timer to gain control of the microcomputer, so *external interrupt capability* permits other devices to do the same. For example, we can design special-purpose circuitry to signal a microcomputer with an interrupt when it is ready to interact with the microcomputer. In this way the microcomputer can undertake other activities knowing that when the time comes for interactions with the special-purpose circuitry, that circuitry will let it know.

If a microcomputer permits several sources of interrupts, we must decide on an appropriate protocol to handle each source adequately. However this is done, the possibility will generally exist for two (or more) sources of interrupts to want the attention of the microcomputer simultaneously. Our job as designers of special-purpose circuitry will be to ensure that reliable operation will ensue in spite of such random delays occurring when our circuitry requests the attention of the microcomputer. For example, we might know that some other task is designed to make interrupts from our circuitry *wait* until a 0.2-ms interval is over. Consequently, although we design our circuitry to initiate interactions with the microcomputer, we must also design it to *wait* until the microcomputer is ready.

Sometimes we might design special-purpose circuitry to employ *flag control* for interactions with a microcomputer. In this case the circuitry might use one line of an input port to the microcomputer as a "flag" input. The microcomputer periodically tests this flag to see if the special-purpose circuitry is ready. If so, the microcomputer will execute an appropriate algorithm of interaction. If not, the microcomputer will go on to do something else.

The handshaking lines of Fig. 2-86 are designed to help in this process of synchronizing the microcomputer with external circuitry. They can support either interrupt control or flag control. Although they do not add a capability that cannot be achieved with two lines of an I/O port, they do provide faster interactions with fewer instructions.

The EPROM programmer of Fig. 1-19 exemplifies *Ready-line control* of interactions between a microcomputer and special-purpose circuitry. It offers hardware simplicity and the fastest possible interaction between the two. However, it halts the operation of the microcomputer until the external circuitry says to resume. For example, whenever the circuit of Fig. 1-19 is written to, it pulls the Ready line low, freezing the microcomputer. This external circuitry takes advantage of the frozen address and data information to negate the need for extra flip-flops to hold on to this information for the 50 ms required to program each address in the EPROM.

While the EPROM programmer makes rather slow and passive use of Ready-line control (in order to simplify hardware), very fast interactions proceed in much the same way. The microcomputer addresses special-purpose circuitry which immediately pulls the Ready line low. As soon as it is ready to release the microcomputer (which might be in 1 to 10 μs for a fast device), it simply raises the Ready line again.

Ready-line control is not an available feature of one-chip microcomputers. It is included in multiple-chip microcomputers built with CPUs such as the Intel 8080 or 8085 or the Zilog Z80. The designers of these chips originally included ready-line control to permit the use of slow memory chips. With no upper limit to the duration of the "wait" state, these CPUs provide a fine interactive capability to designers who use them. In contrast, some other CPUs (such as Motorola's 6800, 6802, and 6809) have a Ready line, but do not permit the CPU to be held up indefinitely. Thus a CPU permitting a maximum wait duration of 10 ms loses a valuable interactive capability.

With this brief overview of the microcomputer as a component, we will move on to other considerations. Later, as we return to the role which a microcomputer plays in the design of specific circuits, we will be particularly interested in the interactions between the microcomputer and our circuitry. At that time we will explore how these interactions affect the implementation.

PROBLEMS

2-1 Binary code. Find the decimal equivalents of each of the following binary numbers:

(*a*) 10000000 (*d*) 00100011
(*b*) 11111111 (*e*) 01000110
(*c*) 10101010 (*f*) 10001100

2-2 Binary code. Find the 8-bit binary equivalents of each of the following decimal numbers:

(*a*) 49 (*d*) 13
(*b*) 200 (*e*) 26
(*c*) 127 (*f*) 52

2-3 Gray code. Introducing a fifth Gray code variable, g_4, extend the table of Fig. 2-1 up to $I = 31$.

2-4 Gray code. Convert the 8-bit Gray code number 01100111 to its binary equivalent.

2-5 Hexadecimal code. Find the hexadecimal equivalents of the following binary numbers:

(*a*) 00010011	(*d*) 111111000000
(*b*) 01100111	(*e*) 010011101101
(*c*) 10100101	(*f*) 101001010010

2-6 Hexadecimal code. Find the binary equivalents of the following hexadecimal numbers:

(*a*) 5A	(*d*) 13
(*b*) CE	(*e*) 26
(*c*) 4F	(*f*) 52

2-7 Hexadecimal code. Find the decimal equivalents of the following hexadecimal numbers:

(*a*) 53	(*d*) 1234
(*b*) FF	(*e*) FFFF
(*c*) 7F	(*f*) 8000

2-8 Binary-coded-decimal code. Express the following decimal numbers using BCD code:

(*a*) 24	(*d*) 999
(*b*) 48	(*e*) 1234
(*c*) 96	(*f*) 1009

2-9 AND function. Make a single truth table analogous to that of Fig. 2-9 showing *all* of the following functions: CBA, $\overline{C}\,\overline{B}\,\overline{A}$, $\overline{C}\,\overline{B}A$, $\overline{C}B\overline{A}$, $\overline{C}BA$.

2-10 OR function. Make a single truth table analogous to that of Fig. 2-9 showing *all* of the following functions: $Z + Y + X$, $\overline{Z} + \overline{Y} + \overline{X}$, $\overline{Z} + \overline{Y} + X$, $\overline{Z} + Y + \overline{X}$, $\overline{Z} + Y + X$.

2-11 Exclusive-OR function. Make a single truth table analogous to that of Fig. 2-9 showing *all* of the following functions: $T \oplus S \oplus R$, $T \oplus S \oplus \overline{R}$, $T \oplus \overline{S} \oplus R$, $\overline{T} \oplus \overline{S} \oplus R$, $\overline{T} \oplus \overline{S} \oplus \overline{R}$, $\overline{T \oplus S \oplus R}$.

2-12 Exclusive-OR function. Evaluate each of the following:

(*a*) $0 \oplus 0 \oplus 1 \oplus 1 \oplus 0 \oplus 0 \oplus 0 \oplus 1$

(*b*) $0 \oplus 1 \oplus 1 \oplus 0 \oplus 0 \oplus 0 \oplus 1$

2-13 Problem formulation. Defining variables "top," "bottom," and "light" as you see fit, construct a truth table to describe the common situation found in house wiring where a light in a stair-

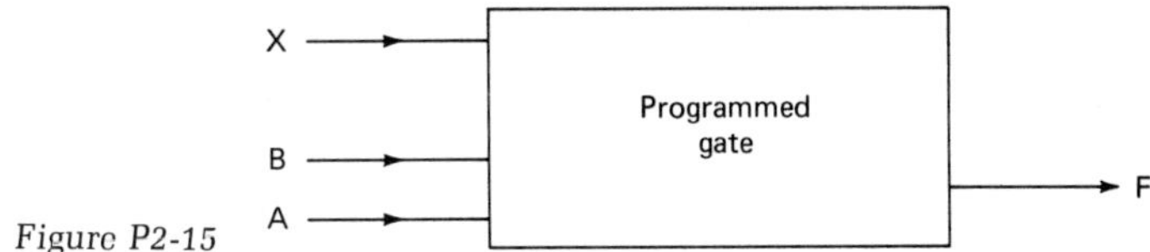

Figure P2-15

well can be turned on or off from a switch at the bottom of the stairs or from a switch at the top of the stairs. Assume that the light is turned off if both switches are in the Down position. Do you recognize the resulting truth table as that of a familiar function?

2-14 Problem formulation. Repeat Prob. 2-13 for the open stairwell of a four-story apartment having light switches SW1, SW2, SW3, and SW4 (one per floor).

2-15 Problem formulation. Define the *programmed gate* shown in Fig. P2-15 with a truth table. If $X = 0$, then $F = A$; if $X = 1$, then $F = B \cdot A$.

2-16 Noise immunity. Determine the guaranteed noise immunity for a low-level output of a TTL gate.

2-17 Noise immunity. A nonstandard TTL-compatible device has its maximum low-level output specified at 0.5 V. What does this do to its low-level guaranteed noise immunity (when used to drive TTL circuitry)?

2-18 Mixed-logic convention. Develop all equivalent representations of a two-input (positive) exclusive-OR gate using polarity indicators on one or both inputs or the output, analogous to Fig. 2-14.

2-19 Mixed-logic convention. Figure 1-19 employs a 74LS32 quad two-input (positive) OR gate. Justify the symbolism used in that figure to represent each gate.

2-20 TTL logic. In Sec. 2-6 mention was made of the use of small 0.01-μF capacitors to prevent the generation of noise on the power-supply line by TTL logic.

(*a*) Why will not a 100-μF electrolytic capacitor in the +5-V power supply serve this same purpose?

(*b*) Why cannot all the 0.01-μF capacitors be located together, like palm trees at an oasis, where the +5-V power comes on to a board from the power supply?

2-21 Small functions. Using gates selected from Fig. 2-20 and minimizing the (fractional) package count (using several different de-

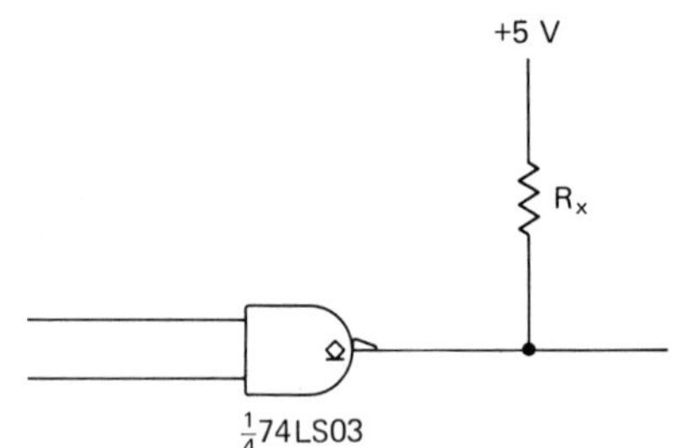

Figure P2-22

vices if this minimizes package count), implement each of the following:

(*a*) Generate RESET-L to be active when T100-H is active and when CLOCK2-H is active.

(*b*) Generate LIGHT-H to be active when COUNT9-H is active and RUN-L is active.

(*c*) Repeat Example 2-12 but generate Test-L.

2-22 Loading rules. A TTL gate with an open-collector output is shown in Fig. P2-22 together with a pull-up resistor R_x. Referring to Figs. 2-11 and 2-25:

(*a*) Determine the maximum value of R_x that will still provide 74LSxxx high-level output drive capability.

(*b*) If the gate has normal 74LSxxx low-level output drive capability, how many 74LSxxx inputs can it drive while at the same time pulling R_x low?

2-23 Loading rules. What is the fan-out capability of a 74Sxxx gate driving 74LSxxx gates?

2-24 Propagation delay. A 74LS14 Schmitt trigger is a circuit with two input threshold voltages, as defined in Fig. 2-70*a* and *b*. Consider a 74LSxxx gate which just barely meets the propagation delay specifications of Fig. 2-28. When it is fully loaded and driving a 74LS14 Schmitt trigger input low, it will have a longer effective propagation delay than for the other normal 74LSxxx gate inputs connected to it. Why is this so?

2-25 Decoders. What inputs are required in order to

(*a*) Make the 8 output (pin 10) of the 74LS42 of Fig. 2-30 go low?

(*b*) Make the lower 0 output (pin 12) of the 74LS139 of Fig. 2-31 go low?

(*c*) Make the 3 output (pin 12) of the 74LS138 of Fig. 2-32 go low?

(*d*) Make the upper 1 output (pin 6) of the 74LS155 of Fig. 2-33 go low?

(*e*) Make the lower 1 output (pin 10) of the 74LS155 of Fig. 2-33 go low?

2-26 Decoder expansion. Using three of the 74LS138s of Fig. 2-32, show their interconnections to achieve the function shown in Fig. P2-26. Label inputs 1, 2, 4, 8, and 16 and outputs 0-L, . . . , 23-L.

2-27 Multiplexers. (a) What inputs are required to make the output of the 74LS152 of Fig. 2-34 active or inactive, depending upon whether the 5 input (pin 13) is active or inactive?

(*b*) In this case, when the 5 input is high, what will the output be?

2-28 Multiplexers. Repeat Prob. 2-27 for both outputs of the 74LS151 of Fig. 2-35.

2-29 Multiplexer symbol. Can the symbol for the 74LS152 of Fig. 2-34 be redefined with an *active-high* output (by also changing input definitions)? If so, show it. If not, why not?

2-30 Multiplexer expansion. Using five of the 74LS152 multiplexers of Fig. 2-34, show their interconnections to achieve the function shown in Fig. P2-30. Label active-high inputs MUX0, . . . , MUX4 and 0, 1, . . . , 31. Also define the output active-high.

2-31 Dependency notation. The 74LS244 of Fig. 2-40 is actually two separate circuits shown with one symbol. Redraw it with a separate symbol for each circuit, labeling pin numbers and using proper dependency symbology.

2-32 Multiplexer expansion. Using four of the 74LS251 multiplexers of Fig. 2-42 as well as one of the two decoders in a 74LS139 chip, implement the function of Fig. P2-30.

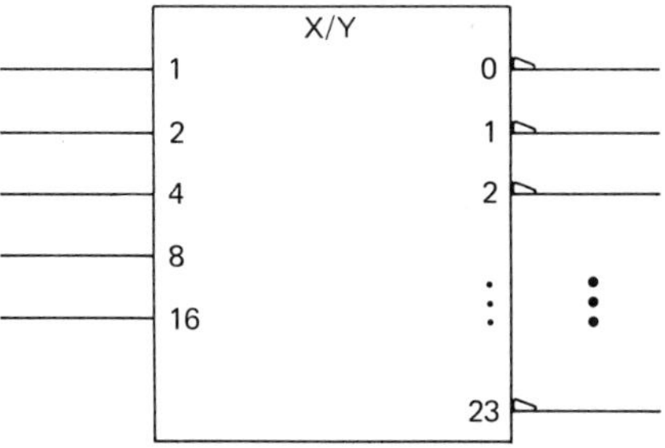

Figure P2-26

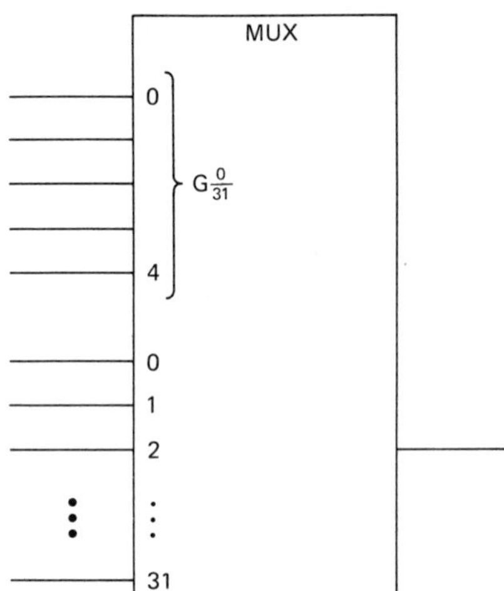

Figure P2-30

2-33 Dependency notation. Explain the difference in *function* between the two multiplexers 74LS151 (Fig. 2-35) and 74LS251 (Fig. 2-42). How is the difference in function reflected in the symbology of the two chips?

2-34 Open-collector output. What is there about the symbol of Fig. 2-43 to distinguish that the comparator output (pin 9) is an open-collector output? Compare this with the output symbolism used for the two devices considered in Prob. 2-33.

2-35 Comparator circuit. Label the outputs of the top two exclusive-OR gates (with active-low outputs) of the comparator in Fig. 2-43 EX12-L and EX34-L. Construct a truth table for an *enabled* four-input version of this comparator, calling the inputs 1-H, . . . , 4-H and the output EQUAL-H. Assume that a pull-up resistor has been added to the output.

2-36 Dot-ORing. (*a*) We want a 6-bit comparator with output labeled UNEQUAL-L. Show a symbol for the 8160 chip (analogous to Fig. 2-43*b*) that will represent this. Use "$P \neq Q$" labeling to represent inequality.

(*b*) Now show the interconnection analogous to Fig. 2-43*c* to implement the UNEQUAL-L output of a 12-bit comparator.

2-37 PROM programming. Complete the next four (missing) rows of PROM Table 1 in Fig. 2-48, using the equations of Fig. 2-47 to define the eight outputs for each row.

2-38 PROM input expansion. Reconfigure the circuit of Fig. 2-51 so that the first 2048 rows of the truth table reside in PROM 1, the second 2048 rows reside in PROM 2, and so on.

2-39 PROM implementation of functions. Show *one* PROM circuit, and the corresponding PROM table, to implement all of the following functions in both active-high and active-low form:

$$\text{AND} = 1 \cdot 2 \cdot 3 \cdot 4 \cdot 5$$

$$\text{OR} = 1 + 2 + 3 + 4 + 5$$

$$\text{EOR} = 1 \oplus 2 \oplus 3 \oplus 4 \oplus 5$$

$$\text{MAJORITY} = 1 \text{ if 3 or more inputs equal 1}$$

2-40 PROM input expansion. (*a*) Show a circuit to implement an equivalent 256 × 1 PROM using a 32 × 8 PROM plus a multiplexer, such that scanning down through successive addresses of the 256 × 1 PROM table is translated into scanning successive bit positions across each row of the 32 × 8 PROM table before going on to the next row. Label "256 × 1 decimal addresses" in the squares of the 32 × 8 PROM table of Fig. 2-53 for addresses 0 to 15 and 240 to 255.

(*b*) Repeat (*a*) but reconfigured so that scanning successive 256 × 1 addresses is translated into scanning all the way down through one column of the 32 × 8 PROM table before going on to the next column.

2-41 FPLA implementation of functions. Using one 74S330 FPLA, implement *all* of the following functions in both active-high and active-low form:

$$\text{AND} = 1 \cdot 2 \cdot 3 \cdot 4 \cdot 5 \cdot 6 \cdot 7 \cdot 8 \cdot 9 \cdot 10 \cdot 11 \cdot 12$$

$$\text{BADOR} = 1 + 2 + 3 + 4 + 5 + 6 + 7 + 8 + 9 + 10 + 11 + 12$$

(implemented using 12 product terms)

$$\text{GOODOR} = 1 + 2 + 3 + 4 + 5 + 6 + 7 + 8 + 9 + 10 + 11 + 12$$

(implemented using *one* product term)

To obtain the latter implementation, *think* in terms of the complementary function, NOTGOODOR (to do the equivalent of the representation of Fig. 2-20).

2-42 FPLA table minimization. Derive an FPLA table equivalent to that of Fig. 2-59 but using as few product terms as possible. In the "Function" column list the original rows (in order) making up each final row.

2-43 FPLA output expansion. (*a*) Consider Example 2-29, in which it was assumed that no more than one product term would be active at the same time. If this assumption is actually violated so that product term 1 (generating coded output 00001) and product term 2 (generating coded output 00010) are both active at the same time, what will the states of OUT4, . . . , OUT19 be?

(*b*) Does it matter which active level is used in the programming of the FPLA outputs? Discuss this as specifically as possible.

2-44 FPLA product-term expansion. What would happen if the scheme of Fig. 2-61 were used, but if we inadvertently employed Signetics 82S100 FPLAs instead of 82S101 units?

2-45 FPLA product-term expansion. (*a*) Draw the interconnection of two FPLAs to obtain an equivalent 12 × 100 × 6 FPLA (using the Texas Instruments units discussed in the text).

(*b*) What is the (qualitative) effect of using passive pull-up devices in translating the loading rules for a single chip into loading rules for the interconnected pair of chips?

2-46 FPLA input expansion. (*a*) Discuss what will happen in Example 2-30 if two of the product terms detected by FPLA 1 actually occur at the same time. Assume that these two product terms are designed to produce coded outputs of 00001 and 00010.

(*b*) Does it matter whether FPLA 1's outputs are programmed to be active-high or active-low? Explain as specifically as possible.

2-47 FPLA input expansion. (*a*) Modify Fig. 2-63 for the case in which the inputs I1, . . . , I5 determine which one of the *eight* extra inputs, I16, . . . , I23, are to be selected. Use a 32 × 8 PROM and a single 8-line–to–1-line multiplexer. What determines the coding of the PROM?

(*b*) Show the PROM table if

I16 is to be looked at for 0–5

I17 is to be looked at for 6–8

I18 is to be looked at for 7–9, 11

I19 is to be looked at for 10, 12

I20 is to be looked at for 13–18

I21 is to be looked at for 19–25

I22 is to be looked at for 26–27

I23 is to be looked at for 28–31

where 0–5 (etc.) represents the state of I5 · · · I1.

2-48 PAL implementation of functions. (*a*) Use a PAL14H4 to implement the two functions AND and GOODOR of Prob. 2-41 in *either* active-high form or active-low form.

(*b*) Obtain the other two forms (e.g., AND-L if AND-H was obtained above) by employing unused capability of the PAL, feeding each output back around to an unused input. Show both the circuit interconnection and the PAL table.

2-49 PAL implementation of functions. Using either a PAL10H8 or a PAL10L8 (whichever is appropriate), implement the decoder shown in Fig. P2-49.

2-50 PAL implementation of functions. Repeat Prob. 2-49 for an identical decoder except that outputs are defined active high.

2-51 Schmitt-trigger clock. Consider the clock circuit of Fig. 2-70e and label the Schmitt-trigger input V_x. Assume that the two input threshold voltages are 1.6 and 0.8 V, as shown in Fig.

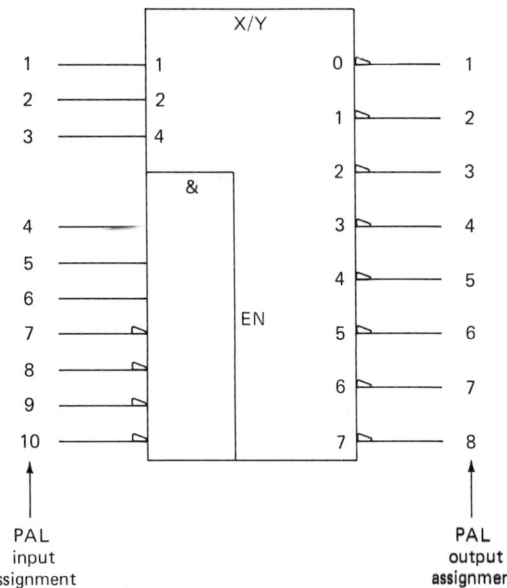

Figure P2-49

2-70*b*. At the moment the CLOCK output has just switched high, to a typical output value of 3.3 V, $V_x = 0.8$ V.

(*a*) With a time scale labeled in units of time constants (1 TC, 2 TC, 3 TC), where TC = R_xC_x, sketch V_x charging exponentially from 0.8 V at time = 0 toward 3.3 V.

(*b*) Where V_x crosses 1.6 V (so that the CLOCK output switches low to a typical value of 0.2 V), sketch V_x discharging exponentially toward 0.2 V.

(*c*) Where V_x crosses 0.8 V, measure the normalized time.

(*d*) With $R_x = 330\ \Omega$, determine C_x to obtain a 1-MHz clock rate.

(*e*) Repeat (*a*), (*b*), and (*c*) with one set of worst-case threshold voltages, 0.5 and 1.9 V.

(*f*) Repeat (*a*), (*b*), and (*c*) with the other worst-case threshold voltages, 1.0 and 1.4 V.

(*g*) With the value of C_x found in (*d*), what is the worst-case range on output frequency due to threshold voltage tolerances?

2-52 Crystal clock. Consider the circuit of Fig. 2-71*d*.

(*a*) Show the range of times during which the falling edge of RUN-H can occur and still yield the same clock waveform.

(*b*) Repeat (*a*) for the rising edge of RUN-H.

(*c*) Is it true that any time the clock is stopped, it will stop with its output high?

(*d*) Is it possible to obtain a "glitch" (i.e., a narrow pulse) on the output of this clock circuit if RUN-H changes at just the "wrong" time?

2-53 Shift registers. List the output sequence of the shift register of Fig. 2-80 if the output of pin 13 is fed back through a 74LS04 inverter to pins 1 and 2 of the shift register. Assume that the shift register is in state 00000000 when you begin.

2-54 Counters. (*a*) Beginning with the circuit of Fig. 2-84, draw a modified circuit (adding as few extra components as necessary) such that after data is loaded into the counter (by making LOAD-L low for a clock period), the counter will count up until it reaches 111111111111, at which point it will remain in this all-1s state until it is loaded again.

(*b*) Discuss why successful results will not be obtained if we try to let COUNT in the circuit of Fig. 2-84 be a function of CARRY12.

2-55 Multiplexed display. (*a*) Shake a digital watch, pocket calculator, or instrument with a light-emitting diode (LED) display.

What can you expect to see the display do if it is a multiplexed display? Why?

(*b*) Some instruments employ LED displays but do not multiplex them because the resulting periodic, and large, LED currents can look like a noisy environment for analog circuitry in the same instrument. Without destroying any laboratory instruments on a "human shake table," can you identify such an instrument among those with which you work?

2-56 Ready-line control. Investigate the data sheet for the CPU of a multiple-chip microcomputer (other than one discussed in Sec. 2-15) to see if it includes a Ready input.

(*a*) Can the CPU be stopped indefinitely with this line (without having it malfunction)?

(*b*) Is this unsynchronized input synchronized in the CPU itself (as in the Zilog Z80 and in the Intel 8085) or in the clock chip (as in Intel's 8224 clock chip for the 8080 CPU), or elsewhere?

REFERENCES

An outstanding contribution to designers looking for a function implemented as an integrated circuit is *IC Master,* published annually by United Technical Publications, Inc., 645 Stewart Avenue, Garden City, NY 11530.

3

DESIGNING FOR MAINTAINABILITY

3-1 SELF-TEST, PUSH-TO-TEST, AND FAULT ISOLATION

The time when we, as designers, should be thinking about ease of maintenance is at the outset of a design project. This is the time when we can develop a *systematic* approach to maintainability. Similarly, in a book on digital design, it is appropriate to consider the implications of designing maintainability into a device *before* considering the design of the device itself. In this way we will develop two areas of awareness:

1 What features must we include in a design for it to be maintainable?
2 What are the implications of this inclusion of maintainability features upon how the rest of the design is to be carried out?

The paramount maintainability question raised by a user of an instrument or device is whether the unit works. If the unit can test itself upon power turn-on and continue to test itself, repeatedly and unobtrusively, during normal operation and warn the user of a malfunction, the unit has included *self-test* capability, a feature of major value to users.

Some parts of the circuitry of an instrument or device do not lend themselves to self-test in that they cannot be exercised at arbitrary times. These include:

1 All inputs, which will generally be driven by external equipment at the moment when an on-going self-test algorithm would otherwise like to exercise them.

2 Some outputs, namely, those which would cause spurious operation of another device if exercised during ongoing operation. For example, exercising the circuitry that drives a built-in printer will be unacceptable to a user if normally printed messages are interspersed with "funny" characters printed to exercise the printer. On the other hand, it may be possible to exercise output circuitry without causing spurious outputs. Thus if the outputs to a thermal printhead are exercised faster than the thermal response time, signal levels can be checked even though no printing takes place.

3 Flip-flops and memory circuitry that hold data being processed by an instrument and "state variables" that define the operating mode of the instrument. Again, users cannot tolerate spurious operation for the sake of self-test. However, it may be possible to find times during the ongoing operation of an instrument, when a self-test algorithm can be executed without disrupting normal operation. For example, an instrument may collect data, process it, produce processed results, and then repeat the cycle. Before beginning another cycle, it should be possible to exercise the data collection circuitry.

Push-to-test capability can be used to augment self-test capability in order to assure a user that even those parts of a design not amenable to self-test do, in fact, work. With this capability, a user first configures inputs appropriately, as specified in the service manual. Then the user initiates "push-to-test," perhaps by depressing a front-panel Test switch. For example, the "signature analyzer" instrument shown in Fig. 3-1 has four inputs, called CLOCK, START, STOP, and PROBE. Before initiating a test, these are connected to the corresponding front-panel test points shown on the right of the instrument. Then the Start, Stop, and Clock pushbutton switches are set as prescribed in the service manual. Finally, the Self-test (really, push-to-test) switch is depressed and the display compared with that given in the service manual for the given configuration of pushbutton switches.

Being able to test the inputs to an instrument is an exceptionally valuable capability for the designer to extend to the user. Inputs represent a "weak link" in that they are the only part of many instruments

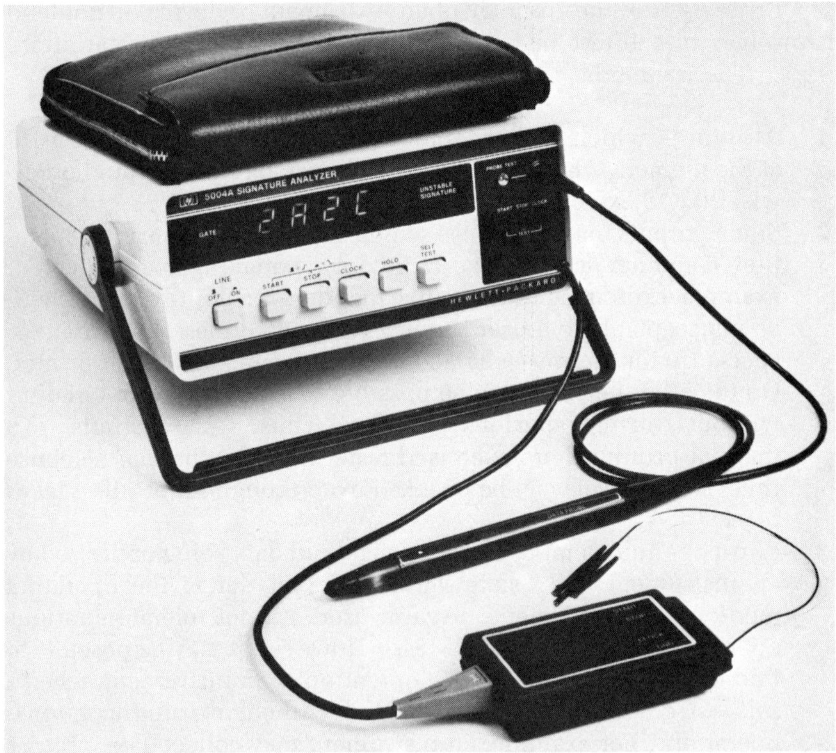

Figure 3-1. Signature analyzer instrument which employs push-to-test capability. (Hewlett-Packard Co.)

accessible under normal use. Because of this accessibility, inputs are also subject to inadvertent abuse due to static discharges or momentary connection to circuits of excessively high voltage.

The modulation analyzer shown in Fig. 3-2 normally expects a radio-frequency input, which it proceeds to characterize. However, it includes a "calibration" output which can be connected to the input to provide both calibration and push-to-test capability. After the connection is made, pressing the Calibration button initiates a measurement that should yield a known result.

In comparison with the single input of the modulation analyzer, the logic state analyzer shown in Fig. 3-3*a* has 32 logic inputs and one clock input. The designers of this unit have put the input circuitry into the external pods shown. In the case of a malfunction of a pod, its cable connector can be quickly disconnected from the logic state analyzer at the socket positions shown in Fig. 3-3*b*. These inputs are exercised by pressing the Performance Verification–Start pushbutton on the rear panel, shown in Fig. 3-3*c*. The user is guided through the test

Figure 3-2. Testing an instrument input with a built-in "calibration" output. (Hewlett-Packard Co.)

of the inputs with directions given on the CRT display. The directions require the user to connect the clock pod to the Clock socket and each of the data pods in turn to the Data socket shown in Fig. 3-3c. Thus even though the input circuitry is extensive, the exercising of the inputs is simple for a user to carry out.

This logic state analyzer also includes a thorough check of keyboard performance. After the rear-panel Performance Verification–

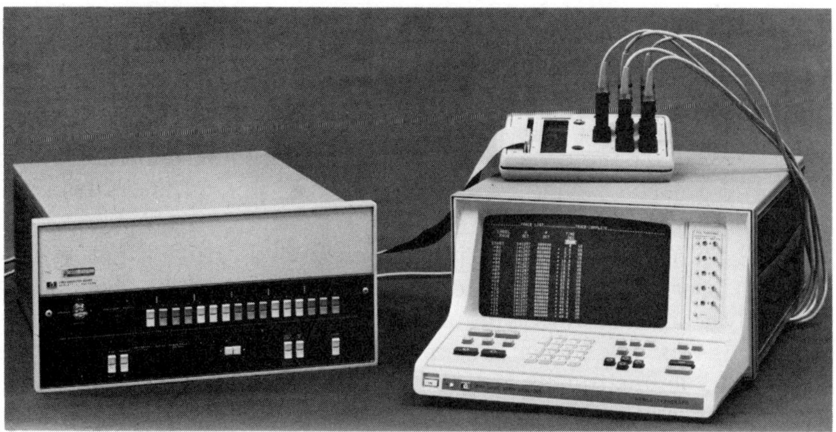

Figure 3-3. Logic state analyzer. (Hewlett-Packard Co.) (a) In use.

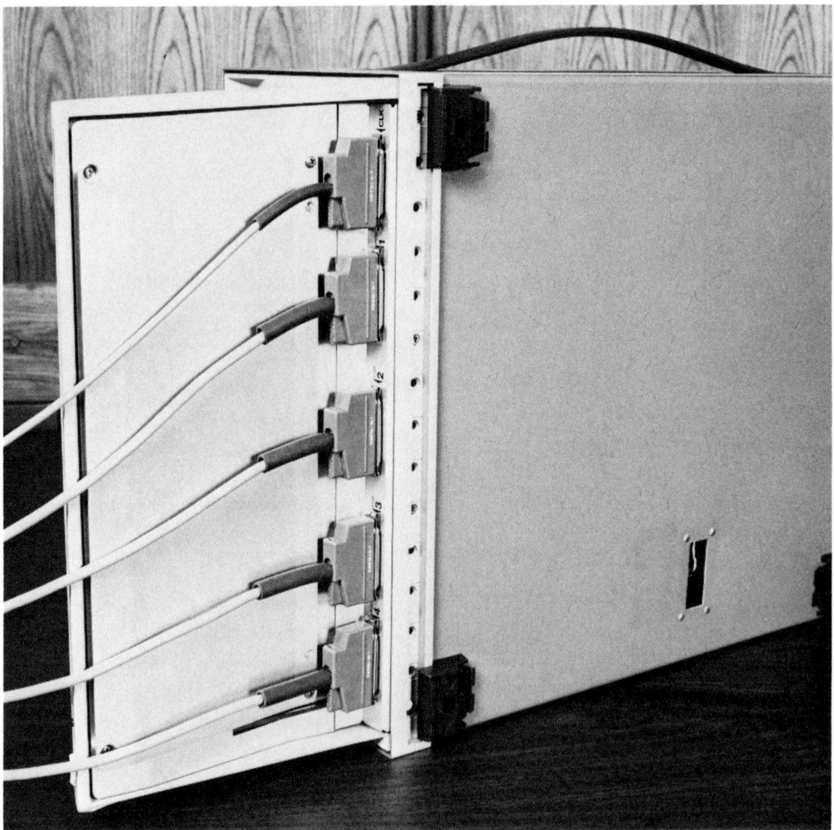

Figure 3-3b. Input-probe-pod cable connections.

Start pushbutton has been pressed, the front panel keyswitch labeled Field Select [ ] is used to select any one of five tests of the push-to-test type, requiring user interaction. The keyboard test is selected and the user is asked to press each key (in no particular sequence), ending with the Field Select [ ] key. If any key has been missed, its "key code" will be shown on the CRT display.

The function of both self-test and push-to-test capability is to provide a user with confidence that an instrument is functioning properly—or that it has malfunctioned. As pointed out earlier, this knowledge is the prime "maintainability" information which the designer of an instrument should be extending to a user. Beyond this, the designer may also support more or less extensive *fault-isolation* capability.

Figure 3-3c. Push-to-test verification of inputs.

Fault isolation can be designed into an instrument or device so as to support one or more of the following *maintenance policies:*

1. When the instrument fails, the user sends the entire unit back to the manufacturer for service.

   In this case the designer only needs to support the user with self-test and/or push-to-test capability which will unequivocally determine the health of the entire unit.
2. When the instrument fails because of the faulty operation of one of its printed circuit boards, the user locates the malfunctioning board and exchanges it. To facilitate speedy repair, a user may keep spare boards or the manufacturer may support overnight, air-express delivery of replacement boards.

   Here, the designer supports the user with the wherewithal to locate a fault down to the board level.
3. Once a bad board has been located and replaced, it may be cheaper to dispose of the bad board than to repair it. This is a controversial service policy which is arising in some quarters as

the price of electronics hardware continues to drop while the cost of personal services continues to rise.

The designer can support this policy by designing in board-level fault-location capability and perhaps by partitioning a design so that some boards are so inexpensive as to warrant being disposable. However, a design that supports board-level fault location can also include fault isolation of bad components for little added cost. The difference lies in the ability of the malfunctioning instrument *itself* to identify a bad board, but not a bad *component* on a board. Fault isolation of a bad component generally requires supporting test equipment such as the signature analyzer of Fig. 3-1, the use of which will be discussed shortly.

4 When the instrument fails, the user is supported in the option of locating and replacing a faulty *component.*

In this case, the designer might employ self-test or push-to-test capability on selected, vulnerable components. For example, any integrated circuits connected directly to instrument inputs are likely to have a higher-than-usual mortality. A push-to-test algorithm might exercise these integrated circuits one by one and display a diagnostic number if one of them fails. Then the service manual can use this diagnostic number to identify which chip malfunctioned.

Going beyond self-test and push-to-test capability for selected components, the designer can build in signature analysis capability. This capability, to be discussed in Sec. 3-5, permits a user to employ the signature analyzer instrument of Fig. 3-1 to locate a bad component—without having to *understand* the functioning of that component, or any component in the instrument.

5 The manufacturer will undertake the repairing of malfunctioning printed circuit boards.

The designer can support this service function by making boards easily *testable.* One means for doing this is, again, to design in signature analysis capability. For more automated testing with an extensive (expensive) PC board tester such as that shown in Fig. 3-4, the designer can aid the development of the test algorithm by including features that will drastically simplify automated testing. These features will be discussed in Sec. 3-8.

As is evident from these five maintenance policies, a good designer can play a significant role in supporting the subsequent maintenance of the equipment he or she designs. One of the rules of thumb upon which electronics test engineers seem to agree is that the average printed circuit board will malfunction and require service *two times* over its lifetime. Although this rule of thumb is undoubtedly high

Figure 3-4. Automatic tester for printed circuit boards. (GenRad.)

when applied to small, simple boards, it is also undoubtedly low for large boards, and for boards that will be subjected to a harsh environment (e.g., static discharges on inputs, or high temperature, or high humidity).

Ed Donn, an engineer with extensive experience in instrument design, instrument marketing, and also the design of automatic test equipment, says: "Testing threatens to become the major cost of digital designs somewhere in the 1980s. At the present snail's pace, testing could hold back the whole digital revolution. I don't think that is going to be allowed to happen." It will not happen because designers are gaining an awareness of the problem and the design techniques that can alleviate it. In addition, the cost of semiconductor technology continues to drop, making self-test, push-to-test, and fault-isolation capability an almost-free feature of an instrument—in the hands of an astute designer.

3-2 HARDWARE ORGANIZATION

While the cost of virtually everything around us rises inexorably, the tools of the trade of the electronics engineer continue to:

- Decrease drastically in price
- Grow ever more sophisticated and powerful
- Get more compact
- Require smaller, simpler power supplies

It is an exciting time to be an electronics designer!

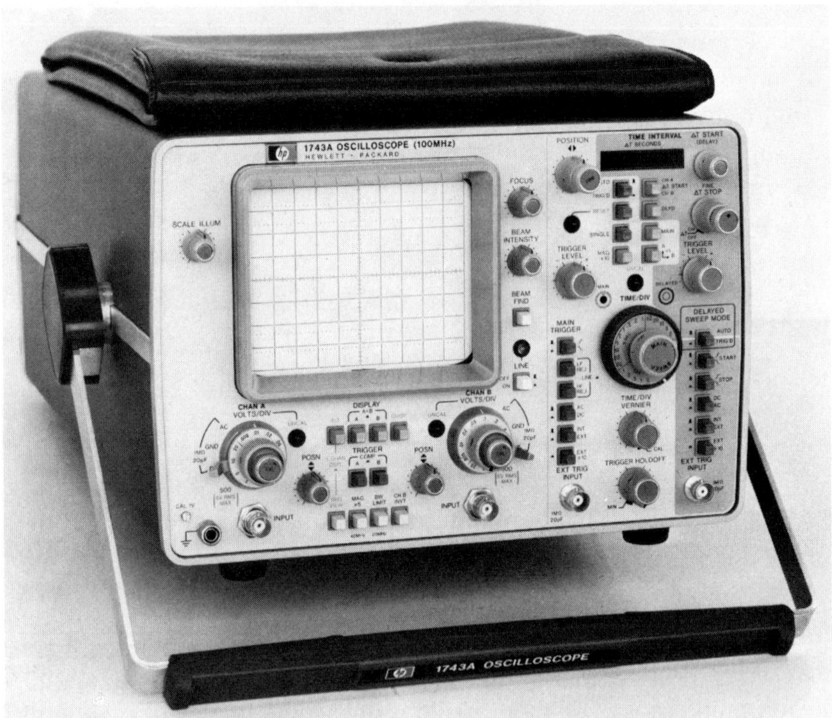

Figure 3-5. Oscilloscope having a labor-intensive front panel. (Hewlett-Packard Co.)

These factors in conjunction with the ever-increasing cost of labor shape how instruments are organized. Labor-intensive front-panel configurations such as that of the top-of-the-line oscilloscope shown in Fig. 3-5 are giving way to the hardware simplicity inherent in a CRT display and keyboard combination, exemplified by the top-of-the-line logic state analyzer shown in Fig. 3-3.

Another way in which hardware simplicity is achieved in many instruments is through a *planar layout* of components, all on one printed circuit board. This is illustrated in Fig. 3-6, which shows the signature analyzer of Fig. 3-1 with the top cover removed. As a more extensive example, Fig. 3-7 shows the planar layout of Intel's PROMPT 48 hardware/software development unit for their 8748 one-chip microcomputer. A planar layout simplifies the manufacture of an instrument. It also simplifies its testing, because of the accessibility of all components and test points.

Many instruments employ so much circuitry as to preclude a planar layout. This is true of the logic state analyzer of Fig. 3-3, which

Figure 3-6. Planar layout of the circuitry of an instrument. (Hewlett-Packard Co.)

(a)

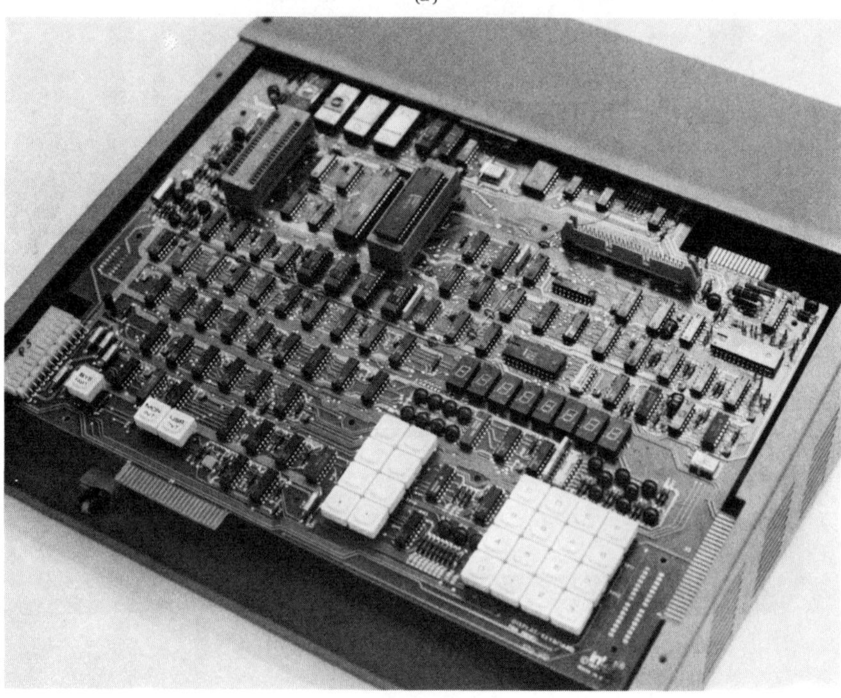

(b)

Figure 3-7. *Planar layout of a microcomputer development unit.* (a) Complete unit; (b) with cover removed. (Intel Corp.)

Figure 3-8. Layout employing a motherboard and daughterboards. (Hewlett-Packard Co.)

is shown opened up in Fig. 3-8. Instead, one printed circuit "motherboard" lies horizontally across the bottom of the instrument and includes PC board edge connectors and their interconnections. The instrument circuitry resides on vertical "daughterboards" which plug into the edge connectors of the motherboard.

This hardware organization offers many possibilities for the coupling of the logic on the different daughterboards. One approach often used (and that used in this logic state analyzer) is to employ a "bus" between all boards, whereby all signals on the bus are common to all of the boards, as in Fig. 3-9. A microcomputer on one board interacts with the logic on other boards by reading from and writing to registers on those boards, treating them as microcomputer memory addresses. In addition to the microcomputer signals, the bus also transmits any other signal communications required between boards.

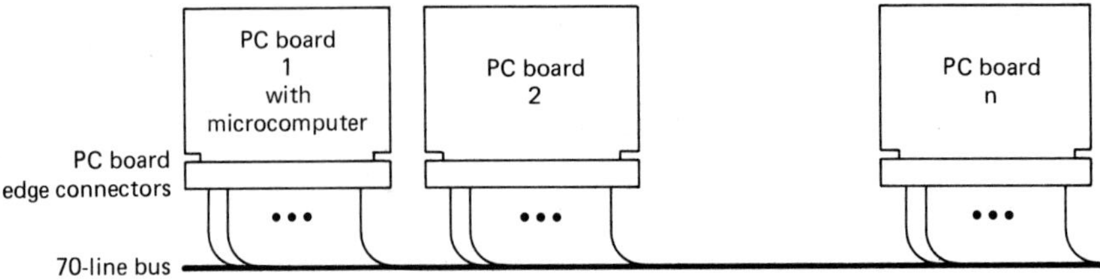

Figure 3-9. Use of a common bus in an instrument.

The use of this bus permits *fast interactions* to take place between boards. It does so subject to the disadvantage of moving myriad signals all over an instrument. For example, the unit of Fig. 3-8 uses edge connectors with 70 contacts, every last one of which has to be a reliable connection. Furthermore, if any of the many *microcomputer* bus lines malfunction, the microcomputer can no longer communicate with anything outside its own board. The user will immediately detect wildly erratic operation, or no operation, of the instrument.

Many of the servicing advantages of a planar layout can be achieved in a motherboard/daughterboard layout by employing a separate microcomputer on each daughterboard. The fast operations required by the functions of each board are handled by that board's microcomputer. Often, these functions can be defined so as not to require exceptionally fast interactions *between* boards. In this case the interactions can be handled *serially*, one bit at a time, easily and automatically by the microcomputers on the separate boards. As will be discussed in Chap. 6, this form of communication between boards can be carried out with just two signal lines, as in Fig. 3-10. If the communication malfunctions, each board can exercise itself with push-to-test capability, by routing the serial output of a board back to the serial input. This organization takes advantage of the microcomputer on each board for executing that board's self-test algorithms. The microcomputer itself

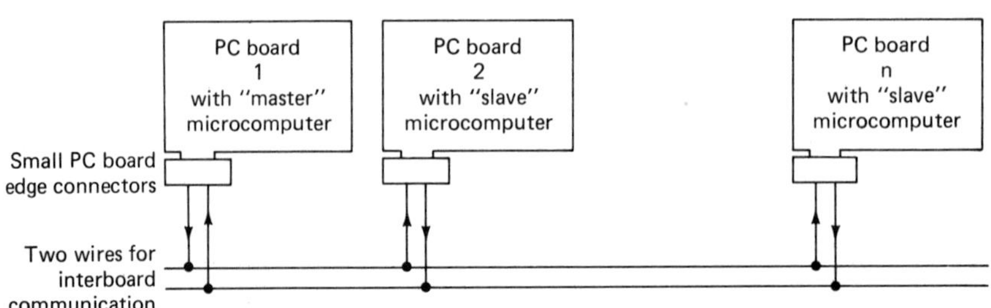

Figure 3-10. Multiboard organization with two-wire serial communication between boards.

might be a one-chip microcomputer like that of Appendix A3. Alternatively, if the resources of a one-chip microcomputer are not adequate, a multiple-chip microcomputer can be employed.

3-3 A DESIGN CRITERION

In this section we will develop a rationale for the following design criterion. This criterion will help us optimize our design choices as we work to meet the specifications for the instrument or device we are designing.

> *While designing to meet the instrument specifications, include testing capability and then minimize package count.*

Testing capability is used here to refer to whatever mix of self-test, push-to-test, and fault-isolation capability makes sense for realizing when the unit malfunctions and for getting it back into operation expeditiously. This is so valuable to *any* user, and adds so little to the cost and complexity of an instrument, that it should be a part of any design.

Minimizing *package count*, the number of integrated circuits employed in the design, has several justifications and several ramifications. The justifications for minimizing package count arise because most of the costs attributable to the logic circuitry of an instrument are proportional to package count. By decreasing package count, we tend to decrease:

- Size of the printed circuit boards
- Size of the resulting instrument package
- Manufacturer's inventory of parts
- Cost of "stuffing" boards with components during manufacture
- Size, weight, and cost of power supply
- Heat dissipated by logic and its adverse effect upon reliability

As a design evolves which tends to minimize package count, we are likely to find that the cost of the integrated circuits themselves will *increase*. This occurs because we tend to employ powerful chips (e.g., a $2.00 PROM) in lieu of a larger number of simple chips (e.g., 10-cent packages of gates). A by-product of this trade-off occurs as we get away from the intricate, but low-cost, gating circuitry which has obscured the design, operation, and troubleshooting of many instruments in the past. The more expensive chips lead to more straightforward designs.

Figure 3-11. Comparison of the size of a 24-pin DIP package versus two 16-pin DIP packages.

Rather than minimizing package count, many designers use the similar criterion of minimizing *package area* taken up by the integrated circuits used in a design. For example, if a 4-line–to–16-line decoder function is needed, many designers will use two 16-pin 74LS138 3-line–to–8-line decoder chips suitably connected together rather than using one 24-pin 74LS154 4-line–to–16-line decoder chip. This choice is made because, as is shown in Fig. 3-11, a "standard"† 24-pin dual-in-line package (DIP) eats up a prodigious amount of board area relative to two 16-pin ICs.

Because 20-pin DIPs are as narrow as 16-pin DIPs, as shown in Fig. 3-12, designers use these longer chips enthusiastically when the four extra pins achieve a function which they need. Thus these parts find extensive use when *eight* lines of data require the same operation and can achieve it with a 20-pin part, such as an *octal* flip-flop or an "*octal* three-state buffer," or an "*octal* universal shift/storage register."

† With the introduction of their 74ASxx and 74ALSxx advanced Schottky TTL families of logic, Texas Instruments has improved upon this "standard," fat, 24-pin DIP. The new 24-pin DIP has a 300-mil-wide package, the same width as a 16-pin IC.

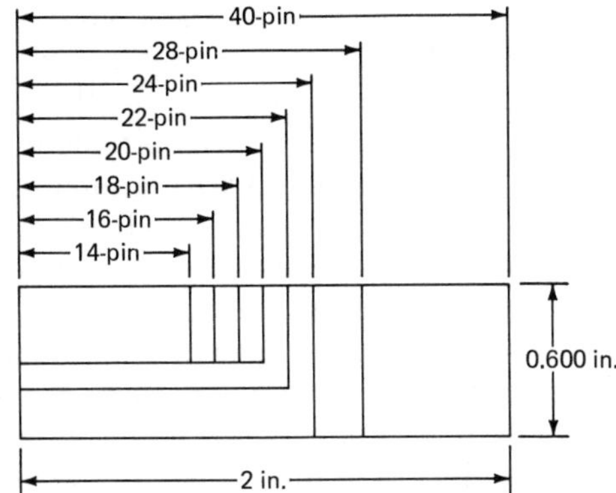

Figure 3-12. Relative size of eight different integrated circuit packages.

One ramification of minimizing package count arises because of the presence of one or more microcomputers in virtually any instrument design. The microcomputer, and its ability to implement arbitrary algorithms in software, gives rise to a remarkable trade-off opportunity, because

1 *Any* digital function can be implemented with digital logic chips organized to serve this sole function.
2 *Any* digital function can be implemented in a microcomputer by acquiring the data involved and then manipulating it appropriately—provided that the functional requirement does not call for results to be generated faster than the microcomputer can generate them.

Because the implementation within a microcomputer offers reduced package count, flexibility, and ease of testing, it is the alternative of choice unless a speed requirement rules it out. In fact, were it not for this speed constraint and for buffering inputs and outputs, the digital circuitry in an instrument would consist of nothing more than a microcomputer.

Another ramification of minimizing package count arises because of the possibility of employing several microcomputers in one design. In many designs organized on several logic boards, as in Fig. 3-9, the multiline bus that couples boards is buffered with "drivers," "receivers," and "tranceivers" on each board. Using multiple microcomputers, as in Fig. 3-10, opened up the possibility of *serial* communication between boards using just two wires, and the attendant elimination of almost all the packages of buffers between boards.

A third ramification of minimizing package count also arises because of the possibility of using multiple microcomputers. Any instrument design benefits by employing a "master" microcomputer as its overall controller, sequencing its orderly operation and the execution of all the tasks required of the instrument, including self-test algorithms. If the speed requirement of any of these tasks strains the ability of this master microcomputer to keep up with the task and carry out its other functions as well, this task might be implemented in special-purpose circuitry. Alternatively, if a "slave" microcomputer (perhaps a one-chip microcomputer) dedicated solely to this task can satisfy the speed requirement, undoubtedly it will result in a reduced chip count. For example, in Chap. 6 we will discuss a CRT display circuit which accepts display information serially on one line and which employs just nine integrated circuits to drive a video monitor and implement the entire display function.

3-4 INFORMATION COMPRESSION

For implementing test algorithms, we need a technique for characterizing massive amounts of data with a concise *signature,* such that

1. If any bits of the data are changed, the signature will almost certainly be changed also.
2. The signature is a relatively small, manageable number.

One commonly used means for obtaining a signature is to compute a "check sum." For example, Fig. 3-13 illustrates a *four-digit signature*

	5	3	4	8
	5	1	6	5
	9	9	2	3
	0	4	0	6
	6	2	0	0
	5	1	3	9
	2	4	9	6
	8	0	3	3
4	2	7	1	0

A four-digit signature = 2710

2 + 7 + 1 + 0 = 1 0

A one-digit signature = 0

Figure 3-13. Formation of check sums.

used to characterize the eight four-digit numbers shown. It is formed by simply adding the four-digit numbers together and keeping only the lower four digits. If these four digits are added together, the least significant digit of the result can be used as a *one-digit signature*.

As is evident from this example, there is a degree of arbitrariness about how signatures are formed. Furthermore, the size of the signature (e.g., 2710 versus 0) is unrelated to the amount of information being compressed. Rather, the size of the signature, as well as the algorithm used to form it, is selected so that a change in the data being compressed will most likely change the signature also.

Notice that the four-digit signature of Fig. 3-13 will change if exactly one digit of the data is changed. This property holds true for the one-digit signature also. On the other hand, both of these signature-forming algorithms fail to detect a variety of multiple-digit changes. For example, if the 8 in the upper right-hand corner is increased to 9 while the 5 just below it is decreased to 4, and if all other digits remain the same, both signatures remain unchanged.

A major weakness of a one-digit signature is that even catastrophic errors, which change many of the digits, have a 10 percent change of producing the same signature. For example, if *all* the digits in Fig. 3-13 are changed to 0, the one-digit signature will still be 0. A signature that has only 10 different values is, for this reason, a weak signature.

The algorithm we will discuss produces a signature that can take on any one of $2^{16} = 65{,}536$ values. Furthermore, random changes of the data will have only 1 chance in 65,536 of producing the same signature. The algorithm operates upon binary data, one bit at a time, to produce a 16-bit, or four-hexadecimal-digit, signature. It is derived from a *pseudo-random binary sequence* (PRBS) generator. It derives excellent error-detecting characteristics from the unusually powerful *randomness* properties† exhibited by the output of a PRBS generator.

A PRBS generator is easily implemented with a shift register and an exclusive-OR gate. With n bits in the shift register, the sequence will have a period of $P = 2^n - 1$ clock periods. For example, Fig. 3-14 shows a 3-bit PRBS generator, how the sequence is generated, and the resulting sequence.

To generate a signature from a binary bit stream, we will use the 16-bit PRBS generator shown in Fig. 3-15*a*, which has been modified with the addition of an extra PROBE input to the exclusive-OR gate. Although there are some other ways in which a 16-bit shift register and an exclusive-OR gate can be interconnected so as to produce a sequence having the required period of $2^{16} - 1$, this configuration is the

† See Golomb, referenced at the end of the chapter.

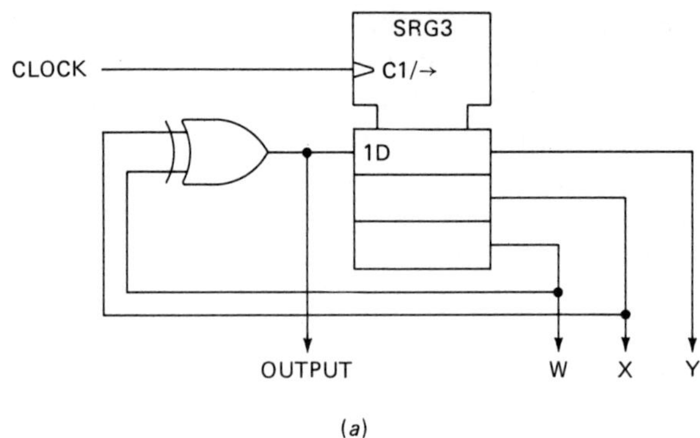

(a)

W	X	Y	OUTPUT
1	1	1	0
1	1	0	0
1	0	0	1
0	0	1	0
0	1	0	1
1	0	1	1
0	1	1	1
1	1	1	0

(The first seven rows are bracketed: Period = $2^3 - 1 = 7$; a dashed line separates them from the last row.)

(b)

··· 0 0 1 0 1 1 1 0 0 1 0 1 1 1 0 0 1 0 ···

(c)

Figure 3-14. PRBS generation. (a) Circuit; (b) sequence generation; (c) generated sequence.

one used by Hewlett-Packard in their 5004A signature analyzer, shown in Fig. 3-1.

To form the signature of a sequence of 1s and 0s, the shift register is first *initialized* to a known state. It happens that the initial state chosen by the Hewlett-Packard designers is the all-0s state. While this is the one state not encountered by the PRBS generator in a full sequence of 65,535 clock periods, this is actually an advantage, as we shall see. The sequence to be characterized is clocked into the circuit of Fig. 3-15*a* via the PROBE input. At the conclusion of the sequence, the state of the shift register *is* the signature, as shown in Fig. 3-15*b*.

With the shift register initialized to all 0s, notice that a zero on the PROBE input will form a 0 on the output of the exclusive-OR gate. Furthermore, if the input sequence consists of *nothing* but 0s (as happens when the Hewlett-Packard unit probes "ground" in a circuit being tested), the shift register hangs up in the all-0s state and termi-

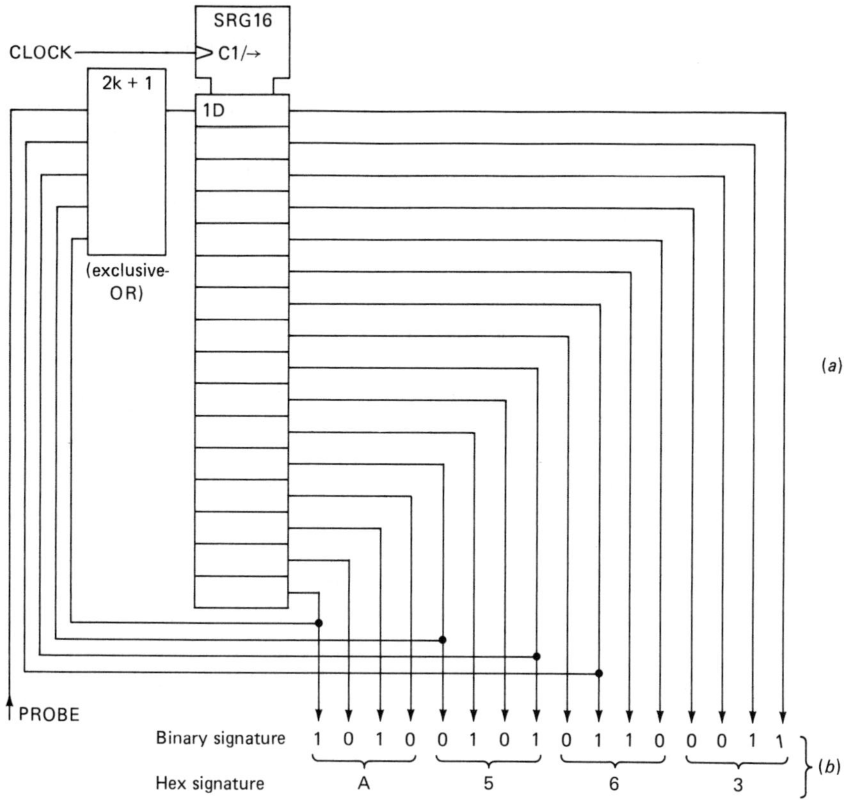

Figure 3-15. PRBS signature-generating circuit. (a) Circuit; (b) signature, obtained at completion of input sequence.

nates with a hexadecimal signature of 0000. Consequently, in using the signature analyzer, if we see 0000 on the display, we can be confident that we are probing a point whose voltage is always 0 V.

Now consider an input sequence consisting of all 0s except for a single 1. Starting from the initial all-0s state, the shift register remains in this state until the single 1 appears on the PROBE input. This kicks the circuit out of the all-0s state to the 0001 state. From this point on, the circuit goes through successive states of the PRBS generator and stops in a unique state. The signature thus depends upon the number of clock periods that occurred between the input bit of 1 and the end of the input sequence.

Finally, consider an arbitrary input sequence. The first 1 appearing on the input kicks the circuit into the PRBS generator sequence. Subsequent 0s permit the PRBS generator to proceed unmolested. However, each subsequent 1 "derails" the train of successive states of the PRBS generator, forcing it into some other one of the 65,536 possible states of the 16-bit shift register.

Since the error-detecting properties of this scheme depend upon this process, we will examine the nature of this "derailment" in some detail. We will see that this PRBS generator algorithm for forming a signature takes advantage of a remarkable "randomness" characteristic.

Consider the simple circuit of Fig. 3-16*a*. Its output (once it is kicked into the PRBS sequence) with 0s on its input is shown in Fig. 3-16*b*. If the three flip-flops making up the shift register are labeled b_4, b_2, and b_1, as in Fig. 3-16*a*, the state of the circuit can be represented as the decimal equivalent of this 3-bit binary number, as in Fig. 3-16*b*. Note that the period of the waveform equals seven clock periods.

Now, consider the derailing effect of a single, randomly placed 1 on the input, as shown in Fig. 3-16*c*. If we compare the output of Fig. 3-16*c* with that of Fig. 3-16*b*, we see that the 1 has produced what a communications engineer calls a *phase hit;* that is, the state of the circuit jumped from 6 to 5, skipping over states 4, 1, and 2. Thus the 1 on the input introduced a phase shift of three clock periods. In Fig. 3-16*d*, the phase shift is shown which results from a phase hit occurring in each possible state of the circuit. We see the remarkable fact that, with a waveform having a period of seven, each of the possible phase shifts of 1, 2, 3, 4, 5, and 6 occurs exactly once. In addition, if the state is 4 when the phase hit occurs, the circuit goes to state 0. Since the circuit remains in this state (until another 1 occurs on the input), we cannot categorize this event by a phase shift.

This *random-phase-shift property* is a characteristic of *any* PRBS generator modified to incorporate an input. Thus the analogous analysis of the circuit of Fig. 3-15 would lead to a listing of 65,535 states and an associated phase shift with each 1. Those phase shifts would include each possible phase shift (1, 2, . . . , 65,534) once and only once.

Returning to our original goal, we want to characterize a long sequence of 1s and 0s with a unique four-hex-digit signature. As we see, each time a 1 occurs on the input sequence, the PRBS generator is thrown out of its normal sequence of states, in effect causing a random-sized phase shift of a waveform having a period of 65,535 clock periods. Errors in the input sequence will produce a *different* set of random-sized phase shifts. The odds that these two sets of random-sized phase shifts will accumulate to produce the same net phase shift, and hence the same signature, is extremely remote, on the order of 1 chance in $2^{16} = 65{,}536$.

Before concluding this section, we might note that this signature-

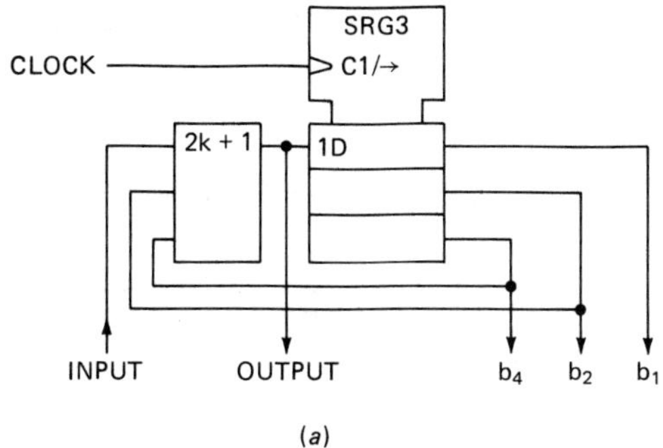

(*a*)

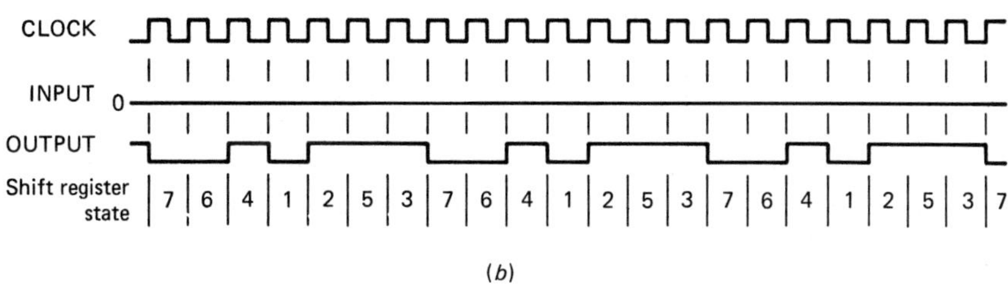

(*b*)

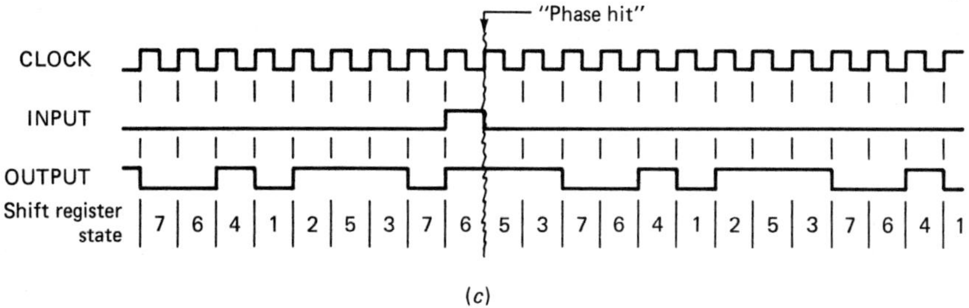

(*c*)

Shift register state when INPUT = 1	Phase shift (clock periods)
6	3
4	X (goes to zero state)
1	2
2	4
5	5
3	1
7	6

(*d*)

Figure 3-16. Random-phase-shift property. (a) Circuit; (b) OUTPUT when INPUT always equals zero; (c) OUTPUT perturbed by INPUT = 1; (d) phase shift.

generating algorithm is almost identical to that used to add a *cyclic redundancy check character* (CRCC) to a record of data stored serially, using magnetic tape or disk storage, or to data transmitted serially. While a *sixteen*-bit PRBS generator is again commonly used for this purpose, the feedback taps used in the PRBS circuit happen to be different from those shown in Fig. 3-15.

We began this section with an example of a simple *check-sum* signature-generating algorithm. With an 8-bit microcomputer carrying out self-test algorithms, a need often arises for a data compression algorithm that operates on data acquired *eight* bits at a time instead of one bit at a time. Since the microcomputer can perform summations of 8-bit *bytes* fast, an algorithm similar to that of Fig. 3-13 might be used. On the other hand, if a slower execution time is not a problem, better error-detecting characteristics can be achieved by using a *software* version of the PRBS algorithm of Fig. 3-15. A short SHIFT subroutine can be prepared which operates upon the contents of two bytes of RAM used to store the "shift register" contents. Each call of the SHIFT subroutine implements the equivalent of one shift of the circuit of Fig. 3-15. Another subroutine called CHECK can take a byte of input data and operate upon its bits with eight successive calls of the SHIFT subroutine. Hence the CHECK subroutine is used to compress each byte of input data, using an unusually potent alternative to a check sum. A faster alternative is presented in Prob. 3-32.

3-5 SIGNATURE ANALYSIS

The signature analyzer of Fig. 3-1 is shown again in Fig. 3-17, being used to isolate a fault in a malfunctioning instrument. The four "grabbers" are used to make Ground, Start, Stop, and Clock connections to appropriate test point lugs in the instrument, as specified in the service manual. For example, the manual might say to connect both the Start and the Stop grabbers to a lug labeled START/$\overline{\text{STOP}}$, the Clock grabber to a lug labeled SA CLOCK, and the Ground grabber to a lug labeled SA GND. Then the manual might say to depress the signature analyzer's Stop pushbutton and leave the Start and Clock pushbuttons extended. These pushbuttons select the edge of each signal to which the signature analyzer will respond.

The configuration described above will create a *window* during which the data on the PROBE input is collected, as shown in Fig. 3-18. This data is compressed, using the algorithm discussed in the last section, and then displayed at the close of the window. The signature is the four-hex-digit contents of the PRBS circuit, coded in the *HP-hex* code shown in Fig. 3-19. For the upper six hex digits (which would

Figure 3-17. Isolating a fault with signature analysis. (Hewlett-Packard Co.)

normally be represented by A, B, C, D, E, and F), this code employs capital letters which can be generated on a low-cost seven-segment display. Such departure from standard hex code is irrelevant. It is only necessary that the signatures given in the service manual correspond to the signatures displayed by the signature analyzer.

A simplified view of the use of signature analysis to locate the source of a malfunction is shown in Fig. 3-20. If pushbutton switch SW1 is depressed, the microcomputer in the instrument under test

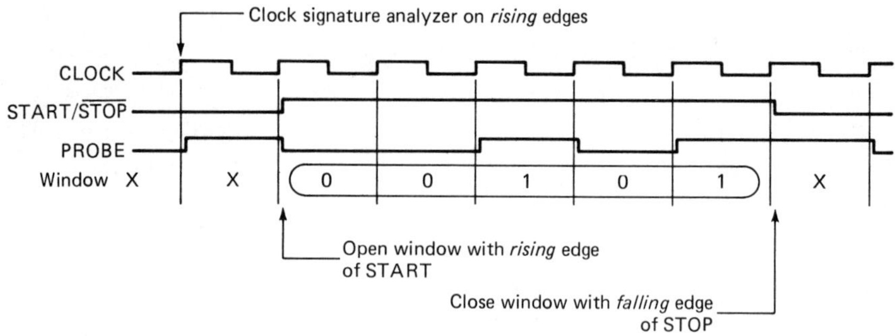

Figure 3-18. Data window of signature analyzer.

senses that it is supposed to lock itself up in a signature analysis routine (until power is turned off and then on again). This routine initializes all the flip-flops in the instrument to a specific state and then pulls the START/$\overline{\text{STOP}}$ line high to open the data window of the signature analyzer. Then the microcomputer, in effect, sprinkles the logic of the instrument with 1s and 0s, thoroughly exercising all of the logic while at the same time putting clock transitions out to the signature analyzer. Finally, the microcomputer pulls the START/$\overline{\text{STOP}}$ line low, to close the data window to the signature analyzer, and jumps back to repeat the entire process. Each time through, the routine must carry out *precisely* the same exercise of the logic. Then each node in the circuitry will produce a unique signature when probed with the signature analyzer.

Finding a faulty component now reduces to locating a component with good signatures on its inputs and at least one bad signature among its outputs. If partition 1 in Fig. 3-20 divides the logic in half, we might check signatures along this partition. If they are good, and if they are generated by the circuitry to the left, the left half of the circuitry must be working properly. Next we might check signatures along partition 2b. If, this time, we find one or more signatures that differ from the values listed in the service manual for the instrument, evidently there is a faulty component between partition 1 and partition 2b. By successive refinement we can thus locate the faulty component.

Notice that this procedure does not require a user to understand the operation of the instrument in order to repair it quickly. However, it does require the designer to partition the circuitry and to provide a guide to its efficient probing.

To illustrate one example of documentation supporting fault isolation by signature analysis, we will consider that provided for debugging the Hewlett-Packard 5004A signature analyzer we have been discussing. Figure 3-21 is provided in the service manual to illustrate

Binary code	HP-hex code
0000	0
0001	1
0010	2
0011	3
0100	4
0101	5
0110	6
0111	7
1000	8
1001	9
1010	A
1011	C
1100	F
1101	H
1110	P
1111	U

Figure 3-19. HP-hex code.

how a functioning signature analyzer is used to debug a malfunctioning signature analyzer. Component locations are identified with Fig. 3-22. The instrument has an internal Normal/Service switch to help isolate malfunctions. Part of the table listing correct signatures for all integrated circuits is shown in Fig. 3-23. Each column corresponds to a specific IC (U1, U2, etc.). Each *pair* of rows within a column lists the two signatures for a specific pin on the IC, one signature

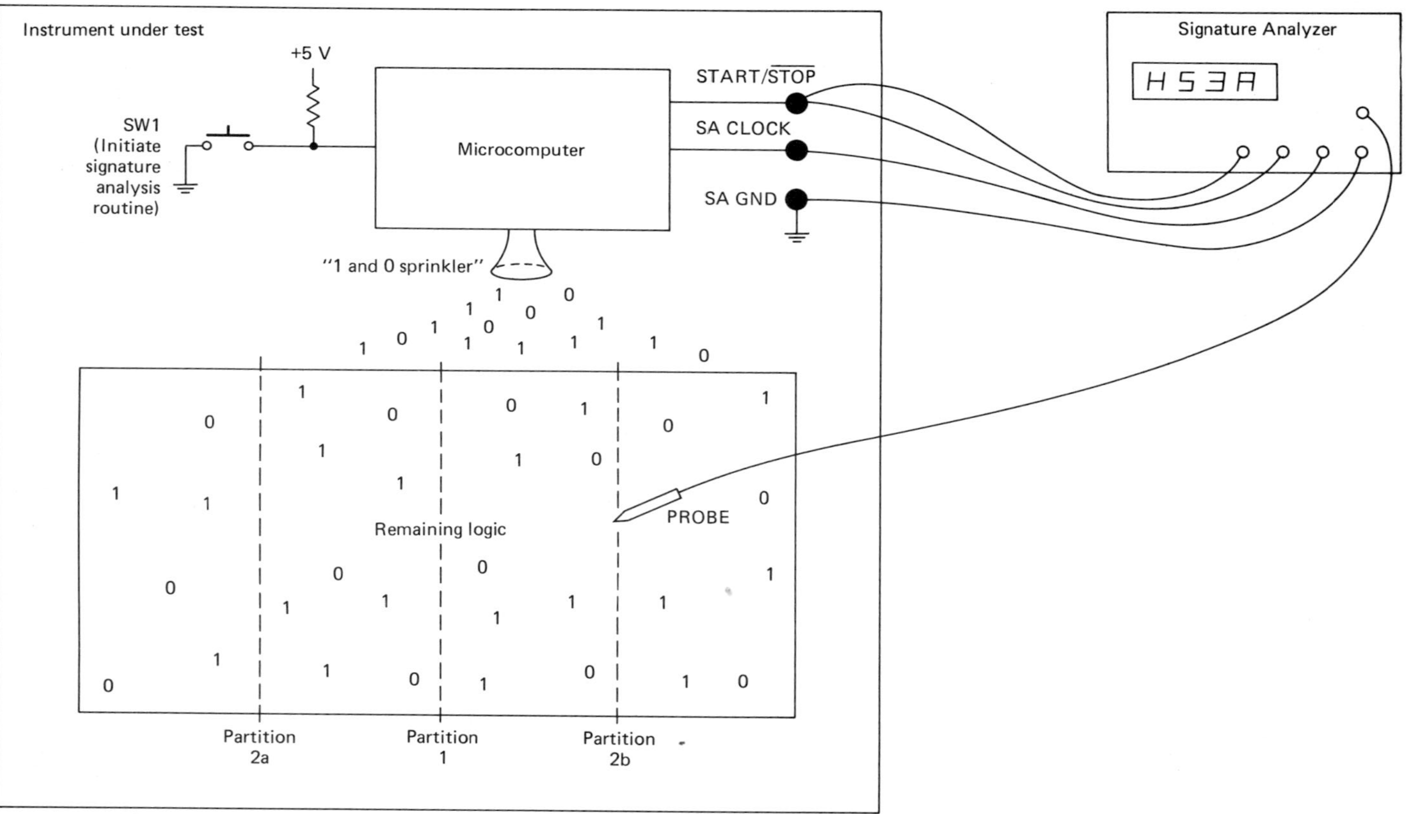

Figure 3-20. Use of signature analysis.

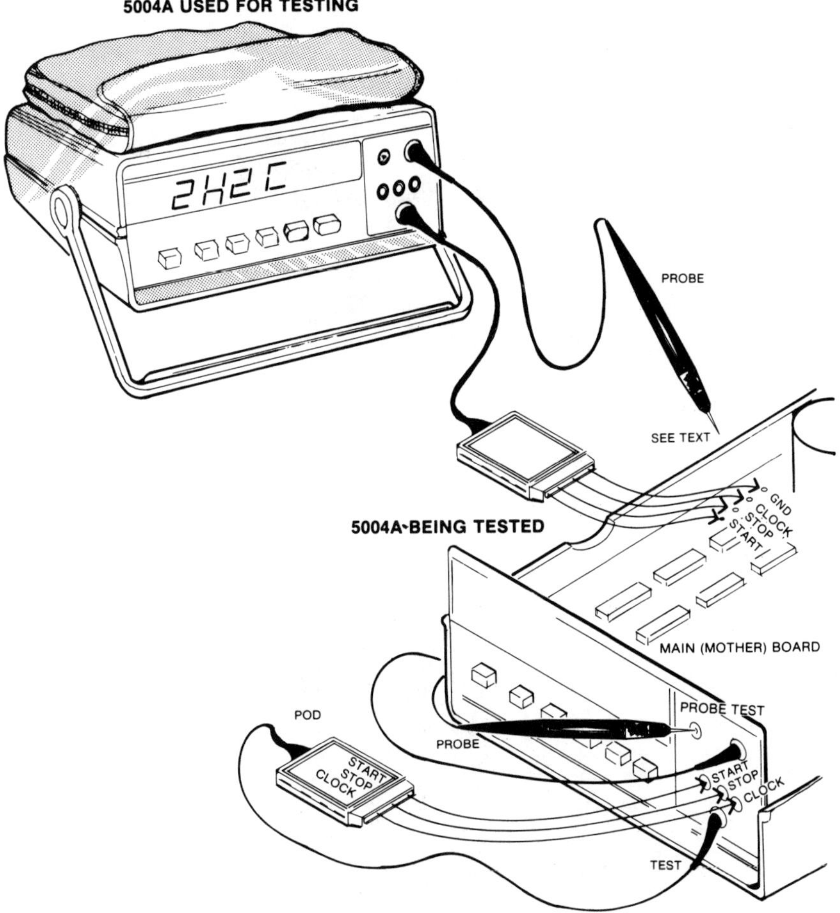

Figure 3-21. Service manual illustration of interconnections for servicing one signature analyzer with another unit. (Hewlett-Packard Co.)

for each position of the Normal/Service switch. In addition to this table, the signatures for nine key test points are given in Fig. 3-24. Finally, the flowchart of Fig. 3-25 guides the user through the sequence of tests to isolate a fault. In effect, this flowchart serves the role of the partitioning discussed in conjunction with Fig. 3-20.

With the probe in place on a pin of an IC, the signature analyzer used for testing should collect the same signature again and again, for each successive pass through the data window. If two successive signatures differ from each other, an "unstable signature" light is blinked, alerting the user to this erratic operation.

Figure 3-22. Service manual identification of component locations. (Hewlett- Packard Co.)

PINS	U1	U2	U3	U4	U5	U6	U7	U8	U9	U10	PIN
1 N	472A	5A22		1H08	5A22	472A	F517	UCP9	472A	7CA7	1
S	472A	94A3		H389	94A3	472A	P7AA	PF43	472A	7CA7	
2 N	A326	A326		09P3	472A	472A	0000	P36F	3F8H	7CA7	2
S	A326	A326		09P3	472A	472A	0000	P36F	3F8H	7CA7	
3 N	P40F	UCP9		1H08		472A	823H	CFF3	7CA7	472A	3
S	P40F	PF43		H389		472A	A080	Ac69	7CA7	472A	
4 N	464F	UCP9		UCP9	P40F	472A	4C4F	CFF3	472A	0000	4
S	464F	PF43		PF43	P40F	472A	125P	AC69	472A	0000	
5 N	13F7	UCP9		UCP9	5829	596F	0F66	66P0	596F	472A	5
S	13F7	PF43		PF43	A427	596F	5574	6606	596F	472A	
6 N	4PF9	3P06		UCP9	H4U0	0147	0000	UCP9	1P46	0000	6
S	4PF9	62CF		PF43	6H73	42U6	0000	PF43	1P46	0000	
7 N	09P3	0000		0000	0000	0000	0000	0000		0000	7
S	09P3	0000		0000	0000	0000	0000	0000		0000	
8 N	0000	0000		C445	66P0	0000	H4U0	472A	0000	13F7	8
S	0000	0000		1669	6606	0000	6H73	472A	0000	13F7	
9 N	0000	5829		5829	5829	0000	HAU1	FUFU		54PH	9
S	0000	A427		A427	A427		HAU1	FUFU		54PH	
10 N		4PF9		P40F	P40F	F944	0F66	0863		464F	10
S		4PF9		P405	P40F	CFU5	5574	0863		464F	
11 N	5829	4PF9		5829	P40F	AUF8	4596	7CA7		0166	11
S	A427	4PF9		A427		HHH5	4596	7CA7		0166	
12 N	3P06	4PF9	54PH	1H08	5A22	2CAU	2946	7A33		0166	12
S	F61C	4PF9	54PH	H389	94A3	6PAH	2946	7A33		0166	
13 N	C445	A326	0166	1H08	P36F	1501	90FP	4596		A446	13
S	2946	A326	0166	H389	P36F	1417	90FP	4596		A446	
14 N	1H08	472A		472A	472A	472A	472A	472A		472A	14
S	H389	472A		472A	472A	472A	472A	472A		472A	
15 N	5A22								472A		15
S	94A3								472A		
16 N	472A								472A		16
S	472A								472A		

N = NORMAL
S = SERVICE position of S7.

To get the signatures given in this table, set the two 5004A's controls as follows:

5004A Being Tested
LINE:OFF; START:OUT; STOP:OUT; HOLD:OUT; SELF-TEST:IN.

5004A Used to Test
Same as above except SELF-TEST:OUT

Make the connections shown between the two 5004A's.

Figure 3-23. Service manual table of integrated circuit signatures. (Hewlett-Packard Co.)

Test Point*	Location	Signature	
		NORMAL	SERVICE
1	U25(11)	FUFU	←
2	U29(1)	54PH	←
3	U29(2)	0166	←
4	U29(3)	A445	←
5	U29(4)	HAU1	←
6	U9(5)	596F	←
7	U11(8)	U36U	6P6F
8	U7(4), U24(9)	4C4F	125P
9	U24(13), U6(10)	F94H	CFU5

Figure 3-24. Service manual table of signatures at nine key test points. (Hewlett-Packard Co.)

In the next section we will consider in more detail what we must do to build signature analysis capability and algorithms into an instrument. We will make this more specific in later chapters by considering various aspects of the design of the signature analyzer itself. The signature analyzer will serve as a good vehicle for illustrating design ideas since it has a limited number of inputs, relatively simple high-speed

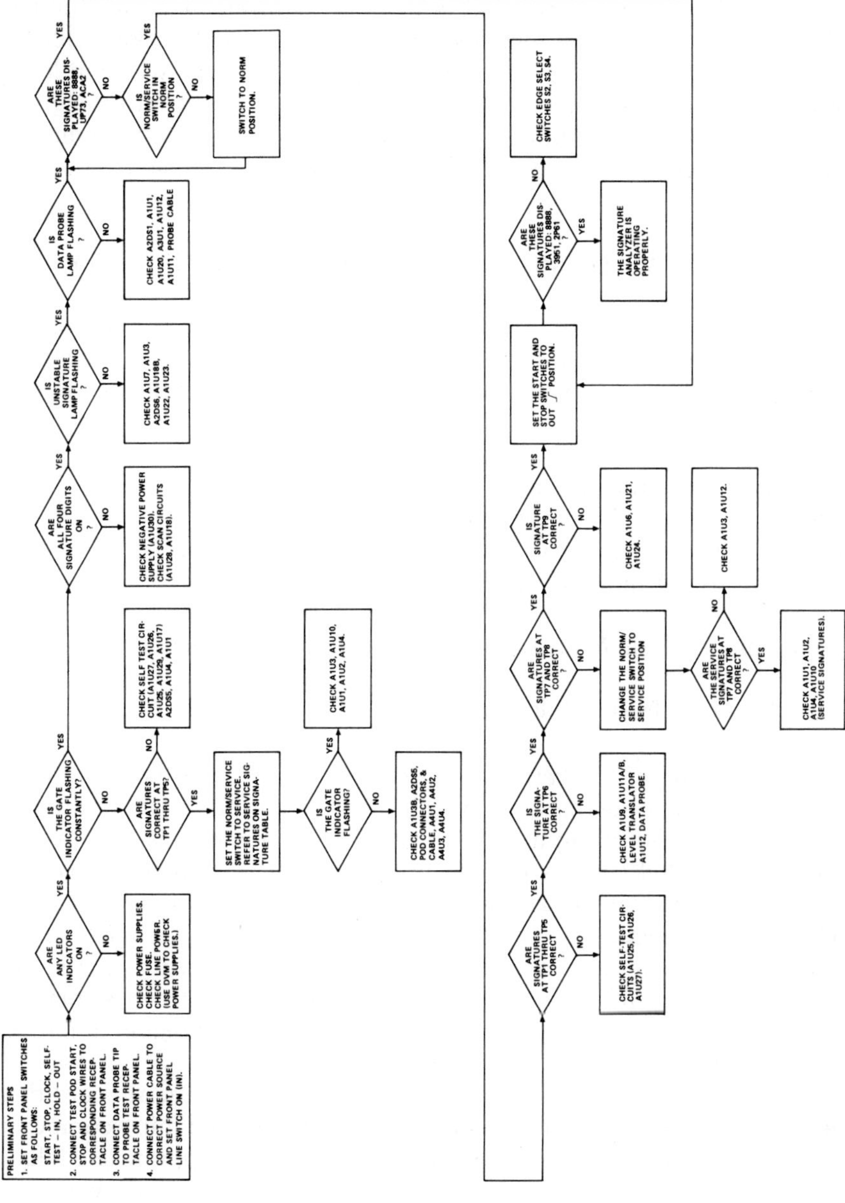

Figure 3-25. Service manual signature analysis flowchart. (Hewlett-Packard Co.)

data acquisition circuitry, simple display requirements, and limited data manipulation requirements. While the Hewlett-Packard 5004A unit is designed entirely out of SSI and MSI chips, we will employ a one-chip microcomputer to reduce the package count rather significantly. The microcomputer will also lend support to the implementation of self-test, push-to-test, and signature analysis capability.

3-6 DESIGN ACCOMMODATIONS FOR MAINTAINABILITY

Whether we are considering the design accommodations required for self-test capability, push-to-test capability, or fault-isolation (via signature analysis) capability, there are four places where our efforts will impact upon a design:

1 Testing of the kernel
2 Controlling alternative inputs
3 Controlling state variables (i.e., flip-flop contents)
4 Observing internal variables

Signature analysis requires one additional design concession:

5 Breaking feedback loops

By *testing of the kernel* we refer to the testing of that minimum number of integrated circuits which must be correctly functioning in order for the microcomputer to execute *testing* algorithms. If any one of the integrated circuits making up the kernel malfunctions, we can immediately narrow down the source of the malfunction to this set of chips. By replacing each of these chips, one at a time, the user can repair the unit. Since we give the user no help in identifying *which* chip in the kernel malfunctioned, we do well to make the kernel as small as possible. We also help the user by employing integrated circuit sockets for *at least* these few ICs.

We can give the user a *one-chip* kernel for any circuit board that employs a one-chip microcomputer. For self-test, the microcomputer will automatically and periodically execute the appropriate algorithms. However, for push-to-test and signature analysis, we must dedicate one or more inputs to the microcomputer so that a user can tell it what to do. For example, Fig. 3-26 illustrates two ways whereby the microcomputer can read an input port and sense that a user has depressed a pushbutton, or alternatively has used a screwdriver to short between two lugs, to initiate a test algorithm.

It is reassuring to a user if the kernel can generate an output

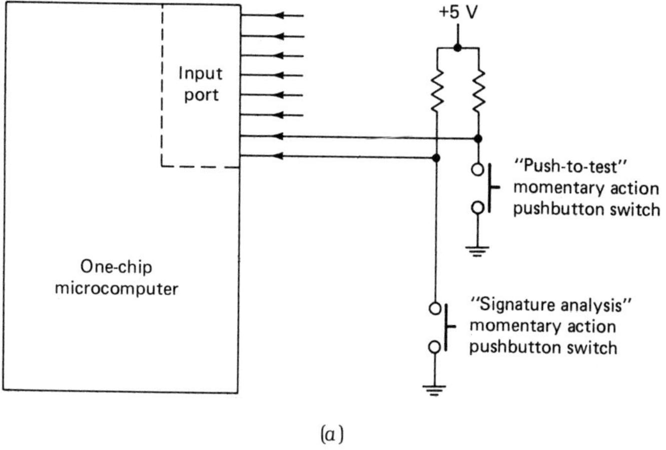

(a)

(b)

Figure 3-26. Initiating push-to-test and signature analysis. (a) Use of pushbuttons; (b) printed circuit board mounted, momentary action pushbutton switch (C & K Components, Inc.).

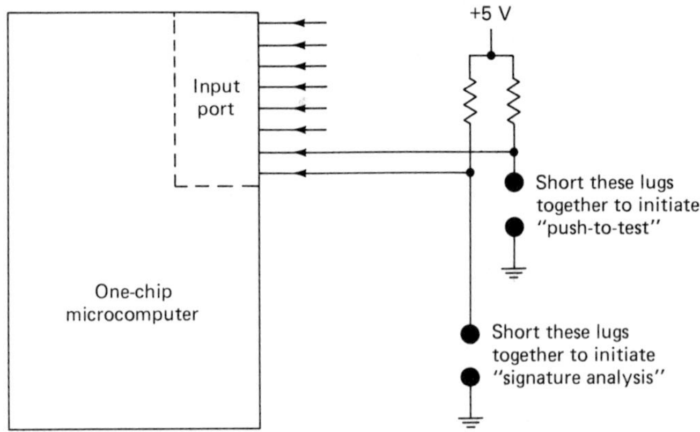

Figure 3-26c. Use of shorting lugs.

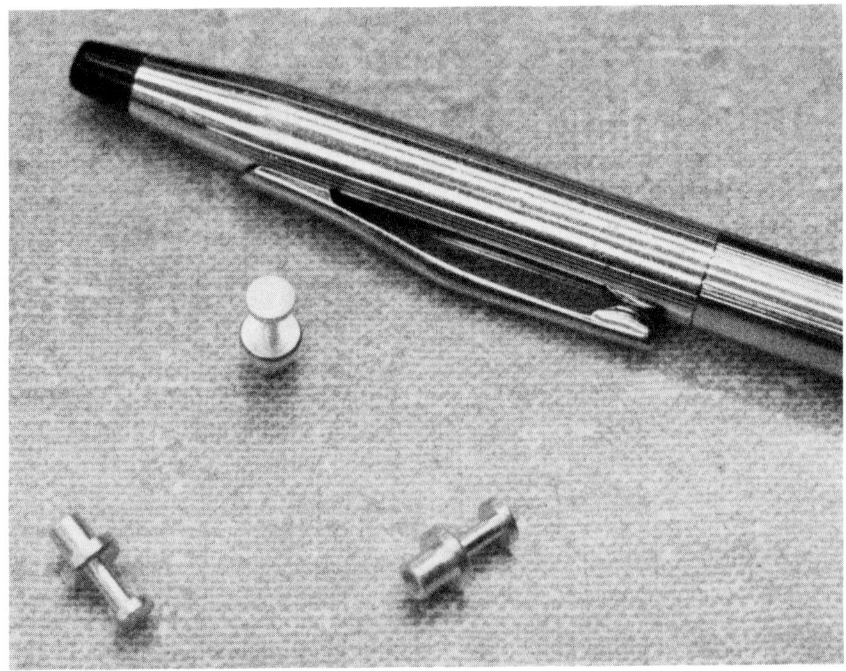

Figure 3-26d. Shorting lugs (Herman H. Smith, Inc.).

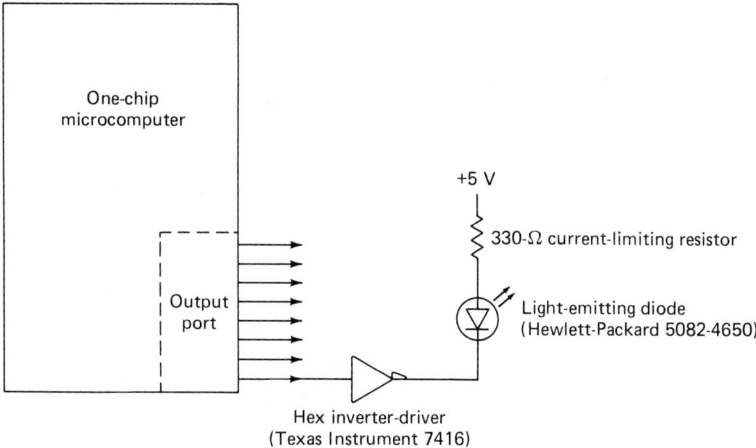

Figure 3-27. Working-kernel indicator circuit.

saying that it is able to execute a test algorithm. Upon power turn-on, it might blink a light-emitting-diode (LED) on-off-on to let a user know that it is a functioning kernel, using the circuit of Fig. 3-27. This driver-LED circuit is not really a part of the kernel. Using a signature analyzer, a user can probe the microcomputer's output which drives the LED driver and ascertain that the kernel works even if the LED itself does not light up.

Often the microcomputer consists of a multitude of chips, including CPU, clock, separate RAM chips, separate ROM chips, and assorted I/O chips. In this case we can add some extra circuitry and removable jumpers to *create* a temporary one-chip "dumb" kernel. As is shown in Fig. 3-28, this temporary kernel is created by removing the jumper dual-in-line packages (DIPs) shown and then putting one of them back into the NOP Programmer socket shown. This will cause the CPU to fetch a NO OPERATION instruction during every instruction cycle. In so doing, the CPU will do nothing but carry out repeated fetches from every address, as follows:

. . . , 0000, 0001, . . . , FFFE, FFFF, 0000, . . .

This is enough to give the signature analyzer something with which to work. It can use the CPU's $\overline{\text{READ}}$ output as an SA CLOCK and its most significant address line as both a START and a STOP input. Now, the signature of each address line can be checked by the user and compared with correct values given in the service manual for this configuration. Next, the ROM outputs can be checked even though they drive nothing (with jumpers 1 and 2 removed). If they are not correct, each

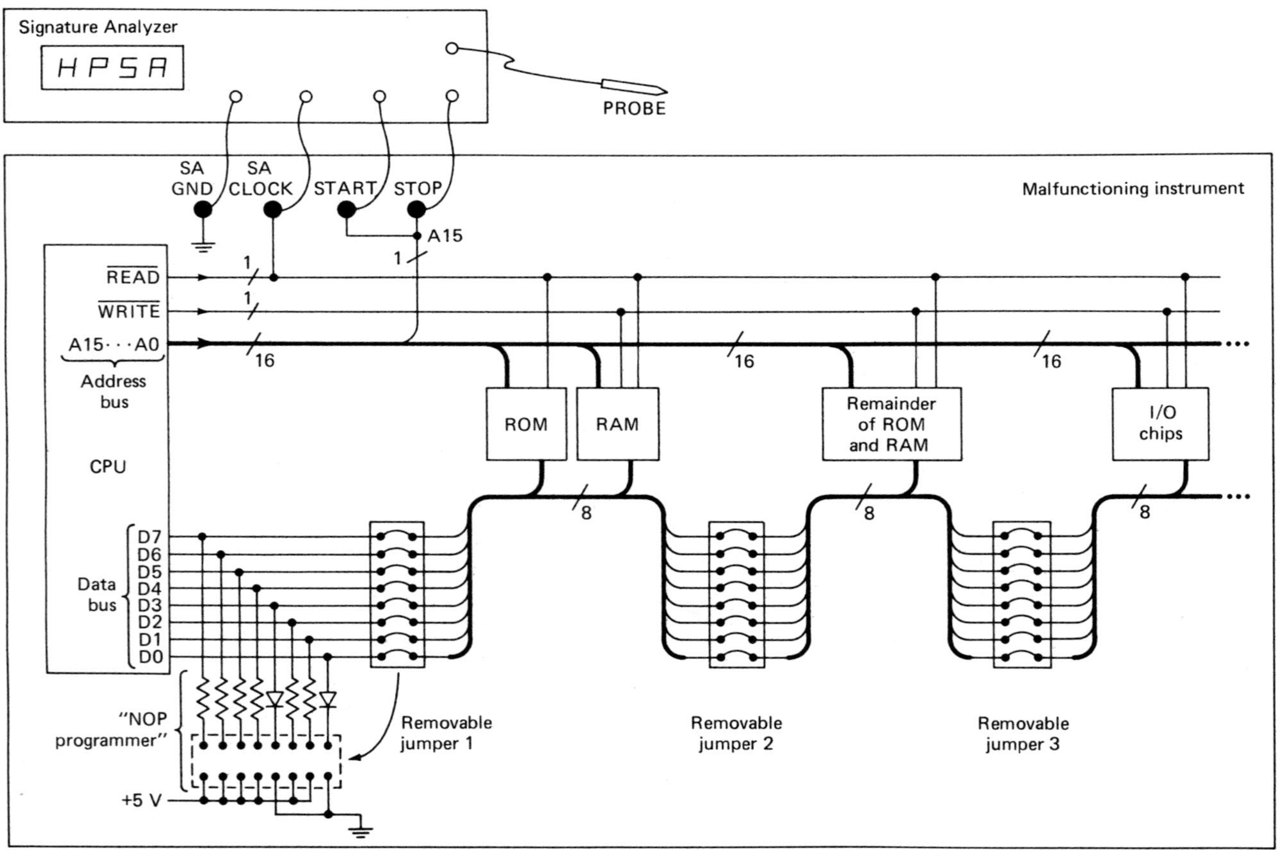

Figure 3-28. Circuitry to support the testing of a growing kernel.

ROM can be removed from its socket, one at a time, and the new signatures for each case compared with the service manual values.

If the ROM signatures are correct when driven by this "dumb" kernel, the NOP Programmer jumper can be removed and jumpers inserted back into the sockets for jumpers 1 and 2. At his point the "dumb" kernel has been expanded to a small, "smart" kernel consisting of CPU and ROM and RAM. The instrument software can be organized to sense when any of the jumpers are removed (by sensing that it cannot write and then read from a carefully selected address) and go to an appropriate signature analysis test routine. This routine can exercise the RAM chips by writing to them and then reading from them. Again, RAM chips can be removed, one by one, in case bad signatures are found. The signatures for each chip configuration can be compared with correct values given in the service manual. In this manner the kernel can be grown successively larger until it includes the entire microcomputer. The jumpers used to grow the kernel might be the inexpensive "programmable shunts" (with all of the shunts left intact) shown in Fig. 3-29. These have the advantage of being easy to locate on a PC board because they do not look like integrated circuits.

Backing up, we note that a microcomputer which employs many chips interconnected on an address bus/data bus structure can require repeated probing of the eight data bus lines with a signature analyzer probe as different jumpers and ICs are pulled. Rather than proceed in this manner, we can organize the signature analyzer routine in the malfunctioning instrument so that the same information can be obtained with the signature analyzer's probe always connected to *one* of the data bus lines, say D7. If the signature analyzer was previously collecting a bit of data every time the CPU executed a READ cycle, then all we need

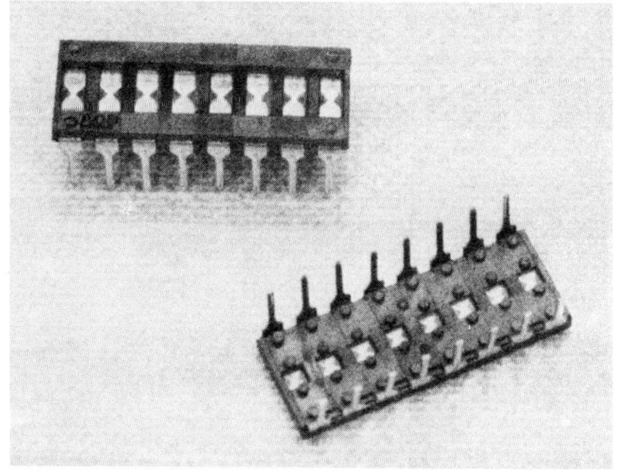

Figure 3-29. Programmable shunt, used as a removable jumper. (AMP, Inc.)

do is make the 8 bits that previously appeared on a read cycle now appear, one by one, on D7. Each time the CPU's accumulator is loaded from the data bus during a read cycle, a ROTATE subroutine can be called which will shift the accumulator left, write this to a RAM location, and read it back from the RAM location (putting the previous D6 bit on the D7 line). The ROTATE subroutine repeats this six more times to make all the bits appear on the D7 line.

With this modification, the testing of the "smart" kernel now amounts to connecting the signature analyzer and then simply comparing its display with that listed in the service manual for assorted configurations, as various ICs and jumpers are removed and replaced. In fact, the testing of a malfunctioning instrument can *begin* with this probing of the D7 data bus line to determine whether or not the kernel is functioning correctly.

Once the kernel is known to function correctly, the user can move ahead to test the rest of the instrument. Testing requires that *known inputs* produce predictable results. For self-test, which is carried out even when the inputs are connected for normal use, we need to bypass these inputs, as in Fig. 3-30*a*. The switch shown might be a reed relay,

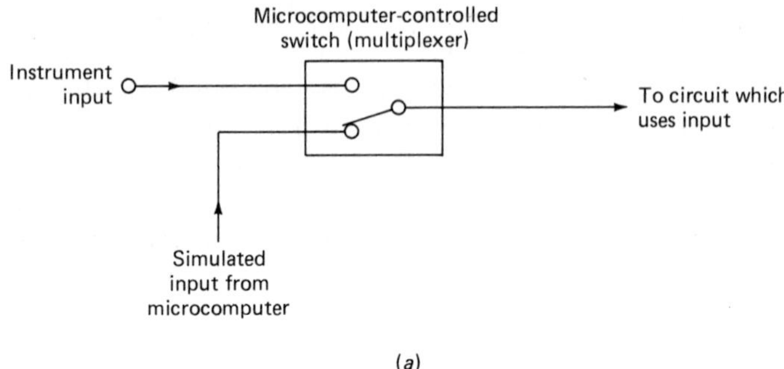

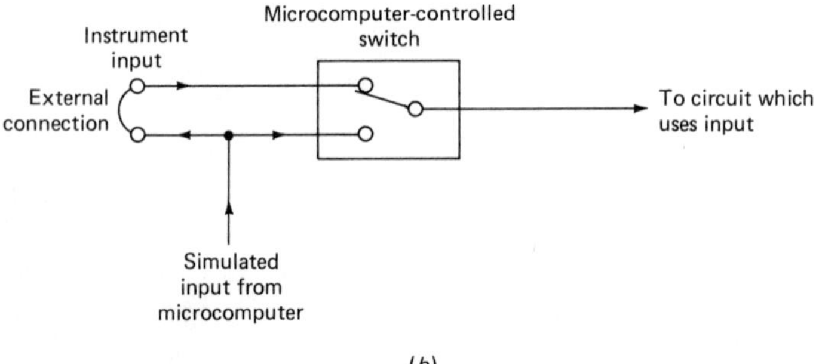

Figure 3-30. Controlling alternative inputs. (a) Control of inputs for (unobtrusive) self-test; (b) control of inputs for push-to-test.

(a)

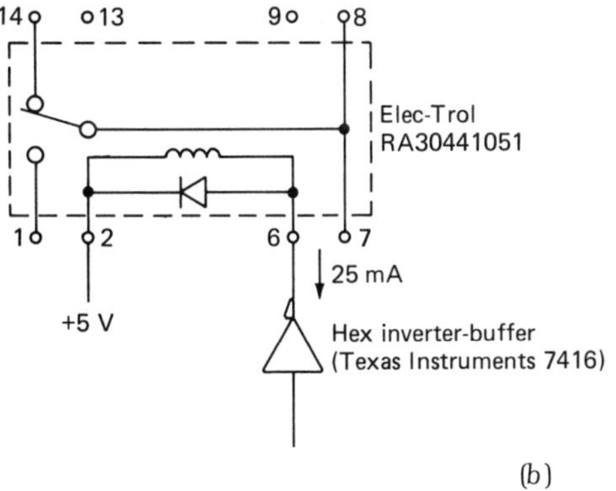

Contact characteristics

On: 0.2 Ω (max.)
0.25 A (max.)
Off: 28 V (max.)
Switching time = 0.25 ms (nominal)
Life: 5×10^6 operations (min.)

(b)

Figure 3-31. *DIP reed relay.* (*a*) *Dual-in-line package;* (*b*) *circuit.* (*Elec-Trol, Inc.*)

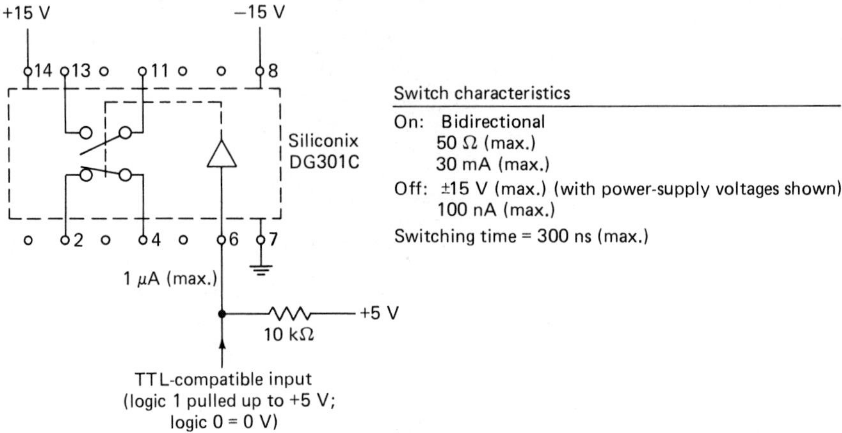

Figure 3-32. CMOS analog switch. (Siliconix Inc.)

such as that of Fig. 3-31, to handle an analog input. Alternatively, for faster switching of an analog input between ±15 V, the CMOS switch of Fig. 3-32 might be used. For the switching of TTL inputs, the quad two-input multiplexer of Fig. 3-33 will handle four inputs per package.

The self-test control of inputs afforded by the approach of Fig. 3-30*a* permits all of the circuitry *after the multiplexer* to be tested. However, the multiplexer input connected to the instrument input can

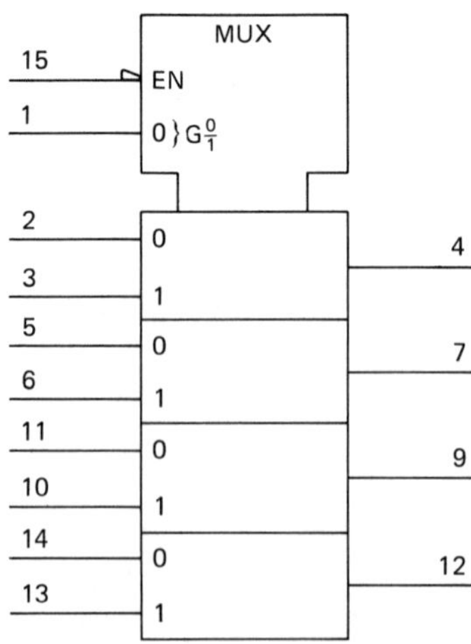

Figure 3-33. Quad two-input multiplexer.

be destroyed, perhaps by a static discharge, and this self-test approach will not catch the malfunction. Catching such malfunctions is one role of push-to-test capability. If the user is given the opportunity to connect inputs to known test signals, as in Fig. 3-30*b*, and then signal the microcomputer that this has been done (with a push-to-test pushbutton switch), the microcomputer can execute virtually the same test routine. The only difference in the routine is that the multiplexer is not switched away from the instrument input.

The third accommodation for maintainability, *controlling state variables*, is required to exercise all of the circuitry of an instrument. Within the microcomputer itself, this step simply means writing data out to assorted registers. Elsewhere we must contend with circuitry that is presumably designed to run fast, with a clock that is independent of the microcomputer's clock. If this were not necessary, the algorithm would have been implemented in software.

Our problem is to design this circuitry so that all of its flip-flops can be loaded, and clocked, by the microcomputer. If a designer takes advantage of the wide variety of medium-scale integrated (MSI) circuits available, this step can demand great ingenuity. We may be able to give the microcomputer control over an asynchronous clear input of flip-flops, counters, and shift registers. From this known state, the circuit *may* be able to be clocked by the microcomputer through its entire repertoire of states without further control.

More generally, much of the circuitry we are called upon to design can take the form of the sequential circuit shown in Fig. 3-34. In this case the complexity of the design might be delegated to general-purpose, programmable, combinational circuits such as programmable read-only memories (PROMs) and field-programmable logic arrays (FPLAs), discussed in Sec. 2-12. We can gain total control of the state, in this case, by using the 74LS195 4-bit parallel-in/parallel-out shift registers of Fig. 3-35 to serve the function of the D-type flip-flops. This modification is illustrated in Fig. 3-36.

The clock to the 74LS195 shift registers can be switched, for testing, between the system clock (SC) used for normal, fast operation and an output port line from the microcomputer. The implementation of this switch requires some careful design, which will be discussed in Chap. 5. At that time we will be concerned with the effects of propagation delay through the switch (if a semiconductor switch is used) and about the control of the switch from its $SC/\overline{TC}$ (SYSTEM CLOCK/TEST CLOCK) input. The *timing* of changes on the $SC/\overline{TC}$ line must be carefully controlled if erratic clocking of the shift registers is to be avoided at the moment of change.

For normal (fast) operation, the circuit of Fig. 3-36 is identical to

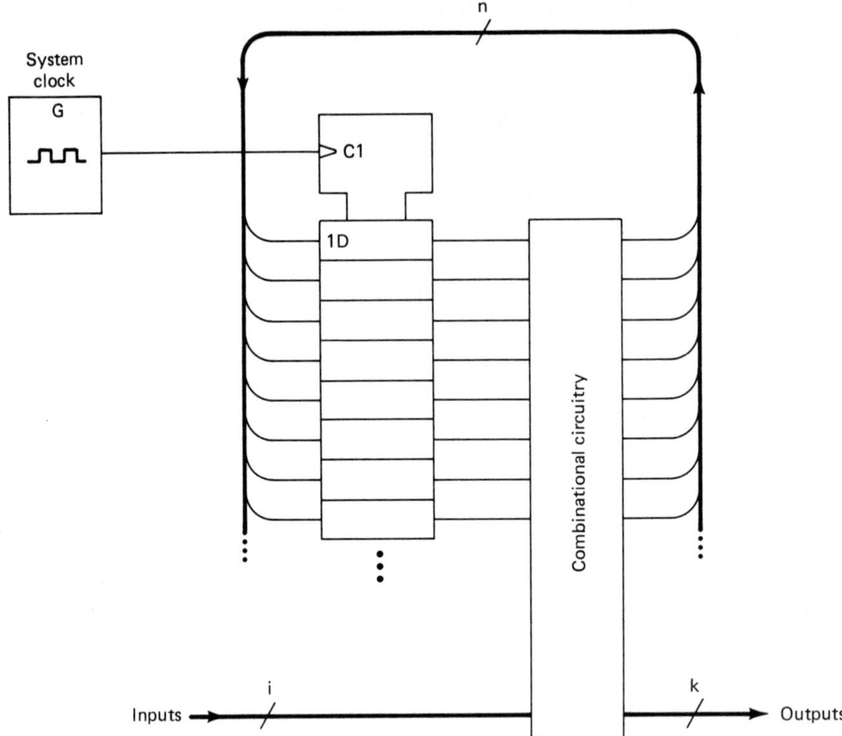

Figure 3-34. Generally applicable implementation of any *sequential circuit.*

that of Fig. 3-34. The microcomputer takes itself out of the picture by setting:

- $SC/\overline{TC}$ high, to select the system clock
- SHIFT low, so the 74LS195s will operate in the parallel mode (i.e., as D-type flip-flops, using the inputs from, and outputs to, the combinational circuitry)

When the microcomputer is ready to execute a self-test routine, it:

1. Pulls $SC/\overline{TC}$ low, to select TEST CLOCK (TC) for testing.
2. Raises SHIFT high, to reconfigure the 74LS195s into a long shift register with input from the SDI (SERIAL DATA IN) input.
3. Shifts initialization data into all the flip-flops, bit by bit, using the SDI and TC lines.
4. Pulls SHIFT low, to run the circuit under control of TEST CLOCK (TC).

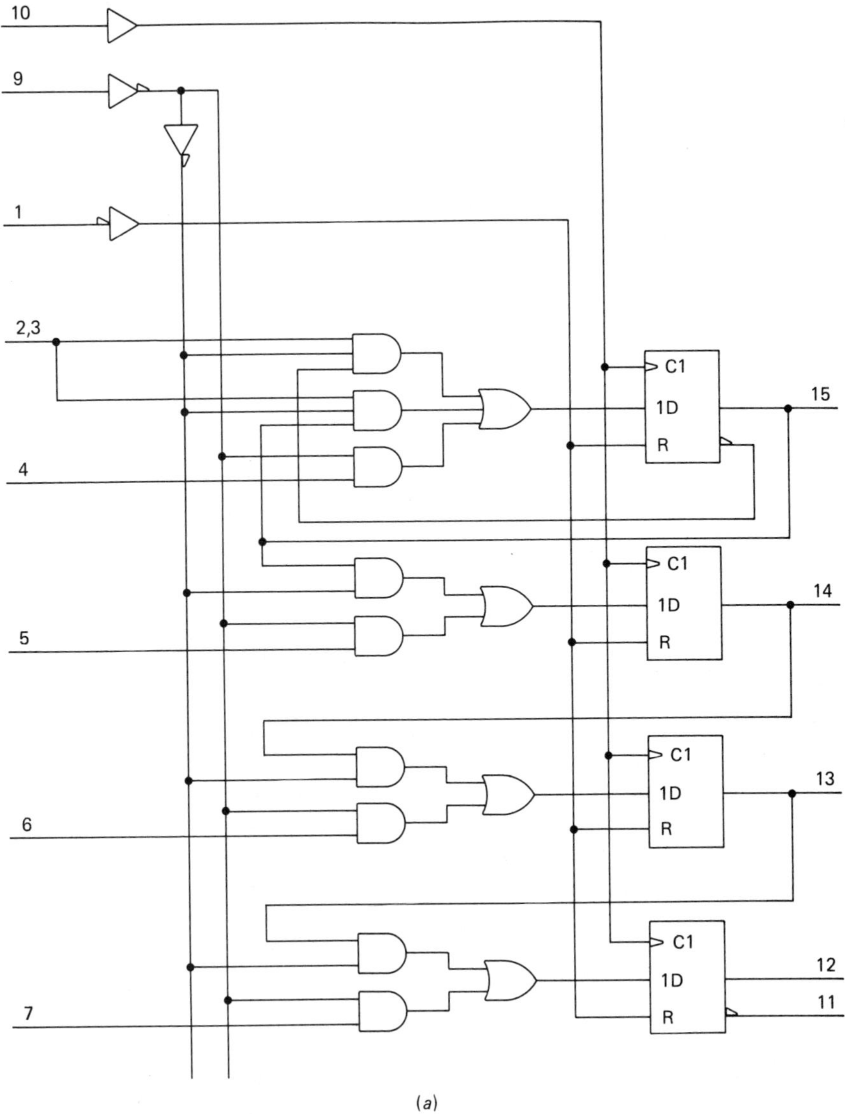

Figure 3-35. 74LS195, 4-bit parallel in/parallel out shift register. (a) *Functional diagram.*

5 Clocks TC.
6 Raises SHIFT high again and shifts the contents of the shift register back into the microcomputer, perhaps compressing it into a signature for comparison with an expected signature.
7 At the same time that step 6 is taking place, *new* initialization data

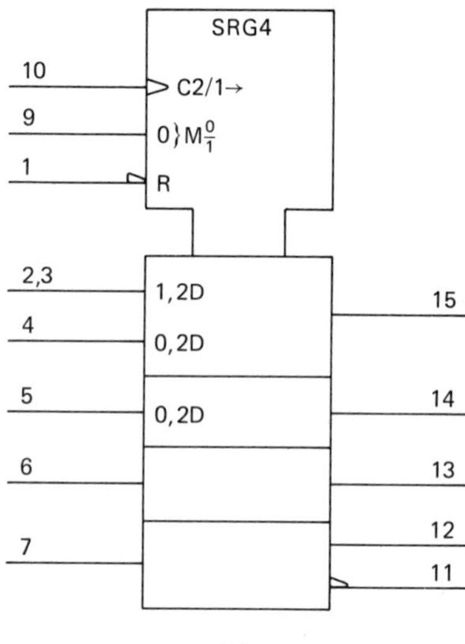

Figure 3-35b. Dependency notation symbol. (Texas Instruments.)

can be shifted out, to begin a *new* exercise of the sequential circuit (i.e., repeating steps 3, 4, 5, and 6).

8 Finally, to return to normal operation, the flip-flops are serially loaded to the desired initial state, SHIFT is pulled low, and SC/$\overline{\text{TC}}$ is raised again, switching back to SYSTEM CLOCK. It is at this moment that we must handle the switching of SC/$\overline{\text{TC}}$ carefully or else the first clocking of the circuit by SYSTEM CLOCK may be garbled. In Chap. 5 we will discuss the *synchronization* of this change in SC/$\overline{\text{TC}}$ to SYSTEM CLOCK in order to preclude such a problem.

The scheme described above represents one (but only one) possibility for controlling state variables (i.e., flip-flop contents). It also represents an unusually powerful means for accomplishing another accommodation for maintainability, *observing internal variables*. Since these flip-flops reach right into the heart of the sequential circuitry, their inputs are vital internal variables that need to be checked to ascertain correct operation. Testing of logic circuitry is so important, and this shift register scheme is so systematic and powerful, that IBM Corporation has designed it into the large-scale integrated (LSI) circuits for their System/38 computer.†

† Neil C. Berglund, Level-Sensitive Scan Design Tests Chips, Boards, System, *Electronics*, March 15, 1979, pp. 108–110.

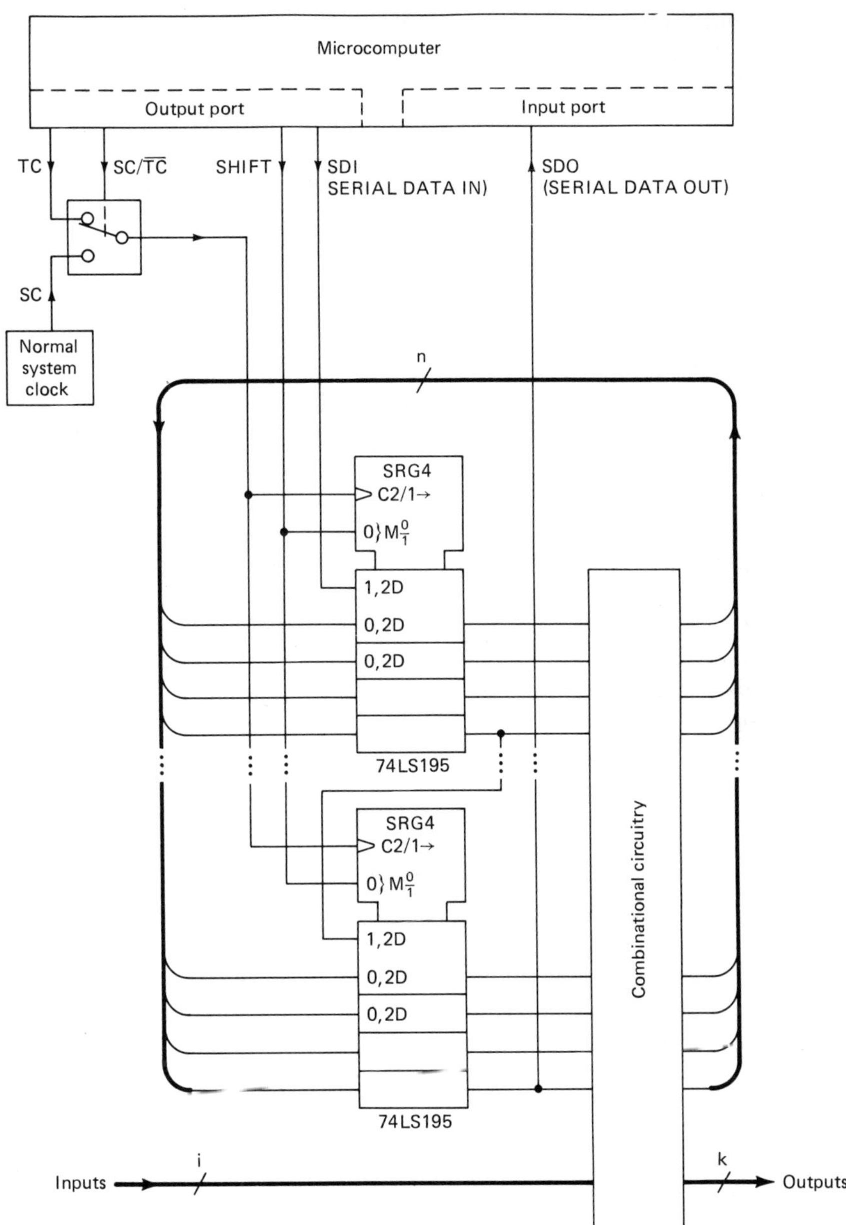

Figure 3-36. Use of a shift register to obtain controllable, observable *flip-flops.*

Often, the function of a sequential circuit is to acquire and massage input data and then to pass the results along to the microcomputer. The shift register scheme of Fig. 3-36 not only fosters testing, it can also handle the transfer of this massaged input data to the microcomputer as an extra, free feature.

Our final accommodation for maintainability consists of *breaking feedback loops.* This is a necessary step in support of signature analysis. As an example of the problem arising from feedback loops, consider Fig. 3-34 again. If one output in the combinational circuitry malfunctions, it will produce bad bits on the input, and then on the output, of one of the D-type flip-flops. These bad bits will feed back into the combinational circuitry and cause bad signatures to appear on the outputs of any circuits that depend upon this input. After many clock periods, we are likely to find that the *signatures* on all the components in the loop are bad even though all *components* but one are good. Consequently, we cannot isolate a faulty component from all the other components in the loop.

In general, the same removable jumpers shown in Fig. 3-29 can be used to break feedback loops. Alternatively, a multiplexer such as that of Fig. 3-33 can be used to break a loop and to substitute suitable test inputs generated by the microcomputer. As a third alternative, the shift register scheme of Fig. 3-36 can be used to break feedback loops. When the 74LS195s are in the serial mode, the loops of Fig. 3-34 are all broken.

3-7 ONE APPROACH TO MAINTAINABLE SEQUENTIAL CIRCUIT DESIGN

In the last section we concluded with one implementation of a general sequential circuit, that shown in Fig. 3-34, and subsequently modified for testing to Fig. 3-36. In this section we will modify that circuit still further and then consider its use for implementing self-test, push-to-test, and signature analysis algorithms.

The circuit will require memory elements that can be switched between two *synchronous* modes of operation, one of which is either internally or externally wired as a shift register. For example, each 74LS195 of Fig. 3-35 is *internally* wired as a shift register. In contrast, consider the 74LS669 shown in Fig. 3-37. It is a 4-bit up/down binary counter which can be (synchronously) parallel-loaded. It can be wired externally so that "parallel-loading" the device will actually cause it to shift. That is, the device can be wired so that when pin 9 is pulled low, each output will be synchronously loaded into the next bit

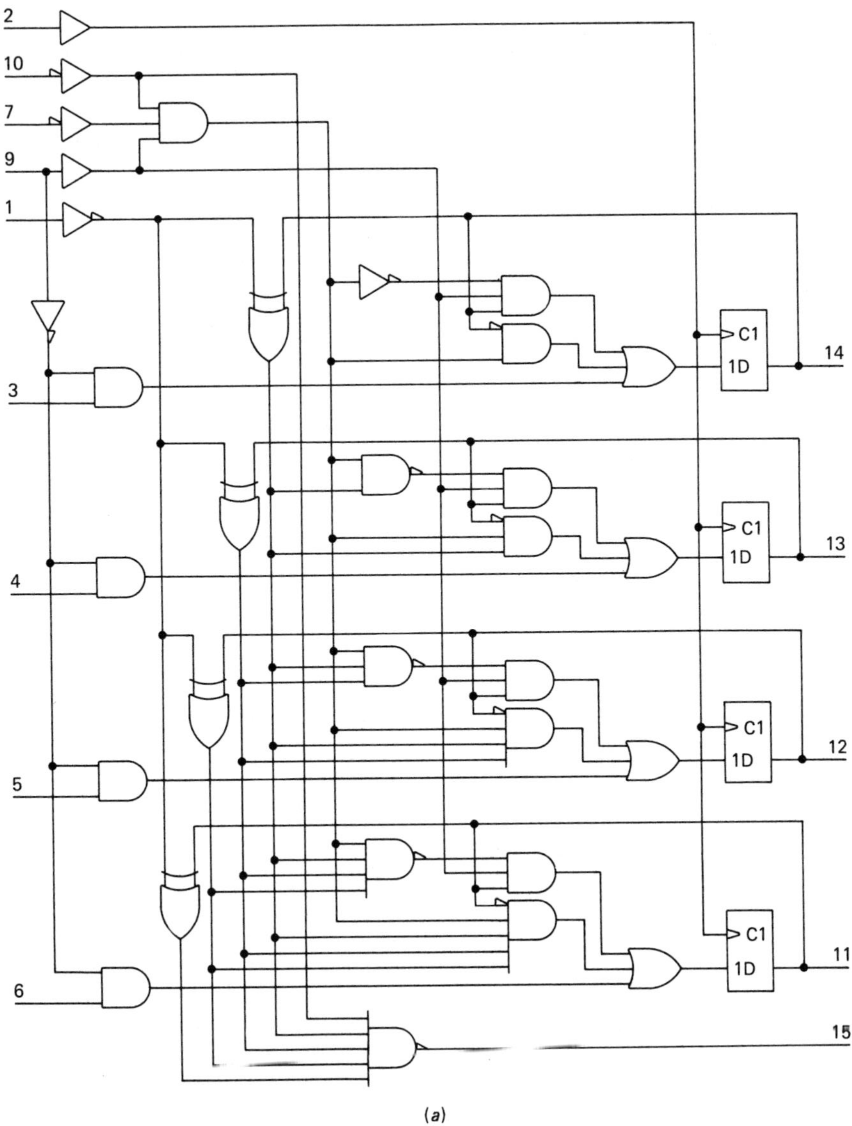

Figure 3-37. 74LS669, 4-bit up/down binary counter. (a) Functional diagram.

position, as in Fig. 3-38. Alternatively, by raising pin 9, the device behaves like a synchronous up/down binary counter.

Given such memory elements, we will interconnect them so that when the signal on a SHIFT line is raised by the microcomputer, all the memory elements will be interconnected into one long shift register.

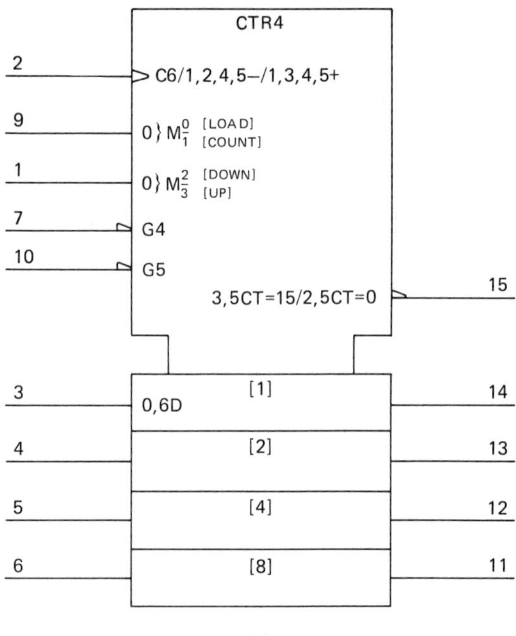

Figure 3-37b. Dependency notation symbol. (Texas Instruments.)

For some memory elements, this may require that SHIFT be inverted. For example, when SHIFT goes high, we want to pull pin 9 *low* on any 74LS669s.

The resulting circuit will look markedly different, depending upon whether SHIFT is high or low. We will use the following terminology to draw a distinction between these two aspects of the same circuit:

1 The *foreground circuit* represents the circuit configuration for carrying out the "real-time" function, clocked by SYSTEM CLOCK. This circuit configuration will also be employed to a limited extent during testing, using TEST CLOCK. The configuration results when the microcomputer pulls the SHIFT line low.

2 The *background circuit* represents the circuit configuration whereby all the flip-flops in the circuit are organized into one long shift register, clocked by TEST CLOCK. This circuit configuration is obtained when the microcomputer raises SHIFT high.

With SHIFT pulled low, the circuit is organized to serve the purposes of the real-time application. Shift registers and other arbitrary

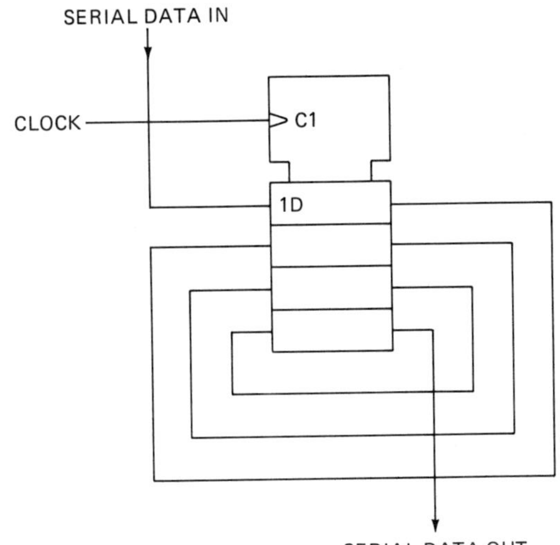

Figure 3-38. Equivalent shift register circuit obtained with external wiring for a 74LS669 4-bit up/down binary counter when pin 9 is pulled low.

sequential circuits can be built from D-type flip-flops, as in Fig. 3-34. Counting-type circuitry can employ MSI counters. All of the flexibility of the memory circuits is still available for normal operation except for the inputs associated with the parallel-load function. Although this may appear to be a handicap, sometimes the handicap is more apparent than real. For example, one of the ways in which the real-time circuit *could* use the parallel-load function, if it were available, would be for *initialization*. However, if this initialization is only required once, at the beginning of one cycle of normal operation, it can be handled by pulling SHIFT low, switching the clock to the microcomputer's TEST CLOCK (TC) shown in Fig. 3-36, and shifting the initialization data from the microcomputer to the memory elements via the long shift register. When the initialization data is in place, SHIFT can be raised and the clock switched back to SYSTEM CLOCK. This "background mode" shifting of data is illustrated in Fig. 3-39.

This approach solves, in a systematic way, one of the problems of organizing the circuitry of an instrument or device whose mode of operation can be selected by a user. User inputs, describing the mode of operation that must be carried out in the foreground circuit, are translated into *initialization data* for the foreground circuit.

Another aspect of sequential circuit design which was glossed over in Figs. 3-34 and 3-36 concerns the circuit inputs. Those figures showed the inputs coming directly into the combinational circuitry. Often the (foreground) circuitry of an instrument will consist of several *distinct* sequential circuits, each of which takes the form of Fig. 3-34 and each of which is clocked by SYSTEM CLOCK. In this case the

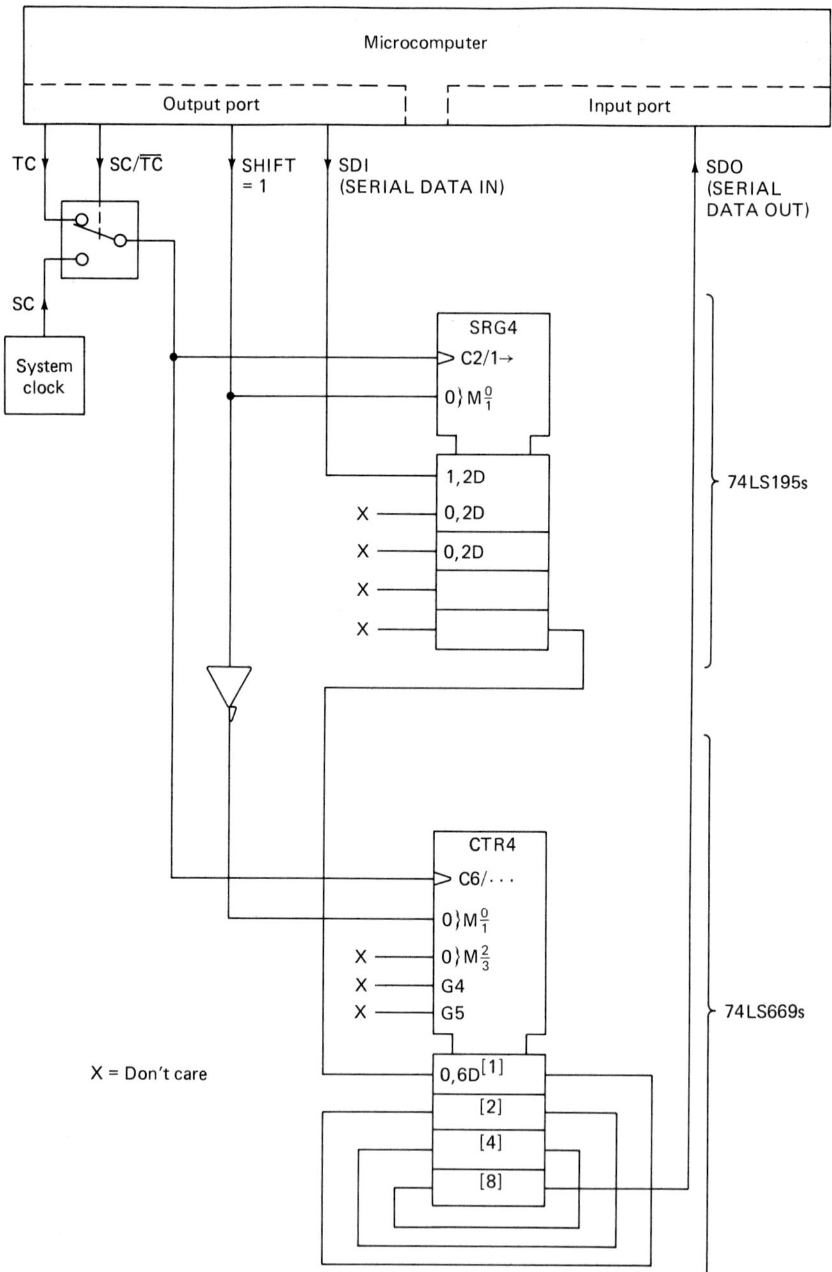

Figure 3-39. Background mode being used for initializing flip-flops before normal system use, and for accessing contents at completion of normal system use.

inputs to one sequential circuit may be the outputs of another sequential circuit, and these inputs can come directly into the combinational circuitry, as in Fig. 3-34.

Inputs arriving from circuitry *external* to the instrument (which is not clocked by SYSTEM CLOCK) must be *synchronized* to SYSTEM CLOCK, or else erratic operation will result. In Chap. 2 we considered input synchronization, in general. We found that input synchronization requires the clocking of unsynchronized data into D-type flip-flops, the outputs of which then form a synchronized version of the input data. If the same 74LS195 parallel in/parallel out shift registers shown in Fig. 3-35 are again used for this function, we will translate the *control of alternative inputs* requirement for maintainability into our foreground/background scheme. This is illustrated in Fig. 3-40. Notice that the input synchronization circuitry can also be used to generate the "Input Test Signals" needed for a push-to-test exercise of inputs. However, since self-test algorithms must ignore actual inputs, the mode of the input synchronization circuitry must be controlled using a separate "SHIFT-IN" signal from the microcomputer. We will see, shortly, how this is used for self-test.

A final modification of this circuit can be made to enhance the maintainability requirement of *observing internal variables.* We already have the means to observe state variables, outputs of the combinational circuitry affecting the next state, and inputs. We also need the ability to observe outputs. The 74LS166 8-bit parallel in/serial out shift register of Fig. 2-82 will serve this purpose well. In the foreground mode, the circuit with this additional modification is shown in Fig. 3-41.

A view of this final circuit while it is operating in the background mode is shown in Fig. 3-42. Although all of the parallel input connections to the memory circuitry have been broken, the memory circuit outputs still drive the remaining circuitry. The flip-flops of the memory circuitry are interconnected in a long shift register stretching from SDI (SERIAL DATA IN) to SDO (SERIAL DATA OUT).

It is this final circuit which we wish to examine in the light of self-test, push-to-test, and signature analysis. In all three, we first switch the clock from SYSTEM CLOCK to TEST CLOCK generated by the microcomputer. TEST CLOCK is used exclusively throughout the testing.

Self-testing this circuit consists of repeating the following three-step sequence of operations over and over again, each time loading the shift register with a different pattern of 1s and 0s. By the end of the test, all possible states of the circuit should have been (exhaustively) tested. Throughout this test SHIFT-IN is raised high so that actual inputs to the circuit are entirely ignored.

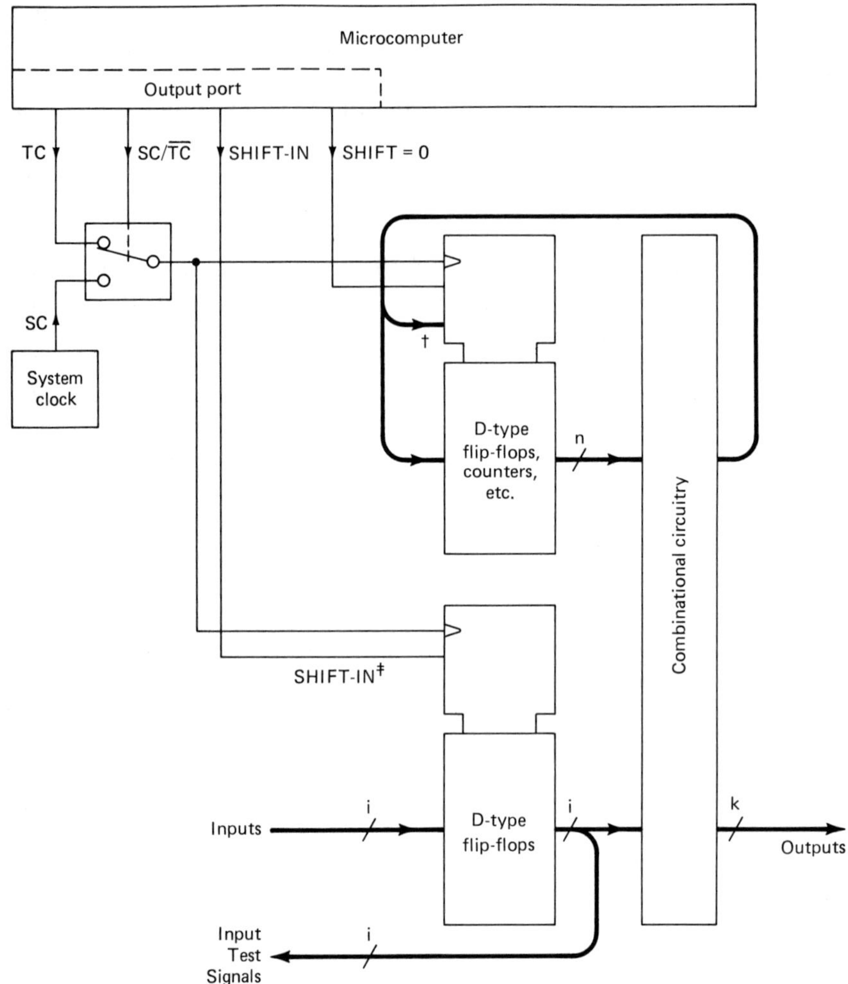

Figure 3-40. Foreground view of circuitry while testing, including input synchronization register.

1 In the background mode (SHIFT = 1) shift an $(n + i)$-bit test pattern of 1s and 0s into the circuit at SDI.
2 Change to the foreground mode (SHIFT = 0) and clock once.
3 Return to the background mode (SHIFT = 1) and shift an $(n + i + k)$-bit result back into the microcomputer from SDO, using the

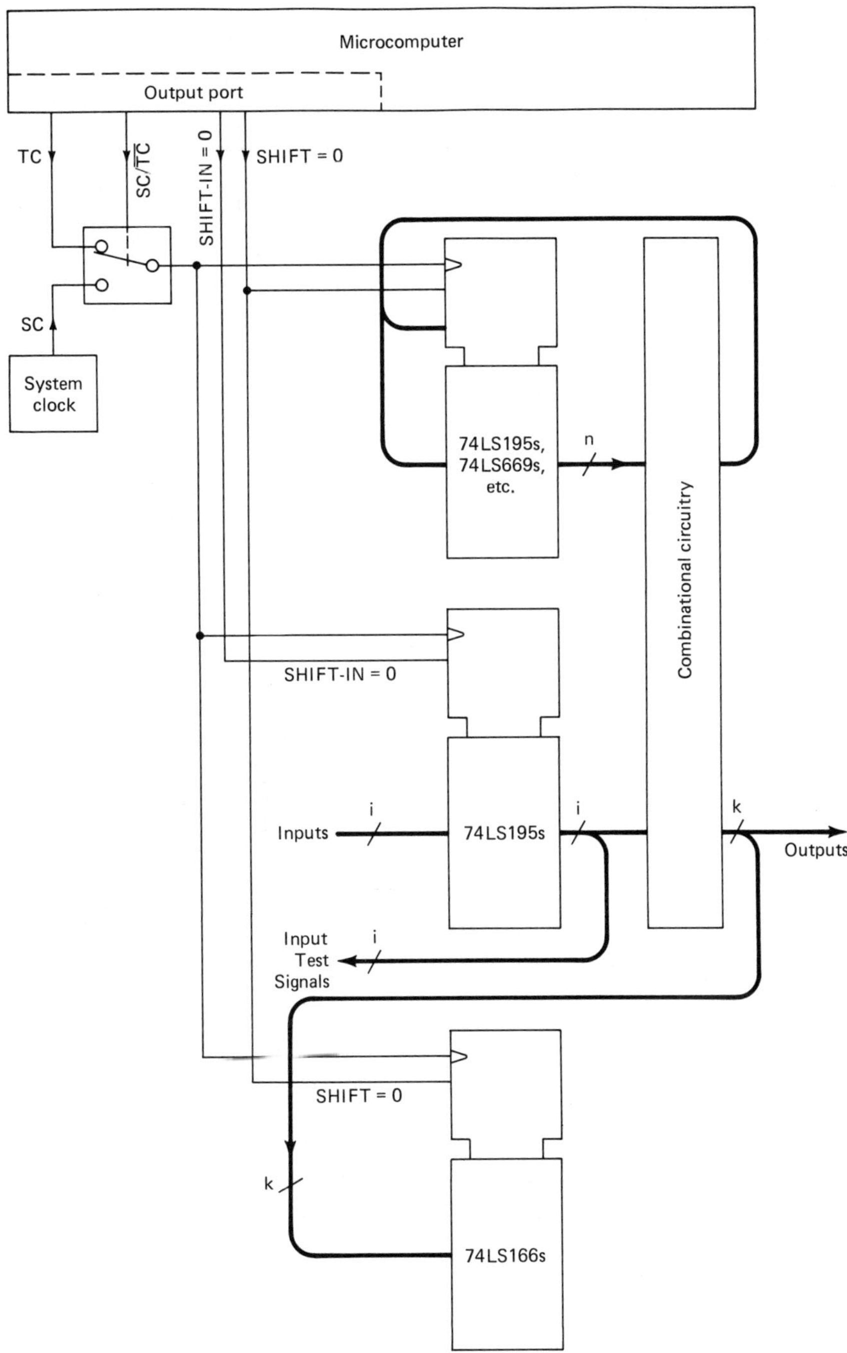

Figure 3-41. Foreground view of final circuit configuration while testing.

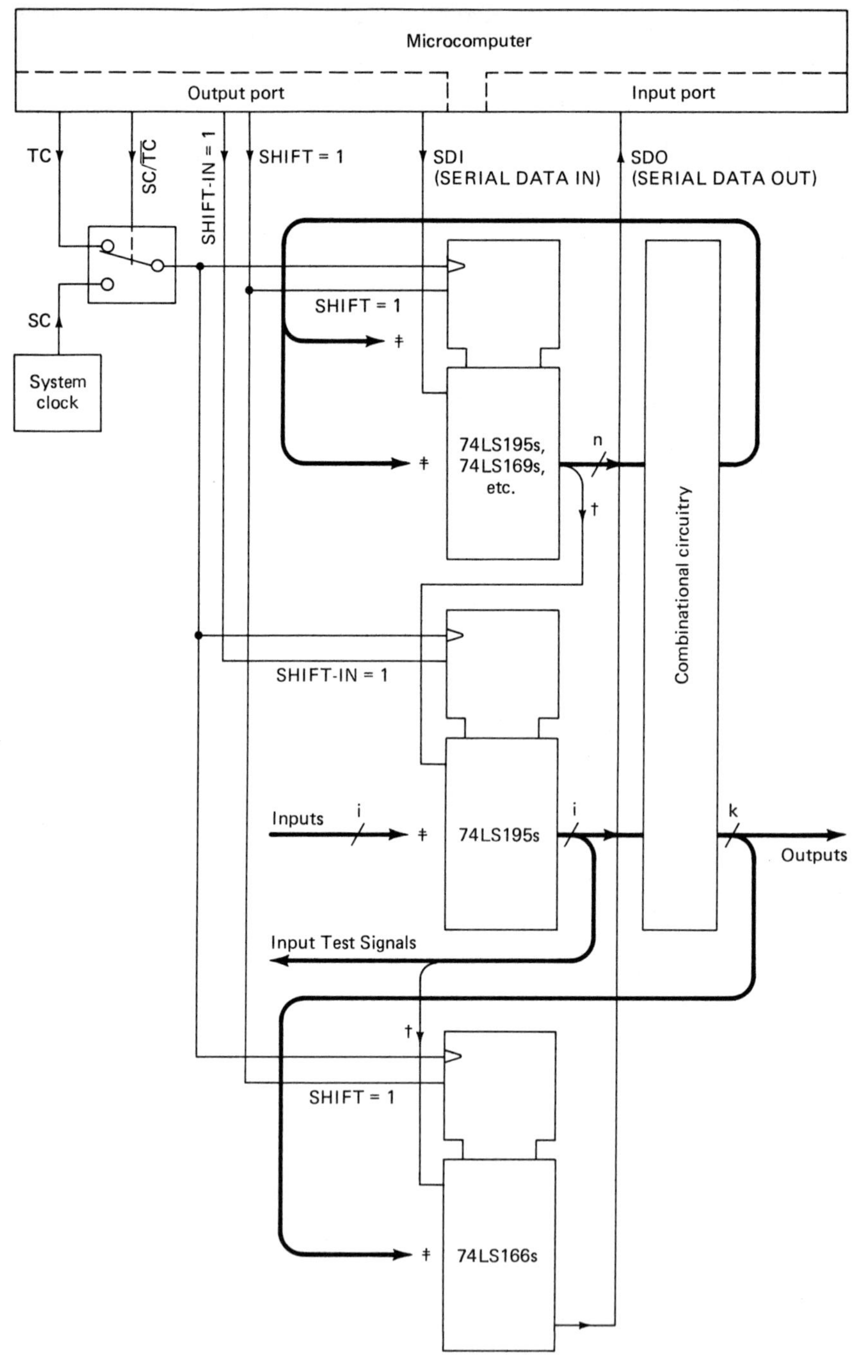

†Last bit of shift register.
‡These are, in effect, broken connections while in the background mode.

Figure 3-42. Background view of final circuit configuration.

SHIFT subroutine discussed at the end of Sec. 3-4 to compress this sequence into an unambiguous signature.

At the conclusion of the test, after all possible states of the circuit have been exercised, the signature obtained is compared with the known, correct value stored in the microcomputer's ROM. If the two are not equal, the user is alerted to a malfunction.

Using this circuit for *push-to-test,* the inputs are connected to the Input Test Signals, in some fashion analogous to what was done for the signature analyzer of Fig. 3-1 or the logic state analyzer of Fig. 3-3*c*. This interconnection must not connect the output of any flip-flop back to its own input. Figure 3-43 shows one possibility.

The push-to-test algorithm can be identical to that for self-test except that SHIFT-IN must always go high when SHIFT goes high, and it must likewise go low when SHIFT goes low. Each time a test pattern is

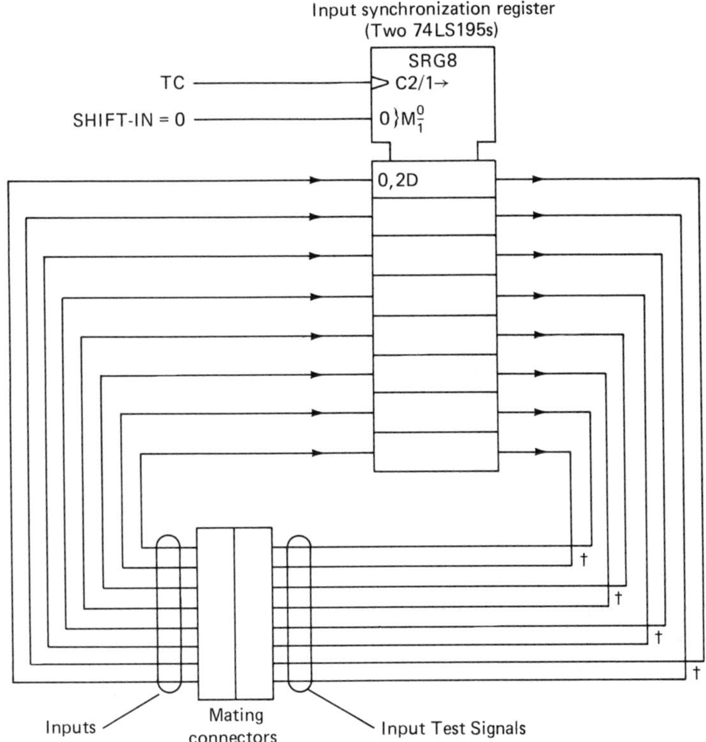

Figure 3-43. Interconnection of Inputs to Input Test Signals.

shifted into the Input Synchronization Register for which adjacent bits differ in value, the wiring shown in Fig. 3-43 will cause both of the adjacent bits to change state. If either flip-flop fails to change, an error will have been detected.

The *signature analysis* algorithm for this circuit requires putting it into the background mode (SHIFT = SHIFT-IN = 1) and leaving it there throughout the test to break all feedback loops. This means that the signature analysis mode can be used to isolate faults everywhere except for the parallel inputs of the registers. If a fault resides there, we will locate it by finding no faults in the signature analyzer mode but detecting an error in the push-to-test mode.

The signature analyzer algorithm can be identical to the repeated application of step 1 of the three-step sequence of operations listed for self-testing, while omitting steps 2 and 3. This will thoroughly exercise the entire circuitry (except as noted above), giving a unique signature to every node.

In concluding this section we should note, again, that there are many ways of organizing the circuitry of an instrument and that this is only *one* of those ways. We have taken the trouble to explore it so thoroughly for two reasons:

1 The regularity of the structure helps to clarify the distinctions between self-test, push-to-test, and signature analysis algorithms.
2 If we can achieve our instrument design goals without undue difficulty using this structure, the testing of the resulting circuit will be straightforward.

We might also note that the combinational circuitry involved in this structure *begs* to be implemented with those superb components for bringing order out of complexity: PROMs and FPLAs.

3-8 DESIGN ACCOMMODATIONS FOR ATE

Automatic test equipment (ATE), such as the unit of Fig. 3-4, presents another dimension to the design problem. It is a dimension that will greatly benefit from the self-test, push-to-test, and signature analysis algorithms we build into an on-board microcomputer. As we do our designing right, the job of applying automatic test to our boards will be drastically simplified.

An automatic board tester's job has two parts:

1 Does a board function correctly?
2 If not, what is the source of the fault?

Any board that includes push-to-test capability has the wherewithal to answer the first question itself. We have only to supply power and to handle any connections needed to see that inputs are routed to the appropriate test signals generated on the board for this purpose.

Any board designed to include signature analysis capability gives *outstanding* support to the fault-locating function of an automatic board tester. A low-cost approach employs the board tester to display messages to a user telling him or her where to probe (with a signature analyzer probe). In effect, the signature analysis flowchart for the board (analogous to the one shown in Fig. 3-25) is simply programmed into the automatic tester. A higher-cost approach requires the tooling of a special test fixture for each kind of board to be tested. The "bed of nails" test fixture shown in Fig. 3-44 permits the automatic tester to probe *all* the points arising in the signature analysis flowchart. Then it can sequence through the flowchart automatically, selecting which probe to look at for each step in the algorithm.

More generally, ATE has been developed to "cover" for all the

(a)

Figure 3-44. "Bed of nails" text fixture for probing a PC board. (a) Closeup of bed of nails.

(b)

(c)

Figure 3-44. (b) *Complete test fixture* (Pylon Co.); (c) *automatic test system employing bed of nails test fixture* (GenRad).

designers in the past who simply have not worried about maintainability when they were carrying out their design work. The increasing complexity of the components on a board has severely burdened the efforts of test engineers trying to program an automatic tester for such boards. It is this state of affairs that has led to the comment of Ed Donn at the close of Sec. 3-1 about testing holding back the whole digital revolution. In this chapter we have explored the problem and looked toward solutions. A designer with forethought for testing can make a far-reaching contribution!

PROBLEMS

The support of maintainability in an instrument should involve interaction between its hardware and the algorithmic processes executed in the software of its microcomputer controller. Some of the problems below are oriented toward the hardware external to the microcomputer and a few are directed toward the algorithmic processes carried out by the microcomputer. The latter are marked with an asterisk and might be handled either with the one-chip microcomputer discussed in Appendix A3 or else by using another microcomputer with which the reader has some familiarity. Or, if the reader's background does not include familiarity with any microcomputer (yet), the problems with asterisks can be bypassed.

3-1 Self-test capability. Consider an instrument with which you have familiarity and which includes a seven-segment display such as that in the signature analyzer of Fig. 3-1.

(*a*) What uppercase letters can be formed on the display?

(*b*) What lowercase letters can be formed on the display?

(*c*) What are some HELPful messages which it might (try to) flash on the display in the event that its self-test routine detects a malfunction?

3-2 Self-test capability. Again consider an instrument with which you have some familiarity.

(*a*) What inputs and outputs are precluded from being self-tested?

(*b*) Are there periodically recurring times during the normal running of the instrument when its microcomputer might be able to take at least a tenth of a second to execute self-test routines? Describe the operation of the instrument enough to describe, further, when self-test algorithms might be executed without arousing the awareness of the user.

(*c*) If a self-test algorithm is broken up into parts, if each part requires less than a tenth of a second to execute, and if a microcomputer executes instructions every 5 μs (on the average), how many instructions can be executed during each part of the algorithm? Would you guess that the microcomputer could build up extensive self-test capability, even given only $\frac{1}{10}$-s slices of time for its execution?

3-3 Push-to-test capability. Continuing with the instrument considered in Prob. 3-2:

(*a*) What special connections might be required by a user to execute a push-to-test exercise of inputs which are precluded from being self-tested?

(*b*) Are there any outputs which should be exercised, but which require the "OK" of a user to exercise them, which should be relegated away from self-test and delegated to push-to-test? If so, describe them. (An example discussed in the text concerned the testing of the output to a printer. We want to know that the instrument can drive the printer. But we do not want self-test "garbage" characters printed in the normal instrument output.)

3-4 Push-to-test capability. The logic state analyzer of Fig. 3-3 includes a push-to-test algorithm to exercise its keyboard, as discussed in the text.

(*a*) Describe an analogous test which might be employed so that a user of the signature analyzer of Fig. 3-1 could test its front-panel switches quickly and easily (without having to refer to the service manual for signatures that are supposed to be displayed for each switch configuration).

(*b*) Assuming that the signature analyzer circuitry included a microcomputer, could it translate any measured signatures into unambiguous diagnostic messages on the display rather than displaying the signatures themselves? With only four switches to be tested (in addition to the power switch and the switch that initiates the tests) and with four seven-segment displays available, what nonstandard (possibly nonalphanumeric) display might be useful in response to depressing and releasing assorted keys?

3-5 Maintenance policies. Consider an instrument with which you are familiar.

(*a*) If it malfunctions, how will you know it?

(*b*) What alternatives will you have for its repair?

(*c*) If the sales and service office of the manufacturer is "only a phone call away," ask what alternatives you have. Is it even possible to do a *fast* board exchange, assuming that you can locate the problem down to the board level and are willing to spend the money required?

(*d*) Does the manufacturer support your own repair of the instrument? Do you have to train yourself in its functioning or are you guided through a repair procedure, such as would be provided for signature analysis?

3-6 Maintenance policies. Ask a manufacturer in your town or nearby city whether their experience supports or refutes the general rule of thumb given in the text that the average board will malfunction and require service two times over its lifetime.

3-7 Hardware organization. If an instrument is available to you having a planar layout, open it up and consider the steps taken to simplify

(*a*) Manufacture
(*b*) Connections for power
(*c*) Connections for input, output, and display
(*d*) Identification of parts for servicing
(*e*) Access to test points, with power turned on for testing

3-8 Hardware organization. Look at the service manual for a multiboard instrument.

(*a*) Does the instrument bus a large number of signals between boards?

(*b*) If so, is the microcomputer's address bus and data bus carried over this bus between boards or is there a separate I/O bus?

(*c*) Can the microcomputer in the instrument function *at all* if the communication between boards has malfunctioned? That is, can test routines be executed in spite of such a malfunction to help locate the source of the malfunction?

(*d*) How is service by a user supported?

3-9 Hardware organization. If the service manual is available to you for an instrument that employs several microcomputers, consider how they interact with each other.

(*a*) Is there one main "master" controller, with the remaining microcomputers being dedicated to specific tasks?

(*b*) If so, what is the nature of these tasks that led the designer to break out the function in this way?

(*c*) How do the microcomputers interact with each other? How many wires are used for this communication?

(*d*) If a serial scheme was not used, do you suppose that it could have been and still have met the speed requirements for the instrument? Discuss.

3-10 Design criterion. Consider the design of a specific instrument which employs a microcomputer but which also employs additional circuitry. What is the function of the additional circuitry, and can you determine why this function was not delegated to the microcomputer?

3-11 Design criterion. Talk to an electronics designer who holds the respect of his or her peers for quality design work.

(*a*) Does minimizing package count make sense?

(*b*) What role does testability play in the design process?

(*c*) What other factors bear upon how a design is organized and what components are used?

(*d*) Under what circumstances does it make sense to use more expensive chips such as PROMs and FPLAs?

(*e*) Does this designer use NOR and NAND gates in much the same way as he or she used them 5 or 10 years ago? Explain.

3-12 Information compression. Consider the PRBS signature-generating circuit of Fig. 3-15. Hewlett-Packard's 5004A signature analyzer uses this configuration, resetting the shift register to zero at the beginning of the sequence. Note that an exclusive-OR gate's output will equal 1 if and only if an *odd* number of 1s appear among the inputs.

(*a*) Show a PROBE input sequence starting at the moment the shift register contains the hexadecimal number shown, A563, which will return the signature to all 0s.

(*b*) What is the minimum number of clock periods that it will take to do this?

(*c*) Will any other PROBE input sequence achieve the same result (over the same interval)?

(*d*) How many different sequences of this length are there all together?

(*e*) If the PROBE input were to receive a *random* sequence of 1s and 0s over this interval, what would be the chances of the signature being 0000 at the end of the interval?

3-13 PRBS generation. Modify the circuit of Fig. 3-14 so as to employ a 4-bit shift register, with the bits labeled W, X, Y, Z and with W again being the last bit in the shift register. In each case below, determine whether or not the connection specified gives rise to a PRBS sequence having the required period of $2^4 - 1 = 15$. Begin with all 1s in the shift register. Compare the sequences generated in any cases where the period is 15. Are they the same? Are they related in any way that you can see?

(*a*) Exclusive-OR gate inputs are W and X.

(*b*) Exclusive-OR gate inputs are W and Z.

(*c*) Exclusive-OR gate inputs are W and Y.

3-14 Random-phase-shift property. Derive a table analogous to Fig. 3-16*d* for any *one* of the circuits of Prob. 3-13 which gives rise to a PRBS sequence (i.e., which does have a period of 15).

(*a*) Do all possible phase shifts arise (once and only once)?

(*b*) Can you detect any pattern in the *sequence* of phase shifts, or does the sequence itself seem to be random?

***3-15 SHIFT subroutine.** (*a*) For a specific microcomputer and minimizing *execution time,* prepare the assembly language SHIFT subroutine defined at the end of Sec. 3-4, but use the easier-to-implement PRBS generator of Fig. P3-15.

(*b*) How long does one call of SHIFT require? Assume that the microcomputer is operating at its maximum clock rate.

***3-16 CHECK subroutine.** Repeat Prob. 3-15 for the CHECK subroutine defined at the end of Sec. 3-4.

3-17 Signature analysis. A general-purpose oscilloscope is useful for servicing an analog instrument. However, for it to be helpful, a user must have a service manual with schematics saying what voltages and waveforms to expect at various nodes throughout the circuitry. Likewise, a signature analyzer can be helpful in locating the source of a malfunction in a digital instrument. If we are test engineers charged with the responsibility of taking a new analog instrument and preparing a service manual test procedure for it, we can proceed to measure voltages and waveforms on a functioning instrument to prepare the service manual. In fact, we can do this even though the analog instrument was not designed with testing in mind. Can we do the same thing for a new digital instrument, to prepare the service manual so that a user can use a signature analyzer to help locate sources of faults? Explain your answer, understanding that the digital instrument was not designed with testing in mind.

3-18 Kernel testing. Is the Push-to-Test switch of Fig. 3-26 and the associated resistor and input port line part of the kernel for carrying out a push-to-test algorithm? Explain.

3-19 Kernel testing. (*a*) For a specific multiple-chip microcomputer organized on an address bus/data bus structure, what is the operation code of a NOP (no operation) instruction?

(*b*) What is the corresponding array of resistors and diodes required in Fig. 3-28 to implement the "dumb" kernel?

(*c*) What would be another instruction that does nothing but READ (i.e., no WRITE) which could be used in place of a NOP instruction and which would minimize the number of diodes required? How many diodes does it require?

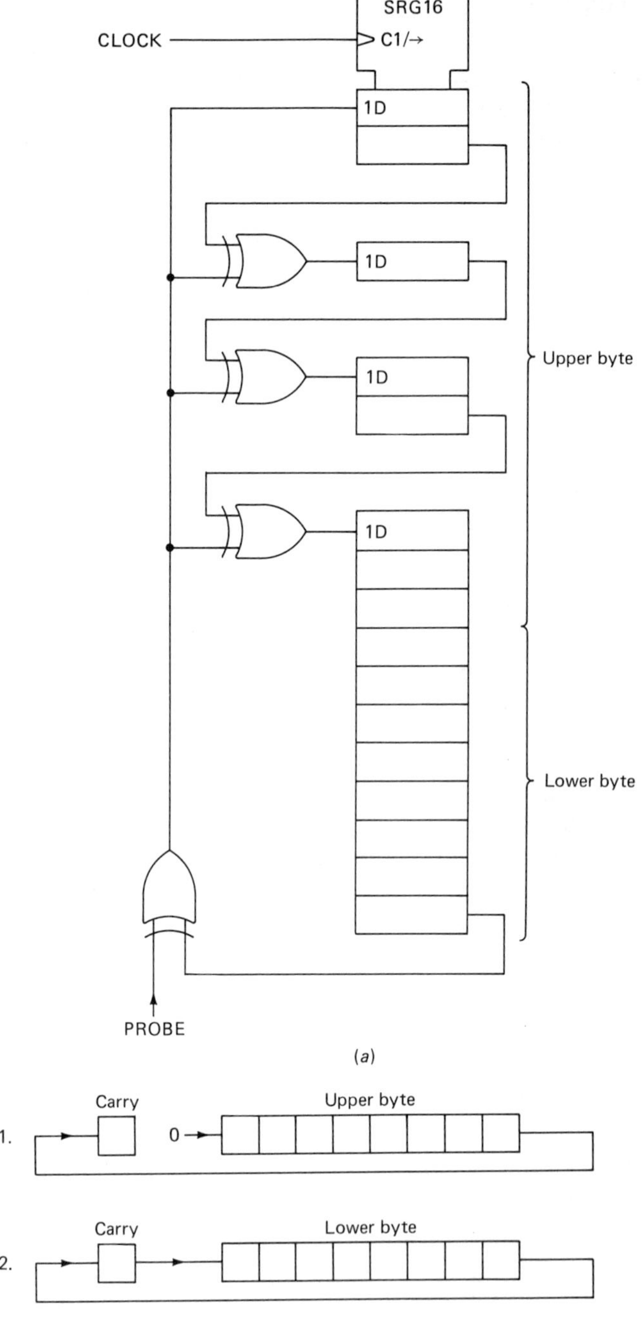

3. Complement carry bit if Probe bit equals 1.

4. Exclusive-OR the upper byte with 10110100 if the new carry bit equals 1.

(b)

Figure P3-15. Alternative PRBS circuit. (a) Hardware implementation; (b) software implementation.

3-20 Kernel testing. Consider the "dumb" kernel circuit of Fig. 3-28 and the connection of the signal analyzer's START and STOP inputs to the most significant address line.

(*a*) Will the signatures on the A14 address line be the same regardless of whether a NOP instruction is used, on the one hand, or a "read data from memory into the accumulator" instruction, on the other (as discussed in Prob. 3-19)? Explain.

(*b*) If the signatures are different for the two situations, does it matter? Explain.

3-21 Kernel testing. Again consider the "dumb" kernel circuit of Fig. 3-28, that is, the circuit with jumpers removed from sockets 1, 2, 3 and with one of them inserted into the NOP Programmer socket. If the ROM between sockets 1 and 2 contains the signature analysis algorithm and if bits of the ROM have suffered from "amnesia" and changed from their intended values, can the signature analyzer detect this by probing the data bus lines between sockets 1 and 2? Explain. (*Note:* As the CPU runs through all 65,536 addresses, this section of the data bus will be in a high-impedance state for many addresses. The signature analyzer input is designed to handle this *unambiguously,* as we shall see when we discuss its design.)

3-22 Kernel testing. If the "dumb" kernel scheme of Fig. 3-28 were carried out on a Motorola 6800 CPU chip, the SA CLOCK would be attached to the CPU's *clock.* This means that the signature analyzer will be clocked during both reads *and writes.* Will the scheme discussed in the text still work for probing only *one* of the data bus lines, say D7, if instead of writing to RAM and then reading it back, the CPU simply writes the data out on the data bus eight times, rotating its contents after each write? Assume that it writes to an unused address. Discuss your answer. Note that if this is possible, it eliminates the need to have a working RAM in order for the scheme to work.

3-23 Clock switching. To change between normal operation and testing, the circuit of Fig. 3-36 employs a switch of some kind on the clock line. If the reed relay of Fig. 3-31 were employed for this function, would any "contact bounce" in the switch contacts affect the operation? Consider each possibility below.

(*a*) When the microcomputer changes to the TC clock, assume that it waits to clock the circuit until after the switch has had a chance to settle.

(*b*) When the microcomputer changes to the SC clock, assume that it waits until the switch has had a chance to settle and then raises a GO signal. The sequential circuitry waits in an initial state until the GO signal (suitably synchronized to the switched clock) is raised.

3-24 Foreground/background circuitry. Consider the use of a 74LS163 4-bit binary counter which can be synchronously reset. The input on pin 9 is used to switch between the foreground and background modes. The two count enable inputs can be employed by the foreground circuitry to control the counter because they are overridden by the pin 9 input. That is, when pin 9 goes low, it does not matter whether the count enable inputs are high or low because they are ignored. Thus when the device is put into the background mode for shifting test data through it, the count enable inputs will be (properly) ignored. Look at the circuitry of the 74LS163 and decide whether the same is true of the pin 1 input. If it is, resetting can also be employed by the foreground circuitry. If not, it cannot.

3-25 Foreground/background circuitry. Refer to Prob. 3-24. For a 74LS194 4-bit bidirectional universal shift register, can *one* of the (S1, S0) mode inputs be used to force the device into the SHIFT RIGHT mode, independent of the other mode input?

3-26 Foreground/background circuitry. Refer to Prob. 3-24. Can a 74LS668 up/down decade counter serve as a decimal version of the 74LS669 in the foreground/background circuit configuration?

3-27 Alternative approaches to maintainable design. In Sec. 3-7 we really did *two* things: we switched the clock source and we set up a "background" shift register circuit. If we chose *not* to constrain ourselves with the shift register circuit, consider the alternative.

(*a*) Would it still be necessary for the microcomputer to get control of the clock line in order to execute test routines?

(*b*) How might it control alternative inputs and state variables?

(*c*) How might it observe internal variables?

3-28 General testable circuit configuration. The configuration of Figs. 3-41 and 3-42 lets us control and observe all the circuitry of an instrument. Consider the merits of implementing a signature analysis algorithm as follows. An $(n + i)$-bit PRBS generator is to be implemented in the software of the microcomputer. Recall from the figures that n is the number of state variables, whereas i is the number of inputs. Together, they are the number of inputs to the combinational circuitry. In the background mode, we make a START/$\overline{\text{STOP}}$ line to the signature analyzer go high, load the

PRBS generator with all 1s, shift its output out on the SERIAL DATA IN line (bit by bit), clock the signature analyzer clock line after each shift, continue until the PRBS generator is back to the all-1s state ($2^{(n+i)} - 1$ shifts later), pull the START/$\overline{\text{STOP}}$ line low to signal the end of the signature analyzer window, and start over again. Assume that in normal operation the combinational circuitry never sees all 0s on its input.

*__3-29 General testable circuit configuration.__ In support of the scheme of Prob. 3-28, the circuits of Fig. P3-29*a* and *b* illustrate two implementations of the same 8-bit PRBS generator. They are the same in that the output sequences are identical since they both implement the difference equation

$$X_n = X_{n-2} \oplus X_{n-3} \oplus X_{n-4} \oplus X_{n-8}$$

However, the implementation in Fig. 3-29*b* can be handled by the simple software algorithm shown in Fig. P3-29*c*.

(*a*) For a specific microcomputer, and minimizing execution

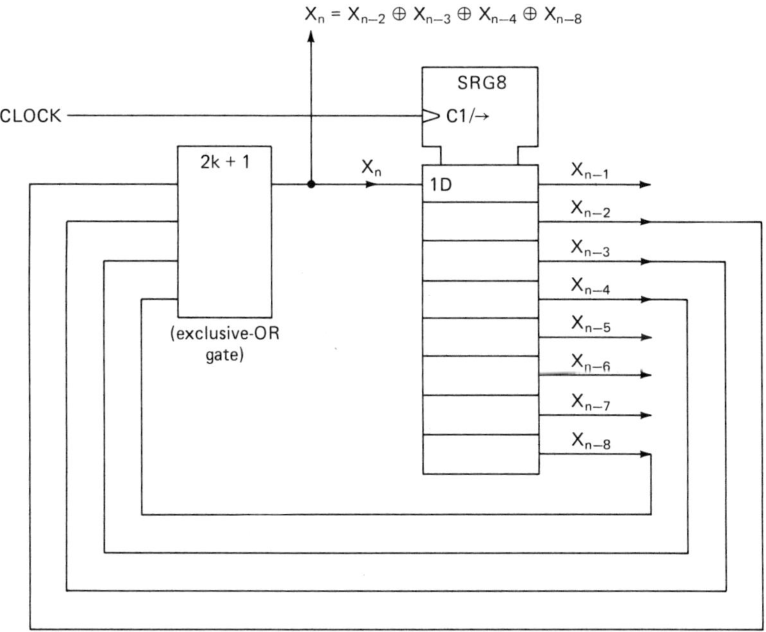

Figure P3-29*a*

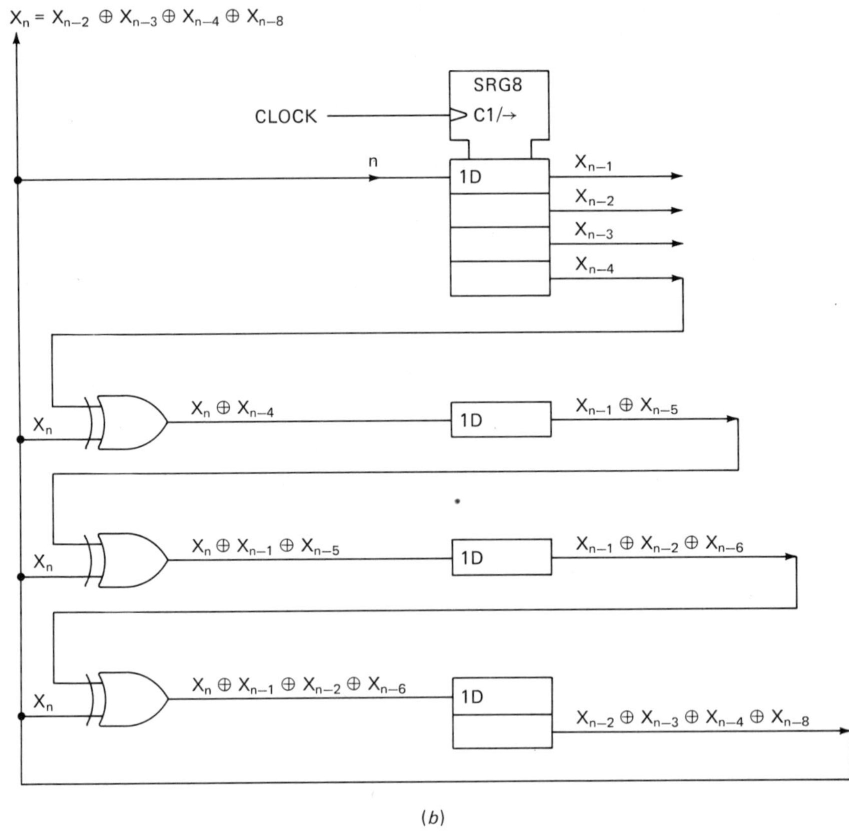

(b)

Figure P3-29b

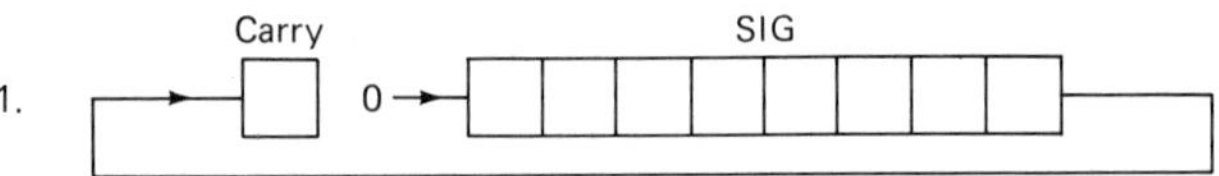

2. Exclusive-OR SIG with 10001110 if the carry bit equals 1.

(c)

Figure P3-29c

time, prepare a PRBS8 assembly language subroutine that will execute the algorithm on a memory location SIG, leaving the output bit in the microcomputer's carry bit.

(b) Assuming the microcomputer is clocked at its maximum rate, how long does a call of this subroutine take?

***3-30 General testable circuit configuration.** Repeat Prob. 3-29 for each of the following PRBS generator equations:

(*a*) PRBS4 subroutine: $X_n = X_{n-3} \oplus X_{n-4}$
(*b*) PRBS6 subroutine: $X_n = X_{n-5} \oplus X_{n-6}$
(*c*) PRBS10 subroutine: $X_n = X_{n-7} \oplus X_{n-10}$
(*d*) PRBS12 subroutine: $X_n = X_{n-2} \oplus X_{n-10} \oplus X_{n-11} \oplus X_{n-12}$
(*e*) PRBS14 subroutine: $X_n = X_{n-2} \oplus X_{n-12} \oplus X_{n-13} \oplus X_{n-14}$
(*f*) PRBS16 subroutine: $X_n = X_{n-11} \oplus X_{n-13} \oplus X_{n-14} \oplus X_{n-16}$
(*g*) PRBS18 subroutine: $X_n = X_{n-11} \oplus X_{n-18}$
(*h*) PRBS20 subroutine: $X_n = X_{n-17} \oplus X_{n-20}$

3-31 PRBS algorithms. (*a*) Add a probe input P_n to the circuit of Fig. P3-29*a* so that

$$X_n = X_{n-2} \oplus X_{n-3} \oplus X_{n-4} \oplus X_{n-8} \oplus P_n$$

(*b*) Show that the circuit of Fig. P3-31 satisfies the same difference equation.

(*c*) Starting from state 11111111, show the next three states of these two circuits if $P_n = 0$ during every clock period.

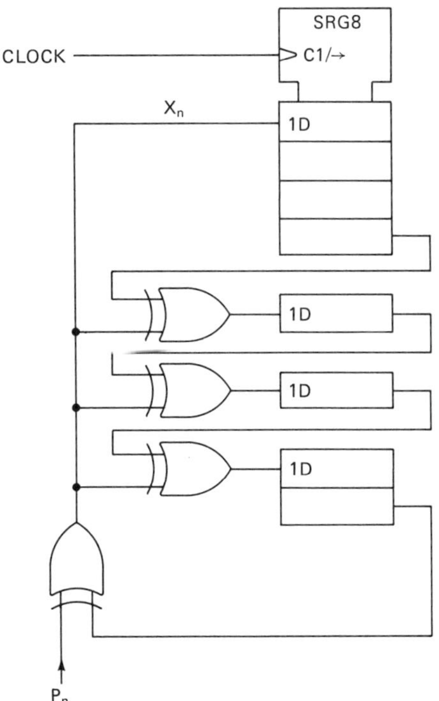

Figure P3-31

(*d*) Even though these two circuits satisfy the same difference equation, are they equivalent signature-generating circuits? That is, will the same input sequence to each one produce identical signatures?

(*e*) Show the Fig. P3-29*b* equivalent of Fig. 3-15. Will this new implementation yield the same signatures as will Fig. 3-15?

(*f*) If we wanted to implement in software the same signature-generating algorithm as is used in the Hewlett-Packard 5004A signature analyzer, could we use the software equivalent of the circuit found in (*e*) and expect to obtain identical signatures?

(*g*) Describe a use of data compression where the software implementation of part (*f*) might be useful.

*3-32 **Byte-handling signature generator.** In looking for a software implementation of a signature-generating algorithm for 8-bit bytes, one design engineer, Chi Sung Row, suggests the scheme shown below for the Motorola 6800 or 6801 microcomputer. This scheme uses *two different* 8-bit PRBS generators (SIG1 and SIG2) shifting in opposite directions to give strong error detection capability. Even related errors in adjacent input bits do not seem to slip through the "egg beater" of this algorithm to go undetected. Show the corresponding hardware implementation.

```
* THIS SIGNAT SUBROUTINE EXPECTS AN INPUT BYTE OF DATA
* TO BE PASSED TO IT IN ACCUMULATOR A.  IT USES TWO SEPARATE
* 8-BIT PRBS GENERATORS, SIG1 AND SIG2, TO FORM A 16-BIT
* SIGNATURE WITH GOOD ERROR DETECTING CHARACTERISTICS.
SIGNAT  PSH A              SET ASIDE A COPY OF THE INPUT BYTE
        EOR A SIG1         EXCLUSIVE-OR THE INPUT WITH ONE SIGNATURE
        LSR A              WHICH USES A RIGHT-SHIFTING PRBS OPERATION
        BCC    SIGN1       SKIP OVER PRBS EXCLUSIVE-ORING IF C=0
        EOR A #%10010101   THIS GENERATOR CHANGES HALF THE BITS
SIGN1   STA A SIG1         STORE THE RESULTING SIGNATURE
        PUL A              GET THE INPUT BYTE AGAIN
        EOR A SIG2         AND EXCLUSIVE-OR IT INTO THE OTHER SIGNATURE
        ASL A              WHICH USES A LEFT-SHIFTING PRBS OPERATION
        BCC    SIGN2       SKIP OVER PRBS EXCLUSIVE-ORING IF C=0
        EOR A #%01100101   THIS SECOND GENERATOR CHANGES HALF THE BITS
SIGN2   STA A SIG2         STORE THE RESULTING SIGNATURE
        RTS                AND RETURN FROM THE SUBROUTINE
```

REFERENCES

The cost of a digital instrument is approximated by its total number of integrated circuits times $16. This rule of thumb is empirically justified by E. S. Donn, Estimate Prices for Electronic Equipment Merely by Counting the ICs, *Electronic Design,* September 27, 1979.

The "randomness" properties of pseudo-random binary sequence generators are discussed by S. W. Golomb, *Digital Communications with Space Applications*, Prentice-Hall, Englewood Cliffs, N.J., 1964, chap. 1. Generators, up to 20 bits long, are defined in Fig. 2.10.

A good overview of the automatic board testers (for both digital and analog boards) of 14 vendors is provided by A. DeSena, Automatic Board Testing: Functional Test Systems, *Electronics Test*, May 1979, pp. 44–69.

Specific steps which a designer can take so that self-test algorithms can support automatic board testing are discussed by M. D. Lippman and E. S. Donn, Design Forethought Promotes Easier Testing of Microcomputer Boards, *Electronics*, January 18, 1979, pp. 113–119.

A more general discussion of design ideas that will greatly ease subsequent testing with an automatic board tester is given by D. Schneider and W. Muller, Design for "Easy" Testability, *Electronics Test*, March 1979, pp. 25–26.

ALGORITHMIC STATE MACHINES

The hardware of an instrument design can be broken down into several parts. One possible organization is illustrated in Fig. 4-1. The microcomputer implements all the tasks it can handle. Thus any input/output (I/O) tasks that do not exceed the microcomputer's speed capability will interact with the microcomputer directly. These tasks may require special-purpose circuitry for buffering the voltage or current requirements of I/O devices, but otherwise the circuitry is generally simple. The microcomputer can take upon itself any timing or interactive complexities required by this circuitry.

Tasks that call for too high a data rate for a microcomputer to handle directly require special-purpose circuitry for their implementation. This circuitry consists of two parts:

1 Data manipulation circuitry.
2 An *algorithmic state machine*† (ASM) which initializes and runs

† A term coined at Hewlett-Packard Company for a systematic description and organization of the control portion of a digital device. See the end-of-chapter reference by C. Clare.

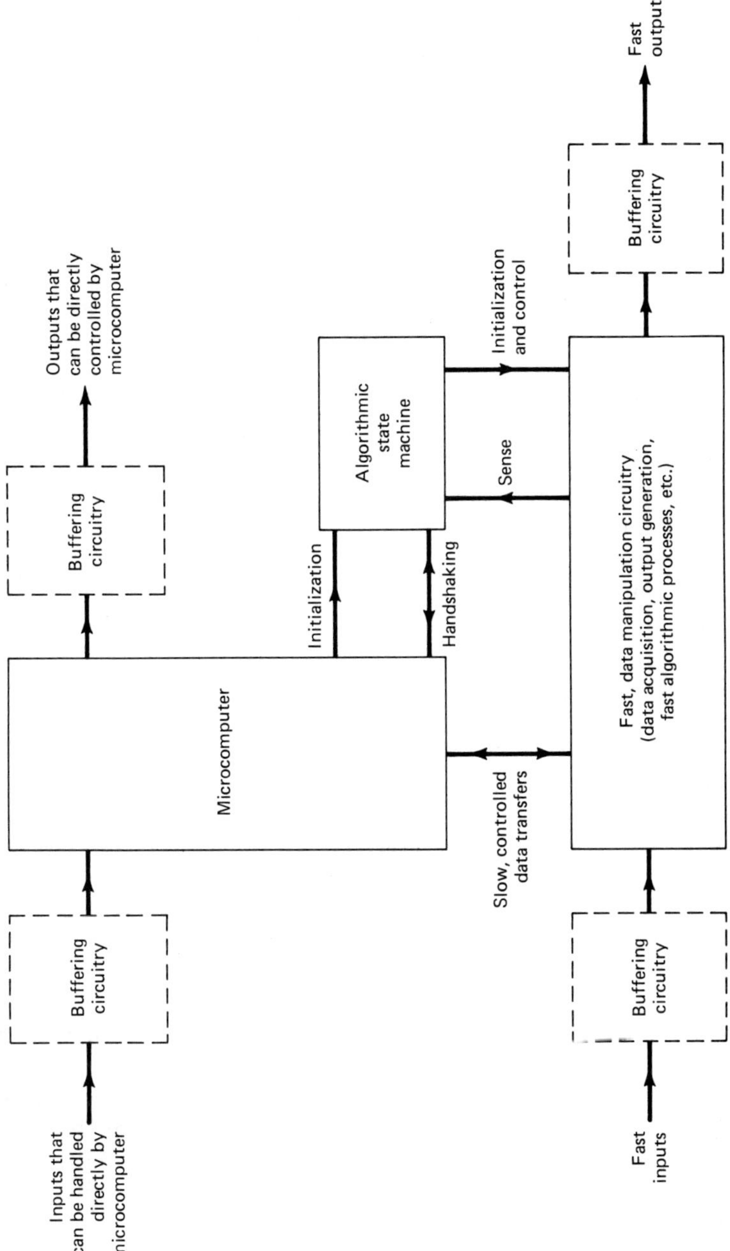

Figure 4-1. Instrument organization.

this data manipulation circuitry and which controls its interactions with the microcomputer.

Our purpose in this chapter will be to explore ASM representation and implementation. However, such a study is rather sterile without a *vehicle* upon which to apply it. Consequently, we will begin by considering the design of the signature analyzer instrument pictured in Fig. 3-1 and discussed extensively in Sec. 3-5.

4-1 DESIGN OF A SIGNATURE ANALYZER

The Hewlett-Packard implementation of the signature analyzer of Fig. 3-1 does not include a microcomputer. It was designed before one-chip microcomputers were the cost-effective (and available) chips they are now. Consequently, we will take the liberty of discussing the design as it might be carried out today.

Our design will proceed in stages. In this chapter, with its emphasis upon algorithmic state machines, we will consider a rudimentary design. Our goal here will be to have the simplest possible vehicle for ASM ideas. Later, we will come back and carry out a redesign that will better handle various features of the instrument, including maintainability.

An overview of the instrument is shown in Fig. 4-2, broken down into five blocks. The *multiplexed display,* shown in detail in Fig. 4-3, generates all the output of the instrument. Its interactions with the microcomputer are handled under the control of the microcomputer's programmable timer. Each digit is turned on for one-fourth of the time, as discussed in Sec. 2-15. To display a 0 on the leftmost digit, DIGIT1-L is made active (i.e., pulled low) while the other digits are turned off. This switches on the bottom of the four PNP transistors, applying about 4.8 V to the anodes of the seven LEDs in the leftmost display. At the same time, all the LED cathodes except *g* are pulled down to ground through 220-Ω current-limiting resistors, under control of the output on port 2. With roughly 2.0 V dropped across each LED, each turned-on resistor sees about 2.5 V, setting the instantaneous LED current to about 10 mA. This gives an average LED current of 2.5 mA due to the multiplexing of the four digits.

The *input circuitry* must handle:

- The edge-selection function (e.g., handle the front-panel switch which selects clocking on either the rising edge or the falling edge of the clock)
- Input loading

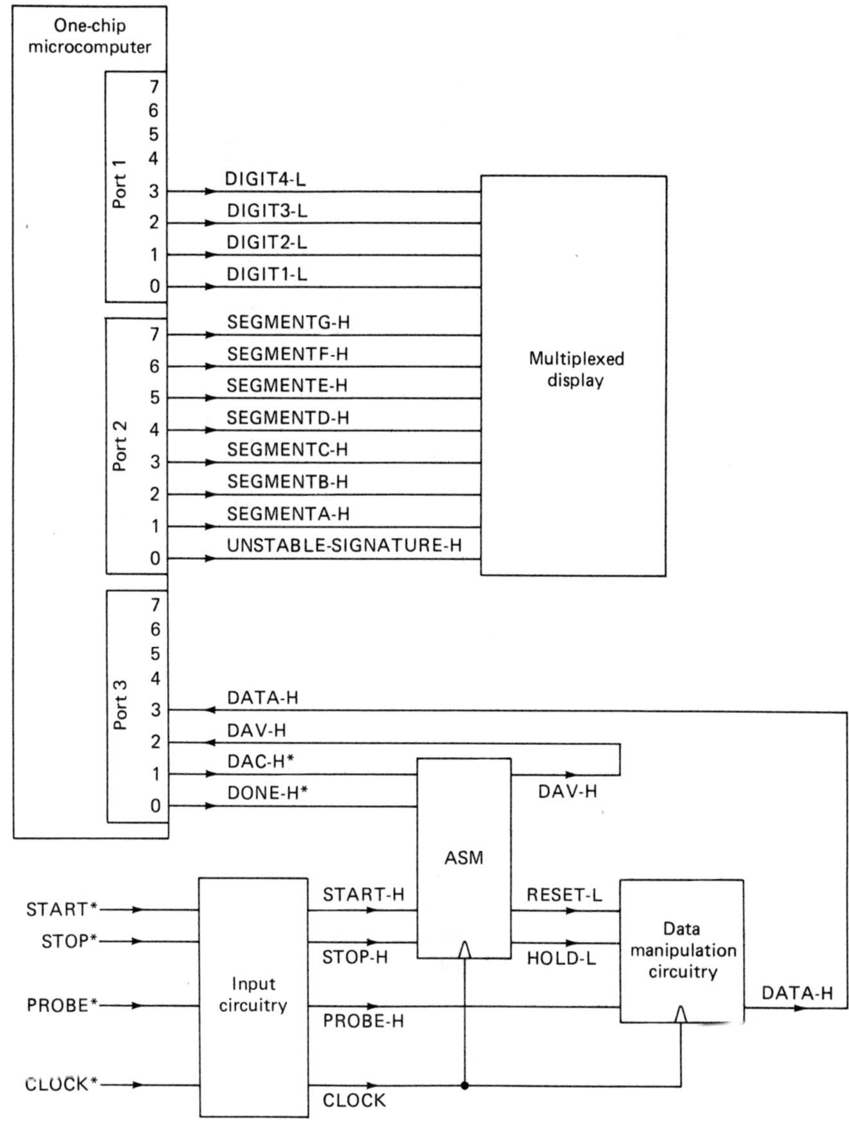

Figure 4-2. Signature analyzer block diagram.

- Input protection
- The maintaining of timing relationships between inputs
- The Schmitt-trigger function of the probe input (so it can probe three-state outputs unambiguously, as will be discussed later)

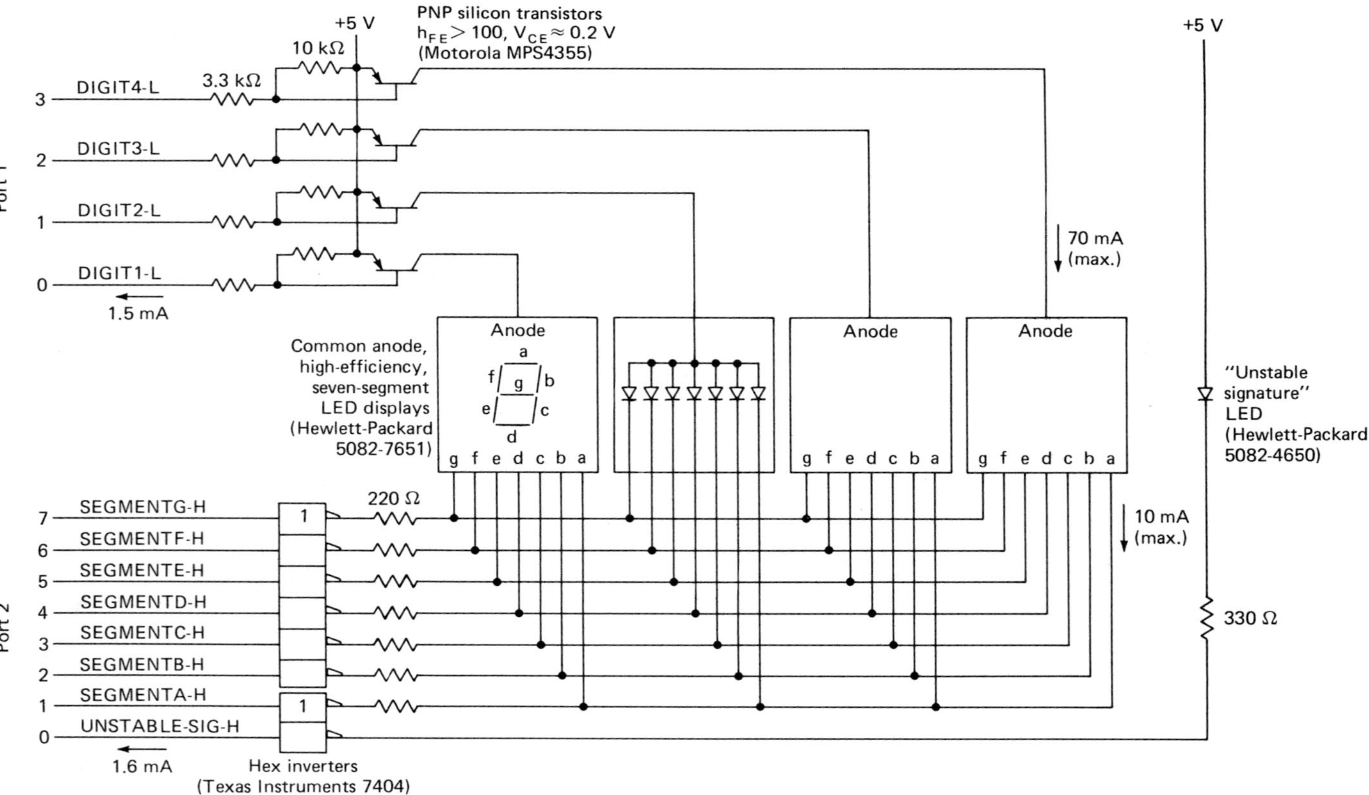

Figure 4-3. Signature analyzer multiplexed display circuitry.

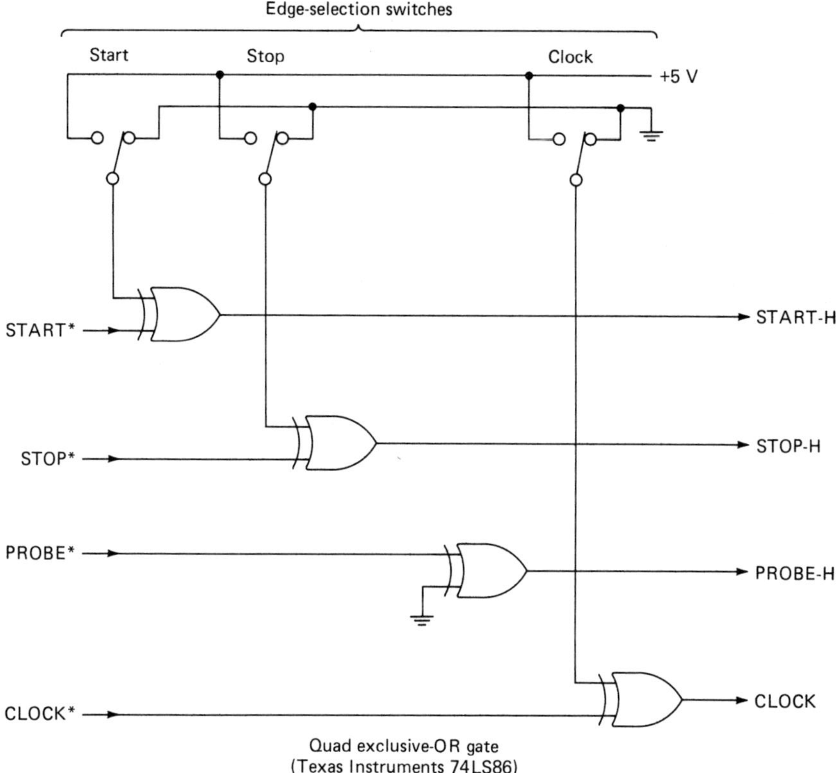

Figure 4-4. Signature analyzer input circuitry.

Of these five aspects of the input circuitry, we will presently handle only the first one, using the circuit of Fig. 4-4. It will generate an output, called CLOCK, which will clock the ASM and the data manipulation circuitry with its *rising edge*. Similarly, the ASM will respond only to the *low-to-high* changes of START-H and STOP-H. The resulting design will be a close *logical* facsimile of the desired signature analyzer.

The *data manipulation circuitry* must implement the PRBS function of Fig. 3-15. Because the device under test (DUT) should be tested at its normal clock rate (within some specified upper limit such as 10 MHz), this function cannot be absorbed by the microcomputer. The implementation must include control inputs for synchronously resetting, holding, or shifting the data in the PRBS shift register. It is illustrated in Fig. 4-5. The implementation employs two 74LS323 "universal" shift registers which can shift in either direction and which permit parallel input or parallel output (but not both during the same clock

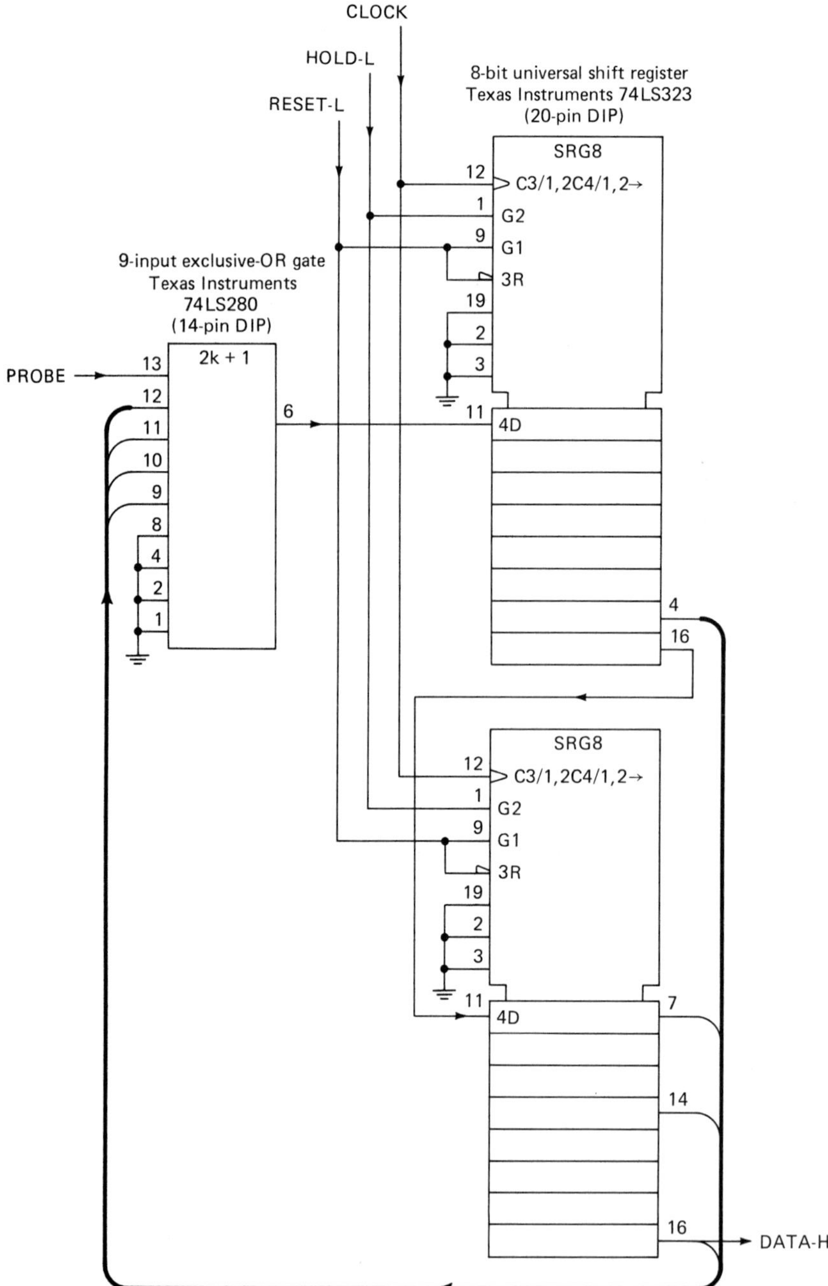

Figure 4-5. Signature analyzer data manipulation circuitry.

period), synchronous resetting, and the hold function. We have tied pins 19, 2, and 3 to ground to eliminate all functions except the three we are using. The simplified representation of Fig. 4-5 shows only this reduced capability. Note the C3-3R CONTROL-dependency for *synchronous* resetting.

The *algorithmic state machine* (ASM) controls the data manipulation circuitry on the basis of its interactions with the START* and STOP* instrument inputs. It also controls the careful transfer of the PRBS shift register contents, bit by bit, to the microcomputer after a signature has been collected so that it can be displayed.

The *microcomputer* runs the display as an autonomous function, as an interrupt service routine under the control of the programmable timer. The timer might be set up to interrupt the CPU every 4 ms so that each of the four digits of the display will be refreshed every 16 ms (i.e., about 60 times per second). Six bytes of the microcomputer's RAM might be set aside for use by the interrupt service routine, with the functions shown in Fig. 4-6. Then, every 4 ms when an interrupt occurs, the CPU's programmable timer interrupt service routine will update the multiplexed display circuitry, shown in Fig. 4-3, as follows:

1 Reinitialize the programmable timer to interrupt again in 4 ms.

2 Turn off the digit that has been displayed for the last 4 ms by writing xxxx1111 to port 1 (where the x's represent DON'T CARE conditions for the unused lines of port 1).

3 Write the contents of the address pointed to by POINTER to port 2 to select appropriate segments of the next hex digit to be displayed. For example, 0111111x would be written to port 2 for displaying a zero.

4 Check the contents of UNSTABLE for zero. If it is zero, do nothing more. Otherwise, decrement it. If the result is 125 or less, write

Address	Contents	Meaning
0	POINTER	Pointer to the next (coded) digit to be displayed (1, 2, 3, or 4)
1	DIGIT1	Encoded seven-segment display data for digit 1
2	DIGIT2	Same for digit 2
3	DIGIT3	Same for digit 3
4	DIGIT4	Same for digit 4
5	UNSTABLE	Number to handle the Unstable Signature light

Figure 4-6. Microcomputer RAM locations.

a 0 to bit 0 of port 2. Otherwise, write a 1 to bit 0 of port 2. This scheme will cause the Unstable Signature light to blink on for half a second and off for half a second every time the microcomputer's main routine stores 250 into the UNSTABLE address.

5 Decode POINTER from its value of 1, 2, 3, or 4 to xxxx1110, xxxx1101, xxxx1011, or xxxx0111, respectively, and write this to port 1, turning on the display.

6 Increment POINTER to its next value (i.e., 1 to 2, 2 to 3, 3 to 4, or 4 to 1).

7 Return to the main program.

In this way, all the main program has to do to display a four-hex-digit number such as OAF3 is to write into its RAM according to the coding shown in Fig. 4-3:

01111110 to DIGIT1 (to generate a 0)

11101110 to DIGIT2 (to generate an A)

11100010 to DIGIT3 (to generate an F)

10011110 to DIGIT4 (to generate a 3)

The other role of the microcomputer is fulfilled by its mainline program. Upon startup, it might turn on all the display segments for a few seconds, and then turn them off again, to permit a user to check for burnt-out segments or drivers. Then it repeatedly tests the DAV-H (data valid) handshaking output of the ASM, waiting for the ASM to raise this line to say that a signature has been collected and that the first bit is sitting on DATA-H (of Fig. 4-2) waiting to be read by the microcomputer. After reading this bit, the microcomputer handshakes by raising the DAC-H* (data accepted) handshaking line and waiting for the ASM to respond by dropping DAV-H. When the microcomputer sees that DAV-H has been dropped, it drops DAC-H* to complete the handshaking input of one bit. This process is continued for all 16 bits of the PRBS shift register.

When the last bit is read by the microcomputer, it raises DONE-H* and then raises DAC-H*. This will handshake DONE-H* back to the ASM, which can look for DONE-H* to be raised when all 16 bits have been transferred. Then the ASM can complete the handshake, reset the PRBS shift register to zero, and begin the acquisition of a new signature.

The microcomputer lowers DAC-H* and DONE-H* after it sees that DAV-H has been lowered, completing the 16-bit transfer. These 16 bits are compared with the last signature acquired. If they are

Address	Contents	Character displayed
DECODE+0	01111110	0
DECODE+1	00001100	1
DECODE+2	10110110	2
DECODE+3	10011110	3
DECODE+4	11001100	4
DECODE+5	11011010	5
DECODE+6	11111000	6
DECODE+7	00001110	7
DECODE+8	11111110	8
DECODE+9	11001110	9
DECODE+10	11101110	A
DECODE+11	01110010	C
DECODE+12	11100010	F
DECODE+13	11101100	H
DECODE+14	11100110	P
DECODE+15	01111100	U

Figure 4-7. Seven-segment display decoder table.

unequal, the UNSTABLE variable of Fig. 4-6 is checked for zero. If it is zero, it is replaced by 250 in order to blink the Unstable Signature light. Otherwise, it is left alone. Finally, the 16-bit number is converted into seven-segment display information, 4 bits at a time, via a decoder function stored in the table of Fig. 4-7. The results are written into DIGIT1, . . . , DIGIT4 (of Fig. 4-6) to be displayed. Now the microcomputer is ready to begin querying DAV-H again to look for a new signature.

With this circuitry as a vehicle, we are now ready to consider algorithmic state machines. We want to develop an unambiguous representation for an ASM function, such as that of the ASM of this section. Then we want to consider alternative implementations.

4-2 ASM BUILDING BLOCKS

Algorithmic state machines are described in terms of the three building blocks of Fig. 4-8. The *state* of the ASM is defined by the state of all the flip-flops in the ASM. For example, Fig. 4-8*a* represents one of 16 possible states for an ASM having flip-flops named S4, S3, S2, and S1. This *state box* says that during any clock period when the ASM is in this state (i.e., when S4 = S1 = 0 and S3 = S2 = 1), the outputs named DAV and HOLD are active. That is, DAV-H will be high and HOLD-L will be low. Notice that it does not matter what the ASM inputs are; these outputs are solely a function of the *state* of the ASM. If it suits our convenience in describing an ASM, we can give names to states. Thus the state of Fig. 4-8*a* is named WAIT.

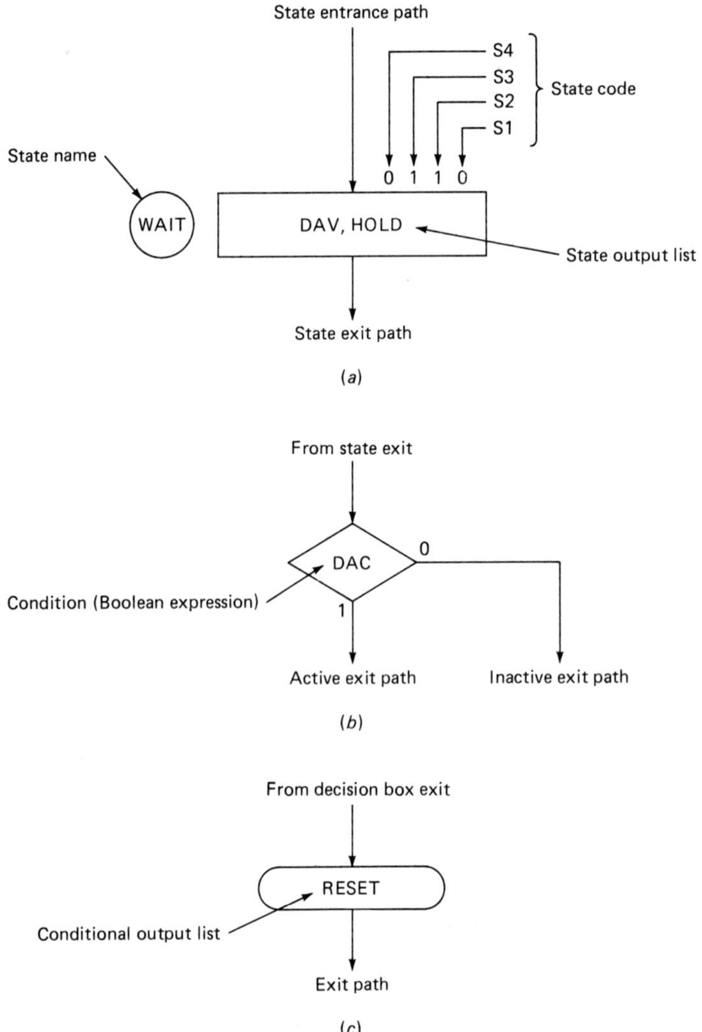

Figure 4-8. ASM building blocks. (*a*) *State box;* (*b*) *decision box;* (*c*) *conditional output box.*

The effect of an input to an algorithmic state machine is represented by a *decision box*. Its use is exemplified in Fig. 4-9. During the clock period when the ASM is in the WAIT state, if DAC is inactive (i.e., 0), then when the next clock transition comes along, the circuit will remain in this same state. On the other hand, if DAC is active during this clock period, when the next clock transition occurs the ASM will go to the SHIFT ONE BIT state (coded arbitrarily as 1000).

A *conditional output box* is used to represent ASM outputs which

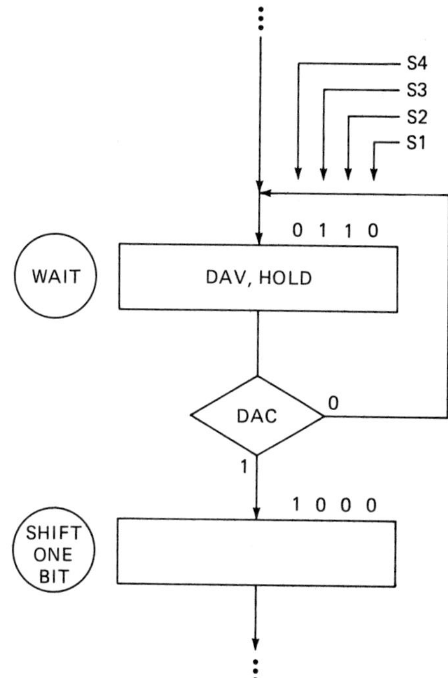

Figure 4-9. Example of a decision box.

depend not only upon the present state but also upon ASM inputs during the *present* clock period. For example, the ASM chart segment of Fig. 4-10*a* represents a circuit in which the output, RESET, will become inactive during the *same* clock period (while in the WAIT FOR START = 1 state) when START becomes active. In contrast, Fig. 4-10*b* illustrates an example where RESET will not become inactive until the clock period *after* START becomes active.

This brief catalog of parts gives us everything we need to represent any algorithmic state machine. In the next section we will represent the ASM for the signature analyzer in these terms.

4-3 ASM CHARTS

A truth table helps us to describe a complicated combinational function one step at a time. At each step we need only decide what the output is supposed to do for one specific set of inputs. By the time we have done this for every row of the truth table, we have obtained an unequivocal definition of the function.

In like manner, we are helped by being permitted to describe an algorithmic state machine one step at a time. Thus although we are

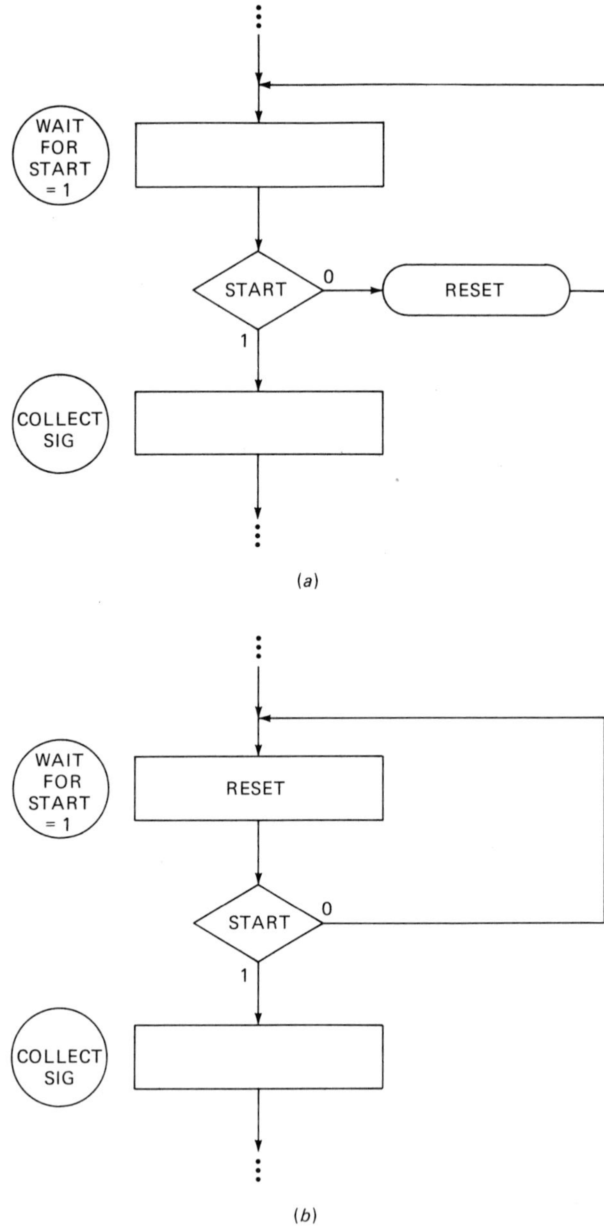

Figure 4-10. Two differently functioning ASM charts. (a) RESET becomes inactive during the same clock period as when START becomes active; (b) RESET becomes inactive during the clock period after the one when START becomes active.

not sure at the outset what the ASM chart for the signature analyzer of Fig. 4-2 will be like, this is irrelevant. We simply start with one state and go from there.

The data window for the Hewlett-Packard signature analyzer is shown in Fig. 3-18. We note that we must begin collecting the probe

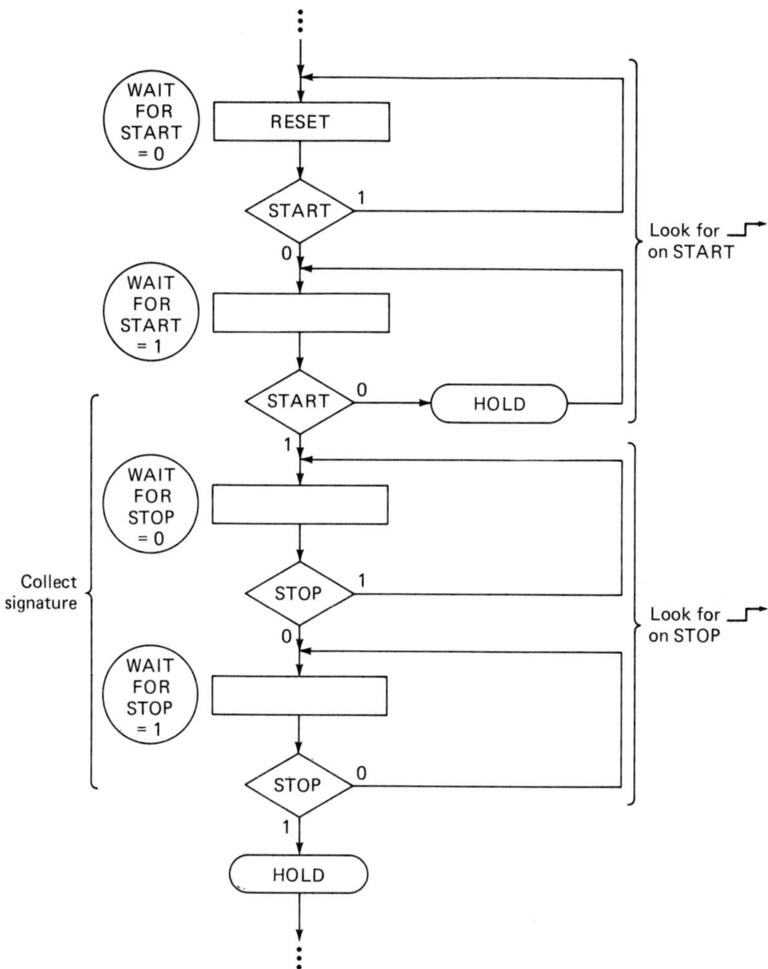

Figure 4-11. Signature acquisition segment of the ASM chart for the signature analyzer.

input during the clock period when START becomes active. Consequently, we need to use the ASM chart segment of Fig. 4-10*a* and *not* that of Fig. 4-10*b*. Next, we note from Fig. 3-18 that we are *not* to collect the probe input during the clock period when STOP becomes active. This leads to the ASM chart segment shown in Fig. 4-11.

Next we must handshake the 16 bits of data, one by one, from the data manipulation circuitry to the microcomputer. Recall that CLOCK is being generated by the device under test. It might be running at 10 MHz. We certainly cannot ask the microcomputer to accept these bits every 100 ns. Handshaking will slow the transfer rate down to a

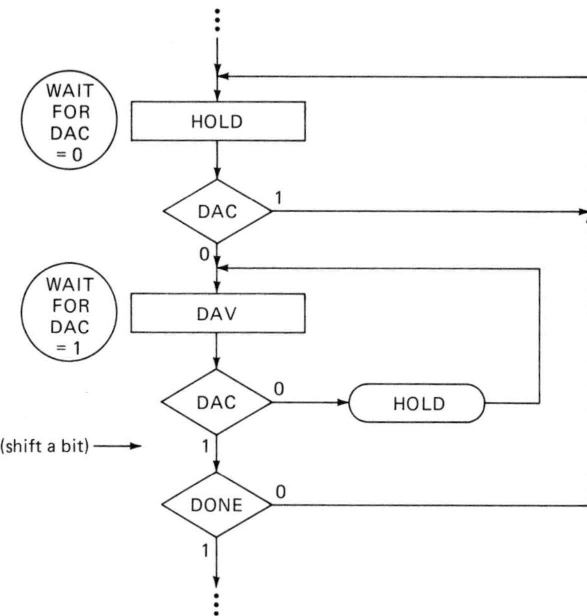

Figure 4-12. Handshaking of data to the microcomputer.

rate which the microcomputer can handle because the rate will, in fact, be determined by the microcomputer.

If CLOCK is only 10 kHz, we are asking the microcomputer to slow the transfer rate down to one determined by the device under test. Again, handshaking will slow the transfer rate down to one determined by the slowest device.

Consider what happens if the microcomputer is halfway through the handshake for one bit of data when the programmable timer strikes in order to refresh the display. The handshake will be suspended while the refresh operation takes place. Then it will pick up again exactly where it left off before the pause that refreshes. Handshaking lets each device wait as long as is necessary to be synchronized with the other device.

At this point we have two options. The ASM can count the number of bits transferred. When it gets to 16, it can discontinue any further transfers and begin the acquisition of a new signature. This will multiply the number of states involved in the ASM's handshake operation by 16. Alternatively, we would prefer to ask the microcomputer to do as much as possible so as to make the ASM circuit as simple as possible. The DONE output from the microcomputer to the ASM in Fig. 4-2 serves just this purpose.

One other consideration arises in our design of the synchronous ASM circuit. We do not have to worry about START* and STOP* in

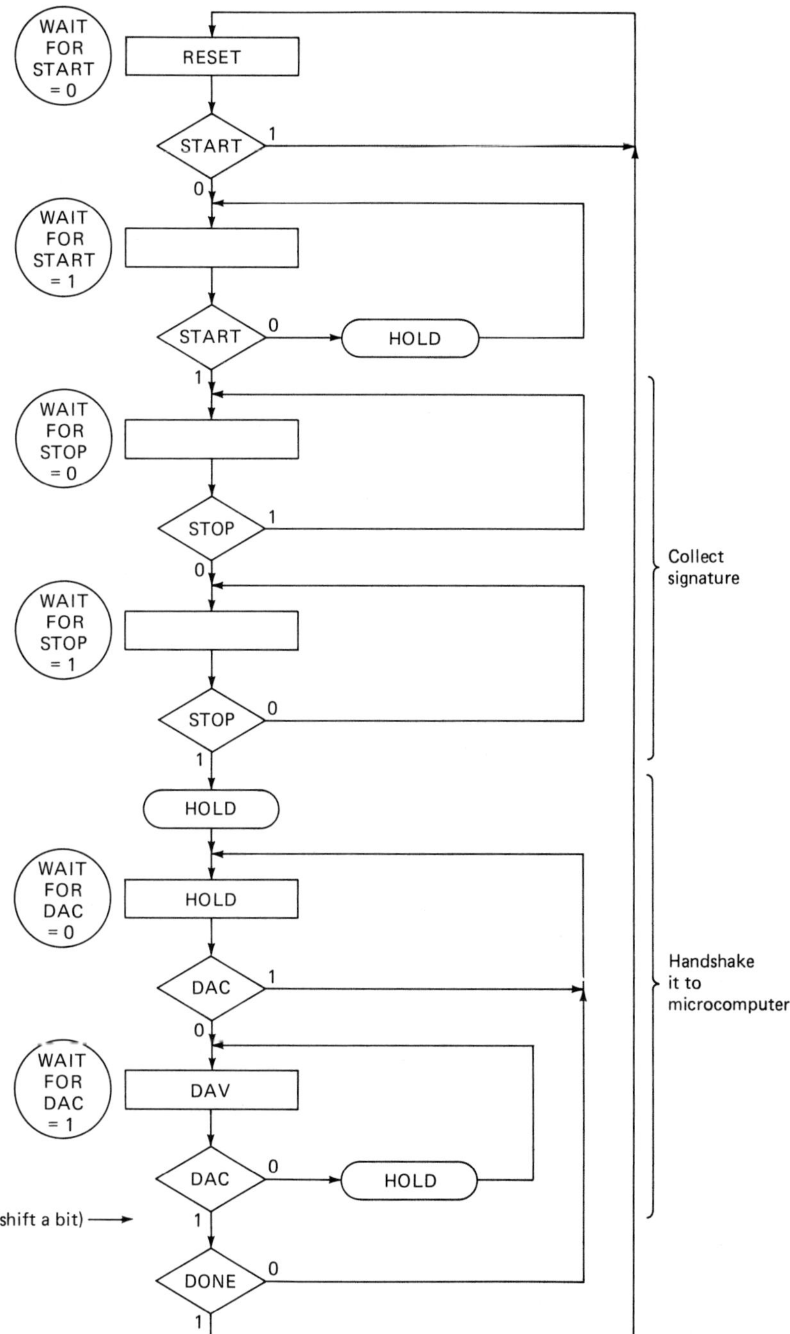

Figure 4-13. Signature analyzer ASM chart.

Fig. 4-2 being synchronized to CLOCK* since they are generated in a device clocked by CLOCK*. Signature analysis depends upon our seeing unambiguous data when we look into the device under test at each active clock transition. On the other hand, inputs to the ASM from the microcomputer are *not* synchronized to CLOCK. Consequently, we must synchronize them. As a reminder, these unsynchronized inputs are labeled DAC-H* and DONE-H* in Fig. 4-2. They will be synchronized in D-type flip-flops whose outputs will be labeled DAC-H and DONE-H.

An ASM chart segment of the handshaking operation is shown in Fig. 4-12, and the complete ASM chart is shown in Fig. 4-13. With six states, it requires three flip-flops (plus the two extra flip-flops needed to synchronize DAC-H* and DONE-H*).

4-4 ALTERNATIVE IMPLEMENTATIONS

We will find that real-life design projects give rise to small-scale algorithmic state machines such as that represented by Fig. 4-13. By the time we transfer as much complexity as possible from a dedicated hardware implementation to the software of a microcomputer, what remains will usually be something without many states, inputs, or outputs. Thus our highest priority task should be to obtain efficient design techniques for small problems.

One excellent approach for small problems is to employ the structure of the general sequential circuit shown in Fig. 2-74. The combinational circuitry can take the form of one of the programmable devices of Sec. 2-12. As applied here, the ASM of Figs. 4-2 and 4-13 reduces to the structure of Fig. 4-14. Note that Fig. 4-2 identifies the number of inputs and outputs required, whereas Fig. 4-13 identifies that three state variables are needed to code the six states.

Our next step is to assign states to the state variables S3, S2, and S1. This is shown in Fig. 4-15. The information in this ASM chart must next be transferred to a table which can then be implemented as a programmable combinational circuit having seven inputs and six outputs. This circuit is small enough to implement with either a 256×8 PROM or a $12 \times 50 \times 6$ FPLA (if there are not too many product terms).

Rather than decide whether to use a PROM or an FPLA at this point, and then fill out the corresponding PROM or FPLA table, we will introduce the intermediate *ASM table* of Fig. 4-16. This is organized to permit us to translate the ASM chart of Fig. 4-15 into a table *with as little change in the form of the information* as possible. Thus we will not worry about whether inputs and outputs are active-high or

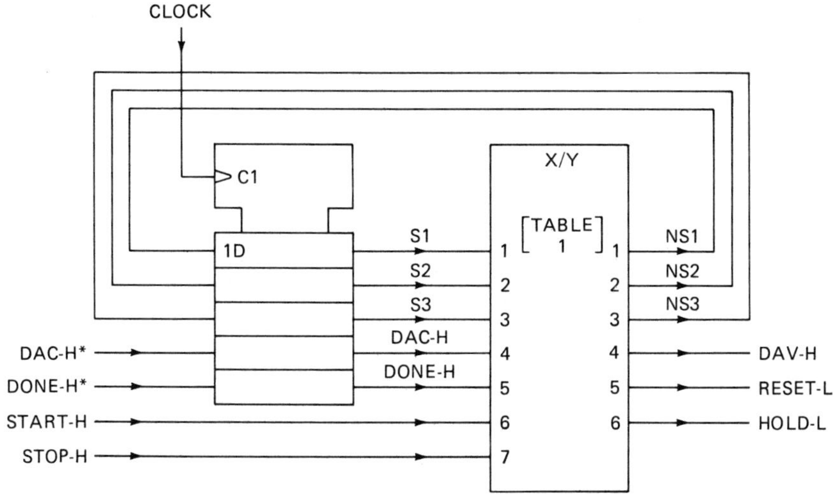

Figure 4-14. Signature analyzer ASM structure.

active-low until later, when this can be indicated in the row at the bottom of the table. We will also permit ourselves to assign columns to inputs and outputs to suit our convenience. Later we can assign the I/O numbers of Fig. 4-14 (i.e., 1 to 7 for inputs and 1 to 6 for outputs) in the other row at the bottom of the table. Finally, we will enter 1s and 0s in the table, corresponding to the 1 and 0 conditions of the ASM chart. Don't care conditions will be left blank (in order to give ourselves one less step in filling out the table). The resulting table for our ASM is shown in Fig. 4-17.

This result can be translated into the form of an FPLA table with very little change. Then an FPLA can be programmed from that table. Alternatively, it can be more arduously translated into the first 128 rows of a 256 × 8 PROM table which can then be used to program a PROM. If this were really our only choice, it would boost our incentive to use FPLAs rather than PROMs! However, with the revolution taking place in PROM (and FPLA) programming, we should be able to interact with a "smart" PROM programmer built around a unit such as that of Fig. 1-18. It should show us an ASM table, permit us to fill in entries, ask us what device we want to use in the implementation (telling us if it is too small), and then *translate the table itself* into the appropriate form and program a chip for us directly. In this way, the 14 rows of the ASM table of Fig. 4-17 do *not* have to be expanded (carefully and somewhat painfully) into 128 rows for PROM programming. The translation becomes even more painful for larger PROMs; yet we do not want to avoid using larger PROMs solely for this reason.

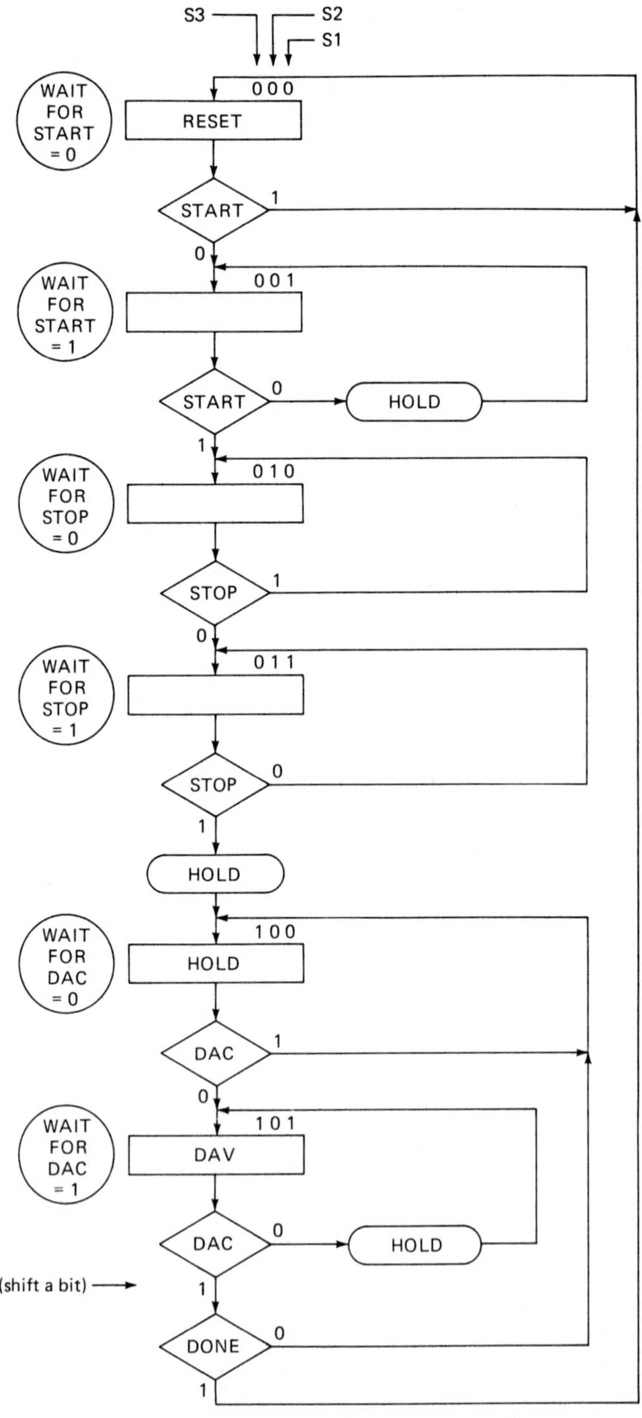

Figure 4-15. Signature analyzer ASM chart with states assigned.

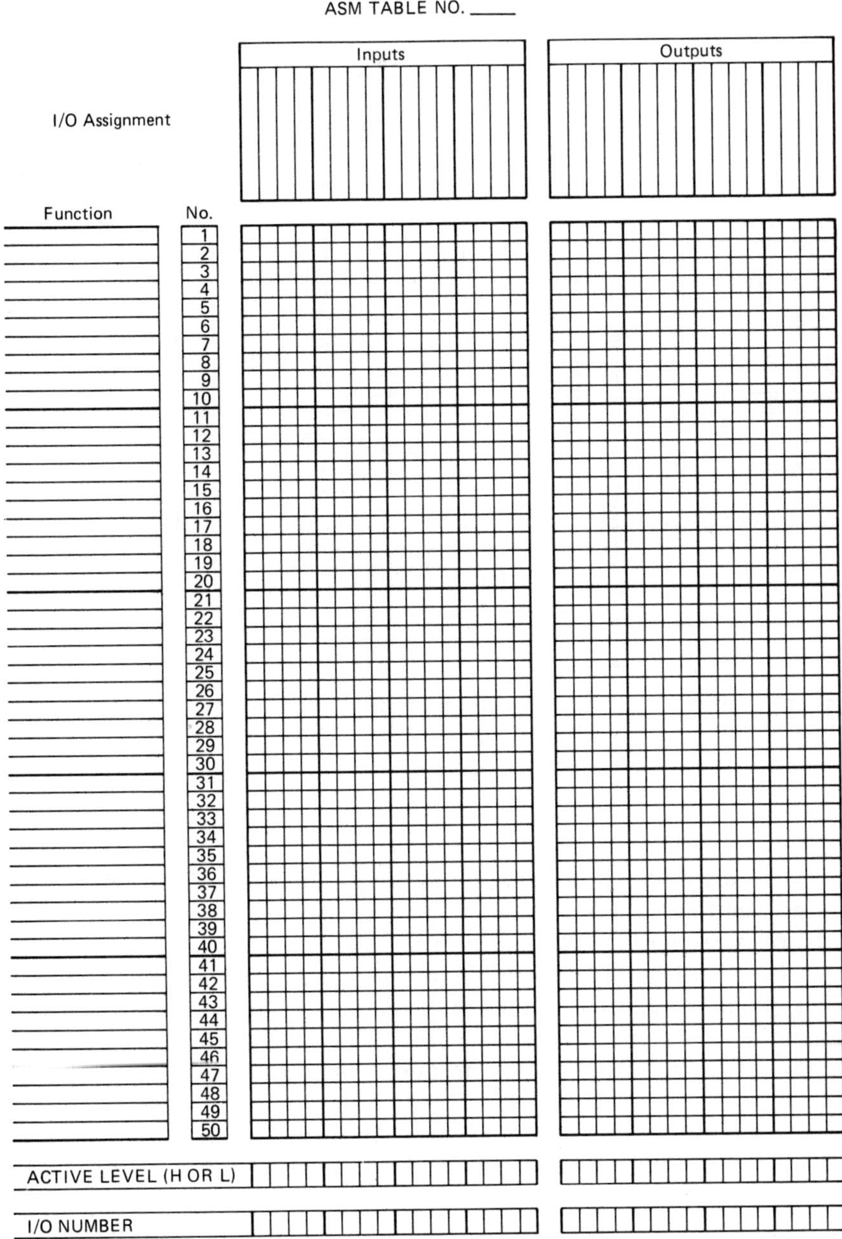

Figure 4-16. *ASM table.*

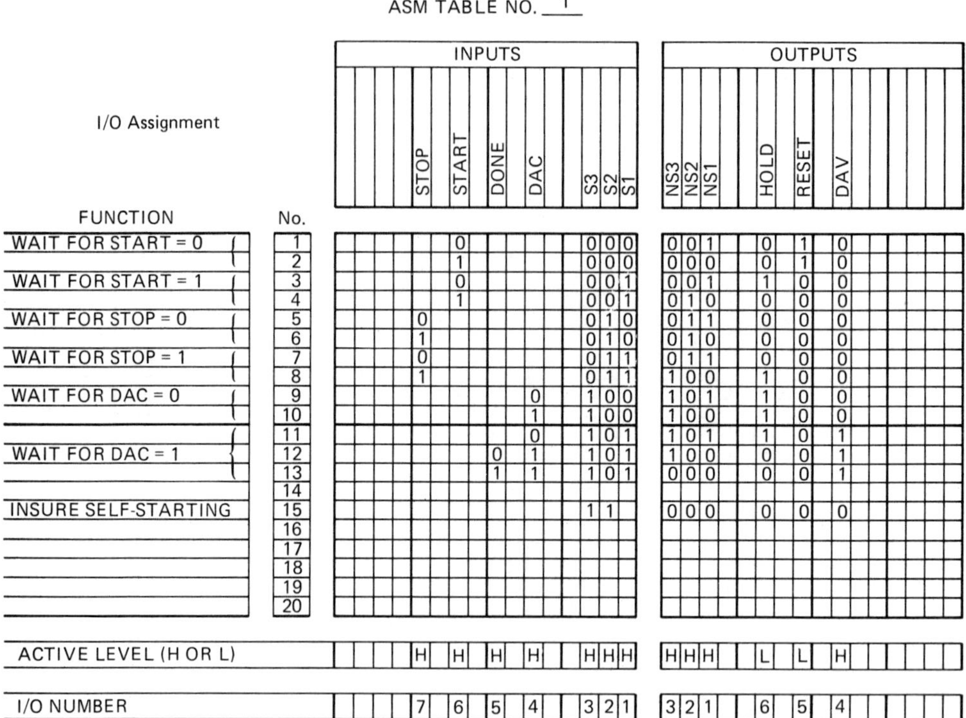

ASM TABLE NO. 1

I/O Assignment

FUNCTION	No.	STOP	START	DONE	DAC	S3	S2	S1	NS3	NS2	NS1	HOLD	RESET	DAV
WAIT FOR START = 0	1		0			0	0	0	0	0	1	0	1	0
	2		1			0	0	0	0	0	0	0	1	0
WAIT FOR START = 1	3		0			0	0	1	0	0	1	1	0	0
	4		1			0	0	1	0	1	0	0	0	0
WAIT FOR STOP = 0	5	0				0	1	0	0	1	1	0	0	0
	6	1				0	1	0	0	1	0	0	0	0
WAIT FOR STOP = 1	7	0				0	1	1	0	1	1	0	0	0
	8	1				0	1	1	1	0	0	1	0	0
WAIT FOR DAC = 0	9				0	1	0	0	1	0	1	1	0	0
	10				1	1	0	0	1	0	0	1	0	0
WAIT FOR DAC = 1	11				0	1	0	1	1	0	1	1	0	1
	12			0	1	1	0	1	1	0	0	0	0	1
	13			1	1	1	0	1	0	0	0	0	0	1
INSURE SELF-STARTING	14													
	15					1	1		0	0	0	0	0	0
	16													
	17													
	18													
	19													
	20													
ACTIVE LEVEL (H OR L)		H	H	H	H	H	H	H	H	H	H	L	L	H
I/O NUMBER		7	6	5	4	3	2	1	3	2	1	6	5	4

Figure 4-17. ASM table for the signature analyzer.

For any ASMs small enough to fit in a PROM or FPLA which we are willing to use, this implementation is fast and direct. Notice that as a "constrained PROM," an FPLA has appropriate constraints to suit it *well* to this task of ASM implementation. In contrast, the PAL devices of Sec. 2-12 are examples of "constrained PROMs" in which the constraints discourage their use for ASM implementation. The output lines are not driven by enough product terms to serve this application well.

Our only further consideration of ASM implementation concerns how to handle those cases where the foregoing approach becomes unwieldy. One alternative is to expand the PROM or FPLA. In particular, the input expansion technique of *selecting* inputs, discussed in Example 2-31, is a powerful one. We can often reconstruct as ASM chart, with the addition of extra states, so that we never look at more than one input per state. Then we can use the state to select among all inputs, as shown in Fig. 4-18.

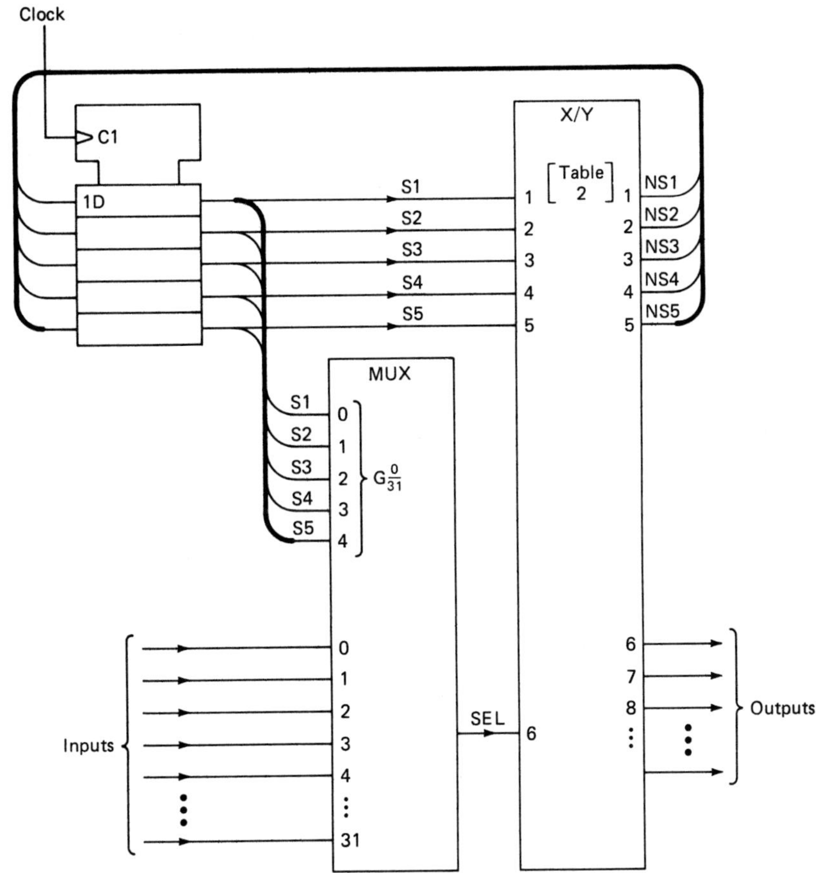

Figure 4-18. ASM input expansion when the construction of the ASM chart has been constrained to permit only one input to be looked at during each state.

Example 4-1. Reconstruct the ASM chart of Fig. 4-15 and implement it with the ASM circuit configuration of Fig. 4-18.

It is only in the "WAIT FOR DAC = 1" state of Fig. 4-15 that we want to look at two states at once. Since we can look at DAC and DONE during two separate clock periods (without affecting the reliability of the handshake), this approach is feasible. The new ASM circuit, ASM chart, and ASM table are shown in Fig. 4-19*a*, *b*, and *c*. Figure 4-19*d* is identical to Fig. 4-19*c* with the four input columns collapsed into one "SEL" column. This table can be implemented with a little 32 × 8 PROM.

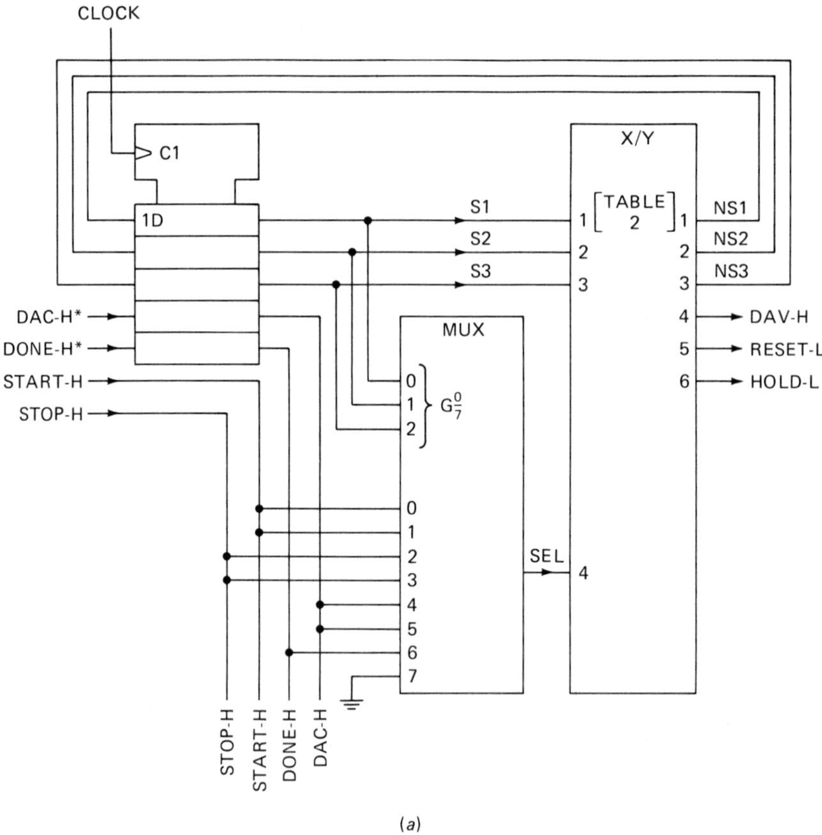

Figure 4-19. Solution to Ex. 4-1; ASM input expansion by input selection. (a) ASM circuit.

ASM output expansion can be carried out by expanding the programmable devices, as discussed in Sec. 2-12. On the other hand, any outputs *which are never conditional* can be decoded from the present-state information, as shown in Fig. 4-20. With 32 or fewer states, expansion can employ one little 32 × 8 PROM for each eight unconditional outputs. We may be able to facilitate this technique by restructuring the ASM chart. Our intent in restructuring is to eliminate conditional outputs by introducing new states. The technique is illustrated in Fig. 4-21. Whether or not it can be applied to a specific conditional output depends upon the nature of the original problem. For example, the signature analyzer's HOLD conditional output from the WAIT FOR START = 1 state can not be converted to an unconditional output without changing the signature that is collected. This restructuring necessarily changes the data window of the signature analyzer.

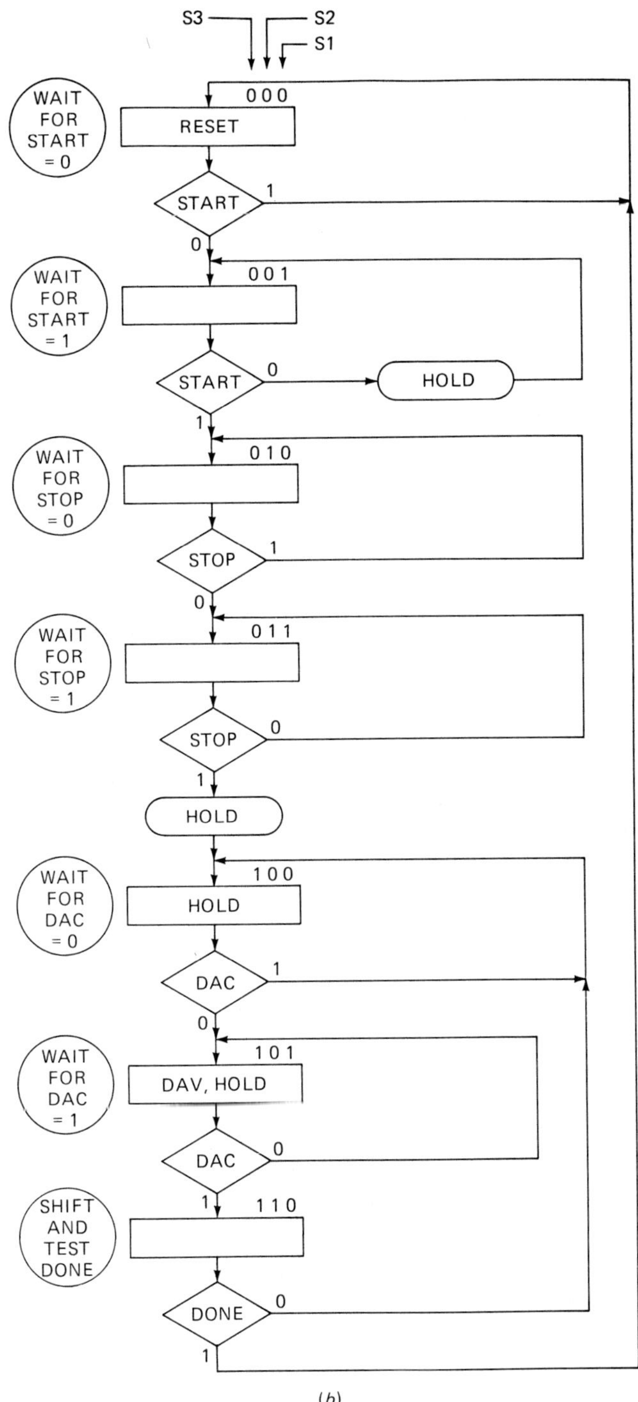

Figure 4-19b. ASM chart.

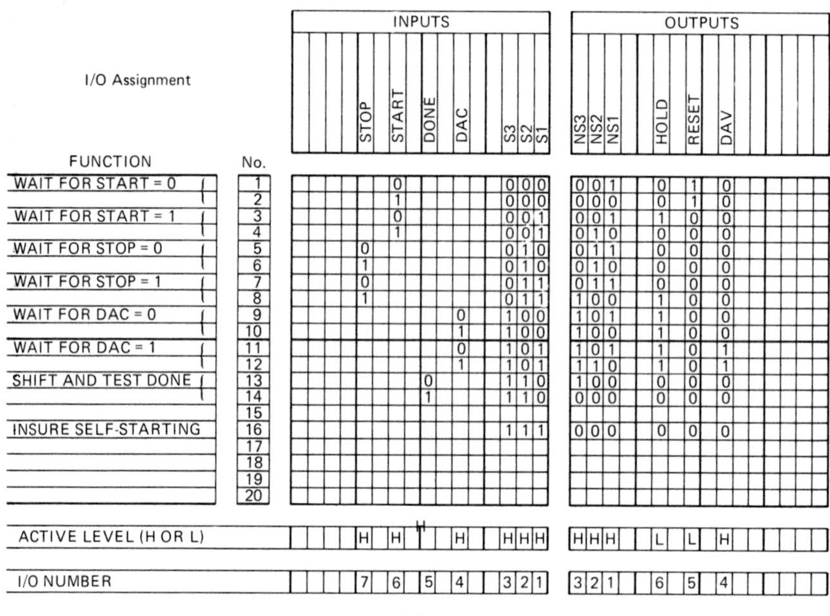

ASM TABLE NO. 1a

I/O Assignment

FUNCTION	No.	STOP	START	DONE	DAC	S3	S2	S1	NS3	NS2	NS1	HOLD	RESET	DAV
WAIT FOR START = 0	1		0			0	0	0	0	0	1	0	1	0
	2		1			0	0	0	0	0	0	0	1	0
WAIT FOR START = 1	3		0			0	0	1	0	0	1	1	0	0
	4		1			0	0	1	0	1	0	0	0	0
WAIT FOR STOP = 0	5	0				0	1	0	0	1	1	0	0	0
	6	1				0	1	0	0	1	0	0	0	0
WAIT FOR STOP = 1	7	0				0	1	1	0	1	1	0	0	0
	8	1				0	1	1	1	0	0	1	0	0
WAIT FOR DAC = 0	9				0	1	0	0	1	0	1	1	0	0
	10				1	1	0	0	1	0	0	1	0	0
WAIT FOR DAC = 1	11				0	1	0	1	1	0	1	1	0	1
	12				1	1	0	1	1	1	0	1	0	1
SHIFT AND TEST DONE	13			0		1	1	0	1	0	0	0	0	0
	14			1		1	1	0	0	0	0	0	0	0
	15													
INSURE SELF-STARTING	16					1	1	1	0	0	0	0	0	0
	17													
	18													
	19													
	20													
ACTIVE LEVEL (H OR L)		H	H	H	H	H	H	H	H	H	H	L	L	H
I/O NUMBER		7	6	5	4	3	2	1	3	2	1	6	5	4

(c)

Figure 4-19c. ASM table.

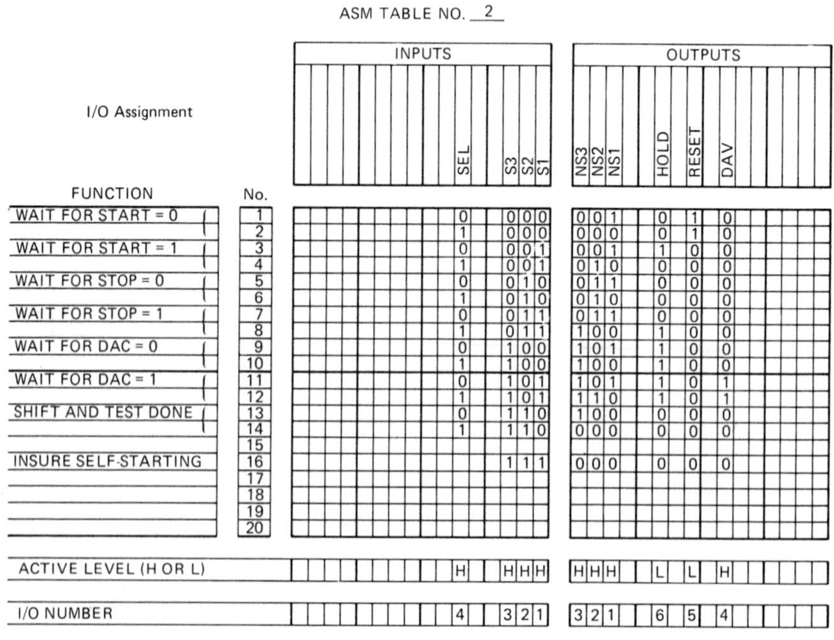

ASM TABLE NO. 2

I/O Assignment

FUNCTION	No.	SEL	S3	S2	S1	NS3	NS2	NS1	HOLD	RESET	DAV
WAIT FOR START = 0	1	0	0	0	0	0	0	1	0	1	0
	2	1	0	0	0	0	0	0	0	1	0
WAIT FOR START = 1	3	0	0	0	1	0	0	1	1	0	0
	4	1	0	0	1	0	1	0	0	0	0
WAIT FOR STOP = 0	5	0	0	1	0	0	1	1	0	0	0
	6	1	0	1	0	0	1	0	0	0	0
WAIT FOR STOP = 1	7	0	0	1	1	0	1	1	0	0	0
	8	1	0	1	1	1	0	0	1	0	0
WAIT FOR DAC = 0	9	0	1	0	0	1	0	1	1	0	0
	10	1	1	0	0	1	0	0	1	0	0
WAIT FOR DAC = 1	11	0	1	0	1	1	0	1	1	0	1
	12	1	1	0	1	1	1	0	1	0	1
SHIFT AND TEST DONE	13	0	1	1	0	1	0	0	0	0	0
	14	1	1	1	0	0	0	0	0	0	0
	15										
INSURE SELF-STARTING	16		1	1	1	0	0	0	0	0	0
	17										
	18										
	19										
	20										
ACTIVE LEVEL (H OR L)		H	H	H	H	H	H	H	L	L	H
I/O NUMBER		4	3	2	1	3	2	1	6	5	4

(d)

Figure 4-19d. Reduced ASM table.

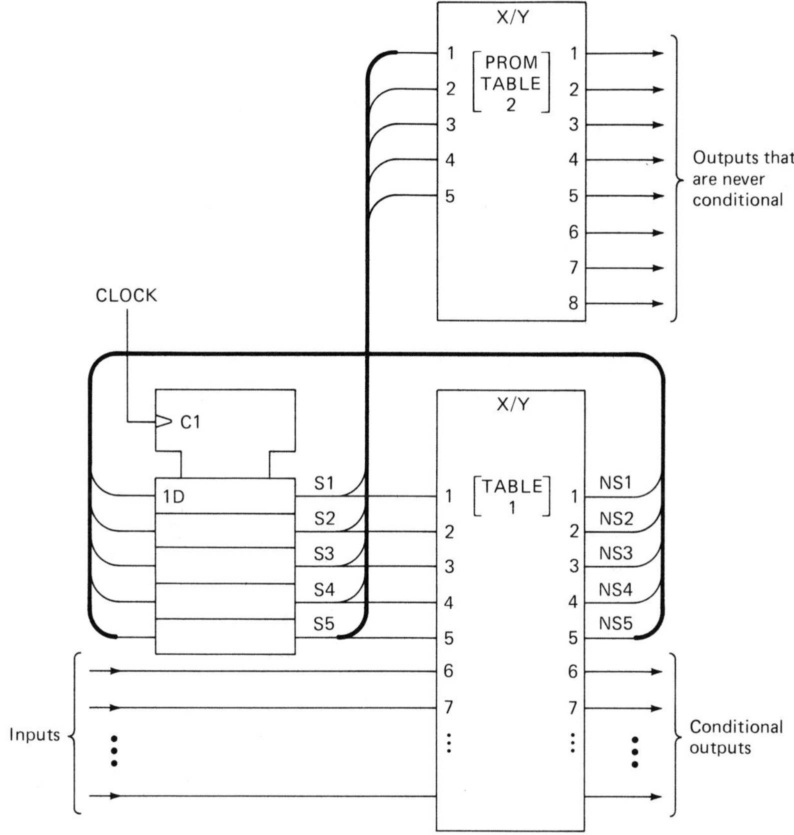

Figure 4-20. Decoding unconditional outputs with a PROM.

Row reduction of an ASM table is of interest if the number of rows in the ASM table precludes the use of a single FPLA, which might otherwise be employed in the implementation. In Sec. 2-12 we discussed a technique for reducing the number of rows in an FPLA table. The only additional point we might note here is that the *coding* of the state information may either hinder or facilitate this reduction technique. If the coding hinders the technique, the state information can be recoded.

Example 4-2. Consider the ASM table of Fig. 4-17 and whether any rows can be eliminated.

We see that rows 5 and 7 of that table differ only in the value of S1. Hence they can be replaced by one row in which the S1 input becomes a don't care condition. However, if the WAIT FOR STOP = 0 state and the

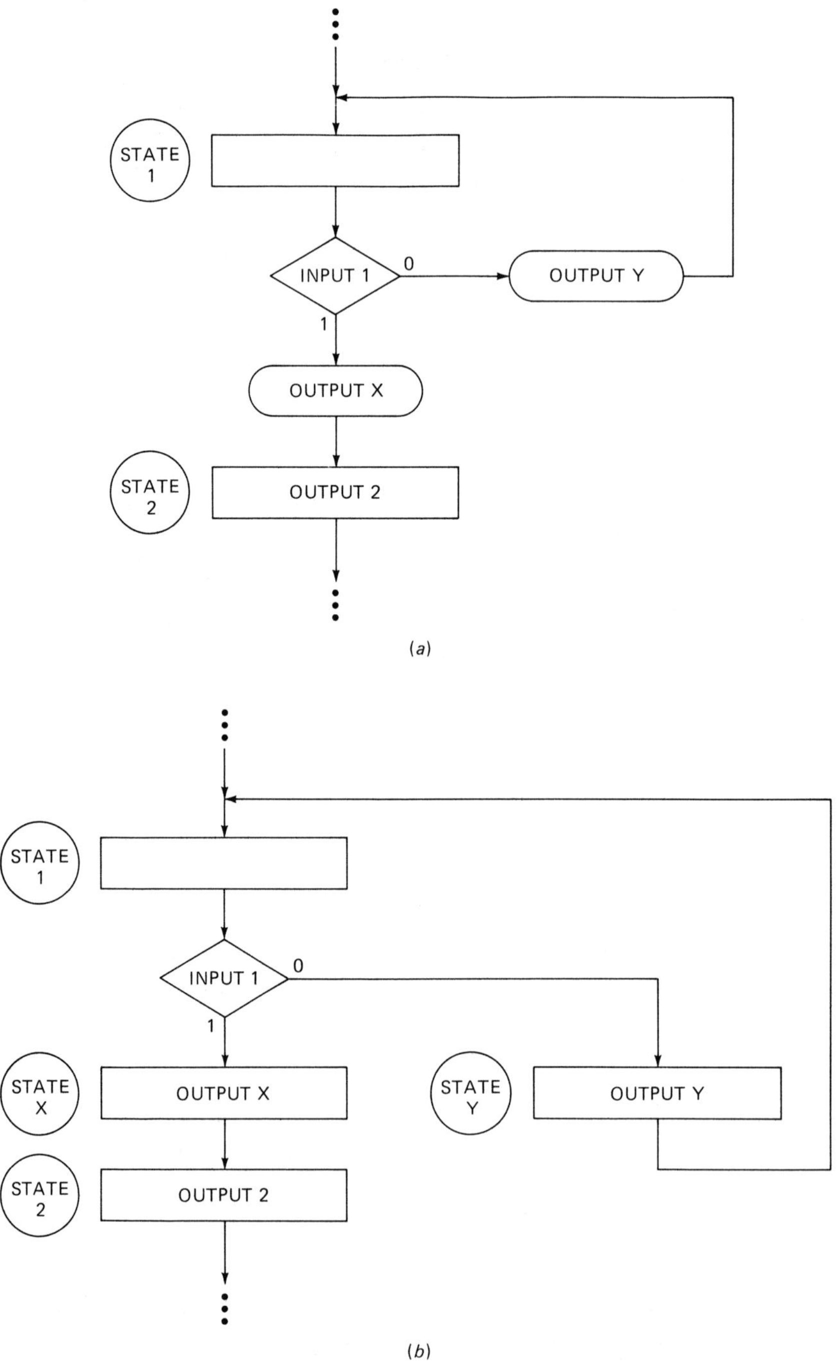

Figure 4-21. Eliminating conditional outputs. (a) Original ASM chart segment; (b) alternative ASM chart segment which generates the same outputs but with delayed timing.

WAIT FOR STOP = 1 state had been coded 010 and 111 (for example) so that both S1 *and* S3 differed, we would not be able to carry out the reduction (without recoding the state).

Generally, row reduction is most effectively achieved by restructuring the ASM circuit, knowing something about what it is doing. For example, the signature analyzer ASM lets the microcomputer do the counting of the bits being transferred. The ASM replaces the counting function by the testing of DONE. If the problem were changed to one where the ASM could not shuck off this counting function, the direct implementation would replace the two WAIT FOR DAC = 0 and WAIT FOR DAC = 1 states of Fig. 4-15 by 16 pairs of these states, leading to a 36-state ASM. The ASM table would have 72 rows, an unfortunately large number for either of the FPLAs we considered in Sec. 2-12. An alternative, shown in Fig. 4-22, uses a separate scale-of-16 binary counter which is controlled by outputs of the ASM to generate a DONE-H input to the ASM.

The *initialization* of an ASM circuit must be implemented either implicitly or explicitly. For example, we might have a reset input to all the flip-flops of the ASM circuit, which is controlled by the microcomputer. In this case we want to make sure that a suitable initial state is coded as all 0s.

We have designed all the ASM circuit alternatives for the signature analyzer to be *self-starting*. That is, regardless of what state the ASM circuit is in when power is turned on, it will not lock up in an undefined state which precludes further interaction. This is why we added a last row to each ASM table. Unused states were defined so as to return to the WAIT FOR START = 0 state.

Before concluding this chapter, we will modify the signature analyzer design. At *no cost* to its design, we will generate significant additional diagnostic capability. There are three ways in which the device under test can thwart the collection of a signature. Since this device is malfunctioning already (or a user would not have the cover off and be trying to use signature analysis on it), a user can benefit from any information available. In particular, we want to tell a user if the CLOCK*, START*, and STOP* signals are functioning. The modification, shown in Fig. 4-23, employs an edge-sensitive (noninterrupting) input on the one-chip microcomputer to sense the presence of a CLOCK input. If none is occurring (over perhaps an interval of a second), the display can be made to show the message "no C." If the clock clip is incorrectly placed so that no clock edges occur, this will immediately point out the problem to the user. As soon as the microcomputer

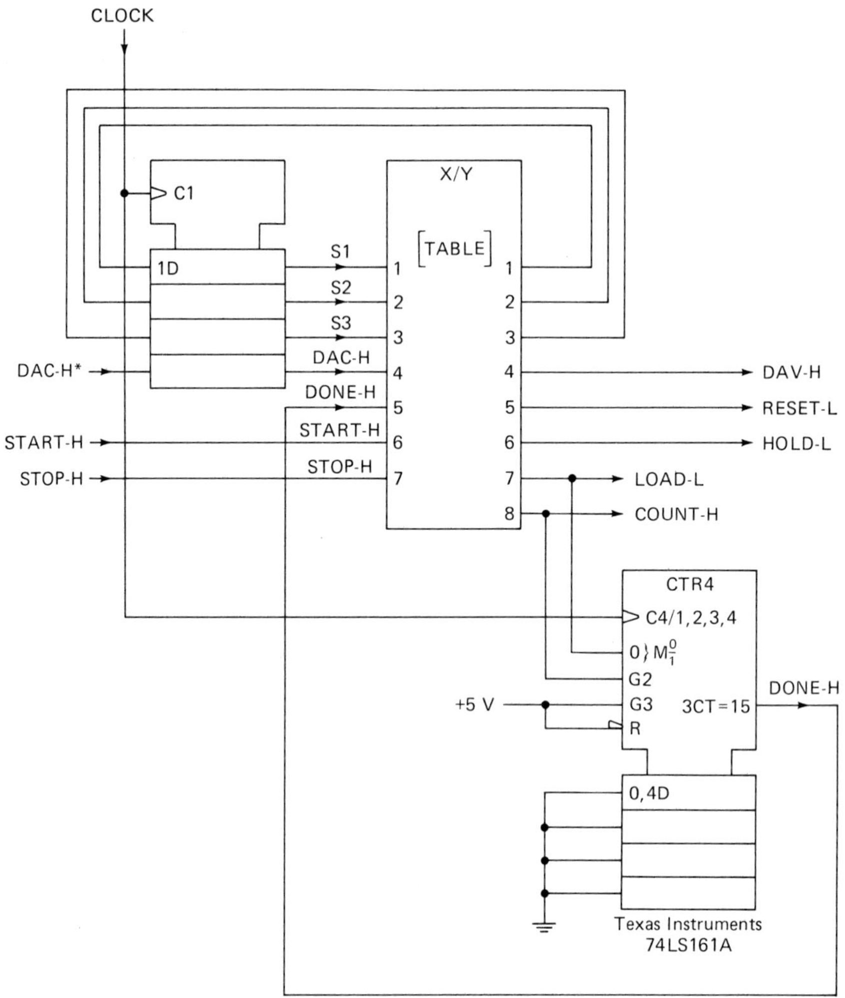

Figure 4-22. Restructuring the signature analyzer ASM to include the counting function, with the help of a separate counter.

senses clock edges, it can remove the "no C" display and collect a signature.

If START* never changes state, the ASM will hang up in either the WAIT FOR START = 0 state or the WAIT FOR START = 1 state. If the microcomputer sees S3 and S2 stuck at 00 over a period of a second (or so), it can turn on the "no G" message shown in Fig. 4-23*b*. When START* is connected to a properly functioning input, the microcomputer can remove this display and collect a signature. In like manner a malfunctioning STOP* input can be detected by S3 and S2 being equal to 01 over a long interval.

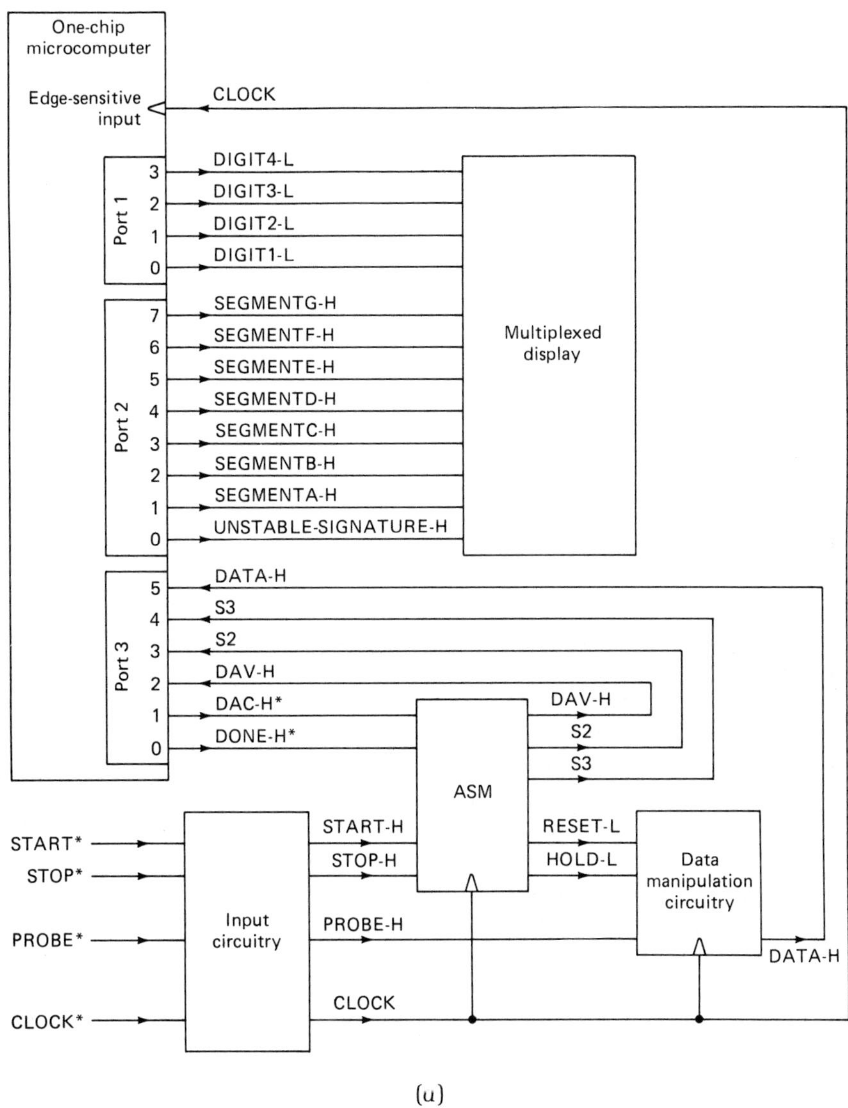

(a)

Figure 4-23. Modification of signature analyzer for checking CLOCK, START*, and STOP* inputs.* (a) Circuit.

PROBLEMS

4-1 Instrument organization. Obtain the service manual for an instrument organized around a microcomputer. Considering the organization of Fig. 4-1, identify the different parts of the design in terms of these blocks.

Display	Meaning
no C	No Clock signal
no G	No "Go," or Start, signal
no H	No "Halt," or Stop, signal

Figure 4-23b. Diagnostic messages. (*b*)

4-2 Multiplexed display. One of the threats to the long life of a multiplexed display is realized when the multiplexing operation is (accidentally) halted with one character still turned on. The instantaneous LED current then becomes the average (or dc) current, which may exceed the current rating of the displays. The high-efficiency units of Fig. 4-3 produce a reasonably bright display with an average current of only 2.5 mA. Their "luminous intensity per segment" is typically 180 μcd at this current level. In comparison, a standard efficiency part (Hewlett-Packard 5082-7751) requires an average current of about 10 mA to achieve the same brightness. The maximum dc current ratings of the two devices are 20 and 25 mA, respectively.

(*a*) Discuss this problem and its impact upon the display choice if we want this amount of brightness from either display.

(*b*) Check the specifications for another manufacturer's seven-segment display to determine its suitability in this application (without extra protection circuitry to shut down the display if multiplexing stops).

4-3 Input circuitry. Considering the circuitry of Fig. 4-4, which side of each switch should be labeled S→ and which side Z→?

4-4 Data manipulation circuitry. The circuit of Fig. 4-5 employs a nine-input exclusive-OR gate. Could the same function have been performed with a 74LS86 quad two-input exclusive-OR gate? If so, show the interconnection. If there are several alternatives, show the one that minimizes the maximum propagation delay of the equivalent five-input exclusive-OR gate. On this logic diagram label all inputs H or L except for the one (which will be labeled H → L or L → H) that produces the worst-case propagation delay, using the data of Fig. P4-4. Comparing this result with the worst-case propagation delay of 50 ns for the 74LS280, which implementation will permit the higher external clock rate, CLOCK* (assuming that this propagation delay is part of the critical path that determines the maximum clock rate)?

4-5 Data manipulation circuitry. Consider the data sheet for the 74LS323 universal shift register. Show (simplified) dependency notation symbolism and pin labeling to achieve the following combinations of functions (assuming that we *never* want to look at the eight flip-flop outputs, but only the one where data is shifted out):

(*a*) Shift, 8-bit parallel load, reset
(*b*) Shift, 8-bit parallel load, reset, hold

4-6 Unstable Signature. How should the software description of Sec. 4-1 be changed if we want the Unstable Signature light to be turned on for half a second each time the signature changes (so that repeated changes occurring more often than every half-second will leave the light continuously turned on)?

***4-7 Microcomputer.** For a specific one-chip microcomputer, show an instruction sequence that will access the ROM table of Fig. 4-7 with a number 0 to 15 located in the accumulator (or other suit-

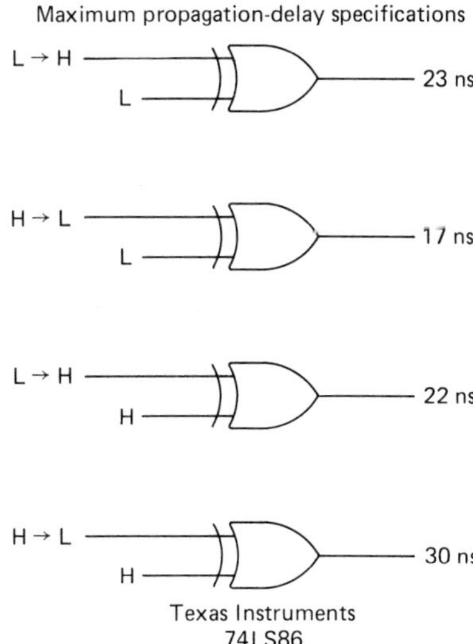

Figure P4-4

able register) and will replace the accumulator contents with the appropriate table entry. Does it matter where in ROM the table is located? If so, show the sequence for an easy location *and* for a more arbitrary location.

4-8 Edge detection. Consider the ASM chart segment of Fig. 4-11. Describe an example of how faulty edge detection could take place if the WAIT FOR START = 0 and WAIT FOR STOP = 0 states were removed.

4-9 Handshaking. Consider the ASM chart segment of Fig. 4-12. Assume that CLOCK* = 10 MHz. Describe how this produces just one shift as DAC goes from low to high to low again over an interval of many clock periods.

4-10 State assignment. The signature analyzer ASM structure of Fig. 4-14, together with the state assignment of Fig. 4-15, led to the ASM table of Fig. 4-17. Either a 256 × 8 PROM or a 12 × 50 × 6 FPLA can be used for the implementation. Can the coding used by the three state variables be changed to some other coding such that the implementation with either PROM or FPLA will be either easier or more difficult? That is, does the complexity of the implementation depend upon how astute we are in assigning states? Explain.

4-11 ASM table-to-PROM table translation. Use a copy of the PROM table of Fig. 2-53 to show the contents of the first 32 addresses of a 256 × 8 PROM used to implement the ASM table of Fig. 4-17. Make sure that the I/O numbers shown in the bottom of Fig. 4-17 correspond to those shown in the PROM table.

4-12 ASM table-to-PROM table translation. Repeat Prob. 4-11 for the ASM table of Fig. 4-19*d*.

4-13 Self-starting ASMs. The Harris semiconductor PROMs discussed in Sec. 2-12 drive all outputs high before they are programmed. That is, they initially hold all ones (given positive-logic definitions). If the last row (row 16) of the ASM table of Fig. 4-19*d* had inadvertently been omitted, and if we only programmed the remaining listed rows into a 32 × 8 Harris PROM, how would the circuit operate when power comes on? Assume that the flip-flops of Fig. 4-19 all happen to power up in their high state.

4-14 ASM output expansion. Using the structure of Fig. 4-20, draw the circuit (labeling lines appropriately) to implement the ASM table of Fig. 4-17 with a 256 × 4 PROM and a 32 × 8 PROM. Do not bother to show the actual PROM contents.

4-15 ASM chart. Construct an ASM chart for the circuit of Fig. 4-22 in which the 16 bits transferred to the microcomputer are counted by the ASM. That is, show LOAD and COUNT as outputs and the new DONE as an input. Make sure that exactly 16 bits are transferred, not 15 or 17.

4-16 Microcomputer. Consider a specific one-chip microcomputer. Does it have a (noninterrupting) edge-sensitive input? If so, what edge does it sense? How can software test whether such an input has occurred? How does the flip-flop in the microcomputer that is set by this edge get reset so that it can sense further edges?

4-17 Diagnostic capability. At the close of Sec. 4-4 we discussed the sensing of edges on the CLOCK*, START*, and STOP* inputs to the signature analyzer. Discuss how the microcomputer might actually implement the testing of these *continuously* so that if any of these ever stops, 1 s later (more or less) the appropriate diagnostic message will appear on the display.

REFERENCES

The algorithmic state machine description and organization of control circuitry is developed by C. Clare, *Designing Logic Systems Using State Machines,* McGraw-Hill, New York, 1973.

While the PAL chips discussed in Sec. 2-12 are not particularly useful for ASM implementation, there are other PAL chips available which include on-board flip-flops and significantly more fusible links. For specifications and applications material, see J. Birkner, *PAL Programmable Array Logic Handbook,* available at cost from Monolithic Memories, Inc., 1165 East Arques Ave., Sunnyvale, CA 94086.

CIRCUITRY WITH A SINGLE CLOCK SOURCE

In this chapter we will discuss the *timing considerations* that must be met to obtain reliable operation from a digital circuit. We will constrain ourselves to circuits having a single clock source, wherein the timing relationships among signals are defined by the clock and by the propagation delays of the digital devices. We will generalize from the single-phase clock of earlier chapters to consider the timing issues raised by the use of a single clock having several clock *phases*.

5-1 TIMING CONSIDERATIONS OF LOGIC

In Sec. 2-13 we used clocked, D-type flip-flops as memory devices. The realm of memory devices is significantly broader than this. Figure 5-1 illustrates a simple *S-R latch* circuit. Just as dependency notation reserves the letter R to designate a RESET input, so it reserves the letter S to designate a SET input. That is, when the S input is active (i.e., low), the latch is set. Furthermore, the ORing of multiple S or R inputs is symbolized as shown in Fig. 5-1*b*. Thus if either pin 2 is active (i.e., pulled low) or pin 3 is active, the top latch will be set. If pin 1 is active, the latch will be reset.

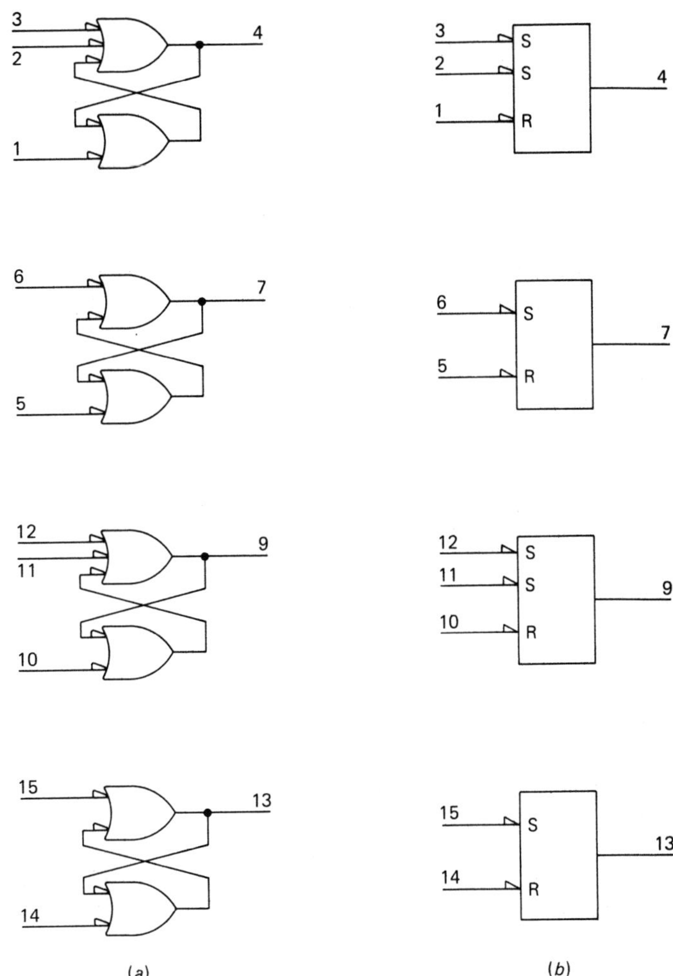

Figure 5-1. 74LS279, quad S-R latch. (a) Functional diagram, (b) symbol. (Texas Instruments.)

The operation of an S-R latch (or S-R clocked flip-flop) is left undefined by the dependency notation standard when both inputs are active at the same time. The *implementation* shown in Fig. 5-1*a* indicates that for *these* latch circuits, the output is actually not ambiguous. With all inputs active (i.e., low), the output is active (i.e., high). The standard also leaves undefined the state of the latch after the S and R inputs *simultaneously* become inactive. This is indeed an ambiguous state. As we design with S-R latches, we must ensure that this ambiguity-producing condition never occurs.

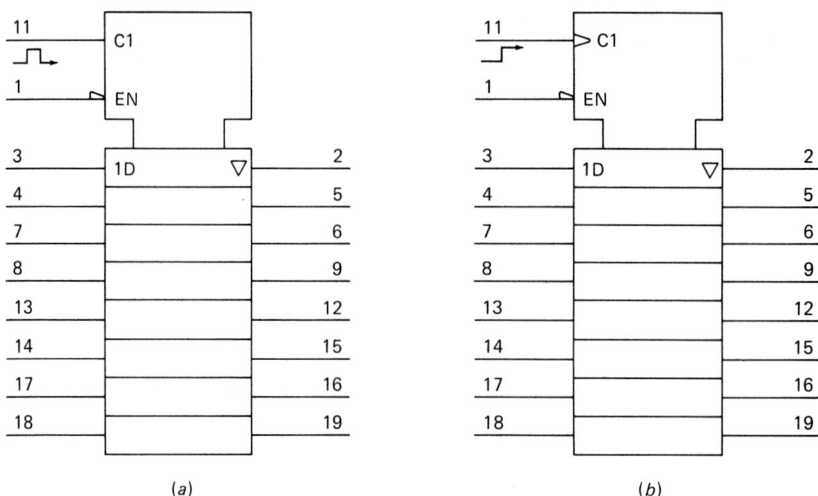

Figure 5-2. Octal D-type devices with three-state outputs. (a) 74LS373, transparent latches; (b) 74LS374, edge-triggered flip-flops. (Texas Instruments.)

A latch is the simplest form of a flip-flop. It is a flip-flop because its output can hold itself in either of two states, and its output can be changed by its inputs. However, the term *latch* signifies a flip-flop with *static* inputs. It is the *level* of the inputs that controls the state of a latch.

To illustrate the distinction between latches and clocked flip-flops, consider the two devices of Fig. 5-2. The D-type latches shown in Fig. 5-2*a* do not employ the dynamic indicator symbol (▷) on the C1 input. Consequently, they use C1 as a static input. As long as C1 is high, the output of each latch follows its input *transparently* (assuming the three-state outputs are enabled, with pin 1 being pulled low). That is, with pin 11 high and pin 1 low, pin 2 will be high as long as pin 3 is high, but it will go low when pin 3 goes low. Each latch remembers the state it is in at the moment that C1 goes low. The output will remain in this state until C1 goes high again, when outputs will again transparently follow inputs.

The D-type edge-triggered flip-flops shown in Fig. 5-2*b* respond to inputs *only* when a rising edge occurs on the C1 input, as symbolized by the presence of the dynamic indicator symbol (▷). This example illustrates the power of the dependency notation symbology. Identical features can be represented identically, while subtle distinctions show up as differences in the symbols. The symbology tells all,

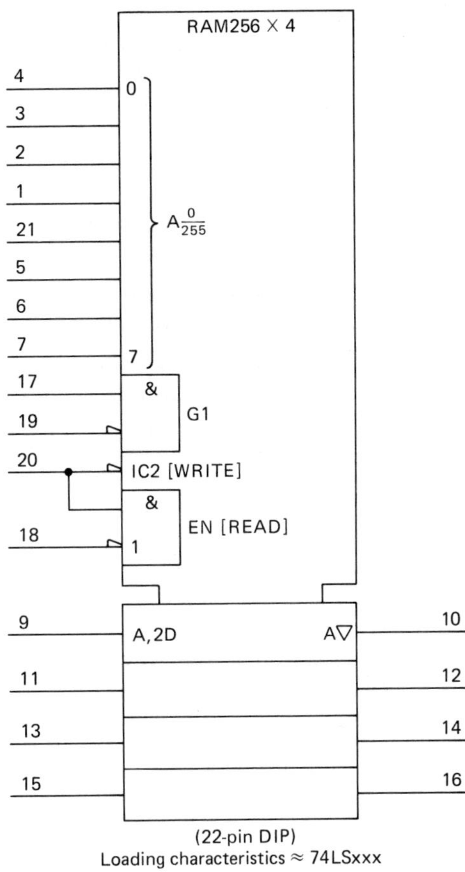

Figure 5-3. 93422, 256 × 4 bipolar RAM with three-state outputs. (a) Symbolic representation.

without our having to refer continually to a data book. But we do have to learn the language of the symbology to gain this advantage.

A *RAM*,† or read/write memory chip, looks like many latches plus an address decoder to help with accessing selected latches. For example, the bipolar RAM symbolized in Fig. 5-3*a* consists of 256 4-bit words. The dependency notation standard reserves the letter A for defining *ADDRESS-dependency*. The labeling of an input or output with the letter A selects the one address picked out by the associated binary grouping symbol and its labeling of $A\frac{0}{255}$. Thus to write 1100 into

† Random-*A*ccess Memory; we will consider only *static* RAMs. A static RAM requires no special provisions in order to retain data (other than power). In contrast, a *dynamic* RAM requires extra *refreshing* circuitry and signals.

Maximum read times:

Access time (address to output),	t_{AA}	= 60 ns
Chip-select time (pin 17 or 19 to output),	t_{ACS}	= 45 ns
Output-enable time (pin 18 to output),	t_{AOS}	= 45 ns

(*b*)

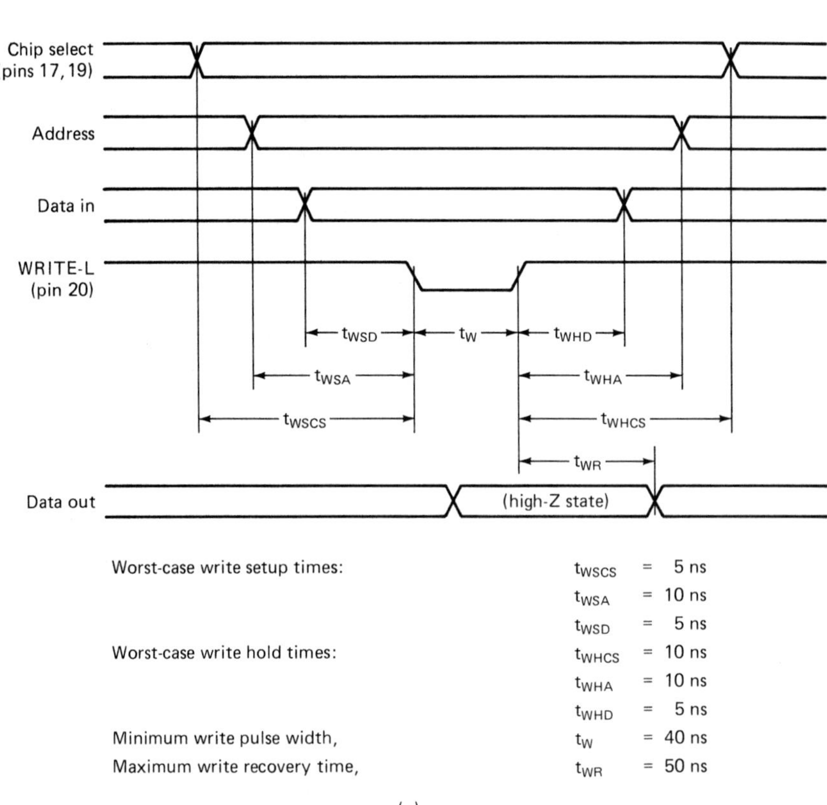

(*c*)

Figure 5-3. (b) Read timing. (c) Write timing. (Fairchild.)

address 3, we would set up the RAM as follows:

Pull pins	2, 1, 21, 5, 6, 7, 19, 9, 11	low
Raise pins	4, 3, 17, 13, 15	high

then drive pin 20 low momentarily (with a ‾‾|_|‾‾ pulse) to strobe the data into the selected address. When pin 20 goes low, the C2–2D dependency, the G1–1 dependency, the A3–A dependency, plus the ANDing implied by A, 2D, says to make the 4 bits of address 3 active or inactive so as to correspond to the 4 input bits on pins 9, 11, 13, and 15.

To *read* from a selected address, EN must be active. Thus pins 17 and 20 must be high while pins 19 and 18 must be low. Notice how pin 20 is represented as *two* inputs, to handle its two distinct roles of writing and inhibiting reading. Finally, notice that the dependency notation standard permits us to label anything (i.e., READ and WRITE) by putting the labels within brackets.

The timing considerations associated with *reading* from a RAM (or a latch) are identical with those associated with reading from a PROM, as discussed in conjunction with Fig. 2-49. For example, Fig. 5-3*b* lists the read timing for the RAM under consideration. Corresponding to the *three* specifications listed there, the octal latch of Fig. 5-2*a* would have just *one* specification, the output enable time (between pin 1 and the outputs). The latches of Fig. 5-1 list none of these read specifications since those latch outputs are always available for reading.

The *write* specifications for a RAM (or a latch) are more involved, as shown in Fig. 5-3*c*. These specifications can be categorized into four groups:

1. *Setup times.* Before the write pulse on pin 20 can be effective, the other inputs that affect writing must be active. The minimum time interval from when the other inputs become active until the *leading edge* of the write pulse occurs defines these setup times. For example, the write setup time for chip selection t_{WSCS} must be at least 5 ns. That is, as long as the chip-select inputs (pins 17 and 19) are enabled more than 5 ns before the write pulse on pin 20 begins, writing will not be delayed by the chip-select inputs.
2. *Pulse width time.* In order for reliable writing to take place (assuming that all other inputs are set up in time so as not to impede writing), the write pulse width t_W must not be less than 40 ns.
3. *Hold times.* For reliable writing to take place, the other inputs that affect writing must hold their levels *after* the trailing edge of the write pulse by the specified hold times. For example, if the address lines were to change in less than the 10 ns specified by t_{WHA} after the trailing edge of the write pulse, we *might* find that data had not been written into the proper address. A more serious threat arises in this case, however. With the address changing while writing is still taking place, *other latches* in the RAM may get "poked" and have *their* contents inadvertently changed.
4. *Recovery time.* Since this RAM disables the output during the

write pulse, the equivalent of a propagation delay between new data being written into the RAM and that data appearing on the output (assuming the output is otherwise enabled) is delayed until the output is no longer in the high-impedance state. The recovery time is a measure of this delay. For a different RAM which does not make output enabling dependent upon the write pulse, the *propagation delay* between the *leading* edge of the write pulse and the time when new data appears on the output would be the corresponding specification.

While these timing requirements may sound extensive, we will find that our handling of them will be reasonably straightforward. We will design circuitry in which RAM chip-select inputs, address, and data settle out during the first part of a clock period. Then, well after this settling out has occurred, if writing is to take place during this clock period, we will strobe the write line with a pulse (‾|_|‾) that begins and ends well within that clock period. Furthermore, we will ensure that none of the inputs to the RAM change until the beginning of the next clock period.

It is important to remember that (most) RAMs are latch-type devices. The latches will follow the inputs all the time writing takes place. Consequently, we cannot use a RAM (or a latch) in a synchronous circuit wherein its inputs are functions of its outputs. Rather, we will employ the multiple-phase clocking (to be discussed in Sec. 5-5) for dealing with RAMs and latches which must be both written into and read from.

Moving on from latch-type flip-flops to clocked flip-flops, we will now consider alternatives to D-type flip-flops. The *J-K* flip-flops of Fig. 5-4*a* illustrate the use of C1−1J and C1−1K CONTROL-dependencies to distinguish between clocked inputs on the one hand and static inputs (i.e., S and R) on the other. Thus the input labeled 1J only has an effect upon the flip-flop when a rising edge occurs on the C1 input. In contrast, whenever the S input is active (i.e., whenever pin 5 is pulled low) the flip-flop is set.

In addition to the reserved letters D, S, and R used to identify flip-flop inputs, the dependency notation standard also reserves the letters J and K. J and K inputs behave in a fashion which is identical to S (set) and R (reset) inputs except where J and K are active at the same time (the corresponding case of S and R inputs being undefined). Thus in Fig. 5-4*a*, if the 1J input is active (because pin 2 is high AND a rising edge is occurring on pin 4) while the other inputs are inactive, the flip-flop will be set. If the 1K input alone is active (with pin 3 pulled low and a rising edge occurring on pin 4), the flip-flop will be reset. If both 1J and 1K are active, the flip-flop will toggle. That is, its output will change state from a 0 to a 1 or from a 1 to a 0.

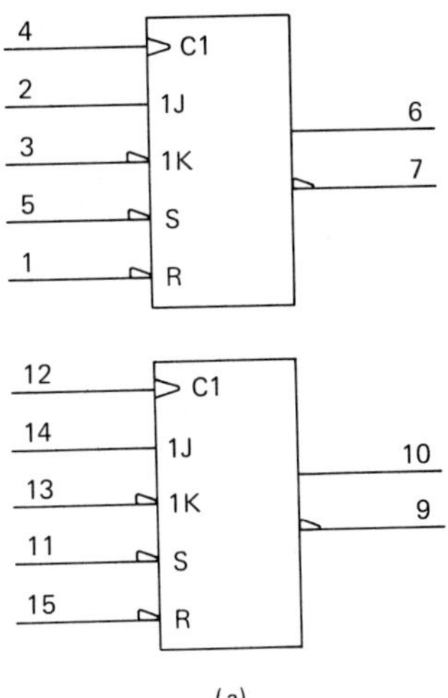

(a)

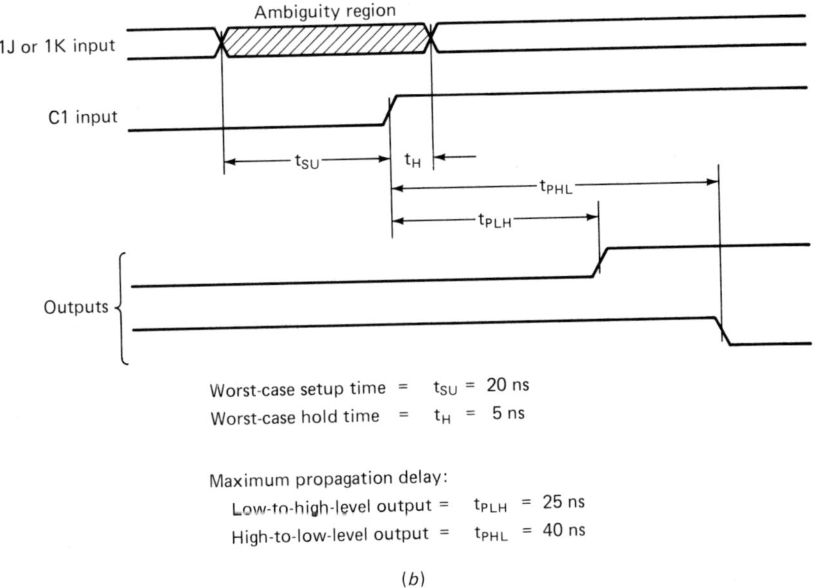

Worst-case setup time = t_{SU} = 20 ns
Worst-case hold time = t_H = 5 ns

Maximum propagation delay:
Low-to-high-level output = t_{PLH} = 25 ns
High-to-low-level output = t_{PHL} = 40 ns

(b)

Maximum propagation delay for S and R inputs:
Low-to-high-level output = 25 ns
High-to-low-level output = 40 ns

(c)

Figure 5-4. *74LS109A, dual J-K edge-triggered flip-flops.* (a) *Symbolic representation;* (b) *timing characteristics for clocked inputs;* (c) *timing characteristics for static inputs.* (*Texas Instruments.*)

The timing characteristics of the flip-flops we have been discussing are shown in Fig. 5-4*b* and *c*. The worst-case setup and hold times given in a data sheet define the two extremes of the *ambiguity region* shown in Fig. 5-4*b*. If we think of the rising edges of C1 as defining the beginning and the end of a clock period, proper operation requires that changes in the J and K inputs settle out, after the clocking that occurred at the beginning of the clock period, *before* this ambiguity region. This will allow the flip-flop time to *set up* to the new values before appropriate action is taken in response to the clock edge at the end of the clock period. The actual setup time of a specific flip-flop (at a specific temperature and power-supply voltage) will be less than this value. However, we can ensure reliable operation under all circumstances by making sure that all 74LS109A flip-flops have a minimum of 20 ns to set up.

We might expect that the worst-case setup time would be listed on a data sheet as a *maximum* setup time if we employ the reasoning above. On the other hand, if we think of the worst-case value as representing the minimum time required to ensure reliable setting up of these inputs under all circumstances, we might expect that the worst-case value would be listed as a *minimum* setup time. In actual fact, it is this latter viewpoint which is used on data sheets. However, no ambiguity arises since a data sheet will list only one extreme value (rather than a minimum value, a typical value, and a maximum value). Obviously, the one extreme value listed is the worst-case value.

The circuitry employed to implement clocked operation within counters has not always been synchronous. However, because of circuit *timing* simplifications which result when all flip-flops in a chip have their clock inputs tied together, and because of the ever-increasing ease of incorporating more logic circuitry in less space in an integrated circuit, the trend is to design new counters as synchronous counters.

The counter of Fig. 5-5 illustrates the *circuit* simplicity of an *asynchronous* binary counter. The clock input to each flip-flop comes from the output of the previous flip-flop. Such a counter is often referred to as a *ripple* counter because of the rippling of the outputs which takes place when the counter rolls over from all 1s to all 0s. Thus (with pin 9 tied to pin 11) pin 9 will first change from 1 to 0 one flip-flop propagation delay after a falling edge occurs on pin 10. One flip-flop propagation delay later, pin 5 will change from 1 to 0. One flip-flop propagation delay later pin 4 will change from 1 to 0. Finally, one more flip-flop propagation delay later, pin 8 will change from 1 to 0.

If we design a circuit that employs a ripple counter and if we employ gating to detect the clock period when the ripple counter is in the

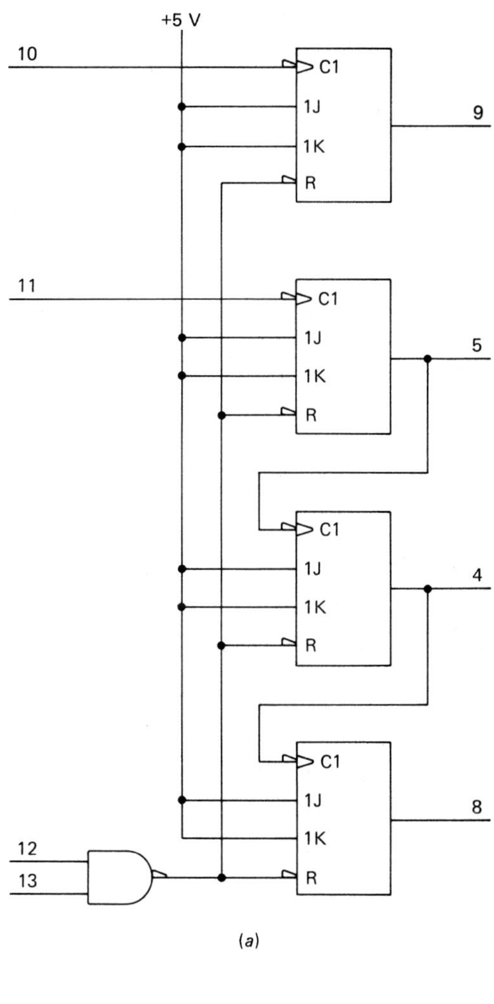

(a)

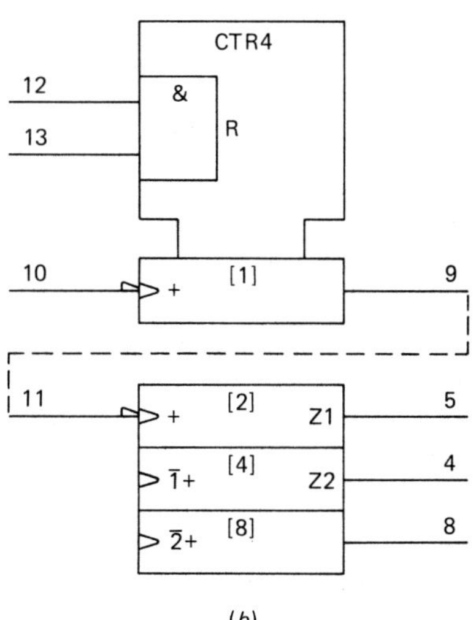

(b)

Figure 5-5. 74LS293, asynchronous 4-bit binary counter. (a) Functional diagram; (b) symbolic representation. (Texas Instruments.)

all-0s state, this rippling of the counter means we must clock the circuit at a slower clock rate than would be permitted if all bits of the counter changed at once. However, if all we want to do is *scale down* a high clock rate to a slower clock rate, the simplicity of an asynchronous counter also makes it fast in such an application. For example, if we have a 100-MHz input to count, a 74S197 asynchronous 4-bit binary counter is one of the few TTL devices available which can be clocked at that high rate. The output from its most slowly changing flip-flop will have a frequency of 100/16 = 6.67 MHz, which can then be used to *clock* other circuitry. It is irrelevant that this output typically changes 24 ns (i.e., about $2\frac{1}{2}$ of the 100-MHz clock periods) after the clock edge that started the ripple process.

The dependency notation symbol of Fig. 5-5*b* illustrates *INTERCONNECTION-dependency*. The letter Z is reserved for this purpose. It is used solely to represent an internal connection in a symbol. Thus a Z1−1 dependency relationship means that the input or output labeled Z1 is connected to the input or output labeled 1. In Fig. 5-5*b* the output on pin 5 is labeled Z1. The input to the next stage of the counter is internally connected, through an inverter, to Z1. This inverter is represented by $\overline{1}$ and serves to represent the same effect as the missing polarity indicator (▷) on the clock input.

Just as new, synchronous counters have largely supplanted older, asynchronous counters, so has *edge-triggered* clocking largely supplanted older clocking approaches. Looking back at the general synchronous sequential circuit of Fig. 2-74, we require that when the 74LS273 flip-flops are clocked, the changing outputs must not feed through the combinational circuitry and back around to the flip-flop inputs faster than the hold time of the flip-flops. Otherwise, we will get unreliable operation. This problem, when it occurs, is called a *race* condition.

An early solution to the race problem arose with the design of the *ones-catching master-slave* flip-flop. The circuit of Fig. 5-6 illustrates this approach. Notice that it consists of two latches plus interconnecting gating. When C1 is high (so that C1−H is high and C1−L is low), the slave latch is connected to the master latch so that their states will be the same. Also at this time the master latch is disconnected from the 1J and 1K inputs. That is, with C1−L low, the input gate outputs will be forced high, in which state they cannot affect the state of the master latch.

When C1 is low, the slave latch is disconnected from the master latch, and the 1J and 1K inputs drive the master latch. Furthermore, because of the two lines feeding back from the outputs of the slave latch to the master input gating, the 1J input can only affect the master latch if the slave latch is *reset*. Likewise, the 1K input has no effect unless

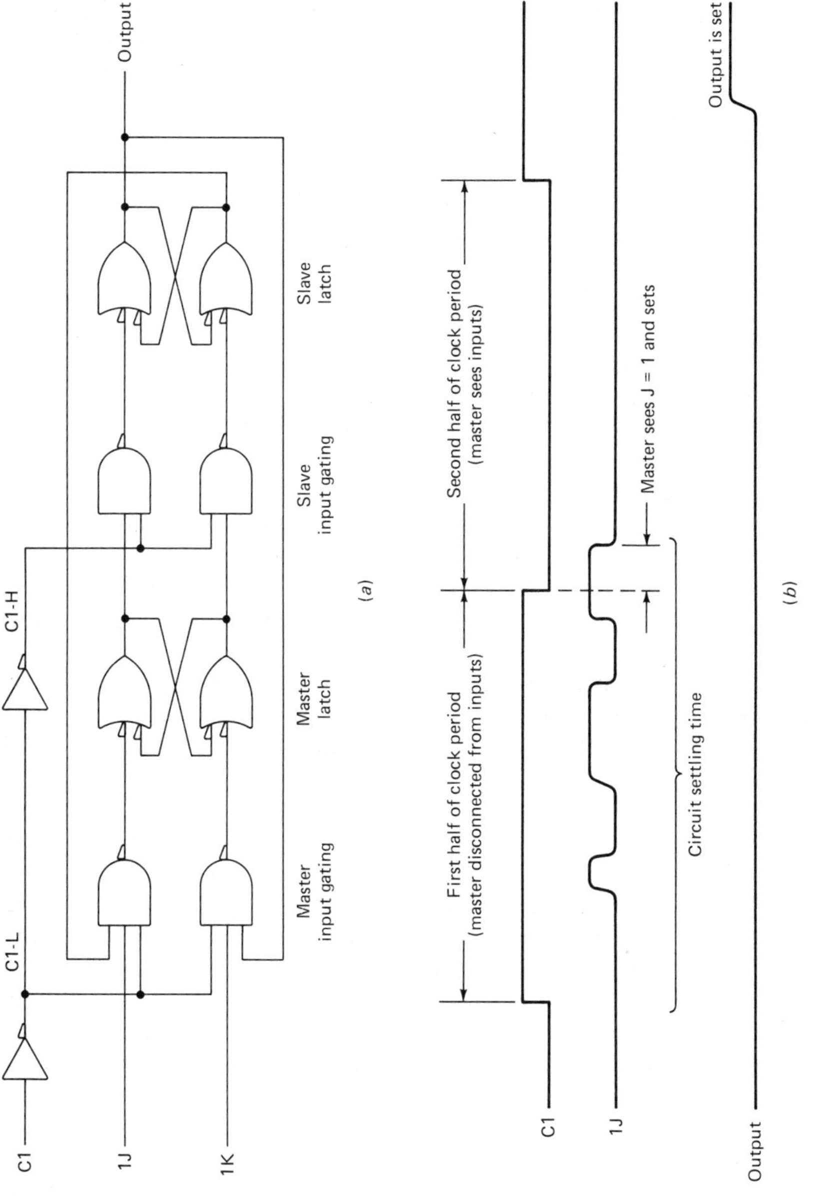

Figure 5-6. *Ones-catching master-slave flip-flop.* (*a*) *Circuit;* (*b*) *the ones-catching problem.*

the slave latch is *set*. If the flip-flop is supposed to be set by the 1J input but it is already set, it does not really matter that the 1J input cannot affect the master latch. If *both* inputs are high, the master latch will change state (i.e., toggle).

Notice that the output of this flip-flop, when it changes, will change as the C1 input changes from low to high. By disabling the inputs at that moment, the flip-flop solves the race problem. Therefore, it can be used in a synchronous circuit employing positive-edge-triggered flip-flops, counters, and shift registers simply by tying its clock input to their clock inputs. However, as is illustrated in Fig. 5-6*b*, the flip-flop inputs must settle out while C1 is high. With a square-wave clock, this means that the inputs must settle out during the first half of the clock period. Otherwise, if the flip-flop is cleared, the 1J input can "poke" the master latch and set it. Once it is set, it will remain set for the rest of the clock period. At the end of the clock period as C1 goes high again, the slave will be set. In comparison, a *positive-edge-triggered* flip-flop ignores the perturbations of the 1J input, looking at its state just nanoseconds before the rising edge of the clock occurs. In the case depicted in Fig. 5-6*b*, we see that a ones-catching master-slave flip-flop and an edge-triggered flip-flop give very different operation.

In effect, the ones-catching master-slave flip-flop of Fig. 5-6 has a setup time equal to the length of time during which C1 is low. For a square-wave clock, this setup time is equal to one-half of the clock period.

From this examination of a ones-catching master-slave flip-flop, we see that it solves the race problem but does so at the expense of poor handling of setup time. One structure for an edge-triggered master-slave flip-flop is shown in Fig. 5-7. It replaces the S-R latches of Fig. 5-6 with transparent D-type latches. Now the master latch will transparently follow the 1D input all the time C1 is low. As long as the 1D input settles out to a stable value some short time before the end of the clock period (when C1 will make a low-to-high transition), proper operation will ensue. When C1 goes high, this settled output of the master latch is transferred to the slave and appears on the flip-flop output.

This example illustrates that it is not the master-slave structure itself which gives rise to a poor setup-time characteristic, but rather the ones-catching feature which was (probably inadvertently) built into that master-slave structure. Furthermore, it is not the use of J-K input gating, rather than D-type input gating, which gives rise to the problem. The positive-edge-triggered J-K flip-flop of Fig. 5-8 appropriately combines 1J and 1K inputs with the flip-flop output to form a 1D

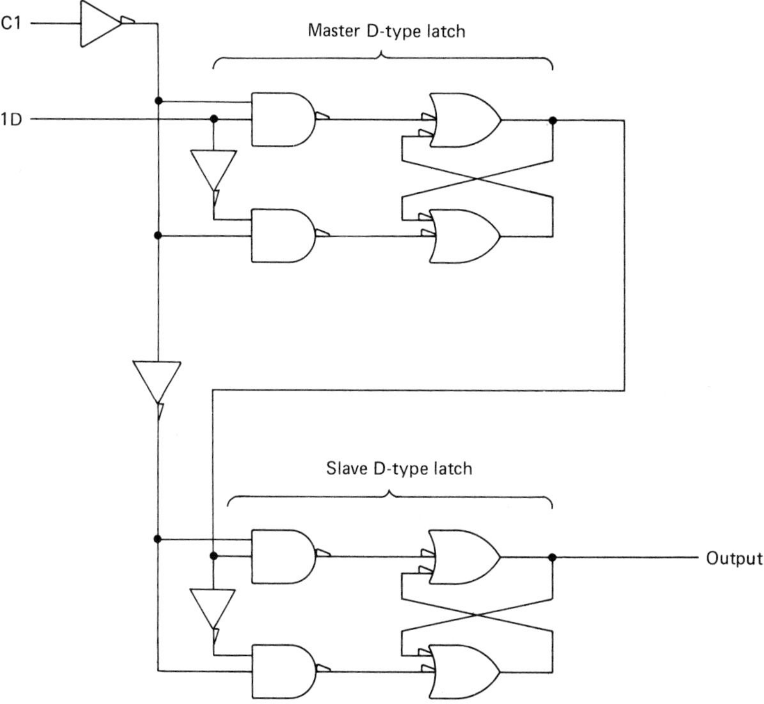

Figure 5-7. Positive-edge-triggered master-slave D-type flip-flop.

input to the remaining structure (which is essentially identical to Fig. 5-7). That is:

1 1D is identical to the flip-flop output as long as 1J and 1K are low.
2 If 1J is high, 1D will go high if the flip-flop output is low.
3 If 1K is high, 1D will go low if the flip-flop output is high.

Consequently, 1J and 1K can still be settling out until just before the end of the clock period and the master latch will transparently follow along, ending up in the correct state. When C1 goes high, this correct state is transferred from master to slave, appearing on the output.

ICs employing the antiquated ones-catching master-slave structure are being replaced by new edge-triggered designs. For example, the 74LS161A 4-bit binary counter of Fig. 2-82 is an edge-triggered ver-

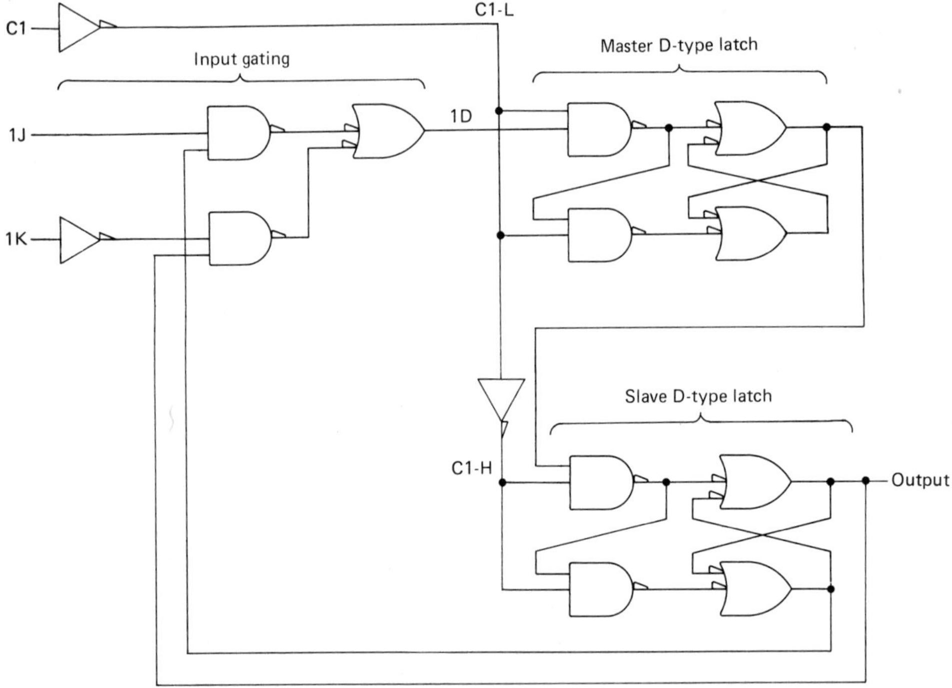

Figure 5-8. Positive-edge-triggered master-slave J-K flip-flop.

sion of a part which was originally designed using ones-catching master-slave clocking, first as a Fairchild 9316 (with poor loading characteristics) and then as a Texas Instruments 74161.

5-2 MAXIMUM CLOCK RATE: SYNCHRONOUS DESIGN

Synchronous design imposes constraints upon our design procedures in order to achieve timing simplicity. Updating the listing of constraints introduced in Sec. 2-13, we require that:

1. All sequential devices (e.g., flip-flops, counters, shift registers) must have outputs that change in response to the same clock edge (e.g., *positive*-edge-triggered devices).
2. All clock inputs must be tied together and to a clock source.

3 Static inputs to all sequential devices (e.g., unclocked reset inputs) must be disabled.

4 No unclocked sequential devices (e.g., latches, RAMs) may be used.

5 Circuit inputs must be synchronized to the clock.

The circuit of Fig. 5-9 meets these constraints by employing only one kind of edge-triggered flip-flop, by disabling its S and R static inputs, by tying all the flip-flop clock inputs together and to a clock source, and by synchronizing inputs. Notice that any of these flip-

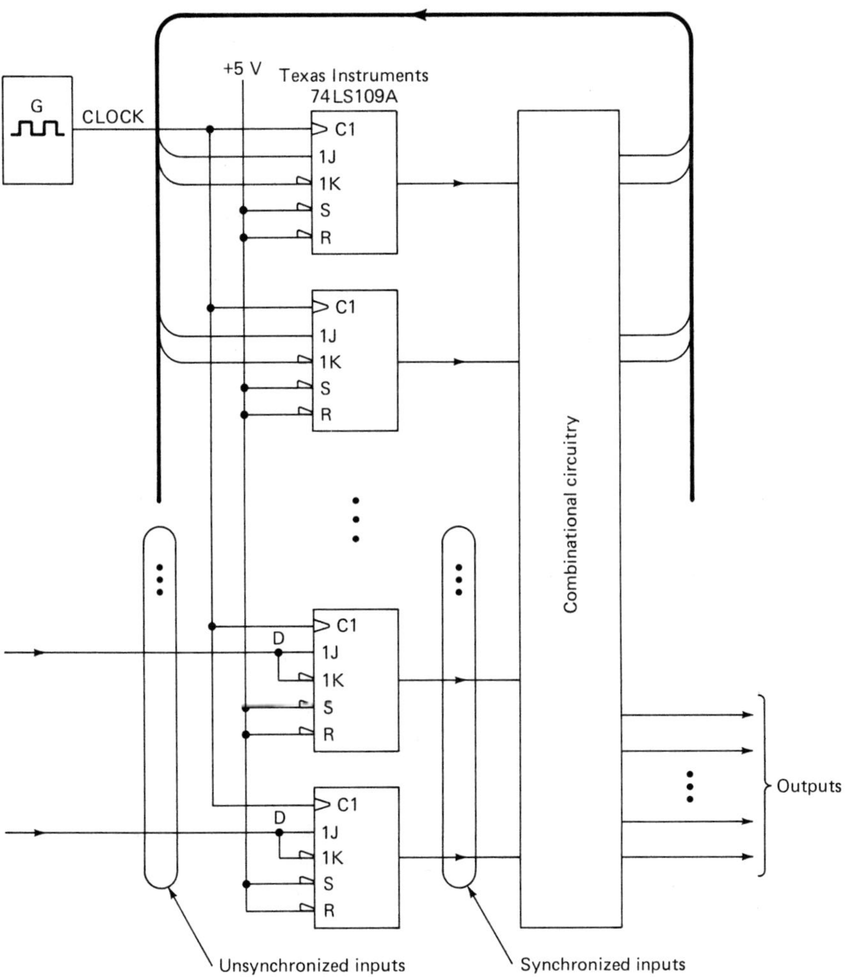

Figure 5-9. Synchronous sequential circuit built with 74LS109A dual J-K flip-flops.

Device	From pin	to pin	Maximum propagation delay (ns)			
			t_{PLH} (low-to-high level output change)		t_{PHL} (high-to-low level output change)	
74LS04			15		15	
74LS251	9, 10, 11	5	45		45	
	4, 3, etc.	5	28		28	
			Maximum three-state enable and disable time (ns)			
			t_{ZH} (high Z to high)	t_{ZL} (high Z to low)	t_{HZ} (high to high Z)	t_{LZ} (low to high Z)
	7	5	45	40	45	25

Figure 5-10. Propagation delays for the 74LS04 inverter and the 74LS251 multiplexer.

flops can be converted to a D-type flip-flop by tying its active-high 1J input to its active-low 1K input.

The maximum clock rate of this circuit is affected by the timing characteristics of the flip-flops and by the *worst-case* propagation delay through the combinational circuitry. In general, our job is to work our way through the gates, decoders, multiplexers, and so on, making up this combinational circuitry and to determine that combination of inputs which, together with *one* changing input, will yield the most slow-to-change output of the combinational circuitry. It is this worst-case propagation delay with which we must be concerned.

Example 5-1. Determine the worst-case propagation delay to the active-high output of the expanded multiplexer circuit of Fig. 2-42.

To handle this problem, we need to know the maximum propagation delays and the three-state enable and disable times of the devices involved. These are listed in Fig. 5-10. The worst-case *path* will be through the inverter, to the lower multiplexer, and on to the output, since this will sum the inverter's propagation delay of 15 ns and the multiplexer's t_{ZH} time of 45 ns to give a worst-case propagation delay of 60 ns. A combination of inputs leading to this result is shown in Fig. 5-11, together with a timing diagram.

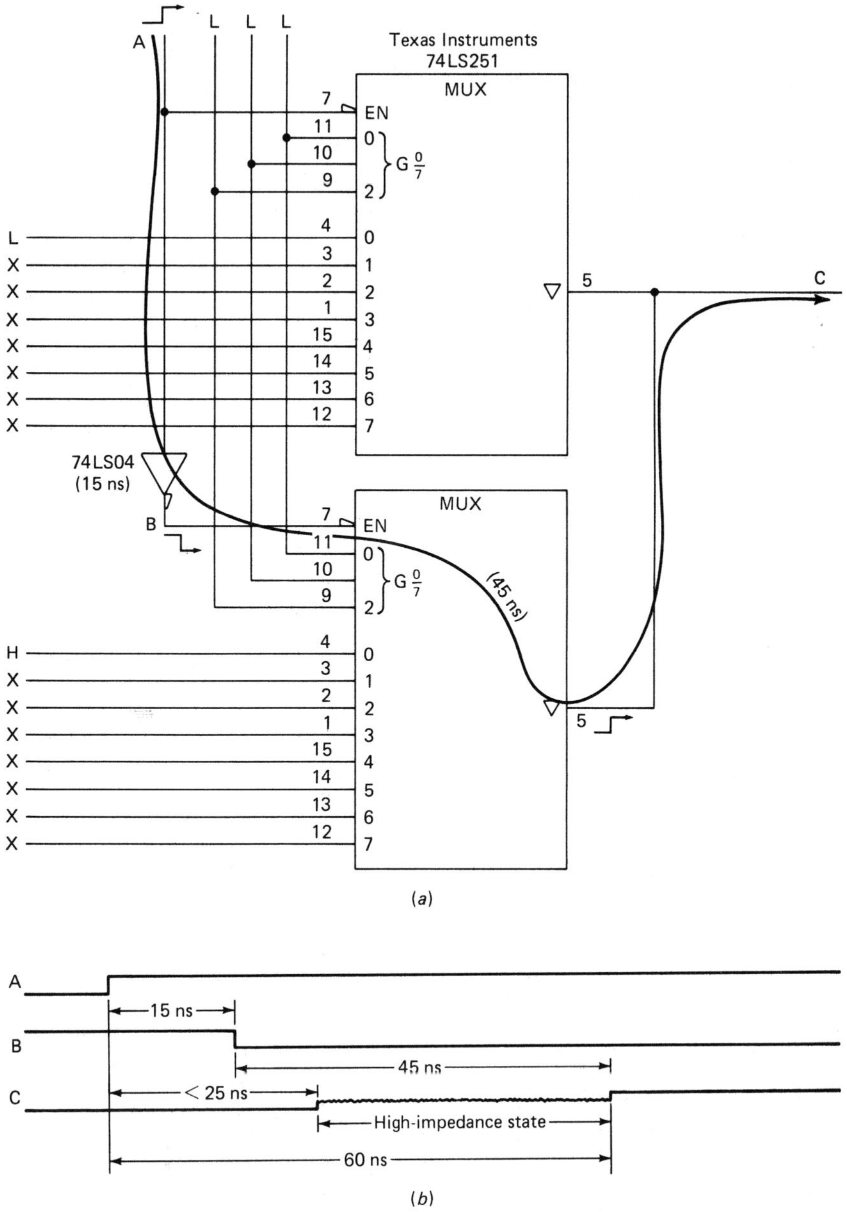

Texas Instruments
74LS251

(a)

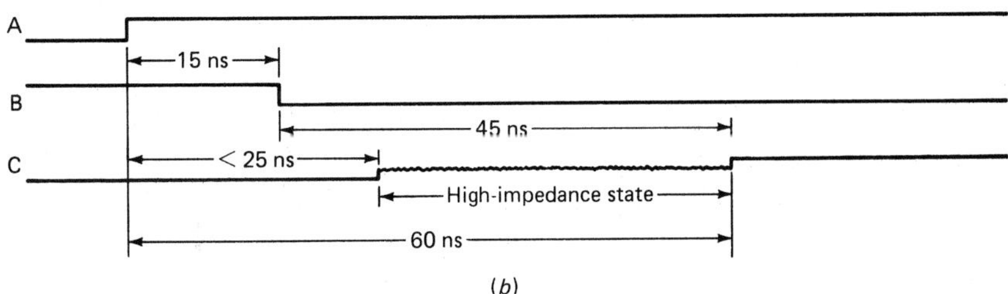

(b)

Figure 5-11. Worst-case propagation delay of circuit of Fig. 2-42. (a) *Worst-case path;* (b) *timing diagram.*

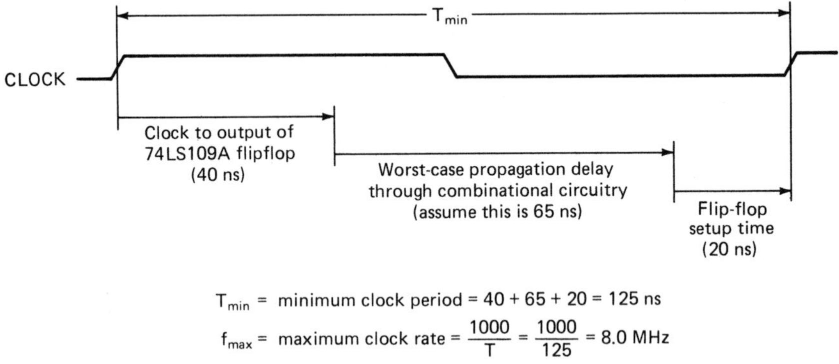

$$T_{min} = \text{minimum clock period} = 40 + 65 + 20 = 125 \text{ ns}$$

$$f_{max} = \text{maximum clock rate} = \frac{1000}{T} = \frac{1000}{125} = 8.0 \text{ MHz}$$

Figure 5-12. Maximum-clock-rate determination for the circuit of Fig. 5-9.

Once we have determined the worst-case propagation delay of the combinational circuitry of Fig. 5-9, we can proceed directly to determine its maximum clock rate. To be concrete, assume that this worst-case propagation delay is 65 ns. Then, as shown in Fig. 5-12, each clock period must allow sufficient time for the following three events to take place:

1 Flip-flop outputs must settle out to their new states in response to being clocked.
2 With these new states as inputs, the combinational circuitry outputs must settle out to their new values.
3 Finally, enough time must remain, before the flip-flops are clocked again, to allow the flip-flops to *set up* to these new outputs of the combinational circuitry.

Notice that in picking the $t_{PHL} = 40$ ns flip-flop propagation delay (rather than $t_{PLH} = 25$ ns), we have assumed that a *high-to-low* flip-flop output change will produce the worst-case propagation delay in the combinational circuitry. If this is so, the resulting 8.0-MHz clock rate obtained represents the maximum reliable clock rate for this circuit. If it is not so, the 8.0-MHz clock rate represents a *conservative maximum* reliable clock rate. That is, the circuit will certainly operate reliably up to 8.0 MHz. We know that it will operate reliably to a higher clock rate but we have not taken the trouble to determine that rate.

Example 5-2. Redetermine the maximum clock rate of the circuit of Fig. 5-9 if, for the combinational circuitry as a whole

t_{PILH} = 65 ns, maximum, with one input changing from low to high

t_{PIHL} = 55 ns, maximum, with one input changing from high to low

With this more complete data, we can now make *two* clock period computations and then pick the longer of the two as the worst-case value. For the case of a low-to-high flip-flop output:

$$\begin{aligned} T_{\min} &= t_{PLH(\text{flip-flop})} + t_{PILH(\text{combinational})} + t_{SU(\text{flip-flop})} \\ &= 25 + 65 + 20 \\ &= 110 \text{ ns} \end{aligned}$$

For the case of a high-to-low flip-flop output:

$$\begin{aligned} T_{\min} &= t_{PHL(\text{flip-flop})} + t_{PIHL(\text{combinational})} + t_{SU(\text{flip-flop})} \\ &= 40 + 55 + 20 \\ &= 115 \text{ ns} \end{aligned}$$

Consequently, the maximum reliable clock rate is determined to be

$$f_{\max} = \frac{1000}{T_{\text{slowest}}} = \frac{1000}{115} = 8.7 \text{ MHz}$$

From the preceding example, we see that the determination of the maximum reliable clock rate for a synchronous design can become complicated for a circuit that employs a *variety* of flip-flops, counters, and shift registers. Each such device may exhibit several propagation delays, depending upon which output is considered and whether the output change is high-to-low or low-to-high. Furthermore, each sequential device may exhibit several setup times, depending upon which input we are considering. Because of this potential for complexity, it is common to partition the calculation of maximum clock rate into three parts, as shown in Fig. 5-13, leading to a conservative (i.e., safe) result. Using the parameters defined in Fig. 5-13, we have

$$T_{\min} = t_{P(\text{sequential})} + t_{P(\text{combinational})} + t_{SU(\text{sequential})} \quad \text{ns}$$

and $$f_{\max} = \frac{1000}{T_{\min}} \quad \text{MHz}$$

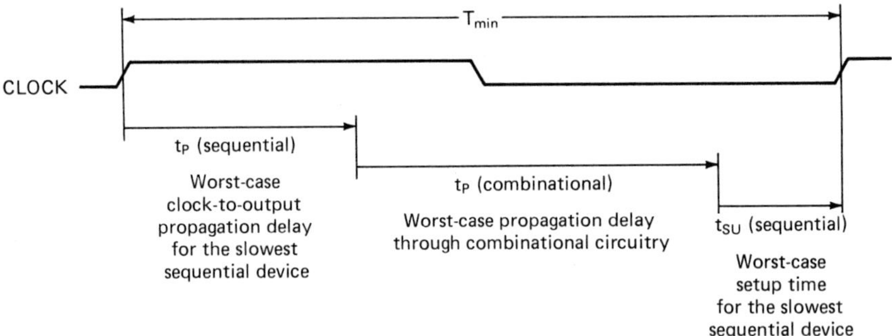

Figure 5-13. Maximum-clock-rate determination for any synchronous circuit.

Example 5-3. Determine the maximum clock rate of a synchronous circuit built with the combinational circuitry just discussed plus 74LS109A dual J-K flip-flops and 74LS273 octal D-type flip-flops (of Fig. 2-73).

For the 74LS273, t_P = 27 ns and t_{SU} = 20 ns. Consequently,

$$t_{P(\text{sequential})} = 40 \text{ ns} \qquad (\text{worst case is 74LS109A } t_{PHL} \text{ time})$$

$$t_{P(\text{combinational})} = 65 \text{ ns}$$

$$t_{SU(\text{sequential})} = 20 \text{ ns}$$

$$T_{\min} = 40 + 65 + 20 = 125 \text{ ns}$$

$$f_{\max} = 8.0 \text{ MHz}$$

Note that this result has not changed from the earlier result. This is a consequence of the 74LS273 flip-flops being no slower that the 74LS109A flip-flops.

Example 5-4. Determine the maximum clock rate of a synchronous circuit built with the same combinational circuitry and 74LS273 octal D-type flip-flops considered in Example 5-3 as well as 74161 binary counters (whose 'LS equivalent is shown in Fig. 2-83). Assume that the carry outputs (pin 15) of the counters are not used. Also assume a square-wave clock waveform.

Whether or not the carry outputs of the counters are used becomes important because of the *combinational* path through the chip from pin 10 to pin 15. In this case we can ignore this path.

The 74161 is designed with ones-catching master-slave flip-flops. Consequently, its setup time is the time during which the clock input is low. With a square-wave clock waveform, its setup time becomes $T_{\min}/2$. In addition, for these counters, t_P = 35 ns. Consequently.

$$t_{P(\text{sequential})} = 35 \text{ ns}$$

$$t_{P(\text{combinational})} = 65 \text{ ns}$$

$$t_{SU(\text{sequential})} = \frac{T_{\min}}{2}$$

$$T_{\min} = 35 + 65 + \frac{T_{\min}}{2}$$

or

$$T_{\min} = 200 \text{ ns}$$

$$f_{\max} = 5.0 \text{ MHz}$$

From Example 5-4 we can see the impact of the inclusion in a design of even a single ones-catching master-slave flip-flop. It slows the maximum clock rate down, even if its other timing characteristics are fast, *if a square-wave clock waveform is being used.* We can help matters by optimizing the clock waveform.

Example 5-5. Determine the optimum waveform, and the resulting maximum clock rate, for Example 5-4.

The data sheet for the 74161 lists a minimum clock pulse width (‾|_|‾) of 25 ns. The 74LS273 lists a minimum value of 20 ns. So, the optimum clock pulse width is 25 ns. The resulting minimum clock period is

$$T_{\min} = 35 + 65 + 25 = 125 \text{ ns}$$

and

$$f_{\max} = \tfrac{1000}{125} = 8 \text{ MHz}$$

The required clock waveform is shown in Fig. 5-14*a*. A circuit to generate it is shown in Fig. 5-14*b*. This circuit employs a fast, asynchronous, *decade* counter. The output on pin 12 is low in states 0, 1, 2, and 3 and is high in state 4. By inverting this, we get the desired waveform. The 40-MHz crystal clock gives the required input frequency, providing easy

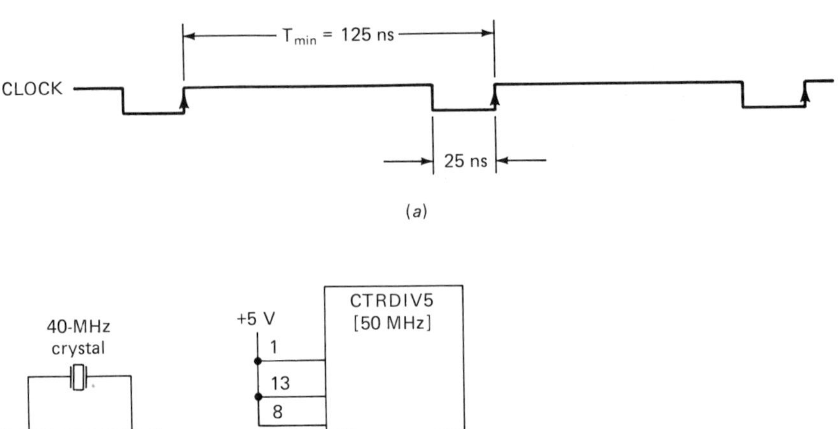

Figure 5-14. Clock for Example 5-5. (a) Clock waveform required; (b) circuit to generate it.

control of both the frequency tolerance and the clock pulse width tolerance. In contrast, an RC-controlled clock would have to run at a lower frequency, or be trimmed with a potentiometer, so that its frequency tolerance would never yield a frequency above 40 MHz.

Example 5-5 illustrates how we can overcome the shortcomings of ones-catching master-slave devices with the help of carefully designed clock circuitry. A better solution is to take advantage of the modern edge-triggered devices and avoid the older ones-catching devices entirely.

Recognizing this problem, we need to be able to *identify* flip-flops and counters which are ones-catching. This is a little tricky. No vendor promotes a part as being ones-catching, except indirectly. We must scan the data sheet description of a counter for words such as "Low-to-high transitions at the load input of the '160 through '163 should be avoided when the clock is low. . . ." Another clue arises in the specifications of setup time and hold time. A setup time listed as

0 ↓ and a hold time listed as 0 ↑ uses the arrow to indicate the clock edge used as a reference. These specs imply a flip-flop or counter whose output changes on the rising edge of the clock and whose inputs can change immediately after this (0 ↑ hold time). However, the inputs must settle out before the clock goes low again (0 ↓ setup time).

We will conclude this section with a rule of thumb generally accepted by designers of high-speed digital circuits:

> *A synchronous design that requires clocking at X MHz needs to employ sequential devices with specified maximum clock frequency of at least 3X MHz.*

Example 5-6. What are the implications of this rule of thumb for the circuitry of Fig. 5-9 employing 74LS109A J-K flip-flops as the sole sequential device?

The 74LS109A data sheet lists a maximum clock frequency of 25 MHz. If the circuit of Fig. 5-9 is clocked at $\frac{25}{3}$ = 8.33 MHz, each clock period will last 120 ns. Subtracting out the flip-flop's worst-case propagation delay of 40 ns and its worst-case setup time of 20 ns leaves *60 ns* as the worst-case permissible propagation delay through the combinational circuitry of Fig. 5-9. If this were implemented with 74LSxxx gates having a worst-case propagation delay of 15 ns, no signal could pass through more than *four* gates between combinational circuit inputs and outputs. Obviously, this three-to-one rule of thumb does not allow much flexibility in the design of the combinational circuitry.

5-3 AVOIDING RACE CONDITIONS

In Sec. 5-1 we defined a race condition. When a synchronous circuit is clocked, we must ensure that each sequential device determines its next state on the basis of inputs as they existed during the previous clock period. If any device sees a changing input, and responds to the changed value, we will have faulty operation. As long as all the sequential devices in a circuit have zero (or negative) hold times, we can be assured that race conditions will not occur (in a synchronous circuit). Even with nonzero hold times, the circuit will operate reliably provided that the *shortest* propagation delay (from clock to output) of the sequential ICs is longer than the *longest* hold time of any of these same ICs.

In the circuit of Fig. 5-9, we are assured of reliable operation if the flip-flop propagation delays are all longer than the worst-case flip-flop hold time of 5 ns. Any propagation delay through the combinational circuitry helps to alleviate potential race conditions. Consequently, the worst-case circuit is one in which an output of one flip-flop is connected to an input of another (as for a shift register).

Evidently, designers have not pressed IC manufacturers hard to specify the *minimum* propagation delay through a device, since this specification is rarely listed on a data sheet. We can surmise that the minimum propagation delay of a 74LS109A must be greater than the 5-ns worst-case hold time. If it were otherwise, some designers' circuits would be malfunctioning because of race conditions. Beyond this we are left to guess how to extrapolate from a maximum t_{PLH} propagation delay of 25 ns and a "typical" t_{PLH} propagation delay of 13 ns to a minimum value (25:13:7??).

One partial resolution to this problem which manufacturers appear to be approaching is to design new sequential ICs with zero hold times. For example, the 74LS161A binary counter of Fig. 2-83 has evolved, as discussed previously, through three generations of design from the original Fairchild 9316 ones-catching part. This generation's part features zero hold time (as well as edge triggering).

This issue would appear to be a required source of compatibility among all parts within a logic family. Thus we would not expect race conditions to arise within a circuit consisting solely of 74LSxxx parts. However, if we design a circuit mixing 74Sxxx parts with 74LSxxx parts, we must be wary of the interconnection shown in Fig. 5-15. For example, the data sheet for a 74S174 hex D-type flip-flop lists

$$t_{PLH} = \begin{cases} 12 \text{ ns maximum} \\ 8 \text{ ns typical} \end{cases}$$

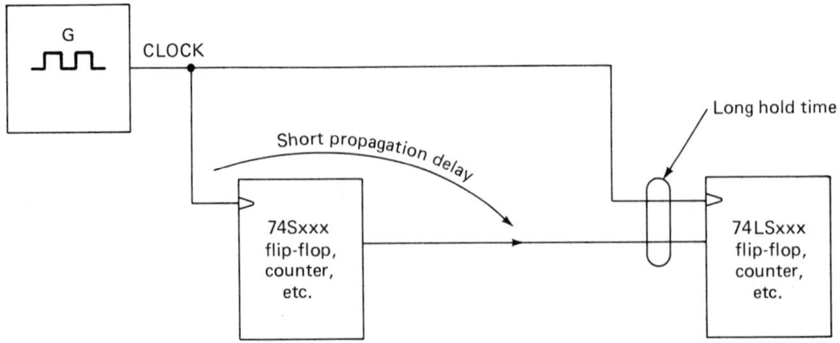

Figure 5-15. Potential source of a race condition.

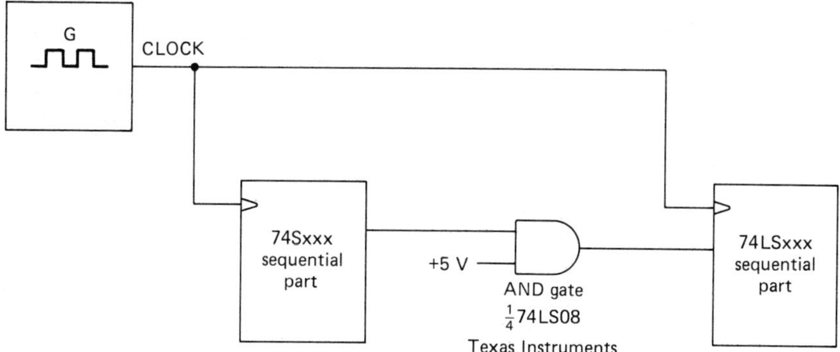

Figure 5-16. Alleviation of the potential race condition of Fig. 5-15.

If an actual, fast 74S174 exhibited $t_{PLH} = 4$ ns and a slow 74LS109A exhibited an actual hold time of 5 ns, their interconnection as in Fig. 5-15 would malfunction due to this race condition.

The solution to this potential problem has two parts:

1 The most difficult part is to remember to look for outputs of 74Sxxx sequential devices which go directly to inputs of 74LSxxx sequential devices *without any intervening logic.*
2 Interpose a gate between the two to increase the propagation delay between the clock input to the 74Sxxx part and the input to the 74LSxxx part. This is illustrated in Fig. 5-16.

5-4 BUFFERING OF SYNCHRONIZED DATA

When successive parallel words of data are transferred between instruments or devices, *synchronization* between the devices becomes a key issue. In Chap. 6 we will deal with this as a problem of communication between two separately clocked circuits. In this section we will consider a special case that satisfies the following timing constraints:

1 The data to be transmitted is synchronized to a clock signal.
2 The transmitted data is a continuous sequence of words, one word every clock period.
3 In addition to the data, the sending device transmits the clock (to which the data is synchronized).

The logic state analyzers of Figs. 1-16 and 3-3 and the signature

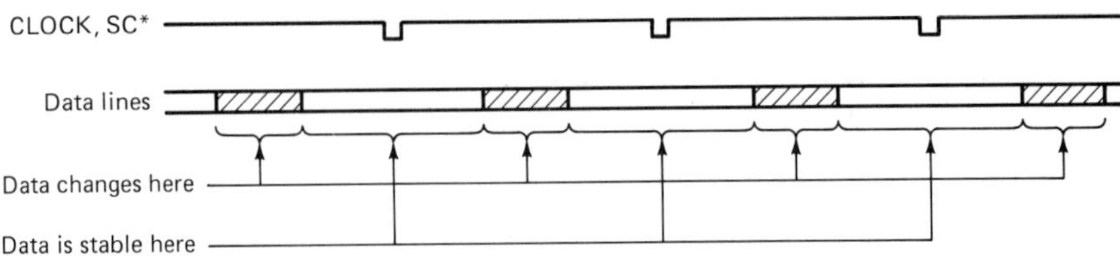

Figure 5-17. Easy-to-handle case of strobed data.

analyzer of Fig. 3-1 exemplify devices which are designed to *receive* such data reliably. The transferred word width of a logic state analyzer depends upon what functions of a device under test a user wishes to examine. For example, the unit of Fig. 1-16 can collect between 1 and 16 bits of data during each clocking whereas the unit of Fig. 3-3 can collect between 1 and 32 bits. In contrast, the signature analyzer employs a word width of 3 bits as it looks at the START*, STOP*, and PROBE* inputs of Fig. 4-2.

The timing relationship between the transmitted data and its clock becomes of paramount importance if we are designing an instrument to receive such data. Sometimes we are in the easy-to-handle position of having *strobed data* which is stable from well before to well after the clock "strobe" pulse, as shown in Fig. 5-17. If this data is to be stored for subsequent manipulation, the receiving instrument can buffer the data inputs (to alleviate any loading problems and to protect inputs against accidently received high voltages) and gate the clock (to start and stop the storage of data) without much difficulty with timing. For example, the received words can be collected using several of the RAM chips of Fig. 5-18 to form a word width which is an arbitrary multiple of the 9-bit word width of the RAM chip.

By driving the address lines with a binary counter, as shown in Fig. 5-19, each successive data word will be written into RAM. The trailing edge of the write pulse will clock the counter to set up for the next address to which data will be written. This scheme will replace the oldest word collected (64 clock periods previously) with a new word. Hence when the clocking is stopped (with the SC/$\overline{\text{TC}}$ input to the multiplexer), the 64 most recently acquired words will be stored in the RAM. Furthermore, the counter will point to the oldest word in the RAM. After the external clock is replaced by the internal clock (TC of Fig. 3-42), no further writing is done into the RAM. The microcomputer can read the successive words out of RAM and manipulate them appropriately. Alternatively, the data can be left in the RAM and accessed as needed. In the latter case, the microcomputer may want to know the *address* of the oldest word. To do this it can read the six counter output lines. Or, it can determine this address indirectly by

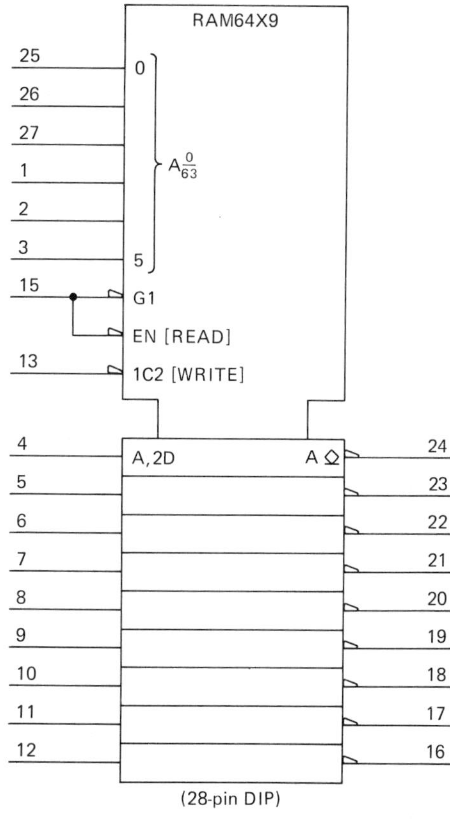

Figure 5-18. 82S09, 64 × 9 bipolar RAM with open-collector outputs. (a) Symbolic representation.

looking at the *one* line labeled 255-H and counting the number of times it must clock the counter until 255-H goes high.

The propagation delay of the multiplexer of Fig. 5-19 is not particularly significant, given the input timing of Fig. 5-17. We do care that the writing into the RAM is completed before the address is changed.

Example 5-7. What is the maximum permissible *difference* in the (low-to-high output) propagation delays between the SC* input to the 74LS158 multiplexer and the outputs, in order for writing into the RAM to occur properly?

The address hold time of the RAM is 5 ns. The clock-to-output propagation delay of the 74LS161A is typically 13 ns. No minimum value is specified. However, *if* a realistic minimum value were 7 ns, we

Input current	$\leqslant$ 0.10 mA at 0.45 V $\leqslant$ 25 μA at 5.5 V
Output current	$\geqslant$ 6.4 mA at 0.5 V (open-collector output)
Power-supply current	$\leqslant$ 190 mA

(*b*)

Access time (address to output), $t_{AA} \leqslant 45$ ns
Chip-select time (pin 15 to output), $t_{ACS} \leqslant 30$ ns

(*c*)

Worst-case write setup times:
- Chip select, t_{WSCS} = 5 ns
- Address, t_{WSA} = 5 ns
- Data, t_{WSD} = 35 ns

Worst-case write hold times:
- Chip select, t_{WHCS} = 5 ns
- Address, t_{WSA} = 5 ns
- Data, t_{WHD} = 5 ns

Minimum write pulse width, t_W = 35 ns
Maximum write propagation delay (pin 13 to output), t_{WD} = 50 ns

(*d*)

Figure 5-18. (b) *Loading characteristics;* (c) *read timing;* (d) *write timing (refer to Fig. 5-3c for timing diagram).* (*Signetics Corp.*)

could be in trouble if the multiplexer output to the counter were more than $7 - 5 = 2$ ns faster than the output to the RAM. In light of this uncertainty, we could hedge, using the approach of Fig. 5-16 to delay counting.

The SC/$\overline{\text{TC}}$ signal which switches the multiplexer is shown in Fig. 5-19 synchronized by SC. This will prevent SC/$\overline{\text{TC}}$ from changing during the middle of an SC* pulse, which could garble the last data word collected. The SC/$\overline{\text{TC}}$ signal was shown being controlled by a microcomputer in Fig. 3-36, where the switching was undertaken to support testing. In the present context, we probably want to switch SC/$\overline{\text{TC}}$ in response to some condition of the received data. For example, a logic state analyzer may be set up to stop collecting data when

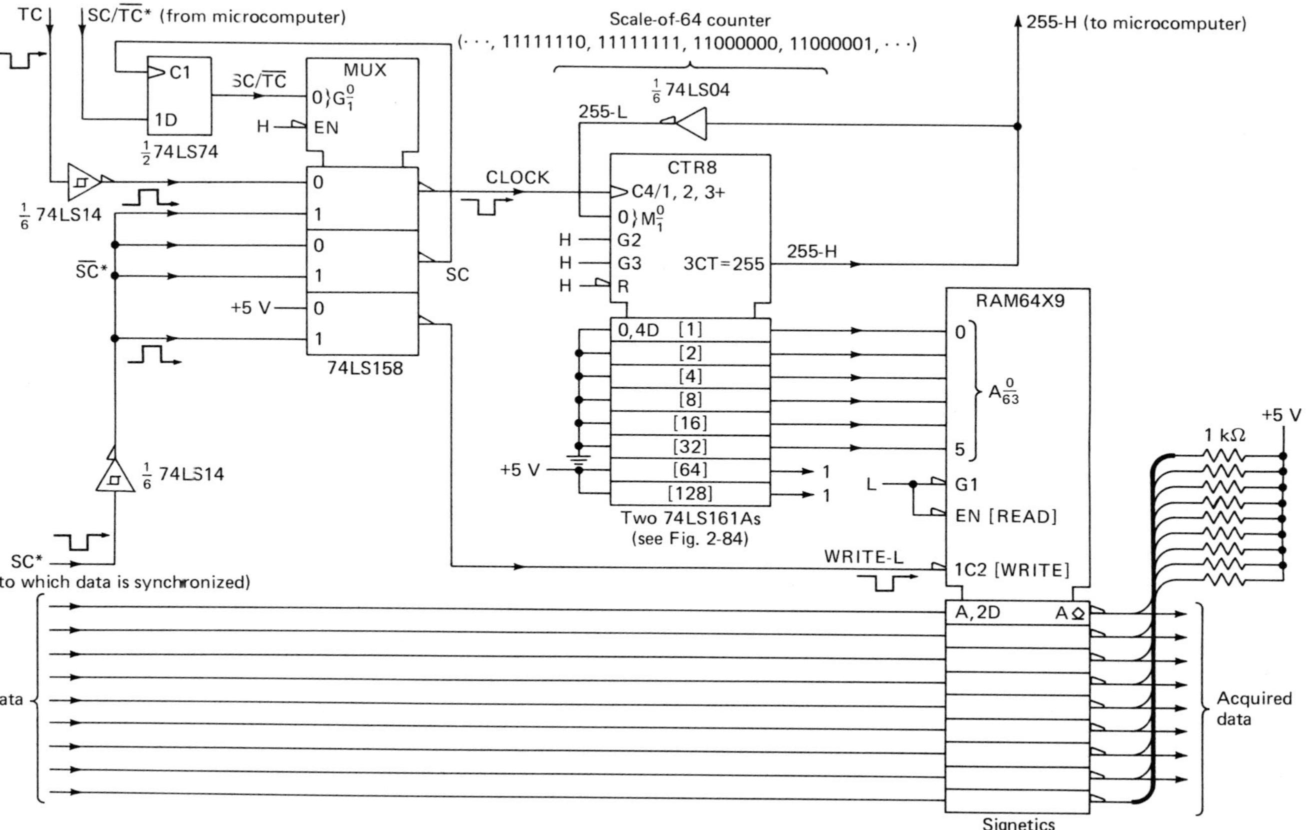

Figure 5-19. Data acquisition circuit.

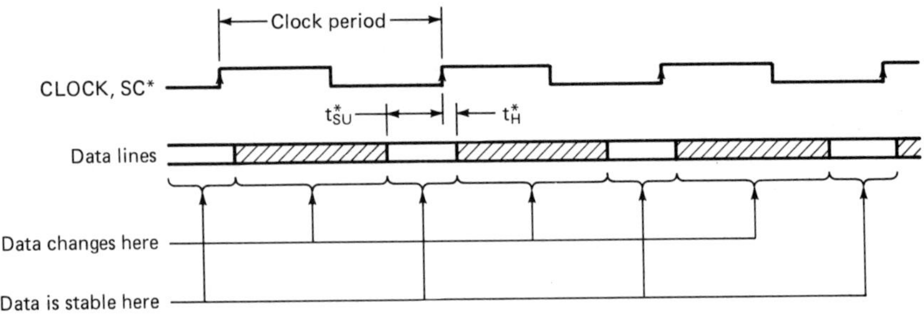

Figure 5-20. Timing in the general case of transmitting synchronized data.

a certain word appears on its input. Whatever variations in performance are desired, we can achieve them with an algorithmic state machine (clocked by CLOCK) which generates SC/$\overline{\text{TC}}$. To handle SC/$\overline{\text{TC}}$ in case the SC* clock ever stops (because of a bad connection or a malfunction), the microcomputer should probably be able to control the state of this ASM with a static reset input (such as that available for the octal D-type flip-flop of Fig. 2-73). The microcomputer can monitor SC*, to sense when this is necessary, using an edge-sensitive input (as shown in Fig. 4-23).

The data acquisition circuit of Fig. 5-19 took advantage of the timing of Fig. 5-17 in which the input data was stable from well before to well after the clock "strobe" pulse. In the general case wherein the sending device is an arbitrary sequential circuit, we have the timing shown in Fig. 5-20. Assuming that the sequential circuit's clock is the clock signal accompanying the transmitted data, the time interval labeled t_H^* is at least as long as the shortest propagation delay through any sequential device in that circuit. The time labeled t_{SU}^* in Fig. 5-20 represents the amount of time during which the receiving device can look at stable data before the clock edge occurs. *If* the receiving device were to use the clock directly to clock the transmitted data into edge-triggered D-type flip-flops, t_{SU}^* and t_H^* define the worst-case setup and hold times which the flip-flops could have and still read the transmitted data reliably.

In the case of Fig. 5-19, the data is not clocked into D-type flip-flops but rather into RAM memory. Also, the clock signal is delayed as it passes through the multiplexer. Assume for the moment that the multiplexer has zero propagation delay. In this case, as soon as WRITE-L goes low, the RAM begins the process of writing the input data into the selected memory address. Since the data is not stable yet (according to Fig. 5-20), incorrect data is being written into the selected address. However, as long as:

1 t^*_{SU} of Fig. 5-20 exceeds the RAM's worst-case write setup time for the data input, $t_{WSD} = 35$ ns
2 The time during which the WRITE-L is low exceeds the RAM's minimum write pulse width, $t_W = 35$ ns
3 t^*_H of Fig. 5-20 exceeds the RAM's data hold time, $t_{WHD} = 5$ ns

the data which *ends up* stored in the selected address will be the correct data.

With this background we are in a position to tackle the general problem of *buffering* data inputs and both *buffering and switching* the clock input. Inputs are buffered:

- To provide negligible loading to the sending circuitry (if this is important).
- To protect them from high voltages (e.g., static discharges or 115 V ac).

We may also wish to incorporate the option of *inverting* selected inputs. For example, the simplified signature analyzer input circuitry of Fig. 4-4 illustrated how exclusive-OR gates could be used to implement this feature.

To clarify our thinking, consider the general input circuitry of Fig. 5-21. Regardless of what these buffering circuits do, for the moment

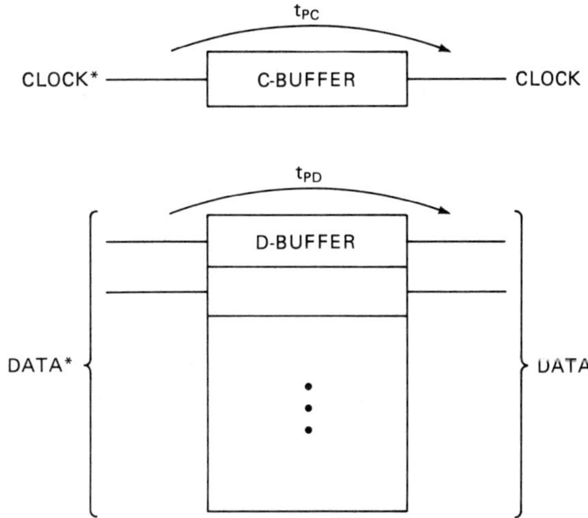

Figure 5-21. General input circuitry.

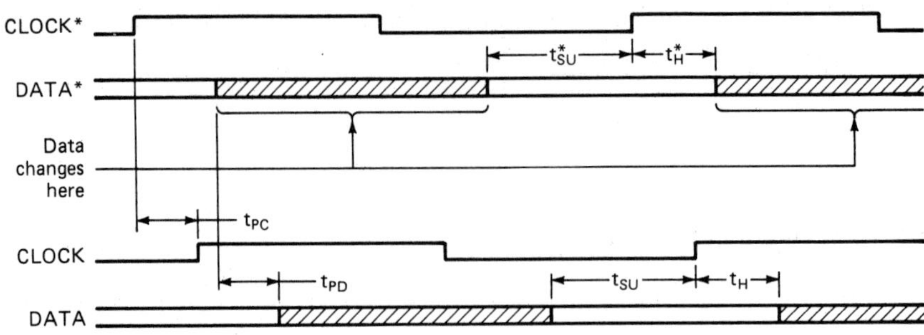

Figure 5-22. Input circuitry translation of timing characteristics when $t_{PC} = t_{PD}$.

we will only consider the effect of the two propagation delays, t_{PC} and t_{PD}, defined in the figure. We have already considered the case wherein these are zero. If they are nonzero *but equal*, the timing relationship between CLOCK and DATA is identical to that for CLOCK* and DATA*. This is illustrated in Fig. 5-22, where

- t_{SU}^* and t_H^* define the sending device's timing characteristics
- t_{SU} and t_H define the receiving device's timing characteristics

We can look upon these times in either of two ways. First (and the way we have been discussing), we can ask what constraints the sender's timing characteristics impose upon the receiver. We are given t_{SU}^* and t_H^*, these are translated (as in Fig. 5-22) into t_{SU} and t_H, and the receiver must live with the resulting timing. As long as the sequential devices in the receiver have setup and hold times which are *less* than these values, the data will be reliably transferred.

Alternatively, we can ask what constraints the receiver's timing characteristics impose upon the sender. This is the viewpoint of the designer of a receiving instrument such as a logic state analyzer or a signature analyzer. To create as useful an instrument as possible, such a designer might like to have inputs which are as close to "ideal" as possible. But what is ideal? We have seen the problems with hold time. Zero hold time t_H^* means that the sending circuitry can change data *immediately* after the clock edge without adverse results, an ideal position. *Zero* setup time t_{SU}^* means that the sending circuitry has the *entire* clock period available for settling time—an ideal position as far as the receiving instrument is concerned. However, since the sending circuitry has its own setup requirements, the receiving instrument

Instrument	t^*_{SU} (ns)	t^*_H (ns)
Hewlett-Packard Model 1602A Logic State Analyzer (Fig. 1-16)	35	0
Hewlett-Packard Model 1610A Logic State Analyzer (Fig. 3-3)	20	0
Hewlett-Packard Model 5004A Signature Analyzer (Fig. 3-1)	25	0

Figure 5-23. Input timing specifications for three instruments.

should probably be designed to impose upon the sender

$$t^*_H = 0$$

t^*_{SU} as small as is reasonably possible

The logic state analyzers and the signature analyzer discussed earlier exhibit the input timing specifications shown in Fig. 5-23.

Even if some of the sequential devices used in the receiving instrument have nonzero hold times, these can be translated into zero-hold-time specifications at the instrument inputs, as shown in Fig. 5-24. It is only necessary to add sufficient *extra* propagation delay to the data inputs, relative to the clock input. However, note that this is done at the expense of increasing the setup time t^*_{SU} by an equal amount. There's no such thing as a free lunch!

Actually, when we buffer inputs, we must expect to introduce *tolerances* on t_{PC} and t_{PD}. These tolerances act so as to make

$$t^*_{SU} + t^*_H < t_{SU} + t_H$$

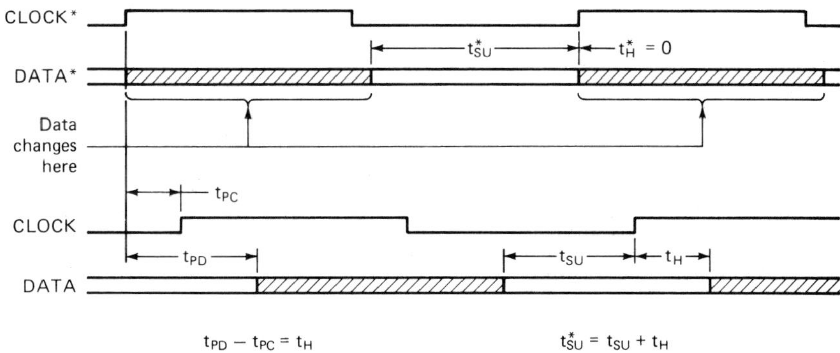

Figure 5-24. Input circuitry translation of timing characteristics to achieve $t^*_H = 0$.

Figure 5-25 illustrates an example in which both t_H^* and t_H have been constrained to equal zero. If we start with given timing characteristics for CLOCK* and DATA* in that figure, CLOCK is shown delayed some arbitrary amount, including a tolerance on that delay. Then DATA is shown delayed a very exact amount so that the range where DATA is unstable begins (due to $t_{PD(\mathrm{minimum})}$) just at the point where the rising edge of CLOCK ends (due to $t_{PC(\mathrm{maximum})}$). As shown in that figure, the net effect is that t_{SU} is reduced from t_{SU}^* by the *total tolerance* on the two propagation delays, t_{PC} and t_{PD}.

In summary, input buffering circuitry can be used to achieve zero-hold-time specifications. However, to achieve this, we must be able to adjust the propagation delay of the clock buffering circuit relative to the propagation delay of the data buffering circuits. Furthermore, the tolerances on the delays, which serve to degrade the setup-time characteristics that can be achieved, should be carefully controlled.

A sloppy way to achieve reliable data transfer is to design input circuitry with t_{PD} much greater than t_{PC}. In effect, this translates $t_H = 0$ into *negative* external hold time ($t_H^* < 0$), a wasted capability for sending circuitry designed to keep data stable until after the clock transition. This wasted capability carries the price of requiring an excessively long setup time t_{SU}^*.

The data acquisition circuit of Fig. 5-19 puts a fundamental limitation upon the achievable value of t_{SU}^* (with $t_H^* = 0$) even *before* input buffering circuitry is taken into account. This is due to the RAM's data setup and hold times of 35 ns and 5 ns, respectively. These times, although quite respectable, will contribute 35 + 5 = 40 ns to t_{SU}^*. If we are willing to pay the price of extra components, we can improve upon this by clocking the input data into fast D-type flip-flops whose outputs then drive the data inputs to the RAM. This is a technique of general value. In effect, the D-type flip-flops transform the longer setup time of the device they drive into a shorter setup-time requirement for the device that drives them. This is illustrated in Fig. 5-26 using three 74S195 4-bit parallel in/parallel out shift registers as D-type flip-flops. Recall from the discussion of their 74LSxxx counterparts (Fig. 3-35) that they are also useful for building testing capability into a design since they can be switched to a "background" mode in which they serve as shift registers.

With this extensive discussion of the *timing* characteristics of input-buffering circuitry behind us, we are ready to consider input-buffering circuitry itself. The hex inverting buffer shown in Fig. 5-27 is an IC which presents extremely low loading to circuits that drive it. This is useful for the design of the inputs to an instrument which must probe arbitrary points in another circuit. It is also useful for permitting

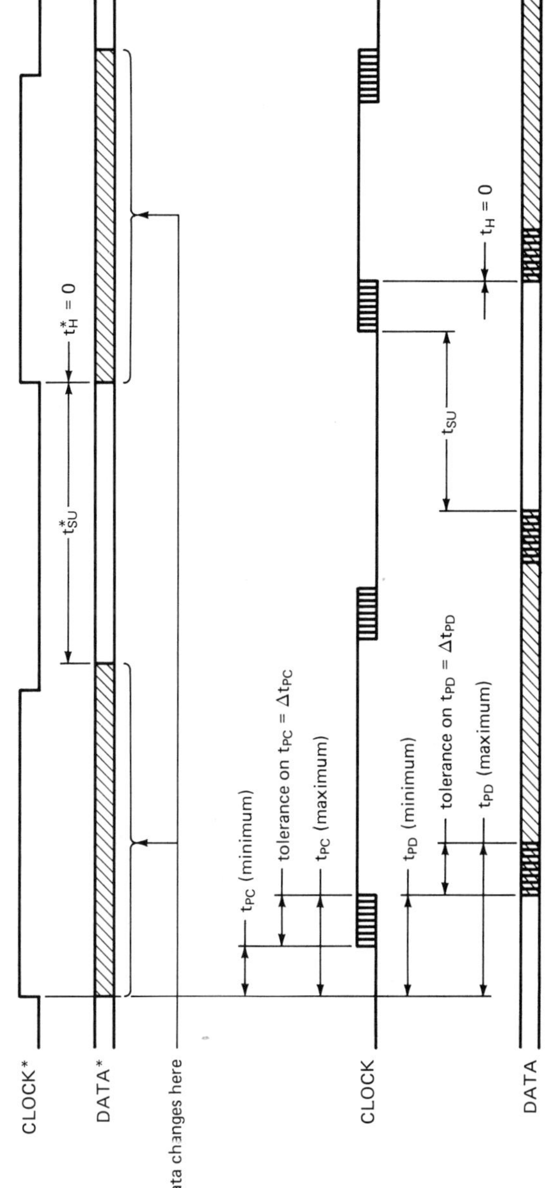

$$t_{SU}^* = t_{SU} + \Delta t_{PC} + \Delta t_{PD}$$

Figure 5-25. Input circuitry translation of timing characteristics to achieve $t_H^* = 0$*, given* $t_H = 0$ *(or vice versa), by adjusting* $t_{PC(maximum)} = t_{PD(minimum)}$.

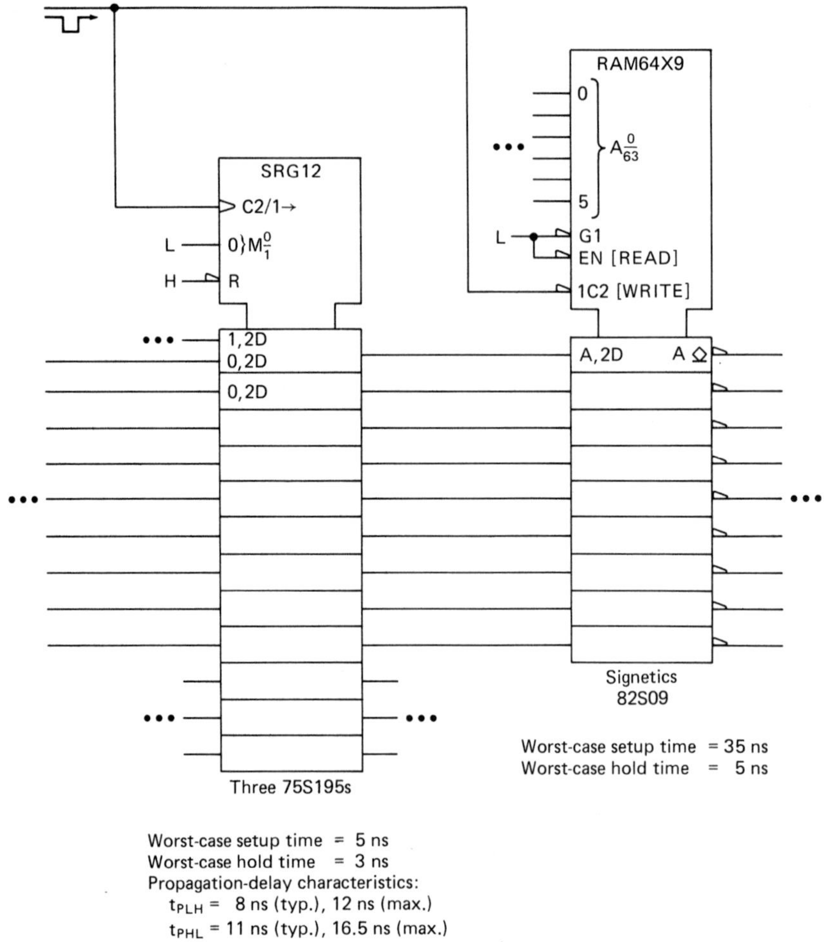

Figure 5-26. Using fast D-type flip-flops as setup-time transformers.

inputs to be protected with a resistor-diode network like that shown in Fig. 5-28.

Example 5-8. What offset voltage will be introduced on the inputs to the buffers of Fig. 5-28 by the 2.2-kΩ input resistors if these buffers draw the maximum input current of 50 μA?

The offset voltage will be 2.2 kΩ × 50 μA = 0.1 V. Hence a "typical" low-level TTL input of 0.2 V will be translated to 0.3 V. Likewise, a "typical" high-level TTL input of 3.3 V will be translated to 3.2 V.

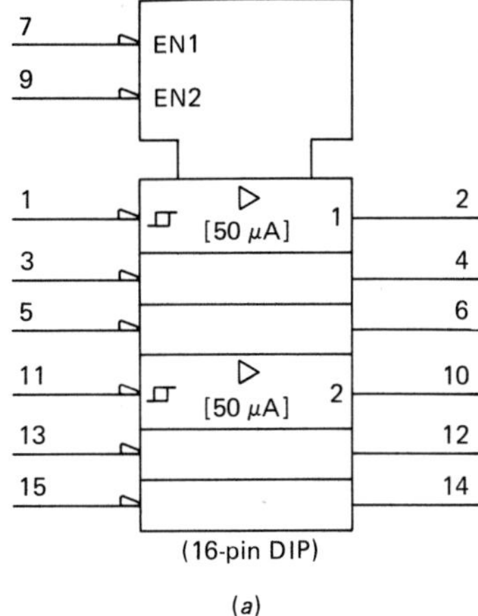

(a)

Input loading:

Schmitt-trigger inputs:	15 μA, typical; 50 μA, maximum
Enable inputs:	< 3.2 mA at 0.4 V; < 80 μA at 2.4 V

Schmitt-trigger-input thresholds (V):

	Minimum	Typical	Maximum
Low	1.05	1.30	1.55
High	1.80	2.25	2.50

Output drive: > 16 mA at 0.4 V; > 400 μA at 2.4 V

Propagation delay (ns):

		Typical	Maximum
Schmitt-trigger inputs:	t_{PHL}	10	30
	t_{PLH}	20	30
Enable inputs:	t_{PHL}	9	15
	t_{PLH}	11	15

(b)

Figure 5-27. 8T37, high-input-impedance hex Schmitt trigger buffer inverters. (a) Symbolic representation; (b) specifications. (Signetics Corp.)

Example 5-9. What will be the peak current through one of the normally back-biased silicon diodes if an input is inadvertently connected to 115 V ac?

The peak voltage is $115\sqrt{2} = 162$ V. The corresponding peak current is 162 V/2.2 kΩ = 74 mA. This is not an unreasonable current for a silicon diode.

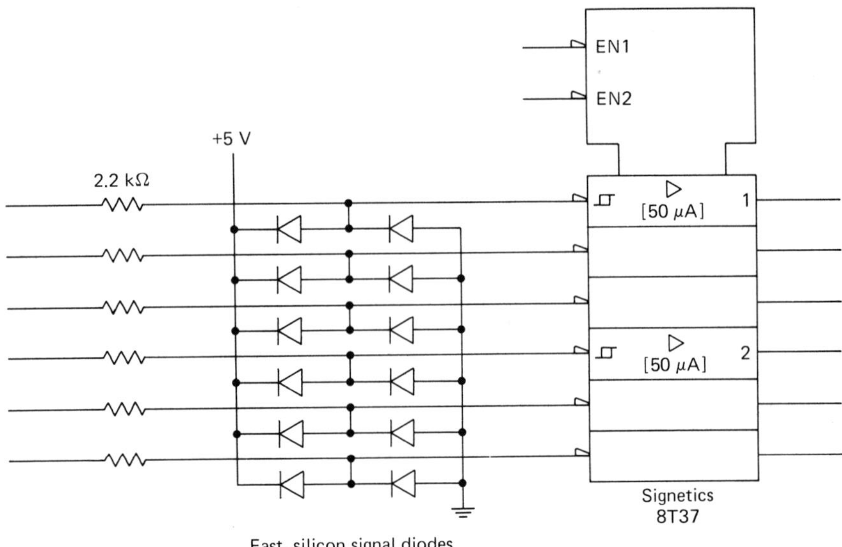

Figure 5-28. Input protection.

If we wish to improve upon the specified tolerance in the propagation delay of the Schmitt-trigger buffers of Fig. 5-27, we can first note that all six buffers within any one chip will be "reasonably" well matched since they have shared identical processing in their production. To match propagation-delay characteristics between chips, we can *test and sort*. This is a particularly fruitful activity if we can live with matched sets of parts, independent of the nominal propagation delay of each set. For example, we might sort 8T37 buffers as follows:

Set 1: 5 ns < propagation delays < 15 ns

Set 2: 10 ns < propagation delays < 20 ns

Set 3: 15 ns < propagation delays < 25 ns

Set 4: 20 ns < propagation delays < 30 ns

Set 5: Everything else (use on another project)

Use of any one of sets 1 to 4 will hold the *tolerance* on t_{PD} discussed earlier down to 10 ns. If the CLOCK*-CLOCK propagation delay t_{PC} can be adjusted with a potentiometer, the *nominal* propagation delay of the buffers is irrelevant.

We will conclude this section on input buffering with another look at the input circuitry for the signature analyzer, previously discussed in conjunction with Fig. 4-4. To achieve high-impedance inputs, input protection, and short propagation delay, the Hewlett-Packard unit employs fast, *emitter-coupled logic* (ECL) voltage comparators on the inputs, followed by ECL-to-TTL translators. The total propagation delay for the pair is less than 11 ns. The Hewlett-Packard unit achieves 0-ns hold-time and 25-ns setup-time specifications by using a few fast components between inputs and the register that resynchronizes them to the clock. Their approach does not require parts selection to achieve these specifications.

We will consider a modification that will permit the switching of the clock for testing purposes. In addition, we will illustrate an approach that employs *trimming* to achieve excellent setup/hold-time characteristics from unselected parts. Trimming offers the possibility of achieving *better* setup/hold-time characteristics for the CLOCK* and DATA* inputs of Fig. 5-21 than those derived from worst-case calculations starting with the setup/hold-time characteristics of CLOCK and DATA. For example, if CLOCK is used to resynchronize DATA in the 74LS195 register of Fig. 3-41, the 74LS195 by itself introduces a 25 ns setup/hold-time ambiguity. By trimming the delay between inputs and resynchronization, we deal with *measured* times rather than with data sheet values (with their attendant tolerances). Of course, trimming introduces a major disadvantage during manufacture. Boards must be assembled and then subjected to a test rig which exercises the inputs and displays the outputs of the resynchronizing register so that trimpots can be optimally adjusted. Such a procedure is characteristic of any analog circuitry in an instrument. It is one of the steps that digital circuitry can usually avoid.

The PROBE* input to the signature analyzer circuit of Fig. 4-2 has a special input requirement. In addition to being a high-impedance, protected input, it needs to detect whether PROBE* is high, low, or *floating*. This is done so that the signature analyzer can obtain unambiguous signatures from three-state outputs. When such an output goes from a high level to the high-impedance state, the signature analyzer treats the high-impedance state during subsequent clock periods as more high-level inputs. When the output goes from a low level to the high-impedance state, the signature analyzer treats the high-impedance state during subsequent clock periods as more low-level inputs. The Schmitt-trigger circuit of Fig. 5-29*a* illustrates one approach. When the input goes from either a low level or a high level to the high-impedance state, the resistor network pulls the input to a voltage between the two threshold levels of the Schmitt trigger. Thus the output of the Schmitt trigger remembers whether the last logic level was high or low.

For the signature analyzer, this Schmitt-trigger approach will give

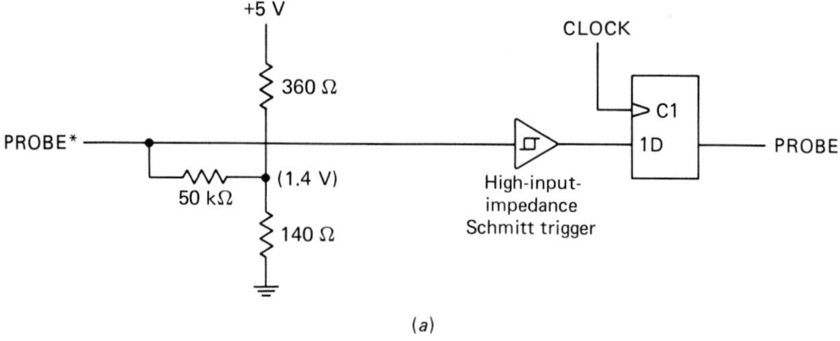

(a)

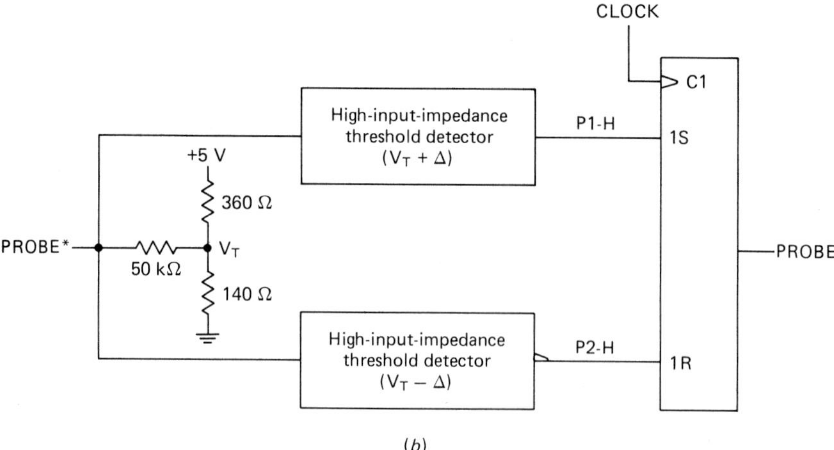

(b)

PROBE*	Logic levels P1-H	Logic levels P2-H	Logic states P1-H	Logic states P2-H	Flip-flop operation
H	H	L	1	0	Set
L	L	H	0	1	Reset
Floating (high Z)	L	L	0	0	No change

(c)

Figure 5-29. Signature analyzer probe input circuitry to handle three-state devices unambiguously. (a) Schmitt-trigger approach; (b) "synchronous Schmitt-trigger" approach; (c) flip-flop operation.

unreliable signatures whenever we probe a three-state output that is momentarily enabled early in a clock period while circuitry is settling out. An output "glitch" in such a case might, or might not, switch the Schmitt trigger depending upon the delays giving rise to the glitch. Whether or not the Schmitt trigger is switched in such a case will give rise to two different signatures, an intolerable situation. A "synchronous Schmitt-trigger" approach used in the Hewlett-Packard unit is shown in Fig. 5-29*b*. It employs two threshold detectors, the outputs of which are looked at only within the setup/hold-time interval of the flip-flop, long past the time in the clock period when glitches might have occurred. As shown in Fig. 5-29*c*, an S-R (or J-K) flip-flop handles the high-impedance state by remaining unchanged.

To facilitate testing, we prefer using a D-type flip-flop so that the circuit configuration of Fig. 3-41 can be implemented. Consequently, we need to convert an S-R input into a D-type input.

Example 5-10. Create an S-R flip-flop from a D-type flip-flop plus gating.

Comparing the two circuits of Fig. 5-30*a*, we see that

If $S = 1$, then D must equal 1

If $R = 1$, then D must equal 0

If $S = R = 0$, then D must equal Q

Consequently,

$$D = S + \overline{R}Q$$

Two implementations are shown in Fig. 5-30*b* and *c*.

Signature analyzer circuitry which will generate these inputs is shown in Fig. 5-31. The outputs P1-L and P2-L yield active-low implementations of the table of Fig. 5-29*c*. They will drive the S-L and R-L inputs of Fig. 5-30*c*. The MECL III† voltage comparator generates complementary ECL outputs which are converted to a TTL output.

The same ECL comparator and ECL-to-TTL translator is used to provide high-impedance, protected inputs for CLOCK*, START*, and

† MECL III is the fastest commercially available logic family. It requires special design rules for proper use. Refer to the following two books available from Motorola: *Motorola MECL High Speed Integrated Circuits* (a data book describing MECL 10,000 and MECL III parts) and *MECL System Design Handbook* (a guide to the "tricks of the trade").

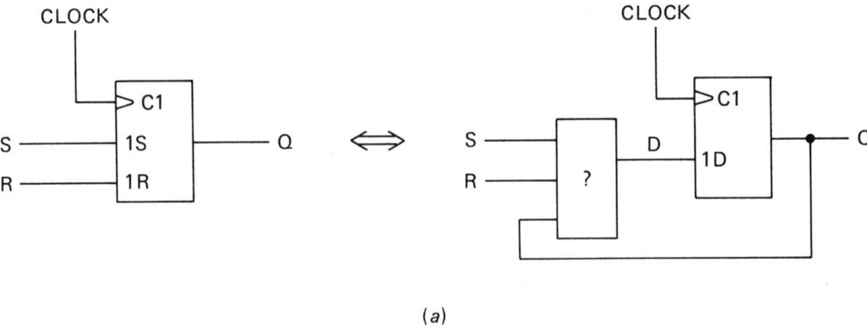

(a)

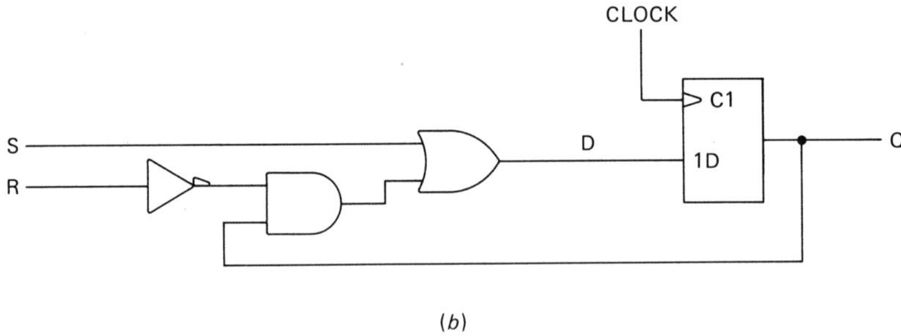

(b)

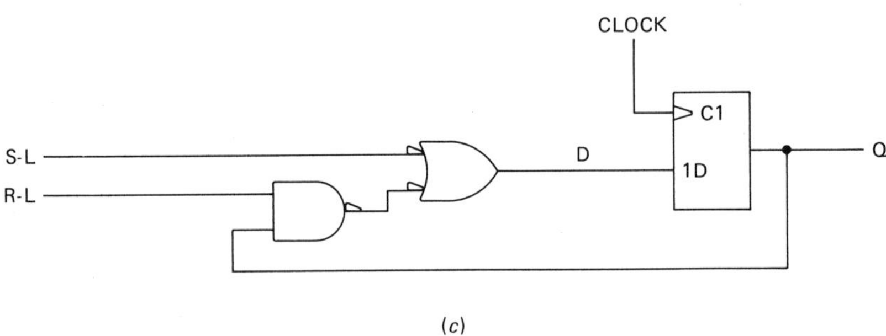

(c)

Figure 5-30. Implementing an S-R flip-flop with a D-type flip-flop plus gating. (a) Required equivalence; (b) implementation with AND-OR-invert gating; (c) implementation with NAND gating and active-low inputs.

STOP*, as shown in Fig. 5-32. The operational amplifier circuit, used in the Hewlett-Packard unit, provides a low-impedance threshold voltage of 1.4 V. Notice that an otherwise unused fourth translator is used to generate $\overline{\text{CLOCK}}'$. This will permit a multiplexer to select either edge without affecting the timing.

These buffered signals (P1-L, P2-L, START′, STOP′, CLOCK′, and $\overline{\text{CLOCK}}'$) are resynchronized in the circuit of Fig. 5-33. This figure il-

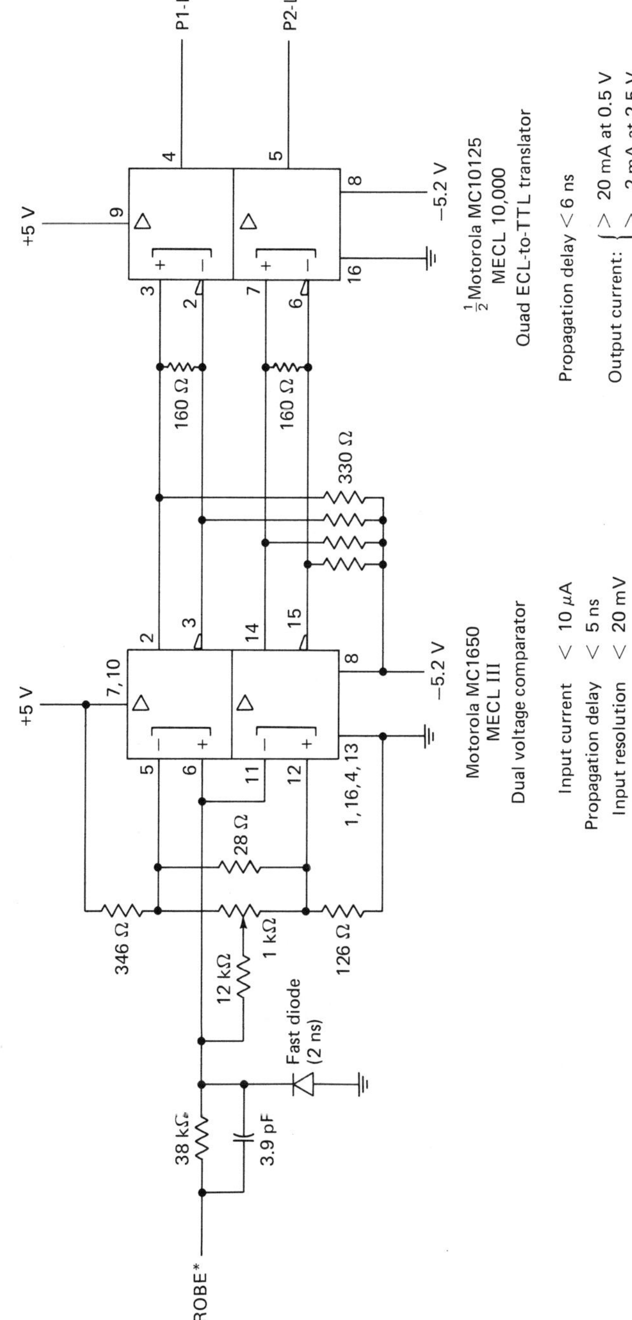

Figure 5-31. *Signature analyzer probe circuitry.*

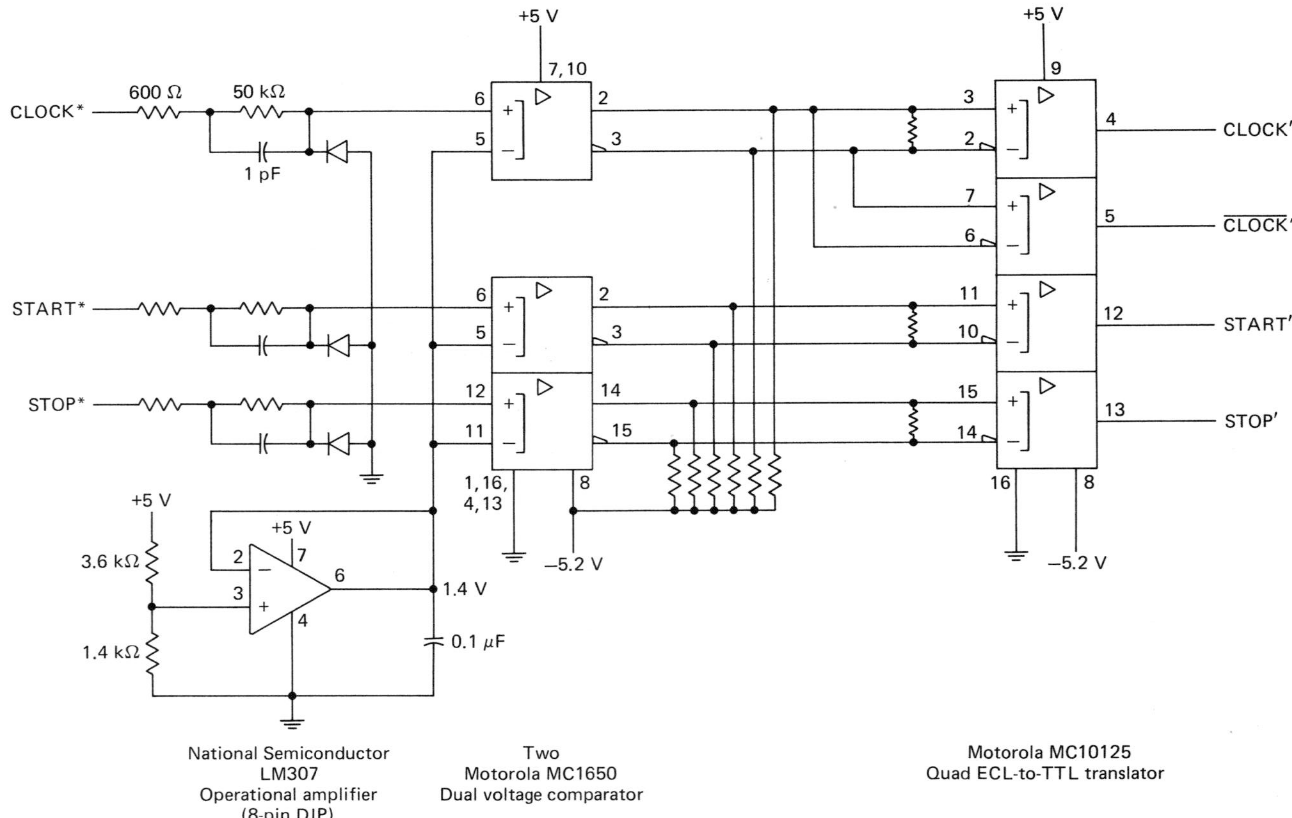

Figure 5-32. Signature analyzer CLOCK, START*, and STOP* input buffering circuitry.*

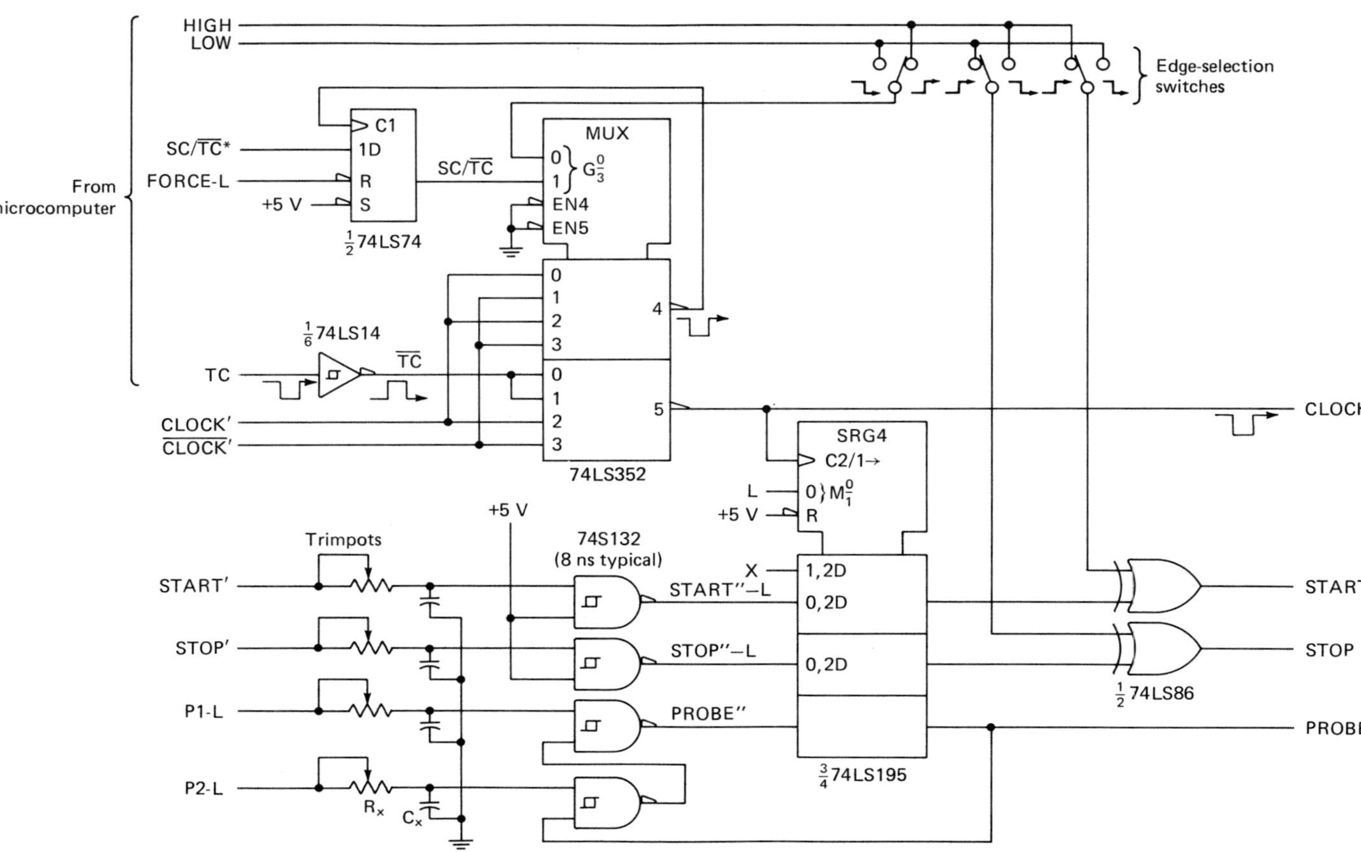

Figure 5-33. Signature analyzer input synchronization circuitry.

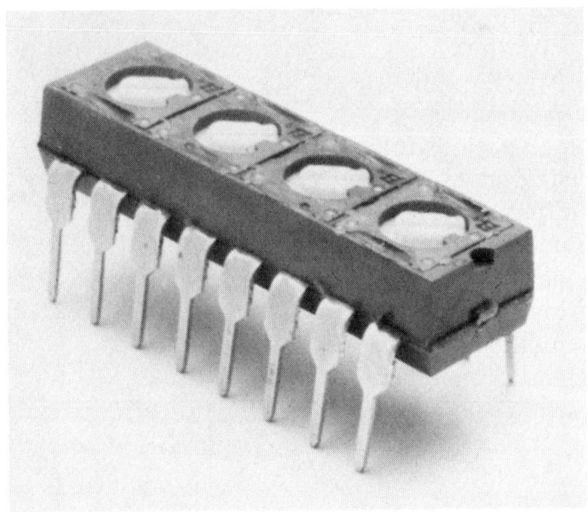

Fig. 5-34. Four trimpots in 16-pin DIP. (Bourns Inc.)

lustrates the use of the 74LS195 parallel in/parallel out shift register operating in the "foreground" mode (discussed in conjunction with Fig. 3-41). It also illustrates the synchronization of SC/$\overline{\text{TC}}$*, used to switch between the external clock and the test clock, whose edges are sharpened up with a Schmitt trigger. The START′, STOP′, P1-L, and P2-L signals are delayed, with variable RC circuits driving Schmitt triggers, to optimize the instrument setup/hold-time characteristics. The trimming potentiometers shown might be implemented with one of the units of Fig. 5-34. Finally, the edge-selection exclusive-OR gates for START and STOP are implemented *after* resynchronization has taken place. This removes their propagation delays from the resynchronization timing. The switch voltages are shown controlled by the microcomputer. During normal operation, HIGH is a high-level voltage and LOW is a low-level voltage. During self-test, both can be made high at the same time (or low at the same time) so that the self-test algorithm can be independent of the switch positions.

5-5 MULTIPLE-PHASE CLOCKING

The synchronous design techniques we have been discussing up to this point support our design efforts by providing reliable timing (within a synchronous sequential circuit) automatically. In this section we will extend our design techniques as required in order to attain reliable timing for inputs to latches and RAMs and for static inputs (e.g., a static reset) to flip-flops, counters, and shift registers.

A *multiple-phase* clock is a clock with several outputs, all of the same frequency but with different phase relationships with respect to each other. For example, consider the multiple-phase clock of Fig. 5-35. We will use the name "CLOCK" to label the one clock phase used to clock synchronous devices. Its rising edges define successive clock periods (assuming we are using sequential devices clocked on a rising edge). We will name the remaining clock phases STATIC*m*/*n*, so that STATIC can serve as a reminder to us that the line describes a clock phase used to provide timing for a static input to a sequential device. The *n* of STATIC*m*/*n* describes the number of equal parts into which the clock period is divided. That part (1, 2, 3, . . .) during which STATIC*m*/*n* is active defines *m*. This labeling scheme is sufficiently general to handle most of our needs. For waveforms that do not fit this framework, we can define other labels as the need arises.

The entire purpose of a multiple-phase clock is to permit us to make static inputs to sequential devices active at times which do not interfere with normal, clocked operation. For example, consider a case in which we wish to reset a sequential circuit every 256 clock periods to start a new cycle of its operation. The 8-bit binary counter of Fig. 5-36*a* generates an output labeled RESET* (once again using an asterisk in the label to indicate a signal whose timing needs to be refined by means of further gating). RESET* goes high for the entire clock period, once every 256 clock periods. It is gated with the STATIC3/4 clock phase to produce the RESET-L waveform shown in Fig. 5-36*b*. When RESET-L is active (i.e., low) all the sequential devices driven by

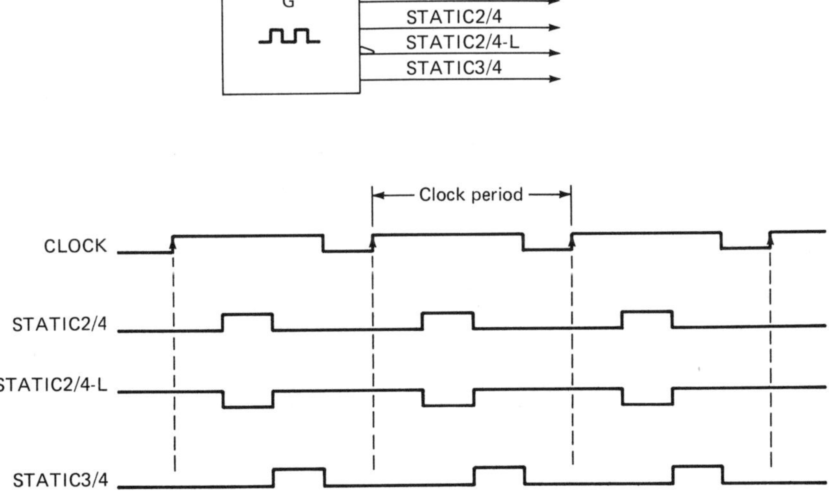

Figure 5-35. Multiple-phase clock and waveforms.

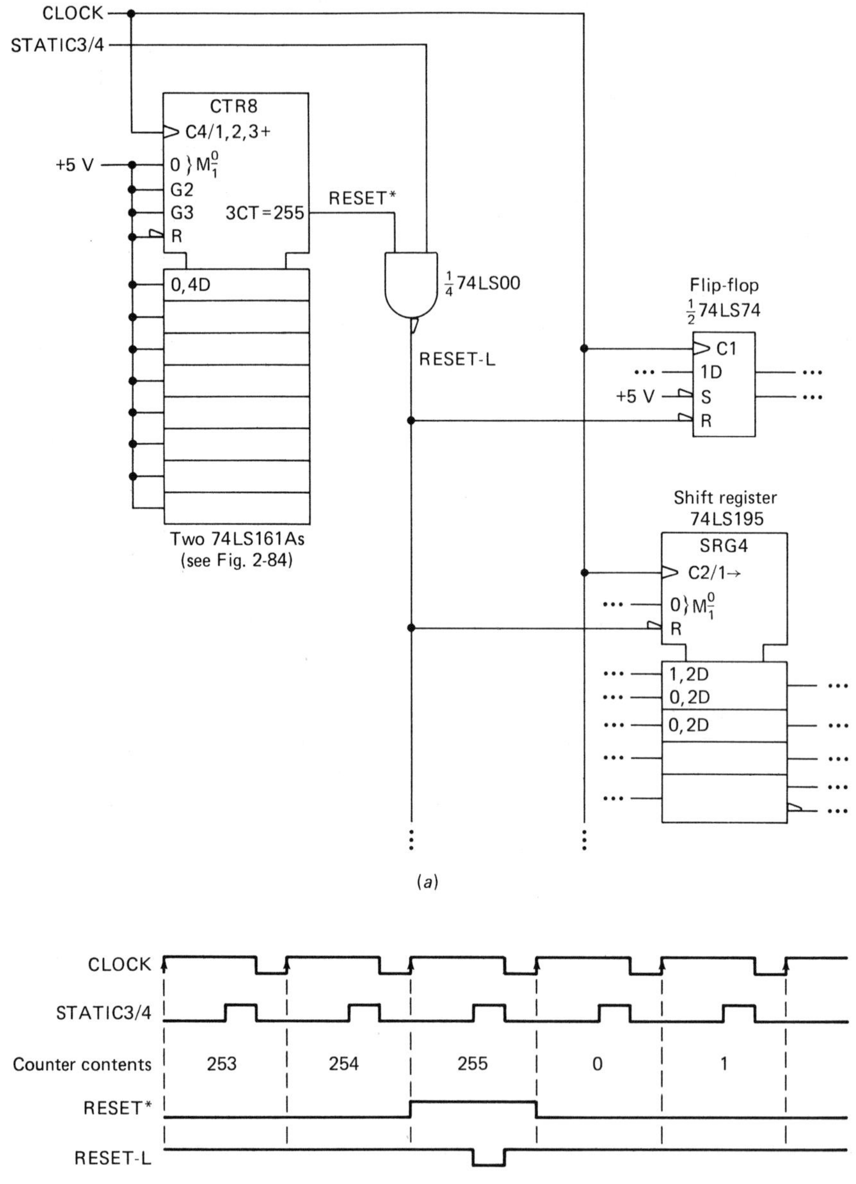

Figure 5-36. Use of multiple-phase clocking for static inputs. (a) Circuit; (b) timing diagram.

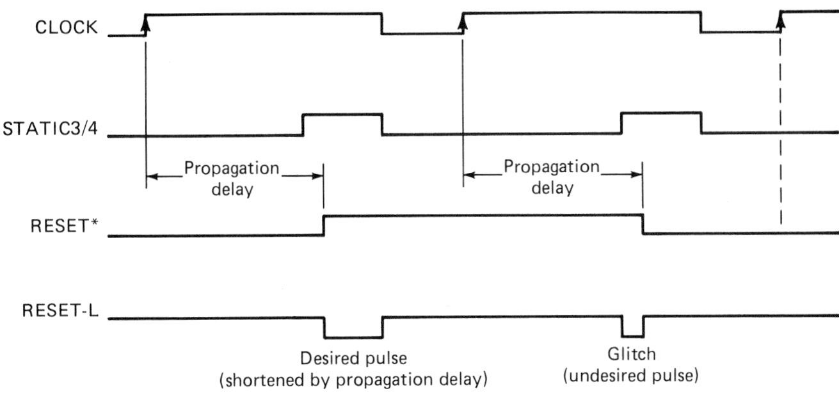

Figure 5-37. Generation of a glitch because of too high a clock rate for the circuit of Fig. 5-36.

it will be reset. This static resetting will begin *as soon as* RESET-L goes low, in the middle of the clock period. For proper operation, the sequential circuitry must settle out before the end of the clock period, in time for all sequential devices to set up for the next rising edge of CLOCK.

Proper operation of the circuit of Fig. 5-36*a* also requires that the 8-bit binary counter generating RESET* settle out *before* STATIC3/4 goes high. That is, whereas most signals in a sequential circuit have essentially the entire clock period to settle out, signals that are gated with a STATIC*m*/*n* clock phase must settle out *before* the clock phase signal becomes active. In the example of Fig. 5-36, RESET* will go high during the clock period when the counter counts up to all 1s. RESET* will remain high after the counter is next clocked, until after the counter flip-flops change state and this change propagates through the gating which generates RESET*. If the clock frequency is so high that STATIC3/4 goes high again during this *next* clock period before RESET* has had a chance to go low again, RESET-L will exhibit a *glitch*, as illustrated in Fig. 5-37. Whether or not the sequential circuit is reset *again* (improperly) during this next clock period depends on the width of the glitch, which in turn depends upon the propagation delays in the circuit. Such a design has not had its timing handled correctly. Circuits built to this design and having slow parts will fail. These timing considerations are summarized in Fig. 5-38.

Even though a RAM is not (usually) synchronously clocked, we can combine a RAM with D-type flip-flops, as in Fig. 5-39, to achieve the equivalent of a synchronous RAM.

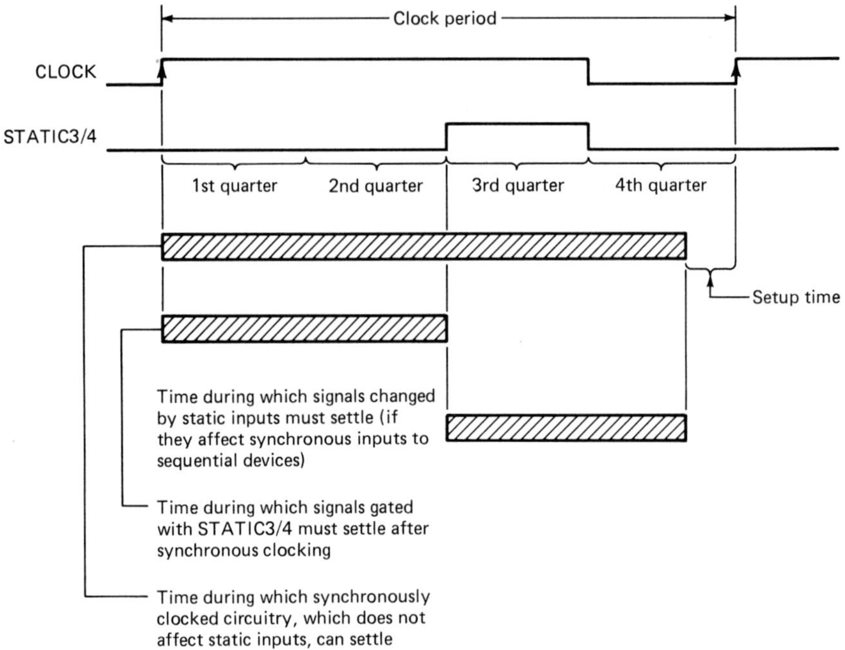

Figure 5-38. General timing considerations for circuitry with a multiple-phase clock.

Example 5-11. What are the timing characteristics of the "synchronous" RAM of Fig. 5-39, created from the 256 × 4 bipolar RAM of Fig. 5-3 and the 74LS195 register (of Fig. 3-35)?

The inputs to the RAM must be set up before the leading edge of STATIC3/4 occurs. Consequently, the setup time is one-half of the clock period, $T/2$. The hold time is $-T/2$. That is, inputs to the RAM can actually change well *before* the clock edge occurs. The propagation delay of interest for synchronous design is that between the clock input to the 74LS195 and its outputs (which is specified as 26 ns maximum) plus $T/2$.

This creation of a "synchronous" RAM permits us to employ it in a "synchronous" sequential circuit like any other sequential device. That is, to design the circuit to step correctly from state to state during successive clock periods, we need only think of what each variable

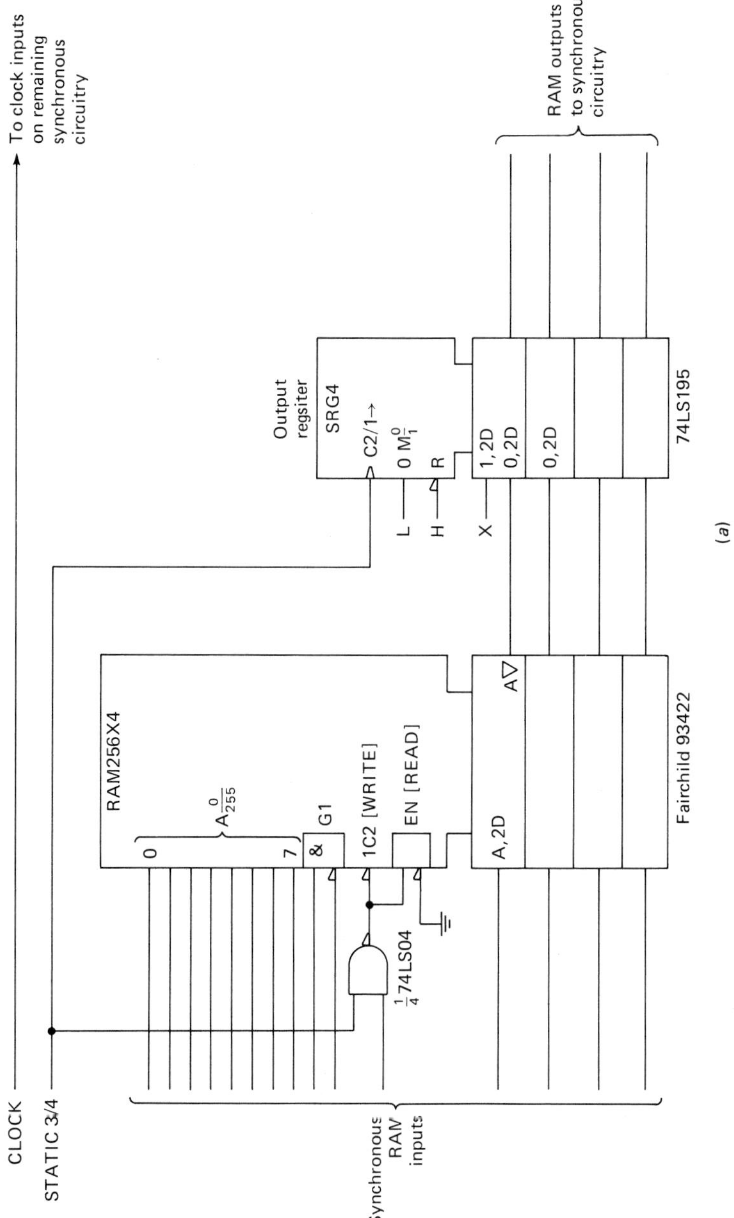

Figure 5-39. Creation of a "synchronous" RAM. (a) Circuit.

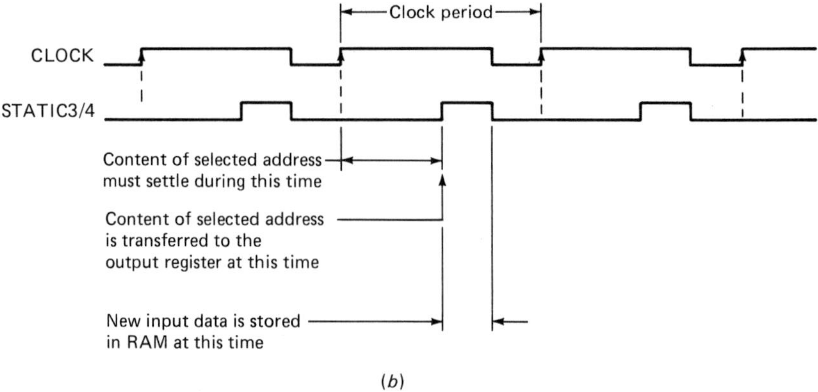

Figure 5-39b. Timing diagram.

should be during each clock period. We need no longer concern ourselves with the output of the RAM itself *within* the clock period.

Few designers use *synchronous* RAMs. Instead, they achieve reliable operation with a RAM by constraining its use so that:

1. The RAM is written to or read from, *but not both,* during any one clock period.
2. Inputs to the RAM are not combinational functions of the outputs of the RAM.

Subject to these constraints, a RAM can be used as shown in Fig. 5-40.

A multiple-phase clock can be designed in any one of several ways. It is necessary to ensure not only that the desired waveforms are generated, but also that the circuitry does not generate glitches on any of the clock phase outputs. The circuit of Fig. 5-41 can generate an output CLOCK frequency up to 8 MHz using 74LS74 dual flip-flops which can be clocked up to 33 MHz. Since a 74S74 can be clocked up to 110 MHz (being one of the fastest 74Sxxx parts available), a 74Sxxx version of this circuit can generate output CLOCK frequencies up to 27 MHz. The circuit avoids glitches because the two Gray code outputs never change at the same time. Consequently, neither of the two gates that look at g_1 and g_2 ever sees one input changing from low to high *at the same time* the other input is changing from high to low, a potential glitch-producing condition.

We may wish to obtain a narrow CLOCK pulse to help alleviate setup-time problems arising from the use of ones-catching sequential devices. In addition, we may want several clock phases so that we *sequence* several statically controlled operations within one clock

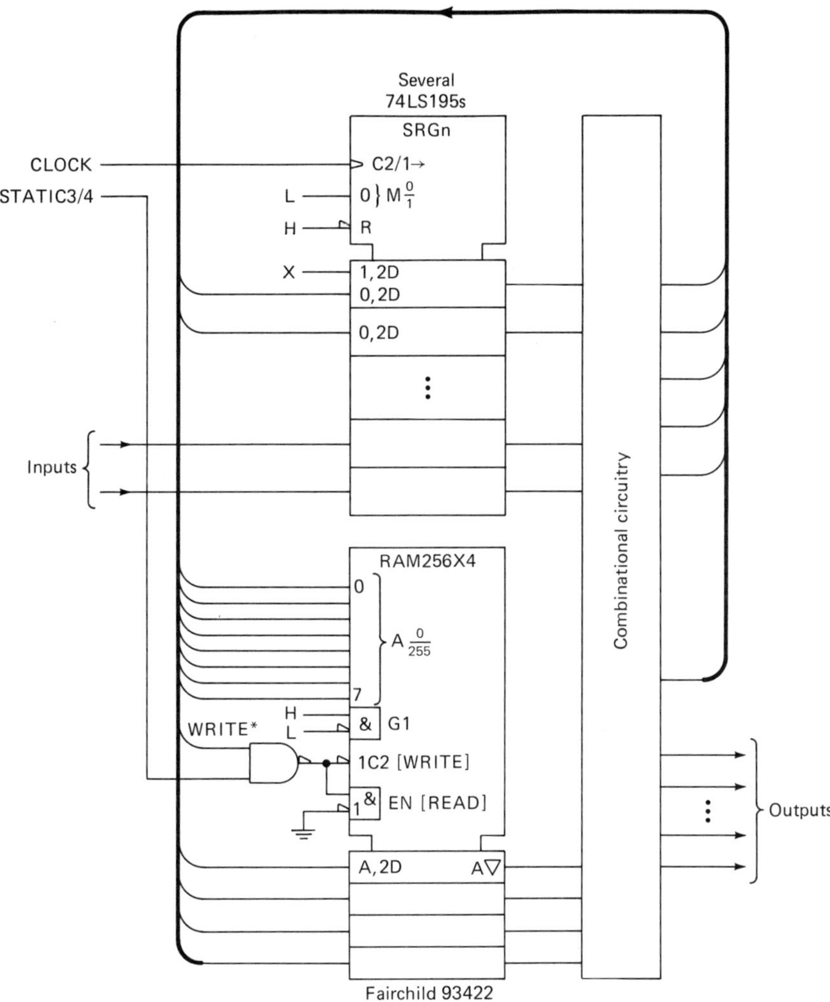

Figure 5-40. Use of a RAM in a sequential circuit.

period. Or, we may want to locate a clock phase within the clock period with finer resolution than can be achieved with the circuit of Fig. 5-41. For any of these reasons we might prefer the circuit of Fig. 5-42. It uses a binary down counter hard-wired to count with an arbitrary scale. For example, it is shown hard-wired to count

$$. \ . \ . \ , 2, 1, 0, 4, 3, 2, 1, 0, 4, 3, \ . \ . \ .$$

This divides the generator clock, f, by five. The decoder decodes

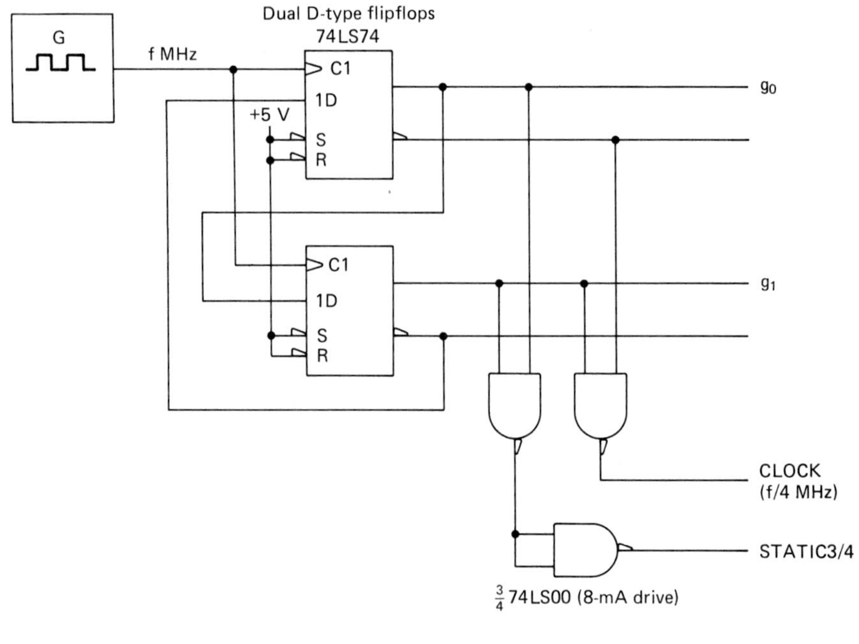

(a)

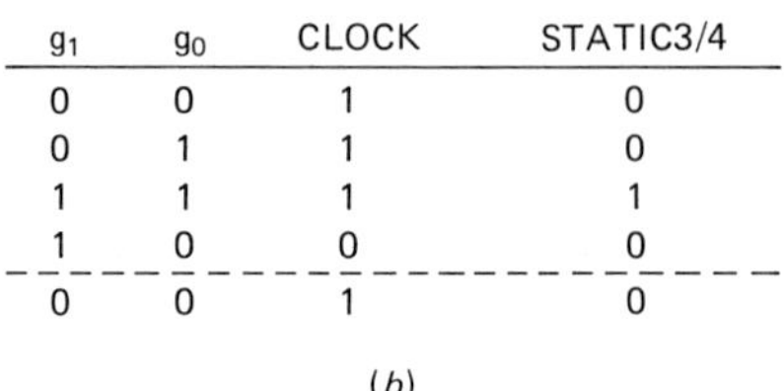

g_1	g_0	CLOCK	STATIC3/4
0	0	1	0
0	1	1	0
1	1	1	1
1	0	0	0
0	0	1	0

(b)

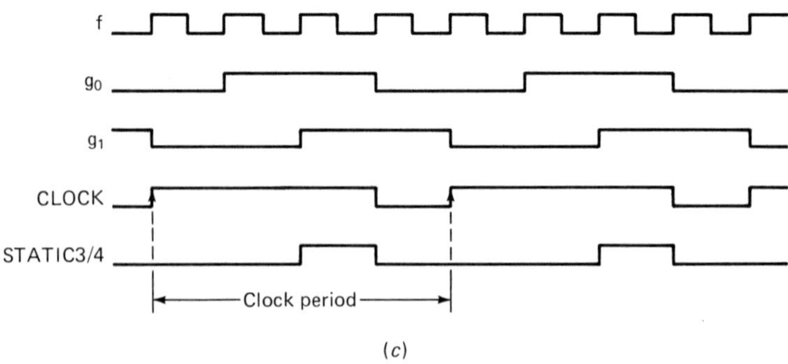

(c)

Figure 5-41. Multiple-phase clock generator built with a 2-bit Gray code counter plus NAND gates. (a) *Circuit;* (b) *count sequence;* (c) *timing diagram.*

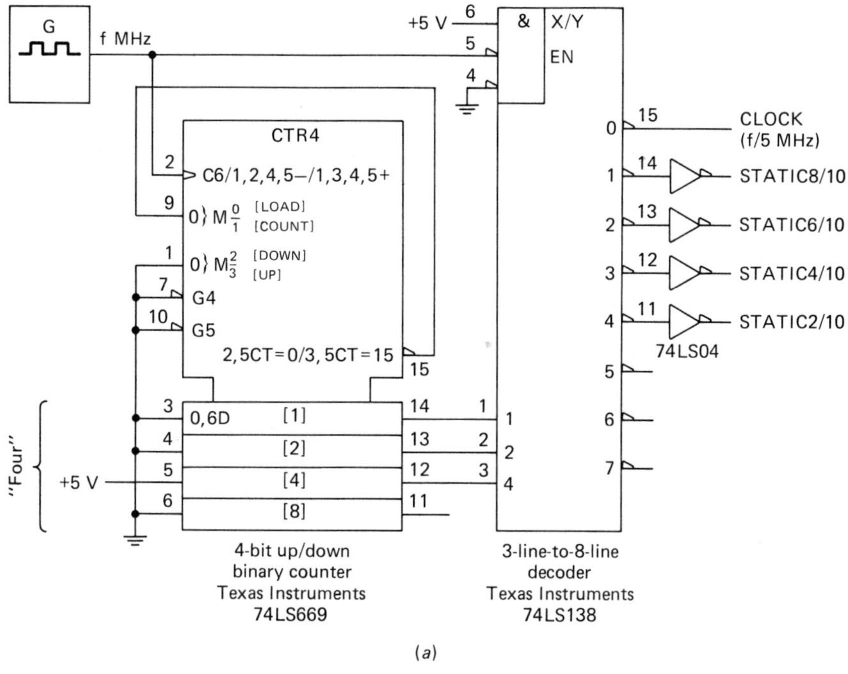

(a)

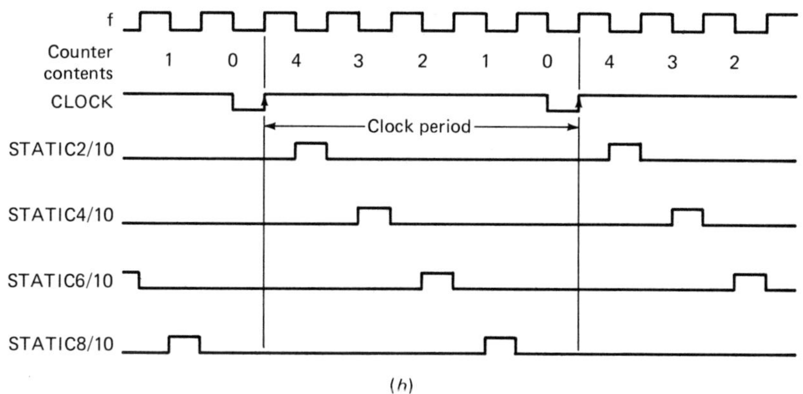

(b)

Figure 5-42. Versatile multiple-phase clock circuit. (a) *Circuit;* (b) *timing diagram.*

these numbers to drive five output lines. Furthermore, by enabling the decoder only during the second half of each clock period of f, any settling going on *within* the decoder during the first part of the clock period (when the counter outputs change) will be blocked out, thus avoiding potential glitches.

5-6 MAXIMUM ALLOWABLE CLOCK SKEW

Earlier in this chapter we found that the hold time for inputs to a sequential device must be less than the clock-to-output propagation delays of the sequential devices which drive them, when both are clocked synchronously. A related problem arises in a system with so many clocked devices that their clock inputs must be split up and driven by parallel buffers such as those of Fig. 2-72b. As long as the propagation delays of the buffers are identical, the operation is the same as if all devices are being driven by one signal. In fact, the rising edges on these signals need not occur at exactly the same time. As long as the edges all occur within the *maximum allowable clock skew* of each other, the sequential devices will behave as if they have been clocked simultaneously.

The circuit of Fig. 5-43 illustrates the worst-case path in a circuit leading to the determination of maximum allowable clock skew. This path must include the outputs of two different clock drivers ($CLOCK_a$ and $CLOCK_b$ in this case), and two sequential devices, one of which drives the other. Furthermore, the *minimum* propagation delay for the driving device minus the worst-case hold time for the driven device must be less than for any other pair of sequential devices in the circuit. This difference defines the maximum allowable clock skew:

$$\text{Maximum allowable clock skew} = t_{P(\text{minimum})} - t_{H(\text{worst-case})}$$

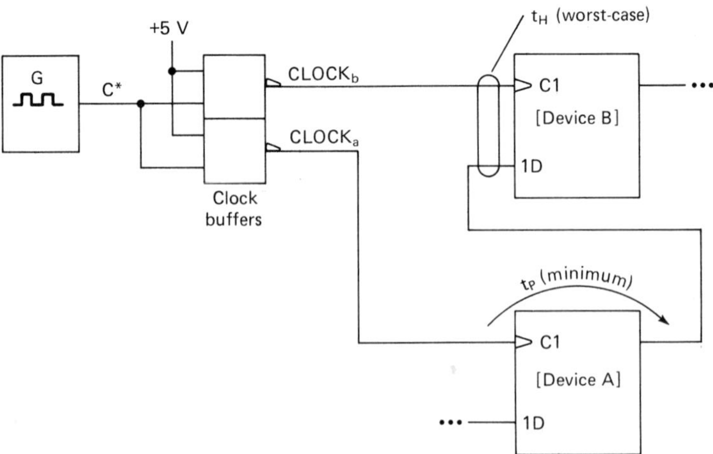

Figure 5-43. Worst-case path leading to the determination of maximum allowable clock skew.

That is, if $CLOCK_a$ occurs earlier than $CLOCK_b$ by *less* than this amount, we can be assured that the devices see their clock inputs as if they occur simultaneously.

Example 5-12. Assume that the specifications for device A in Fig. 5-43 list a minimum propagation delay of 8 ns. Assume that the worst-case hold time of device B is specified as 5 ns. What is the maximum allowable clock skew in this case?

Maximum allowable clock skew $= 8 - 5 = 3$ ns. That is, as long as the *difference* between the two clock buffer propagation delays is less than 3 ns, we can be assured that the changing data on the output of device A will remain long enough (after $CLOCK_b$) to satisfy device B's hold requirements.

The unfortunate fact arises again here, just as it did earlier, that *minimum* propagation delays are not usually specified by IC manufacturers. Consequently, while it is one thing to understand the *nature* of maximum allowable clock skew, it is quite another thing to *determine* it for a given circuit.

5-7 PSEUDOSYNCHRONOUS CLOCKING

On occasion it is useful to derive *gated* clock signals in addition to the normal CLOCK signal. We must pay careful attention to the timing involved so that the rising edges of the gated clock signals coincide with the rising edges of CLOCK. Because of this coincidence of separate clock edges, the circuitry that utilizes these separate *pseudo-synchronous* clock signals will benefit from the same timing simplicity that arises with synchronous design.

This technique will permit us, in effect, to add a clock-enable input to any sequential device. For example, the quad two-input multiplexer with storage, shown in Fig. 5-44*a*, consists of four D-type flip-flops which are driven by a quad 2-line–to–1-line multiplexer. Each time a clock transition occurs, the data in the four flip-flops will be *replaced* by one of the two sets of four inputs. We cannot hold the data. By *gating* the clock, we obtain the equivalent of the device shown in Fig. 5-43*b*, which *does* hold the data in the flip-flops if the input labeled G2 is inactive when the clock transition occurs.

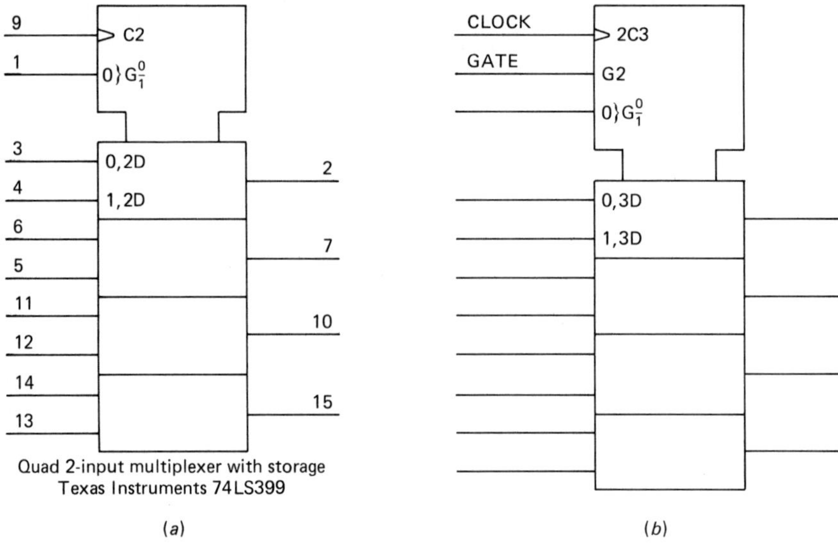

Figure 5-44. Creation of equivalent parts by gating the clock. (a) Actual device; (b) equivalent device after gating the clock.

To gate the clock inputs to sequential devices which are sensitive to *low-to-high* transitions, we need to use an AND gate with active-low output, such as either device of Fig. 5-45. This will let us form a pulse whose *trailing edge* defines the end of the clock period.

Pseudosynchronous clocking of a circuit is illustrated in Fig. 5-46. All rising edges on CLOCK, CLOCK1, and CLOCK2 occur one propagation delay after the falling edge on C*, the oscillator's output which drives the buffers. Consequently, the difference between these

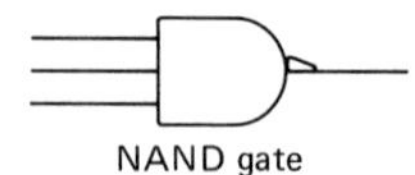

Figure 5-45. Gates that are suitable for gating the clock input to positive-edge-triggered sequential devices.

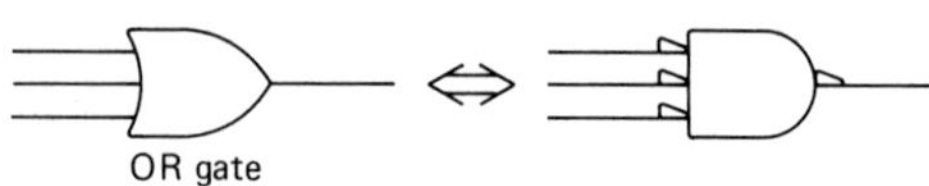

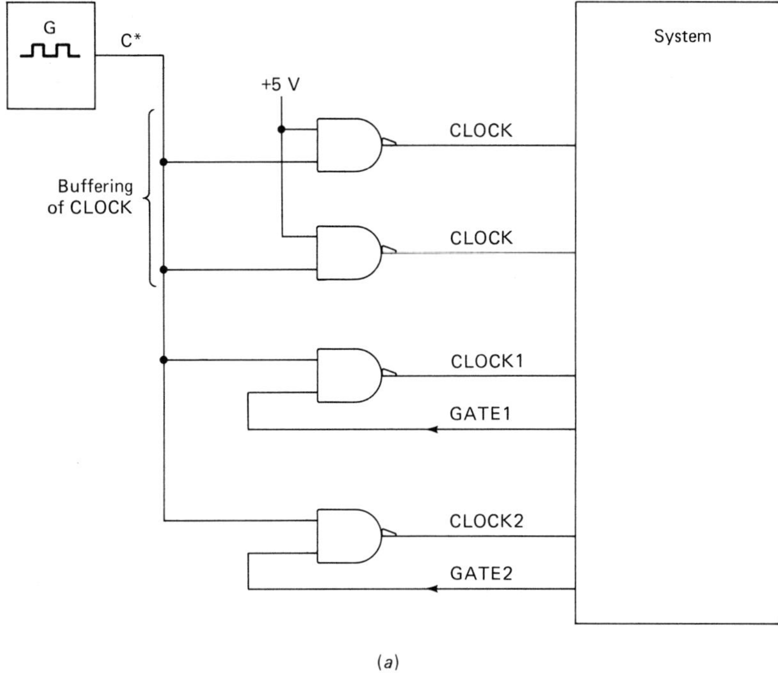

(a)

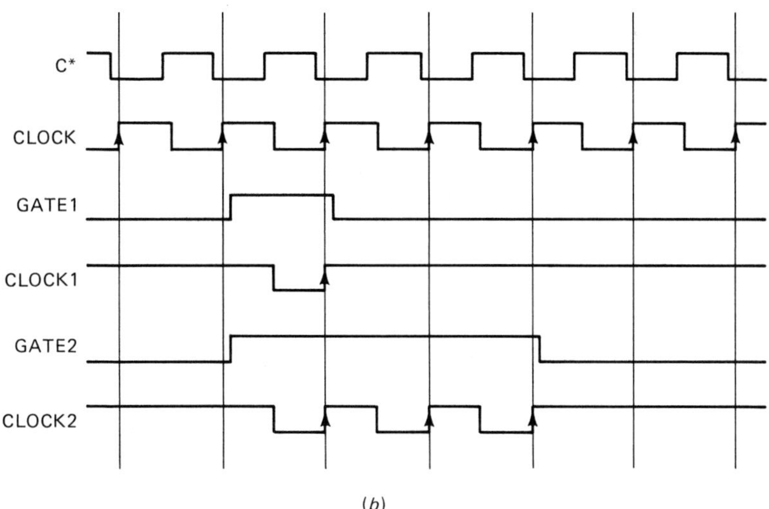

(b)

Figure 5-46. Pseudosynchronous clocking. (a) *Circuit;* (b) *timing diagram.*

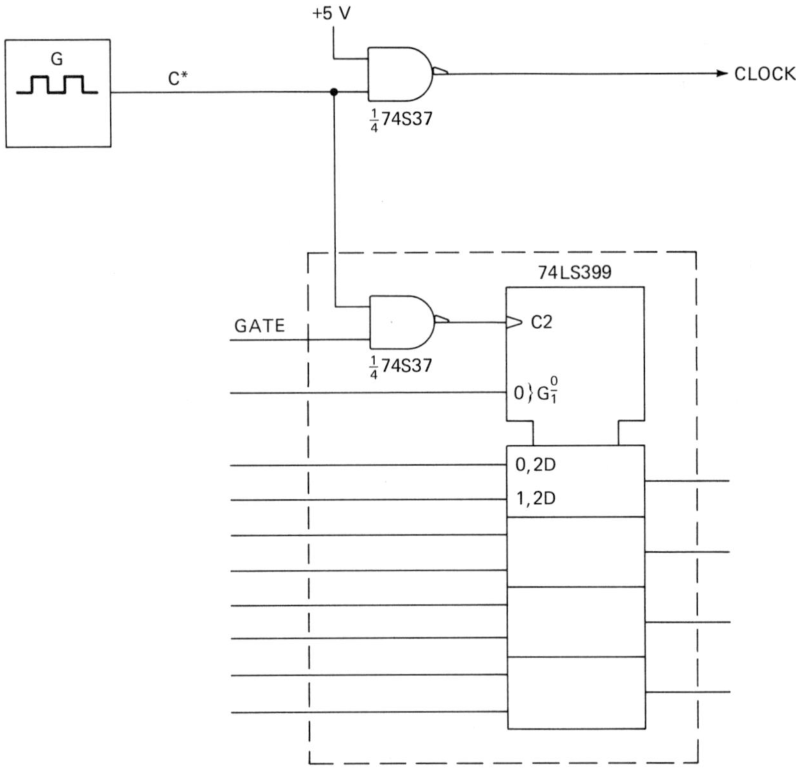

Figure 5-47. Implementation of Fig. 5-44b.

propagation delays must be less than the maximum allowable clock skew permitted by the system circuitry.

Since GATE1 (used to generate CLOCK1) comes from the pseudo-synchronously clocked circuit, its changes will occur (when they occur) *early* in a clock period, when C* has already gone low. Thus with C* low during the first half of each clock period, any settling out taking place on GATE1 and GATE2 during this time is irrelevant.

We will conclude by implementing the gated clock of Fig. 5-43. If we employ the 74S37 quad NAND buffer of Fig. 2-72*b* for clock drivers, we will tend to minimize clock skew since they are all fast and since they were manufactured together (and therefore shared identical IC processing). The circuit is shown in Fig. 5-47. If C* is a square wave, GATE must settle out before C* goes high, halfway into the clock period. This sets a constraint upon the maximum clock rate which must be met in addition to the constraints imposed by the rest of the synchronously clocked circuitry.

PROBLEMS

5-1 Latch circuit. Construct a latch circuit with NOR gates. Show the circuit and symbol, including pin numbers, for a latch built with two of the four NOR gates in a 74LS02, analogous to Fig. 5-1.

5-2 Transparency. A counter with a static load input can be used to combine a count function with a multiplexer function. However, we must be willing to destroy the counter contents when we want to drive the output lines from another source. For example, a 74LS191 up/down binary counter will let its four flip-flop outputs be driven directly by the four data inputs if pin 11 is pulled low. When pin 11 is high, these inputs are disconnected and the device behaves like a synchronous up/down counter.

(*a*) Draw a dependency notation symbol for this counter.

(*b*) Describe an example of how this counter might be used transparently during normal operation but as a counter during testing.

5-3 Transparency. Is the RAM of Fig. 5-3 transparent? If so, explain. If not, redraw the symbol as it would look for a RAM that is identical in every respect except for being transparent.

5-4 RAM characteristics. For a bipolar RAM for which you have data (other than one of the two described in this chapter), show the symbolic representation, read timing, and write timing in the form of Fig. 5-3.

5-5 Latch timing characteristics. Repeat Prob. 5-4 for the octal latch of Fig. 5-2*a*, using timing specifications taken from a manufacturer's data book. Use the same timing specification names (e.g., t_{WSD}) as in Fig. 5-3.

5-6 Edge-triggered RAM. Consider the data sheet for the Texas Instruments 74LS208 256 × 4 positive-edge-triggered RAM (available in Texas Instruments' *Bipolar Microcomputer Components Data Book for Design Engineers*). Discuss this RAM's setup/hold-time characteristics and the consequences of using this RAM in a synchronous system designed with 74LSxxx parts if the system clock is tied to the WRITE input (pin 14).

5-7 J-K flip-flops. Using as little extra gating as possible, figure out and show how to convert one of the J-K flip-flops of Fig. 5-4 into each of the following. Redraw the symbol in each case, labeling pin numbers.

(*a*) A D-type flip-flop with active-high D-type input.

(*b*) A T-type, toggle flip-flop which, when the clock transition occurs, will toggle if T is high and do nothing if T is low.

(*c*) A J-K flip-flop with active-low J input and active-high K input.

5-8 Ripple counters. For the TTL 4-bit asynchronous binary counter with the fastest clock rate for which you have data:

(*a*) Show a circuit to make an 8-bit counter.

(*b*) Determine the worst-case propagation delay between clock input and output.

(*c*) If a 74S30 8-input NAND gate is used to detect the all-1s state, what is the maximum input clock rate that can be used if the gate output must be stable 20 ns (worst-case) before the input clock transition occurs which counts the counter back to the all-0s state?

5-9 Ones-catching devices. Look at the data sheet for the 74LS191 up/down binary counter. Is it a ones-catching part? How do you know?

5-10 Flip-flop structure. If the 1K input to the flip-flop of Fig. 5-6 is connected to the 1J input through an inverter, will the resulting D-type flip-flop be ones-catching? Explain.

5-11 Flip-flop structure. Show how one of the 74LS109A flip-flops of Fig. 5-4 (complete with static inputs) might be implemented with a modification of the structure of Fig. 5-8.

5-12 Maximum propagation delay. Using the Signetics 82S100 FPLA access-time data from the table in Fig. 2-67, and implementing a 16-input multiplexer with the circuit of Fig. 2-42, determine the worst-case path and the maximum propagation delay of the circuit of Fig. 2-63.

5-13 Maximum propagation delay. Repeat Prob. 5-12 using a large (24-pin DIP) 74150 16-input multiplexer.

5-14 Maximum clock rate. (*a*) Using PROM access-time data from the table of Fig. 2-49, a 74LS151 multiplexer, and 74LS195 shift registers (operating in the parallel-load mode), determine the maximum reliable clock rate of the circuit of Fig. 4-19. Assume that START-H and STOP-H come directly from 74LS195 outputs.

(*b*) Determine the worst-case propagation delay between the clock edge and HOLD-L. This is useful for maximum clock rate calculations for the ASM circuit that looks at HOLD-L.

5-15 Maximum clock rate. Assuming that PROBE is generated as the output of a 74LS195 shift register, determine the maximum reliable clock rate of the signature analyzer data acquisition circuitry of Fig. 4-5.

5-16 Maximum clock rate. Using PROM access-time data from the table of Fig. 2-49 and assuming that all registers are 74LS195 parts (operating in the parallel-load mode), determine the maximum reliable clock rate of the circuit of Fig. 4-22. Assume that START-H and STOP-H come directly from 74LS195 outputs.

5-17 Maximum clock rate. Using a square-wave clock and a ones-catching 74161 counter, repeat Prob. 5-16.

5-18 Maximum clock rate. Comment on the application of the rule of thumb discussed at the end of Sec. 5-2 to

(*a*) Prob. 5-14 (*b*) Prob. 5-15
(*c*) Prob. 5-16 (*d*) Prob. 5-17

5-19 Race conditions. Looking through Texas Instruments' *TTL Data Book for Design Engineers* for 74LSxxx clocked sequential devices:

(*a*) What is the longest hold time you find?

(*b*) What is the shortest "typical" clock-to-output propagation delay you find?

(*c*) *If* the following were a valid way to extrapolate to minimum propagation delay from typical and maximum values, could the parts above be used together in a synchronous circuit?

$$\frac{\text{Maximum}}{\text{Typical}} = \frac{\text{typical}}{\text{minimum}}$$

5-20 Setup/hold-time input specifications. Check the operating and service manual(s) for an instrument that operates upon input data synchronized to a clock.

(*a*) What is the worst-case setup-time specification for the inputs?

(*b*) What is the worst-case hold-time specification for the inputs?

(*c*) Is this achieved with fast, but standard, front-end parts? Or with selected parts? (How might you tell this?) Or with trimmed propagation delays? Discuss.

5-21 Translation of input timing characteristics. Reconsider the positive-edge-triggered RAM of Prob. 5-6.

(*a*) Minimizing package count and showing the resulting circuit, augment the inputs to the RAM appropriately so as to achieve "zero-hold-time" specifications. Assume that you have available to you both 74LS04 hex inverters and 74LS08 quad two-input AND gates which have been sorted into the following sets (assuming a load of two or less 74LSxxx inputs and 15-pF capacitance).

74LS04(4 − 8) and 74LS08(4 − 8):
4 ns < propagation delay < 8 ns
74LS04(6 − 10) and 74LS08(6 − 10):
6 ns < propagation delay < 10 ns
74LS04(8 − 12) and 74LS08(8 − 12):
8 ns < propagation delay < 12 ns
74LS04(10–14) and 74LS08(10–14):
10 ns < propagation delay < 14 ns
74LS04(other) and 74LS08(other):
all others

(*b*) List the timing specifications for the derived RAM circuit (including the augmenting parts).

5-22 Instrument input design. Assume that we can ensure zero hold time on the clocked data inputs to an instrument by adding pairs of 74LS04 inverters (in series) to each data line.

(*a*) If we use unselected 74LS04s, what is the effect of this approach upon the input setup-time specifications?

(*b*) Discuss the specific role played by the propagation delay tolerance of the 74LS04s upon the problem.

5-23 Setup-time transformer. Consider the register and RAM circuit of Fig. 5-26.

(*a*) What are the critical specifications *between* the two parts needed to achieve reliable operation?

(*b*) If this condition were not met, show how (minimal) extra circuitry (e.g., 74LS04s and/or 74LS08s) could be used to provide reliable operation.

5-24 Input buffers. The Signetics 8T37 hex buffer shown in Fig. 5-27 is remarkable for its high input impedance and short propagation delay. Can you discover any other +5-V-powered devices with shorter maximum propagation delay which also present minimal loading to 74LSxxx parts?

5-25 Protection diodes. If a manufacturer of SIP resistor packages (like those of Fig. 2-38) were to make a SIP *diode* package to meet the opportunity afforded by "everybody's input protection problem" shown resolved in Fig. 5-28, then aside from the width of the package (e.g., 10 pins for 8 diode pairs), would there be a market for parts having different diode characteristics? Or could one set of characteristics serve all? What diode characteristics are important to this application?

5-26 Propagation-delay trimming procedure. (*a*) Discuss the signals you can apply to the CLOCK* and START* inputs of Fig. 5-32 so as to adjust the Start trimpot in Fig. 5-33.

(*b*) Show circuitry to generate these signals.

(*c*) What would you display on an oscilloscope and how would you adjust the trimpot to achieve exactly zero hold time? Note that the setup/hold-time ambiguity region of Fig. 5-4*b* reduces to zero for this measurement.

(*d*) How might you determine a rough calibration of the trimpot so that this ambiguity region might be backed off by 7 ns (so that aging, power-supply voltage variations, and so on, can have ±7-ns tolerance and still meet zero-hold-time, 15-ns setup-time specifications?

(*e*) Alternatively, what inputs could have been applied to CLOCK* and START* to achieve this 7-ns setup time directly? How might they be generated?

(*f*) Could the same procedure also be used to set the trimpots for STOP* and PROBE*?

5-27 Three-state input circuitry. (*a*) If the 8T37 of Fig. 5-27 were used in the circuit of Fig. 5-29*a*, determine the maximum value of R_x which can be used in the circuit of Fig. P5-27. The trimpot shown permits an adjustment so that a disconnected PROBE*

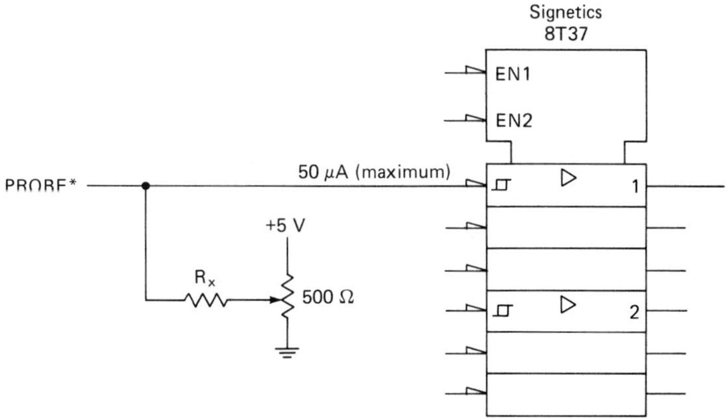

Figure P5-27

input will float at 1.4 V. This is done to compensate for a "fixed" bias current into (or out of) the 8T37 which might be as large as 50 μA.

(*b*) Assuming that this bias current is independent of the input voltage on PROBE*, what is the input impedance to this circuit?

(*c*) Redesign the circuit to provide the protection of Fig. 5-28 and as high an input impedance as is possible.

5-28 Multiple-phase clocking. What is the maximum reliable clock rate for the circuit of Fig. 5-36 which will ensure that the glitch of Fig. 5-37 will not occur? Assume that the circuit of Fig. 5-41 is used to generate CLOCK and STATIC3/4.

5-29 RAM use. For the circuit of Fig. 5-40, describe what will happen if we try to read from and write to the RAM during the same clock period. Will the data last written into the selected address during previous clock periods be the data read out during the present clock period? Explain.

5-30 Multiple-phase clock generator. Describe why a Gray-code counter serves better in the circuit of Fig. 5-41 than a binary counter would.

5-31 Multiple-phase clock generator. (*a*) The 74LS669 counter of Fig. 5-42 lists a maximum clock rate of 25 MHz for counting. However in the connection shown, the counter must parallel-load when it is in state 0. Working with data book specifications for this part, determine its maximum reliable clock rate in this application.

(*b*) Repeat this problem, replacing the 74LS669 with the similar, but faster, 74S169.

5-32 Narrow-pulse-width clock generator. We want only a single-phase clock, but we wish to control the duty cycle to improve the setup time of ones-catching master-slave flip-flops. Use just the 74LS669 of Fig. 5-42 but connect pins 10 and 2 together and to the generator output labeled f.

(*a*) Will the counter now count?

(*b*) Will it parallel-load correctly to roll over from 0 to 4?

(*c*) Will CLOCK exhibit glitches?

(*d*) Draw a timing diagram.

(*e*) Modify the design so that CLOCK is low for one-twentieth of the clock period.

5-33 Maximum allowable clock skew. Modify the CLOCK output circuitry of Fig. 5-41 to drive a heavier load. Assume that the clock load is larger than can be handled with a single 74S37 NAND buffer.

5-34 Pseudosynchronous clocking. Does it matter whether t_{PHL} is essentially equal to t_{PLH} for the NAND gates of Fig. 5-46? Explain.

5-35 Pseudosynchronous clocking. The rising edges of CLOCK, CLOCK1, and CLOCK2 are shown occurring at exactly the same time at the end of the second clock period of the timing diagram of Fig. 5-46*b*.

(*a*) What event(s) in the circuit gives rise to these three edges?

(*b*) Does the exact timing of either edge of GATE1 affect the timing of the rising edge of CLOCK1?

5-36 Gating the clock to a sequential device. The circuit of Fig. 5-47 assumes that GATE is derived from a single-phase, pseudosynchronously clocked circuit. If, in fact, GATE is derived from the output of a counter that is statically reset, show the timing relationship required between C* and the STATICm/n clock phase used for resetting so that the settling of GATE will not produce a glitch (which might clock the 74LS399).

SEPARATELY CLOCKED CIRCUITS

Two factors have drastically altered the way in which instruments are being organized:

1. The *density* of logic has reached the point where the hardware to implement an *extensive* task, plus the microcomputer to control it, can all fit on a single PC board.
2. The rapidly decreasing cost of microcomputers encourages designs that employ *several* microcomputers if this will simplify other aspects of the design (e.g., communication between boards, testing, simultaneous control of several devices).

The problem of organizing an instrument around several microcomputers is part of the larger problem of ensuring reliable interactions between separately clocked circuits. In this chapter we will consider a variety of ways of doing this.

6-1 SWITCHING BETWEEN CLOCK SOURCES

The foreground/background scheme of instrument organization discussed in Sec. 3-7 utilized two clocks. The system clock SC ran at normal speed, doing the job of the instrument. Periodically, the mode

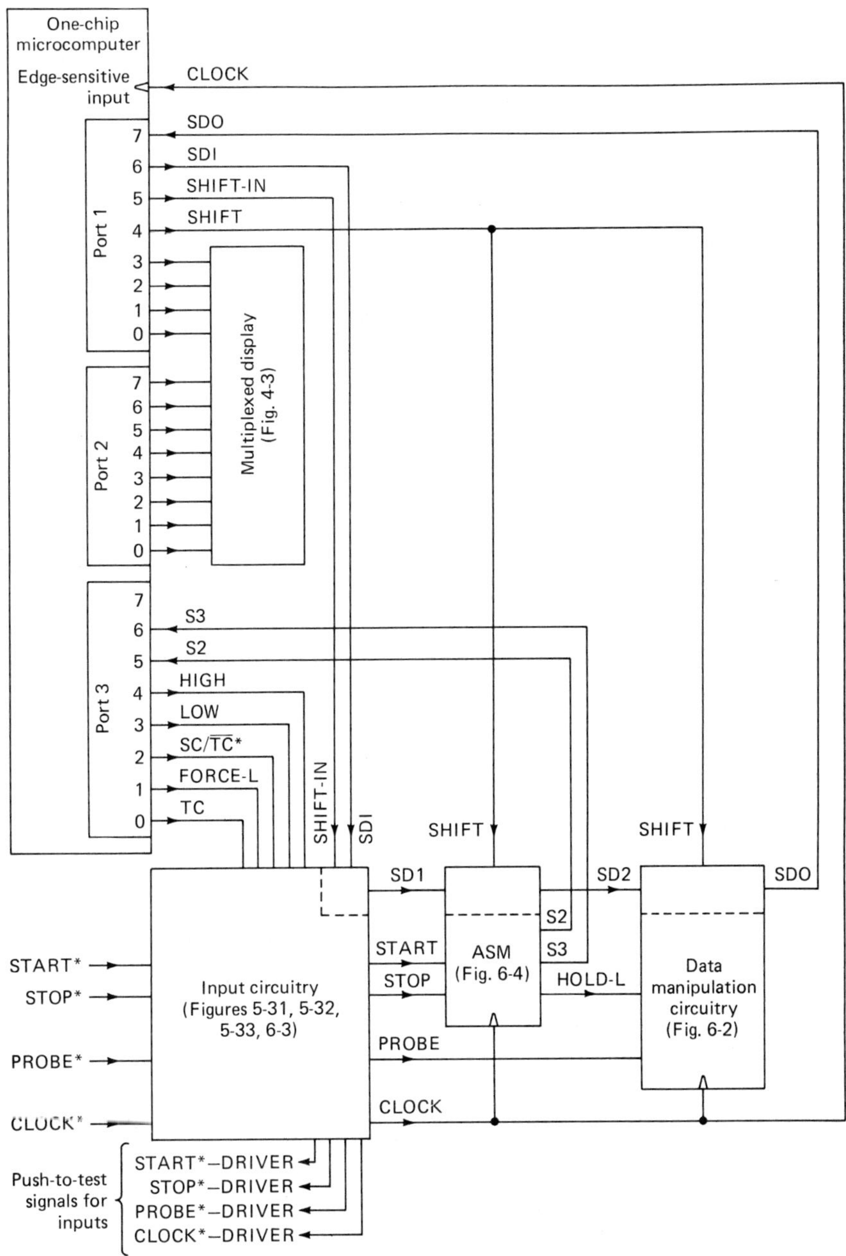

Figure 6-1. Signature analyzer block diagram for the switched-clock design.

was changed so that all the sequential devices became organized into a shift register. The clock for all these sequential devices was switched from the fast system clock to a test clock TC generated by the microcomputer. As long as the interactions between the separately clocked circuits can be delayed until the mode can be switched in this way, this organization, which aids testing, also aids interactions between the microcomputer and the separately clocked hardware.

In this section we will use the signature analyzer design which we have been developing as a vehicle for exploring the possibilities of this approach. Reconsider the block diagram of Fig. 4-23*a*. The multiplexed display circuitry, shown in detail in Fig. 4-3, consists solely of the displays plus the buffering circuitry to drive them. Since it is *already* driven by the microcomputer, the microcomputer has no problem in communicating with it. In contrast, the input circuitry, ASM, and data manipulation circuitry are clocked by the externally derived CLOCK. In Chap. 4 we handled the interactions between the microcomputer and this externally clocked circuitry by handshaking. Here, the handshaking lines will be replaced by the data and control lines for handling the foreground/background scheme, shown in Fig. 6-1.

The foreground/background scheme includes provision for *initializing* all foreground sequential devices. The desired initial values are *shifted* into all flip-flops as the last step before switching from the background mode to the foreground mode. This will permit a modification of the data manipulation circuitry, shown in Fig. 6-2, since we no longer need a reset input to the 16-bit shift register. The 16-bit shift register will be reset by shifting 16 zeros into it while it is still in the background mode. As a consequence, the shift register capability that we need is reduced to a serial in/parallel out device with enabled clock. However, we need to be able to switch the clock enable input and also the data input with the SHIFT line from the microcomputer that controls the mode (SHIFT = 1 in the background mode; SHIFT = 0 in the foreground mode).

To accentuate the background mode interconnections, Fig. 6-3 illustrates these. It also shows the variables which are loaded into the shift register for a push-to-test exercise of the instrument, including inputs connected to test signals. The mode is switched from background to foreground for one clock period. Then it is returned to the background mode. In this way a test condition can be serially loaded from the microcomputer into all the flip-flops of the system. This test condition propagates through all the combinational circuitry and back around to the parallel-load inputs to the flip-flops. Clocking once in the foreground mode (SHIFT = SHIFT-N = 1) loads these values so that they can be shifted back to the microcomputer (in the background mode again) for conversion into a test signature.

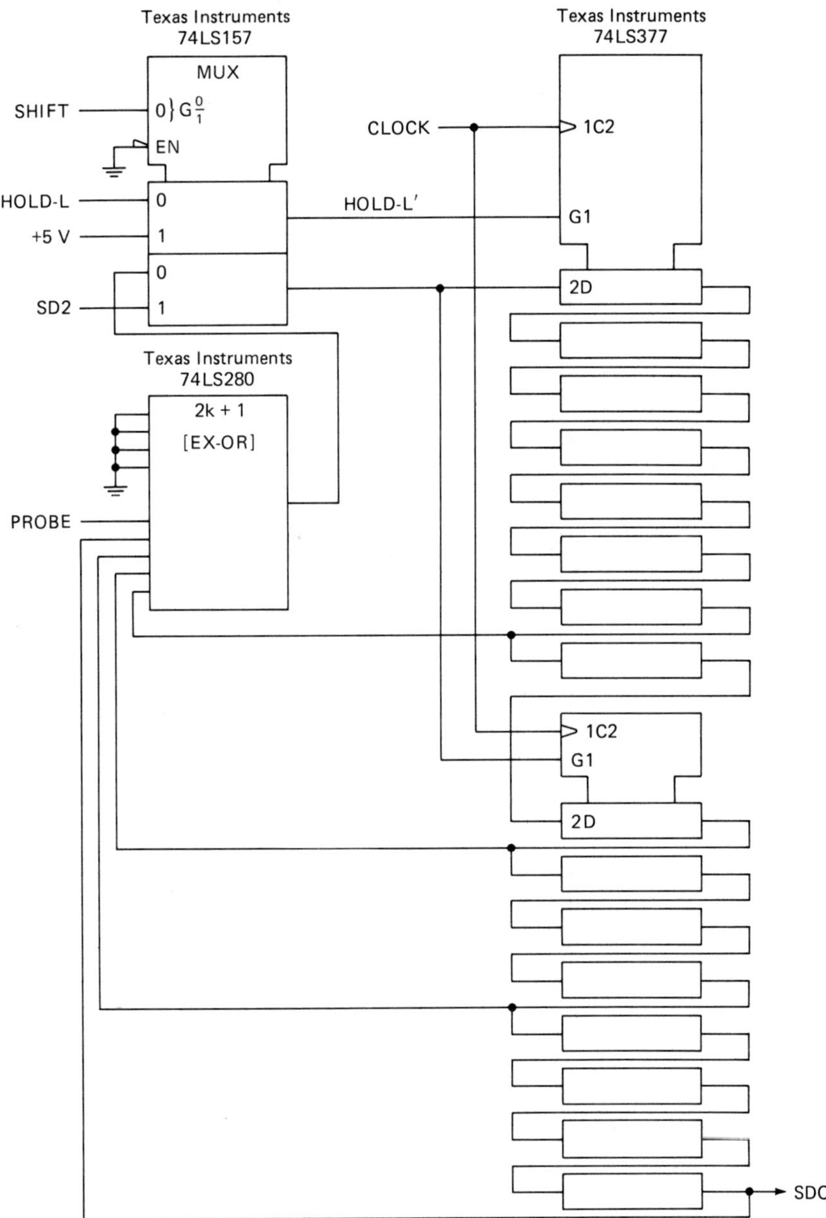

Figure 6-2. Signature analyzer data manipulation circuitry (modification of Fig. 4-5 for foreground/background control by SHIFT).

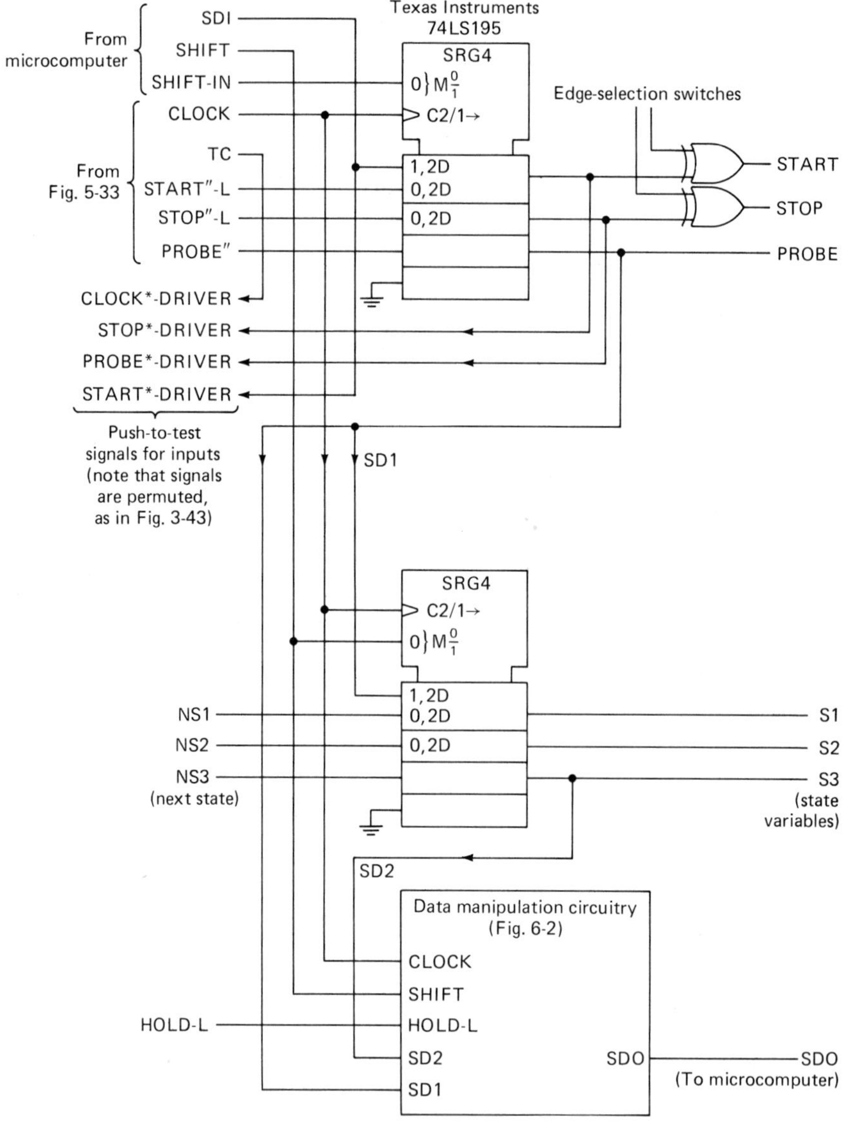

Figure 6-3. Background view of signature analyzer (SHIFT = SHIFT-IN = 0).

For self-test, the same scheme is used except that SHIFT-IN is left in the background mode (SHIFT-IN = 0) throughout. This permits a test signature to be obtained which is independent of the ambiguity that would arise from actual instrument inputs.

For signature analysis, the circuit is never switched to the foreground mode. Instead, we can use the highly time-efficient PRBS generator scheme of Prob. 3-28 to push a continuous pseudo-random binary sequence through the background mode shift register. The PRBS6 subroutine of Prob. 3-30(b) will *completely* exercise every possible input and state combination of the ASM in 63 successive shifts. In the process, the data manipulation circuitry will also be completely tested.

Notice that signature analysis can be used to isolate faults anywhere in the circuit *except for* the parallel-loading of the 74LS195 shift registers. By never parallel-loading these registers, we break all feedback loops in the circuit. Although we cannot check the parallel-loading itself via signature analysis, we do get a check on every signal that *would* be parallel-loaded (e.g., NS3 of Fig. 6-3). As a consequence, we should include a push-to-test algorithm which performs a separate check of the parallel loading of each 74LS195 and which blinks a diagnostic message (e.g., CHP1 or CHP2) if chip 1 or chip 2 (the two 74LS195s) will not parallel-load correctly.

The ASM chart shown in Fig. 6-4 is simpler than that discussed in Fig. 4-13 because the states required to handshake with the microcomputer are no longer necessary. States have been carefully assigned so that the microcomputer can look at only two of the three state variables (S2 and S3) and tell when a signature has been successfully collected (S3=1) of it it is hung up waiting for START* (S3=0, S2=0) or waiting for STOP* (S3=0, S2=1).

At this point we should count the cost of enhancing maintainability by taking this foreground/background approach. The two 74LS195 4-bit shift registers replace one octal flip-flop part. The multiplexer in the data manipulation circuitry is the second extra package. On the other hand, the ASM circuit can now be implemented with a small 32 × 8 PROM (plus flip-flops) since it has only two inputs and three state variables. The input circuitry of Fig. 5-33 includes the clock-switching circuitry. If this were removed, three packages (74LS74, 74LS153, and 74LS14) could be saved. However, presumably this would be offset to some extent by providing testing capability in some other way. Whether or not we use the foreground/background approach, we might still want to switch the clock so that the microcomputer can clock everything during testing.

6-2 COMMUNICATION VIA RAM

Direct memory access† (DMA) control of a RAM is a common way for external circuitry to communicate with a microcomputer. A DMA

† Refer to the author's *Microcomputer-Based Design*, McGraw-Hill, New York, 1977, sec. 3-8.

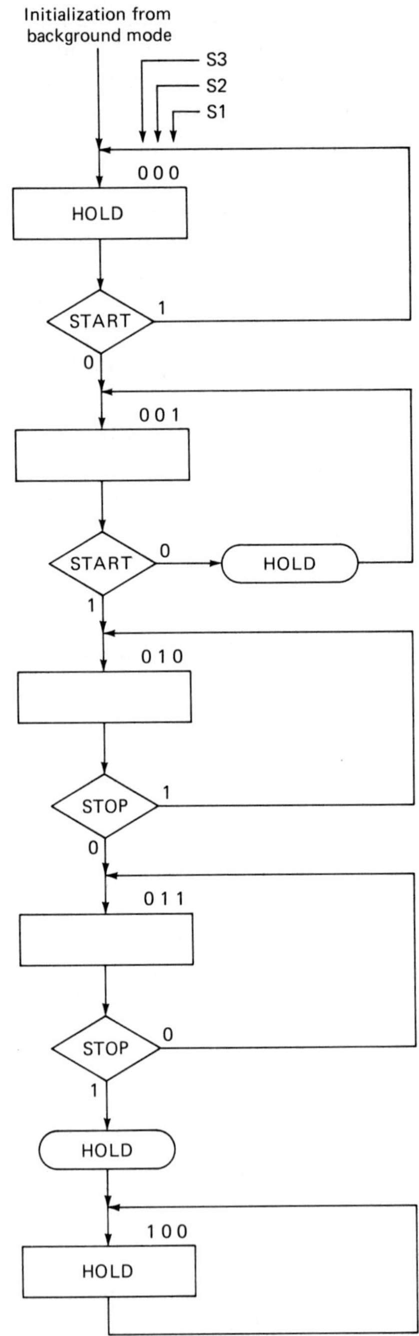

Figure 6-4. Signature analyzer ASM chart for the switched-clock design.

channel is first set up by the microcomputer. Then, every time the external circuitry signals the microcomputer's DMA controller that it is ready to access the next word in memory, the microcomputer stops what it is doing and the DMA controller does an automatic read from memory to the external circuitry (or an automatic write to memory from the external circuitry).

The technique described above is useful where an array of data in successive RAM locations is to be accessed (perhaps repeatedly accessed). This occurs in the refreshing of a CRT video display. It accounts for the DMA approach being used in many video display circuits.

Another approach to the sharing of RAM between separately clocked circuits is to use a two-port RAM. This approach is useful where the amount of data to be shared is small, since the largest two-port RAMs tend to be *much* smaller than the largest one-port RAMs. For example, the 16 × 4 two-port RAM shown in Fig. 6-5 is one of the largest units available, yet it only contains a 64-bit RAM (plus latches on all 8 outputs). The "1A, 3D" labeling of pins 2, 1, 27, and 26 indicates that the data on these pins will be written into the 1A address selected by the inputs on pins 4, 5, 6, and 7 when C3 is active (i.e., when pins 25 and 3 are pulled low). The "1A-4D" labeling says that when C4 is active, the contents of the 1A address will be strobed into the transparent latches driving output pins 10, 12, 15, and 17. These three-state outputs are enabled by pulling pin 19 low. The four latches driving pins 11, 13, 16, and 18 are reset if pin 8 is pulled low. The contents of the 2A address are written into these four latches if C4 is active.

As a means for communicating between two separately clocked circuits, this RAM can be usefully simplified as shown in Fig. 6-5*b*. Here the latches are made transparent and the outputs on pins 10, 12, 15, and 17 are ignored. This RAM is written into by one of the circuits. Completely independently, a separately clocked circuit can read data out of an arbitrary address. Of course, if that address is being written into at the moment of reading, the data read out might be the old data, the new data, or a little bit of both. Consequently, this approach to moving data between separately clocked circuits is appropriate only for applications that are insensitive to this problem.

A smaller 4 × 4 two-port RAM, packaged in a 16-pin DIP, is shown in Fig. 6-6. It does the job of Fig. 6-5*b*, but for only four addresses instead of 16. One of these RAMs is used in the Hewlett-Packard design of the signature analyzer we have been discussing. It buffers between the externally clocked ASM and data manipulation circuitry and the internally clocked multiplexed display. The refresh circuitry for the display reads one character at a time out of the RAM and

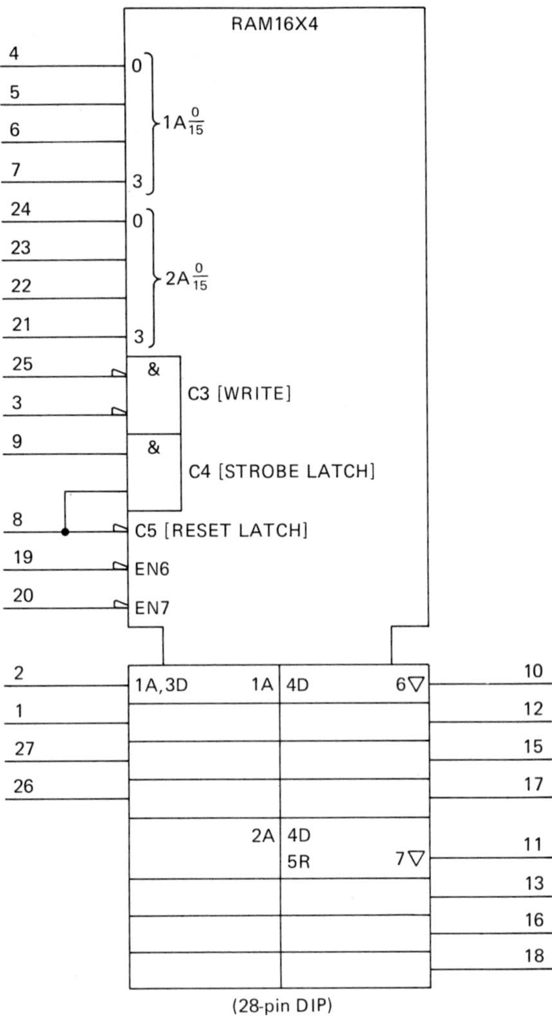

Figure 6-5. 29705, 16 × 4 two-port RAM. (Advanced Micro Devices, Inc.) (a) Full representation.

drives one digit of the display with it. By sequencing through the four successive characters faster than the eye's blink rate, the refresh circuitry gives the desired visual output. If a garbled character is displayed when the RAM is updated with a new signature, it will only be garbled for one refresh—faster than the blink of an eye.

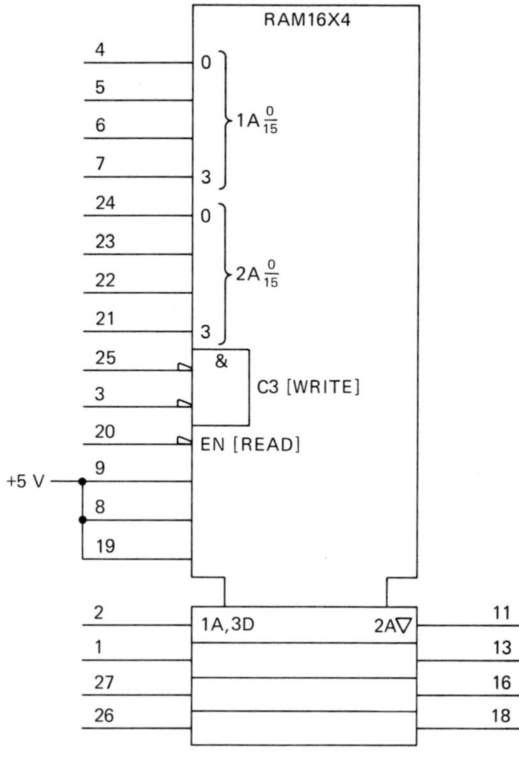

Figure 6-5b. Simplified representation.

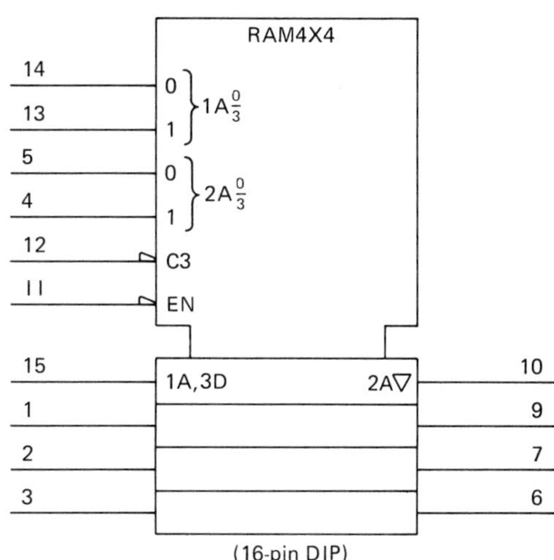

Figure 6-6. 74LS670, 4 × 4 two-port RAM. (Texas Instruments.)

6-3 HANDSHAKING

In Chap. 4 we utilized handshaking to provide reliable data transfer between a microcomputer and the data manipulation circuitry of the signature analyzer. Although only one line of data was transferred in that case, the handshaking operation demonstrated there was as thorough and complete as it would be for handling *many* lines during each transfer.

Generally, handshaking is thought of as a process of ensuring reliable data transfer from a talker to a listener. The talker raises a data valid (DAV) flag when it has put a new word of valid data on the data transfer lines AND when it sees that the listener has lowered its data accepted (DAC) flag, whereby it completed the previous handshake. The talker will lower DAV when it sees DAC raised again, signifying that the listener has accepted the new word of valid data.

Handshaking can be usefully employed to provide reliable data transfer not only from a talker to a listener but also from a listener back to a talker. In fact, this is exactly what was happening in the ASM for the signature analyzer (Fig. 4-13) when the ASM looked simultaneously at the DAC flag and at DONE. While DONE might be thought of as a second flag, it is more general to think of it as representing *any* data being transferred back from the listener to the talker. Reliable data transfer only requires that DONE (or in general any listener-to-talker data) be valid, or stable, *before* the DAC flag is raised. In the block diagram of Fig. 4-2 we saw that DONE and DAC came from the same port 3 of the microcomputer. The temptation is to save a couple of instructions and raise DONE and DAC together (to signify that the last data transfer has been completed). Most of the time this will work. However, once in a while the externally generated clock edge will occur just as these are both being raised. If DAC is read as its new value while DONE is read as its old value, a faulty handshake of DONE will have occurred.

Example 6-1. What will happen, given the ASM chart of Fig. 4-13, if DONE is misread in this fashion?

The ASM will return to the WAIT FOR DAC = 0 state. The microcomputer will lower DAC and DONE, knowing that it has collected the complete 16-bit signature. The ASM will then see DAC lowered and raise DAV. Although no new signature has been collected, the new 16-bit contents of the data manipulation circuitry's shift register will be handshaken to the microcomputer. That is, the microcomputer will think it is getting a properly collected new signature. Since this new signature will (almost certainly) not agree with the last signature, the microcomputer will blink the "unstable signature" light to the user. The signature analyzer has not only goofed, but it tells the world about its goof!

The use of DONE by the signature analyzer design of Chap. 4 exemplifies a worthy feature for *any* ASM design. If the ASM communicates with a microcomputer, we should let the microcomputer do as much as possible (such as counting the number of bits transferred) so that the ASM can do as little as possible. In a more general case, the microcomputer might look at the data that has been transferred and then handshake back a multiple-line response telling the ASM which of several alternative actions to begin next.

6-4 SERIAL DATA TRANSMISSION

A common way to transmit data between separately clocked circuits is to use *asynchronous serial data transmission.*† For example, a computer terminal uses this technique to transmit a character to a computer over a single line (plus ground), perhaps using the format shown in Fig. 6-7. Each time a terminal key is depressed, the line that had been high (while idle) goes low for one *bit time* (i.e., for the *start bit*) followed by the data bits coding the character. At the completion of the data bits, the line is raised for a *stop bit.* This ensures that the beginning of the next character can be identified by the next high-to-low transition on the line. As shown in Fig. 6-7*a*, if successive characters are being transmitted at less than the maximum data rate, the time between the end of the stop bit and the next start bit is filled with high, idle bits. Thus the start of the next character will again produce a high-to-low transition upon which the receiver can synchronize.

The receiver reads the serial data by synchronizing upon the high-to-low transition initiated by the start bit. Then it reads the line at $\frac{3}{2}$ bit times, $\frac{5}{2}$ bit times, $\frac{7}{2}$ bit times, and so on, to pick up successive data bits. Since the receiver (normally) uses its own clock to measure bit times, its measure of the duration of each bit time must be close to the actual bit time generated by the transmitter.

We will explore the specific characteristics of the serial data transmission used by the Motorola 6801 one-chip microcomputer of Fig.

† Refer to the author's *Microcomputer-Based Design*, McGraw-Hill, New York, 1977, sec. 5-9.

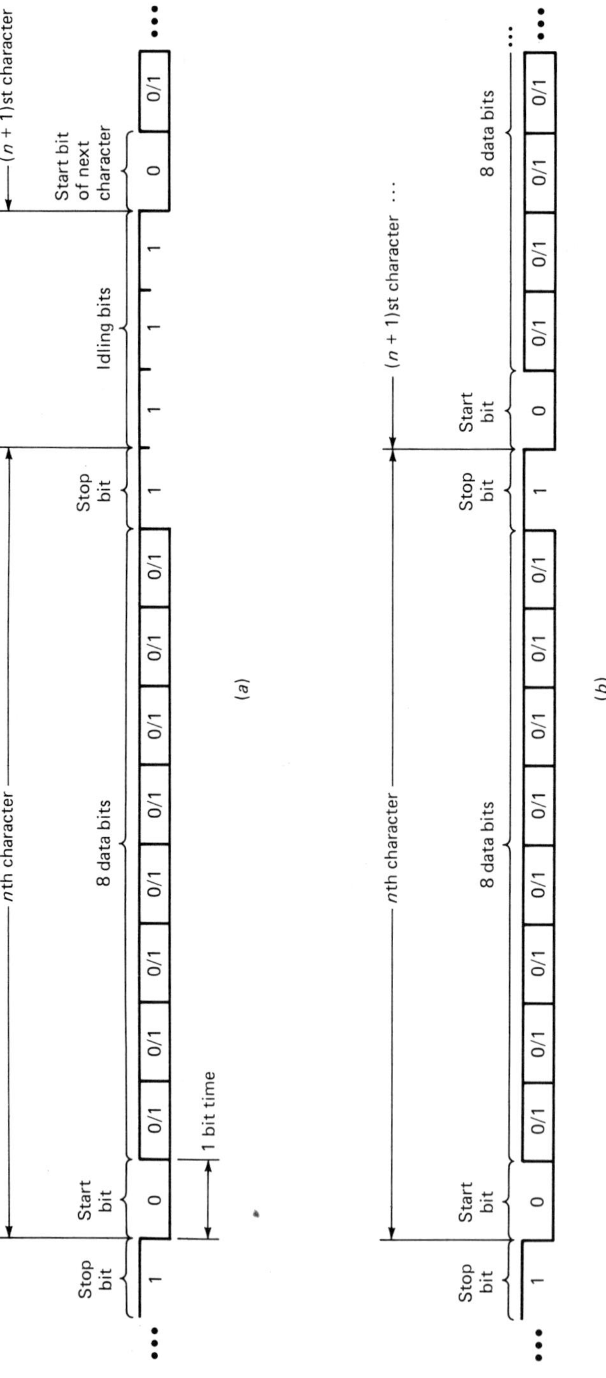

Figure 6-7. *Asynchronous serial data format.* (*a*) *Less than maximum data rate;* (*b*) *maximum data rate.*

1-2. This unit includes a built-in *UART*, or *universal asynchronous receiver transmitter*. Any time a character is written to hex address 13, it will be transmitted serially on bit 4 of port 2. Likewise, any time a character is received serially on bit 3 of port 2, it will be automatically written into hex address 12. This assumes that these two lines have been set up for this purpose under program control. We are particularly interested in this microcomputer's serial data transmission capability, since it superbly supports the coupling of several microcomputers together within an instrument, as will be discussed in the next section.

The format shown in Fig. 6-7 is exactly that used by the Motorola 6801. With a 4-MHz crystal, the 6801 offers a programmable choice of four bit times: 16 μs, 128 μs, 1.024 ms, and 4.096 ms. The transmitter and receiver clocks can be mismatched by as much as ±3.75 percent and still maintain proper synchronization.

It is common to append a *parity bit* to each character so that the receiver will have a check on the correctness of the received character, in spite of the idiosyncrasies of the transmission path, which might include acoustic couplers, telephones, and miles of telephone line. Because the Motorola 6801's serial data transmission capability was optimized for another purpose (i.e., for coupling several 6801s together within a single instrument), the designers of the 6801 opted to do without a parity bit (and the extra circuitry, and extra transmission time, required by it).

If an instrument employs several 6801s, each on a separate board and each with its own 4-MHz crystal, the tolerance on the transmitter and receiver clocks of ±3.75 percent is easily attainable. However, an instrument may include a microcomputer not having this built-in serial data transmission capability. In this case, the serial data transmission can be achieved with a software routine. This will be facilitated by the *biphase format* of data transmission shown in Fig. 6-8, which is also supported by the 6801 (as an alternative setup under program control). In this format, a *transition* is generated at every bit time. Another transition is generated at the center of every bit time during which a 1 is

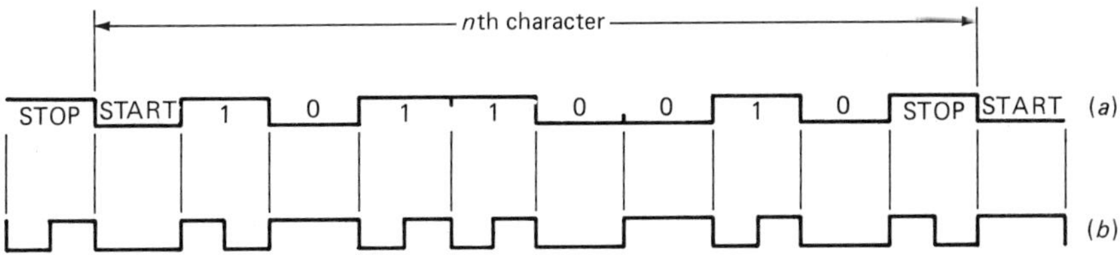

Figure 6-8. Alternative Motorola 6801 serial data formats. (a) *NRZ* (*nonreturn to zero*) *format;* (b) *biphase format.*

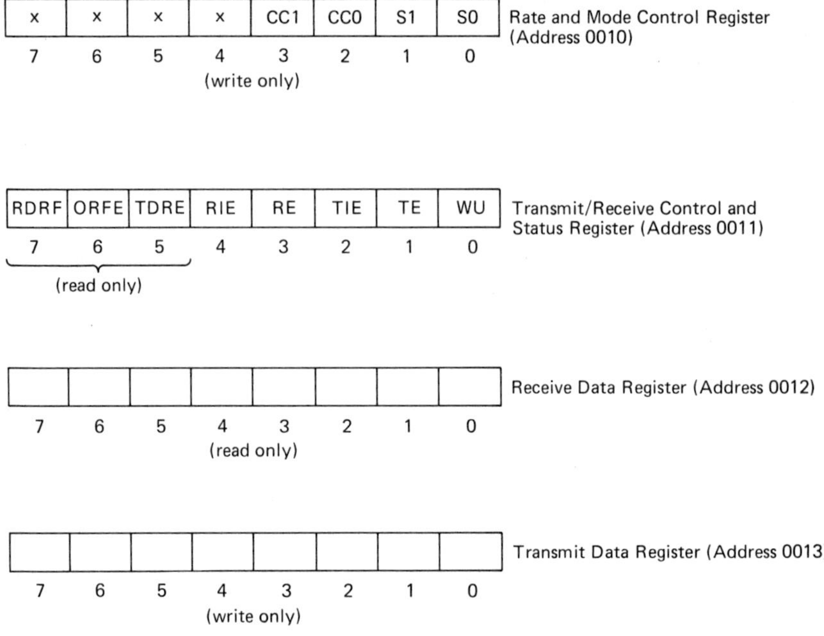

Figure 6-9. Register addressing for the Motorola 6801's UART.

being transmitted. Because no bit time goes by without a transition, the receiver can resynchronize on these transitions and maintain reliable data reception as long as its estimate of the bit time is within ±25 percent of the actual bit time.

The four Motorola 6801 registers associated with UART operation are shown in Fig. 6-9. Each is accessed by means of the hexadecimal address shown in that figure. The Rate and Mode Control Register must be written to initially, to set up the UART. The alternatives provided are shown in Fig. 6-10. Note that standard baud rates like 300 baud, 1200 baud, and 9600 baud are attainable if we use a 4.9152-MHz crystal. For serial data transmission between microcomputers, we would tend to select the highest rate easily available. With a 4-MHz crystal, this will result in a byte of data appearing in hex address 12 of a receiving 6801 roughly 160 μs after it is written into hex address 13 of a transmitting 6801. The data format alternatives are also shown in this figure.

The Transmit/Receive Control and Status Register contains five control bits and three read-only status bits, defined in Fig. 6-11. The TE and RE bits can be set if we wish to allocate bits 3 and 4 of port 2 to the UART function (rather than use them as general I/O bits). The

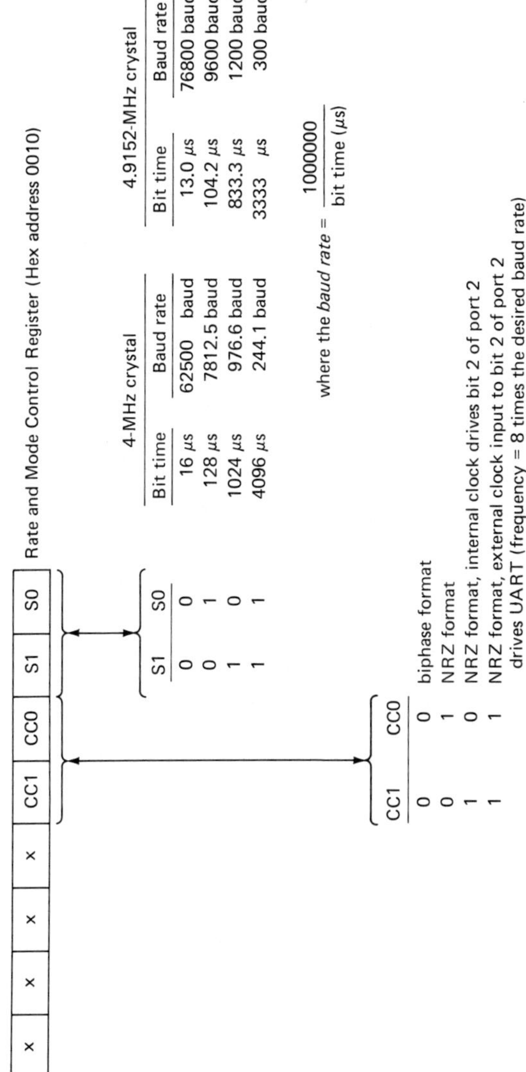

Figure 6-10. Motorola 6801 UART's Rate and Mode Control Register.

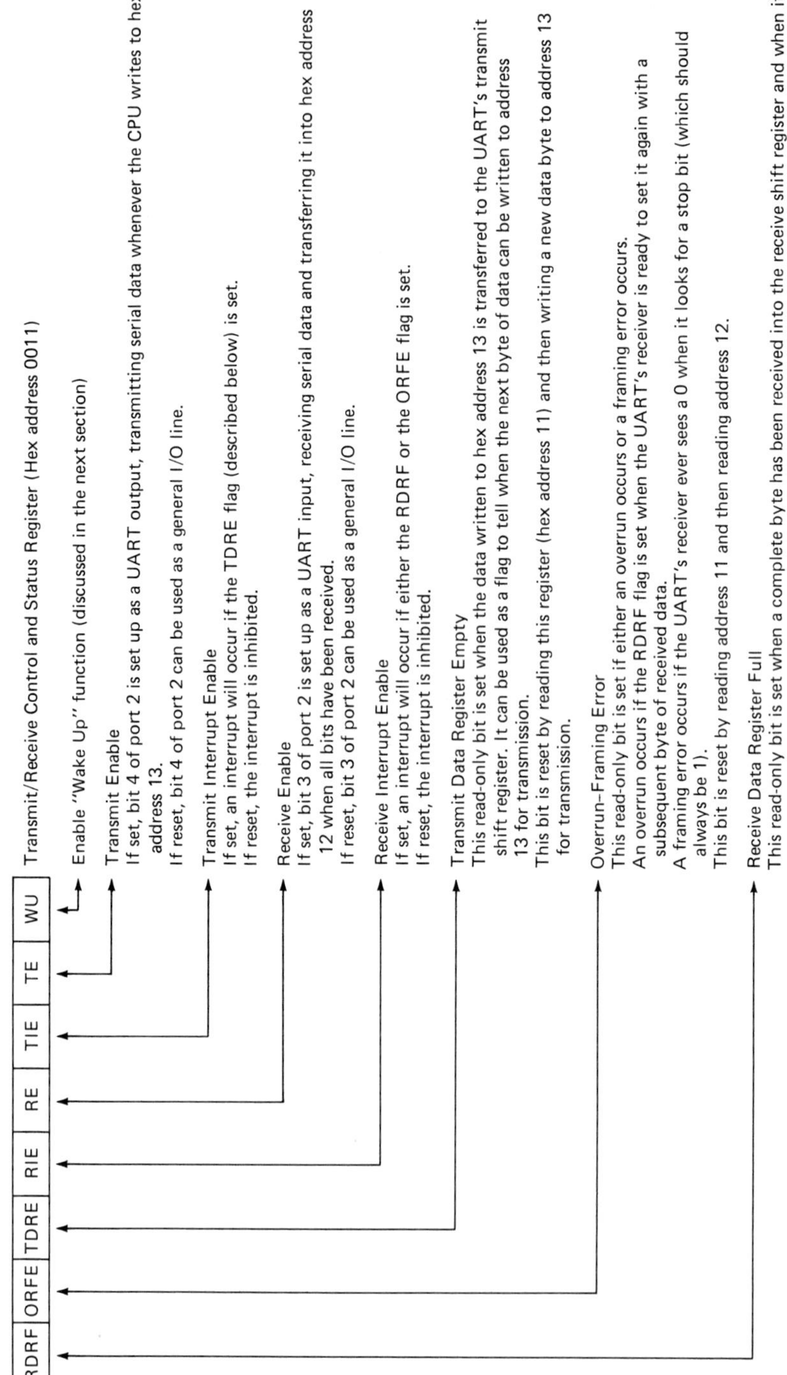

Figure 6-11. Motorola 6801 UART's Transmit/Receive Control and Status Register.

states of the interrupt enable bits are chosen so as to interact with the UART under either "interrupt control" or "flag control," as will be discussed in the next two sections. The TDRE and RDRF status flags serve as handshaking flags between a 6801 program trying to transmit or receive successive bytes of data and the UART which performs these functions.

The net effect of this capability is to permit computing power to be distributed among the different boards of an instrument. These microcomputers can communicate easily with each other, yet *only two* pins on each one will be tied up by the communication process. The designers of the 6801 microcomputer have produced a unit which encourages the inevitable revolution toward a computer on every board in an instrument.

6-5 INTERCONNECTED MASTER-SLAVE "SMART" SUBSYSTEMS

As an instrument design outgrows the possibility of organization with a planar layout (e.g., Figs. 3-6 and 3-7) and instead requires several daughterboards interconnected with a motherboard (e.g., Fig. 3-8), new design decisions arise. The instrument of Fig. 3-8 exemplifies a design with one microcomputer distributed throughout the instrument. The CPU's address bus and data bus extend out from the CPU board to all the other boards. This organization permits the CPU to carry on *high-speed* interactions with registers located on other boards. Each such register looks to the CPU like a memory location that it can read from or write to. However, if any component malfunctions so as to cause a "stuck at 1" or "stuck at 0" fault on any of the address or data bus lines, nothing in the instrument will work. Instructions cannot even be fetched to execute test routines (without modifying the configuration of the instrument, perhaps with an extender board wired especially for testing).

This organization is commonly encountered with the variety of general-purpose CPU, RAM, EPROM, and I/O boards available both from IC manufacturers and from various "systems" companies. It is flexible, permitting a designer to configure a system design quickly, with prebuilt, tested, and documented boards. However, it does raise testing difficulties.

An alternative organization, which again employs a single microcomputer, constrains the microcomputer to reside entirely on one board. An I/O bus, separate from the CPU's address bus/data bus structure, extends out to the other boards. Consequently, a fault among the I/O bus lines does not preclude the execution of test rou-

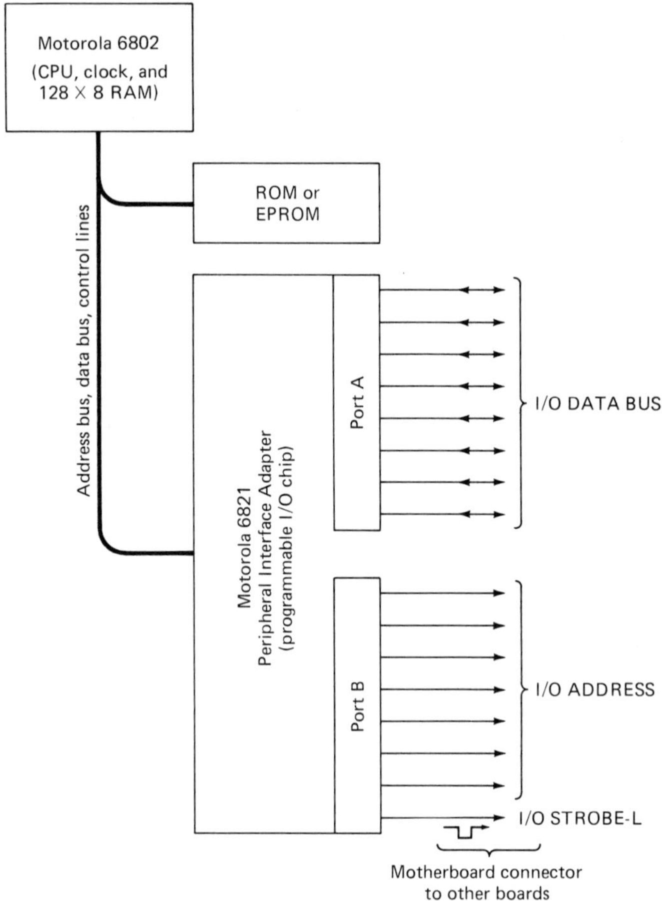

Figure 6-12. I/O bus structure.

tines. As one example, Fig. 6-12 illustrates a configuration employing a three-chip kernel. An alternative configuration, with a one-chip kernel, would consist of a one-chip microcomputer, two of whose ports drive an I/O bus. The configuration of Fig. 6-12 benefits from having an I/O chip whose I/O lines can each drive eight 74LSxxx devices. This is a reasonable number for many instruments if each board on the bus presents a load of only one 74LSxxx input to each line.

Communications between the CPU and registers on other boards are significantly slower than in the case discussed previously. In effect, all communications are squeezed through the keyhole afforded by the I/O bus. However, this is not all bad. Slower data transfers mean that the I/O bus lines do not need special buffering to handle the capacitive loading presented by the distributed bus, since signals may have 5 to 10 μs to settle out. In contrast, the CPU's data bus must settle out in 200 to 500 ns (more or less).

The transfers themselves can be aided by the preparation of an INPUT and an OUTPUT subroutine. Then a call of INPUT might load the CPU's accumulator with 8 bits accessed from the I/O address passed to the INPUT subroutine in one of the CPU's scratchpad registers (or accumulator B in the case of the Motorola 6802 system of Fig. 6-12). The INPUT subroutine itself:

1 Sets up the I/O port that drives the I/O data bus as an input port.
2 Transfers the I/O address from the CPU scratchpad register holding it to the output port which drives the I/O bus address lines.
3 Drives the I/O STROBE-L line low.
4 Reads the I/O data bus into the accumulator.
5 Drives the I/O STROBE-L line high again.

As we have discussed, the instrument organization of Fig. 6-12 supports maintainability by reducing the size of the kernel. If the I/O bus malfunctions, this reduced kernel can run test routines to help us locate the problem. Beyond this, the CPU can exercise the logic throughout the instrument, albeit through the keyhole presented by the I/O bus. Once this point in the test routines is reached, an instrument organized around an I/O bus does not differ in any essential way from that of an instrument organized around a distributed CPU address bus and data bus (except that the latter can execute test routines faster).

An alternative instrument organization employing a separate microcomputer on each board of an instrument achieves a variety of desirable ends:

1 Communication between boards can be reduced to two lines, facilitating the maintainability of this communication.
2 By dedicating a separate microcomputer to the tasks undertaken on each board, those tasks can obtain a faster response from the microcomputer.
3 Tasks requiring simultaneous computer processing are more effectively handled with separate microcomputers than with a fast vectored priority-interrupt structure or with a slower real-time operating system, if these latter two alternatives reside within one microcomputer.
4 Self-testing during the ongoing activities of an instrument is facilitated because each microcomputer can engage its own self-test

routines as idle moments arise in *its own* activities. Other microcomputers on other boards may be working furiously at the same time, doing normal instrument activities.

5 By distributing several tasks among separate microcomputers, each one may be small enough to fit within a one-chip microcomputer which can then become a one-chip kernel for testing this part of the instrument circuitry.

6 Communication between boards can be *drastically* reduced, from the detailed commands needed to execute an involved task, to a command such as "execute task 5."

7 An instrument organization which can employ a one-chip microcomputer on each board will be an organization which significantly reduces the package count (and even the package area) of a design.

As the one-chip microcomputer becomes an all-pervasive low-cost component, we want to be armed with techniques for exploiting these advantages. In the remainder of this section we will explore an instrument organization in which a *master* microcomputer controls the overall job of the instrument by initiating tasks in *slave* microcomputers and subsequently collecting results of these tasks back from them.

Consider the connection of Motorola 6801 one-chip microcomputers shown in Fig. 6-13. The UART output (bit 4 of port 2) of the master microcomputer drives the UART inputs (bit 3 of port 2) of all the slave microcomputers. As we will see shortly, the master can direct a message to one specific slave. A slave can reciprocate and send a message back to the master only upon command from the master. For example, the master may want to receive a status byte from a specific slave. To initiate this transfer, the master must send the slave a message telling it to enable the three-state output of bit 4 on port 2 by setting the TE (transmit enable) bit of the UART's Transmit/Receive Control and Status Register and then writing the status byte into its Transmit Data Register (address 13). At the same time, all other slaves must disable the three-state output of their port 2, bit 4, by:

1 Clearing their TE bit.

2 Writing a 0 to bit 4 of address 01 (the data direction register for port 2), converting bit 4 of port 2 to an input and thereby putting it into a high-impedance state.

This relationship between the master microcomputer and its slaves is not unlike the relationship between the microcomputer in

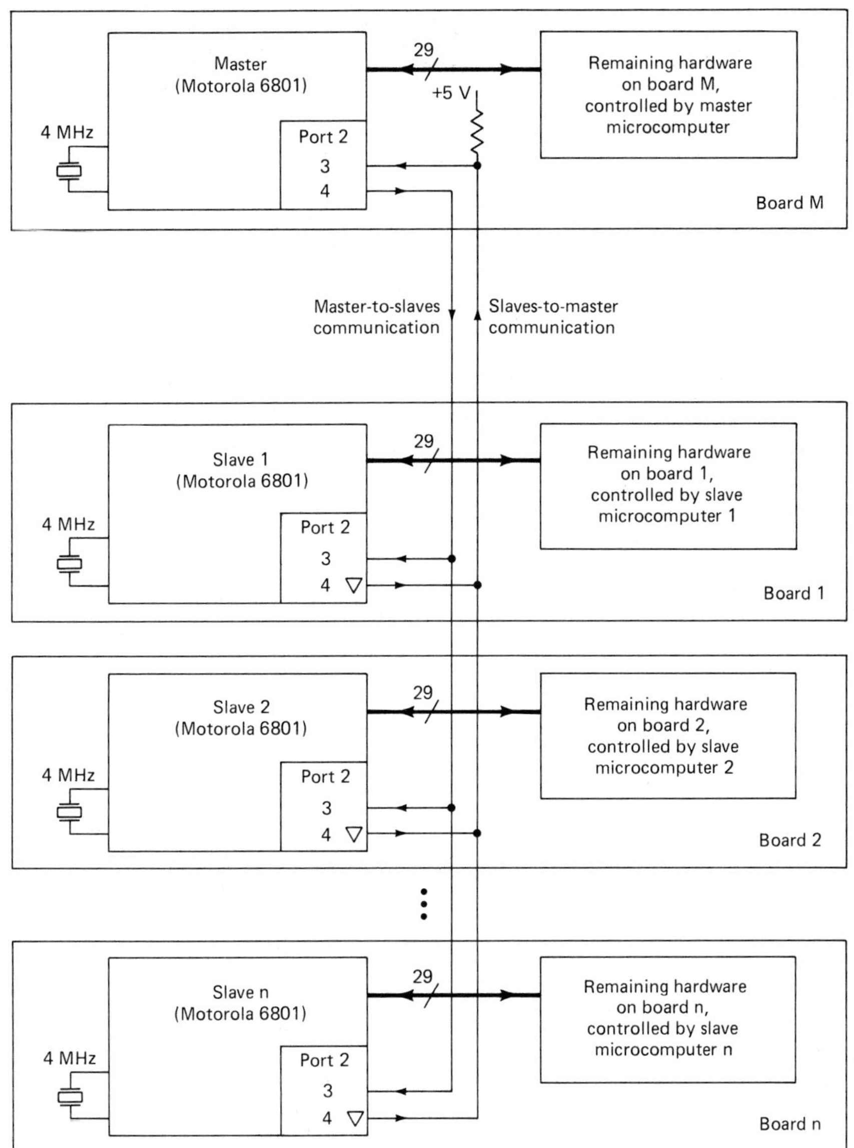

Figure 6-13. Instrument organization with multiple Motorola 6801 microcomputers.

a single-microcomputer instrument and the registers it accesses throughout the instrument. It loads data into registers and reads status information back from registers as it sees fit. In effect, the master runs the instrument under flag control, polling each slave for status information. If the status information indicates that a slave requires further interactions, the master can initiate them. Because each slave *is* a microcomputer, it can *buffer* data in its RAM while it awaits servicing by the master. We will examine an example of buffering in detail in the next section.

If flag control of the slaves does not provide sufficient speed, Fig. 6-14 illustrates interrupt control. When one of the slaves requires service, it sets up bit 2 of port 2 as an output and then writes a 0 to port 2 as an active-low interrupt output to the master's IRQ1-L interrupt input. Each slave *initializes* bit 2 of port 2 as an *input* by writing a 0 into bit 2 of the data direction register (address 01) for port 2. Each slave might be sent commands from the master enabling or disabling the slave's interrupt capability. That is, we might prepare the software in a slave 6801 so that it will not pull bit 2 of port 2 low until after it receives an "interrupt enable" command from the master. The master can subsequently send an "interrupt disable" command addressed to a specific slave, which turns off its permission to interrupt.

When the master receives an interrupt, it queries the enabled slaves to determine who caused the interrupt and therefore requires service. As part of its response to the master, saying that it did indeed cause the interrupt, the slave must write a 0 to bit 2 of address 01 (the data direction register for port 2), converting bit 2 of port 2 to an input and thereby releasing the interrupt line.

Thus far we have dealt with the problem of how slaves communicate with the master in spite of sharing one line for this communication. The master has a related problem in that it needs the ability to send an *addressed message* to one specific slave and have the remaining slaves ignore it. In addition, it needs the ability to send a *universal command* to all slaves and have none of the slaves ignore it. The Motorola 6801 supports this capability superbly with its "wake-up" mode. When power is first turned on, each slave initializes its UART by writing 00011000 to hex address 11, the UART's Transmit/Receive Control and Status Register (refer to Fig. 6-11), setting the Receive Enable bit and the Receive Interrupt Enable bit in this register.

When the master sends a byte of data out to the slaves, they will all be interrupted by the reception of this character. As shown in Fig. 6-15, the master sends *messages* consisting of one or more bytes. The end of one message is followed by 10 or more idle bits before the next message is allowed to begin. Each message begins with a Message Control Byte, which might be coded as shown in Fig. 6-15*b*. This scheme permits the master to utilize this first byte to send up to 16 different addressed commands to a specific slave (e.g., 20, 21, 22, . . . , 2F to slave 2). If more than 16 different addressed commands are desired, the first byte might serve to say that the second byte is to be interpreted as further command information. For example, a

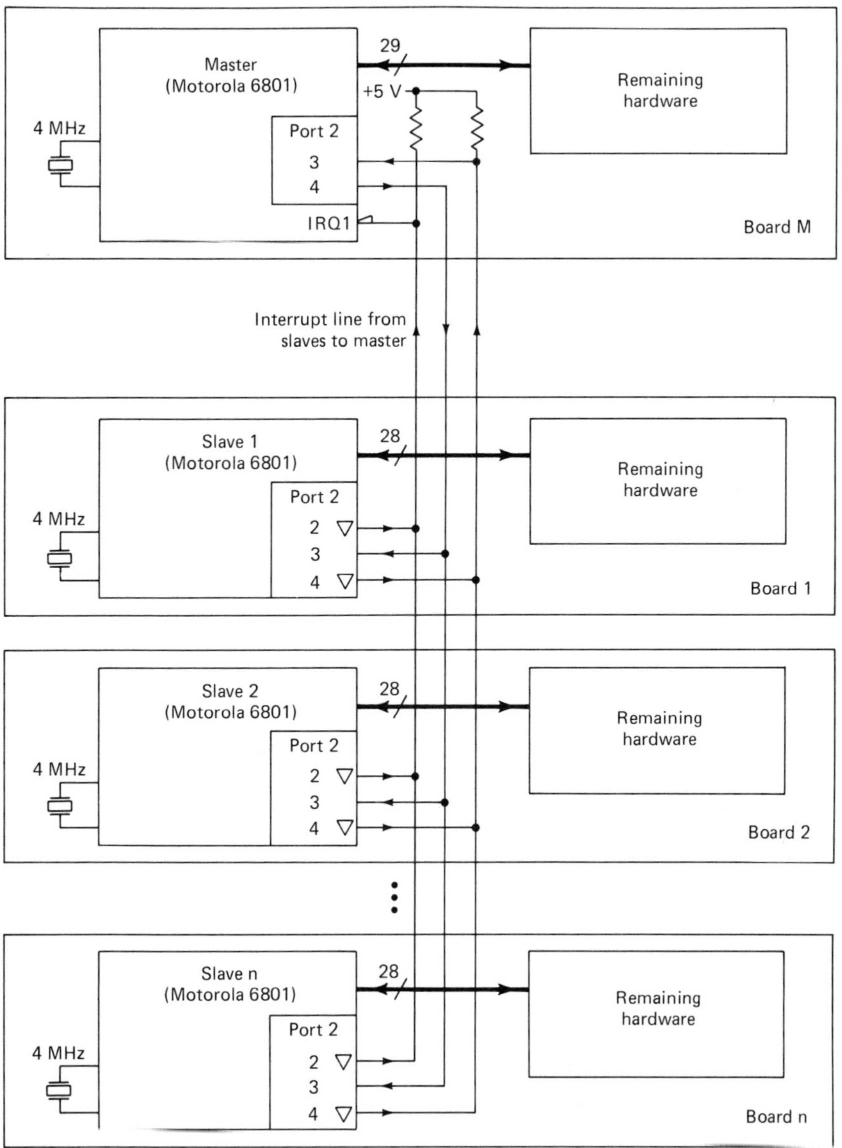

Figure 6-14. Instrument organization with multiple Motorola 6801 microcomputers, wherein slaves can interrupt the master to request service.

first byte of 2F might be used to tell slave 2 that the second byte of the message represents one of up to 256 further commands.

If the addressed command implies that more bytes must be received to complete the message, the slave interprets the remaining bytes accordingly. This addressed slave must be able, in one way or

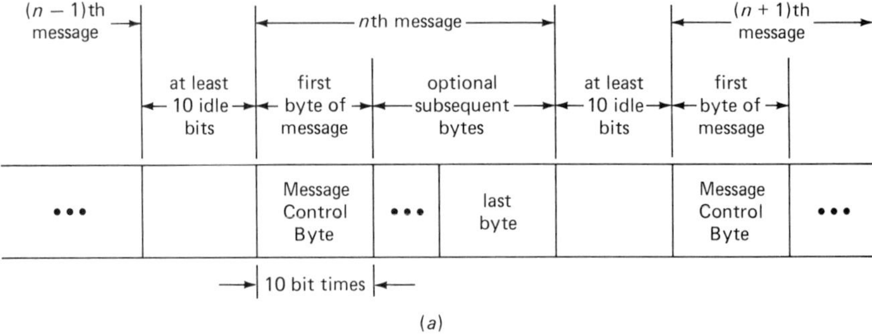

(a)

Binary contents	Hexadecimal contents	Meaning
0000xxxx	00-0F	Addressed messages to slave 0
0001xxxx	10-1F	Addressed messages to slave 1
0010xxxx	20-2F	Addressed messages to slave 2
0011xxxx	30-3F	Addressed messages to slave 3
0100xxxx	40-4F	Addressed messages to slave 4
0101xxxx	50-5F	Addressed messages to slave 5
0110xxxx	60-6F	Addressed messages to slave 6
0111xxxx	70-7F	Addressed messages to slave 7
1000xxxx	80-8F	Addressed messages to slave 8
1001xxxx	90-9F	Addressed messages to slave 9
1010xxxx	A0-AF	Addressed messages to slave 10
1011xxxx	B0-BF	Addressed messages to slave 11
11xxxxxx	C0-FF	Universal commands

(b)

Figure 6-15. One possible format for messages from master to slaves. (a) Format of successive messages; (b) definition of Message Control Byte.

another, to tell when the message has been completed so that it will respond correctly to the Message Control Byte of the next message.

If the Message Control Byte is a hexadecimal number between C0 and FF, *all* slaves are to carry out the universal command associated with this number. For example, C0 might be used as the code whereby the master tells all slaves to disable their interrupt capability (i.e., the capability to pull bit 2 of their port 2 low, interrupting the master).

If the Message Control Byte is an addressed command, all unaddressed slaves set the "wake-up" bit (refer to Fig. 6-11). This has the effect of inhibiting all subsequent interrupts as each subsequent byte of the message is received from the master. Consequently, *all* slaves respond to the first byte of a message, but only the addressed slave will see the remaining bytes of the message. At the completion of the message, the master must ensure that a new message is not sent for at least 10 bit-times so that 10 idle bits (i.e., 1s) will be sent to all slaves. These 10 consecutive 1s are detected within each UART and reset the wake-up bit. As a result, all slaves will be interrupted by the reception of the first byte of the next message.

A slightly different way to organize messages is to code all bytes after the first byte with the commonly used ASCII code (American Standard Code for Information Interchange), in much the same way as is done for messages transferred between instruments on the General Purpose Interface Bus (GPIB). Since all ASCII characters require only 7 bits, the most significant bit might be used to identify the last character of a message (as the EOI line can be used by GPIB messages). To give an idea of the versatility of this approach, Fig. 6-16 shows the

MEASUREMENT DATA FORMAT

B1 ... sets Hexadecimal
B2 ... sets Decimal
B3 ... sets Octal
B4 ... sets Binary
P1 ... sets positive logic polarity
P2 ... sets negative logic polarity
C1 ... sets positive clock edge
C2 ... sets negative clock edge
Wx ... sets word width = x; $2 \leq x \leq 16$
Fx ... sets coded subfield width = x; $2 \leq x < \text{word width}$

TRACE SPECIFICATION

M1 ... sets Start Trace on Trigger + Delay.
M2 ... sets End Trace on Trigger + Delay.
Dx ... sets Delay = x; $0 \leq x \leq 65535_{10}$
Tx ... sets Trigger = x; x must fit current format exactly.
Ex ... sets Delay by Trigger Events = x; $0 \leq x \leq 65535_{10}$

EXECUTE

R ... causes Trace execution and configures 1602A to transmit unformatted data as in U. Aborts any previous Trace in progress.
Z ... causes Trace Trigger Events (TRACE E) execution and configures 1602A to transmit unformatted data as in U. Aborts any previous Trace in progress.
H ... halts any Trace in progress.

OUTPUT

Nx ... configures 1602A to transmit formatted data in memory Word Number = x; $0 \leq x \leq 63_{10}$ (at conclusion of Trace).
U ... configures 1602A to transmit unformatted data from data memory at conclusion of any Trace in progress
S ... configures 1602A to transmit Status Byte (8 bits).
L ... configures 1602A to transmit "Learn" message that defines its measurement configuration.
V ... Verify; causes 1602A to execute self-test and power-on initialize (except HP-IB status); configures 1602A to transmit self-test result (0 = passed, 16_{10} = failed).

OTHER

I ... Initialize; causes 1602A to go to power-on configuration (except HP-IB status).

Figure 6-16. GPIB commands for the logic state analyzer of Fig. 1-16.

GPIB commands for the logic state analyzer of Fig. 1-16. The advantage of this approach results when one message is used to transfer a string of characters representing *several* commands. For example, the character string

B4C1W5T10000R

sends *five* distinct commands

B4, C1, W5, T10000, and R

to the logic state analyzer. The last command, R, is analogous to the command of the master asking a slave to return data. Similarly, the S command of Fig. 6-16 parallels the manner in which a master obtains status information from a slave. That is, when an addressed slave receives such a message, it sends an appropriate status character back to the master.

Testing a board with a 6801 microcomputer on it should include the testing of its UART. The inclusion of a miniature triple-pole, double-throw switch on the board in the configuration of Fig. 6-17 will permit the 6801 to carry out push-to-test capability. If we dedicate bit 2 of port 2 to this function, then actuating the test switch grounds this bit to signal the microcomputer to initiate a UART test. When the microcomputer senses that this switch has been closed, it can transmit characters and check that each received character is identical to the corresponding transmitted character.

The master-slave interconnection of microcomputers has been optimized somewhat differently by Intel with their 8041A/8741A universal peripheral interface. Engineers familiar with Intel's 8048/8748 one-chip microcomputer† are familiar with most aspects of this slave microcomputer. It differs from the 8048/8748 in that it has the registers, flags, and instructions needed for reliable communication with a master microcomputer. It ties up 12 of its 40 pins to effect *fast* data transfers between itself and the master. Ten other pins are used for power, crystal, resetting, programming, and testing. This leaves 18 pins for I/O, in the form of two 8-bit I/O ports and two flag inputs, T0 and T1, which can be tested. T1 can also serve as an input to a counter or as an interrupt input, just as in the 8048/8748. The 8041A contains a 1024 × 8 mask-programmed ROM, whereas the 8741A contains a 1024 × 8 ultraviolet erasable EPROM.

† Refer to the author's *Microcomputer-Based Design*, McGraw-Hill, New York, 1977, app. A9.

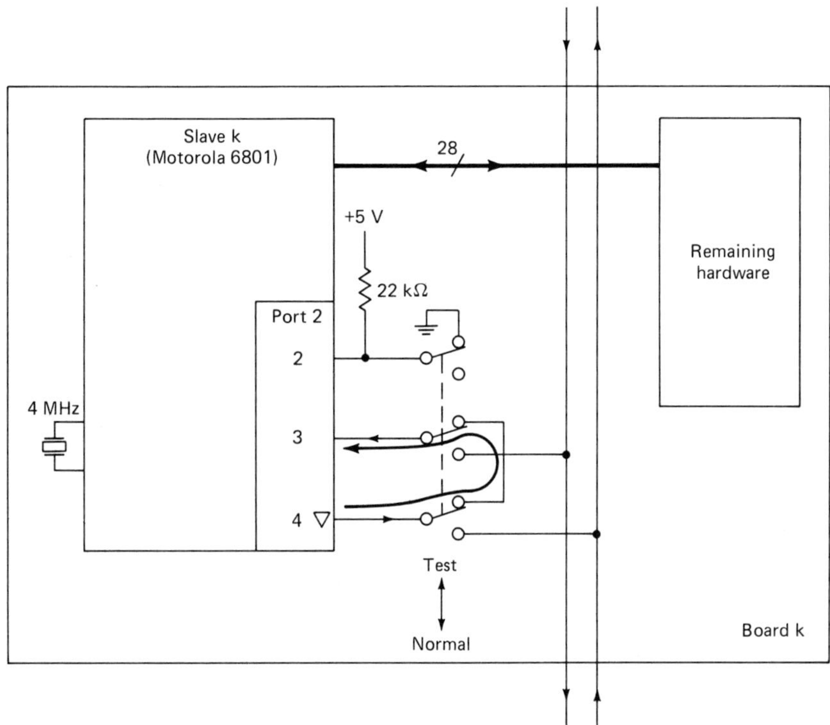

Figure 6-17. Addition of a switch to facilitate testing of the Motorola 6801's UART.

This slave microcomputer is shown interfaced to Intel's 8085 CPU chip in Fig. 6-18. The 8085 can access up to 256 I/O ports with instructions of the form

$$\text{IN } n \quad \text{and} \quad \text{OUT } n \qquad \text{where } 0 \leqslant n \leqslant 255$$

The port address is shown being decoded from the upper eight address lines, where it appears during the execution of an I/O instruction. With the interconnections shown, the registers of the 8041A/8741A are accessed as hex addresses 00 and 01.

This slave microcomputer has the three interface registers of Fig. 6-19 for interacting with a master microcomputer. Both data and commands are written by the master to the slave into DBBIN. By writing data bytes to address 0 and command bytes to address 1, the master resets or sets the F1 bit in the Status register, in addition to writing the byte into DBBIN. In either case, the IBF handshaking flag in the Status register is also set.

If we wish to employ interrupt control within the slave for

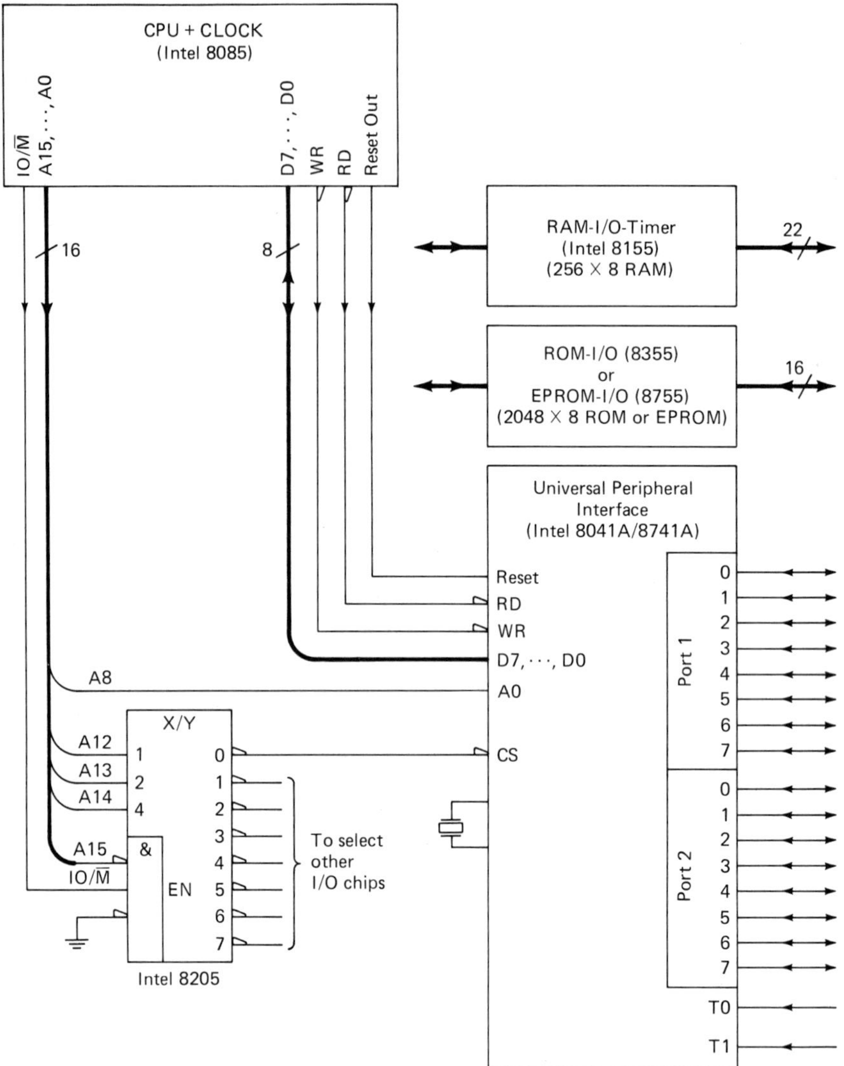

Figure 6-18. Interconnection of the Intel 8041A/8741A universal peripheral interface to a master microcomputer.

responding to byte transfers from the master, the instruction

EN I

enables an interrupt to occur when IBF is set. On the other hand,

DIS I

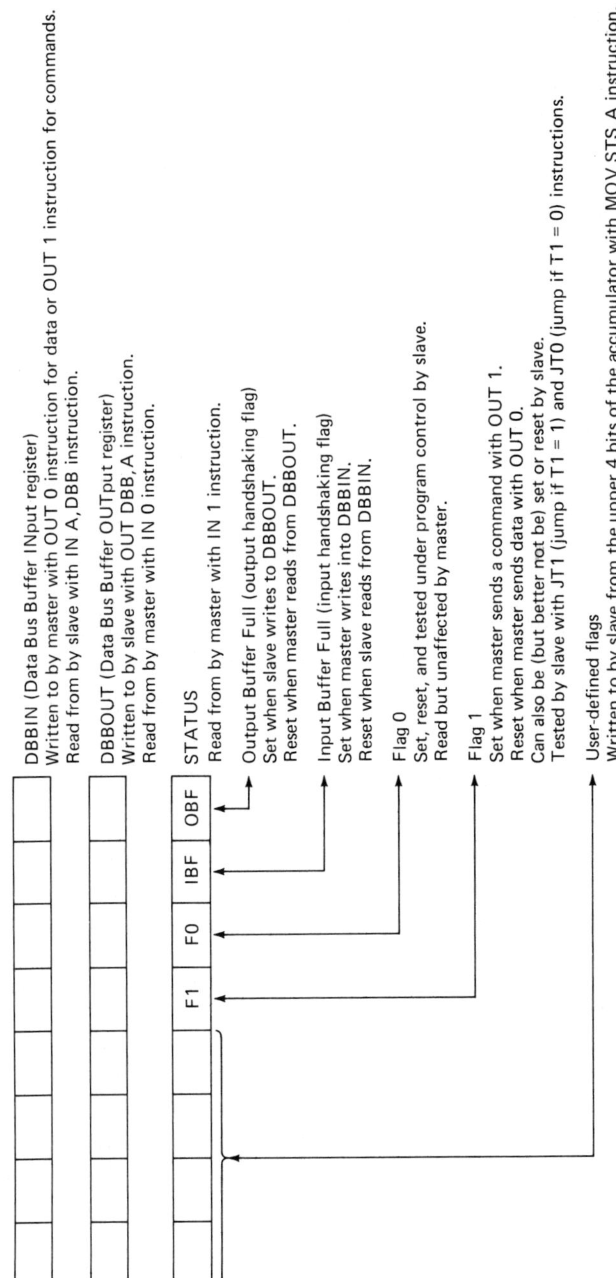

Figure 6-19. Registers within Intel 8041A/8741A slave which interface with Intel 8085 master.

disables this source of interrupts. If IBF interrupts are enabled, the setting of IBF will produce the same response within an 8041A/8741A which the $\overline{\text{INT}}$ input produces in the 8048/8748. That is, a subroutine call is made to address 003, which must therefore be used as the starting address of the interrupt service routine.

If we prefer to employ flag control within the slave, for responding to byte transfers from the master, the slave can test its IBF flag with a

JNIBF address

instruction. This will cause a jump to the indicated address (on the same page of ROM) if IBF = 0. The IBF flag is automatically cleared when the slave transfers the byte from DBBIN to the accumulator with an

IN A,DBB

instruction. Before transferring another byte to the slave, the master can sense that the last byte was read out of the DBBIN register (by the slave) by reading the Status register (address 01) and testing the IBF bit. In this way, the master handshakes successive data and command bytes to the slave.

The slave transfers bytes to the master by first checking the OBF flag in the Status register to make sure that the master has read the previous byte which the slave wrote into DBBOUT. If the OBF flag is reset, the slave uses an

OUT DBB,A

instruction to transfer the accumulator contents to the DBBOUT register, which automatically sets the OBF flag. When the master sees that this flag is set, it reads the DBBOUT register, which automatically resets the OBF flag. Successive bytes are handshaken from slave to master in this way.

The 8041A/8741A can provide the *immediate* access of 4 bits of user-defined status information to the master via the upper 4 bits of the STATUS register. These are write-only bits for the slave, which executes a

MOV STS,A

instruction to transfer the upper 4 bits of the accumulator into these Status register bits (leaving the lower four bits of the Status register un-

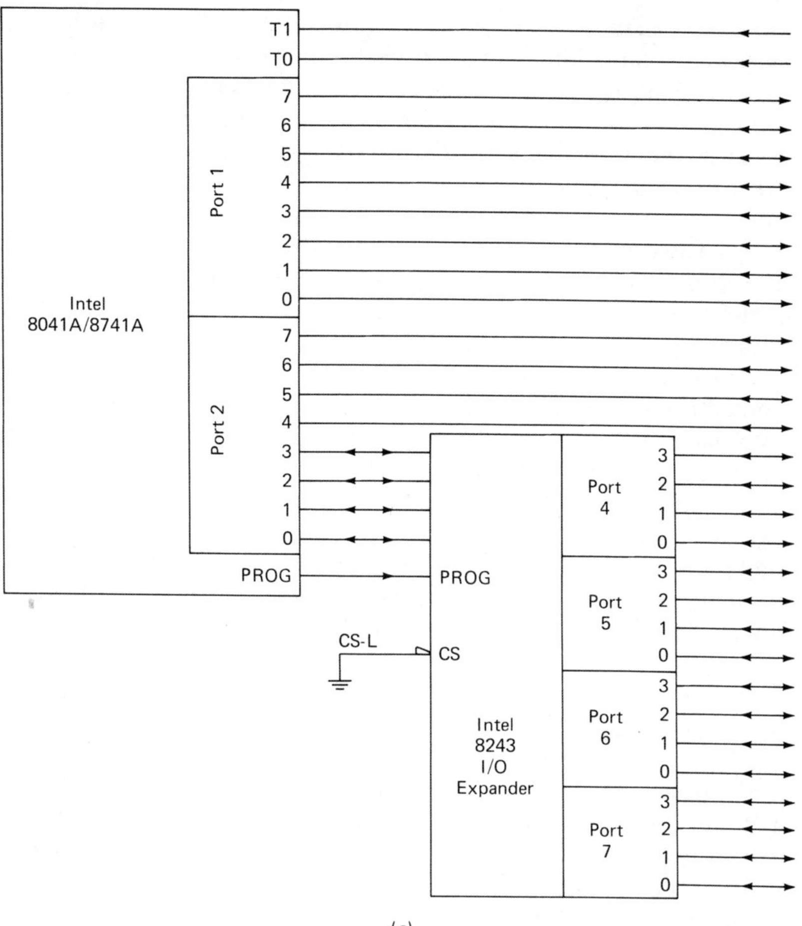

(*a*)

Instruction		Meaning
MOVD	Pp,A (where p = 4, 5, 6, or 7)	Pp ← bits 3-0 of accumulator
ANLD	Pp, A (where p = 4, 5, 6, or 7)	Pp ← Pp AND bits 3-0 of accumulator
ORLD	Pp, A (where p = 4, 5, 6, or 7)	Pp ← Pp OR bits 3-0 of accumulator

(*b*)

MOVD	A,Pp (where p = 4, 5, 6, 7)	bits 3-0 of accumulator ← Pp; clear bits 7-4 of accumulator

(*c*)

Figure 6-20. Intel 8243, I/O port expander for the Intel 8041A/8741A (or the Intel 8048/8748). (a) Circuit interconnections; (b) output instructions; (c) input instructions.

changed). The slave receives no indication of when the master has seen these status bits (which are read-only bits for the master), so they must be used in a manner whereby such feedback is unnecessary.

At the cost of two bits (4 and 5) of port 2, the 8041A/8741A can be set up so that these lines mirror the OBF flag and the complement of the IBF flag. Consequently, they can be used to interrupt the master, if interrupt-driven response is desired for the master microcomputer.

To augment the limited number of I/O lines on the 8041A/8741A, Intel provides the 8243 I/O expander, shown in Fig. 6-20. This unit contains four 4-bit ports. The lower 4 bits of the accumulator are transferred to or loaded from one of these ports with one of the instructions shown in Fig. 6-20*b* or *c*. More 8243 I/O expanders can be used by connecting them *all* as shown in Fig. 6-20*a* and then decoding other outputs of the 8041A/8741A to chip select (CS-L) only one 8243 before one of the instructions of Fig. 6-20*b* or *c* is executed.

Multiple-byte messages between master and Intel 8041A/8741A slaves can be organized in one of the same ways as was discussed for the Motorola 6801 (e.g., with ASCII characters and GPIB-like organization). However, since the addressing of slaves by the master is hardwired, no initial address byte is required.

6-6 BUFFERING DATA TRANSFER RATES

The transfer of information between separately clocked circuits is often facilitated if the transfer rate desired by the sender does not have to match the transfer rate desired by the receiver. The *long-term* average transfer rates must be identical, or else information is being lost or created by the transfer process. However, short-term transfer rates can be quite different. Consider the following two examples.

1 A circuit that samples and collects data may need to carry out extensive manipulations after a batch of data has been collected. Then it may want to emit the results in a fast burst of data transfers to another circuit so that it can get back to sampling and collecting a new batch of data. A buffering problem arises if the receiver cannot keep up with the sender's burst rate of data transfer.
2 A slave microcomputer may need to transfer an array of data to its master microcomputer. Both are capable of fast data transfers. However, a buffering problem arises if the master is tied up at the exact moment when the slave wishes to carry out the transfers.

We will consider two approaches to this buffering problem. A *FIFO*, or first-in/first-out memory, represents a hardware solution. An

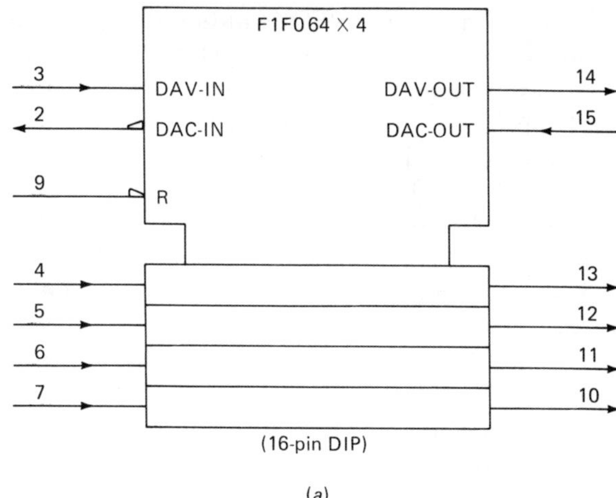

(a)

Input and output data transfer rates = 10 MHz (max.)

$T_{\text{ripplethrough}}$ = 3 μs, typical

Worst-case setup time = 5 ns

Loading characteristics ≈ 74xxx

(b)

Figure 6-21. 67401, bipolar 64 × 4 FIFO. (a) Device (nonstandard symbol); (b) characteristics. (Monolithic Memories, Inc.)

interrupt-driven *queue* in a microcomputer represents a software solution.

The 64 × 4 FIFO of Fig. 6-21 is optimized for high-speed applications. Handshaking circuits on input and output are independent of each other to provide reliable data transfer into and out of the chip, at handshaking rates of up to 10 MHz. Data is handshaken into the FIFO by raising the DAV-IN handshaking line. The FIFO responds by pulling DAC-IN-L low. When DAV-IN is pulled low again, the FIFO responds by raising DAC-IN-L. If successive 4-bit "nibbles" are entered into the FIFO with none taken out, the FIFO will indicate that it is full by *not* raising DAC-IN-L in response to DAV-IN being pulled low after the last transfer. Finally, when data is removed from the FIFO, it will complete the handshake.

The first nibble of data entered into the FIFO will appear on the output within 3 μs, causing the DAV-OUT pin to go high. Subsequent nibbles pile up behind this first nibble. As nibbles are handshaken out of the FIFO, they are emitted in the same order in which they were received (i.e., first in, first out).

Internally, the data in the FIFO ripples through 64 stages of asynchronously coupled flip-flops. This accounts for the relatively long "ripple through" time of 3 μs listed in Fig. 6-21.

Expansion of a FIFO is aided by parts designed with explicit expansion control lines. Thus the Fairchild 9423, another 64 × 4 bipolar FIFO, is packaged in a 400-mil-wide 24-pin DIP. It can be expanded as wide and as deep as desired with no extra parts (other than the requisite number of FIFOs). The resulting composite FIFO is guaranteed to handshake reliably. In addition, the Fairchild unit can accept or emit either parallel or serial data. For example, two units might be combined (for a width of 8 bits) to accept a high-speed burst of handshaken serial data which could then be handshaken out in the form of 8-bit bytes.

The FIFO solution to data-rate buffering is appropriate to use in applications that are too fast to handle within a microcomputer. In contrast, the master-slave interconnection of several microcomputers gives rise to a ready-made application of *queues* (i.e., software FIFOs). We will use the nine-chip video display circuit† of Fig. 6-22 as a vehicle for carrying on an explicit discussion of the role of a queue in the master-slave multiple-microcomputer organization of an instrument.

A CRT display, such as the small 5-in. black-and-white unit shown in Fig. 6-23, offers a flexible I/O device for an instrument. The nine-chip display circuit can be conveniently mounted on the frame of the display itself, forming a complete, self-testable module and requiring only a four-wire cable (+5 V, ground, serial data and commands in, and serial status out) to the rest of an instrument.

This unit can display instrument output data in both alphanumeric and graphic form. It can, at the same time, display the mode of operation of the instrument that produced this output. This is especially valuable in a keyboard-driven or GPIB-driven instrument, where the mode of operation might not otherwise be apparent. The display can also assist with the setting up of the instrument by giving a user a menu of choices. It can be used to help implement "soft keys" like those of Fig. 1-15*b*, where the function of a key is redefined, depending upon the present mode of the instrument, with a label on the CRT.

The circuit of Fig. 6-22 will display 16 lines of 32 characters per line. If a color TV or color monitor is used in place of the black-and-white unit of Fig. 6-23, the circuit will intermix a limited set of eight-color-semigraphics with a standard 64-character ASCII set. Inverse video is permitted on all characters. Alternatively, by driving the $\overline{A}/G$ line of Fig. 6-22 high, a 64 × 64 point, four-color graphic display is obtained.

The Motorola 6801 (or the 68701 EPROM version) microcomputer can operate in any one of eight different modes, most of which are used

† Edward J. Rupp, MC6801/6805 Single-Chip Microcomputer Family, *1979 WESCON Convention Record,* Session 21.

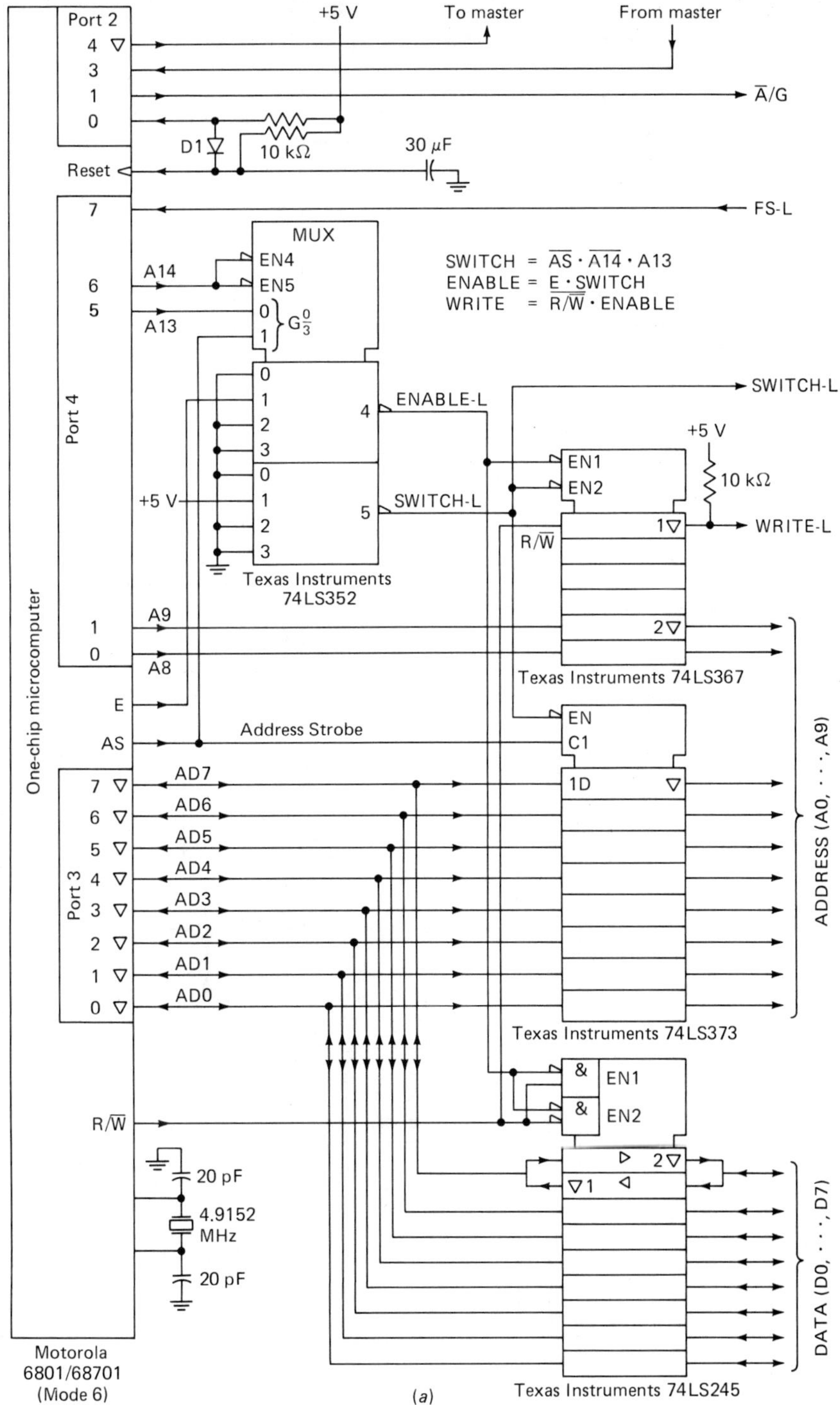

Figure 6-22. Nine-chip CRT display. (Edward J. Rupp, Motorola.) (a) Derivation of address bus/data bus structure.

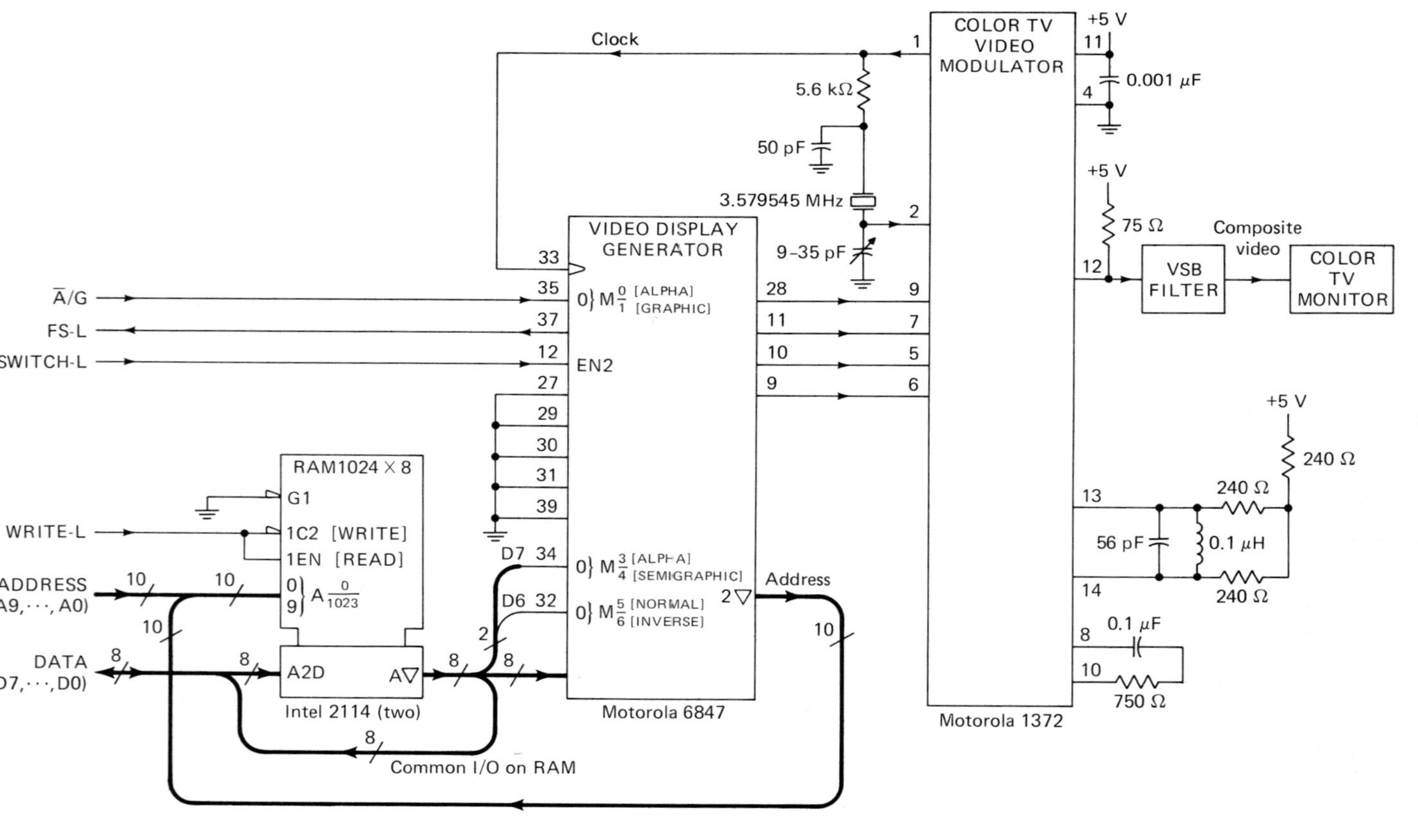

Figure 6-22b. RAM, video display generator, modulator, and TV monitor.

Figure 6-23. 5-in. black-and-white CRT display. (Motorola, Inc.)

for testing the chip. The mode is determined, when power is first turned on to the chip, by which of bits 0, 1, and 2 of port 2 are pulled low at that time. For example, the one-chip microcomputer configuration (mode 7) is obtained by pulling none of these lines low at startup. The diode, D1, connected from bit 0 of port 2 to the Reset line in Fig. 6-22 forces the microcomputer into mode 6, the "expanded, multiplexed" mode. In this mode the 6801 can access any of the external addresses shown in Fig. 6-24. To do this, the lower 8 bits of the address bus are multiplexed with the data bus on port 3, as shown by the timing diagram of Fig. 6-25. Consequently, a full-blown address bus/data bus structure can be obtained at the cost of one chip, the 74LS373 octal latch shown in Fig. 6-22*a*. The upper 8 bits of the address are strobed into this latch by AS, an address strobe generated specifically for this purpose. The AS and R/$\overline{\text{W}}$ (Read/$\overline{\text{Write}}$) lines of mode 6 are the port 3 I/O control lines of mode 7 (the one-chip microcomputer mode). Also, any unused port 4 I/O lines can be used as

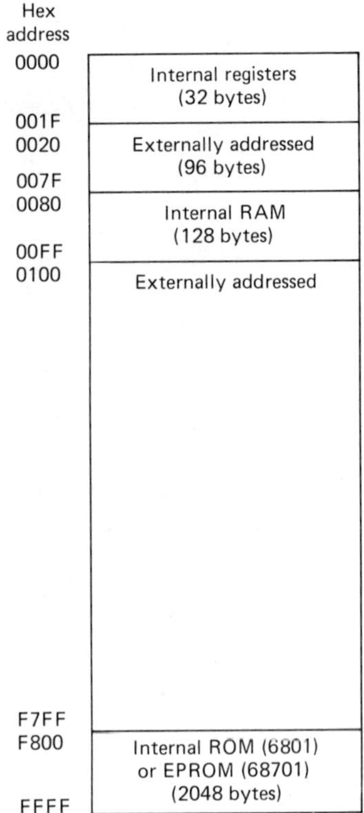

Figure 6-24. Motorola 6801, Mode 6 memory map.

inputs. It is only necessary to write 0s into the corresponding bits of the data direction register (address 5) for this port.

In this application, the address latch must have three-state outputs, as must address lines A8 and A9 and the data bus, since they are multiplexed with other three-state drivers. That is, these lines are used to write into and read out of the RAM shown in Fig. 6-22*b*. At all other times, the video display generator reads character codes out of the RAM and translates this information into a video signal.

Whenever the 6801 wants to update a character code in RAM, it waits until the FS-L (field synchronization) signal is low. When it is, the 6801 writes to the RAM, knowing that the video display generator has completed the refresh of one frame and is waiting for the vertical synchronization pulse. By writing into the RAM only at this time, we avoid generating "snow" on the screen. However, this means that while serial data can enter the 6801 at any time, the display produces a wait of up to roughly $\frac{1}{60}$ s. Hence the circuit has a data-rate buffering problem.

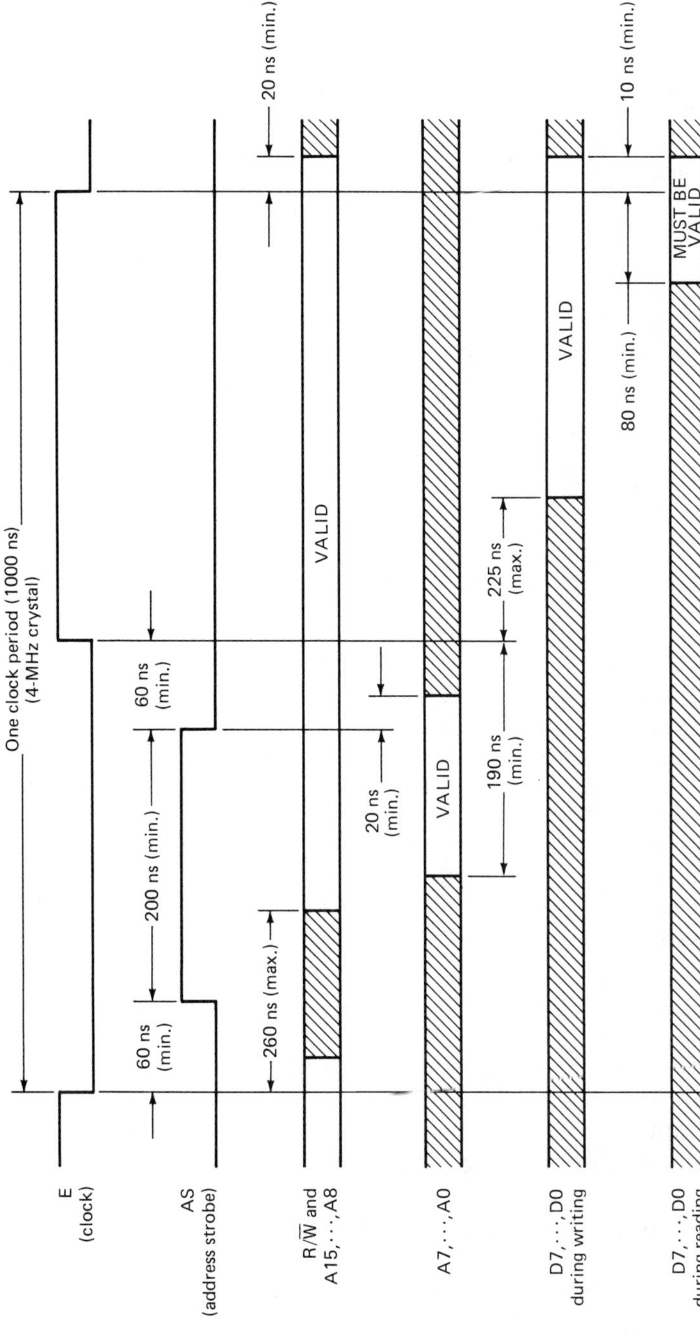

Figure 6-25. Timing diagram for the Motorola 6801, in the expanded, multiplexed mode (Mode 6).

Example 6-2. What addresses does the 6801 use to access the 1024 × 8 display RAM?

This RAM is accessed, either to write into it or to read from it, by making SWITCH-L active. The 74LS352 multiplexer makes this line active when

$$\overline{\mathrm{AS}} \cdot \overline{\mathrm{A14}} \cdot \mathrm{A13} = 1$$

Furthermore, looking at the memory map of Fig. 6-24, we see that when the internal ROM is accessed,

$$\mathrm{A14} \cdot \mathrm{A13} = 1$$

When the internal RAM is accessed,

$$\overline{\mathrm{A14}} \cdot \overline{\mathrm{A13}} = 1$$

Consequently, *any* binary address of the form

x01xxxxxxxxxxxxx

will access *some address* in the RAM and will not access anything else. In particular, we might use hex address 2000 to access the lowest address in the RAM and 23FF to access its highest address.

Incidently, note the use of the timing signal $\overline{\mathrm{AS}}$ to disable SWITCH-L while the upper address lines are settling and yet to get the entire address out to the RAM *before* the write pulse occurs (when the timing signal E goes high). Also note the use of the multiplexer and the upper part of the 74LS367 to implement the three timing functions ENABLE-L, SWITCH-L, and WRITE-L.

Display characters and CRT control characters (e.g., for cursor control) enter this display circuitry serially, whenever the master microcomputer transmits these. If the master updates the display at its maximum rate, this slave display will receive a new character every 130 μs. At this rate, 100 or so characters might be received before the electron beam of the display has worked its way down to the bottom of the active display area, at which time the first character received can be written into the display RAM. Furthermore, the display circuit only has so much time before FS-L goes high again, indicating that it is time to stop updating the display RAM if we do not want to put "snow" on the display.

To forestall these problems, we can define two addressed commands from the master to the display. One addressed command is used when the master wants the display to return its status. The status information sent will be the number of bytes remaining before the display's queue is filled. With this information, the master can use the other addressed command to send a string of characters to the display. It can send any message that does not overflow the queue and be done with it. A longer message can be sent in parts, filling the queue, checking the status again, filling the queue again, and so on, until the entire message has been sent.

The display's slave microcomputer will have a mainline program which simply takes a character from the queue, interprets it appropriately (i.e., is it a cursor control or is it a display character?), and then carries out the needed operation upon the display RAM. When done, it goes back to the queue and gets the next character. When the queue has been emptied, the mainline program does nothing further, waiting for the queue to receive a new entry. We will define a variable, QLEN, to keep track of the length of the queue. When the queue has been emptied out, QLEN will equal zero.

Commands from the master can be handled well in this scheme under interrupt control. Each time the display's microcomputer receives a byte from the master, it will be interrupted. It will set aside whatever it is doing, handle the received byte appropriately, and then return to what it was doing. If the received byte is a character to be displayed or a cursor control character, it will be put into the queue, for subsequent removal and handling by the mainline program.

A queue is a rather simple structure to implement in software. It requires that an area of RAM be allocated to it and that two pointers, which we will designate QIN and QOUT, be defined. QIN points to the location where the next entry into the queue is to go. QOUT points to the location from which the next byte is to be removed.

The example of Fig. 6-26 illustrates the operation of a queue. In this case, the maximum length of the queue (which we will designate as QLENMX) is three because only three RAM locations have been allocated for use by the queue. Upon initialization (Fig. 6-26*a*), QOUT and QIN point to the same location and QLEN = 0. If we are ready to remove data from the queue at this time, we check QLEN, find that it is zero, and realize that there is no data to remove. When the first byte, B1, is ready for entering into the queue, it is stored in the address pointed to by QIN. Then QIN and QLEN are incremented, leading to the state shown in Fig. 6-26*b*. Successive entries and removals are shown in successive parts of Fig. 6-26. Note how the pointers must correctly "increment" from the highest RAM address allocated to the queue back to the lowest.

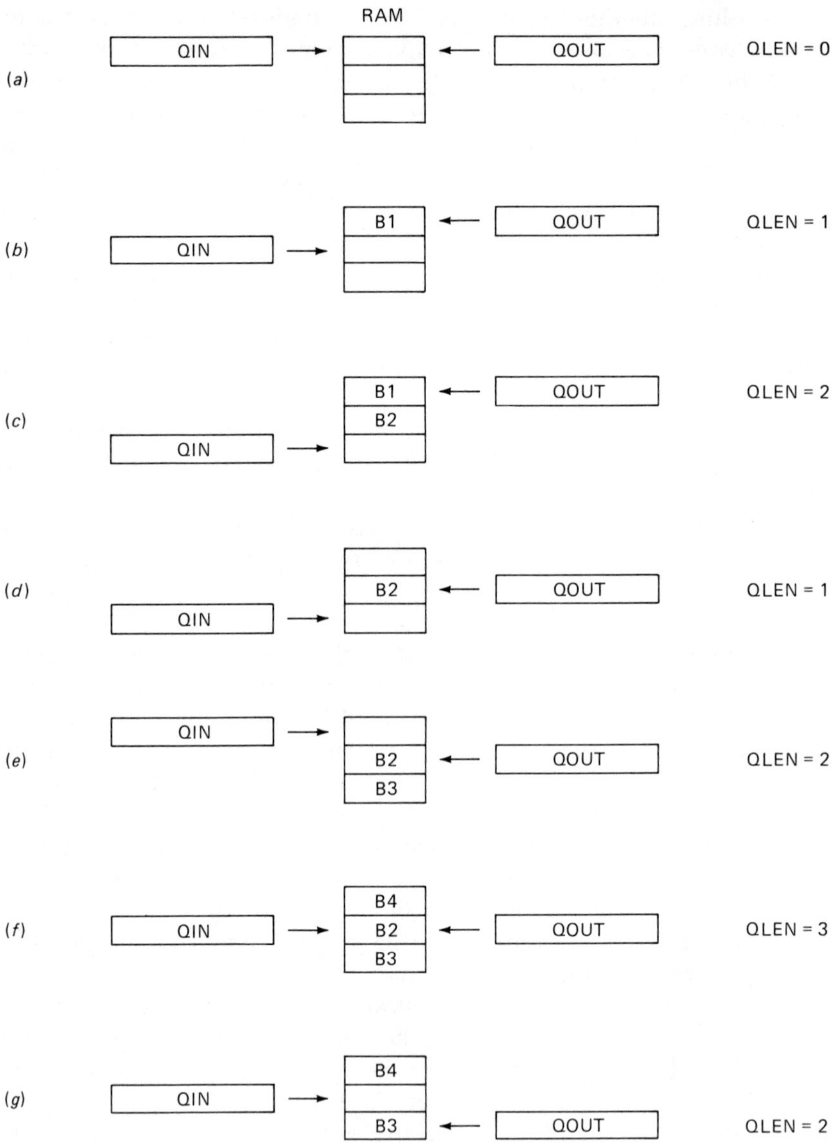

Figure 6-26. Operation of a queue. (a) *Initially empty queue;* (b) *put B1;* (c) *put B2;* (d) *get B1;* (e) *put B3;* (f) *put B4;* (g) *get B2.*

A Motorola 6801 implementation of a queue is shown in Fig. 6-27. Also shown is the interrupt service routine for handling messages from the master microcomputer. The two messages to which the display is to respond are:

1 The one-byte addressed command labeled DSTAT (which is shown encoded as the hex number 10, one of the slave 1 message control bytes of Fig. 6-15). Upon receiving this message, the display's microcomputer is to transmit the number of bytes left unused in its queue, namely QLENMX − QLEN. The master can then transmit a message with this many characters for the queue (or fewer) and know that the queue will not overflow.

2 The multiple-byte, addressed command having the format

DSPLY (Message Control Byte)

First character for display queue

Second character for display queue

. . . .

Last character for display queue

End of String character (00)

The display is to ignore any other messages.

Not shown in Fig. 6-27 is the mainline program which initializes everything when power is first turned on (although Fig. 6-27*c* shows that *part* of the initialization sequence of instructions needed to set up the queue) and which takes bytes out of the queue and interprets them appropriately. For example, in addition to handling the characters to be displayed, the microcomputer might respond to the following control characters:

- Clear screen and home cursor
- Clear line with cursor and move cursor to beginning of line
- Cursor left, right, up, or down
- Carriage return, line feed (and scroll)
- Clear all tabs, set tab, go to next tab
- Enter or exit from graphics mode

The display should be set up to execute a self-test routine during otherwise idle times. The INTRPT routine of Fig. 6-27*g* should be modified to respond to an addressed command asking whether self-test indicates that the unit is operating satisfactorily.

Figure 6-27. Parts of the 6801 software for the CRT display. (*a*) *Definition of labels;* (b) *allocation of RAM variables;* (c) *initialization of the queue;* (d) *INCX subroutine;* (3) *PUTQ subroutine;* (*f*) *GETQ subroutine;* (g) *INTRPT interrupt service routine.*

```
DSTAT     EQU    $10         MESSAGE CONTROL BYTE—STATUS MESSAGE
DSPLY     EQU    DSTAT+1     MESSAGE CONTROL BYTE—CHARACTER STRING MESSAGE
DDR2      EQU    $0001       DATA DIRECTION REGISTER FOR PORT 2
TRCS      EQU    $0011       UART'S TRANSMIT/RECEIVE CONTROL AND STATUS REGISTER
RXDATA    EQU    $0012       RECEIVE DATA REGISTER
TXDATA    EQU    $0013       TRANSMIT DATA REGISTER
QLENMX    EQU    100         MAXIMUM LENGTH OF QUEUE
EOS       EQU    $00         END-OF-STRING CHARACTER WHICH TERMINATES DSPLY MESSAGE
```

(*a*)

```
          ORG    $0080       START OF 6801 ON-CHIP RAM
QIN       RMB    2           ADDRESS OF LAST CHARACTER ENTERED INTO QUEUE
QOUT      RMB    2           ADDRESS OF LAST CHARACTER REMOVED FROM QUEUE
QLEN      RMB    1           LENGTH OF QUEUE
Q         RMB    QLENMX      RESERVE QLENMX BYTES FOR QUEUE
MESBYT    RMB    1           STATE VARIABLE USED BY INTRPT
```

(b)

```
INITQ     LDX    #Q          GET ADDRESS OF START OF QUEUE
          STX    QIN         AND STORE IT IN QIN
          STX    QOUT        AND IN QOUT
          CLR    QLEN        LENGTH OF QUEUE IS ZERO, INITIALLY
          CLR    MESBYT      INITIALIZE STATE VARIABLE USED BY INTRPT
```

(c)

```
******  INCX IS A SUBROUTINE WHICH INCREMENTS THE INDEX REGISTER X TO POINT
*       TO THE NEXT CHARACTER POSITION IN THE QUEUE.  IT ROLLS OVER FROM
*       Q+QLENMX TO Q.
INCX      INX                       INCREMENT X
          CPX    #Q+QLENMX          HAVE WE GONE PAST THE END OF THE RESERVED AREA?
          BNE    INC1               IF NOT, THEN RETURN
          LDX    #Q                 IF SO, THEN RESET POINTER TO Q
INC1      RTS                       RETURN FROM SUBROUTINE
```

(*d*)

```
******  PUTQ IS A SUBROUTINE WHICH PUTS THE CONTENTS OF ACCUMULATOR A INTO
*       THE QUEUE AND THEN INCREMENTS QLEN
PUTQ      LDX    QIN                GET NEXT QUEUE ENTRY ADDRESS
          STA A  0,X                PUT CHARACTER INTO QUEUE USING X AS A POINTER
          BSR    INCX               INCREMENT POINTER
          STX    QIN                SAVE POINTER
          INC    QLEN               INCREMENT LENGTH OF QUEUE
          RTS                       AND RETURN FROM SUBROUTINE
```

(*e*)

```
******  GETQ IS A SUBROUTINE WHICH IS NOT TO BE CALLED UNLESS QLEN IS GREATER
*       THAN ZERO.  IT LOADS ACCUMULATOR A WITH A CHARACTER FROM THE QUEUE
*       AND THEN DECREMENTS QLEN.
GETQ      LDX    QOUT               GET NEXT QUEUE EXIT ADDRESS
          LDA A  0,X                GET CHARACTER FROM QUEUE USING X AS A POINTER
          BSR    INCX               INCREMENT POINTER
          STX    QOUT               SAVE POINTER
          DEC    QLEN               DECREMENT LENGTH OF QUEUE
          RTS                       AND RETURN FROM SUBROUTINE
```

(*f*)

(Continued)

Figure 6-27 (continued)

```
******  INTRPT IS THE INTERRUPT SERVICE ROUTINE.  IT LOOKS FOR THE FIRST
*       BYTE OF A MESSAGE TO BE EITHER DSTAT OR DSPLY.  OTHERWISE, IT SETS
*       THE WAKE-UP BIT AND GOES TO SLEEP FOR THE REMAINDER OF THE MESSAGE.
*       IF IT SEES THE ONE-BYTE-LONG MESSAGE, DSTAT, IT RETURNS THE NUMBER
*       OF UNFILLED LOCATIONS IN THE QUEUE TO THE MASTER.
*       IF IT SEES DSPLY, THEN THE NEXT BYTE RECEIVED WILL BE LOADED INTO
*       THE QUEUE.  SUBSEQUENT BYTES RECEIVED ARE ALSO QUEUED UP UNTIL THE
*       "END-OF-STRING" CHARACTER (00) IS RECEIVED, SIGNIFYING THAT THE
*       MESSAGE IS COMPLETE.
*       INTRPT USES A STATE VARIABLE, MESBYT, TO KEEP TRACK OF WHICH BYTE
*       OF A MESSAGE THE NEXT BYTE RECEIVED WILL BE, DEFINED AS FOLLOWS:
*                 MESBYT = 0       FIRST BYTE OF MESSAGE
*                 MESBYT = 1       SUBSEQUENT BYTES OF MESSAGE
INTRPT    LDA A  TRCS              CLEAR THE RECEIVER INTERRUPT
          LDA A  RXDATA            AND GET CHARACTER
          TST    MESBYT            TEST STATE  VARIABLE
          BNE    ONE               BRANCH IF THIS IS NOT THE FIRST BYTE OF THE MESSAGE
ZERO      CMP A  #DSPLY            IS THIS THE DSPLY ADDRESSED COMMAND?
          BNE    ZERO1             IF NOT, THEN BRANCH
          INC    MESBYT            IF SO, THEN SET MESBYT TO 1
          RTI                      AND RETURN FROM INTERRUPT
ZERO1     CMP A  #DSTAT            IS THIS THE DSTAT ADDRESSED COMMAND?
          BNE    ZERO3             IF NOT, THEN BRANCH
ZERO2     LDA A  #%00011010        IF SO, THEN SET TRANSMIT ENABLE BIT
          STA A  TRCS
          LDA A  QLENMX            COMPUTE QLENMX - QLEN
          SUB A  QLEN
          STA A  TXDATA            AND SEND IT TO THE MASTER
          RTI                      AND RETURN FROM INTERRUPT
```

```
ZERO3   LDA A  #%00011001   SET WAKE-UP BIT
        STA A  TRCS
        LDA A  #%00000100   DISABLE UART OUTPUT
        STA A DDR2          BY MAKING BIT 4 AN INPUT
        RTI                 AND RETURN FROM INTERRUPT
ONE     CMP A #EOS          HAS EOS CHARACTER BEEN RECEIVED?
        BNE    ONE1         IF NOT, THEN BRANCH
        CLR    MESBYT       IF SO, THEN REINITIALIZE MESBYT FOR A NEW MESSAGE
        RTI                 AND RETURN FROM INTERRUPT
ONE1    BSR    PUTQ         QUEUE THE RECEIVED CHARACTER
        RTI                 AND RETURN FROM INTERRUPT
```

(g)

6-7 ONE-SHOTS

A *one-shot,* or *monostable multivibrator,* is a device that converts a transition into a pulse. The pulse width of the output is set by an *RC* time constant, and can range from less than 100 ns to seconds. A *nonretriggerable* one-shot generates its output pulse, of prescribed duration, independent of what the input does *after* the input transition that triggers the one-shot. At the completion of the output pulse, and after a short recovery time, the one-shot can be triggered again. This operation is illustrated in Fig. 6-28.

A *retriggerable* one-shot reinitializes the timing of the output pulse each time the prescribed transition occurs on the input. For example, the output of a retriggerable one-shot with a 1-s pulse width will remain continuously on as long as the one-shot sees input transitions occurring more often than once per second, as illustrated in Fig. 6-29. This is sometimes used to provide a malfunction indication to an instrument user. A retriggerable one-shot drives a LED indicator which remains turned off as long as normal operation continues to trigger the one-shot. If normal operation ever ceases, the transitions to the one-shot cease and the indicator light turns on.

Two popular dual one-shots are shown in Figs. 6-30 and 6-31. While they can both be used with $C_x < 1000$ pF, the pulse width (PW) equations given are reasonably accurate only for larger values of C_x.

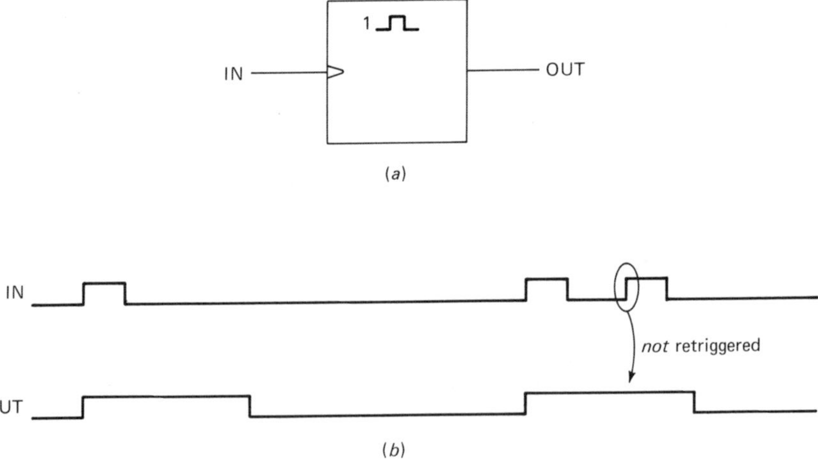

Figure 6-28. Nonretriggerable one-shot. (a) General symbol (positive-edge-triggered); (b) timing diagram.

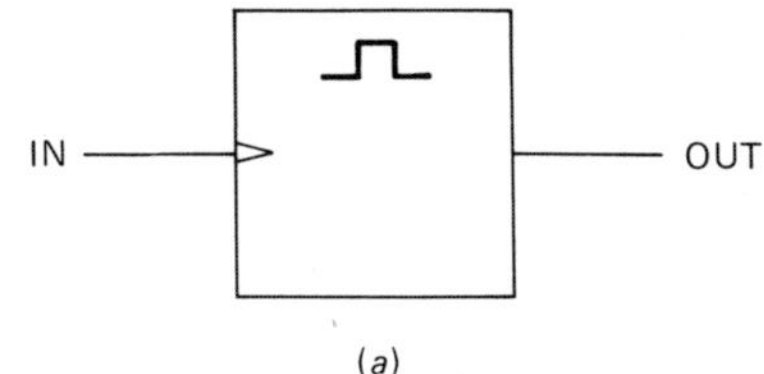

(a)

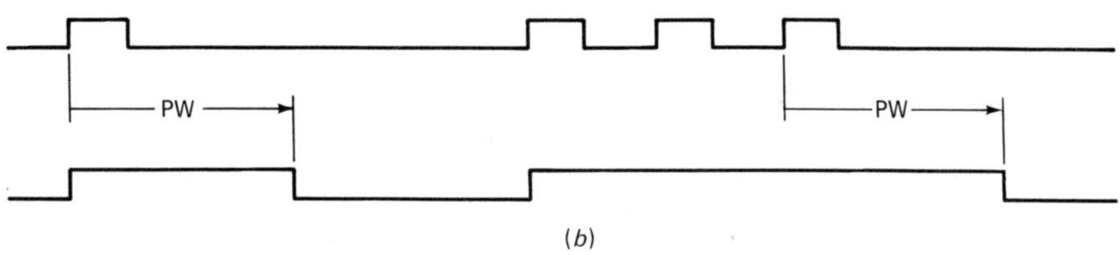

(b)

Figure 6-29. Retriggerable one-shot. (a) General symbol (positive-edge-triggered); (b) timing diagram.

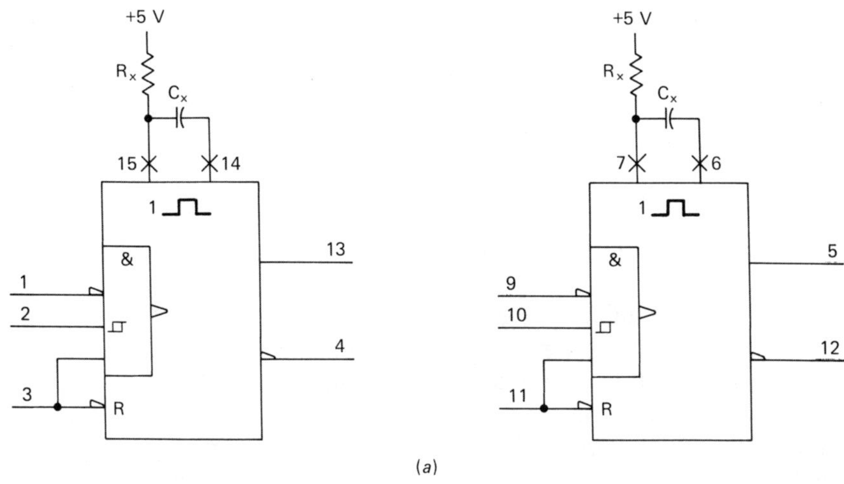

(a)

$$PW = 0.7R_xC_x$$

$$1.4\ k\Omega < R_x < 100\ k\Omega$$

$$0 < C_x < 1000\ \mu F$$

(b)

Figure 6-30. 74LS221, dual nonretriggerable one-shots with Schmitt-trigger input. (a) Symbolic representation; (b) timing circuit characteristics. (Texas Instruments.)

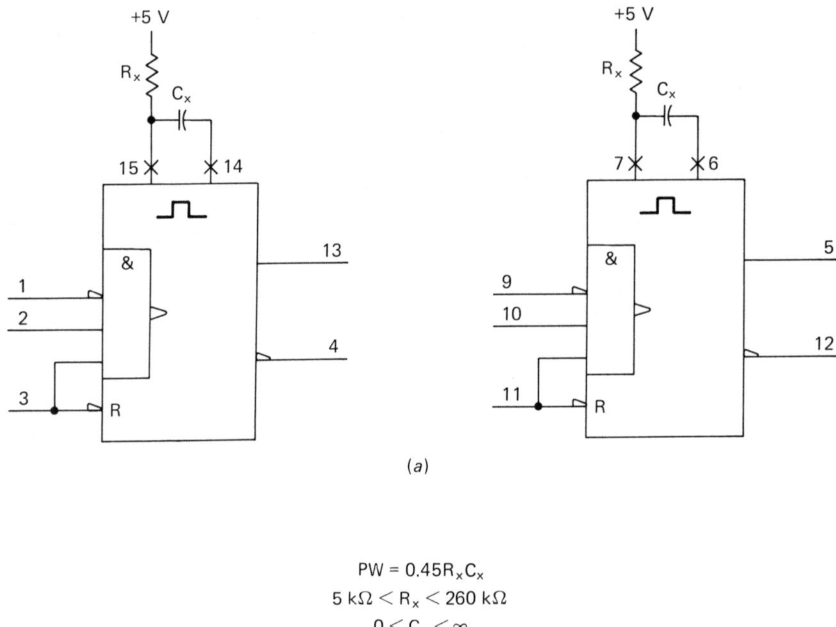

(b)

Figure 6-31. 74LS123, dual retriggerable one-shots. (Texas Instruments.) (a) Symbolic representation; (b) timing circuit characteristics.

For many applications, the Reset input is disabled (i.e., tied to + 5 V). One of the other two inputs is normally used as the transition input, selecting the one that will give the edge sensitivity desired. The other input can then be either permanently enabled or else used as an input enable. An example is shown in Fig. 6-32.

Because it generates a transition (i.e., the trailing edge of the output pulse) which is unsynchronized to the clock, a one-shot can introduce all the problems of an unsynchronized input from a separately clocked circuit. Consequently, a one-shot is wisely used to solve only a few specialized problems.

One of the most common uses of a one-shot is to provide protective, backup timing. For example, consider the multiplexed display of Fig. 4-3. Recall that to obtain an average LED current of 2.5 mA, we drove a turned-on LED with 10 mA for one-fourth of each refresh cycle and turned it off for the other three-fourths of the refresh cycle. If the microcomputer is stopped because of a malfunction, because a board in

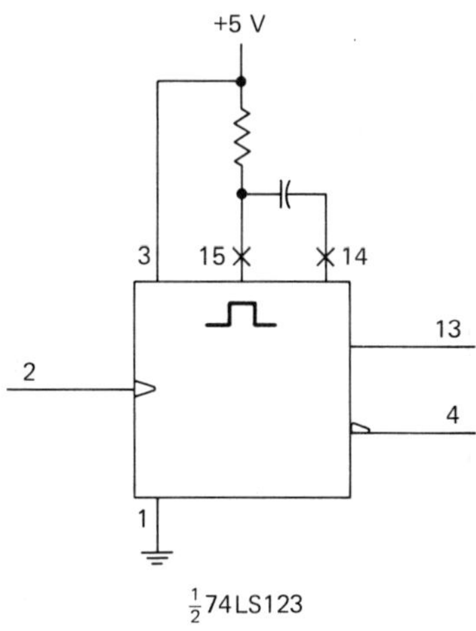

Figure 6-32. Simplified representation of a one-shot.

an instrument is removed during servicing or for any other reason, some LEDs are likely to be left turned on constantly with 10 mA. The seven-segment displays of Fig. 4-3 actually list a maximum dc current rating of 20 mA, so no problem would ensue. More generally, however, we might use the same approach to multiplex 16 seven-segment displays instead of just four. We might change the drive circuitry to that shown in Fig. 6-33. As long as the microcomputer keeps running the display, the one-shot will continuously retrigger and enable the display. However, if the multiplexing ever stops, so does the one-shot, turning off the display and protecting it. The fact that the one-shot timing is derived from a rather inaccurate *RC* timing circuit is irrelevant in this application.

As another application, consider the protection of the printhead of a thermal printer. Thermal printheads are designed to have a low thermal time constant so they can be heated quickly to print one dot in a character dot matrix and then cool down again so that the printhead can be moved to a new position without smearing the printing. It is common to *overdrive* the printhead with a current which, if left on continuously, would quickly burn out the printhead.

Suppose that the printer of Fig. 6-34 requires a 20-ms pulse on the PRINT input. If we drive PRINT *directly* from an output of the microcomputer, as in Fig. 6-34*a*, we can use the crystal clock and built-in programmable timer to control the pulse width of PRINT precisely. However, if the microcomputer ever stops with PRINT high, . . . smoke! Alternatively, we might be tempted to forget the use of

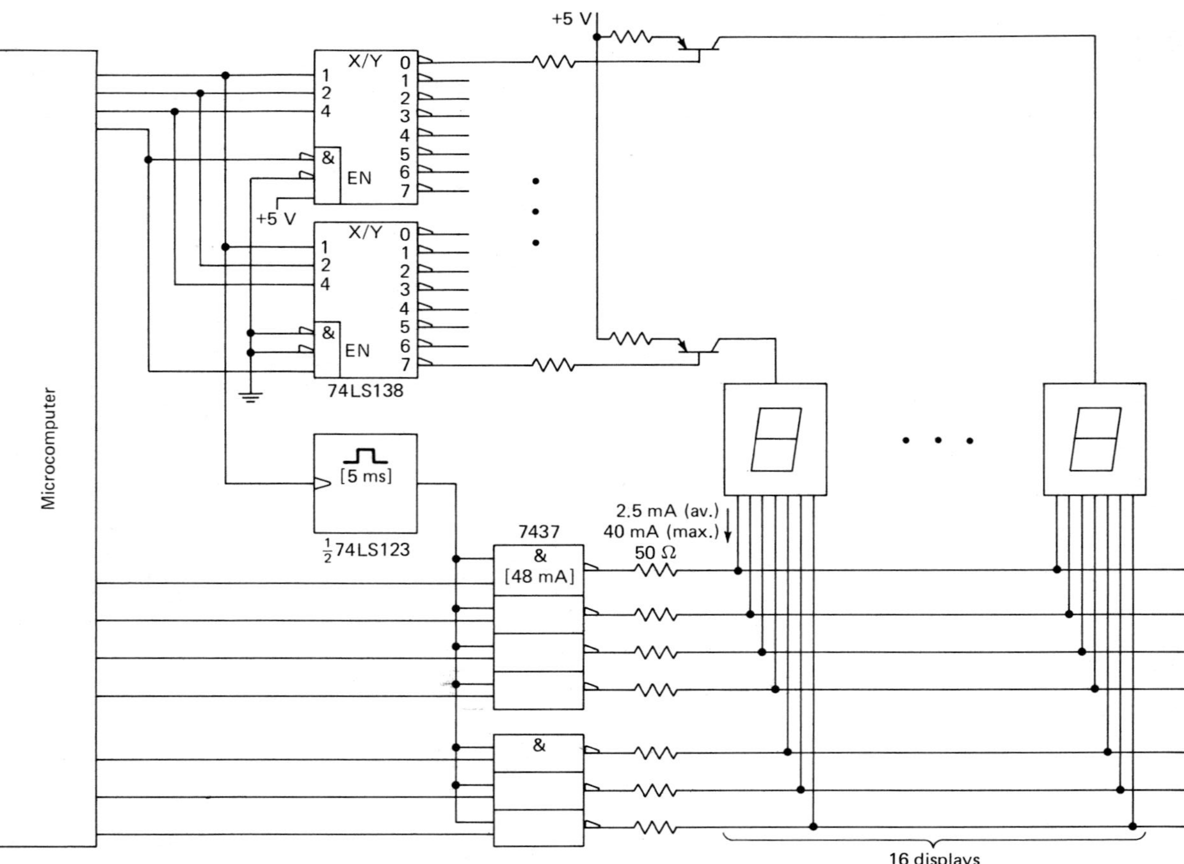

Figure 6-33. Use of a one-shot to provide protective backup.

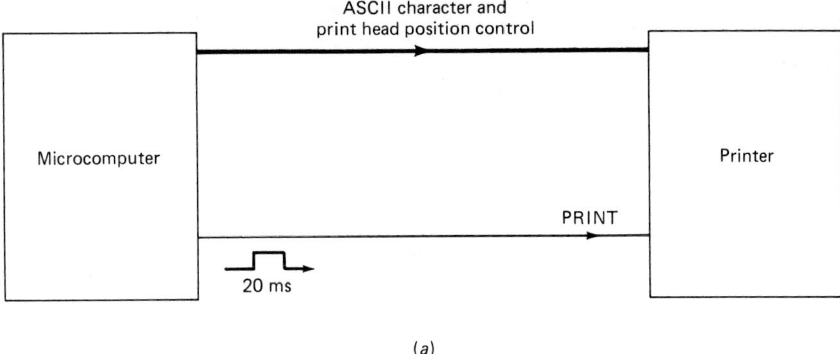

(a)

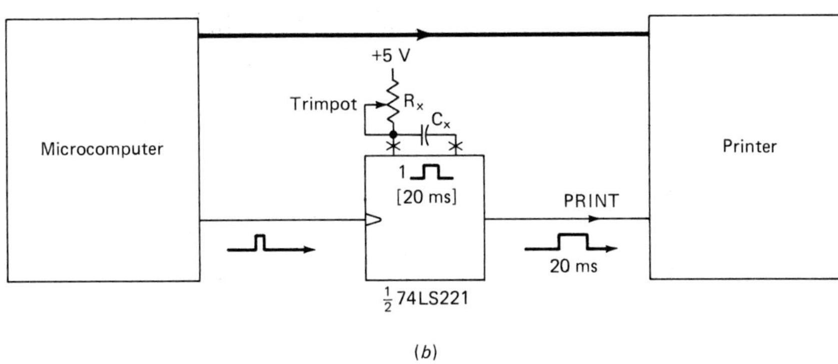

(b)

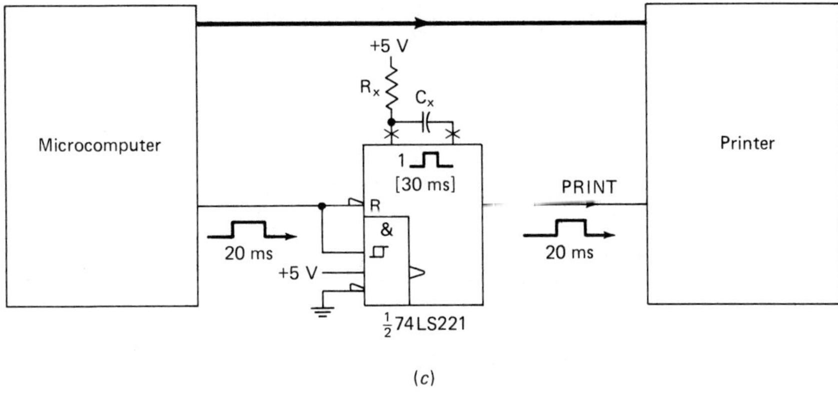

(c)

Figure 6-34. One-shot protection of a thermal printhead. (a) Timing from microcomputer; (b) timing from one-shot; (c) timing from microcomputer, protection from one-shot.

the programmable timer and derive the PRINT timing directly from a one-shot, as in Fig. 6-34*b*. The microcomputer need only raise the output line with one instruction and lower it with the next instruction, knowing that the one-shot will do the rest. Unfortunately, this leaves us with a design that requires a special test setup and the tweaking of a trimpot during manufacture. It also places the printer at the mercy of any users who decide to *darken* the printing by turning the trimpot (out of spec), not realizing the effect they are having upon the life of the printhead.

The good third alternative is to derive precise timing for PRINT from the microcomputer but to use a one-shot as a backup, protective device, as in Fig. 6-34*c*. If we require a 20-ms pulse, we can use *fixed* R_x and C_x values. The one-shot pulse width need only be longer than 20 ms and short enough to shut down PRINT quickly in case of a microcomputer malfunction. By using the pin 11 input, the one-shot will

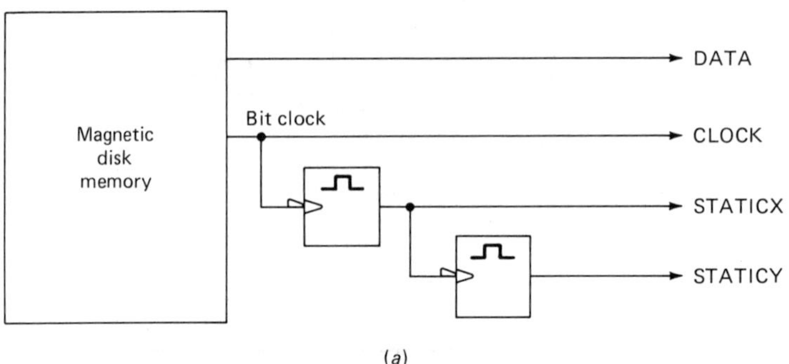

(*a*)

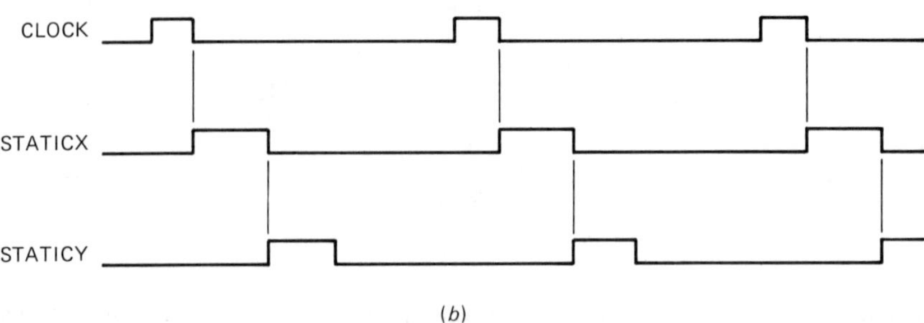

(*b*)

Figure 6-35. Derivation of a multiple-phase clock. (a) Circuit; (b) timing diagram.

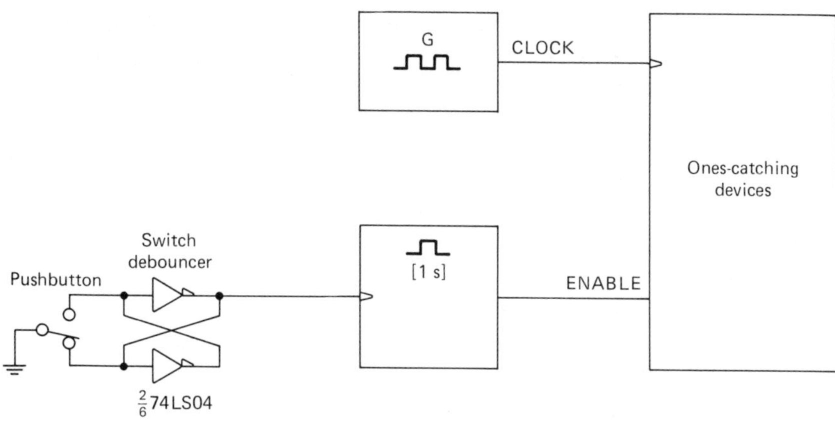

Figure 6-36. Example of the bad use of a one-shot.

be triggered by the leading edge of the 20-ms pulse output from the microcomputer and statically reset when the trailing edge of this pulse pulls the reset input low.

Another application of one-shots arises if we need to obtain a multiple-phase clock from an externally obtained clock source. For example, data from a magnetic disk memory might be synchronized to a "bit clock" taken from a separate clock track on the disk. If we need a multiple-phase clock to use with this data, the one-shot circuit of Fig. 6-35 will provide it.

In each of these applications, the one-shot has avoided the introduction of any timing ambiguity into a circuit in spite of the unsynchronized trailing edge of its output pulse. In contrast, consider the bad example of Fig. 6-36. Perhaps we want to make a circuit pause for 1s whenever a pushbutton is depressed. The one-shot can be trimmed to give a 1-s pulse. If its output is used as an input to a separately clocked circuit, there is no telling when it is likely to change relative to CLOCK. Any ones-catching devices that look at this unsynchronized input will behave erratically. Even edge-triggered devices will have difficulty when occasionally the input changes just before the CLOCK transition, during the setup/hold-time ambiguity region of some sequential devices in the circuit. Some flip-flops may see the new value of ENABLE, while others may respond to the old value, yielding erratic operation.

It is this type of application that has given the one-shot a bad image in the minds of many designers. Our job is to capitalize on the strengths of this device and use it where it is appropriate. At the same time, we want to be wary of the timing that arises from the trailing edge of a one-shot, because this edge is not synchronized to anything else in our circuitry.

PROBLEMS

6-1 Foreground/background scheme. Minimizing package count, redesign the data manipulation circuitry of Fig. 6-2 using four 74LS195s in place of the two 74LS377s. Label all inputs and outputs.

6-2 Switched-clock ASM design. The microcomputer in Fig. 6-1 looks at outputs S2 and S3 of the ASM (described in Fig. 6-4) which are synchronized to the external CLOCK* while in the foreground mode. Even though this is a separately clocked circuit, the microcomputer wants to read S2 and S3 unambiguously. Can it do so? Explain.

6-3 Two-port RAM. The two-port RAMs of Figs. 6-5*b* and 6-6 permit the orderly transfer of data between two separately clocked circuits. One circuit can take permanent hold of the WRITE input data and address lines while another can take permanent hold of the READ output data and address lines. Discuss the possibility of achieving this same function with the 256 × 4 RAM of Fig. 5-3 if two of the multiplexers of Fig. 2-36 are used to multiplex a WRITE-address input and READ-address input into the RAM's address input.

6-4 Handshaking. Consider two separately clocked circuits that handshake data bilaterally. For example, consider the signature analyzer design of Fig. 4-2 in which the microcomputer and the ASM exchanged DATA and DONE.

(*a*) Is there complete symmetry in the handling of the data between the circuit that controls the DAV line and the circuit that controls the DAC line?

(*b*) Is there complete symmetry in the handling of the DAV and DAC lines? That is, could one circuit control a DAV-DAC-1 line and the other control a DAV-DAC-2 line such that either one could initiate the handshaking process with the other? Discuss.

6-5 Gray code. An unusual opportunity for reliably transmitting data between two separately clocked circuits arises in the use of a Gray code shaft-angle encoder, like that of Fig. 2-2. As the shaft rotates, its output changes at times which are unsynchronized to the clock in the system which uses this output.

(*a*) Considering the unit-distance property of Gray code, discussed in conjunction with Fig. 2-1, can the output of a Gray code encoder *ever* be read erroneously (by a separately clocked circuit)? Explain.

(*b*) While the Gray code–to–binary code converter circuits of Figs. 2-10 and 2-47 appear to represent good solutions to the conversion problem, discuss their use in light of the problem of reliably reading their outputs into a microcomputer. If there is a reliability problem, then discuss a satisfactory alternative.

(*c*) Some high-speed analog-to-digital converters generate a Gray code output which follows an analog input continuously (just as the Gray code shaft-angle encoder output follows the shaft position continuously). Is there a reliability advantage which arises because the output is Gray code rather than binary code? Explain.

6-6 Serial data transmission. The UART built into the Motorola 6801 does not handle a parity bit.

(*a*) Can the 6801 detect parity errors in received data, each byte of which consists of a 7-bit ASCII character plus a parity bit, by employing a software routine for this purpose?

(*b*) Can the 6801 transmit bytes of data, each one of which consists of a 7-bit ASCII character to which a parity bit has been added in a software routine?

6-7 Serial data transmission. For the multiple-microcomputer instrument organization of Fig. 6-13, what is the *range* of crystal frequencies that will provide satisfactory operation when used with slave 2 if the crystals of the other microcomputers are all exactly 4 MHz?

6-8 CRT display. Consider the timing diagram of Fig. 6-25 and the circuit of Fig. 6-22.

(*a*) Is there a bus contention problem on the address bus driven by both the 74LS373 three-state latch and the 6847 video display generator? What data do you need to answer this precisely?

(*b*) Is there a bus contention problem on the data bus driven by both the 74LS245 three-state transceivers and the 2114 RAMs? What data do you need to answer this precisely?

6-9 Queues. What would be the nature of the impact upon the operation of the CRT display of Fig. 6-22 if the maximum length of the queue had been chosen to be 50 bytes instead of 100 bytes?

6-10 One-shots. The 74LS221 one-shot has been designed so that the variance in output pulse width from device to device is typically less than ± 0.5 percent for given external timing components. Mica capacitors of ± 1 percent (and even ± 0.5 percent) are commonly available up to 0.1 μF. Cermet film resistors of ± 1 percent are commonly available up to 10 MΩ. What is the implication of this data for the manufacture of protection circuits like those of Fig. 6-34*b* and *c* as well as the multiple-phase clock circuit of Fig. 6-35?

REFERENCES

To obtain a detailed description and a software listing for the CRT terminal from which the nine-chip CRT display was derived, write its astute designer, Ed Rupp, Motorola, Inc., NMOS Design Group, 3501 Ed Bluestein Blvd., Austin, TX 78721.

In general, a good vehicle for applying the design techniques of this chapter can be obtained by studying the service manual for the digital portion of any instrument. In addition to gaining the insight of a designer's overall approach to an instrumentation task, we can carry out one more iteration upon the design. We can build in the foreground/background scheme, switching the clock between the normal clock and a test clock. Or we can reorganize the design using master and slave "smart" subsystems.

APPENDIX A1

LOGIC SYMBOLOGY AND DEPENDENCY NOTATION

Frederic A. Mann†

A1-1 INTRODUCTION

The International Electrotechnical Commission (IEC) has been developing a very powerful symbolic language that can show the relationship of each input of a digital logic circuit to each output without showing explicitly the internal logic. At the heart of the system is dependency notation, which will be explained in Sec. A1-4.

The system was introduced in the United States in a rudimentary form in IEEE/ANSI Standard Y32.14-1973. Lacking at that time a complete development of dependency notation, it offered little more than

† Manager, Commercial Product Specifications, Semiconductor Group, Texas Instruments Incorporated, MS84, P. O. Box 225012, Dallas, Texas 75265. Member, IEEE Committee SCC 11.9 and IEEE representative to IEC Technical Committee TC-3, Working Group 2.

‡ Taken by permission from Texas Instruments' *TTL Data Book for Design Engineers*, 3d edition, now in preparation. To purchase the symbol standards (as they become available), write to the American National Standards Institute, Inc. (1430 Broadway, New York, NY 10018) for IEC Publication 617-12 and to the Institute of Electrical and Electronics Engineers, Inc. (345 East 47th Street, New York, NY 10017) for the *revised* IEEE Std 91/ANSI Y32.14.

a substitution of rectangular shapes for the familiar distinctive shapes for representing the basic functions of AND, OR, negation, etc. This is no longer the case.

Internationally, Working Group 2 of IEC Technical Committee TC-3 is preparing a new document (Publication 617-12) that will consolidate the original work started in the mid-1960s and published in 1972 (Publication 117-15) and the amendments and supplements that have followed. Similarly for the United States, IEEE Committee SCC 11.9 is revising the publication IEEE Std 91/ANSI Y32.14. Texas Instruments is participating in the work of both organizations and this third edition of the TTL Data Book introduces new logic symbols in anticipation of the new standards. When changes are made as the standards develop, future editions of this book will take those changes into account. Unfortunately, time and publication schedules have prevented the preparation of symbols for all the devices. This work will continue.

The following explanation of the new symbolic language is necessarily brief and greatly condensed from what the standards publications will finally contain. This is not intended to be sufficient for those people who will be developing symbols for new devices. It is primarily intended to make possible the understanding of the symbols used in this book; comparing the symbols with functional block diagrams and/or function tables will further help that understanding.

A1-2 SYMBOL COMPOSITION

A symbol comprises an outline or a combination of outlines together with one or more qualifying symbols. The shape of the symbols is not significant. As shown in Fig. A1-1, general qualifying symbols are used to tell exactly what logical operation is performed by the elements. Table A1-1 shows the general qualifying symbols used in this data book. Input lines are placed on the left and output lines are placed on the right. When an exception is made to that convention, the direction of signal flow is indicated by an arrow, as shown in Fig. A1-11.

All outputs of an element always have identical internal logic states determined by the function of the element except when otherwise indicated by an associated qualifying symbol inside the element. The outlines of elements may be joined or embedded, in which case the following conventions apply. There is no logic connection between the elements when the line common to their outlines is in the direction of information flow. There is at least one logic connection between the elements when the line common to their outlines is perpendicular to the direction of information flow. The number of logic connections

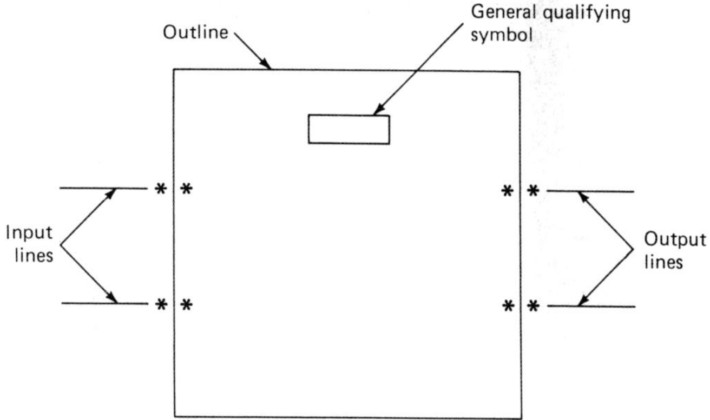

Figure A1-1. Symbol composition.

between elements will be clarified by the use of qualifying symbols and this is discussed further under that topic. If no indications are shown on either side of the common line, it is assumed there is only one connection.

When a circuit has one or more inputs that are common to more than one element of the circuit, the common-control block may be used. This is the only distinctively shaped outline used in the IEC system. Figure A1-2 shows that, unless otherwise qualified by dependency notation, an input to the common-control block is an input to each of the elements below the common-control block.

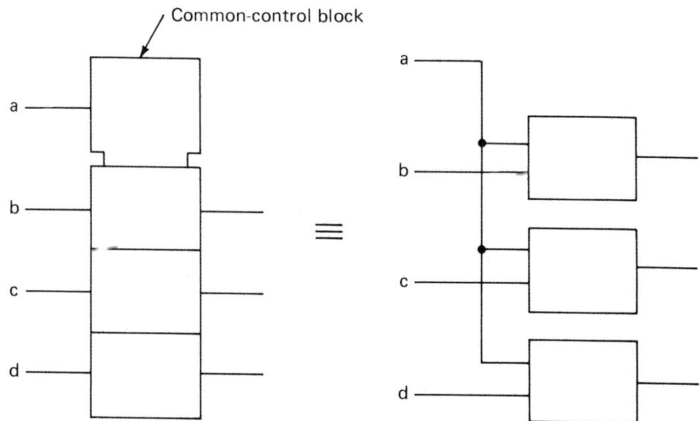

Figure A1-2. Illustration of common-control block.

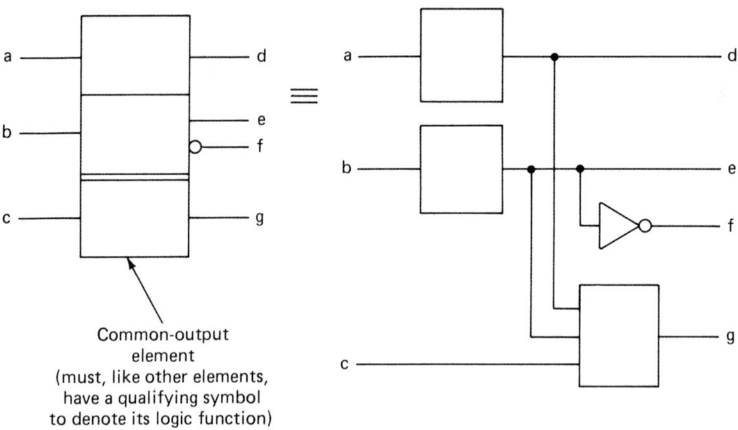

Figure A1-3. Illustration of common-output element.

A common output depending on all elements of the array can be shown as the output of a common-output element. Its distinctive visual feature is the double line at its top. In addition the common-output element may have other inputs as shown in Fig. A1-3. The function of the common-output element must be shown by use of a general qualifying symbol.

A1-3 QUALIFYING SYMBOLS

Table A1-1 shows the general qualifying symbols used in this data book. Qualifying symbols for inputs and outputs are shown in Table A1-2 and will be familiar to most users, with the possible exception of the logic polarity indicators. The older logic negation indicator means that the external 0 state produces the internal 1 state. The internal 1 state means the active state. Logic negation may be used in pure logic diagrams; in order to tie the external 1 and 0 logic states to the levels H (high) and L (low), a statement of whether positive logic (1 = H, 0 = L) or negative logic (1 = L, 0 = H) is being used is required or must be assumed. Logic polarity indicators eliminate the need for calling out the logic convention and are used in this data book in the symbology for actual devices. The presence of the triangular polarity indicator indicates that the L logic level will produce the internal 1 state (the active state) or that, in the case of an output, the internal 1 state will produce the external L level. Note how the active direction of transition for a dynamic input is indicated in positive logic, negative logic, or with polarity indication.

Table A1-1. General Qualifying Symbols

≥ 1	OR
&	AND
$=1$	Exclusive-OR
$=$	All inputs at same state
$2k$	Even number of inputs active
$2k+1$	Odd number of inputs active
1	One input active
▷	Buffer, driver, amplifier
⎍	Schmitt trigger
X/Y	Coder, code converter, BCD/DEC, BIN/BCD, etc.
MUX	Multiplexer
DMUX	Demultiplexer
Σ	Adder
P-Q	Subtracter
CPG	Look-ahead carry generator
π	Multiplier
COMP	Magnitude comparator
ALU	Arithmetic logic unit
⎍	Retriggerable monostable
1⎍	Nonretriggerable monostable
G ⎍⎍	Astable element. Showing ⎍⎍ is optional.
!G ⎍⎍	Synchronously starting astable
G! ⎍⎍	Astable element stopping with completed pulse
SRGm	Shift register (m = number of bits)
CTRm	Counter (m = number of bits)
CTRDIVm	Counter with cycle length = m
ROM	Read-only memory
RAM	Random-access memory

The internal connections between logic elements abutted together in a symbol may be indicated by the symbols shown. Each logic connection may be shown by the presence of qualifying symbols at one or both sides of the common line and if confusion can arise about the numbers of connections, use can be made of one of the internal connection symbols.

The internal (virtual) input is an input originating somewhere else in the circuit and is not connected directly to a terminal. The internal (virtual) output is likewise not connected directly to a terminal. The application of internal inputs and outputs requires an understanding of dependency notation, which is explained in Sec. A1-4.

In an array of elements, if the same general qualifying symbol and the same qualifying symbols associated with inputs and outputs would

Table A1-2. Qualifying Symbols for Inputs and Outputs

Symbol	Description		
	Logic negation at input	external 0 = internal 1	
	Logic negation at output	internal 1 = external 0	
	Logic polarity	external LOW produces internal 1	

Symbol	Positive logic	Negative logic	Polarity indication	
	1 → 0 or	1 → 0	not used	= internal 1
	not used	not used	H → L	= internal 1
	0 → 1 or	0 → 1 or	L → H	= internal 1

Symbol	Description
	Internal connection
	Internal connection with negation
	Internal dynamic connection
	Internal input (virtual input)
	Internal output (virtual output)

appear inside all the elements of the array, these qualifying symbols are usually shown only in the first element. This is done to reduce clutter and to save time in recognition.

A1-3.1 Symbols Inside the Outline Table A1-3 shows some symbols used inside the outline. Note particularly that open-collector, open-emitter, and three-state outputs have distinctive symbols. Also note that an EN input affects all of the outputs of the circuit and has no effect on inputs. When an enable input affects only certain outputs and/or does affect one or more inputs, a form of dependency notation will in-

Table A1-3. Symbols Inside the Outline

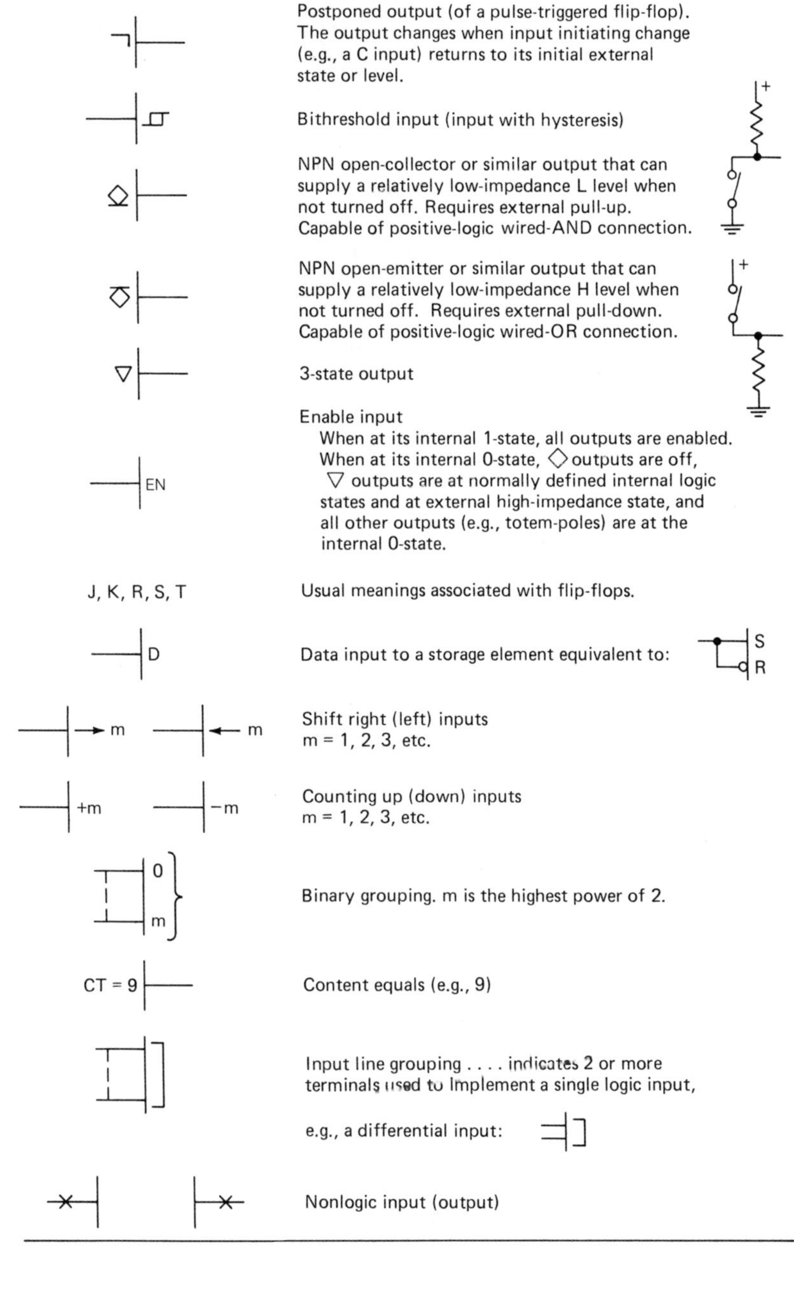

Symbol	Description
	Postponed output (of a pulse-triggered flip-flop). The output changes when input initiating change (e.g., a C input) returns to its initial external state or level.
	Bithreshold input (input with hysteresis)
	NPN open-collector or similar output that can supply a relatively low-impedance L level when not turned off. Requires external pull-up. Capable of positive-logic wired-AND connection.
	NPN open-emitter or similar output that can supply a relatively low-impedance H level when not turned off. Requires external pull-down. Capable of positive-logic wired-OR connection.
	3-state output
EN	Enable input When at its internal 1-state, all outputs are enabled. When at its internal 0-state, ◇ outputs are off, ▽ outputs are at normally defined internal logic states and at external high-impedance state, and all other outputs (e.g., totem-poles) are at the internal 0-state.
J, K, R, S, T	Usual meanings associated with flip-flops.
D	Data input to a storage element equivalent to: S R
→ m ← m	Shift right (left) inputs m = 1, 2, 3, etc.
+m −m	Counting up (down) inputs m = 1, 2, 3, etc.
0 … m	Binary grouping. m is the highest power of 2.
CT = 9	Content equals (e.g., 9)
	Input line grouping . . . . indicates 2 or more terminals used to implement a single logic input, e.g., a differential input:
	Nonlogic input (output)

dicate this. The effects of the EN input on the various types of outputs are shown.

It is particularly important to note that a D input is always the data input of a storage element. At its internal 1 state, the D input sets the storage element to its 1 state, and at its internal 0 state it resets the storage element to its 0 state.

The binary grouping symbol is important. Binary-weighted inputs are arranged in order and the binary weights of the least-significant and the most-significant lines are indicated by numbers. In this data book weights of input and output lines will be represented by powers of 2 only when the binary grouping symbol is used; otherwise, decimal numbers will be used. The grouped inputs generate an internal number on which a mathematical function can be performed or that can be an identifying number for dependency notation. See Fig. A1-24. A frequent use is in addresses for memories.

Reversed in direction, the binary grouping symbol can be used with outputs. The concept is analogous to that for the inputs, and the weighted outputs will indicate the internal number assumed to be developed by the circuit.

Other symbols are used inside the outlines in this catalog in accordance with the IEC/IEEE standard but are not shown here. Generally these are associated with arithmetic operations and are self-explanatory.

When nonstandardized information is shown inside an outline, it is usually enclosed in square brackets [like these].

A1-4 DEPENDENCY NOTATION

A1-4.1 General Explanation Dependency notation is the powerful tool that sets the IEC symbols apart from previous systems and makes compact, meaningful, symbols possible. It provides the means of denoting the relationship between inputs, outputs, or inputs and outputs without actually showing all the elements and interconnections involved. The information provided by dependency notation supplements that provided by the qualifying symbols for an element's function.

In the convention for the dependency notation, use will be made of the terms "affecting" and "affected." In the case where it is not evident which inputs must be considered as being the affecting or the affected ones (e.g., if they stand in an AND relationship), the choice may be made in any convenient way.

So far, ten types of dependency have been defined and all of these are used in this data book. They are listed below in the order in which they are presented and are summarized in Table A1-4 in Sec. A1-4.11.

Section	Dependency type or other subject
A1-4.2	G, AND
A1-4.3	General rules for dependency notation
A1-4.4	V, OR
A1-4.5	N, negate, exclusive-OR
A1-4.6	Z, interconnection
A1-4.7	C, control
A1-4.8	S, set and R, reset
A1-4.9	EN, enable
A1-4.10	M, mode
A1-4.11	A, address
A1-4.12	Use of a coder to produce affecting inputs
A1-4.13	Use of binary grouping to produce affecting inputs
A1-4.14	Sequence of input labels
A1-4.15	Sequence of output labels

A1-4.2 G (AND) Dependency A common relationship between two signals is to have then ANDed together. This has traditionally been shown by explicitly drawing an AND gate with the signals connected to the inputs of the gate. The 1972 IEC publication and the 1973 IEEE/ANSI standard showed several ways to show this AND relationship using dependency notation. While nine other forms of dependency have since been defined, the ways to invoke AND dependency are now reduced to one.

In Fig. A1-4 input *b* is ANDed with input *a* and the complement of *b* is ANDed with *c*. The letter G has been chosen to indicate AND relationships and is placed at input *b*, inside the symbol. An arbitrary number (1 has been used here) is placed after the letter G and also at each affected input. Note the bar over the 1 at input *c*.

In Fig. A1-5, output *b* affects input *a* with an AND relationship. The lower example shows that it is the internal logic state of *b*, unaffected by the negation sign, that is ANDed. Figure A1-6 shows input *a* to be ANDed with a dynamic input *b*.

The rules for G-dependency can be summarized thus: When a G*m* input or output (*m* is a number) stands at its internal 1 state, all inputs and outputs affected by G*m* stand at their normally defined internal

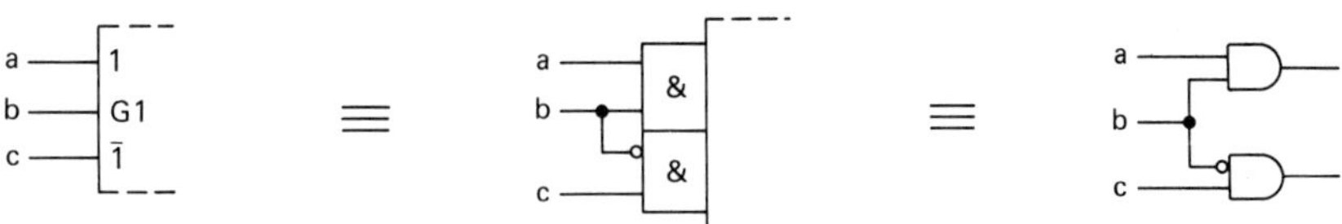

Figure A1-4. G dependency between inputs.

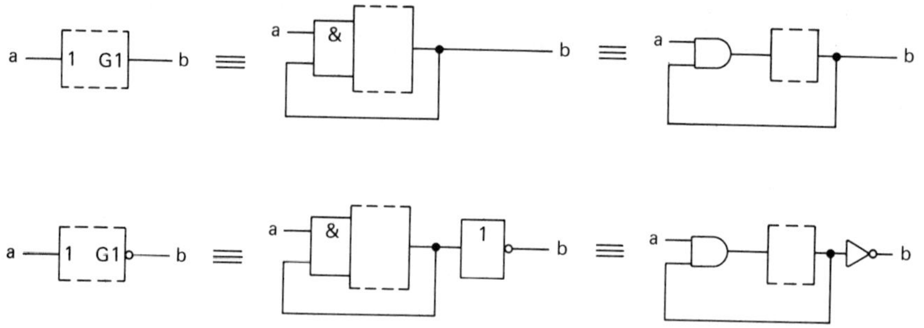

Figure A1-5. G dependency between outputs and inputs.

logic states. When the Gm input or output stands at its 0 state, all inputs and outputs affected by Gm stand at their internal 0 states.

A1-4.3 Conventions for the Application of Dependency Notation in General The rules for applying dependency relationships in general follow the same pattern as was illustrated for G-dependency.

Application of dependency notation is accomplished by:

1. Labeling the input (or output) *affecting* other inputs or outputs with a letter symbol indicating the relationship involved (e.g., G for AND) followed by an identifying number, arbitrarily chosen.
2. Labeling each input or output *affected* by that affecting input (or output) with that same number.

If it is the complement of the internal logic state of the affecting input or output that does the affecting, then a bar is placed over the identifying numbers at the affected inputs or outputs. See Fig. A1-4.

If the affected input or output requires a label to denote its function (e.g., D), this label will be *prefixed* by the identifying number of the affecting input. See Fig. A1-12.

If the affected input or output already has a label denoting its function (e.g., D), this label will be *prefixed* by the identifying number of the affecting input. See Fig. A1-12.

If an input or output is affected by more than one affecting input, the identifying numbers of each of the affecting inputs will appear in the label of the affected one, separated by commas. The left-to-right

Figure A1-6. G dependency with a dynamic input.

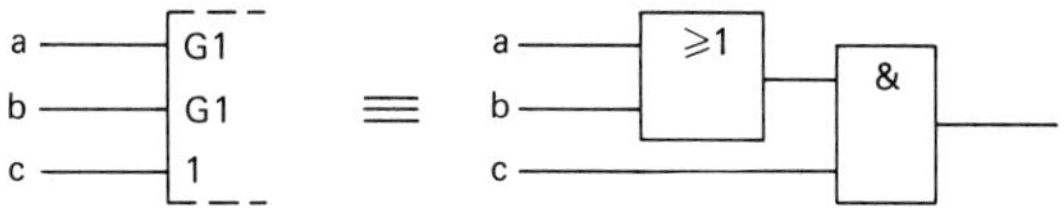

Figure A1-7. OR'ed affecting inputs.

Figure A1-8. Substitution for numbers.

sequence of these numbers is the same as the sequence of the affecting relationships. See Fig. A1-12.

If the labels denoting the functions of affected inputs or outputs must be numbers, the identifying numbers to be associated with both affecting inputs and affected inputs or outputs will be replaced by another character selected to avoid ambiguity (e.g., Greek letters). See Fig. A1-8.

A1-4.4 V (OR) Dependency The symbol denoting OR-dependency is the letter V. See Fig. A1-9.

When a V*m* input or output stands at its internal 1 state, all inputs and outputs affected by V*m* stand at their internal 1 states. When the V*m* input or output stands at its internal 0 state, all inputs and outputs affected by V*m* stand at their normally defined internal logic states.

A1-4.5 N (Negate) (X-OR) Dependency The symbol denoting negate dependency is the letter N. See Fig. A1-10. Each input or output affected by an Nm input or output stands in an exclusive-OR relationship with the Nm input or output.

When an N*m* input or output stands at its internal 1 state, the in-

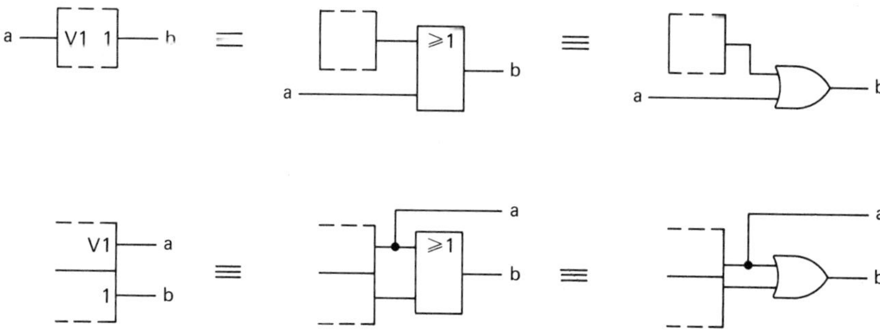

Figure A1-9. V(OR) dependency

If a = 0, c = b
If a = 1, c = $\overline{b}$

Figure A1-10. *N (Negate) (X-OR) dependency.*

ternal logic state of each input and each output affected by N*m* is the complement of what it would otherwise be. When an N*m* input or output stands at its internal 0 state, all inputs and outputs affected by N*m* stand at their normally defined internal logic states.

A1-4.6 Z (Interconnection) Dependency The symbol denoting interconnection dependency is the letter Z.

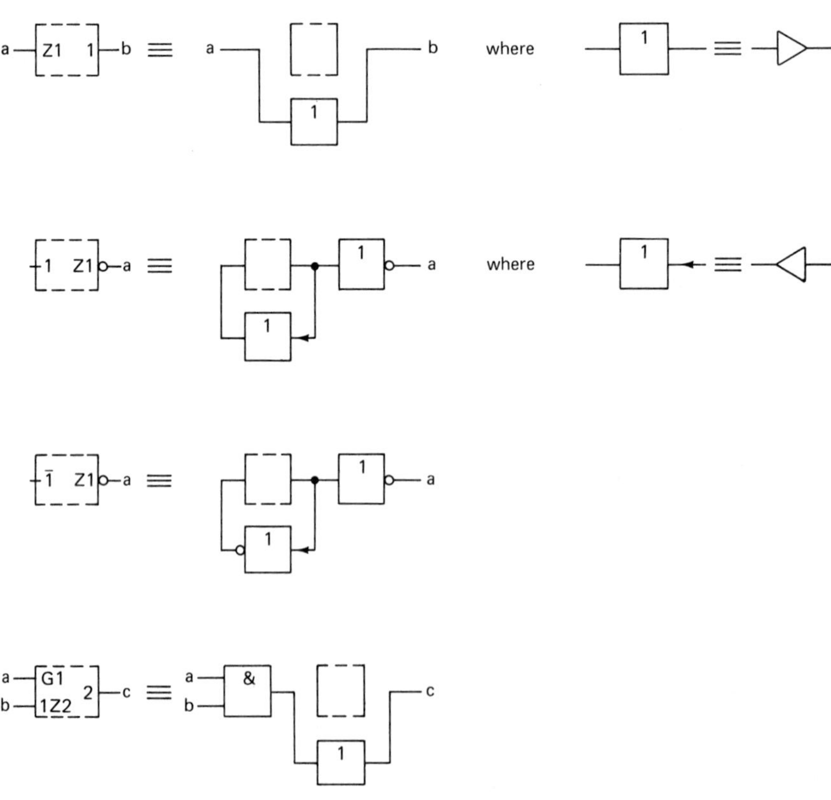

Figure *A1-11.* Z (interconnection) dependency.

Interconnection dependency is used to indicate the existence of internal logic connections between inputs, outputs, internal inputs, and/or internal outputs.

The internal logic state of an input or output affected by a *Zm* input or output will be the same as the internal logic state of the *Zm* input or output. See Fig. A1-11.

A1-4.7 C (Control) Dependency The symbol denoting control dependency is the letter C.

Control inputs are usually used to enable or disable the D (data) inputs of storage elements. They may take on their internal 1 states (be active) either statically or dynamically. In the latter case the dynamic input symbol is used as shown in the third example of Fig. A1-12.

When a C*m* input or output stands at its internal 1 state, the inputs affected by C*m* have their normally defined effect on the function of the element (i.e., these inputs are enabled). When a C*m* input or output

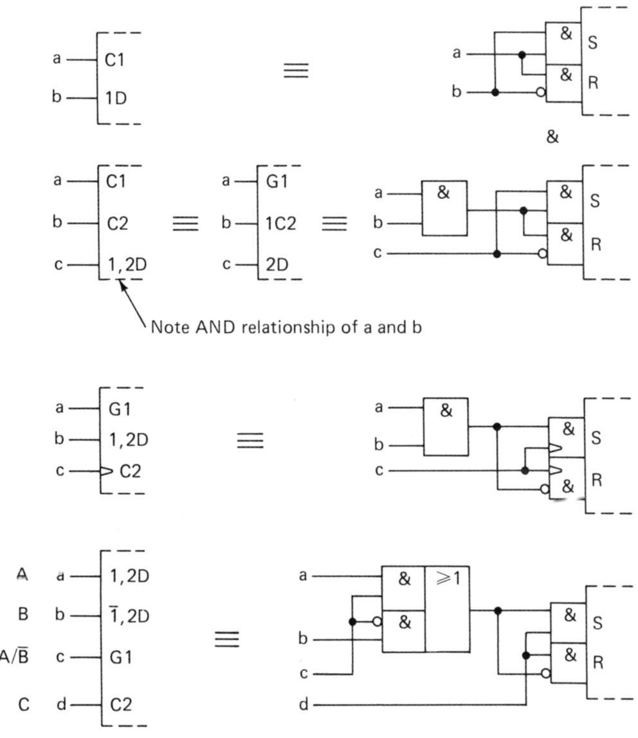

Figure A1-12. C (control) dependency.

stands at its internal 0 state, the inputs affected by C*m* are disabled and have no effect on the function of the element.

A1-4.8 S (Set) and R (Reset) Dependencies The symbol denoting set dependency is the letter S. The symbol denoting reset dependency is the letter R.

Set and reset dependencies are used if it is necessary to specify the effect of the combination R = S = 1 on a bistable element. Case 1 in Fig. A1-13 does not use S or R dependency.

When an S*m* input is at its internal 1 state, outputs affected by the S*m* input will react, regardless of the state of an R input, as they normally would react to the combination S = 1, R = 0. See cases 2, 4, and 5 in Fig. A1-13.

When an R*m* input is at its internal 1 state, outputs affected by the R*m* input will react, regardless of the state of an S input, as they normally would react to the combination S = 0, R = 1. See cases 3, 4, and 5 in Fig. A1-13.

When an S*m* or R*m* input is at its internal 0 state, it has no effect.

Note that the noncomplementary output patterns in cases 4 and 5 are only pseudo stable. The simultaneous return of the inputs to S = R = 0 produces an unforeseeable stable and complementary output pattern.

A1-4.9 EN (Enable) Dependency The symbol denoting enable dependency is the combination of letters EN.

An EN*m* input has the same effect on outputs as an EN input (see Sec. A1-3.1), but it can affect less than all of the outputs. It can also affect inputs. By contrast, an EN input affects all outputs and no inputs. The effect of an EN*m* input on an affected input is identical to that of a C*m* input. See Fig. A1-14.

When an EN*m* input stands at its internal 1 state, the inputs affected by EN*m* have their normally defined effect on the function of the element and the outputs affected by this input stand at their normally defined internal logic states, i.e., these inputs and outputs are enabled.

When an EN*m* input stands at its internal 0 state, the inputs affected by EN*m* are disabled and have no effect on the function of the element, and the outputs affected by EN*m* are also disabled. Open-collector outputs are turned off, three-state outputs stand at their normally defined internal logic states but externally exhibit high impedance, and all other outputs (e.g., totem-pole outputs) stand at their internal 0 states.

A1-4.10 M (Mode) Dependency The symbol denoting mode dependency is the letter M.

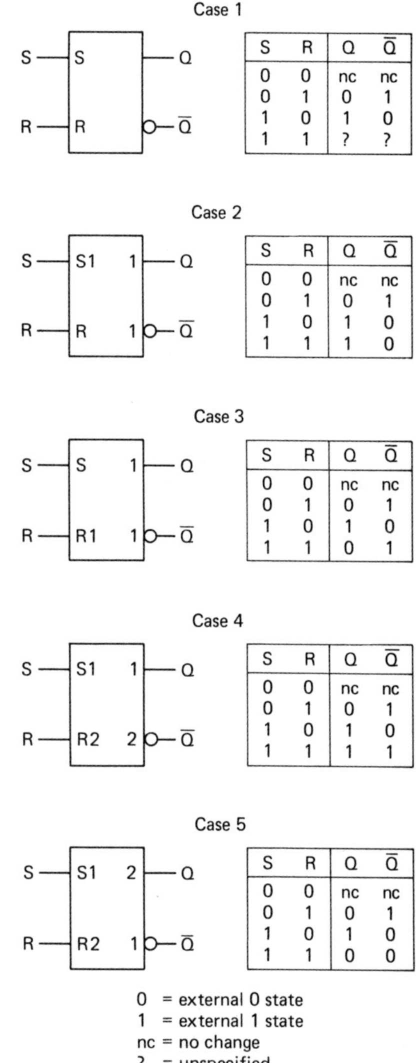

Case 1

S	R	Q	$\overline{Q}$
0	0	nc	nc
0	1	0	1
1	0	1	0
1	1	?	?

Case 2

S	R	Q	$\overline{Q}$
0	0	nc	nc
0	1	0	1
1	0	1	0
1	1	1	0

Case 3

S	R	Q	$\overline{Q}$
0	0	nc	nc
0	1	0	1
1	0	1	0
1	1	0	1

Case 4

S	R	Q	$\overline{Q}$
0	0	nc	nc
0	1	0	1
1	0	1	0
1	1	1	1

Case 5

S	R	Q	$\overline{Q}$
0	0	nc	nc
0	1	0	1
1	0	1	0
1	1	0	0

Figure A1-13. S (set) and R (reset) dependencies.

Mode dependency is used to indicate that the effects of particular inputs and outputs of an element depend on the mode in which the element is operating.

If an input or output has the same effect in different modes of operation, the identifying numbers of the relevant affecting M*m* inputs will appear in the label of that affected input or output between parentheses and separated by commas. See Fig. A1-19.

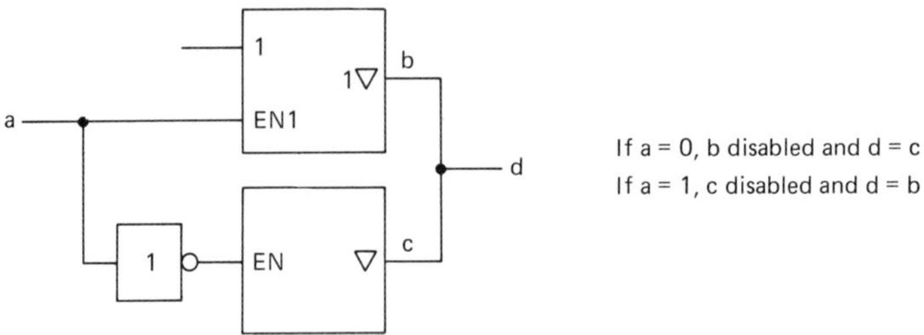

Figure A1-14. EN (enable) dependency.

M Dependency Affecting Inputs M dependency affects inputs the same as C dependency. When an M*m* input or M*m* output stands at its internal 1 state, the inputs affected by this M*m* input or M*m* output have their normally defined effect on the function of the element, i.e., the inputs are enabled.

When an M*m* input or M*m* output stands at its internal 0 state, the inputs affected by this M*m* input or M*m* output have no effect on the function of the element. When an affected input has several sets of labels separated by slashes, any set in which the identifying number of the M*m* input or M*m* output appears has no effect and is to be ignored. This represents disabling of some of the functions of a multifunction input.

The circuit in Fig. A1-15 has two inputs, *b* and *c*, that control which one of four modes (0, 1, 2, or 3) will exist at any time. Inputs *d*, *e*, and *f* are D inputs subject to dynamic control (clocking) by the *a* input. The numbers 1 and 2 are in the series chosen to indicate the modes so inputs *e* and *f* are only enabled in mode 1 (for parallel loading) and input *d* is only enabled in mode 2 (for serial loading). Note that input *a* has three functions. It is the clock for entering data. In mode 2, it causes right shifting of data, which means a shift away from the control block. In mode 3, it causes the contents of the register to be incremented by one count.

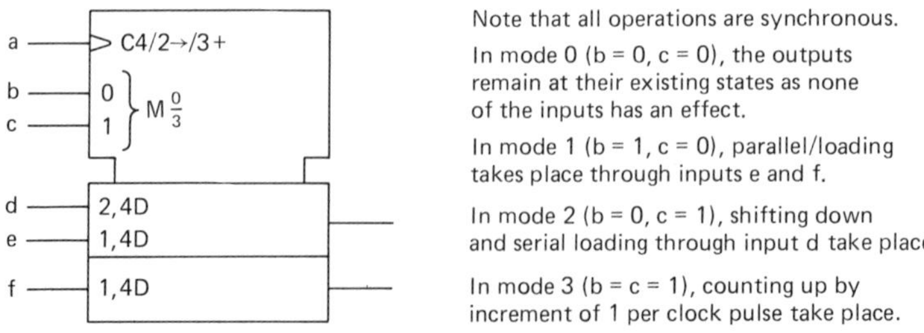

Figure A1-15. M (mode) dependency affecting inputs.

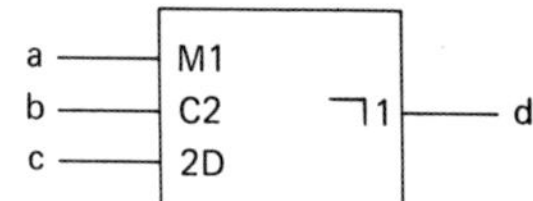

Figure A1-16. Type of flip-flop determined by mode.

M (Mode) Dependency Affecting Outputs When an M*m* input or M*m* output stands at its internal 1 state, the affected outputs stand at their normally defined internal logic states, i.e., the outputs are enabled.

When an M*m* input or M*m* output stands at its internal 0 state, at each affected output any set of labels containing the identifying number of that M*m* input or M*m* output has no effect and is to be ignored. When an output has several different sets of labels separated by slashes (e.g., C4/2→/3+), only those sets in which the identifying number of this M*m* input or M*m* output appears are to be ignored.

In Fig. A1-16, mode 1 exists when the *a* input stands at its internal 1 state. The delayed output symbol is effective only in mode 1 (when input $a = 1$) in which case the device functions as a pulse-triggered flip-flop. See Sec. A1-5. When input $a = 0$, the device is not in mode 1 so the delayed output symbol has no effect and the device functions as a transparent latch.

In Fig. A1-17, if input *a* stands at its internal 1 state establishing mode 1, output *b* will stand at its internal 1 state when the content of the register equals 9. Since output *b* is located in the common-control block with no defined function outside of mode 1, this output will stand at its internal 0 state when input *a* stands at its internal 0 state, regardless of the register content.

In Fig. A1-18, if input *a* stands at its internal 1 state establishing mode 1, output *b* will stand at its internal 1 state when the content of the register equals 15. If input *a* stands at its internal 0 state, output b will stand at its internal 1 state when the content of the register equals 0.

In Fig. A1-19 inputs *a* and *b* are binary weighted to generate the numbers 0, 1, 2, or 3. This determines which one of the four modes exists.

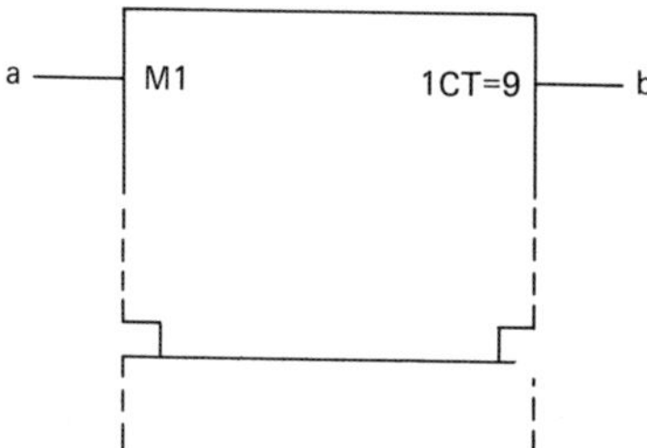

Figure A1-17. Disabling an output of the common-control block.

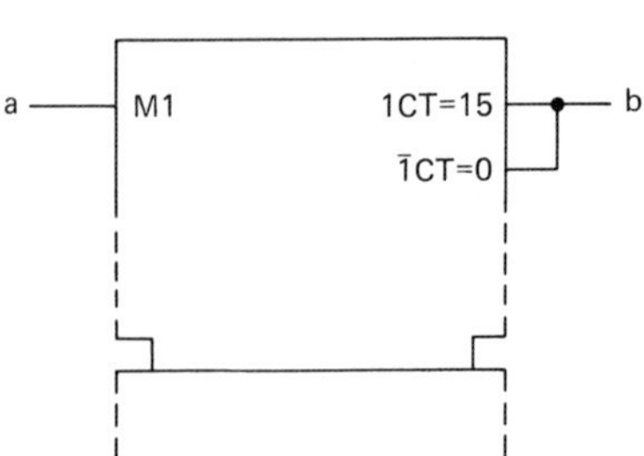

Figure A1-18. Determining an output's function.

At output e the label set causing negation (if $c = 1$) is effective only in modes 2 and 3. In modes 0 and 1 this output stands at its normally defined state as if it had no labels.

At output f the label set has effect when the mode is not 0 so output e is negated (if $c = 1$) in modes 1, 2, and 3. In mode 0 the label set has no effect so the output stands at its normally defined state. In this example, $\bar{0}$,4 is equivalent to (1/2/3)4.

At output g there are two label sets. The first set, causing negation (if $c = 1$), is effective only in mode 2. The second set, subjecting g to AND dependency on d, has effect only in mode 3.

Note that in mode 0 none of the dependency relationships have any effect on the outputs, so e, f, and g will all stand at the same state.

A1-4.11 A (Address) Dependency The symbol denoting address dependency is the letter A.

Address dependency is used to obtain a clear representation of those elements, particularly memories, that use address control inputs to select specified sections of a multidimensional array. Such a section of a memory array is usually called a word. The purpose of address dependency is to allow a symbolic presentation of only a single general case of the sections of the array, rather than requiring a symbolic presentation of the entire array. An input of the array shown at a particular element of this general section is common to the corresponding elements of all selected sections of the array. An output of the array shown at a particular element of this general section is the result of the OR function of the outputs of the corresponding elements of selected sections. If the label of an output of the array shown at a particular element of this general section indicates that this output is an open-circuit output

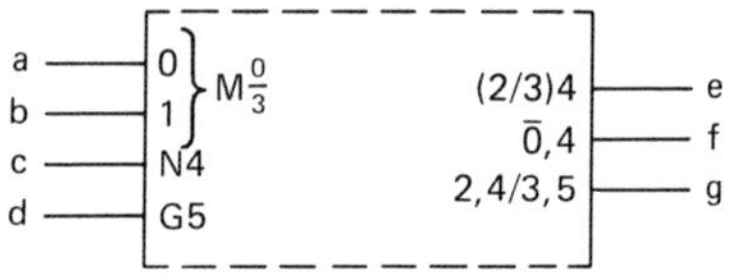

Figure A1-19. Dependent relationships affected by mode.

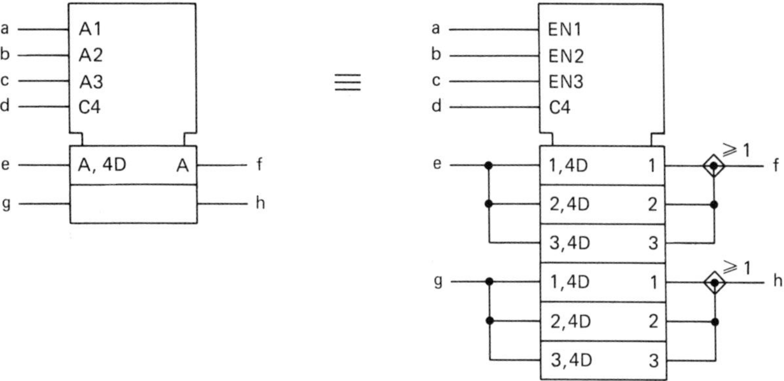

Figure A1-20. A (address) dependency.

or a three-state output, then this indication refers to the output of the array and not to those of the sections of the array.

Inputs that are not affected by any affecting address input have their normally defined effect on all sections of the array, whereas inputs affected by an address input have their normally defined effect only on the section selected by that address input.

An affecting address input is labeled with the letter A followed by an identifying number that corresponds with the address of the particular section of the array selected by this input.

Within the general section presented by the symbol, inputs and outputs affected by an A*m* input are labeled with the letter A, which stands for the identifying numbers, i.e., the addresses, of the particular sections.

Fig. A1-20 shows a 3-word by 2-bit memory having a separate address line for each word and uses EN dependency to explain the operation. To select word 1, input *a* is taken to its 1 state, which establishes mode 1. Data can now be clocked into the inputs marked 1,4D. Unless words 2 and 3 are also selected, data cannot be clocked in at the inputs marked 2,4D and 3,4D. The outputs will be the OR functions of the selected outputs, i.e., only those enabled by the active EN functions.

The identifying numbers of affecting address inputs correspond with the addresses of the sections selected by these inputs. They need not necessarily differ from those of other affecting dependency-inputs (e.g., G, V, N, . . .), because in the general section presented by the symbol they are replaced by the letter A.

If there are several sets of affecting A inputs for the purpose of independent and possibly simultaneous access to sections of the array, then the letter A is modified to 1A, 2A. . . . Because they have

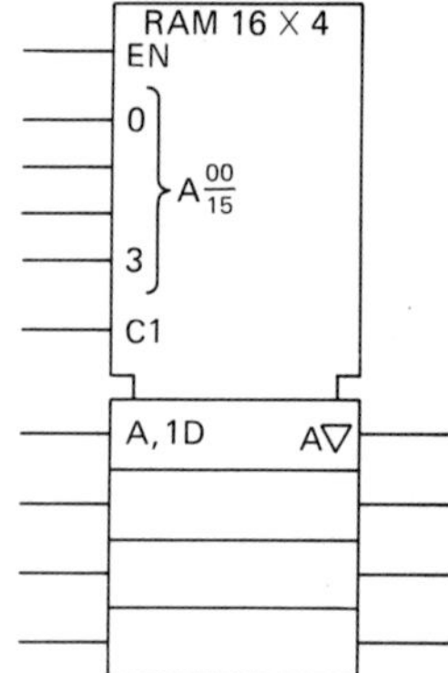

Figure A1-21. Array of 16 sections of four transparent latches with three-state outputs. This comprises a 16-word × 4-bit random-access memory.

access to the same sections of the array, these sets of A inputs may have the same identifying numbers. Figure A1-21 is another illustration of the concept. Table A1-4 summarizes the dependency notation.

A1-4.12 Use of a Coder to Produce Affecting Inputs It often occurs that a set of affecting inputs is produced by decoding the signals on certain inputs to an element. In such a case one can use the symbol for a coder as an embedded symbol. See Fig. A1-22.

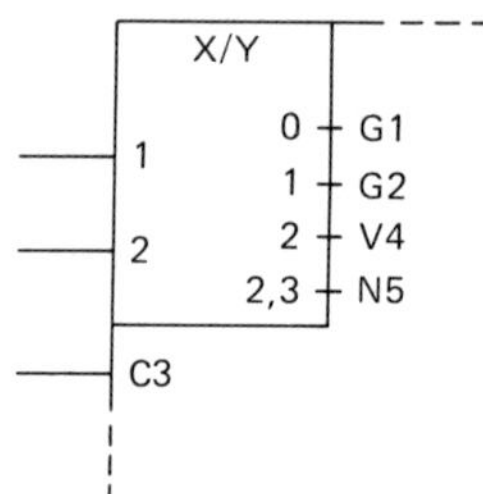

Figure A1-22. Producing various types of dependencies.

If all affecting inputs produced by a coder are of the same type and their identifying numbers correspond with the numbers shown at the outputs of the coder, Y (in the qualifying symbol X/Y) may be replaced by the letter denoting the type of dependency. The indications of the affecting inputs should then be omitted. See Fig. A1-23.

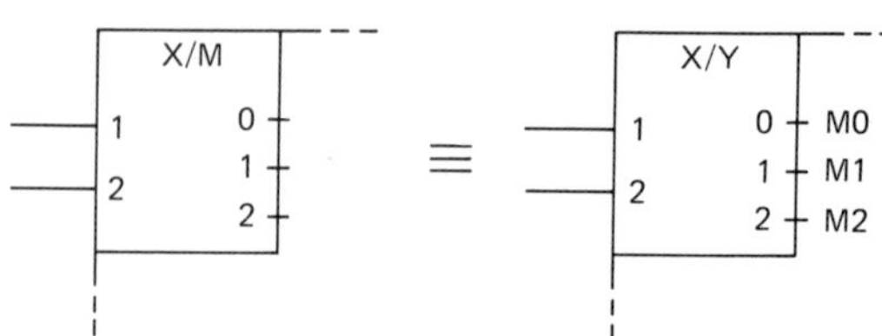

Figure A1-23. Producing one type of dependency.

Table A1-4. Summary of Dependency Notation

Type of dependency	Letter symbol*	Affecting input at its 1 state	Affecting input at its 0 state
Address	A	Permits action (address selected)	Prevents action (address not selected)
Control	C	Permits action	Prevents action
Enable	EN	Permits action	Prevents action of inputs ◇ Outputs off ▽ Outputs at external high impedance, no change in internal logic state Other outputs at internal 0 state
AND	G	Permits action	Imposes 0 state
Mode	M	Permits action (mode selected)	Prevents action (mode not selected)
Negate (X-OR)	N	Complements state	No effect
Reset	R	Affected output reacts as it would to $S = 0$, $R = 1$	No effect
Set	S	Affected output reacts as it would to $S = 1$, $R = 0$	No effect
OR	V	Imposes 1 state	Permits action
Interconnection	Z	Imposes 1 state	Imposes 0 state

* These letter symbols appear at the *affecting* input (or output) and are followed by a number. Each input (or output) *affected* by that input is labeled with that same number. When the labels EN, R, and S appear at inputs without the following numbers, the descriptions above do not apply. The action of these inputs is described under "Symbols Inside the Outline." See Table A1-3.

A1-4.13 Use of Binary Grouping to Produce Affecting Inputs If all affecting inputs produced by a coder are of the same type and have consecutive identifying numbers not necessarily corresponding with the numbers that would have been shown at the outputs of coder, use can be made of the binary grouping symbol (Table A1-3). It is followed by the letter denoting the type of dependency followed by $\frac{m1}{m2}$. The $m1$ is to be replaced by the smallest identifying number and the $m2$ by the largest one, as shown in Fig. A1-24.

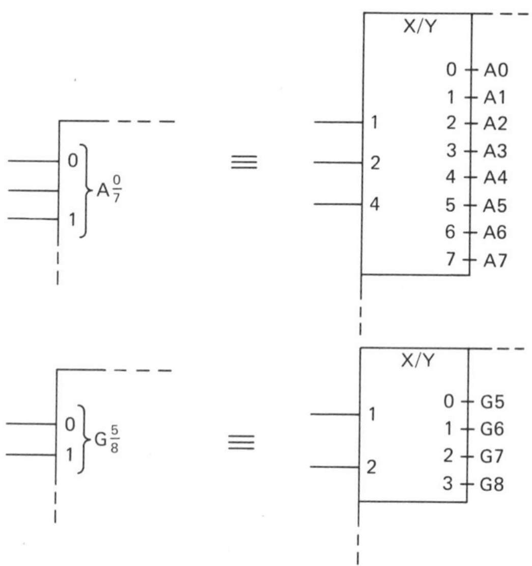

Figure A1-24. Use of the binary grouping symbol.

A1-4.14 Sequence of Input Labels If an input having a single functional effect is affected by other inputs, the qualifying symbol (if there is any) for that functional effect is preceded by the labels corresponding to the affecting inputs. The left-to-right order of these preceding labels is the order in which the effects or modifications must be applied. The affected input has no functional effect on the element if the logic state of any one of the affecting inputs, considered separately, would cause the affected input to have no effect, regardless of the logic states of other affecting inputs.

If an input has several different functional effects or has several different sets of affecting inputs depending on the mode of action, the input may be shown as often as required. See Fig. A1-25. However, there are cases in which this method of presentation is not advantageous. In those cases the input may be shown once with the different sets of labels separated by slashes. No meaning is attached to the order

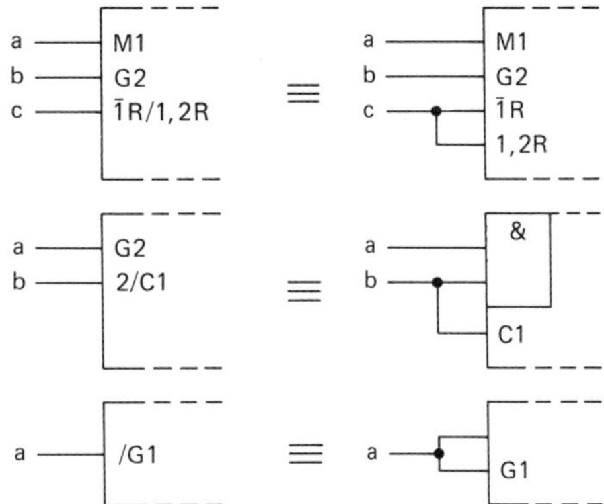

Figure A1-25. Input labels.

of these sets of labels. If one of the functional effects of an input is that of an unlabeled input of the element, a slash will precede the first set of labels shown.

If all inputs of a combinational element are disabled (caused to have no effect on the function of the element), the internal logic states of the outputs of the element are not specified by the symbol.

If all inputs of a sequential element are disabled, the content of this element is not changed and the outputs remain at their existing internal logic states.

A1-4.15 Sequence of Output Labels If an output has a number of different labels, regardless of whether they are identifying numbers of affecting inputs or outputs or not, these labels are shown in the following order:

1 If the postponed output symbol has to be shown, this comes first, if necessary preceded by the indications of the inputs to which it must be applied.

2 Followed by the labels indicating modifications of the internal logic state of the output, such that the left-to-right order of these labels corresponds with the order in which their effects must be applied.

3 Followed by the label indicating the effect of the output on inputs and other outputs of the element.

Symbols for open-circuit outputs or three-state outputs, where applicable, are placed just inside the outside boundary of the symbol adjacent to the output line. See Fig. A1-26.

If an output needs several different sets of labels that represent alternative functions (e.g., depending on the mode of action), these sets

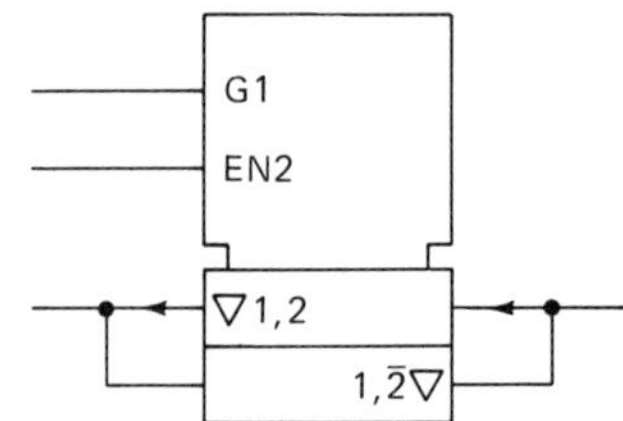

Figure A1-26. Placement of three-state symbols.

may be shown on different output lines that must be connected outside the outline. See Fig. A1-27. However, there are cases in which this method of presentation is not advantageous. In those cases the output may be shown once with the different sets of labels separated by slashes.

Two adjacent identifying numbers of affecting inputs in a set of labels that are not already separated by a nonnumeric character should be separated by a comma.

If a set of labels of an output not containing a slash contains the identifying number of an affecting M*m* input standing at its internal 0 state, this set of labels has no effect on that output.

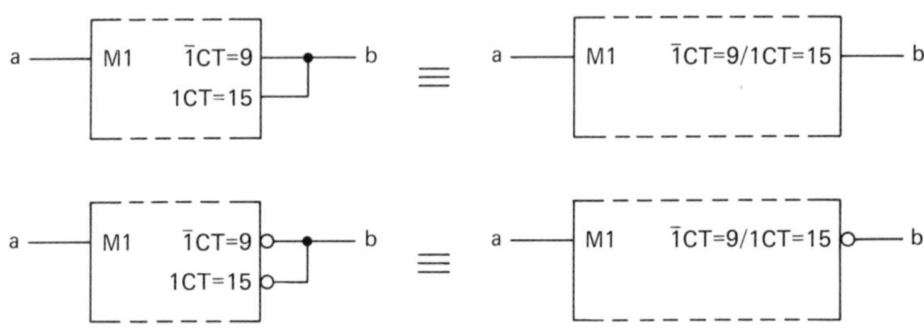

Figure A1-27. Output labels.

A1-5 BISTABLE ELEMENTS

The dynamic input symbol, the postponed output symbol, and dependency notation provide the tools to differentiate four main types of bistable elements and make synchronous and asynchronous inputs easily recognizable. See Fig. A1-28. The first column shows the essential distinguishing features; the other columns show examples.

Transparent latches have a level-operated control input. The D

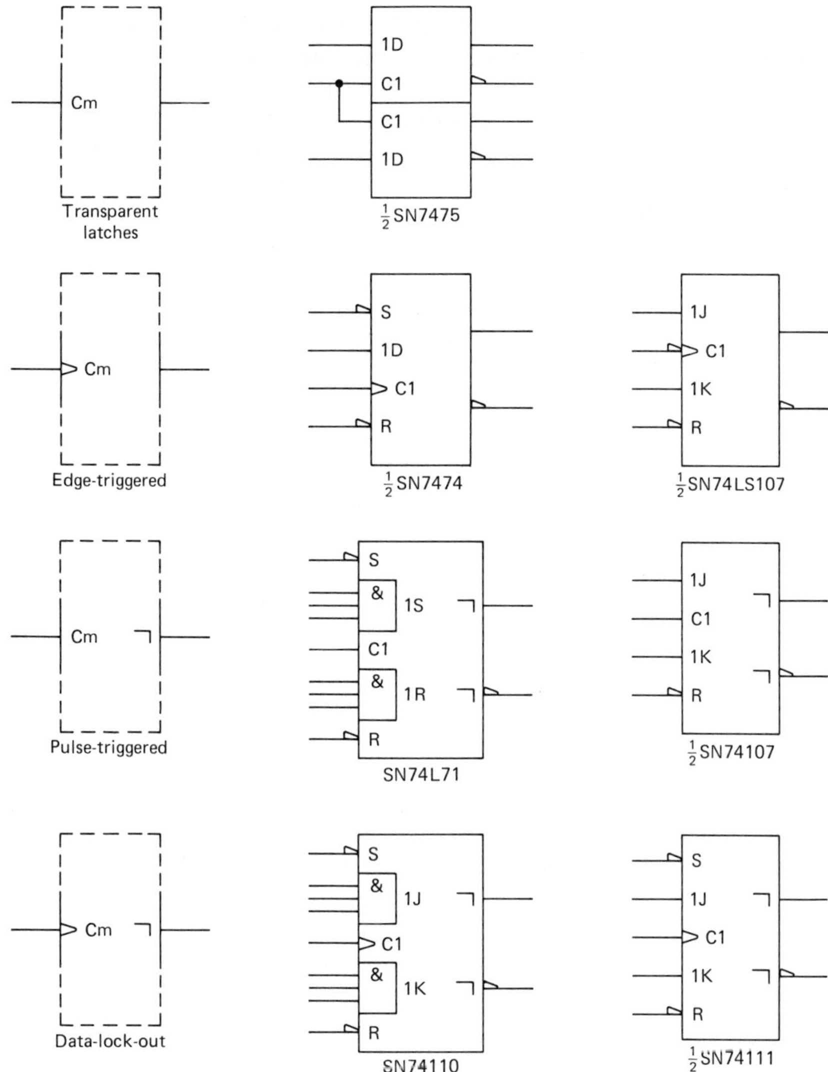

Figure A1-28. Four types of bistable circuits.

input is active as long as the C input is at its internal 1 state. The outputs respond immediately. Edge-triggered elements accept data from D, J, K, R, or S inputs on the active transition of C. Pulse-triggered elements require the setup of data before the start of the control pulse; the C input is considered static since the data must be maintained as long as C is at its 1 state. The output is postponed until C returns to its 0 state. The data-lockout element is similar to the pulse-triggered version except that the C input is considered dynamic in that shortly after C goes through its active transition, the data inputs are disabled and data does not have to be held. However, the output is still postponed until the C input returns to its initial external level.

Notice that synchronous inputs can be readily recognized by their dependency labels (1D, 1J, 1K, 1S, 1R) compared to the asynchronous inputs (S, R), which are not dependent on the C inputs.

APPENDIX A2

SYSTEM IMPLEMENTATION

Both prototype development and small quantity production can benefit from a *wire-wrapped* approach to system implementation. The general-purpose board shown in Fig. A2-1 is unusual in that it will accept any size DIP socket with wire-wrap posts, whether 300 mil wide, 400 mil wide, or 600 mil wide. Although it is designed to slide into a card cage, the two nylon ejector clips can be removed and the board used for a planar design.

With the tool shown in Fig. A2-2, wire wrapping has become a low-cost, reliable means for putting together circuits fast and for changing them easily. The ground and power planes of the board in Fig. A2-1 provide a low-noise environment for up to 120 sixteen-pin DIPs (or somewhat fewer packages when the mix of ICs includes some larger DIPs).

For interconnecting the parts of a design, flat cable and connectors such as those of Fig. A2-3 are unmatched in convenience and versatility. For example, the simple EPROM programmer of Fig. A2-4 uses a flat cable with a mating pair of connectors on one end to connect to the EPROM programmer board. The other end has a PC board edge connector for mating to a computer such as the one shown in Fig. 1-18.

Figure A2-1. Versatile development board. (Cambridge Thermionic Corp.)

These connectors support development work by being available as separate parts. Cable making requires nothing more than a vise, or a special hand tool, which squeezes the parts together so that they pierce the flat cable appropriately and make solid connections.

To power an instrument, modular power supplies give outstanding performance in a small package. The switching supply shown in Fig. A2-5 achieves an exceptionally high current rating for such a small package. For an instrument that includes low-level analog circuitry, a linear supply is usually preferred in lieu of a low-level-noise-generating switcher.

If an instrument is going to be bothered by power line interference, this problem can be met with an RFI filter, such as one of those shown in Fig. A2-6, on the 115-V ac line. The combined switch and circuit breaker of Fig. A2-7 solves the problem of protecting circuitry somewhat more usefully than with a separate fuse holder. The user

Figure A2-2. Wire-wrapping. (OK Machine & Tool Corp.)

has no incentive to replace a blown fuse with "anything available." These units are available with 11 different current ratings between 0.1 and 15 A.

An instrument employing a planar design can be enclosed in a small desktop console, such as one of those shown in Fig. A2-8. A more extensive design can be packaged with several universal wire-wrap socket terminal boards such as that in Fig. A2-9, mounted in a drawer assembly such as that in Fig. A2-10. This can then be mounted in an instrument case such as one of those shown in Fig. A2-11.

An instrument that uses several power-supply voltages can self-destruct if one of the supplies dies while the remaining supplies continue operation. For example, the EPROM programmer of Fig. A2-4 includes an on-board +25-V supply. The +5 V for the board comes from the computer to which the board is cabled. To ensure that the +25-V supply will not be turned on unless the EPROM programmer

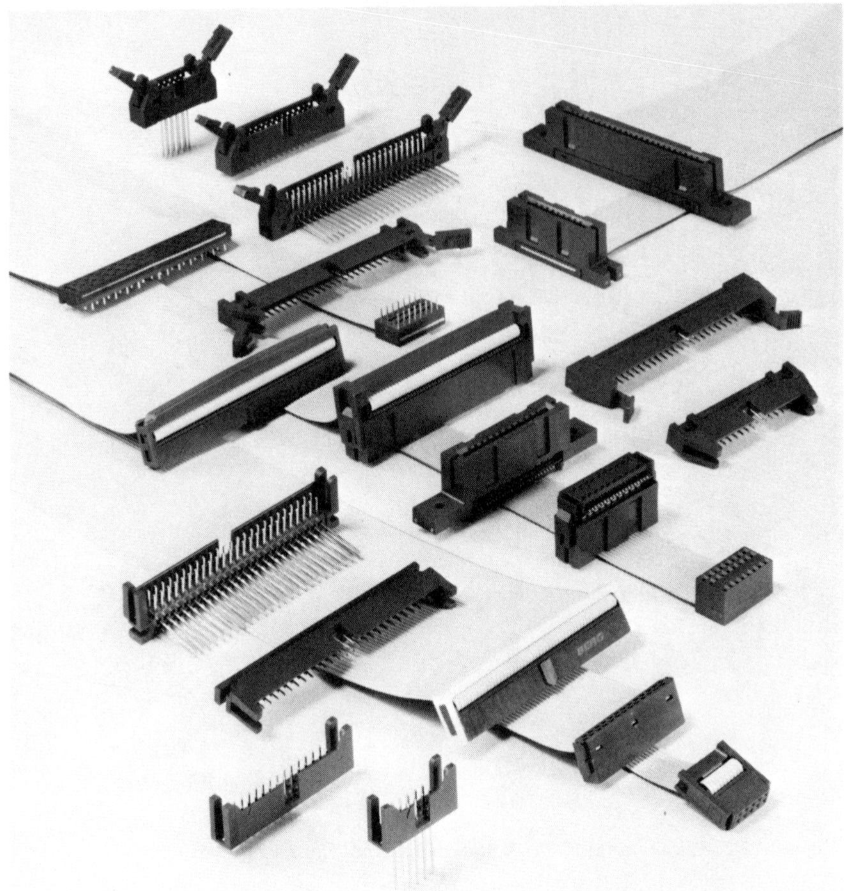

Figure A2-3. Flat cable and connectors. (*Berg Electronics.*)

board is connected to the computer and the computer is turned on, the circuit of Fig. A2-4 includes an optically coupled triac to control the power to the +25-V supply, as shown in Fig. A2-12.

The microcomputer and (relatively) slow I/O portion of a design can be simplified by using the standard boards and packaging hardware available from IC manufacturers or from independent "systems" houses. For example, Fig. A2-13 shows one chassis/power supply/card cage configuration. It can employ a "monoboard microcomputer" with clock, CPU, EPROM, RAM, I/O ports, and serial interface all on one board. The EPROM, RAM, and I/O ports can be expanded by plugging in appropriate extra boards. A wide variety of I/O boards handle digital I/O, analog I/O, and GPIB I/O. Wire-wrap boards can be used to implement fast, special-purpose functions which cannot be met by the microcomputer itself.

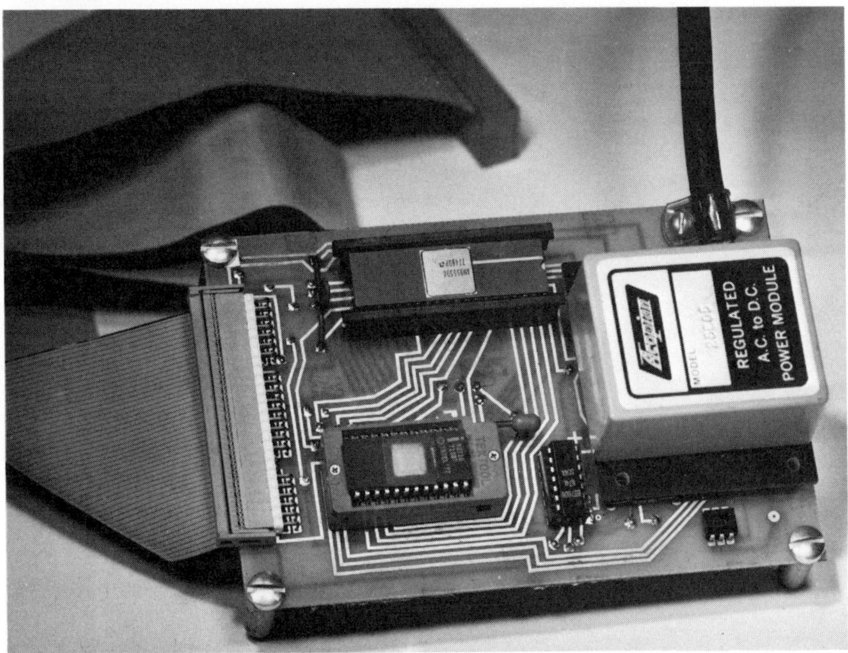

Figure A2-4. EPROM programmer. (Rafael Hernandez.)

Figure A2-5. 5 V at 5 A high-efficiency switching power supply with built-in overvoltage and short-circuit protection and RFI shielding in a 3.5 × 2.5 × 1.25 in. package. (Computer Products Inc.)

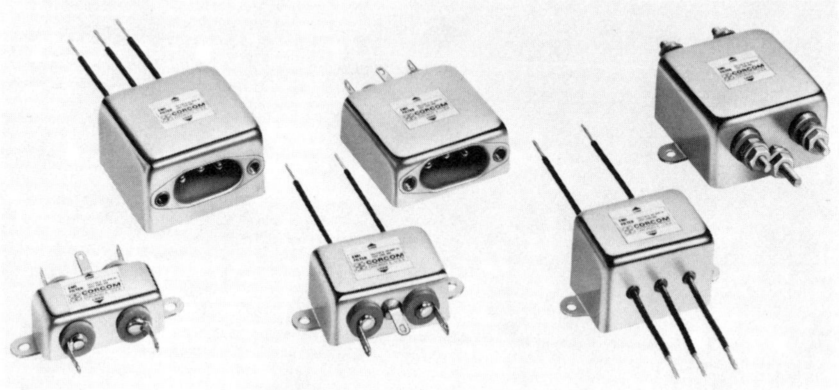

Figure A2-6. RFI filters for eliminating power line interference. (Corcom Inc.)

Figure A2-7. Combined power switch and circuit breaker. (*Airpax, Cambridge Div.*)

Figure A2-8. Desktop consoles. (*Hammond Manufacturing Co.*)

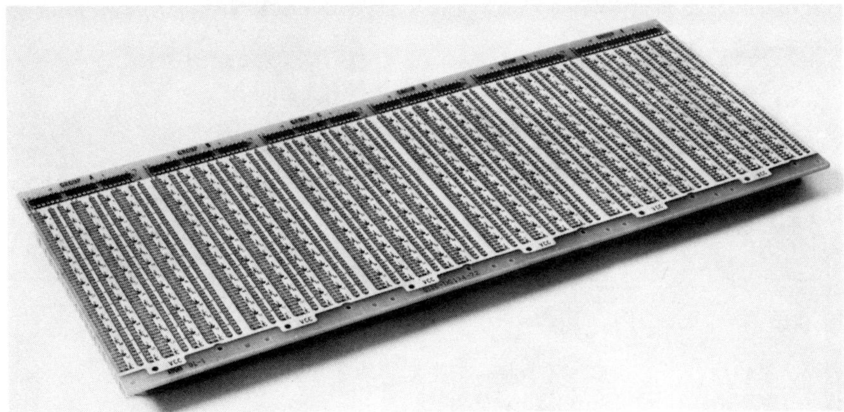

Figure A2-9. *Universal wire-wrap socket terminal board.* (Augat Inc.)

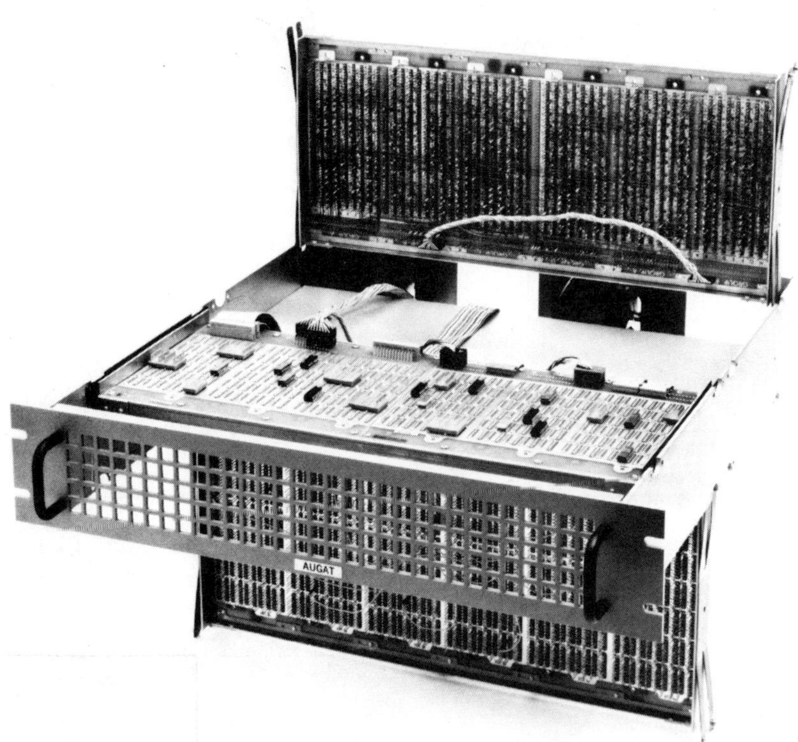

Figure A2-10. *Drawer assembly.* (Augat Inc.)

Figure A2-11. Instrument cases. (Optima Div., Scientific Atlanta.)

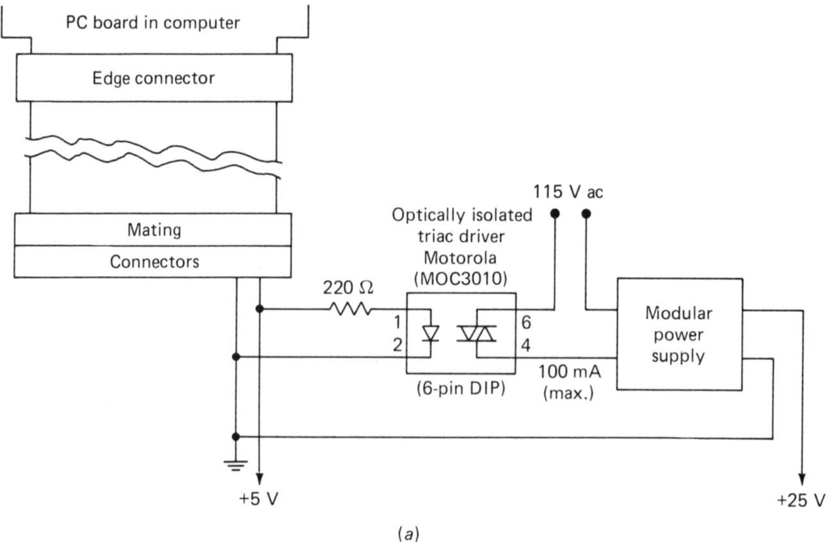

Figure A2-12. Control of one power supply by another. (a) Low ac current load.

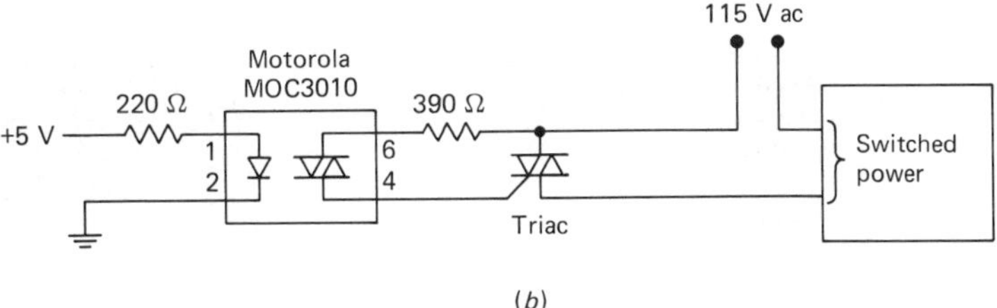

Figure A2-12b. Higher load.

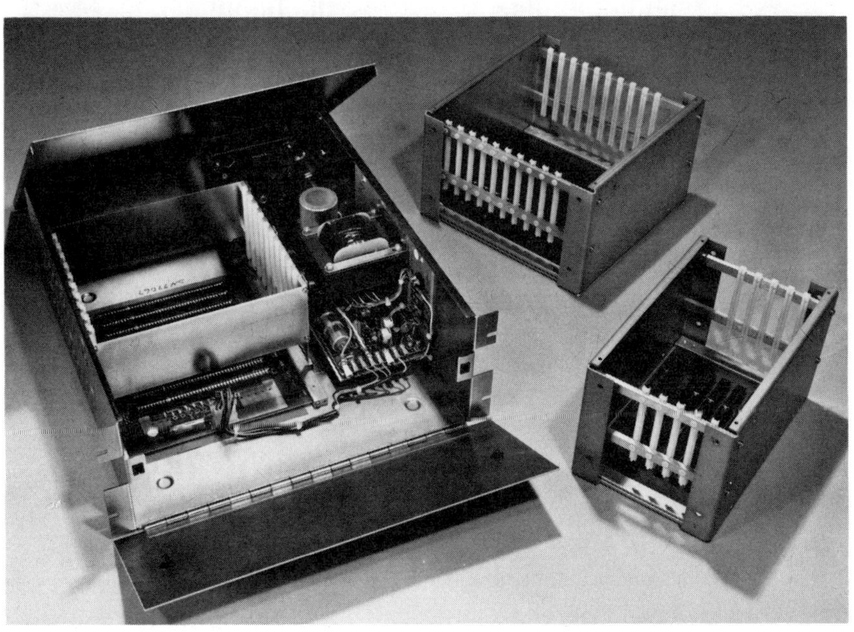

(a)

Figure A2-13. Off-the-shelf hardware design support. (Motorola Inc.) (a) Chassis, power supply, and 10-slot card cage.

(b)

(c)

Figure A2-13. (b) Monoboard microcomputer; (c) analog multiplexer and A/D converter board.

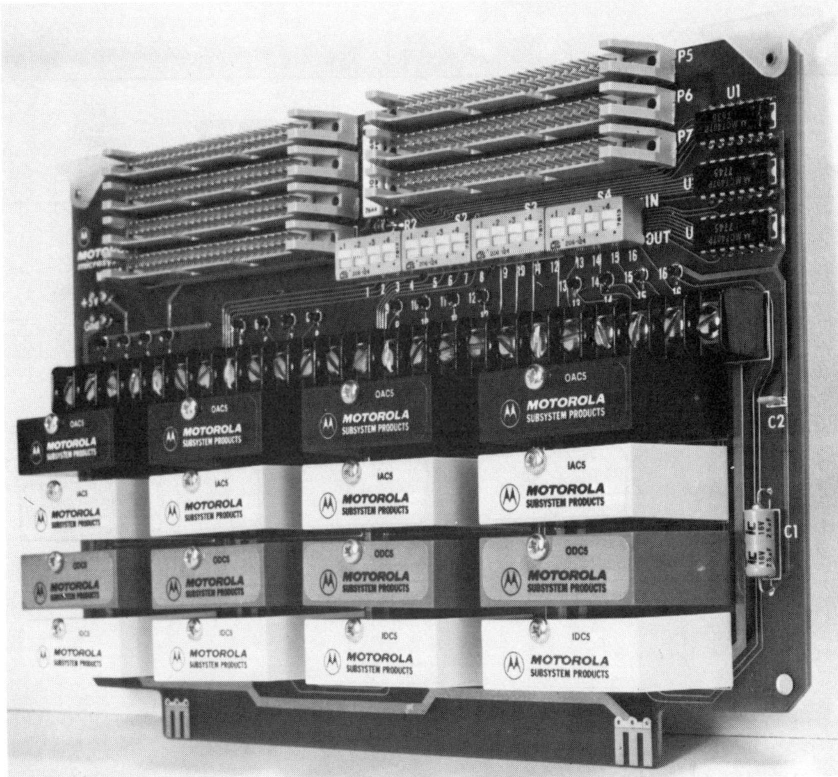

(d)

(e)

Figure A2-13. (d) *Optically isolated I/O board and I/O modules;* (e) wire-wrap board.

APPENDIX A3

MOTOROLA 6801/68701 ONE-CHIP MICROCOMPUTER

In this appendix we will consider the register structure, instruction set, and on-chip resources of the versatile Motorola 6801/68701 microcomputer. The essential difference between the 6801 and the 68701 is that the 6801 incorporates a 2048-byte ROM while the 68701 incorporates a 2048-byte EPROM. Both operate from a single +5-V power supply.

As shown in Fig. A3-1, the CPU includes two 8-bit accumulators (A and B) which are concatenated together into one 16-bit accumulator (D) for some instructions, a 16-bit index register (X), six internal flag flip-flops (H, I, N, Z, V, and C) located in a condition code (CC) register, a 16-bit program counter (PC), and a 16-bit stack pointer (SP). Of the internal flags, C is the normal carry bit, while H is a "half-carry" bit used with BCD operations during the execution of a "decimal adjust" instruction. N is set by certain instructions when the most-significant bit of the result of an operation equals one. Following arithmetic operations upon signed numbers coded in 2s-complement code, the N bit indicates whether or not the result of the operation is negative. V, the overflow flag, will be set if an overflow has occurred during a 2s-complement addition or subtraction. The I flag disables interrupts when it is set.

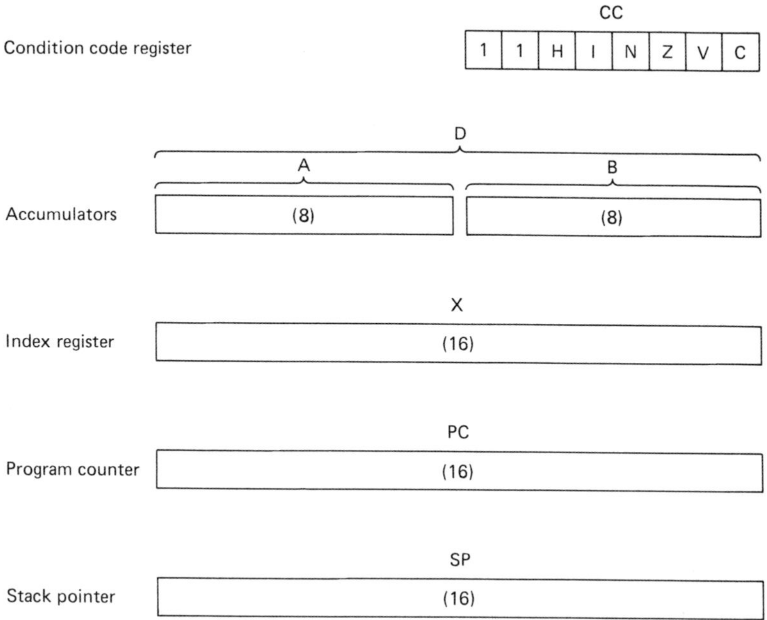

Figure A3-1. Motorola 6801/68701 CPU registers.

The 6801 instruction set is given in Fig. A3-2. If the register involved in an instruction is labeled A(B), either accumulator A or accumulator B can be designated for use with the instruction. Where D is designated, a 16-bit operand is indicated which employs accumulator B to hold the lower 8 bits and accumulator A to hold the upper 8 bits, just as is implied by Fig. A3-1.

The columns of Fig. A3-2 labeled "Bytes/Cycles" indicate how many bytes make up an instruction and how many clock cycles are required to execute the instruction for each appropriate addressing mode. For example, a LDAA instruction loads accumulator A from memory. The memory location employed can be the second byte of the instruction (immediate addressing), it can be a hexadecimal address between 0000 and 00FF (direct addressing), it can be identified with a full 16-bit address (extended addressing) or it can be obtained by temporarily adding the second byte of the instruction to the contents of the index register to form a pointer to the desired address (indexed addressing).

The unconditional branch instruction (BRA), the unconditional branch to subroutine instruction (BSR), and all of the conditional branch instructions (BCS, BCC, etc.) employ relative addressing. That is, the second byte of the instruction is treated as a 2s-complement

Operation	MNE	REG	Description	Inherent	Immediate	Direct	Extended	Indexed	Flags C Z N V	Not available in 6800
				← Bytes/Cycles →						
Move	LDA	A(B)	A ← M		2/2	2/3	3/4	2/4	– ↕ ↕ 0	
	STA	A(B)	M ← A			2/4	3/5	2/5	– ↕ ↕ 0	
	LDD		D ← M		3/3	2/4	3/5	2/5	– ↕ ↕ 0	*
	STD		M ← D			2/4	3/5	2/5	– ↕ ↕ 0	*
	TAB		B ← A	1/2					– ↕ ↕ 0	
	TBA		A ← B	1/2					– ↕ ↕ 0	
	PSH	A(B)	Stack ← A	1/3					– – – –	
	PUL	A(B)	A ← Stack	1/4					– – – –	
	PSH	X	Stack ← X	1/4					– – – –	*
	PUL	X	X ← Stack	1/5					– – – –	*
	CLR		M ← 00				3/6	2/6	0 1 0 0	
	CLR	A(B)	A ← 00	1/2					0 1 0 0	
	LDX		X ← M		3/3	2/4	3/5	2/5	– ↕ ① 0	
	LDS		SP ← M		3/3	2/4	3/5	2/5	– ↕ ① 0	
	STX		M ← X			2/4	3/5	2/6	– ↕ ① 0	
	STS		M ← SP			2/4	3/5	2/6	– ↕ ① 0	
	TXS		SP ← X – 1	1/3					– – – –	
	TSX		X ← SP + 1	1/3					– – – –	
	TPA		A ← CC	1/2					– – – –	
	TAP		CC ← A	1/2					↕ ↕ ↕ ↕	
Increment	INC		M ← M + 1						– ↕ ↕ ②	
	INC	A(B)	A ← A + 1	1/2			3/6	2/6	– ↕ ↕ ②	
	INX		X ← X + 1	1/3					– ↕ – –	
	INS		SP ← SP + 1	1/3					– – – –	
Decrement	DEC		M ← M – 1				3/6		– ↕ ↕ ③	
	DEC	A(B)	A ← A – 1	1/2					– ↕ ↕ ③	
	DEX		X ← X – 1	1/3					– ↕ – –	
	DES		SP ← SP – 1	1/3					– – – –	
Set carry	SEC		C ← 1	1/2					1 – – –	
Clear carry	CLC		C ← 0	1/2					0 – – –	
Set overflow	SEV		V ← 1	1/2					– – – 1	
Clear overflow	CLV		V ← 0	1/2					– – – 0	
Complement	COM		M ← $\overline{M}$				3/6	2/6	1 ↕ ↕ 0	
	COM	A(B)	A ← $\overline{A}$	1/2					1 ↕ ↕ 0	
Add	ADD	A(B)	A ← A + M		2/2	2/3	3/4	2/4	↕ ↕ ↕ ↕	
	ABA		A ← A + B	1/2					↕ ↕ ↕ ↕	
Add with carry	ADC	A(B)	A ← A + M + C		2/2	2/3	3/4	2/4	↕ ↕ ↕ ↕	
Decimal adjust acc. A	DAA		Correct BCD addition	1/2					④ ↕ ↕ ↕	
Add, 16-bit	ADD	D	D ← D + M		3/4	2/5	3/6	2/6	↕ ↕ ↕ ↕	*
	ABX		X ← X + B	1/3					– – – –	*
Subtract	SUB	A(B)	A ← A – M		2/2	2/3	3/4	2/4	↕ ↕ ↕ ↕	
	SBA		A ← A – B	1/2					↕ ↕ ↕ ↕	
Subtract with carry	SBC	A(B)	A ← A – M – C		2/2	2/3	3/4	2/4	↕ ↕ ↕ ↕	
Negate	NEG		M ← 00 – M				3/6	2/6	⑤ ↕ ↕ ②	
	NEG	A(B)	A ← 00 – A	1/2					⑤ ↕ ↕ ②	
Subtract, 16-bit	SUB	D	D ← D – M		3/4	2/5	3/6	2/6	↕ ↕ ↕ ↕	*
Multiply	MUL		D ← A × B	1/10					⑦ – – –	*
AND	AND	A(B)	A ← A AND M		2/2	2/3	3/4	2/4	– ↕ ↕ 0	
Exclusive-OR	EOR	A(B)	A ← A ⊕ M		2/2	2/3	3/4	2/4	– ↕ ↕ 0	
OR (inclusive)	ORA	A(B)	A ← A OR M		2/2	2/3	3/4	2/4	– ↕ ↕ 0	
Compare (only flags are affected)	CMP	A(B)	A – M		2/2	2/3	3/4	2/4	↕ ↕ ↕ ↕	
	CBA		A – B	1/2					↕ ↕ ↕ ↕	
	TST		M – 00				3/6	2/6	0 ↕ ↕ 0	
	TST	A(B)	A – 00	1/2					0 ↕ ↕ 0	
	CPX		X – (M, M + 1)		3/4	2/5	3/6	2/6	– ↕ ① ↕	
	BIT	A(B)	A AND M		2/2	2/3	3/4	2/4	– ↕ ↕ 0	

(Continues)

Figure A3-2. Motorola 6801 instruction set.

Operation	MNE	REG	Description	Inherent (Bytes/Cycles)	Immediate	Direct	Extended	Indexed	Flags C Z N V	Not available in 6800
Rotate left	ROL		C ← M, A, or B ← C				3/6	2/6	↕ ↕ ↕ ⑥	
	ROL	A(B)		1/2					↕ ↕ ↕ ⑥	
Rotate right	ROR		C → M, A, or B → C				3/6	2/6	↕ ↕ ↕ ⑥	
	ROR	A(B)		1/2					↕ ↕ ↕ ⑥	
Arithmetic shift left	ASL		C ← M, A, or B ← 0				3/6	2/6	↕ ↕ ↕ ⑥	
	ASL	A(B)		1/2					↕ ↕ ↕ ⑥	
	ASL	D	C ← D ← 0	1/3					↕ ↕ ↕ ⑥	*
Arithmetic shift right	ASR		M, A, or B → C				3/6	2/6	↕ ↕ ↕ ⑥	
	ASR	A(B)		1/2					↕ ↕ ↕ ⑥	
Logic shift right	LSR		0 → M, A, or B → C				3/6	2/6	↕ ↕ 0 ⑥	
	LSR	A(B)		1/2					↕ ↕ 0 ⑥	
	LSR	D	0 → D → C	1/3					↕ ↕ 0 ⑥	*
Set interrupt mask	SEI		I ← 1	1/2					– – – –	
Clear interrupt mask	CLI		I ← 0	1/2					– – – –	
No operation	NOP		PC ← PC + 1	1/2					– – – –	

Operation	MNE	Description	Inherent (Bytes/Cycles)	Relative	Direct	Extended	Indexed	Flags C Z N V
Jump unconditionally	JMP	PC ← M				3/3	2/3	– – – –
Branch unconditionally	BRA	PC ← PC + M		2/3				– – – –
if carry set	BCS	if C = 1		2/3				– – – –
if carry clear	BCC	if C = 0		2/3				– – – –
if equal zero	BEQ	if Z = 1		2/3				– – – –
if not equal zero	BNE	if Z = 0		2/3				– – – –
if minus	BMI	if N = 1		2/3				– – – –
is plus	BPL	if N = 0		2/3				– – – –
if overflow set	BVS	if V = 1		2/3				– – – –
if overflow clear	BVC	if V = 0		2/3				– – – –
if ≥ zero	BGE	if N ⊕ V = 0		2/3				– – – –
if > zero	BGT	if Z + (N ⊕ V) = 0		2/3				– – – –
if ≤ zero	BLE	if Z + (N ⊕ V) = 1		2/3				– – – –
if < zero	BLT	if N ⊕ V = 1		2/3				– – – –
if higher	BHI	if C + Z = 0		2/3				– – – –
if lower or same	BLS	if C + Z = 1		2/3				– – – –
Jump to subroutine	JSR	Stack ← PC; PC ← M			2/5	3/6	2/6	– – – –
Branch to subroutine	BSR	Stack ← PC; PC ← PC + M		2/6				– – – –
Software interrupt	SWI	Stack ← PC, X, A, B, CC; I ← 1; PC ← M	1/12					– – – –
Wait for interrupt	WAI	Stack ← PC, X, A, B, CC; halt	1/9					– – – –
Return from subroutine	RTS	PC ← Stack	1/5					– – – –
Return from interrupt	RTI	CC, B, A, X, PC ← STACK	1/10					↕ ↕ ↕ ↕

Notes on flags (set flag if test is true; otherwise clear flag):

① Does bit 15 = 1?
② Does result = 10000000?
③ Does result = 01111111?
④ Is most significant digit greater than nine? (Do not clear if previously set)
⑤ Does result ≠ 00000000?
⑥ Does N ⊕ C = 1?
⑦ Does bit 7 of accumulator B = 1?

Figure A3-2 (continued).

number and added to the contents of the program counter to form the new program counter contents. Consequently, these instructions can branch "nearby" (up to about ±128 addresses from the present address). A jump to an address which is farther away than this can employ the corresponding 3-byte jump instruction. On the other hand, if NEXT is a nearby address, then

```
BRA    NEXT
```

and

```
JMP    NEXT
```

will both result in the address of the instruction labeled NEXT being in the program counter after instruction execution.

The 6801 clock rate is typically 1.0 MHz (unless a "standard" baud rate is desired for the built-in UART; see Fig. 6-10). The external, low-cost 4.0-MHz crystal is connected to an internal oscillator whose output is counted down to 1.0 MHz. At this clock rate, the LDAA instruction will take 2, 3, or 4 μs to execute, depending upon the addressing mode used.

Those flag bits of the condition code which can be tested are shown in the Flags column of Fig. A3-2. The effect of each instruction upon these flags is shown as:

- \- No effect
- ↕ Set or cleared, depending upon the result of the instruction
- 1 Set
- 0 Cleared
- ①, ②, etc. See comments at the bottom of Fig. A3-2

The 6801 uses a stack, located in RAM, to handle subroutine return addresses automatically during subroutine call and return instructions. Enough bytes of RAM must be set aside for the stack so that use of the stack will never write over other data stored in the RAM. When data is pushed onto the stack, the data is *first* moved, and *then* the stack pointer is *decremented*. Consequently, when power is first turned on, the stack pointer must be initialized to the highest address reserved for the stack. Since the 6801 has RAM extending between the hexadecimal addresses 0080-00FF, the stack can be located in the top of RAM by initializing the stack pointer to 00FF.

As indicated by the right-most column of Fig. A3-2, 10 instructions have been added to the 6801 which were not available in its multiple-chip ancestor, the popular 6800:

1 The index register can be temporarily stored on, and retrieved from, the stack. These 1-byte instructions, PSHX and PULX, facilitate the use of the single index register X for operations which involve more than one pointer.
2 An 8-bit (unsigned) binary number in accumulator B can be added to the contents of the index register using the ABX instruction. This pointer-manipulation instruction is exceedingly valuable for accessing tables.
3 The two 8-bit (unsigned) binary numbers in accumulators A and B can be multiplied together with the fast MUL instruction. The resulting product resides in the 16-bit D accumulator made up of the A and B accumulators. Because MUL is an *unsigned* multiply instruction, subroutines to multiply larger numbers are short and fast.
4 The 16-bit D accumulator can be loaded, stored, added, subtracted, and shifted.

The 6801 can be operated in any one of eight modes, several of which are provided to aid the testing of the chip. When power is first turned on, the CPU reads a 3-bit binary number on bits 0, 1, and 2 of port 2. On the basis of this 3-bit number at that moment, the 6801 thereafter operates in the selected mode. For example, the one-chip mode (mode 7) is selected by making sure that all of these three bits of port 2 are high when the RESET-L input sees a rising edge.

As shown in Fig. A3-3, this one-chip mode can be achieved easily if bits 0, 1, and 2 of port 2 are used as *outputs* (so that external circuitry will not ever pull them low). This eliminates the possible use of a minor capability of the UART (i.e., the use of bit 2 to accept an *external* clock). It also eliminates the sometimes valuable capability of the programmable timer to measure an input pulse width to a resolution of 1 μs. However, it does leave the timer free to carry out a major function, which will be discussed shortly. If either of these features is desired, then its input signal to port 2 can pass through a three-state buffer so that it can be disabled at the time of reset.

In the one-chip mode, the 6801 has the memory map shown in Fig. A3-4. The data direction register for each port permits each bit of the port to be set up as an input or an output, independent of the other bits of the port. A zero (one) written to a selected bit position in a data direction register sets up the corresponding bit position of the port as an input (output). Thus, the assembly language sequence

```
LDAA  #%00000111
STAA  $0000
```

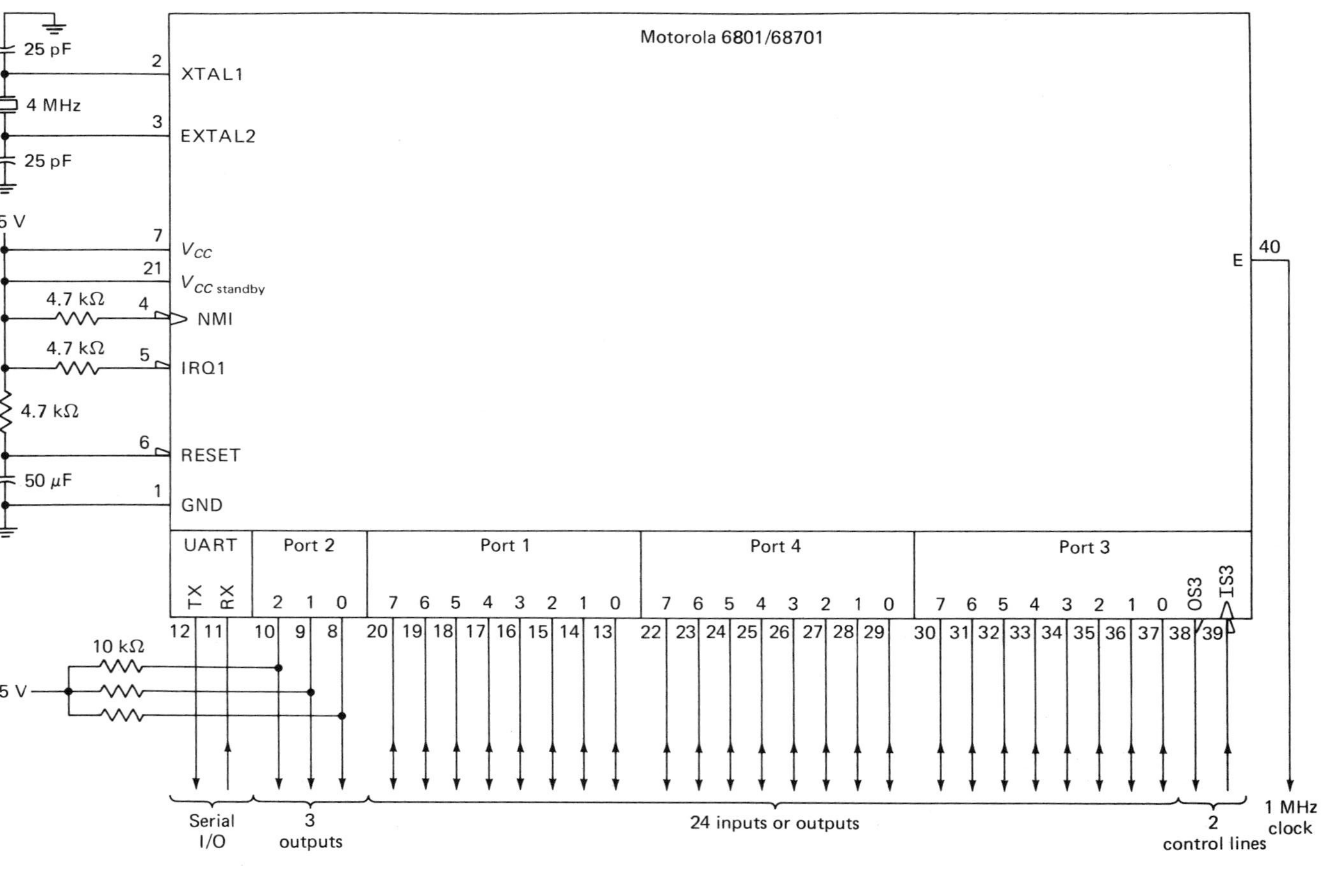

Figure A3-3. Motorola 6801/68701 one-chip microcomputer (Mode 7).

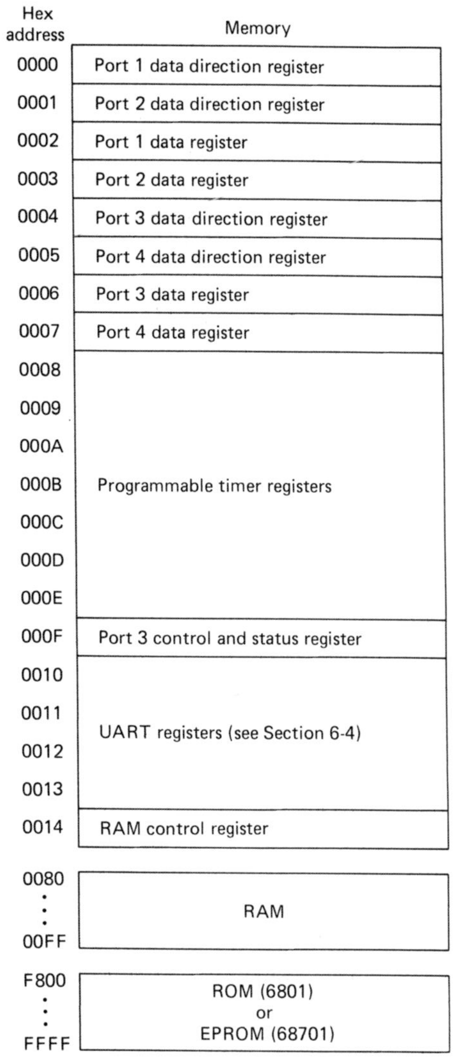

Hex address	Memory
0000	Port 1 data direction register
0001	Port 2 data direction register
0002	Port 1 data register
0003	Port 2 data register
0004	Port 3 data direction register
0005	Port 4 data direction register
0006	Port 3 data register
0007	Port 4 data register
0008 0009 000A 000B 000C 000D 000E	Programmable timer registers
000F	Port 3 control and status register
0010 0011 0012 0013	UART registers (see Section 6-4)
0014	RAM control register
0080 ⋮ 00FF	RAM
F800 ⋮ FFFF	ROM (6801) or EPROM (68701)

Figure A3-4. 6801/68701 memory map for the one-chip mode.

loads the binary number 00000111 first into accumulator A, and from there into hexadecimal address 0000, the data direction register for port 1. Bits 0, 1, and 2 of port 1 are thereby set up as outputs while bits 3 to 7 of port 1 are set up as inputs. The CPU can read these inputs at any subsequent time with a

```
LDAA   $0002
```

instruction. This instruction will also read whatever was last written out to the three output bits (without changing these lines). Correspondingly, a *write* to port 1,

STAA $0002

will transfer the lower three bits of accumulator A to the output bits 0 to 2 of port 1. The bits of the port which have been set up as inputs (bits 3 to 7) are oblivious to the execution of this instruction.

Notice that by locating all of these port addresses on page zero, the designers of the 6801 have created 2-byte I/O instructions (using direct addressing). In contrast, a typical 6800 multiple-chip microcomputer configuration employs 3-byte I/O instructions (using extended addressing).

As shown in Fig. A3-3, the 6801 (when operated in the one-chip mode) provides 24 I/O lines of general applicability on ports 1, 3, and 4. It provides five additional I/O lines on port 2, which we can allocate to a UART (as discussed in Sec. 6-4, and as shown in Fig. A3-3), to a programmable timer, or as more general I/O (preferably output) lines. Port 3 also has associated with it the two control lines, IS3-L and OS3-L, whose operation is defined in Fig. A3-5. These lines are defined in this way *only* in the one-chip microcomputer mode.

One of several possible multiple-chip microcomputer modes (mode 6) is shown in Fig. A3-6. In this mode, pins 38 and 39 (which were the port 3 control lines of the one-chip mode) automatically become a READ/$\overline{\text{WRITE}}$ (R/$\overline{\text{W}}$) output and an ADDRESS STROBE (AS) output. As was shown in the timing diagram of Fig. 6-25, the address strobe serves to latch up the lower 8 address bits which are available on pins 30 to 37 early in each clock period. During the latter part of each clock period, pins 30 to 37 become a data bus. The clock output E is a timing signal used to enable all peripheral chips during the second half of each clock cycle, when all other signals from the CPU to the peripheral chips have settled out to stable values. During any clock period when the CPU is not accessing an external chip (e.g., during the execution of an instruction to shift the contents of accumulator *A*), it puts hex address FFFF on the address bus. In mode 6 this address is reserved for use by the internal ROM or EPROM and thus peripheral chips can remain deselected by this address. The memory map for mode 6 is identical to that for mode 7 shown in Fig. A3-4, except that the CPU can access registers in peripheral chips with hex addresses 0004-0007, 000F, 0020-007F, and 0100-F7FF.

This configuration of Fig. A3-6 forms an extremely powerful multiple-chip microcomputer for the design of instruments which can give outstanding support to self-test capability. The 6801 can, upon startup, exercise itself without reaching outside of itself to access a

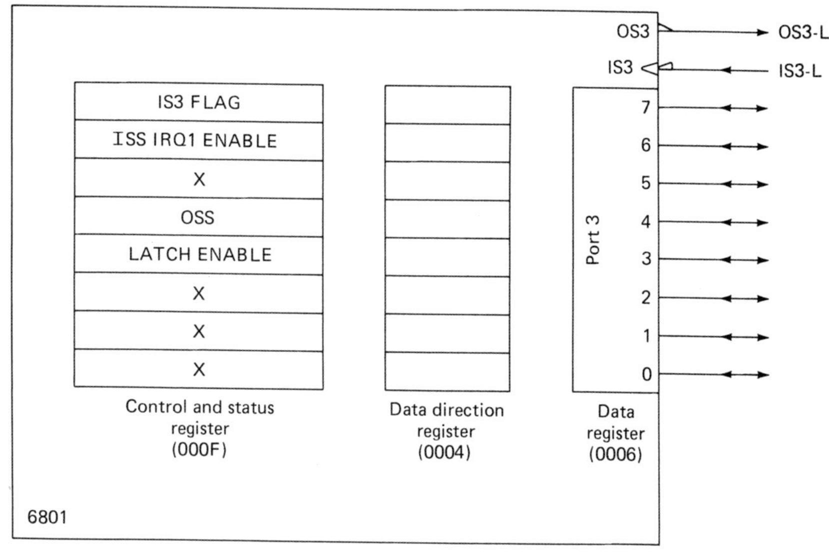

(*a*)

OS3-L is an active-low pulse output which occurs in response to either a CPU read from, or a CPU write to, port 3 (address 0006). If OSS = 0 then reading port 3 produces a one-clock-period pulse on OS3-L. If OSS = 1 then writing to port 3 produces a one-clock-period pulse on OS3-L.

(*b*)

IS3-L is a high-to-low edge-sensitive input which sets the read-only bit, IS3 FLAG. This flag is cleared by a read from the control and status register (address 000F) followed by either a read from, or a write to, port 3 (address 0006).

If IS3 IRQ1 ENABLE = 1, then setting IS3 FLAG will pull the IRQ1-L line to the CPU low, achieving the same effect as when an external device pulls pin 5 (IRQ1-L) low. This provides an edge-sensitive alternative to the IRQ1-L input.

If LATCH NEABLE = 1, then a falling edge on the IS3-L input will latch the data on any lines of port 3 set up as inputs. Port 3 lines set up as outputs are unaffected. The latch circuitry is reinitialized by a read of the port (address 0006). If LATCH ENABLE = 0, then this latch circuitry is transparent, so that a read of the port reads the data present at that moment.

(*c*)

Figure A3-5. Port 3 operation. (*a*) *Registers;* (*b*) *OS3-L operation;* (*c*) *IS3-L operation.*

self-test routine. It forms a one-chip kernel in a multiple-chip microcomputer! Even if the external address bus/data bus structure malfunctions, the *internal* buses are isolated so that *internal* fetches will be carried out successfully.

The 6801 can test each external ROM before using it, perhaps

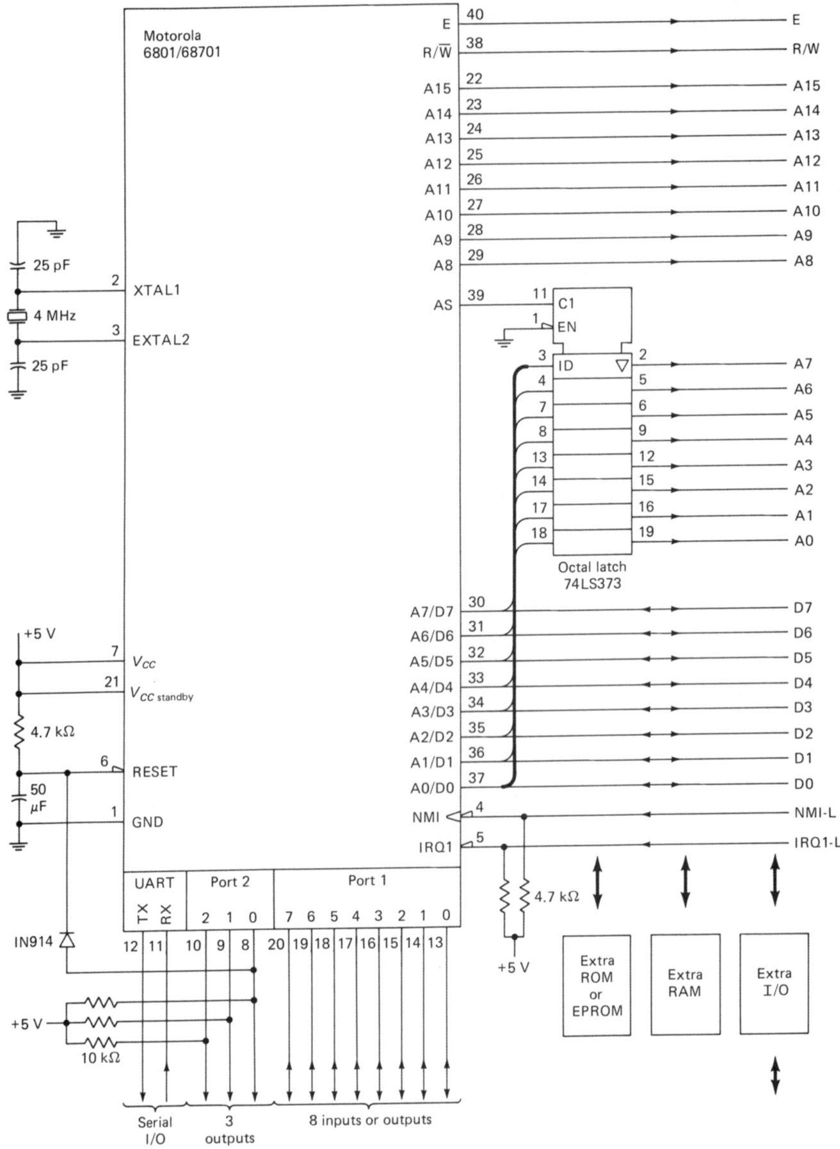

Figure A3-6. Motorola 6801/68701 expansion (Mode 6).

using Row's algorithm of Prob. 3-32 to generate and check a signature for each one. This not only checks the ROM but also checks accesses on the address bus/data bus structure. It can go on to check external RAM before using it. Output ports can be self-tested by writing to them and then reading from them (assuming programmable I/O chips, such as Motorola's 6821 Peripheral Interface Adapter chip, are being used which permit this capability). Input ports need the help of external circuitry to support self-test.

If any malfunction occurs, the 6801 can use a dedicated output of port 1 or 2 to signal a user with a buzzer or a flashing light, further supporting the one-chip kernel capability. In addition to all this, the 6801 gives users the popular 6800 instruction set (augmented by ten new instructions) and a built-in and self-testable programmable timer and UART.

The 6801 includes a significant amount of hard-wired initialization capability. While RESET-L (pin 6) is held low:

1 Instruction execution is suspended.
2 The I bit of the condition code register is set, disabling interrupts initially.
3 Nonmaskable interrupts are disregarded.
4 The E clock output is active.
5 All data direction registers are cleared (initializing all ports as input ports).
6 The port 3 control and status register is cleared.
7 The UART and programmable timer are initialized to suitable states so that nothing further need be done if they are to be left unused.

When RESET-L goes high, the CPU completes its reset sequence by reading bits 0, 1, and 2 of port 2, latching the operating mode of the chip (and configuring the chip accordingly), loading the program counter with the "reset vector" contained in hex addresses FFFE and FFFF, and then beginning instruction execution from this address.

Both internal and external interrupts are supported by the 6801. Each of eight interrupt sources has its own interrupt vector, shown in Fig. A3-7. As shown, resetting has the highest priority, initiating the sequence of operations just described. Nonmaskable interrupts have the next highest priority. A falling edge on pin 4 (NMI-L) will be sensed by the CPU at the completion of the present instruction. Regardless of what the CPU is doing at this time (assuming it is not being reset), the CPU will:

1 Stack all CPU registers (other than the stack pointer).
2 Set the I flag in the condition code register of Fig. A3-1, disabling all lower priority interrupts.
3 Vector to the interrupt service routine whose starting address is stored in FFFC and FFFD.

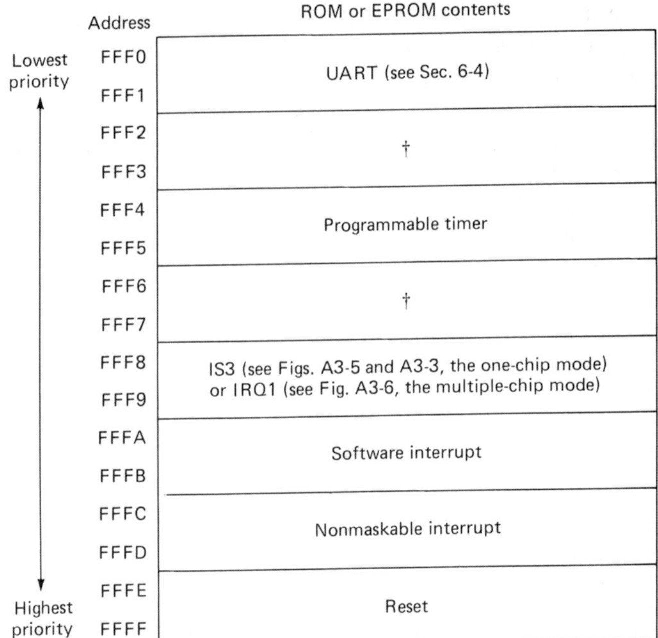

Figure A3-7. Interrupt vectors.

At the completion of this service routine, a return from interrupt RTI instruction is executed. This restores all of the registers in the CPU just as they were when the interrupt occurred. Notice that the I flag is also restored. Since this I flag can disable all of the interrupts whose vectors reside in addresses FFF0-FFF9, the restoration leaves these interrupt sources either reenabled or still disabled, just as they were before the interrupt occurred.

Use of the nonmaskable interrupt input (pin 4) requires care. We must ensure that this input *cannot possibly* see a falling edge after reset has taken place and before the stack pointer is initialized. Otherwise, the CPU registers will be "stacked" off into limbo. At the end of the NMI service routine, the program counter will be restored with garbage (unless "limbo" just happened to be RAM). Almost certainly, program execution from this point on will not give the desired performance.

Some designers use NMI-L as an extra vectored priority interrupt input from a programmable I/O chip in the multiple-chip microcomputer configuration of Fig. A3-6. Motorola's 6821 Peripheral Interface

Adapter (PIA) handles this well. One of its control inputs can be used to sense an input transition and to set a flag bit in one of the PIA's registers. Furthermore, if an interrupt enable bit in the PIA is set, then the setting of this flag bit will drive a PIA output line low. This output can be used as an NMI-L input. Finally, the RESET-L input on the PIA can be used to ensure that a nonmaskable interrupt will not take place prematurely since it clears the PIA's interrupt enable bit.

The power of this nonmaskable interrupt relative to the other interrupts of the 6801 is that it can immediately interrupt anything going on, even another interrupt service routine. In contrast, the lower priority interrupts are turned off by *any* interrupt since they are not invoked if the I bit of the condition code register is set. Furthermore, if one of the interrupt service routines wants to re-enable higher priority interrupts while leaving lower priority interrupts disabled, it must write into the control register associated with each of the lower priority interrupts and disable it individually and then clear the I bit in the condition code register. Then at the end of the interrupt service routine, it must re-enable any of these lower priority interrupts (which were enabled previously) before executing the return from interrupt RTI instruction.

With this restriction upon interrelated interrupts, it is useful to consider the meaning associated with the "lowest priority–highest priority" scale of Fig. A3-7. A more usual way to handle 6801 interrupts is to let one interrupt leave other interrupts turned off (by leaving the I bit set for the entire duration of its service routine). Upon execution of the RTI instruction, all interrupts are re-enabled (as the I bit is automatically cleared). At *that* moment, the CPU looks among any interrupts which are *pending* (i.e., which have occurred during the time I was set) and invokes the one with the highest priority.

The software interrupt is invoked by the SWI instruction, independent of the I flag. In effect, it is a 1-byte subroutine call which sets all CPU registers aside, disables lower priority interrupts by setting I, and vectors to the service routine with starting address stored in hex addresses FFFA-FFFB.

The interrupt vector at FFF8-FFF9 is shared. In the multiple-chip mode of Fig. A3-6 this vector is invoked by external chips like the 6821 PIA which we have just discussed, which can pull the IRQ1-L line low. The IRQ1-L input on the 6801 is level-sensitive and not edge-sensitive. Consequently, the 6801 benefits from the 6821's mechanism for sensing an edge, setting a flag, driving an output line low, and for subsequently clearing the flag and raising the output line again with instructions in the interrupt service routine.

In the one-chip mode, this same mechanism is still available, but it loses much of its power because of the extra circuitry required which is no longer freely available in an otherwise needed I/O chip. Accordingly, the designers of the 6801 have provided the built-in edge-sensitive input on IS3-L described in Fig. A3-5, which gives all of the capability described above without external chips.

The programmable timer is designed to facilitate several tasks:

1 It can measure the time interval between transitions occurring on the input to bit 0 of port 2 with a resolution of 1 μs (assuming a crystal frequency of 4 MHz).

2 It can output periodic pulses, square waves, etc., from bit 1 of port 2 with a timing resolution of 1 μs.

3 It can interrupt the CPU after a specified time interval.

For our purposes here, we will ignore tasks 1 and 2 and concentrate on task 3. This will leave bits 0 and 1 of port 2 uncommitted to the programmable timer and may thereby simplify the initialization of the *mode* of the chip (which is determined by the state of bits 0, 1, and 2 of port 2 at reset). More importantly, this third task will let us employ interrupt control of the timing of external events on *any* I/O lines. For example, we can initiate a 20-ms pulse on an output line of a port, set the programmable timer to cause in interrupt in 20 ms, and then complete the 20-ms pulse when the interrupt occurs.

The registers involved in this subset of the programmable timer's capabilities are shown in Fig. A3-8. The 16-bit free-running counter is automatically clocked by the CPU every clock cycle. With a 1-MHz clock (i.e., a 4-MHz crystal), it repeats every 65.536 ms. This counter can be reliably read with the instruction

```
LDD     $0009
```

This will first read the upper byte in hex address 0009 and then the lower byte in 000A. In spite of the fact that both bytes are not actually read simultaneously, the circuitry is suitably buffered so that the resulting value read represents the contents of both addresses at the time the content of 0009 was read. This 16-bit counter should be written to cautiously since it is used to generate the UART's timing as well as that for the programmable timer. Furthermore, the counter ignores the data written to it and simply initializes itself to FFF8.

To generate an interrupt after a time interval of less than 65 ms, we can load *D* with the desired number of microseconds and then call the following TIMER subroutine, assuming interrupts are initially disabled (i.e., EOCI = 0).

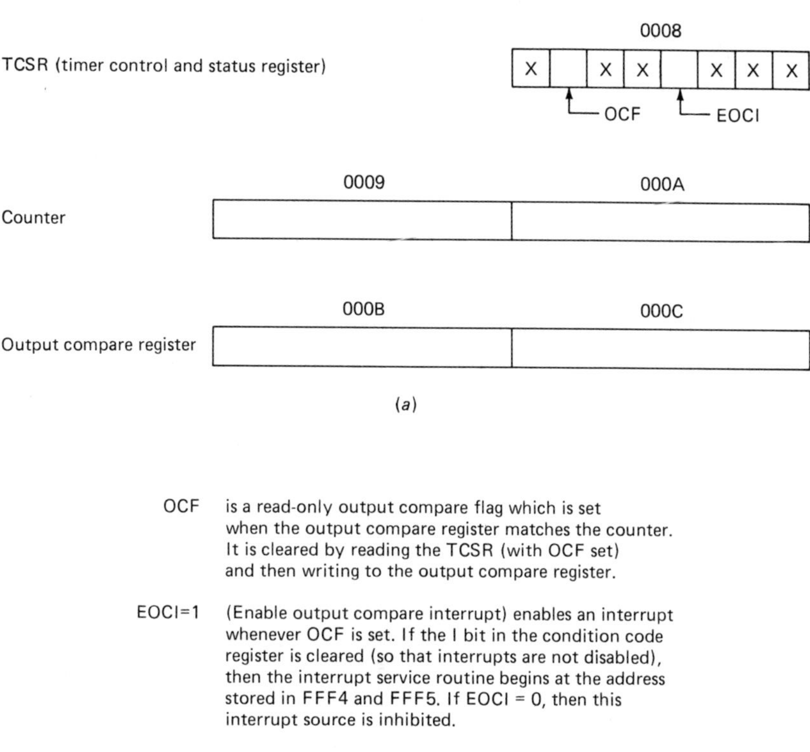

Figure A3-8. Programmable timer. (a) Registers; (b) TCSR bit definitions.

```
TCSR      EQU     $0008          DEFINE LABELS
CTR       EQU     $0009
OCR       EQU     $000B
****** TIMER SUBROUTINE ******
* THIS SUBROUTINE INITIATES PROGRAMMABLE TIMER USE.
* THE NUMBER OF MICROSECONDS (UP TO 65535) OF DELAY
* ARE PASSED TO THE TIMER SUBROUTINE IN D.
TIMER     ADDD    CTR            ADD COUNTER + TIME INTERVAL
          STD     OCR            STORE FOR LATER COMPARISON
          CMPA    TCSR           RESET OUTPUT COMPARE FLAG
          STD     OCR            (IF IT HAPPENS TO BE SET)
          LDAA    #%00001000     SET EOCI BIT
          STAA    TCSR           TO ENABLE INTERRUPTS
          CLI                    ALSO ENABLE CPU
          RTS                    AND RETURN
```

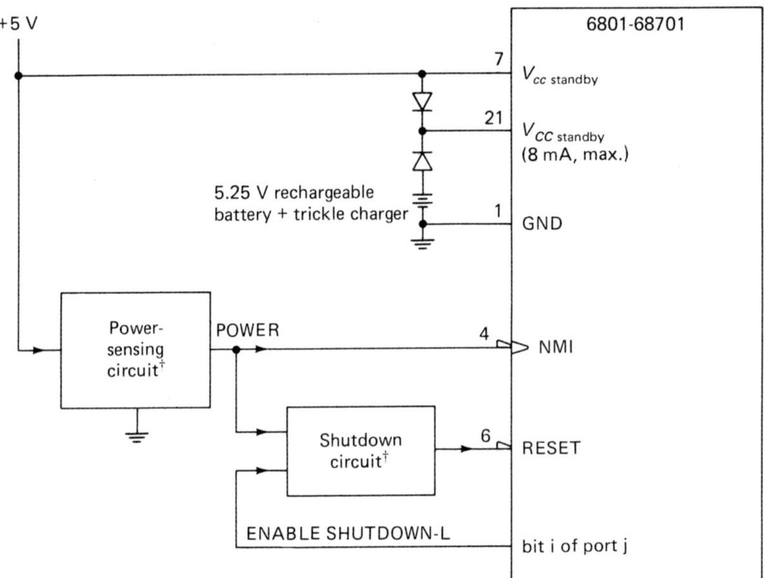

†Refer to the author's *Microcomputer-Based Design*, McGraw-Hill, New York, 1977 sec. 4-3.

Figure A3-9. Power-standby circuitry.

Thus, to obtain an interrupt after 20 ms:

```
LDD    #20000    PASS 20000 (DECIMAL)
JSR    TIMER     TO THE TIMER SUBROUTINE
```

To handle time intervals T longer than 65 ms, we might first load the integer part of T/65536 into an address in RAM labeled LTIME (long time). Then *D* is loaded with the remainder. Then TIMER is called. The interrupt service routine for the programmable timer can decrement LTIME if it does not equal zero. Then it can return from the interrupt. When LTIME does equal zero, the interrupt service routine can clear the EOCI bit defined in Fig. A3-8 (to disable further interrupts) and do whatever is supposed to be done after this longer time interval.

The 6801 includes several features which facilitate the implementation of power-standby capability, using the circuitry of Fig. A3-9:

1 A nonmaskable interrupt input can be used to sense a falling edge from a power-sensing circuit which detects when the +5-V power drops below a specified level.
2 The power-down service routine can store the stack pointer in

RAM so that, when power is subsequently restored, the microcomputer can begin again where it left off (if that is desired). The routine should then write 10000000 to the RAM control register (address 0014) of Fig. A3-4. The 0 in bit 6 disables the internal RAM (which will be automatically re-enabled upon reset). Bit 7 can be tested when power is restored. If it is 0, then $V_{CC\ standby}$ (pin 21) has dropped below an acceptable minimum value and the RAM content is suspect. If this bit is 1, then we can feel confident that the "standby RAM" (hex addresses 0080-00BF) has retained its data.

3 Finally, the power-down service routine can drive an output bit of a port low (labeled ENABLE SHUTDOWN-L in Fig. A3-9), which will activate a "shutdown circuit," resetting the CPU. With the RESET-L input held low, instruction execution is suspended.

4 The power-sensing circuit detects when power is restored. Its output, labeled POWER in Fig. A3-9, goes high and tells the shutdown circuit to drive RESET-L high, regardless of the value of ENABLE SHUTDOWN-L. The CPU can restore the stack pointer, reinitialize ports, etc., and then execute a return from interrupt RTI instruction to continue operation exactly where it left off when power failure was sensed.

INDEX